BRITISH RAIL MOTIVE POWER

COMBINED VOLUME

LONDON

IAN ALLAN LTD

1989

BRITISH RAIL LOCOMOTIVES

LONDON

IAN ALLAN LTD

INTRODUCTION

The serious railway enthusiast will realise that 1988 saw further major changes to BR's traction. Locomotives are extremely costly and where a multiple-unit can be introduced, as is the case with all Network SouthEast and Provincial Sector services, this is being implemented as quickly as practicable. InterCity is concentrating its future on electric locomotives operating push-pull trains on the East Coast and West Coast main lines. The tighter control of resources permitted by Sector management has led to an overall reduction in the locomotive fleet.

A brief analysis of 1988 and the programme for 1989 indicates that Class 03 will be reduced to one operating on the mainland, but two will continue to operate on the Isle of Wight. The Parcels Sector will require fewer shunters as the maintenance of its van fleet is concentrated on two depots. No major overhauls are being carried out on Class 20 locomotives and they will gradually be displaced, but they will make history early in 1989 when up to eight will enter private ownership with Hunslet-Barclay for hire to the operators of special purpose trains such as weedkillers. Another side effect of the stricter adherance of locomotive operation to the financing Sector's duties has been the reduction of the maximum operating speed of many in the Freight and Departmental fleets. This also reduces the frequency of routine maintenance and helps reduce the quantity of spares required. Many Class 31/1s are due to become surplus over the next year. Refurbishment of the Class 37 fleet will cease with the entry to traffic of the last Class 37/7 conversion in February 1989. Further Class 47s will also gradually become surplus. The last Class 40 has been replaced as the celebrity Charter Sub-Sector locomotive by the final Class 45/1. Overhauls have also ceased on Class 50, and by October many should be replaced by the Class 47/7 fleet displaced from Scotland by new Class 158 DMUs. Railfreight runs a substantial number of petroleum, construction (stone and aggregates) and steel trains that require the uneconomic double-heading of heavy trains. It is therefore due to take delivery of the first of 100 Class 60 locomotives in June, thus gradually eliminating, from 1990, over 200 of the current fleet.

Commencing in May 1989 the first 10 Class 91 locomotives will be available to haul King's Cross-Leeds services. This will release some Class 43 IC125 power cars for mid-life re-engining whilst InterCity determines the long-term future of those displaced by the East Coast main line electrification. There are no plans to displace those on InterCity Midland, Western or Cross-Country services. The gradual introduction of Class 90 locomotives and push-pull operation of West Coast main line services will also allow the withdrawal of Classes 81, 83 and most of Class 85. An accident at Newcastle caused two IC125 coaches to be withdrawn. Although new Mk 4 coaches are to be introduced on the East Coast route, other IC125 routes require additional or strengthened rakes to cater for traffic growth, but no significant cascading is envisaged until May 1990.

Roger Wood, January 1989

Important Note

A significant number of changes, particularly relating to Sector allocation codes, were announced by BR after this book went to press. Where possible these have been incorporated. A complete summary by sub-Sector and a 'Late News' amendment list corrected to February 1989 appear later in this book. Our modern scene magazine *Motive Power Monthly*, produces a fully detailed and up-to-date guide to changes as advised by BR.

Equipment and Special Characteristics

This year's format has been further revised as part of our policy of continued improvement and clarity for users. Equipment that is standard to a locomotive class is shown in the heading and special characteristics (variations) are indicated by a symbol against the individual locomotive number. An innovation this year is the inclusion of the official BRB DMEE locomotive diagram code which is made up of locomotive class, sub-class, an alphabetical variation code, and a train brake type code (A=air, V=vacuum or X=dual air and vacuum). The variations can apply to weight, train heating, maximum speed and major components fitted and are indicated in the class headings. Characteristic codes used comply where possible with those used officially by BR.

Locomotives:

B Cab-to-shore radio communication (BR telephone network)
C Refurbished cab (Classes 08 and 09)
H Drawbar tested for emergency haulage of IC125 trains (to be advised)
K* Snowplough brackets for fitting three-part miniature snowploughs
L Fixed beam headlight/spotlight
M Driver-only operation equipment
N* Remote control radio (experimental)
P Push-pull operation by Time Division Multiplex system
R Radio Electronic Token Block
S Slow Speed Control
T Transponder code transmitter (locomotive number to shore)
U Electric train heating equipment non-operational
X Additional fuel capacity (see class heading for tank capacity)
Z* Remote control (for MGR trains at equipped power stations; out of use experiment)
60, 75 or 80mph maximum operating speed, long-term restrictions

InterCity 125 Coaches:

P Public payphone
R Refurbished interiors

Locomotive Liveries

BR has announced its intention to standardise liveries to five main variations, although standard blue still predominates at this time. Colour photographs in this booklet generally indicate the following styles. Minor variations to styles are not indicated here but special liveries are indicated in class headings.

I **InterCity.** Classes 43, 86, 87, 89, 90 and 91 are authorised to carry the branding 'INTERCITY' and swallow emblem. Other InterCity Sector locomotives carry the livery without the branding and emblem. The number is to be placed on the cabside, near the bottom, by the driving position. Parcels Sector diesel locomotives of Classes 31/4 and 47/4, and electric locomotives, are intended to carry this unbranded livery with the number below the cab window.
Is **InterCity.** Old style with red waistband and ScotRail lettering.
Ps **Provincial.** Old style InterCity with blue waistband and ScotRail lettering.
Pt **Provincial.** Trans-Pennine two-tone blue.
F **Railfreight.** Old grey livery, later examples with red band round sole-bar.
F **Railfreight.** New two-tone grey livery, without sub-Sector symbols.
Fa **Railfreight Construction.** Blue and yellow rectangles.
Fe **Railfreight Coal.** Black diamonds on yellow background.
Fg **Railfreight Distribution.** Red diamonds on yellow background.
Fm **Railfreight Metals & Automotive.** Blue and yellow chevrons.
Fp **Railfreight Petroleum.** Blue ripple lines on yellow background.
Fx **Railfreight General.** Red and yellow rectangles.
N **Network SouthEast.** Classes 47 and 50 only.
D **Departmental.** Falcon grey livery.
★ **Special livery.** See class heading.

Coupling of Locomotives

Main line diesel locomotives can be operated in multiple (driven only from leading locomotive) with locomotives fitted with compatible control equipment. Classes 20, 31, 33 and 37 have electro-pneumatic control and carry a 'blue star' symbol above each buffer. Class 50 locomotives carry an 'orange square' symbol and can only multiple with others of this class, whilst Classes 56 and 58 are in the 'red diamond' code group. Other classes, and these when not electronically compatibly coupled, are able to operate in tandem — a separate driver controlling each locomotive. Multiple-working restrictions applicable to electronic locomotives are indicated in the appropriate class headings. When operating in multiple or tandem, restrictions applicable to one locomotive (maximum speed etc) must be adhered to by the assisting locomotive(s).

Level of Repair and Maintenance Facility

In April 1987 BR introduced a new maintenance policy for all traction and coaching stock. Under the scheme, depots and workshops are classified on a scale of 1 to 6, called Levels, determined by the facilities available and work effected at each location.

The larger establishments, Level 5, normally have separate workshops to carry out this category of repair and are not necessarily answerable to the Sector which 'owns' the main depot.

Definition

Level	*Facility*	*Description*
1	Fuel point	Facility for dispensing fuel, oil and water to diesel locomotives and/or DMUs. Minor servicing to EMUs. Manned by unskilled staff.
2	Servicing	Capable of undertaking 'A' exam work and occasional 'B' exams on locomotives and multiple-units together with work arising and brake blocking also full maintenance for diesel shunter locomotives. For coaching stock some cleaning, chemical emission toilet disposal, environmental checks, two daily exams, weekly exams and brake blocking. The facility will have a covered pit, a small store and be manned by skilled staff.
3	Maintenance	This facility will have a Traction and Rolling Stock allocation and be capable of carrying out all levels of exams and the majority of repairs arising. It will have covered pits, staff accomodation, light lifting and jacking facilities. A full range of equipment will be available to meet all exam requirements. Multiple-units and coaching stock all levels of exams, code 'C' cleaning, patch painting and some body repair.
4	Maintenance and repair	As for level 3 but having an additional capability for heavier repairs. The depot will be well equipped with cranes and/or heavy lifting jacks for bogie removal and possibly a wheel lathe.
5	Heavy repair	A facility capable of undertaking unplanned heavy repairs and collision damage arising at lower-level facilities. May also have the facility for lower level of classified repair, limited component refurbishment and half life component exchange. Fuelling facilities are not necessarily provided.
6	Workshop	A main workshop with full facilities for undertaking all levels of classified and unclassified repairs.

Depot Codes

	Level			Main Sector(s)	Full Maintenance
	Loco	*HST*		*(Locomotives)*	*Classes Allocated*
AB	2	2	Aberdeen HS	P/I	08/0
AF	2		Ashford, Chart Leacon T&RSMD	N	08/0, 09
AN	2		Allerton SD	F	08/0
AY	2		Ayr TMD	F	08/0
BD	1		Birkenhead North EMUD	P	03, 97/7
BI	2		Brighton T&RSMD	N	—
BL	2		Blyth (Cambois) SD	F	—
BM	2		Bournemouth West EMUD	N	—
BN	2	4	Bounds Green T&RSMD	I/R	—
BR	4	5	Bristol Bath Road TMD	I/R	08/0, 47/4
BS	3		Bescot TMD	D	08/0, 31/1, 31/4
BW	1		Barrow	F	—
BX	2		Buxton TMD	F	—
BY	2		Bletchley TMD	N	08/0
BZ	2		St Blazey SD	F	—
CA	2		Cambridge (Coldhams Lane) TMD	R	08/0
CD	4		Crewe TMD	I/F	08/0, 31/1, 31/4, 47/0, 47/3, 47/4, 97/2, 97/4
CE	4		Crewe ETD	F	85
CF	4		Cardiff Canton TMD	F	08/0, 09, 37/0, 37/5, 37/7, 37/9, 47/0, 47/3, 47/9, 56, 97/8
CH	1		Chester TMD	P	—
CL	2		Carlisle Upperby	P	08/0
CR	2		Colchester SD	F	—
DL	5		Doncaster Major Depot, BRML	D	08
DR	2		Doncaster TMD	F	08/0
DY	2	4	Derby, Etches Park T&RSMD	I	08/0
EC		4	Edinburgh, Craigentinny T&RSMD	I	43
ED	4		Eastfield, Glasgow TMD	I/P/F	08/0, 20, 26/0, 26/1, 37/0, 37/4, 47/0, 47/4, 47/7
EH	4		Eastleigh T&RSMD	D/F/N/R	08/0, 09, 33/0, 33/1
EX	2		Exeter St Davids SD	F/N	—
FH	2		Frodingham T&RSMD	F	—

	Level Loco	HST		Main Sector(s) (Locomotives)	Full Maintenance Classes Allocated
FW	1		Fort William	P/F	—
GD	2		Gateshead TMD	F	08/0
GL	2		Gloucester SD	F	08/0
GM	2		Grangemouth SD	F	—
GW	4		Glasgow, Shields EMD	I	81
HA	2		Haymarket TMD	F	08/0
HD	1		Holyhead SD	F	—
HO	2		Holbeck SD	F	08/0
HT		4	Heaton T&RSMD	I/P	43
IL	2		Ilford EMD	I/N	—
IM	4		Immingham TMD	F	08/0, 20, 37/0, 37/3, 47/0, 47/3, 47/4
IP	1		Ipswich HS	F	—
IS	4		Inverness TMD	P	08/0, 37/0, 37/4, 47/4
KY	2		Knottingley SD	F	—
	1		Kings Lynn	F	—
LA	5	4	Laira TMD	I/N	08/0, 37/4, 37/5, 43, 50, 50/1
LE	2	2	Landore TMD	F	08/0, 08/9
LG	2		Longsight EMD	I	—
LO	2		Longsight TMD	R	08/0
LR	2		Leicester SD	F	—
MG	2		Margam FP	F	—
ML	3		Motherwell TMD	F	08/0, 20, 37/0, 37/3
MR	2		March SD	D	—
NC	2		Norwich, Crown Point T&RSMD	P	08/0
NH	1		Newton Heath TMD	P	—
NL	4	5	Neville Hill T&RSMD	I	08/0, 43
OC/OO	4	4	Old Oak Common T&RSMDs	N/I	08/0, 43, 47/4, 50
PB	2		Peterborough SD	F	—

Depot Codes

	Level			Main Sector(s)	Full Maintenance
	Loco	*HST*		*(Locomotives)*	*Classes Allocated*
PH	1		Perth LIP	R	08/0
PM		4	St Phillips Marsh HSTD	I	43
PZ	1	2	Penzance SD	I	—
RG	2		Reading TMD	R	08/0
RL	2		Ripple Lane SD	F	—
RY	1		Ryde, Isle of Wight EMD	D	03, 97/8
SB	2		Shirebrook SD	F	—
SF	4		Stratford TMD	F	08/0, 31/1, 37/0, 37/3, 37/7, 47/0, 47/3, 47/4
SG			Slade Green T&RSMD	D	97/8
SL	4		Stewarts Lane T&RSMD	I/F	33/0, 33/2, 73/0, 73/1
SP	2		Springs Branch, Wigan TMD	F	08/0
SR	5		Stratford Major Depot		—
SU	2		Selhurst T&RSMD	N	08/0, 09
SY	1		Saltley LIP	F	—
TE	4		Thornaby TMD	F	08/0, 20, 31/1, 37/0, 37/5, 47/0, 47/3, 47/4
TI	4		Tinsley TMD	F	08/0, 31/1, 31/4, 37/0, 37/3, 37/5, 47/0, 47/3
TJ	2		Thornton SD	F	—
TO	4		Toton TMD	F	08/0, 20, 56, 58
TS	2		Tyseley TMD	R	—
WN	4		Willesden TMD	I	86/1, 86/2, 86/4, 86/5, 87/0, 87/1
WY	2		Westbury Loco SD	F	—
YK	2		York LIP (Wagon Works)	F	08/0
ZG	6		Eastleigh BRML	D	08/0
ZH	5		Springburn BRML	D	08/0
ZN		5	Wolverton BRML	D	08/0

	Level Loco	Level HST		Main Sector(s) (Locomotives)	Full Maintenance Classes Allocated
BREL Works					
ZC	6		Crewe	C	08/0
ZD		6	Derby Carriage	C	—
ZE	6	6	Derby Locomotive	C	08/0
ZR			York Carriage	C	—
Private Works					
ZB	5		RFS Engineering Doncaster	C	08/0

British Railways Board

ZQ BRB Headquarters
(Traction on acceptance and Private Owner stock)

Sectors:

C: Private owner
D: Departmental (HQ)
F: Railfreight
I: InterCity
N: Network SouthEast
P: Provincial
R: Parcels

CLASS 03 SHUNTER 0-6-0

Built: British Rail 1959-62.
Engine: Gardner 8L3 8cyl, 4-stroke, 204hp (152kW).
Weight: 31 tonnes.
Brake force: 13 tonnes.
Maximum tractive effort: 15,300lb (68.1kN).
Power/control equipment: Mechanical. Wilson-Drewry type CA5 R7 five-speed epicyclic gearbox; Vulcan-Sinclair type 23 fluid coupling.
Dimensions: *Diagram* 03-OBX 26ft L × 8.5ft W × 12.2ft H. *Diagram* 03-ODX 26ft L × 8.5ft W × 11.8ft H
Route availability: 1.
Fuel: 300gal.
Maximum operating speed: 28.5mph.
Train brakes: Dual Air and Vacuum.
Standard equipment: Sanding gear.

Sectors:
Network SouthEast: **NXXA:** General
Provincial: **PXXA:** General.
Railfreight: **FGZZ:** Distribution (Speedlink). **FTZZ:** Chemicals.
Special livery: *Green:* 03162.
Note: 03162 carries pre-TOPS number D2162.

Loc No	*Dia*	*SC*	*Liv*	*Pool*	*Dep*
03073	BX			*PXXA*	BD
03162	BX		★	*FTZZ*	BD
Birkenhead South 1879-1985					
03170	BX			*FGZZ*	BD
03179	DX			*NXXA*	RY

CLASS 08/0 SHUNTER 0-6-0

Built: British Rail 1953-62.
Engine: English Electric 6cyl, 6KT of 400hp (315kW).
Weight: 49 tonnes.
Dimensions: 29.3ft L × 8.5ft W × 12.7ft H.
Brake force: 19 tonnes.
Maximum tractive effort: 35,000lb (156kN).
Power/control equipment: Two English Electric EE 506 traction motors; double reduction gear drive; main generator EE 801.
Route availability: 5.
Fuel: 668gal.

Diagram	*Train Brake*	*Max Speed*	*Voltage*
08-0AV	Vacuum	20mph	90
08-0BX	Dual	20mph	110
08-0CA	Air	20mph	90
08-0DV	Vacuum	15mph	90
08-0EX	Dual	15mph	90
08-0FA	Air	15mph	90
08-0KX	Dual	15mph	110

Standard equipment: Sanding gear.

Sectors:

Private owner: (unofficial codes): **CBRE:** BREL '88, **CRFS:** RFS Engineering.

Departmental: **DBMS:** BRML. **DCMB:** DCE Midland. **DCSB:** DCE Southern. **DRTC:** Research. **DWCS:** DMEE.

InterCity: **IANB:** Anglia. **ICCA:** Cross Country. **ICHA:** Charter. **IECA:** East Coast route. **IMLA:** Midland Lines. **IWCA:** West Coast route. **IWRA:** Western Region.

Network SouthEast: **NXXA:** General.

Parcels: **RXLA:** General.

Provincial: **PXXA:** General.

Railfreight: **FAZZ:** Construction. **FEZZ:** Coal (MGR). **FGZZ:** Distribution (Speedlink). **FHZZ:** Coal. **FMZZ:** Metals. **FPZZ:** Petroleum. **FTZZ:** Chemicals. **FVZZ:** Automotive. **FXXA:** General. **FXXL:** General. **LNRS:** Distribution (Freightliner).

Special liveies: *Black:* 08601, 08730, 08867, 08907.

Great Eastern blue: 08833.

Green: 08011, 08556, 08604, 08772/93, 08869, 08944.

Loc No	*Dia*	*SC*	*Liv*	*Pool*	*Dep*
08011	DV		★	*DCWA*	BY
Haversham					
08182	DV			*CBRE*	ZR
D3236					
08202	AV			*FHZZ*	CF
08250	DV			*FXXL*	NC
08258	DV			*DWCS*	CA
08308	DV			*RXLA*	TI
08309	DV			*RXLA*	HO
08335	DV			*CRFS*	ZB
Terence					
08375	AV			*FHZZ*	CF
08388	FA	C		*FGZZ*	IM
08389	FA	C		*FGZZ*	NL
08390	FA			*FHZZ*	LE
08393	FA	C		*DWCS*	SF
08397	FA	C		*FGZZ*	IM
08399	FA			*FGZZ*	DY
08401	FA			*FXXL*	IM
08402	FA			*FHZZ*	AN
08405	FA	C		*FGZZ*	IM
08407	FA			*FGZZ*	NC
08410	FA	E		*FGZZ*	BR
08411	FA			*DWCS*	TE
08413	FA			*LNRS*	SF
08414	CA			*LNRS*	SF
08415	EX			*LNRS*	AN
08416	FA			*FQZZ*	TO
08417	FA			*DWCS*	SF
08418	FA			*FGZZ*	DR
08419	FA			*FGZZ*	KD
08421	FA			*FHZZ*	GD
08428	FA			*FHZZ*	DY
08434	DV			*FEZZ*	TI
08436	DV			*FEZZ*	TI
~~08440~~	FA			*DWCS*	SF
08441	FA			*FHZZ*	GD
08442	FA			*FHZZ*	GD
08445	FA	C		*FGZZ*	IM
08447	FA			*FGZZ*	KD
08448	FA			*FGZZ*	DY
08449	FA			*FTZZ*	HO
~~08451~~	EX	C		*IWCA*	WN
08454	EX			*FGZZ*	WN
08460	FA			*FGZZ*	NC
08463	FA			*FTZZ*	DY
08466	FA	C	F	*FGZZ*	BS
08468	DV			*PXXA*	SP
08470	DV			*CBRE*	ZC
08472	FA			*LNRS*	CD
08479	DV			*FXXL*	CF
~~08480~~	FA			*IWRA*	OC
Old Oak Common 1882-1982					

Loc No	Dia	SC	Liv	Pool	Dep
08481	EX	c		*FGZZ*	CF
08482	FA			*FPZZ*	AN
08483	FA			*IWRA*	BR
08484	FA			*DBMS*	ZN
08485	FA			*FMZZ*	AN
08489	FA			*FGZZ*	GD
08492	FA	c		*FGZZ*	TI
08493	FA			*FHZZ*	CF
08495	EX			*FGZZ*	CA
Bury					
08496	FA			*FGZZ*	CA
08498	FA			*FGZZ*	NC
08499	FA			*FXXL*	YK
08500	EX	c		*FXXL*	YK
Thomas 1					
08506	FA			*DWCS*	TE
08507	FA	c		*FGZZ*	GD
08508	DV			*FXXL*	TI
08509	FA			*FHZZ*	TI
Wath ETD 41F					
08510	FA	c		*FGZZ*	DR
08511	FA			*FTZZ*	DY
08512	FA			*FHZZ*	GD
08514	FA			*FGZZ*	DR
08515	FA			*FHZZ*	GD
08516	FA			*DWCS*	HO
08517	FA			*FGZZ*	BS
08519	FA	c		*FGZZ*	TE
08521	FA			*FXXL*	GD
08523	EX			*FGZZ*	OC
08525	KX	c		*FXXL*	YK
08526	KX			*FGZZ*	CA
08527	KX			*RXLA*	SF
08528	KX			*DWCS*	CA
08529	KX			*DWCS*	CA
08530	KX			*DWCS*	NC
08531	KX			*FXXL*	SF
08532	KX			*FAZZ*	AN
08533	KX			*FGZZ*	SF
08534	KX			*RXLA*	SP
Edge Hill					
08535	KX	c	F	*FHZZ*	BS
George					
08536	KX			*IMLA*	DY
08537	KX	c	F	*FXXL*	IM
08538	KX			*RXLA*	CA
08539	KX			*DWCS*	CA
08540	KX	c		*DWCS*	CA
08541	KX			*FXXL*	SF
08542	KX			*FXXL*	SF
08543	KX			*FHZZ*	TI
Rotherwood					
08544	KX			*FXXL*	GD
08556	AV		★	*ICHA*	OC
08561	EX	c		*DWCS*	AY
08562	EX			*RXLA*	DR
The Doncaster Postman					
08565	EX			*DWCS*	ML
08567	EX			*DWCS*	YK
08568	EX	c		*ICCA*	ML
08569	EX	c		*FGZZ*	AN
08570	EX			*FGZZ*	HA
08571	EX			*ICCA*	HA
08573	EX			*DCMB*	WN
08575	EX	c		*FXXL*	TE
08576	EX			*DWCS*	LA
08577	EX	K		*FXXL*	GD
08578	EX			*RXLA*	GD
08580	EX			*FGZZ*	CA
08581	EX	CK		*FAZZ*	ML
08582	FA	c		*FGZZ*	TE
08583	EX			*FXXL*	YK
08584	EX			*DWCS*	LA
08585	EX			*RXLA*	CD
08586	FA			*DWCS*	AY
08587	EX			*DWCS*	GD
08588	EX	c		*FXXL*	TE
08589	EX	c		*FGZZ*	CF
08590	EX	c		*FGZZ*	NL
08591	EX	K		*FGZZ*	AY
08593	EX			*FXXL*	SF
08594	EX			*FXXL*	CA
Ely					
08595	EX			*FXXL*	YK
08597	EX			*RXLA*	TO
08599	EX	c		*FGZZ*	CD

Loc No	Dia	SC	Liv	Pool	Dep
08601	EX	C	★	*FVZZ*	BS
Spectre					
08603	EX			*FMZZ*	BS
08604	EX	C	★	*FMZZ*	BS
Phantom					
08605	EX	C		*DWCS*	YK
08607	EX	C		*FGZZ*	DR
08609	EX			*IWCA*	WN
08610	EX	C		*FEZZ*	BS
08611	EX			*RXLA*	LO
08612	EX			*DCMB*	WN
08613	EX			*FHZZ*	CD
08614	EX	C		*RXLA*	WN
08615	EX			*FMZZ*	AN
08616	EX	C		*PXXA*	BS
08617	EX			*RXLA*	WN
08618	EX			*FXXL*	GD
08619	EX			*DCMB*	LO
08620	EX			*FGZZ*	ML
08622	EX			*RXLA*	DY
08623	EX	C		*FHZZ*	TO
08624	EX			*FXXL*	LO
08625	EX			*RXLA*	WN
08627	FA			*FGZZ*	SF
08628	EX			*DCMB*	BY
08629	EX			*DBMS*	ZN
Wolverton					
08630	EX			*FGZZ*	ML
08631	EX	C	N	*FGZZ*	CA
Eagle					
08632	EX	C		*RXLA*	IM
08633	EX			*RXLA*	CD
08634	EX			*RXLA*	OC
08635	EX			*IWCA*	CD
08637	EX	C		*FGZZ*	CF
08638	EX			*DWCS*	CA
Cambridge					
08641	KX	E		*ICCA*	LA
08642	BX			*DBMS*	ZG
08643	KX	E		*IWRA*	BR
08644	KX	E	I	*ICCA*	LA
Ponsendane					

Loc No	Dia	SC	Liv	Pool	Dep
08645	KX	E		*IWRA*	LA
Friary					
08646	KX			*FXXL*	LE
08647	KX			*DBMS*	DL
08648	BX			*IWCA*	WN
08649	KX			*FGZZ*	OC
08650	BX			*FXXL*	EH
08651	KX	E		*IWRA*	OC
08652	KX	K		*FXXL*	CF
08653	BX			*DWCS*	SU
08654	KX	CK		*FGZZ*	CF
08655	BX			*FXXL*	SF
08656	FA			*FGZZ*	BY
08657	FA			*DWCS*	YK
08658	EX			*IANB*	NC
08659	FA			*LNRS*	HO
08660	DV			*FHZZ*	CF
08661	FA			*FGZZ*	NL
08662	EX	C		*FXXL*	YK
08663	FA	E		*FTZZ*	LA
08664	EX	C		*FGZZ*	CF
08665	EX	C		*FXXL*	IM
08666	EX			*DCMB*	LO
08667	EX			*FGZZ*	NL
08668	EX	C		*FXXL*	CF
08669	FA			*LNRS*	AN
08670	FA			*LNRS*	WN
08672	FA			*FGZZ*	BS
08673	EX		I	*ICCA*	LO
Piccadilly					
08675	EX	C		*FGZZ*	AY
08676	EX			*RXLA*	LO
08677	EX	C		*IWCA*	WN
08680	KX			*IWCA*	AB
Northern Lights					
08682	EX	C		*DWCS*	DR
08683	EX			*IWCA*	WN
08685	EX			*FXXL*	NC
08686	FA			*FHZZ*	AN
08688	FA			*FVZZ*	AN
08689	FA			*DWCS*	SF
08690	EX			*FGZZ*	KD
08691	EX			*FHZZ*	TI
Escafeld					

Loc No	Dia	SC	Liv	Pool	Dep
08692	EX	c		DWCS	BS
08693	EX			FGZZ	AY
08694	EX			FMZZ	CD
08695	EX			FGZZ	CD
08696	FA			NXXA	WN
08697	EX			RXLA	TO
08698	FA			DWCS	SF
08699	EX			FGZZ	CD
08700	FA			FGZZ	BS
08701	EX			FXXL	HO
08702	EX			DCMB	CD
08703	FA			FGZZ	AN
08704	EX			RXLA	BY
08705	FA			FGZZ	CA
08706	EX	c		FGZZ	HO
08707	FA			FHZZ	HO
08708	FA			LNRS	NC
08709	EX			FXXL	SF
08710	EX			DWCS	HA
08711	EX	c		FGZZ	CA
08712	EX			DWCS	PH
08713	FA			FGZZ	CA
08714	EX			FXXL	CA
08715	DV			FXXL	SF
08716	DV			DWCS	CA
08717	EX			IWCA	IS
08718	EX			IWCA	HA
08719	EX			DWCS	YK
08720	FA	c	P	PXXA	HA
08721	EX		R	RXLA	LO
Starlet					
08723	EX			RXLA	DR
08724	EX	c		FGZZ	SF
08725	EX			FGZZ	ML
08727	EX			FHZZ	AY
08729	FA			FHZZ	DR
08730	EX		★	RXLA	HA
08731	EX			PXXA	ML
08732	EX	c		FGZZ	ML
08733	EX	c		DWCS	ML
08734	EX	c		RXLA	IM
08735	EX	c		FHZZ	AY
08737	KX			FGZZ	CD
08738	KX	c		FGZZ	ML
08739	KX			FGZZ	CD
08740	KX			FXXL	SF
08741	KX	c		IECA	GD
08742	KX			RXLA	CD
08743	KX	c		RXLA	IM
08744	KX			RXLA	SP
08745	KX			FXXL	IM
08746	KX			RXLA	CD
08747	KX			FXXL	GD
08748	KX			RXLA	NC
08749	KX			FXXL	TI
Great Central					
08750	KX	c		FGZZ	SF
08751	KX	c		FXXL	IM
08752	KX			IANB	NC
08753	KX			PXXA	IS
Kinnoul K.D					
08754	KX			FGZZ	IS
08755	KX	c		FGZZ	HA
08756	KX			FXXL	LE
08757	KX	c		DWCS	CA
08758	KX			FXXL	SF
08759	KX			FMZZ	BS
08760	BX			FXXL	EH
08761	KX			PXXA	HA
08762	KX			PXXA	PH
08763	KX			DWCS	HA
08765	KX		★	IWCA	BS
08766	KX			DWCS	NL
08767	KX			DWCS	NC
08768	KX	c		IWCA	KD
08769	DV			FHZZ	LE
08770	FA			DWCS	TE
08771	KX			FXXL	YK
08772	EX		★	DWCS	NC
Camulodunum					
08773	EX			FHZZ	HO
08775	EX			DWCS	NC
08776	FA	c		FHZZ	HO
08777	EX			DWCS	YK
08778	EX			FGZZ	GL
08780	EX	c		FGZZ	LE
08781	EX			FGZZ	GL
08782	FA			FHZZ	HO
08783	EX			FXXL	HO
08784	EX			DCMB	CD

Loc No	Dia	SC	Liv	Pool	Dep
08785	FA	E		FHZZ	CF
08786	FA	C		FGZZ	TE
08787	EX			FXXL	CF
08788	EX			FPZZ	DY
Caergybi					
08789	FA			DCMB	BY
08790	EX			PXXA	LO
08791	FA			FEZZ	HA
08792	EX	C		FGZZ	LA
08793	FA		★	DWCS	HA
08794	EX			FXXL	NL
08795	EX	C		FGZZ	GL
08796	FA			FHZZ	CF
08797	EX			DWCS	GD
08798	EX	C		DWCS	LE
08799	EX			FGZZ	GL
08800	EX			FGZZ	BR
08801	EX			FXXL	BZ
08802	EX	C		FGZZ	GD
08803	EX	C		FGZZ	RG
08804	EX	C		FXXL	OC
08805	EX	C	F	RXLA	BS
08806	FA		F	FXXL	HO
08807	EX			RXLA	BY
08808	EX			IWCA	CL
08809	EX			FHZZ	AN
08810	FA			DWCS	NC
08811	CA			LNRS	WN
08813	FA	C		DWCS	DR
08814	FA			DRTC	DY
08815	EX			DCMB	SP
08817	EX	C		FXXL	TE
Thornaby					
08818	EX	C		FHZZ	CF
08819	EX	C		FGZZ	BR
08820	FA			LNRS	LO
08821	EX			RXLA	OC
08822	EX			RXLA	CF
08823	FA			LNRS	CD
08824	FA			FHZZ	DR
08825	FA			FGZZ	WN
08826	FA			FGZZ	CL
08827	FA			FGZZ	CL
08828	FA			DWCS	SF
08829	FA			FQZZ	TO
08830	BX			NXXA	EH
08831	BX			DCSB	EH
08832	KX	C	F	FGZZ	BS
08833	BX	C	★	IECA	SF
Liverpool Street Pilot					
08834	KX	C	FG	FGZZ	SF
08835	KX	E		FXXL	CF
08836	KX			RXLA	CF
08837	BX			DCSB	SU
08838	KX			DCMB	SP
08839	KX			DWCS	LA
08840	KX			RXLA	LA
08841	KX			IWCA	BS
08842	KX			RXLA	DY
08843	KX			DCMB	CD
Holyhead					
08844	KX	C		RXLA	CL
08845	BX			NXXA	EH
08846	KX			IWCA	AN
08847	BX			DCSB	EH
08848	KX			FXXL	CF
08849	KX			FGZZ	LA
08850	KX			FXXL	RG
08851	KX			PXXA	ML
08853	KX	CR		FGZZ	ML
08854	BX			ICCA	SU
08855	KX			RXLA	AB
Hatton Castle					
08856	KX			FGZZ	AN
08857	KX	C		RXLA	TI
Darnall					
08858	KX			IWCA	AN
08859	KX			DWCS	NC
08865	EX			RXLA	CA
08866	EX			DWCS	DR
08867	EX	C	★	RXLA	TE
Ralph Easby					
08868	EX			IANB	NC
08869	EX		★	FXXL	NC
The Canary					

Loc No	Dia	SC	Liv	Pool	Dep
08870	EX			FHZZ	TI
	Millhouses 41C				
08871	EX			FXXL	IM
08872	KX	C		IECA	GD
08873	KX		I	FXXL	SF
08874	KX	E		IECA	NL
08875	KX			RXLA	NL
08876	KX			DWCS	DR
08877	KX	C		DWCS	IM
08878	KX			FXXL	TI
	Grimesthorpe 41B				
08879	KX	C		RXLA	TI
	Earles				
08880	KX			FXXL	TI
	Mexborough 41F				
08881	KX			FGZZ	HA
08882	KX			FGZZ	AB
	Bennachie				
08883	KX			DBMS	ZH
08884	KX			FVZZ	AN
08885	KX			DWCS	DR
08886	KX			FXXL	GD
08887	KX			FGZZ	WN
08888	KX			IECA	GD
08889	KX			DWCS	CA
08890	KX			RXLA	WN
08891	KX			FXXL	LO
08892	BX			DBMS	ZG
08893	KX	C	F	FEZZ	BS
08894	KX			DCMB	SP
08895	KX	C		FXXL	LE
08896	KX			FXXL	LE
08897	KX			RXLA	LE
08898	KX			RXLA	LE
08899	KX			RXLA	DY
08900	KX			DWCS	BR
08901	KX			IWCA	BS
08902	KX			FVZZ	AN
08903	KX			FHZZ	DR
08904	KX			FGZZ	WN
08905	KX			FGZZ	WN
08906	KX			RXLA	TE
08907	KX		★	DWCS	CD
08908	KX			DWCS	NL
08909	KX			RXLA	BY
08910	KX			DWCS	CL
08911	KX			FGZZ	CL
08912	KX	C		FGZZ	CL
08913	KX			DWCS	CD
08914	KX			RXLA	BY
08915	KX			FXXL	LO
08916	KX			FPZZ	AN
08917	KX			FAZZ	AN
08918	KX			RXLA	AN
08919	KX	C		DWCS	TI
	Cadeby 41A				
08920	KX			FMZZ	BS
08921	KX			DWCS	CD
08922	KX			DCMB	BY
08923	KX			FXXL	SF
08924	KX			PXXA	AN
08925	KX			DCMB	SP
08926	KX			IWCA	WN
08927	KX			DCMB	BY
08928	KX	C	F	FXXL	TS
08929	BX			DWCS	AF
08930	KX			RXLA	SF
08931	KX			DWCS	GD
08932	KX			DWCS	CF
08933	BX			DWCS	EH
08934	KX			IWCA	WN
08935	KX			FGZZ	BR
08936	KX			DWCS	NC
08937	KX			FGZZ	LA
08938	KX	CR		FGZZ	ML
08939	KX			FGZZ	AN
08940	KX			FXXL	CF
08941	KX			DWCS	LA
08942	KX			DWCS	CF
08944	KX		★	RXLA	OC
08945	KX			FXXL	LA
08946	KX			FHZZ	RG
08947	KX			IXXA	OC
08948	KX	C		FGZZ	OC
08949	KX	C		IWRA	BR
08950	KX			RXLA	BR
08951	KX			RXLA	BR
08952	KX			FMZZ	ML

Loc No	Dia	SC	Liv	Pool	Dep
08953	KX			FGZZ	LA
Plymouth					
08954	KX			FXXL	LA
Penwithers					
08955	KX	c		RXLA	LA
08956	KX			FGZZ	NC
08957	KX			IECA	SF
08958	KX			FGZZ	SF

CLASS 08/9 SHUNTER 0-6-0

Built: British Rail 1958-59.
Details as Class 08/0 except height reduced to 11ft 10ins for operation of Cwm Mawr line (BPGV).

Diagram	Train Brake	Max Speed	Voltage
08-9CX	Dual	15mph	90
08-9DA	Air	15mph	90

Standard equipment: Refurbished cab (C), Headlight (L), and Sanding gear.

Sector:
Railfreight: **FHZZ:** Coal.

Loc No	Dia	SC	Liv	Pool	Dep	
08993	CX			FHZZ	LE	*Ashburnham*
08994	DA		F	FHZZ	LE	*Gwendraeth*
08995	DA		Fc	FHZZ	LE	*Kidwelly*

CLASS 09 SHUNTER 0-6-0

Built: British Rail 1959-62.
Engine: English Electric 6cyl, 4-stroke, 6KT of 400hp (315kW).
Weight: 50 tonnes.
Dimensions: 29.3ft L × 8.5ft W × 12.7ft H.
Brake force: 19 tonnes.
Maximum tractive effort: 25,000lb (112kN).
Power/control equipment: Two English Electric EE 506 traction motors; double reduction gear drive; main generator EE 801.
Route availability: 5.
Fuel: 668gal.
Train brakes: Dual Air and Vacuum.
Maximum operating speed: 27.5mph.
Diagram: 09-0AX.
Standard equipment: Sanding gear.

Sectors:
Departmental: **DCSB:** DCE Southern.
InterCity: **ICCA:** Cross Country. **IVGA:** Gatwick Express.
Network SouthEast: **NXXA:** General.
Railfreight: **FGZZ:** Distribution (Speedlink). **FMZZ:** Metals. **FXXL:** General.
Parcels: **RXLA:** General.
Special livery: *Light blue:* 09026.

Loc No	*Dia*	*SC*	*Liv*	*Pool*	*Dep*
09001		C		*FGZZ*	EH
09002				*RXLA*	AF
09003		C		*DCSB*	SU
09004				*DCSB*	SU
09005		C		*DCSB*	SU
09006				*NXXA*	SU
09007				*DCSB*	SU
09008				*FMZZ*	CF
09009				*DCSB*	SU
09010		C		*FGZZ*	SU
09011		C		*DCSB*	AF
09012			I	*IVGA*	SU
Dick Hardy					
09013				*FMZZ*	CF

Loc No	*Dia*	*SC*	*Liv*	*Pool*	*Dep*
09014				*DCSB*	SU
09015		C		*FGZZ*	EH
09016				*NXXA*	SU
09018				*FXXL*	AF
09019		C		*DCSB*	AF
09020				*ICCA*	SU
09021				*DCSB*	AF
09022		C		*FGZZ*	AF
09023				*NXXA*	AF
09024				*FGZZ*	AF
09025		C		*FGZZ*	EH
Victory					
09026		C	★	*DCSB*	EH

CLASS 20 TYPE 1 BO-BO

Built: English Electric 1957-68.
Engine: English Electric 8cyl, 4-stroke, 8SVT Mk2 of 1,000hp (746kW).
Weight: 73-74 tonnes.
Dimensions: 46.8ft L × 8.8ft W × 12.6ft H.
Brake force: 35 tonnes.
Maximum tractive effort: 42,000lb (187kN).
Power/control equipment: Four English Electric traction motors (see below); main generator EE819/3C.
Route availability: 5.
Fuel: 380gal, except *SC* 'x' 1,040gal.
Maximum operating speed: 60mph (originally 75mph).

Standard equipment: AWS, Multiple working (Blue star), Guard's emergency brake, Sanding gear, Single cab.
Special characteristics: Slow speed control (S), Transponder code transmitter (T), Snowplough brackets (K), One man operation (M), Radio Electronic Token Block (R), Remote control radio, experimental (N), Headlight (cab front only) (L) as shown.

Diagram	*Train Brake*	*Traction Motors*
20-0BX	Dual	EE526/5D
20-0DX	Dual	EE526/8D
20-0FX	Dual	EE526/8D

Sectors:

Departmental: **DCEA:** DCE Eastern. **DCMA:** DCE Midland. **DWCQ:** DMEE, General.

Railfreight: **FEGA:** Coal, Fife. **FEND:** Coal, East Midlands. **FENW:** Coal, West Coast route (Crewe). **FGXX:** Distribution, General (Speedlink). **FMGA:** Metals (Steel), Glasgow. **FMYI:** Metals (Steel), Immingham. **FTYT:** Chemicals, Thornaby.

Special livery: *Green:* 20030/64.

Loc No	Dia	SC	Liv	Pool	Dep
20004	BX	STM		FENW	TO
20005	BX	SM		DCMA	TO
20006	BX	STM		FENW	TO
20007	BX	SM		FENW	TO
20008	BX			FTYT	TE
20009	BX	M		FPLI	IM
20010	BX	SM	F	FENW	TO
20013	BX	SM		FENW	TO
20016	BX	STM		FENW	TO
20019	BX	SM		FENW	TO
20020	BX	STM		FENW	TO
20021	BX	SM		FENW	TO
20023	BX	SM	F	FENW	TO
20025	BX	M		FMYI	IM
20026	BX	STM		FEND	TO
20028	BX	SM		FMYT	TE
Bedale					
20029	BX	KM		DCMA	TO
20030	BX	KM	★	DCEA	IM
20031	BX	KM		FMYI	IM
20032	BX	SKM		DCMA	TO
20034	BX	SKM		DCMA	TO
20035	BX	M		FPLI	IM
20040	BX	SM		FENW	TO
20041	BX	STM		DCMA	TO
20042	BX	M		DCMA	TO
20043	BX	M		FMYI	IM
20044	BX	M		FMYI	IM
20045	BX	SM		FENW	TO
20046	BX	M		FMYI	IM
20047	BX	SM		FEND	TO
20048	BX	M		DCMA	TO
20051	DX	SM		FENW	TO
20052	DX	STM		FENW	TO
20053	DX	STM		FENW	TO
20054	DX	M		DCMA	TO
20055	DX	SM		FENW	TO
20056	DX	SM		FENW	TO
20057	DX	SM		FENW	TO
20058	DX	SMR		FENW	TO
20059	DX	SM	F	FEND	TO
20060	DX	SM		DCMA	TO
20061	DX	M		FMYI	IM
20063	DX	M		DCMA	TO
20064	DX	M	★	DCEA	IM
20065	DX	STM		FENW	TO
20066	DX	M		DWCQ	ED
20069	DX	M		FMYI	IM
20070	DX	SKM		DCMA	TO
20071	DX	SKM		FEND	TO
20072	DX	STKM		DCMA	TO
20073	DX	SKM		FENW	TO
20075	DX	SKM		FENW	TO
20078	DX	SKM		FENW	TO
20080	DX	STKM		FENW	TO
20081	DX	STKM		FEND	TO
20082	DX	STKM		FEND	TO
20083	DX	STKM		FGXX	TO
20084	DX	SXKM		FEND	TO
20085	DX	SKM		FEND	TO
20087	DX	SMKR		FENW	TO
20088	DX	SKM	F-	FEND	TO
20090	DX	SKM	F	FENW	TO
20092	DX	KM		FMYI	IM
20093	DX	KM		FMYI	IM
20094	DX	SKM		FEND	TO
20095	DX	KM		FMYI	IM
20096	DX	KM		DCEA	IM
20097	DX	KM		DCMA	TO
20098	DX	KM		FMYI	IM
20099	DX	STKM		DCMA	TO
20100	DX	KM		FGXX	TO
20101	DX	STK		DCMA	TO
20102	DX	KM		FMYI	IM
20103	DX	SKM		FEND	TO
20104	DX	SKM	F	FEND	TO
20105	DX	STKM		FEND	TO

Loc No	Dia	SC	Liv	Pool	Dep
20106	DX	SKM		FENW	TO
20107	DX	KM		FMYI	IM
20108	DX	SKM	F	FEND	TO
20110	DX	KM		FMYI	IM
20112	DX	KM		FMYI	IM
20113	DX	STKM		FENW	TO
20114	DX	KMRL		DCHB	ED
20117	DX	SKM		FENW	TO
20118	DX	KM		FTYT	TE
	Saltburn-on-the-Sea				
~~20119~~	DX	KM		FTYT	TE
20120	DX	SKM		FENW	TO
20121	DX	SKM		FENW	TO
20122	DX	KM	F	FTYT	TE
	Cleveland Potash				
20124	DX	K		DCMA	TO
20126	DX	KM		FMYI	IM
20127	DX	KMRL		DCHB	ED
20128	DX	SKM		FEND	TO
20129	FX	SKM		FEND	TO
20130	FX	SKM		FENW	TO
20131	FX	SKM		FEND	TO
20132	FX	SKM	F	FENW	TO
20133	FX	SKM		FEND	TO
20134	FX	SKM		FEND	TO
20135	FX	SKM		FENW	TO
20136	FX	SKM		FEND	TO
20137	FX	KM	F	FTYT	TE
	Murray B. Hofmeyr				
~~20138~~	FX	KMRL	F	DCHB	ED
20139	FX	K		DCMA	TO
20140	FX	SKM		FEND	TO
20141	FX	SKM	F	FENW	TO
20142	FX	SKM		FEND	TO
20143	FX	SKM		FENW	TO
~~20144~~	FX	K		FTYT	TE
20145	FX	KM		FPLI	IM
20146	FX	K		DWCQ	ED
20147	FX	SKM		DCMA	TO
20148	FX	KM		DWCQ	ED
20151	FX	SKM		FEND	TO
20154	FX	SKM		FEND	TO
20156	FX	KM	F	FTYT	TE
	HMS Endeavour				

Loc No	Dia	SC	Liv	Pool	Dep
20157	FX	SKM		FEND	TO
20158	FX	SKM		DCMA	TO
20159	FX	SKM		FENW	TO
20160	FX	SK		DCMA	TO
20163	FX	SKM	F	FEND	TO
20165	FX	K	F	FTYT	TE
	Henry Pease				
~~20166~~	FX	SKM		FEND	TO
20168	FX	SKM		FENW	TO
20169	FX	SKM		FENW	TO
20170	FX	SKM	F	FEND	TO
20171	FX	KM		FPLI	IM
20172	FX	SKM		FMYT	TE
	Redmire				
20173	FX	SKM		FGXX	TO
20175	FX	SKM	F	FENW	TO
20176	FX	K		DCMA	TO
20177	FX	SKM		FEND	TO
20178	FX	SKM		FENW	TO
20179	FX	SKM	F	FEGA	ED
20182	FX	SKM		FEND	TO
20183	FX	SKM		FENW	TO
20185	FX	K		FGXX	IM
20186	FX	SKM		FEND	TO
20187	FX	SK		FEND	TO
20188	FX	SKM		FENW	TO
20189	FX	M		FGXX	TO
20190	FX	SKM		FEND	TO
20192	FX	SKM		FEGA	ED
20193	FX	SKM		FEGA	ED
20194	FX	SKM		FEND	TO
20195	FX	SK		DCMA	TO
20196	FX	SKM		FEND	TO
20197	FX	SKM		FENW	TO
20198	FX	SKM		FEGA	ED
20199	FX	SKM		FEGA	ED
20202	FX	SKM		DCEA	ED
20203	FX	SKM		FEGA	ED
20204	FX	SKM		DWCQ	ED
20205	FX	SKM		FEGA	ED
20206	FX	SKM		FEGA	ED
20208	FX	SKML		FEGA	ED
20209	FX	SK		DCMA	TO
20210	FX	SKM		FEND	TO
20211	FX	SKM		FEGA	ED

Loc No	Dia	SC	Liv	Pool	Dep
20212	FX	SKM		FEGA	ED
20213	FX	SKM		FEGA	ED
20214	FX	SKM		FEND	TO
20215	FX	SKM	F	FEND	TO
20217	FX	SKM		DCMA	TO
20218	FX	KM		FGXX	TO
20219	FX	SKM		FGXX	TO
20224	FX	KM		FGXX	TO
20225	FX	SKM		FGXX	TO
20226	FX	KM		FPLI	IM
20227	FX	KM	F	DWCQ	ED
20228	FX	KML		FGXX	IM

CLASS 26/0 TYPE 2 BO-BO

Built: Birmingham RC&W Ltd 1958-59.
Engine: Sulzer 6cyl, 4-stroke, 6LDA28B of 1,160hp (865kW).
Weight: 75-77 tonnes.
Dimensions: 50.8ft L × 8.8ft W × 12.7ft H.
Brake force: 35 tonnes.
Maximum tractive effort: 42,000lb (187kN).
Power/control equipment: Four Crompton Parkinson C171 A1 traction motors; main generator Crompton Parkinson CG391 A1.
Route availability: 6.
Fuel: 500gal.
Train brakes: Dual Air and Vacuum.
Maximum operating speed: 75mph.
Diagram: 26-0AX.
Standard equipment: Multiple working (Blue star), One man operation (M), Sanding gear.
Special characteristics: Slow speed control (S) as shown.

Sectors:
Departmental: **DCHA:** DCE Scottish Region. **DWCQ:** DMEE, General.
Railfreight: **FEGB:** Coal, Lothians.

Loc No	Dia	SC	Liv	Pool	Dep
26001	AX	S	F	FEGB	ED
26002	AX	S	F	FEGB	ED
26003	AX	S	F	FEGB	ED
26004	AX	S	F	FEGB	ED
26005	AX	S	F	FEGB	ED
26006	AX	S	F	FEGB	ED
26007	AX	S	F	FEGB	ED
26008	AX		F	FEGB	ED
26010	AX		F	DWCQ	ED
26011	AX			DCHA	ED
26014	AX			DCHA	ED
26015	AX			DCHA	ED

CLASS 26/1 TYPE 2 BO-BO

Built: Birmingham RC&W Ltd 1959.
Engine: Sulzer 6cyl, 4-stroke, 6LDA28B of 1,160hp (865kW).
Weight: 75 tonnes.
Dimensions: 50.8ft L × 8.8ft W × 12.7ft H.
Brake force: 35 tonnes.
Maximum tractive effort: 42,000lb (187kN).

Power/control equipment: Four Crompton Parkinson C171 A1 traction motors; main generator Crompton Parkinson CG391 A1.
Route availability: 5.
Fuel: 500gal.
Train brakes: Dual Air and Vacuum.
Maximum operating speed: 75mph.
Standard equipment: Multiple working (Blue Star), One man operation (m). Sanding gear, Snowplough brackets (k).
Diagram: 26-1CX.

Sectors:
Departmental: **DCHA:** DCE Scottish Region. **DWCQ:** DMEE, General.
Railfreight: **FGWS:** Distribution (Speedlink), Eastfield.

Loc No	*Dia*	*SC*	*Liv*	*Pool*	*Dep*
26021	DX			*DCHA*	ED
26023	DX			*DCHA*	ED
26024	DX			*DCHA*	ED
26025	DX		F	*FGWS*	ED
26026	DX		F	*DCHA*	ED
26027	DX			*DCHA*	ED
26028	DX			*DCHA*	ED
26031	DX		F	*FGWS*	ED
26032	DX		F	*FGWS*	ED
26034	DX		F	*FGWS*	ED
26035	DX		F	*DCHA*	ED
26036	DX			*DCHA*	ED
26037	DX		F	*FGWS*	ED
26038	DX		F	*FGWS*	ED
26039	DX			*DCHA*	ED
26040	DX		F	*FGWS*	ED
26041	DX		F	*FGWS*	ED
26042	DX			*DWCQ*	ED
26043	DX			*DWCQ*	ED
26046	DX			*DWCQ*	ED

CLASS 31/1 TYPE 2 A1A-A1A

Built: Brush Traction 1959-62.
Engine: English Electric 12cyl, 4-stroke, 12SVT of 1,470hp (1,097kW).
Weight: 49 tonnes.
Dimensions: 56.8ft L × 8.8ft W × 12.6ft H.
Power/control equipment: Four Brush traction motors TM73-68, main generator Brush TG160-48.
Route availability: 5.
Fuel: 530gal except *SC* 'x' 1,230gal.
Train brake: Dual Air and Vacuum.
Maximum operating speed: 75mph. (Diagram 31-1GX originally 80mph, others 90mph).
Train heating: Not operational. (Diagram 31-1CX retains Spanner Swirlyflow Mk 1 1,500lb/hr steam generator isolated and 100gal boiler fuel tank.)
Water tank: 600gal.
Standard equipment: AWS, Multiple Working (Blue star), One man operation (M), Sanding gear.
Special characteristics: Snowplough brackets (K), Headlight (L) as shown.

Diagram	*Weight*	*Maximum Tractive Effort*	
31-1CX	111 tonnes	35,900lb	(Boiler fitted)
31-1FX	108 tonnes	35,900lb	
31-1GX	108 tonnes	42,800lb	

Sectors:

Departmental: **DCAA:** DCE Anglia. **DCEA:** DCE Eastern. **DCMA:** DCE Midland. **DWCQ:** DMEE General.

Railfreight: **FALG:** Construction, Stone, Stratford. **FAMA:** Construction, Stone, Thornaby. **FGWC:** Distribution (Speedlink), Tinsley. **FHHA:** Flask, Crewe. **FPLI:** Petroleum, Immingham. **FTLC:** Chemicals, Crewe.

Loc No	*Dia*	*SC*	*Liv*	*Pool*	*Dep*
31101	FX			*DWCQ*	IM
31102	FX	L	F	*FGWC*	TI
31105	GX		F	*DWCQ*	SF
31106	GX			*DWCQ*	BS
31107	FX		F	*DCMA*	BS
31108	FX		F	*FGWC*	TI
31110	FX		F	*FGWC*	TI
31112	GX		F	*DCMA*	BS
31113	FX		F	*FGWC*	TI
31116	FX	L	F	*FALG*	SF
31118	FX	K		*DCEA*	TE
31119	FX		F	*DCMA*	BS
31120	FX	K	F	*FHHA*	CD
31123	FX	K		*DCEA*	TE
31124	FX			*DCMA*	BS
31125	FX	K	F	*FGWC*	TI
31126	FX	LK	F	*FGWC*	TI
31127	CX			*DCAA*	SF
31128	FX		F	*FALG*	SF
31130	FX	L	F	*FHHA*	CD
31131	CX			*DWCQ*	TE
31132	FX	LK	F	*FGWC*	TI
31134	FX		F	*FALG*	SF
31135	FX		F	*DWCQ*	BS
31138	FX			*DCMA*	BS
31141	FX			*DCMA*	BS
31142	FX	K	F	*FGWC*	TI
31143	FX		F	*FGWC*	TI
31144	FX		F	*FGWC*	TI
31145	FX		F	*FGWC*	TI
31146	FX	LK	F	*FGWC*	TI
31147	FX		F	*FGWC*	TI
31149	FX		F	*DCMA*	BS
31152	CX			*DCMA*	BS
31154	FX		F	*FPLI*	IM
31155	FX		F	*FGWC*	TI
31156	FX			*FPLI*	IM
31158	FX		F	*FGWC*	TI
31159	FX		F	*FGWC*	TI
31160	FX	LK	F	*FGWC*	TI
31162	CX			*DCMA*	BS
31163	FX		F	*FGWC*	TI
31164	FX	LK	F	*FGWC*	TI
31165	FX			*DCAA*	SF
31166	FX		F	*FGWC*	TI
31168	CX			*DCMA*	BS
31170	CX			*DCEA*	IM
31171	FX	L	F	*FGWC*	TI
31173	CX			*DCAA*	SF
31174	FX		F	*FGWC*	TI
31178	FX		F	*DCMA*	BS
31180	FX		F	*FGWC*	TI
31181	FX		F	*DCAA*	SF
31184	FX	L	F	*FAMA*	TE
31185	FX		F	*FPLI*	IM
31186	FX		F	*DCAA*	SF
31187	FX		F	*DCAA*	SF
31188	FX		F	*FPLI*	IM
31189	CX			*DWCQ*	SF
31190	FX		F	*DCAA*	SF
31191	FX		F	*DCAA*	SF
31196	FX		F	*DWCQ*	IM
31198	FX		F	*FALG*	SF
31199	FX		F	*FPLI*	IM
31200	FX	K	F	*FHHA*	CD
31201	FX		F	*FPLI*	IM
31203	FX	L	F	*FPLI*	IM
31205	FX		F	*DWCQ*	IM
31206	FX			*DWCQ*	IM
31207	FX	L	F	*FPLI*	IM
31208	CX			*DCEA*	IM
31209	FX		F	*FALG*	SF
31210	FX	K	F	*FPLI*	IM
31212	CX			*FPLI*	IM
31215	FX		F	*FAMA*	TE
31217	FX		F	*FHHA*	CD
31219	FX		F	*DCAA*	SF
31221	FX			*DCEA*	IM

Loc No	Dia	SC	Liv	Pool	Dep
31223	CX			*FPLI*	IM
31224	FX		F	*DCAA*	SF
31225	CX			*FPLI*	IM
31226	FX		F	*FALG*	SF
31227	FX			*FPLI*	IM
31229	FX	LK	F	*FAMA*	TE
31230	GX	L	F	*DWCQ*	BS
31231	CX			*DCAA*	SF
31232	FX		F	*DWCQ*	IM
31233	FX		F	*FPLI*	IM
31234	FX		F	*FALG*	SF
31235	FX		F	*DCMA*	BS
31237	FX		F	*DCMA*	BS
31238	FX		F	*FPLI*	IM
31240	FX		F	*FALG*	SF
31242	FX		F	*DCEA*	IM
31243	FX		F	*FPLI*	IM
31247	FX		F	*DCEA*	IM
31248	FX		F	*FGWC*	TI
31249	CX			*FPLI*	IM
31250	FX		F	*DCAA*	SF
31252	FX		F	*DWCQ*	BS
31255	FX		F	*DWCQ*	BS
31257	CX			*DCMA*	BS
31259	CX	K		*FGWC*	TI
31260	FX			*DWCQ*	TE
31263	FX		F	*DCAA*	SF
31264	CX			*DWCQ*	TE
31268	FX		F	*DCAA*	SF
31270	FX	LK	F	*FHHA*	CD
31271	FX	K	F	*DCMA*	BS
31272	FX		F	*DWCQ*	SF
31273	FX	K	F	*FPLI*	IM
31275	FX	K	F	*FHHA*	CD
31276	FX		F	*FHHA*	CD
Calder Hall Power Station					
31278	FX			*DCEA*	TE
31281	FX			*DCEA*	TE
31282	FX		F	*DCEA*	TE
31283	FX			*DCEA*	TE
31284	FX			*DCEA*	TE
31285	FX		F	*DCEA*	TE
31286	CX			*DWCQ*	TE
31288	FX			*DCMA*	BS
31289	FX			*DCMA*	BS
31290	FX	L	F	*DWCQ*	BS
31292	FX			*DWCQ*	BS
31293	CX			*DCMA*	BS
31294	FX	K	F	*FALG*	SF
31296	FX	L	F	*DCMA*	BS
Trên Nwyddau Amlwch, Amlwch Freighter					
31299	FX		F	*FPLI*	IM
31301	FX		F	*DCMA*	BS
31302	FX		F	*FPLI*	IM
31304	FX	LK	F	*FPLI*	IM
31305	CX			*DCMA*	BS
31306	FX	L	F	*FALG*	SF
31308	FX		F	*FALG*	SF
31309	CX			*LNRD*	TI
Cricklewood					
31311	FX			*DCMA*	BS
31312	FX	K	F	*FHHA*	CD
31317	FX	LK	F	*DCMA*	BS
31319	FX	LK	F	*FPLI*	IM
31320	FX			*DCAA*	SF
31322	FX			*DCMA*	BS
31323	CX			*DWCQ*	SF
31324	FX		F	*FHHA*	CD
31327	FX		F	*FALG*	SF
Phillips-Imperial					

CLASS 31/4 TYPE 2 A1A-A1A

Built: Brush Traction 1959-62.
Engine: English Electric 12cyl, 4-stroke, 12SVT of 1,470hp (1,097kW).
Brake force: 49 tonnes.
Maximum tractive effort: 35,900lb.
Dimensions: 56.8ft L × 8.8ft W × 12.6ft H.

Power/control equipment: Four Brush traction motors TM73-68, main generator Brush TG160-48.
Route availability: 5.
Fuel: 530gal.
Train brake: Dual Air and Vacuum.
Maximum operating speed: 90mph.
Train heating: Brush electric alternator BL100-30 driven by main engine 320kW.
ETH Index: 66.
Water tanks: 600gal.
Standard equipment: AWS, Multiple working (Blue star), One man operation (M), Sanding gear.
Special characteristics: Headlights (L) as shown.

Diagram	*Weight*
31-4CX	109 tonnes

Sectors:
Departmental: **DCEA:** DCE Eastern. **DCMA:** DCE Midland. **DCQA:** DCE BRB HQ. **DWCQ:** DMEE General.
Railfreight: **FGWC:** Distribution (Speedlink), Tinsley. **FPLI:** Petroleum, Immingham.
Provincial: **PXXA:** General.
Parcels: **RXLB:** General.
Special livery: Dark blue 31413/430

Loc No	*Dia*	*SC*	*Liv*	*Pool*	*Dep*
31400	CX			*RXLB*	CD
31402	CX			*FGWC*	TI
31403	CX			*DCWA*	OC
31404	CX			*RXLB*	CD
31405	CX	L		*RXLB*	CD
31406	CX			*RXLB*	CD
31407	CX			*RXLB*	CD
31408	CX			*RXLB*	CD
31409	CX			*RXLB*	CD
31410	CX			*RXLB*	CD
31411	CX			*DCMA*	CD
31412	CX	L		*DCQA*	CD
31413	CX		★	*DWCQ*	BS
Severn Valley Railway					
31414	CX	L		*DCQA*	CD
31415	CX			*DWCQ*	BS
31416	CX			*DCQA*	CD
31417	CX			*DWCQ*	BS
31418	CX			*RXLB*	CD
31419	CX			*RXLB*	CD
31420	CX			*DCMA*	BS
31421	CX			*RXLB*	CD
31422	CX			*RXLB*	CD
31423	CX	L		*RXLB*	CD
31424	CX			*RXLB*	CD
31425	CX			*RXLB*	CD
31426	CX			*DCQA*	CD
31427	CX			*RXLB*	CD
31428	CX			*RXLB*	CD
North Yorkshire Moors Railway					
31429	CX			*RXLB*	CD
31430	CX		★	*DCMA*	BS
Sister Dora					
31431	CX			*DCEA*	IM
31432	CX			*DCEA*	IM
31433	CX			*DCMA*	BS
31434	CX			*DCMA*	BS
31435	CX			*DCMA*	BS
31437	CX			*DCMA*	BS
31438	CX			*RXLB*	CD
31439	CX			*DCEA*	IM
31441	CX			*DCEA*	IM
31442	CX			*RXLB*	CD
31443	CX			*RXLB*	CD
31444	CX			*DCEA*	IM
Keighley and Worth Valley Railway					
31445	CX			*DCMA*	BS
31446	CX			*DCMA*	BS
31447	CX	L		*DCEA*	IM
31448	CX	L		*RXLB*	CD

Loc No	Dia	SC	Liv	Pool	Dep
31449	CX	L		*DCEA*	IM
31450	CX	L		*RXLB*	CD
31451	CX	L		*RXLB*	CD
31452	CX	L		*DCEA*	IM
31453	CX	L		*DCEA*	IM
31454	CX	L		*RXLB*	CD
31455	CX	L		*RXLB*	CD
31456	CX			*DCEA*	IM
31457	CX			*DWCQ*	IM
31458	CX			*DCEA*	IM
31459	CX			*RXLB*	CD

Loc No	Dia	SC	Liv	Pool	Dep
31460	CX			*DCEA*	IM
31461	CX			*DWCQ*	IM
31462	CX			*DCWA*	OC
31463	CX			*DCWA*	OC
31464	CX			*RXLB*	CD
31465	CX			*DWCQ*	BS
31466	CX			*FGWC*	TI
31467	CX			*FGWC*	TI
31468	CX			*DCMA*	CD
31469	CX	L		*DCEA*	IM

CLASS 33/0 TYPE 3 BO-BO

Built: Birmingham RC&W Ltd 1960-62.
Engine: Sulzer 8cyl, 4-stroke, 8LDA28 of 1,550hp (1,156kW).
Weight: 77 tonnes.
Dimensions: 50.8ft L × 9.3ft W × 12.7ft H.
Brake force: 35 tonnes.
Maximum tractive effort: 45,000lb.
Power/control equipment: Four Crompton Parkinson C171C2 traction motors; main generator Crompton Parkinson CG391B1.
Route availability: 6.
Fuel: 750gal.
Train brake: Dual Air and Vacuum.
Maximum operating speed: 85mph.
Train heating: Electric generator Crompton Parkinston CAG392A1 driven by engine, 235kW at 750V dc for heating only Mk 1, Mk 2a, b, c, d stock. *SC* 'U': Not maintained in working order.
ETH Index: 48 (except *SC* 'U').
Diagram: 33-0AX.
Standard equipment: Multiple working (blue star), One man operation (M), Snowplough brackets (K), Sanding gear.
Special characteristic: Train heating isolated (U).

Sectors:
Departmental: **DCSA:** Civil Engineer, Southern.
Railfreight: **FALS:** Construction, Stone, Southern. **FPXX:** Petroleum, General. **FXXA:** General.
Network SouthEast: **NSSB:** Solent and Sarum.
Special livery: *Green:* 33008.

Loc No	Dia	SC	Liv	Pool	Dep
33002	AX	U		*DCSA*	EH
33004	AX			*DCSA*	SL
33006	AX			*DCSA*	EH
33008	AX		★	*FALS*	EH
Eastleigh					
33009	AX			*FALS*	EH

Loc No	Dia	SC	Liv	Pool	Dep
33011	AX			*FALS*	SL
33012	AX			*FALS*	EH
33013	AX	U		*DCSA*	EH
33015	AX			*DCSA*	EH
33016	AX			*FALS*	SL
33019	AX			*FXXA*	SL
33020	AX			*FALS*	EH

Loc No	Dia	SC	Liv	Pool	Dep
33021	AX		FA	FALS	SL
33022	AX			FALS	SL
33023	AX			DCSA	EH
33025	AX			DCSA	EH
33026	AX			DCSA	EH
33027	AX			FALS	SL
Earl Mountbatten of Burma					
33029	AX			FALS	SL
33030	AX			DCSA	EH
33031	AX			FALS	SL
33033	AX			FALS	SL
33035	AX			FXXA	SL
33039	AX			FXXA	SL
33040	AX			FALS	SL
33042	AX	U		FALS	SL
33046	AX	U		FXXA	SL
33047	AX	U		FALS	SL
33048	AX			DCSA	SL
33050	AX		FA	FALS	SL
Isle of Grain					
33051	AX		FA	FALS	SL
Shakespeare Cliff					
33052	AX			FXXA	SL
Ashford					
33053	AX		FA	FALS	SL
33055	AX			FALS	SL
33056	AX	U	FA	FALS	SL
The Burma Star					
33057	AX	U		FALS	SL
33058	AX			FXXA	SL
33060	AX			FALS	SL
33063	AX	U		FXXA	SL
33064	AX		FA	DCSA	EH
33065	AX			DCSA	EH

CLASS 33/1 TYPE 3 BO-BO

Specification as Class 33/0 above except as follows:
Built: 1960-61.
Weight: 78 tonnes.
Diagram: 33-1AX.
Standard equipment (additional): Buck-eye couplings (E), Flashlight adaptor (for Weymouth Quay line).

Special Characteristics: Push-Pull cabling for working in multiple with Buck-eye coupling fitted dc EMUs and Class 438 stock (P).

Sectors:
Departmental: **DCSA:** Civil Engineer, Southern.
Network SouthEast: **NSSB:** Solent and Sarum.
Parcels: **RXLA:** General.

Loc No	Dia	SC	Liv	Pool	Dep
33101	AX	P		NSSB	EH
33102	AX	PU		NSSB	EH
33103	AX	P		NSSB	EH
33106	AX	P		NSSB	EH
33107	AX	U		DCSA	EH
33108	AX	P		RXLC	EH
33109	AX	P		RXLC	EH
33110	AX	PU		DCSA	EH

Loc No	Dia	SC	Liv	Pool	Dep
33111	AX	P		RXLC	EH
33113	AX	P		RXLC	EH
33114	AX	P		NSSB	EH
Sultan					
33115	AX	P		RXLC	EH
33116	AX	P		RXLC	EH
33117	AX	P		DCSA	EH
33118	AX	P		DCSA	EH
33119	AX	P		RXLC	EH

CLASS 33/2 TYPE 3 BO-BO

Specification as Class 33/0 above except as follows:
Built: 1962.
Weight: 77 tonnes.
Dimensions: 50.8ft L × 8.7ft W × 12.7ft H.
Diagram: 33-2AX.
Standard equipment (additional): Slow speed control,(s).

Sectors:
Departmental: **DCSA:** Civil Engineer, Southern.
Railfreight: **FALS:** Construction, Stone, Southern. **FGWD:** Distribution (Speedlink), Dover Linkspan.
Footnote: 33205 was numbered 33302 for a few months during 1988.

Loc No	Dia	SC	Liv	Pool	Dep
33201	AX			DCSA	SL
33203	AX		FG	FGWD	SL
33204	AX			DCSA	SL
33205	AX		FG	FGWD	SL
33206	AX		FG	FGWD	SL
33207	AX			DCSA	SL
33208	AX			FALS	SL
33209	AX			DCSA	SL
33211	AX			FALS	SL

CLASS 37/0 TYPE 3 CO-CO

Built: English Electric 1960-65.
Engine: English Electric 12cyl, 4-stroke, 12CVST of 1,750hp (1,306kW).
Weight: see below.
Dimensions: 61.5ft L × 8.8ft W *Height:* First series 12.9ft (except *SC* 'h'), Second series 13.1ft.
Brake force: 50 tonnes.
Maximum tractive effort: 55,500lb (247kN).
Power/control equipment: Six English Electric traction motors EE538/A; main generator EE Type 822/10G.
Train heating: Not operational. (Some retain Clayton RO2500 Steam General, 2,500lb/hr, isolated and 800gal water tank — see below.)
Train brakes: Dual air and vacuum.
Route availability: 5.
Fuel: see below.
Maximum operating speed: 80mph (originally 90 mph).
Standard equipment: AWS, Multiple working (Blue star), One man operation (M), Sanding gear.

Special characteristics: Radio electronic token block (R), Snowplough brackets (K), Headlight or spotlight (L), Revised height 13.1ft (H) as shown.

First series built with end doors and two part route indicator boxes, some since replaced with sealed end and two marker lights. Second series built with electrical variations, four character route indicator boxes, now used for marker lights, and roof mounted horns.

Diagram	*Series*	*Weight*	*Fuel*
37-0CX	First	105 tonnes	890gal*
37-0DX	First	103 tonnes	890gal
37-0EX	Second	105 tonnes	890gal
37-0GX	Second	107 tonnes	890gal*
37-0JX	First	106 tonnes	1,690gal
37-0KX	Second	108 tonnes	1,690gal

*Steam generator fitted.

Sectors:

Departmental: **DCAA:** DCE Anglia. **DCHA:** DCE Scotland. **DCWA:** DCE Western.

Railfreight: **FEGA:** Coal, Fife. **FGWB:** Distribution (Speedlink), Tinsley. **FGXX:** Distribution (Speedlink), General. **FMCA:** Metals (Steel) Cardiff. **FMCH:** Metals (Steel), Cardiff (for HGR at Crewe Works). **FMGM:** Metals (Ore) Hunterston. **FMYI:** Metals (Steel), Immingham. **FMYT:** Metals, Thornaby. **FPGE:** Petroleum and Chemicals, Eastfield. **FPLW:** Petroleum, South Wales. **FQLC:** Distribution (Speedlink), Coal, Cardiff.

Freightliner: **LNRA:** General, Stratford.

Renumbering note: Locomotives 37310-26 are in the process of reverting to former numbers as follows: 37310 = 37152, 37311 = 37156, 37312 = 37137, 37313 = 37145, 37314 = 37190, 37320 = 37026, 37321 = 37037, 37322 = 37049, 37323 = 37088, 37324 = 37099, 37325 = 37108, 37326 = 37111.

Locomotives 37303, 37304, 37306 and 37308 will also be renumbered to Nos 37271-74 respectively.

Loc No	*Dia*	*SC*	*Liv*	*Pool*	*Dep*
37002	JX	XL	F	*FMYI*	IM
37003	JX	X		*FGWB*	TI
37004	DX			*LNRA*	SF
37009	JX	X		*FGWB*	TI
37010	DX			*FMGM*	ML
37012	CX	K		*LNRA*	SF
~~37013~~	JX	X		*FGWB*	TI
37015	JX	XL		*FGWB*	TI
37019	DX			*LNRA*	SF
37023	DX			*DCHA*	ED
37025	CX	K		*DCHA*	ED
37026					
37029	JX	X		*FGWB*	TI
37031	JX	XK		*FGWB*	TI
37035	CX	K		*FPGE*	ED
37037					
37038	DX			*LNRA*	SF
37040	DX			*FMGM*	ML
37042	JX	X		*FMYI*	IM
37046	DX			*FMYT*	TE
37047	CX			*LNRA*	SF
37048	DX			*FMYI*	IM
37049	CX			*FMGM*	ML
	Imperial				
37050	CX			*FMCH*	CF
37051	CX	K		*FMGM*	ML
37053	DX			*LNRA*	SF
37054	CX			*FMYI*	IM
37055	DX			*LNRA*	SF
~~37057~~	DX			*LNRA*	SF
37058	JX	X		*FGWB*	TI
37059	JX	X	FG	*LNRA*	TI
	Port of Tilbury				
37062	JX	X		*FGWB*	TI
37063	JX	X		*FGWB*	TI
~~37065~~	JX	X		*FGWB*	TI
37066	JX	X		*FGWB*	TI
37069	JX	X	F-	*FMYT*	TE
	Thornaby TMD				

Loc No	Dia	SC	Liv	Pool	Dep
37070	DX		FG	FGXX	IS
37071	JX	X		FGWB	TI
~~37072~~	JX	X		FGWB	TI
37073	JX	Xh		FGWB	TI
37074	DX	h		LNRA	SF
37075	DX		F-	FGWB	SF
37077	DX	K		LNRA	SF
~~37078~~	JX	X		FPLW	CF
37080	DX			FPGE	ED
37083	JX	X		FMYI	IM
37087	CX			LNRA	SF
37088					
37092	CX			FMGM	ML
37095	JX	X		FGWB	TI
37096	JX	X		FGWB	TI
37097	DX			DCHA	ED
37098	JX	X		FGWB	TI
37099					
37100	JX			LNRA	SF
~~37101~~	JX	X		FGWB	TI
37104	DX		Fx	LNRA	SF
37106	JX	X		FMYI	IM
37107	CX			LNRA	SF
37108					
37109	CX			FGXX	IS
37110	CX			FGXX	IS
37111					
37113	DX			FPGE	ED
37114	CX	TLK		FGXX	IS
	Dunrobin Castle				
37116	CX			LNRA	SF
~~37128~~	EX	K		LNRA	SF
37131	KX	X		FQLC	CF
37133	EX			DCWA	CF
37137					
~~37138~~	EX	TL		FALG	SF
37139	KX	X		FQLC	CF
~~37140~~	EX	TL		DCAA	SF
37141	EX			DCWA	CF
37142	EX			DCWA	CF
37144	EX	TL		FALG	SF
37145					
37146	EX			DCWA	CF
37152					
37153	EX	K		DCHA	IS
37154	EX	K		LNRA	SF

Loc No	Dia	SC	Liv	Pool	Dep
37156					
37158	EX	K		DCWA	CF
37162	KX	X		FQLC	CF
37167	KX	X		FQLC	CF
37170	EX	K		DCHA	ED
37174	EX	K		DCWA	CF
37175	EX	LK		DCHA	IS
37178	GX	K		LNRA	SF
37184	GX	K		FPGE	ED
37185	KX	XK		FGWB	TI
37188	GX	LK		FPGE	ED
	Jimmy Shand				
37190	GX	LK		FMGM	ML
	Dalzell				
37191	GX	LK		FPGE	ED
37194	KX	XK		FGWB	TI
37196	EX	K	F	FGXX	IS
37197	KX	XK		FMCA	CF
37198	KX	XK		FGWB	TI
37201	EX	K		FMGM	ML
37202	EX	K		FMYI	IM
37203	EX	K		FMYI	IM
37207	EX	K		DCWA	CF
37209	EX	K		LNRA	SF
~~37211~~	EX	K		FAWC	CF
37212	KX	XK		FQLC	CF
37213	KX	K		FQLC	CF
37214	KX	XK		FQLC	CF
37215	EX	K		DCWA	CF
37216	KX	XTLK		DCAA	SF
37217	KX	XK		FQLC	CF
~~37218~~	EX	K		FAWC	CF
37219	EX	TLK		FALG	SF
37220	KX	XK		FPLW	CF
37221	EX	K		FQLC	SF
37222	KX	XK		FQLC	CF
~~37223~~	KX	XK		FQLC	CF
37225	KX	XK		FMYI	IM
37227	KX	XK		FQLC	CF
37229	KX	XK	F-	FEGA	ED
37230	KX	XK		FQLC	CF
37232	EX	K		FPGE	ED
37235	KX	XK		FQLC	CF
	Coal Merchants' Association of Scotland				

Loc No	Dia	SC	Liv	Pool	Dep
37238	EX	K		LNRA	SF
37239	KX	XK		FQLC	CF
37240	KX	XK		FEGA	ED
37241	EX	K		FMYI	IM
37242	KX	XK		FGWB	TI
37244	KX	XK		FQLC	CF
37245	EX	K		FPGE	ED
37248	KX	XK		FPLW	CF
37250	KX	XK	F	FEGA	ED
37251	KX	XK		FGWB	TI
37252	EX	K		LNRA	SF
37254	KX	XK		FMCA	CF
37255	KX	XK	F	FMYI	IM
37258	KX	XK		FMYI	IM
37260	GX	TLK		FGXX	IS
Radio Highland					
37261	GX	TLK		DCHA	IS
Caithness					
37262	GX	TLK		DCHA	IS
Dounreay					
37263	GX	K		DCWA	CF
37264	GX	LK		DCWA	CF
37275	KX	XK		FMYI	IM
37278	KX	XK		FMCA	CF
37280	KX	XK		FPLW	CF
37285	KX	XK	F-	FGWB	TI
37293	KX	XK		FMCA	CF
37294	KX	X		FQLC	CF
37298	KX	XK		FGWB	TI

Loc No	Dia	SC	Liv	Pool	Dep
37303	KX	XK		FGWB	TI
37304	KX	XK		FGWB	TI
37306	KX	XK		FPLW	CF
37308	KX	K		FQLC	CF
37310	EX	K		FMGM	ML
British Steel Ravenscraig					
37311	EX	K		FMGM	ML
British Steel Hunterston					
37312	EX			FMGM	ML
Clyde Iron					
37313	EX			FMGM	ML
37320	KX	XLK		FMGM	ML
Shap Fell					
37321	CX	LK		FMGM	ML
Gartcosh					
37323	CX	L		FMGM	ML
Clydesdale					
37324	CX	L		FMGM	ML
Clydebridge					
37325	CX	LK		FMGM	ML
Lanarkshire Steel					
37326	CX	K		FMGM	ML
Glengarnock					

CLASS 37/3 TYPE 3 CO-CO

Specification as Class 37/0 but fitted with refurbished bogies during 1987/88 at BREL Crewe.

Diagram	Series	Weight	Fuel
37-3AX	First	103 tonnes	890gal
37-3BX	First	106 tonnes	1,690gal
37-3CX	Second	105 tonnes	890gal
37-3DX	Second	108 tonnes	1,690gal

Sectors:
Departmental: **DCWA:** DCE Western Region.
Railfreight: **FAMM:** Construction (Stone), Motherwell. **FAMT:** Construction (Stone), Tinsley. **FGWB:** Distribution (Speedlink), Tinsley. **FMYI:** Metals (Steel) Immingham. **FPLX:** Petroleum, North Thames, Ripple Lane. **FQLC:** Distribution (Speedlink), Coal, Cardiff.
Special livery: *Green:* 37350.

Loco No	*Former No*	*Dia*	*SC*	*Liv*	*Pool*	*Dep*
37350	(37119)	BX	X	★	*FPLX*	SF
37351	(37002)					
37352	(37008)	BX	X	F	*FGWB*	TI
37353	(37032)	BX	X	F	*FGWB*	TI
~~37354~~	(37043)	AX	K	FA	*FALG*	SF
~~37355~~	(37045)	BX	X	F	*FGWB*	TI
37356	(37068)	BX	X	F	*FGWB*	TI
	Grainflow					
37357	(37079)	BX	X	F	*FGWB*	TI
37358	(37091)	AX			*LNRA*	SF
	P & O Containers					
37359	(37118)	CX	L	F	*FPGE*	ED

Loc No	*Former No*	*Dia*	*SC*	*Liv*	*Pool*	*Dep*
37370	(37127)	CX		F	*FAMM*	ML
37371	(37147)	DX	X	F	*FPLW*	CF
37372	(37159)	CX		F	*DCWA*	CF
37373	(37160)	CX		F	*FAMM*	ML
37374	(37165)	DX		F	*FQLC*	CF
37375	(37193)	DX		F	*FQLC*	CF
37376	(37199)	DX	XK	F	*FQLC*	CF
37377	(37200)	DX	XK	F	*FMYI*	IM
37378	(37204)	DX	XK	F	*FGWB*	TI
37379	(37226)	CX	K	F	*FAMM*	ML
37380	(37259)	CX	K	F-	*FAMT*	TI
37381	(37284)	DX	XK	FM	*FMYI*	IM

CLASS 37/4 TYPE 3 CO-CO

Built: English Electric 1965, ETH fitted 1985/86.
Engine: as Class 37/0.
Weight: 107 tonnes.
Dimensions: as Class 37/0 Second series.
Brake force, Maximum tractive effort, Train brakes, Route availability, Maximum operating speed: As Class 37/0.
Power/control equipment: Six English Electric traction motors EE538/A, main alternator Brush BA100SA.
Train heating: Electric, Brush alternator BAH 701.
ETH Index: 30.
Fuel: 1,689gal.
Diagram: 37-4AX.
Standard equipment: AWS, Headlight (L), Multiple working (Blue star), One man operation (M), Sanding gear, Snowplough brackets (K).
Special characteristics: Radio Electronic Token Block (R).

Sectors:
Departmental: **DCHA:** DCE Scotland.
Railfreight: **FAWC:** Construction (Stone), Cardiff. **FGXX:** Distribution (Speedlink), General. **FMGA:** Metals, Glasgow.
InterCity: **ICHA:** Charter. **IWCA:** West Coast main line.
Provincial: **PXXA:** General.

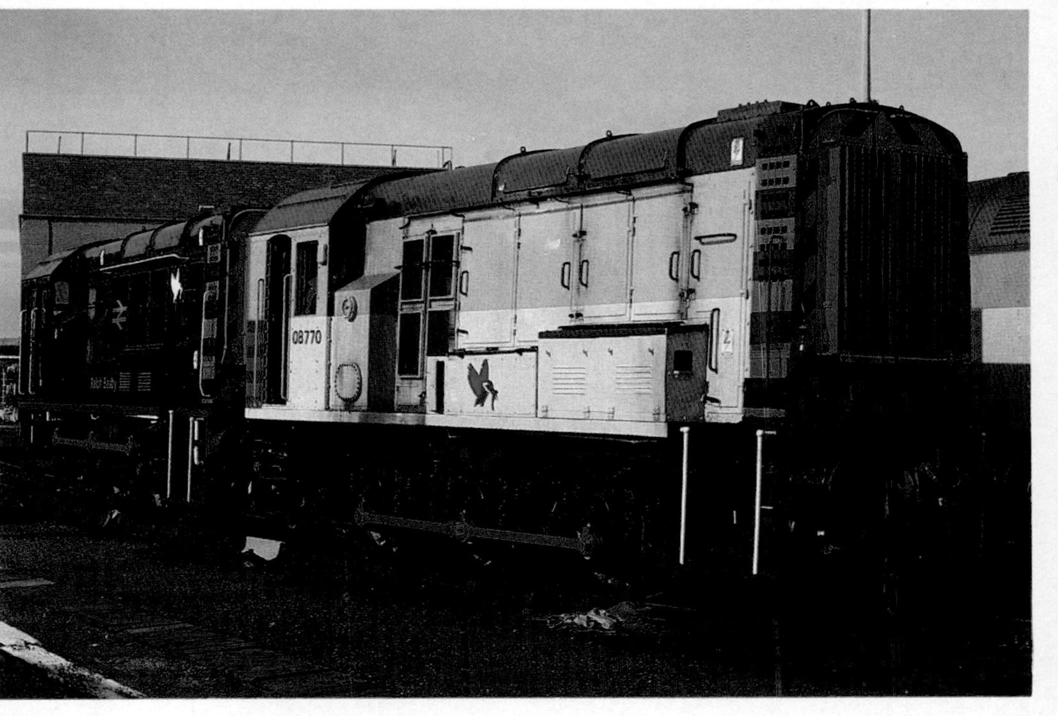

Class 08 0-6-0 No 08770 is seen carrying Railfreight livery, with No 08867 *Ralph Easby* behind. *Thomas Silsbury*

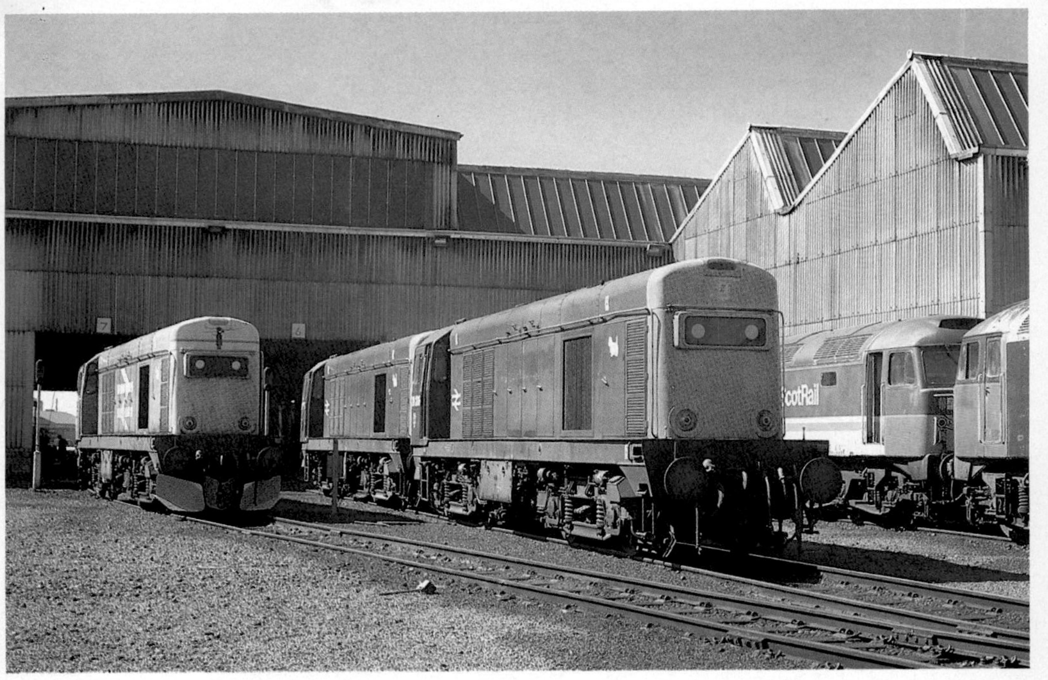

Eastfield TMD plays host to Class 20 B0-B0s Nos 20206, 20138 (in Railfreight livery) and 20211 on 12 June 1988.
Hugh Ballantyne

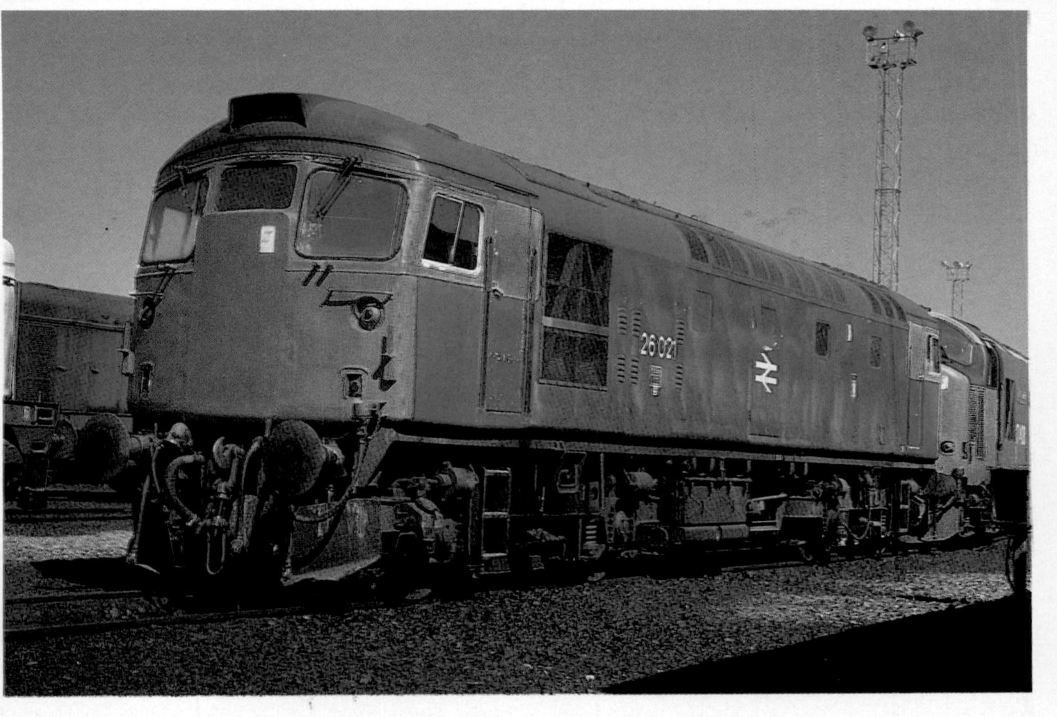

Class 26/1 B0-B0 No 26021 is seen at Eastfield TMD on 12 June 1988. *Hugh Ballantyne*

Class 31/1 A1A-A1A No 31196 still carried 'red stripe' Railfreight livery when it was photographed at Bristol Temple Meads on 22 December 1987. *John Chalcraft*

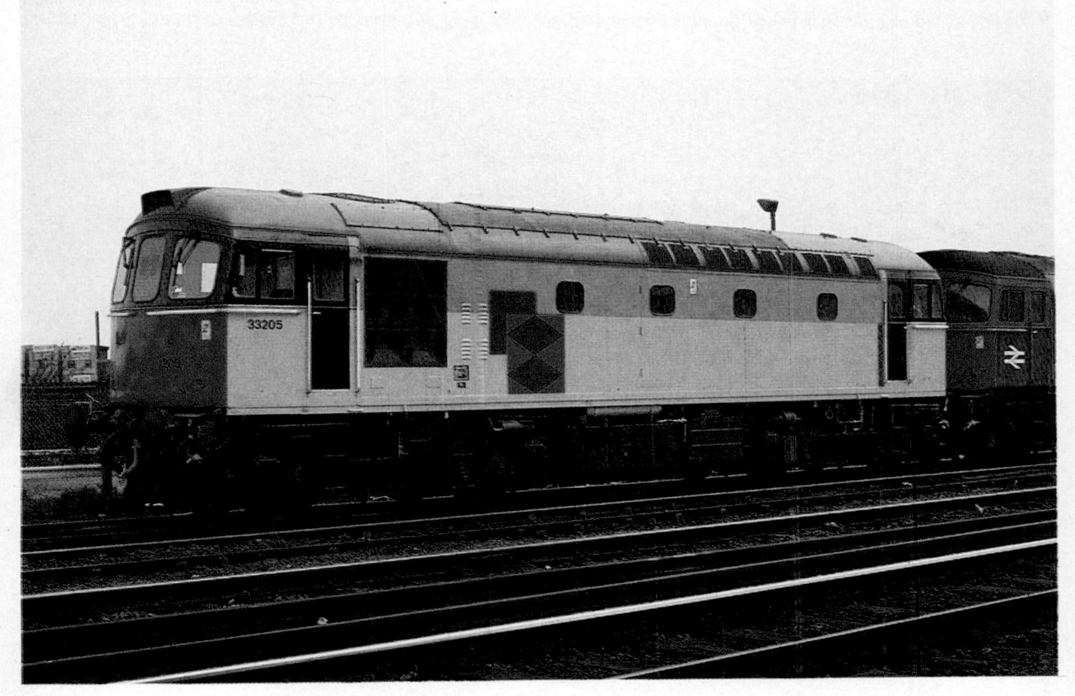

Class 33/2 B0-B0 No 33205 in Railfreight livery. *Brian Morrison*

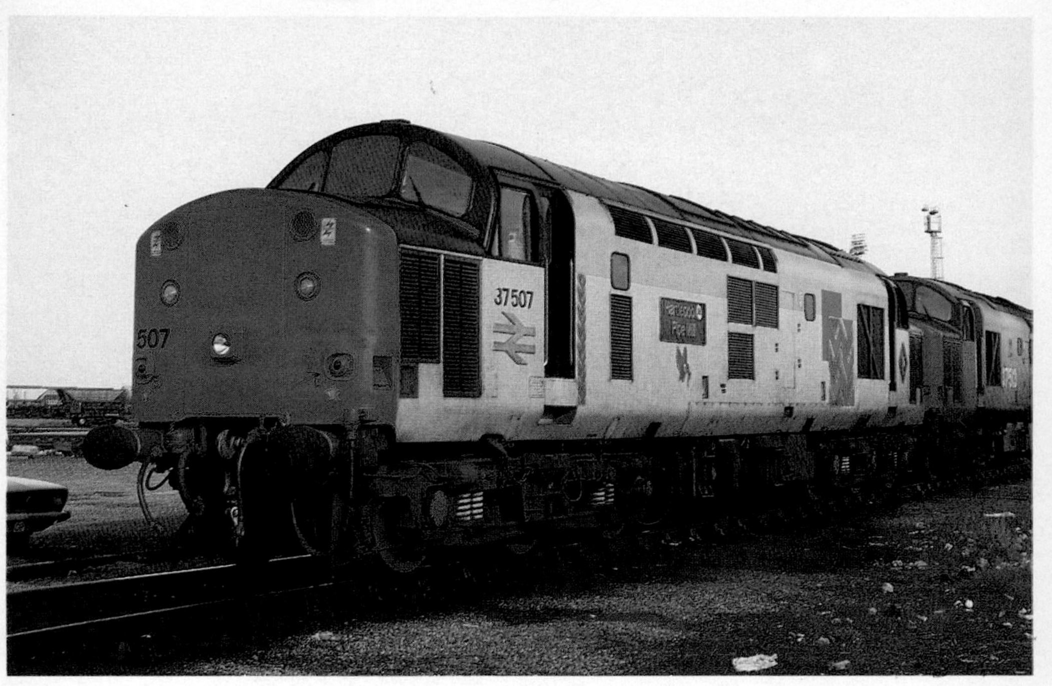

Class 37/5 C0-C0 No 37507 *BSC Hartlepool Pipe Mill* displays the latest Railfreight livery with Metals & Automotives sub-Sector symbols at Thornaby on 18 February 1988. *Barry Nicolle*

Class 45/1 'Peak' 1C0-C01 No 45106 is retained by the InterCity Sector for charter work, and is seen here at Wigan Springs Branch on 18 September 1988. The locomotive has been repainted in green livery, although the large nose-end numerals have since been painted out. *Hugh Ballantyne*

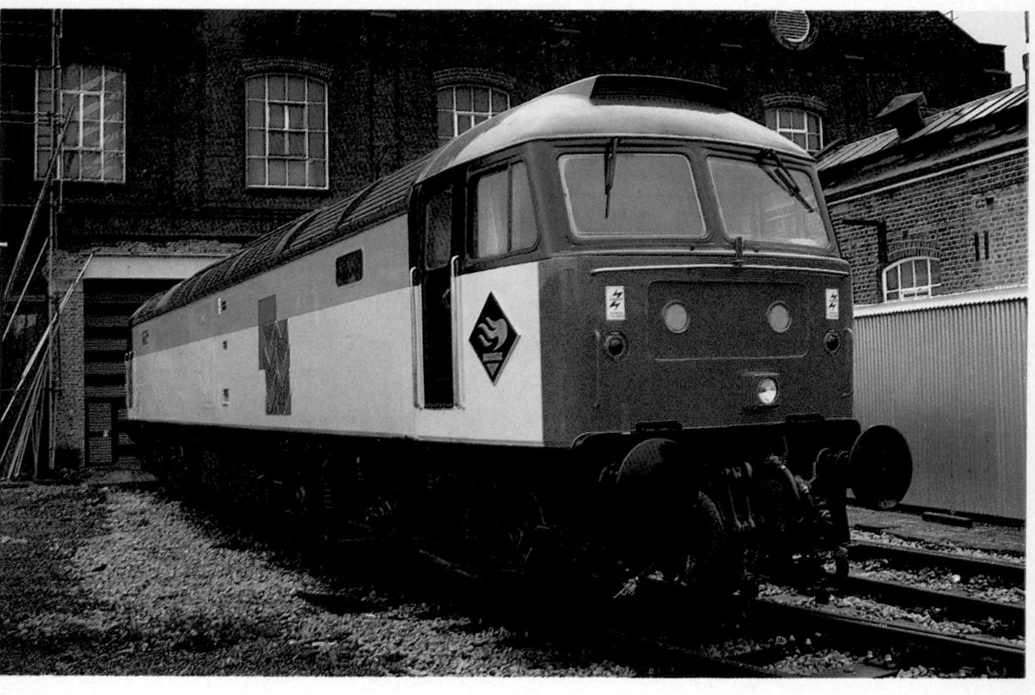

Class 47/0 No 47079 in Railfreight livery

The unique Class 50/1 C0-C0 No 50149 *Defiance* passes Golant with a china clay working to Carne Point on 4 May 1988.
Hugh Ballantyne

Class 56 C0-C0 No 56001 at Stratford. *John Augustson*

Model of the forthcoming Class 60 heavy freight locomotive. *Courtesy of Brush Traction*

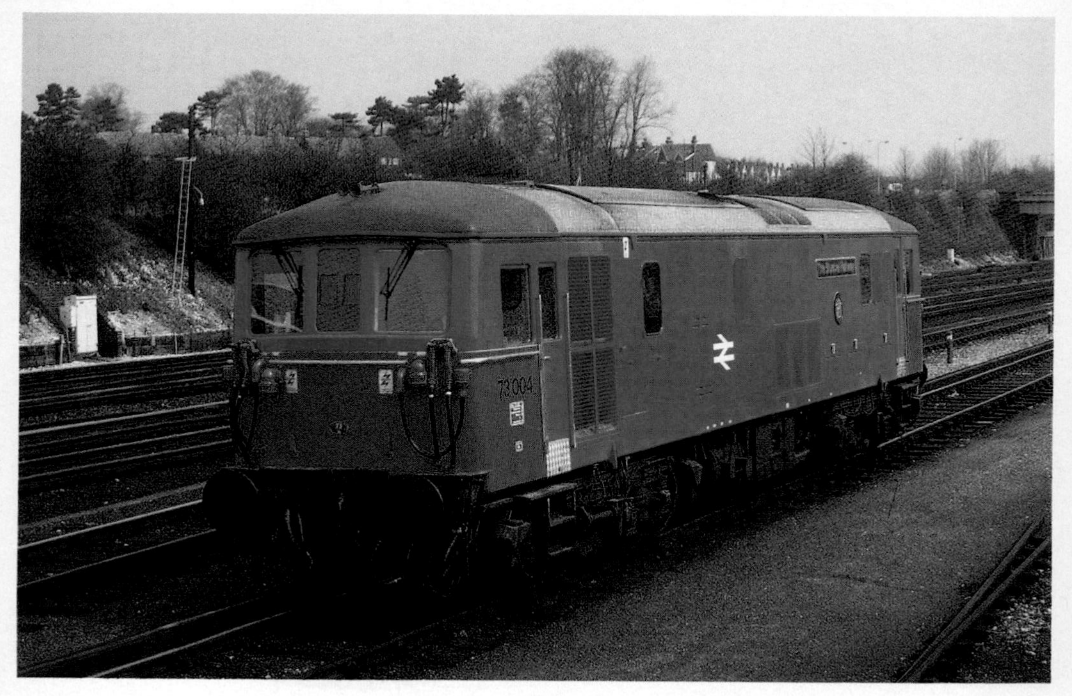

Class 73/0 electro-diesel No 73004 *The Bluebell Railway* at Basingstoke on 5 April 1988. The Mid-Hants Railway has since been commemorated on No 73005. *John Chalcraft*

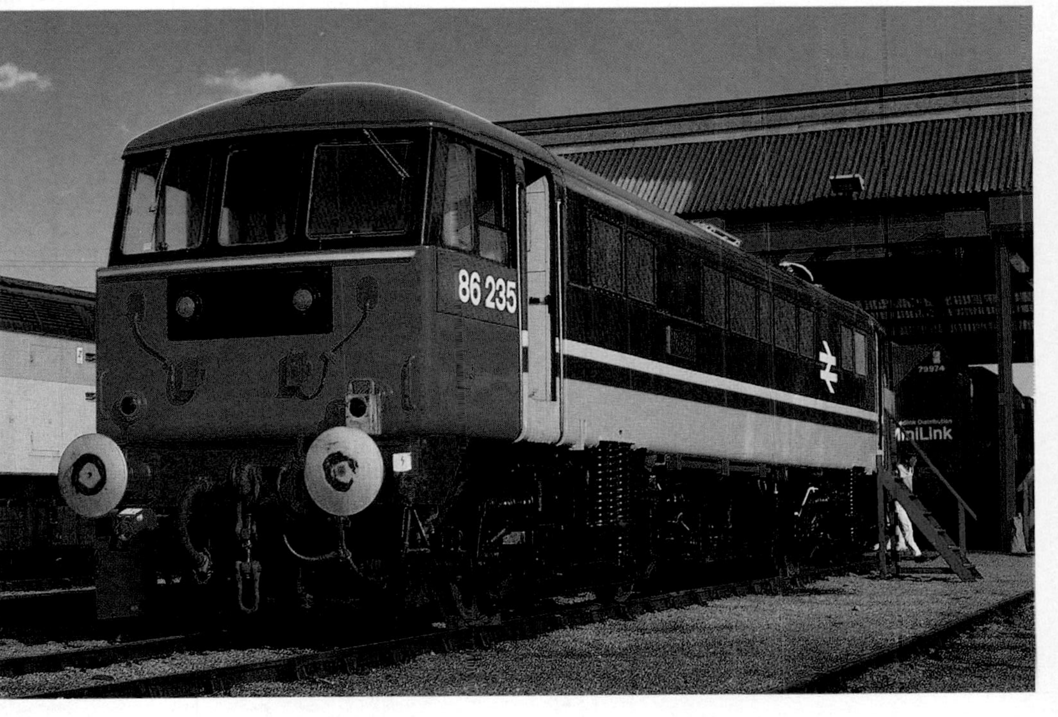

Class 86/2 B0-B0 No 86235 *Novelty* on display at Ripple Lane on 17 October 1987. *John Augustson*

Class 90 B0-B0 No 90005 is stabled in Platform 10 at Crewe station between test workings on 10 August 1988. *Kieran J. Platt*

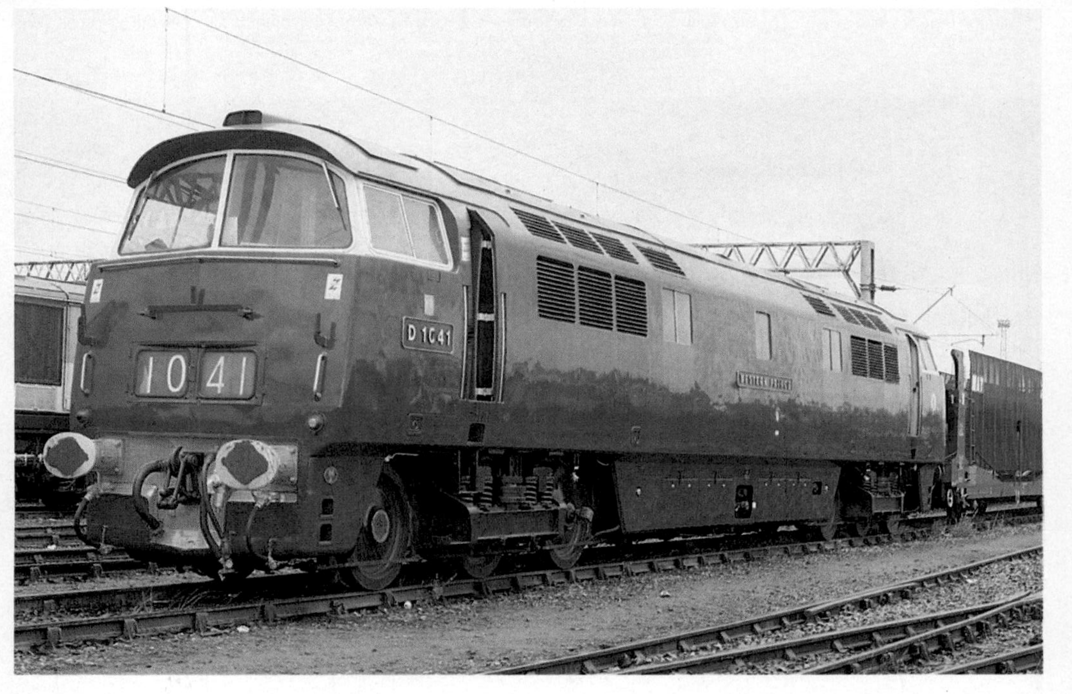

One of the star attractions at Bescot open day on 9 October 1988 was immaculately-preserved Class 52 'Western' C-C No D1041 *Western Prince*. *John Robinson*

HST power car No 43004, in the latest InterCity 'Swallow' livery with enlarged yellow end panel, passes Aller Junction with the 14.30 Penzance-Paddington on 9 August 1988. *Peter J. Robinson*

Loc No	Dia	SC	Liv	Pool	Dep	Name
37401	AX	RK	I	IWCA	ED	*Mary Queen of Scots*
37402	AX	RK		DCHA	ED	*Oor Wullie*
37403	AX	RK		PXXA	ED	*Glendarroch*
37404	AX	RK		FGXX	ED	*Ben Cruachan*
37405	AX	RK		PXXA	ED	*Strathclyde Region*
37406	AX	RK		FGXX	ED	*The Saltire Society*
37407	AX	RK		PXXA	ED	*Loch Long*
37408	AX	RK		PXXA	ED	*Loch Rannoch*
37409	AX	RK		ICHA	ED	*Loch Awe*
37410	AX	RK		FGXX	ED	*Aluminium 100*
37411	AX	RK		PXXA	ED	*Institution of Railway Signal Engineers*
37412	AX	RK		PXXA	ED	*Loch Lomond*
37413	AX	RK		FGXX	ED	*Loch Eil Outward Bound*
37414	AX	RK		PXXA	IS	
37415	AX	RK		PXXA	IS	
37416	AX	RK		PXXA	IS	
37417	AX	RK		PXXA	IS	*Highland Region*
37418	AX	RK		PXXA	IS	*An Comunn Gaidhealach*
37419	AX	RK		PXXA	IS	
37420	AX	RK		PXXA	IS	*The Scottish Hosteller*
37421	AX	RK		PXXA	IS	
37422	AX	RK		DCHA	ED	
37423	AX	RK	FM	FMGA	ED	*Sir Murray Morrison 1874-1948*
37424	AX	RK		ICHA	ED	*Isle of Mull*
37425	AX	RK		PXXA	ED	*Sir Robert MacAlpine, Concrete Bob*
37426	AX	K		FAWC	CF	*Y Lein Fach, Vale of Rheidol*
37427	AX	RK		PXXA	CF	*Bont Y Bermo*
37428	AX	RK		PXXA	CF	*David Lloyd George*
37429	AX	RK		PXXA	CF	*Eisteddfod Genedlaethol*
37430	AX	K		FAWC	CF	*Cwmbran*
37431	AX	K		FAWC	CF	*County of Powys, Sir Powys*

CLASS 37/5 TYPE 3 CO-CO

Built: English Electric 1960-65, refurbished BREL Crewe 1986-88.
Engine: English Electric 12cyl, 4-stroke, 12 CVST of 1,750hp (1,306kW).
Weight: 106-107 tonnes.
Dimensions, Brake force, Maximum tractive effort, Train brakes, Route availability: As Class 37/0.
Power/control equipment, Fuel, Standard equipment: As Class 37/4.
Train heating: Not equipped.
Maximum operating speed: 80mph.
Special characteristics: Slow speed control (s) as shown.

Diagram	*Series*
37-5AX	First
37-5CX	Second

Sectors:
Railfreight: **FAMT:** Construction, Stone, Tinsley. **FHCC:** Coal, Trainload, Cardiff. **FMYT:** Metals, Thornaby. **FTLL:** China clay, Laira.
Special livery: *British Steel blue:* 37501.

Loc No	*Former No*	*Dia*	*SC*	*Liv*	*Pool*	*Dep*
37501	(37005)	AX		★	*FMYT*	TE
	Teesside Steelmaster					
37502	(37082)	AX		F	*FMYT*	TE
	British Steel Teesside					
37503	(37017)	AX		F	*FMYT*	TE
	British Steel Shelton					
37504	(37039)	AX		F	*FMYT*	TE
	British Steel Corby					
37505	(37028)	AX		F	*FMYT*	TE
	British Steel Workington					
37506	(37007)	AX		F	*FMYT*	TE
	British Steel Skinningrove					
37507	(37036)	AX		FM	*FMYT*	TE
	BSC Hartlepool Pipe Mill					
37508	(37090)	AX		F	*FMYT*	TE
37509	(37093)	AX		F	*FMYT*	TE
37510	(37112)	AX		F	*FMYT*	TE
37511	(37103)	AX		FM	*FMYT*	TE
	Stockton Haulage					
37512	(37022)	AX	D	F	*FMYT*	TE
	Thornaby Demon					
37513	(37056)	AX		F	*FMYT*	TE
37514	(37115)	AX	S	F	*FMYT*	TE
37515	(37064)	AX	S	F	*FMYT*	TE
37516	(37086)	AX	S	F	*FMYT*	TE
37517	(37018)	AX	S	F	*FMYT*	TE
37518	(37076)	AX		F	*FMYT*	TE
37519	(37027)	AX		F	*FMYT*	TE
37520	(37041)	AX		F	*FMYT*	TE
37521	(37117)	AX		FM	*FMYT*	TE

Loc No	*Former No*	*Dia*	*SC*	*Liv*	*Pool*	*Dep*
37667	(37151)	CX	S	FM	*FMYT*	TE
	Wensleydale					
37668	(37257)	CX	S	FM	*FMYT*	TE
	Leyburn					
37669	(37129)	CX		F	*FTLL*	LA
37670	(37182)	CX		F	*FTLL*	LA
37671	(37247)	CX		F	*FTLL*	LA
	Tre Pol and Pen					
37672	(37189)	CX	S	F	*FTLL*	LA
	Freight Transport Association					
37673	(37132)	CX		FG	*FTLL*	LA
37674	(37169)	CX		F	*FTLL*	LA
37675	(37164)	CX	S	F	*FTLL*	LA
	William Cookworthy					
37676	(37126)	CX		F	*FAMT*	TI
37677	(37121)	CX		F	*FAMT*	TI
37678	(37256)	CX		F	*FAMT*	TI
37679	(37123)	CX		F	*FAMT*	TI
37680	(37224)	CX		F	*FAMT*	TI
37681	(37130)	CX		F	*FAMT*	TI
37682	(37236)	CX		F	*FAMT*	TI
37683	(37187)	CX		F	*FAMT*	TI
37684	(37134)	CX		F	*FAMT*	TI
37685	(37234)	CX		F	*FAMT*	TI
37686	(37172)	CX		F	*FAMT*	TI
37687	(37181)	CX		F	*FAMT*	TI
37688	(37205)	CX		FA	*FAMT*	TI
	Great Rocks					
37689	(37195)	CX	S	F	*FHCC*	CF
	Coedbach					
37690	(37171)	CX	S	F	*FHCC*	CF
37691	(37179)	CX	S	F	*FHCC*	CF

Loc No	Former No	Dia	SC	Liv	Pool	Dep
37692	(37122)	CX	s	F	*FHCC*	CF
37693	(37210)	CX	s	F	*FHCC*	CF
37694	(37192)	CX	s	F	*FHCC*	CF
37695	(37157)	CX		F	*FHCC*	CF
37696	(37228)	CX	s	F	*FHCC*	CF
37697	(37243)	CX	s	F	*FHCC*	CF
37698	(37246)	CX	s	F	*FHCC*	CF
37699	(37253)	CX	s	F	*FHCC*	CF

CLASS 37/7 TYPE 3 CO-CO

Built: English Electric 1961-65, refurbished and fitted with ballast weights on bogies at BREL Crewe 1986-89.
Engine: English Electric 12cyl, 4-stroke, 12 CVST of 1,750hp (1,306kW).
Dimensions, Brake force, Train brakes, Route availability: As Class 37/0.
Maximum tractive effort: ?
Power/control equipment: Six English Electric traction motors EE538/A; main alternator Brush BA 100 SA or GEC 564 (see below).
Train heating: Not equipped.
Fuel, Maximum operating speed, Standard equipment: As Class 37/5.
Special characteristics: Slow speed control (s).

Diagram	*Series*	*Alternator*
37-7AX	First	Brush
37-7BX	First	GEC
37-7CX	Second	Brush
37-7DX	Second	GEC

Sectors:
Railfreight: **FECA:** Coal, Trainload, Aberthaw. **FMCH:** Metals, Steel, Cardiff. **FPLX:** Petroleum, North Thames, Ripple Lane.

Loc No	Former No	Dia	SC	Liv	Pool	Dep
37701	(37030)	AX	SK	F	*FECA*	CF
37702	(37020)	AX	SK	F	*FECA*	CF
37703	(37067)	AX	SK	F	*FECA*	CF
37704	(37034)	AX	SK	F	*FECA*	CF
37705	(37060)	AX	K	FP	*FPLX*	SF
37706	(37016)	AX	K	FP	*FPLX*	SF
37707	(37001)	AX	K	FP	*FPLX*	SF
37708	(37089)	AX	K	FP	*FPLX*	SF
37709	(37014)	AX	K	FP	*FPLX*	SF
37710	(37044)	AX	K	FM	*FMCH*	CF
37711	(37085)	AX	K	FM	*FMCH*	CF
Tremorfa Steel Works						
37712	(37102)	AX	K	FM	*FMCH*	CF
Cardiff Rod Mill						
37713	(37052)	AX	K	FM	*FMCH*	CF
37714	(37024)	AX	K	FM	*FMCH*	CF
37715	(37021)	AX	K	FM	*FMCH*	CF
37716	(37094)	AX		FM	*FMCH*	CF
37718	(37084)	AX		FM	*FMCH*	CF
37719	(37033)	AX		FM	*FMCH*	CF
37796	(37105)	BX	s	F	*FECA*	CF
37797	(37081)	BX	s	F	*FECA*	CF
37798	(37006)	BX	s	F	*FECA*	CF
37799	(37061)	BX	s	F	*FECA*	CF
Sir Dyfed-County of Dyfed						
37800	(37143)	DX	s	F	*FECA*	CF
Glo Cymru						
37801	(37173)	DX	s	F	*FECA*	CF
Aberddawan, Aberthaw						

Loc No	Former No	Dia	SC	Liv	Pool	Dep
37802	(37163)	DX	s	F	*FECA*	CF
37803	(37208)	DX	s	F	*FECA*	CF
37883	(37176)	CX		FM	*FMCH*	CF
37884	(37183)	CX		FM	*FMCH*	CF
37885	(37177)	CX		FM	*FMCH*	CF
37886	(37180)	CX		FM	*FMCH*	CF
37887	(37125)	CX	s	FP	*FECA*	CF
37888	(37135)	CX		FP	*FPLX*	SF
	Petrolea					
37889	(37233)	CX	s	FP	*FECA*	CF
37890	(37168)	CX		FP	*FPLX*	SF
37891	(37166)	CX		FP	*FPLX*	SF
37892	(37149)	CX		FP	*FPLX*	SF
	Ripple Lane					
37893	(37237)	CX		FP	*FPLX*	SF
37894	(37124)	CX	s	F	*FECA*	CF
37895	(37283)	CX	s	F	*FECA*	CF
37896	(37231)	CX	s	F	*FECA*	CF
37897	(37155)	CX	s	F	*FECA*	CF
37898	(37186)	CX	s	F	*FECA*	CF
37899	(37161)	CX	s	F	*FECA*	CF

CLASS 37/9 TYPE 3 CO-CO

Built: English Electric 1963/64, rebuilt to present design at BREL Crewe 1986.
Engine: Mirrlees MB275T or GEC Ruston RK270T, 12cyl, 4-stroke of 1,800hp (1,343kN).
Weight: 120 tonnes.
Dimensions: As Class 37/0 Second Series.
Brake force: ?
Maximum tractive effort: ?
Power/control equipment: Six English Electric traction motors EE538/A; main alternator Brush BA100SA or GEC 564.

Train heating: Not equipped.
Train brakes: Dual Air and Vacuum.
Route availability: 7.
Fuel: 1,689gal.
Maximum operating speed: 80mph.
Standard equipment: As Class 37/4.
Special characteristics: Slow speed control (s) as shown.

Diagram	*Engine*	*Alternator*
37-9AX	Mirrlees	Brush
37-9BX	GEC	GEC

Sector:
Railfreight: **FMCC:** Metals (Steel), Cardiff.

Loc No	Dia	SC	Liv	Pool	Dep
37901	AX		F	*FMCC*	CF
Mirrlees Pioneer					
37902	AX		FM	*FMCC*	CF
37903	AX		FM	*FMCC*	CF
37904	AX		FM	*FMCC*	CF
37905	BX	s	F	*FMCC*	CF
Vulcan Enterprise					
37906	BX	s	FM	*FMCC*	CF

CLASS 43 TYPE 4 BO-BO

INTERCITY 125 POWER CARS

Built: BREL Crewe 1976-82.
Dimensions: 58.4ft L (except Diagram *43-OFA*: 59.9ft) ×8.9ft W ×12.8ft H.
Weight: 70 tonnes.
Engine: Paxman Valenta 12cyl, 4-stroke, 12RP200L, V type or Mirrlees Blackstone 12cyl, 4-stroke, MP190, 2,250hp (1,680kW).
Power/control equipment: Four traction motors Brush THM68-46 or GEC417AZ frame mounted; main alternator BA1001B.
Train brake: Air.
Locomotive brake: Air.
Brake Force: 50 tonnes.
Maximum operating speed: 125mph.
Maximum tractive effort: 17,900lbs (80kN).
Route availability: 5.
Fuel: 1,000gal.
Standard equipment: Driver/Guard communication.
Special characteristics: Cab/shore radio (B), One man operation (M).

Diagram	*Type**	*Power unit*	*Traction motors*
43-OAA	DMB	Paxman	Brush
43-OBA	DMB	Paxman	GEC
43-OCA	DM	Paxman	Brush
43-ODA	DM	Paxman	GEC
43-OEA	DM	Mirrlees	Brush
43-OFA	DM/TV	Paxman	Brush

*DMB: Driving Motor Brake (Guard's accommodation retained); DM: Driving Motor (Guard's accommodation removed); DM/TV: Driving Motor Trailer Van (Equipped with TDM Push-Pull equipment and nose-end buffers).

Train heat: Electric from alternator (for IC125 stock only).

Sectors:
INTERCITY: **ICCP:** Cross Country; **IECP:** East Coast main line; **IMLP** Midland main line; **IWRP:** Western Region main line.

Livery: INTERCITY. Those marked 'I' carry the latest style with Swallow emblem.

Loc No	*Dia*	*SC*	*Liv*	*Pool*	*Dep*
43002	CA		I	*IWRP*	00
	Top of the Pops				
43003	CA		I	*IWRP*	00
43004	CA		I	*IWRP*	00
43005	CA		I	*IWRP*	00
43006	CA			*IWRP*	00
43007	CA			*IWRP*	00
43008	CA	B		*IWRP*	LA
43009	CA			*IWRP*	LA
43010	CA			*IWRP*	LA
43011	CA			*IWRP*	LA
43012	CA		I	*ICCP*	LA
43013	FA			*IECP*	BN
	University of Bristol				
43014	FA			*IECP*	BN
43015	CA			*IWRP*	LA
43016	CA			*ICCP*	LA
43017	CA			*IWRP*	LA
	HTV West				
43018	AA			*IWRP*	PM
43019	CA			*ICCP*	LA
	Dinas Abertawe. City of Swansea				
43020	CA			*IWRP*	LA
43021	AA			*IWRP*	LA
43022	CA			*IWRP*	LA
43023	CA			*IWRP*	LA
43024	CA			*IWRP*	LA
43025	CA	B		*IWRP*	LA
43026	CA			*IWRP*	LA
	City of Westminster				

Loc No	Dia	SC	Liv	Pool	Dep
~~43027~~	CA			IWRP	LA
	Westminster Abbey				
~~43028~~	CA			IWRP	LA
43029	CA			IWRP	LA
43030	CA			IWRP	PM
~~43031~~	CA			IWRP	PM
~~43032~~	CA			IWRP	PM
43033	CA			IWRP	PM
~~43034~~	CA			IWRP	PM
43035	CA		I	ICCP	PM
43036	AA		I	ICCP	PM
43037	CA	B	I	ICCP	PM
43038	CA			IMLP	NL
	National Railway Museum. The First Ten Years 1975-1985				
~~43039~~	CA			IMLP	NL
43040	CA	M		IECP	EC
~~43041~~	CA	M		IECP	EC
~~43042~~	CA			IECP	BN
43043	CA	M		IECP	BN
43044	AA	M		IMLP	NL
43045	CA	M		IMLP	NL
	The Grammar School Doncaster AD 1350				
~~43046~~	CA		I	IMLP	NL
~~43047~~	CA			IMLP	NL
	Rotherham Enterprise				
~~43048~~	CA	B	I	IMLP	NL
43049	CA			IMLP	NL
	Neville Hill				
43050	CA	M		IMLP	NL
~~43051~~	CA	M	I	IMLP	NL
	The Duke and Duchess of York				
~~43052~~	AA	BM		IECP	NL
	City of Peterborough				
~~43053~~	CA			IECP	NL
	County of Humberside				
~~43054~~	CA	BM		IECP	NL
~~43055~~	CA	M		IMLP	NL
~~43056~~	CA	M		IECP	BN
	University of Bradford				
43057	CA	BM		IECP	BN
	Bounds Green				
43058	CA	BM	I	IECP	NL
~~43059~~	CA			IECP	NL
43060	CA			IMLP	NL
	County of Leicestershire				
~~43061~~	CA	BM	I	IMLP	NL
	City of Lincoln				
~~43062~~	CA	M		IECP	BN
~~43063~~	CA			IECP	BN
~~43064~~	CA			IMLP	NL
	City of York				
~~43065~~	FA		I	IMLP	NL
~~43066~~	CA	B		IMLP	NL
~~43067~~	CA	M	I	IECP	EC
~~43068~~	CA	M	I	IECP	EC
~~43069~~	CA	M		IECP	EC
~~43070~~	CA	M		IECP	EC
~~43071~~	CA			IECP	EC
~~43072~~	CA		I	IMLP	NL
~~43073~~	CA			IMLP	NL
~~43074~~	CA			IECP	BN
~~43075~~	CA			IECP	BN
43076	CA	M		IMLP	NL
~~43077~~	CA	M		IMLP	NL
	County of Nottingham				
~~43078~~	CA		I	IECP	EC
	Shildon, County Durham				
~~43079~~	CA			IECP	EC
~~43080~~	AA			IECP	BN
~~43081~~	CA	M		IECP	BN
~~43082~~	CA	M		IECP	BN
43083	CA	M		IECP	BN
~~43084~~	FA		I	IECP	BN
	County of Derbyshire				
43085	AA			IECP	BN
	City of Bradford				

Loc No	Dia	SC	Liv	Pool	Dep
43086	CA			IECP	EC
43087	CA	M		IECP	EC
43088	CA	M		IECP	EC
XIII Commonwealth Games, Edinburgh 1986					
43089	CA			IECP	EC
43090	CA	M	I	IECP	EC
43091	AA			IECP	EC
Edinburgh Military Tattoo					
43092	CA		I	IECP	EC
Highland Chieftain					
43093	CA		I	IECP	EC
York Festival '88					
43094	CA			IECP	EC
43095	CA			IECP	HT
Heaton					
43096	AA		I	IECP	HT
The Queen's Own Hussars					
43097	CA	M	I	IECP	HT
The Light Infantry					
43098	CA		I	IECP	HT
Tyne & Wear Metropolitan County					
43099	AA			IECP	HT
43100	AA	M	I	IECP	EC
Craigentinny					
43101	CA		I	IECP	EC
Edinburgh International Festival					
43102	CA		I	IECP	HT
City of Wakefield					
43103	CA		I	IECP	HT
John Wesley					
43104	AA		I	IECP	HT
County of Cleveland					
43105	CA		I	IECP	HT
Hartlepool					

Loc No	Dia	SC	Liv	Pool	Dep
43106	AA			IECP	BN
43107	AA	M		IECP	BN
City of Derby					
43108	AA			IMLP	NL
43109	AA			IMLP	NL
43110	AA	M		IECP	HT
Darlington					
43111	CA		I	IECP	NL
43112	AA	M		IECP	NL
43113	AA	M		IECP	HT
City of Newcastle upon Tyne					
43114	AA	M		IECP	BN
43115	AA			IECP	BN
43116	AA	M		IECP	NL
City of Kingston upon Hull					
43117	AA			IECP	NL
43118	CA		I	IECP	NL
Charles Wesley					
43119	AA	M		IECP	NL
43120	CA			IECP	NL
43121	CA			IECP	NL
West Yorkshire Metropolitan County					
43122	AA			IECP	NL
South Yorkshire Metropolitan County					
43123	FA			IECP	BN
43124	DA			IWRP	PM
BBC Points West					
43125	DA		I	IWRP	PM
Merchant Venturer					
43126	DA		I	ICCP	PM
City of Bristol					
43127	DA			IWRP	PM
43128	DA		I	IWRP	PM
43129	BA			IWRP	PM
43130	BA			IWRP	PM
43131	DA		I	IWRP	PM
Sir Felix Pole					

Loc No	Dia	SC	Liv	Pool	Dep
43132	CA		I	IWRP	PM
	Worshipful Company of Carmen				
43133	DA		I	IWRP	PM
43134	DA		I	IWRP	PM
43135	DA		I	IWRP	PM
43136	DA		I	IWRP	PM
43137	DA			IWRP	PM
43138	BA			IWRP	PM
43139	DA			IWRP	OO
43140	BA		I	IWRP	OO
43141	DA			IWRP	OO
43142	DA			IWRP	OO
	St Mary's Hospital Paddington				
43143	DA			IWRP	OO
43144	DA			IWRP	OO
43145	BA		I	IWRP	OO
43146	DA		I	IWRP	OO
43147	BA		I	IWRP	OO
43148	BA		I	IWRP	OO
43149	BA		I	IWRP	PM
	BBC Wales Today				
43150	BA		I	IWRP	PM
	Bristol Evening Post				
43151	DA			IWRP	PM
	Blue Peter II				
43152	DA			IMLP	NL
	St Peter's School York AD 627				
43153	CA			IMLP	NL
	University of Durham				
43154	CA			IECP	NL
43155	CA			IECP	NL
	BBC Look North				
43156	CA			IECP	NL
43157	CA			IECP	NL
	Yorkshire Evening Post				
43158	CA			IMLP	NL
43159	CA			IECP	NL
43160	CA			IECP	NL
43161	CA			IMLP	NL

Loc No	Dia	SC	Liv	Pool	Dep
43162	CA			IMLP	NL
	Borough of Stevenage				
43163	CA		I	ICCP	LA
43164	CA	B		ICCP	LA
43165	CA			ICCP	LA
43166	CA			ICCP	LA
43167	EA	B		IWRP	PM
43168	EA			IWRP	PM
43169	EA	B		IWRP	PM
43170	EA			IWRP	PM
43171	CA		I	ICCP	PM
43172	CA			ICCP	PM
43173	CA			ICCP	PM
43174	CA			ICCP	PM
43175	CA			ICCP	PM
43176	CA			IWRP	PM
43177	CA			ICCP	LA
43178	CA		I	ICCP	LA
43179	CA			ICCP	LA
43180	CA			IWRP	OO
43181	CA			ICCP	LA
43182	CA			ICCP	LA
43183	CA			ICCP	LA
43184	CA			ICCP	LA
43185	CA		I	ICCP	LA
43186	CA		I	ICCP	LA
43187	CA			IWRP	LA
43188	CA			IWRP	LA
	City of Plymouth				
43189	CA		I	IWRP	LA
43190	CA		I	IWRP	LA
43191	CA			IWRP	LA
43192	CA			IWRP	LA
43193	CA			IMLP	NL
	Yorkshire Post				
43194	CA		I	IECP	NL
	Royal Signals				
43195	CA			IECP	NL
43196	CA			IECP	NL
	The Newspaper Society				
43197	CA			IECP	NL
43198	CA			IECP	NL

CLASS 45/1 TYPE 4 1CO-CO1

Built: British Rail 1961.
Engine: Sulzer 12cyl 12LDA28-B of 2,500hp (1,865kW).
Weight: 135 tonnes.
Dimensions: 67.9ft L × 9.1ft W × 12.8ft H.
Brake force: 63 tonnes.
Maximum tractive effort: 55,000lb.
Power/control equipment: Six Crompton Parkinson C172A1 traction motors; main generator Crompton Parkinson CG426A1.
Route availability: 6.
Fuel: 790gal.
Train brake: Dual Air and Vacuum.
Maximum operating speed: 90mph.
Diagram: 45-1AX.
Standard equipment: Sanding gear, Headlight (L).
Train heating: Electric alternator, Brush BL100-30 Mk II driven by main engine.
ETH Index: 66

Sector:
InterCity: **ICHA:** Charter.
Special livery: *Green:* 45106.

Loc No	*Dia*	*SC*	*Liv*	*Pool*	*Dep*
45106	AX			*ICHA*	TI

CLASS 47/0 TYPE 4 CO-CO

Built: British Railways and Brush Engineering Ltd 1962-67.
Engine: Sulzer 12cyl, 4-stroke, 12LDA28C of 2,580hp (1,925kW).
Power/control equipment: see below.
Weight: see below.
Dimensions: 63.6ft L × 9.2ft W × 12.8ft H.
Brake force: 60 tonnes.
Maximum tractive effort: 62,000lb (267kN).
Route availability: 6.
Train brake: Dual Air and Vacuum.
Maximum operating speed: 75mph (originally 95mph).
Train heating: (see also below): Steam generator, where fitted, isolated. *Types:* **B:** Clayton Mk II, 2,500lb/hr; **C:** Stone Vapor 4625, 2,750lb/hr; **D:** Spanner Swirlyflow Mk III, 1,850lb/hr; **O:** Not fitted. Boiler water (see below)*: Water tanks have not been retained by all locomotives, but this data is not available from published DMEE specifications.
Standard equipment: Headlights (L); One man operation (M).
Special characteristics: Cab-shore radio (B); Snowplough brackets (K); Extra 250gal fuel tank (X).

Diagram	Weight tonnes	Main Generator Brush	Traction Motors Six Brush	Fuel (gal)	Train Heat/ Boiler Water
47-0BX	120.6	TG160-60 Mk 2	TM64-68 Mk 1	720	D.1,250gal
47-0EX	120.4	TG160-60 Mk 4	TM64-68 Mk 1A	720	D.1,200gal
47-0GX	119.1	TG172-50 Mk 1	TM64-68 Mk 1A	720	C.1,200gal
47-0HX	118.8	TG172-50 Mk 1	TM64-68 Mk 1A	720	B.1,200gal
47-0LX	111.5	TG172-50 Mk 1	TM64-68 Mk 1A	720	0.1,200gal*
47-0MX	119.3	TG160-60 Mk 2	TM64-68 Mk 1	720	0.1,250gal*
47-0NX	118.8	TG172-50 Mk 1	TM64-68 Mk 1A	970	0.1,200gal*

Sectors:

Departmental: **DCHA:** DCE Scotland. **DCMA:** DCE Midland.

Railfreight: **FAME:** Construction (Stone), Eastfield. **FAWC:** Construction (Stone) Cardiff Canton. **FGWA:** Distribution (Speedlink). **FPLC:** Petroleum, Stanlow. **FPLI:** Petroleum, Immingham. **FPLW:** Petroleum, South Wales. **FTLC:** Chemicals, Crewe.

Freightliner: **LNRB:** Anglia, Stratford. **LNRC:** General, Crewe.

Loc No	Dia	SC	Liv	Pool	Dep
47002	MX	B		FGWA	TI
47003	BX	BK		DCMA	ED
47004	BX	BK		FAME	ED
47005	MX	B		FGWA	TI
47006	MX	BK		FAME	ED
47007	MX			LNRB	SF
Stratford					
47008	BX			LNRC	CD
47009	BX	B		LNRC	CD
47010	MX	B		FPLC	CD
47012	BX			FGWA	TI
47014	MX			LNRB	SF
47016	MX			FGWA	TI
The Toleman Group					
47017	DX	BK		FAME	ED
47018	MX	K		DCMA	ED
47019	MX			LNRC	CD
47033	LX	B		FAWC	CF
47049	GX			FGWA	TI
47050	LX			FTLC	CD
47051	LX			LNRC	CD
47052	LX			FGWA	TI
47053	GX	K		DCMA	ED
47054	HX			FPLI	IM
47060	HX		FG	FGWA	TI
Halewood Silver Jubilee 1988					
47063	LX	B		FAWC	CF
47079	LX	B	FM	FAWC	CF
47085	HX	B	FP	FPLC	CD
Conidae					
47094	LX			FPLW	CF
47095	LX			FGWA	TI
47096	BX			LNRB	SF
47097	MX			FGWA	TI
47098	MX	B		FGWA	TI
47099	MX			LNRB	SF
47100	MX			LNRB	SF
47101	BX	B		LNRC	CD
47102	BX			FGWA	TI
47105	BX			LNRB	SF
47107	LX			FGWA	TI
47108	BX	B		LNRB	SF
47110	MX	B		FGWA	TI
47112	MX			LNRB	SF
47114	EX	B		FALG	SF
47115	BX			FGWA	TI
47116	BX			LNRB	SF
47117	BX	BK		FGWA	TI
47118	BX	K		DCMA	ED
47119	MX		FP	FPLC	CD
Arcidae					
47120	BX			FGWA	TI
RAF Kinloss					

Loc No	Dia	SC	Liv	Pool	Dep
47121	BX	B		LNRB	SF
47123	BX			LNRB	SF
47124	BX			LNRC	CD
47125	LX		FP	FPLC	CD
	Tonnidae				
47142	LX	B	F	FGWA	TI
	The Sapper				
47143	LX	B		FGWA	TI
47144	EX			FGWA	TI
47146	EX	B		FGWA	TI
47147	LX	B		FGWA	TI
47150	EX	B		FGWA	TI
47152	EX	B		FGWA	TI
47156	EX			FGWA	TI
47157	LX		F	FGWA	TI
47186	LX		F	FMCA	CF
47187	GX	B		FMCA	CF
47188	LX			FGWA	TI
47190	LX		FP	FPLC	CD
	Pectinidae				
47193	LX		FP	FPLC	CD
	Lucinidae				
47194	GX		FP	FPLC	CD
	Bullidae				
47195	GX	B	FP	FPLC	CD
	Muricidae				
47196	LX		FP	FPLC	CD
	Haliotidae				
47197	GX			FPLW	CF
47198	LX	B		FPLW	CF
47200	GX	B		FGWA	TI
47201	GX	B		FGWA	TI
47203	GX			FGWA	TI
47204	LX			FGWA	TI
47205	GX			FGWA	TI
47206	GX	K		FGWA	TI
47207	LX	B	FG	FGWA	TI
	Bulmers of Hereford				
47209	GX			FGWA	TI

Loc No	Dia	SC	Liv	Pool	Dep
47210	GX	BK		FAME	ED
47211	LX	B	F	FGWA	TI
47212	NX	XB		FPLI	IM
47213	LX	B	F	FGWA	TI
47214	LX			FGWA	TI
	Tinsley Traction Depot				
47215	LX		F	FGWA	TI
47217	GX			FGWA	TI
47218	LX			FGWA	TI
47219	GX	B		FGWA	TI
47220	LX		F	FGWA	TI
47221	LX			FPLC	IM
47222	LX	B		FPLI	IM
	Appleby Frodingham				
47223	GX	B		FPLI	IM
47224	LX	B		FPLI	IM
47225	LX	B		FGWA	TI
47226	LX			FGWA	TI
47227	LX	B	F	FTLC	CD
47228	HX			FTLC	CD
47229	LX	B		FTLC	CD
47231	LX		FG	FGWA	TI
	The Silcock Express				
47233	LX		FP	FPLC	CD
	Strombidae				
47234	LX			FGWA	TI
47235	LX		F	FGWA	TI
47236	LX		F	FGWA	TI
47237	LX		F	FGWA	TI
47238	LX			FGWA	TI
	Bescot Yard				
47241	LX			FGWA	TI
47245	LX			FGWA	TI
47249	LX		F	FGWA	TI
47256	LX	B		FGWA	SF
47258	LX	B		FGWA	TI
47270	LX	B		FGWA	TI
47276	NX	XB		FPLI	IM
47277	LX	B		FPLI	IM
47278	LX	P	FP	FPLC	CD
47279	HX	B	FG	FGWA	TI
47280	LX		F	FGWA	TI
	Pedigree				

Loc No	Dia	SC	Liv	Pool	Dep
47281	LX	B		FMCA	CF
47283	LX		FG	FGWA	TI
Johnnie Walker					
47284	LX			FGWA	TI
47285	LX		F	FGWA	TI
47286	LX	B		FGWA	TI
47287	LX			FGWA	TI
47288	LX			FGWA	TI
47289	LX			FGWA	TI
47290	HX		F	FGWA	TI

Loc No	Dia	SC	Liv	Pool	Dep
47291	LX		F	LNRB	SF
The Port of Felixstowe					
47292	LX			FGWA	TI
47293	LX	B		FGWA	TI
47294	LX	B		FPLC	IM
47295	NX	XB		FPLI	IM
47296	LX			FGWA	TI
47297	LX			FGWA	TI
47298	HX			FGWA	TI
47299	NX	XB		FPLI	IM

CLASS 47/3 TYPE 4 CO-CO

Built: Brush Engineering Ltd 1964/65.
Engine, Dimensions, Maximum tractive effort, Brake force, Route availability, Train brakes: As Class 47/0.
Power/control equipment: Six Brush TM64-68 Mk 1A traction motors; main generator TG172-50 Mk 1.
Train heat, Boiler water: Not equipped.

Diagram	Fuel (gal)
47-3AX	720
47-3BX	970

Standard equipment: Headlights (L); One man operation (M); Slow speed control (S), Sanding gear.
Special characteristics: Cab-shore radio (B).

Sectors:
Departmental: **DCAA:** DCE Anglia Region. **DCEA:** DCE Eastern Region. **DCMA:** DCE Midland Region.
Railfreight: **FALG:** Construction, (Stone) Stratford. **FAWC:** Construction (Stone), Cardiff Canton. **FGWA:** Distribution (Speedlink). **FMCA:** Metals (Steel), Cardiff Canton. **FMYT:** Metals (Steel), Thornaby. **FPLI:** Petroleum, Immingham. **FPLW:** Petroleum, South Wales. **FTLC:** Chemicals, Crewe.
Freightliner: **LNRC:** General, Crewe.

Loc No	Dia	SC	Liv	Pool	Dep
47301	AX			FTYT	TE
47302	AX	B		FTYT	TE
47303	AX	B	FX	FTYT	TE
47304	AX	B		FTYT	TE
47305	AX	B	FP	FTYT	TE
47306	AX			FGWA	TI
47307	AX			FGWA	TI
47308	AX		F-	FGWA	TI
47309	AX			FGWA	TI
47310	AX	B		FGWA	TI

Loc No	Dia	SC	Liv	Pool	Dep
47311	AX		FG	FGWA	TI
Warrington Yard					
47312	AX			FGWA	TI
47313	AX	B		FGWA	TI
47314	AX			FGWA	TI
47315	AX			FGWA	TI
47316	AX	B		FGWA	TI
47317	AX	B	FG	FGWA	TI
Willesden Yard					

Loc No	Dia	SC	Liv	Pool	Dep
47318	AX	B	F	*FPLW*	CF
47319	AX		FG	*FPLI*	IM
	Norsk Hydro				
47320	AX		F	*FALG*	SF
47321	AX			*FGWA*	TI
47322	AX			*FTLC*	CD
47323	AX	B		*FTLC*	CD
47324	AX	B	FP	*FPLC*	CD
	Glossidae				
47325	AX	B	F	*FTLC*	SF
47326	AX			*FPLW*	CF
47327	AX	B	F	*FPLW*	CF
47328	AX	B		*FALG*	SF
47329	AX	B		*DCEA*	IM
47330	AX	B		*LNRC*	CD
47331	AX	B	F	*DCEA*	IM
47332	AX	B		*DCEA*	IM
47333	AX	B		*DCMA*	OC
47334	AX	B		*FPLW*	CF
47335	AX	B		*LNRC*	CD
47336	AX			*FPLI*	IM
47337	AX		F	*FGWA*	TI
	Herbert Austin				
47338	AX	B		*FGWA*	TI
47339	AX	B		*DCMA*	CD
47340	AX			*DCMA*	CD
47341	AX	B		*DWCA*	OC
47342	AX			*LNRC*	CD
47343	AX	B		*DCMA*	CD
47344	AX			*DCEA*	IM
47345	AX	B		*LNRC*	CD
47346	AX		F	*DCAA*	SF
47347	AX			*FMYT*	TE
47348	AX	B	F	*DCEA*	IM
	St Christopher's Railway Home				
47349	AX	B		*LNRC*	CD
47350	AX	B	F	*LNRC*	CD
	British Petroleum				
47351	AX	B		*LNRC*	CD
47352	AX	B		*DCEA*	IM
47353	AX			*DCMA*	CD
47354	AX	B		*LNRC*	CD
47355	AX			*LNRC*	CD
47356	AX	B	F	*DCMA*	CD
47357	AX			*DCMA*	CD
47358	AX		F	*DCMA*	CD
47359	AX	B	FM	*FMCA*	CF
47360	AX			*FGWA*	TI
47361	AX	B		*FTYT*	TE
	Wilton Endeavour				
47362	AX	B	F	*FTYT*	TE
47363	AX	B	F	*FTYT*	TE
	Billingham Enterprise				
47364	AX	B		*LNRC*	CD
47365	AX	B	F	*FTLC*	CD
	Diamond Jubilee				
47366	AX	B	F	*DCAA*	SF
	The Institution of Civil Engineers				
47367	AX		F	*FALG*	SF
47368	AX	B	F	*FPLC*	CD
	Neritidae				
47369	AX			*FPLW*	CF
47370	AX		F	*FGWA*	TI
47371	AX		F	*FGWA*	TI
47372	AX			*FGWA*	TI
47373	AX		F	*FPLI*	IM
47374	AX	B	F	*FPLI*	IM
47375	AX	B		*FGWA*	TI
47376	AX			*FGWA*	TI
47377	AX	B		*FGWA*	TI
47378	AX	B	F	*FGWA*	TI
47379	AX	B	F	*FPLI*	IM
	Total Energy				
47380	BX	XB	FP	*FPLI*	IM
	Immingham				
47381	AX		F-	*FPLW*	CF

CLASS 47/4 TYPE 4 CO-CO

Built: British Railways and Brush Engineering Ltd 1962-67.
Engine, Dimensions, Brake force, Train brake: As Class 47/0.
Route availability: 7
Power/control equipment: see below.
Weight and Fuel: see below.
Maximum operating speed: 95mph (except *SC* '75' see below).
Train heating: (see also below): *Electric types:* **H&K:** Brush Electric Generator TG160-16; **E, M** and **N:** Brush Alternator BL100-30. (see *SC* 'U')
Steam generator types: where fitted, isolated. **E** and **H:** not fitted. **K:** Spanner Swirlyflow Mk IV, 2,500lb/hr. **M:** Spanner Swirlyflow Mk III, 1,850lb/hr. **N:** Stone Vapor 4,625, 2,750lb/hr.
Boiler water:* see Class 47/0.
ETH Index: 66. (400amps, except § (see below), 600amps).
Standard equipment: Headlights (L); One man operation (M).
Special characteristics: Cab-shore radio (B); Snowplough brackets (K); Phosphor brake blocks, maximum speed 75mph (75); Electric alternator isolated (U).

Diagram	Weight tonnes	Traction Motors Brush	Main Generator Brush	Fuel (gal)	Train Heat/ Boiler Water
47-4AX	121.4	TM64-68 Mk 1	TG160-60	720	K.1,250gal
47-4BX	122.6	TM64-68 Mk 1	TG160-60 Mk 2	720	M.1,250gal
47-4CX	120.4	TM64-68 Mk 1	TG160-60 Mk 2	720	E.1,250gal*
47-4DX	121.9	TM64-68 Mk 1A	TG160-60 Mk 4	720	M.1,250gal
47-4EX	121.0	TM64-68 Mk 1A	TG160-60 Mk 4	720	E.1,250gal*
47-4FX	123.6	TM64-68 Mk 1A	TG172-50 Mk 1	720	M.1,250gal
47-4GX	125.1	TM64-68 Mk 1A	TG172-50 Mk 1	720	N.1,200gal
47-4HX	122.6	TM64-68 Mk 1A	TG172-50 Mk 1	720	E.1,200gal
47-4JX	123.4	TM64-68 Mk 1A	TG172-50 Mk 1	720	M.1,200gal
47-4KX§	122.6	TM64-68 Mk 1A	TG172-50 Mk 1	720	E.1,200gal
47-4LX	120.4	TM64-68 Mk 1	TG160-60	720	H.—*
47-4MX§	122.6	TM64-68 Mk 1A	TG172-50 Mk 1	1,295	E.—

Note: *Locomotives to Diagram 47-4MX may be reclassified 47/8, and renumbered from 47850.*
Sectors:
Departmental: **DCHA:** DCE Scottish Region. **DCWA:** DCE, Western Region.
Railfreight: **FGWA:** Distribution (Speedlink). **FMYT:** Metals, Thornaby. **FTLC:** Chemicals, Crewe.
InterCity: **ICCA:** Cross Country. **ICHA:** Charter. **IWCA:** West Coast main line. **IWRA:** Western Region.
Network SouthEast: **NNEA:** Northeast. **NSSA:** Solent and Sarum. **NWRA:** Western Region.
Provincial: **PTPA:** Trans-Pennine, North. **PXXA:** General.
Parcels: **RXLD:** General.
Special liveries: *GWR Brunswick Green:* 47484, 47500, 47628.
LNER Apple Green: 47522.

Loc No	Dia	SC	Liv	Pool	Dep
47401	LX			RXLD	IM
47402	AX	B		RXLD	IM
47406	AX			PCRA	IM
47407	LX	B		PCRA	IM
47411	AX			FGXX	IM
47413	LX			PCRA	IM
47417	AX			DCEA	IM
47418	AX	B		DCEA	IM
47421	BX	75		FGWA	TI
47422	BX			PTPA	CD
47423	BX	B		FTLC	CD
47424	CX	B		PTPA	CD
The Brontes of Haworth					
47425	BX			FTLC	CD
Holbeck					
47426	BX			DCMA	CD
47427	CX	B		DCMA	CD
47428	CX			DCMA	CD
47430	BX	B	IS	LNRB	SF
47431	CX			DCMA	CD
47432	CX			DCMA	CD
47433	CX	75		FGWA	TI
47434	CX	B		PTPA	CD
47435	DX	B		RXLD	SF
47436	EX	B		DCMA	CD
47438	EX	B		DCMA	CD
47439	EX	B		FTLC	CD
47440	EX			FTLC	CD
47441	EX			FTLC	CD
47442	EX	B		FTLC	CD
47443	EX			PTPA	CD
47444	EX	B		PTPA	CD
University of Nottingham					
47445	EX			FTLC	CD
47446	EX	B		FTLC	CD
47447	EX	B		FTLC	CD
47448	EX	B		PTPA	CD
47449	EX	B		FTLC	CD

Loc No	Dia	SC	Liv	Pool	Dep
47450	EX			DCMA	CD
47451	EX			LNRC	CD
47452	EX			LNRB	SF
47453	EX	B		DCMA	CD
47454	EX	B		FTLC	CD
47455	HX			RXLD	SF
47456	HX			FTLC	CD
47457	FX			LNRC	CD
Ben Line					
47458	HX	B		RXLD	SF
47459	HX			IWCA	CD
47460	FX	BK		PXXA	IS
47461	HX	BK	PS	PXXA	IS
Charles Rennie Mackintosh					
47462	HX	B		LNRB	SF
47463	HX	B		DCWA	CD
47465	HX	B		RXLD	SF
47466	HX	B		RXLD	BR
47467	HX	BK		DCHA	IS
47468	HX			RXLD	BR
47469	HX	BK	IS	PXXA	IS
Glasgow Chamber of Commerce					
47470	HX	BK		ICCA	ED
University of Edinburgh					
47471	HX	B	I	IECA	CD
Norman Tunna G.C.					
47473	HX			NSSA	LA
47474	HX	75		FGWA	TI
47475	HX			PTPA	CD
47476	HX	B		RXLD	BR
47477	HX			RXLD	BR
47478	HX			ICCA	CD
47479	HX			LNRC	CD
47481	HX	B		LNRC	OC
47482	HX	B		RXLD	SF
47483	HX	B		IWCA	CD

Loc No	Dia	SC	Liv	Pool	Dep
47484	HX	B	★	DWCC	OC
Isambard Kingdom Brunel					
47485	CX	B		FTLC	CD
47487	CX		I	FTLC	CD
47488	CX			PTPA	CD
Rail Riders					
47489	HX			RXLD	BR
47490	HX	B	I	RXLD	BR
47491	HX			FTLC	CD
Horwich Enterprise					
47492	HX	BK	Is	PXXA	IS
The Enterprising Scot					
47500	HX		★	ICHA	BR
Great Western					
47501	HX	B	I	RXLD	BR
Craftsman					
47503	HX			PTPA	CD
47508	HX		I	ICHA	BR
S.S. Great Britain					
47509	HX	B	I	ICHA	CD
Albion					
47512	HX	B		ICCA	CD
47513	HX			DWCA	OC
Severn					
47515	HX		I	RXLD	ED
Night Mail					
47517	KX	B		IWCA	CD
Andrew Carnegie					
47518	HX			DCHA	ED
47519	HX			ICCA	BR
47520	GX	B		ICCA	CD
47521	GX	B		ICCA	CD
47522	HX			RXLD	SF
Doncaster Enterprise					
47523	GX			RXLD	SF

Loc No	Dia	SC	Liv	Pool	Dep
47524	GX	B		RXLD	ED
47525	HX	B	I	ICCA	BR
47526	HX			RXLD	BR
Northumbria					
47527	GX	B		ICCA	CD
47528	GX	B		RXLD	BR
47530	HX			IWCA	CD
47531	HX	B		FTLC	CD
47532	HX	B		FTLC	CD
47533	HX			RXLD	BR
47534	HX	B		RXLD	BR
47535	HX			RXLD	BR
University of Leicester					
47536	HX			RXLD	BR
47537	HX	B		RXLD	BR
Sir Gwynedd. County of Gwynedd					
47538	HX			RXLD	BR
47539	HX	B		RXLD	BR
Rochdale Pioneers					
47540	HX			DCWA	OC
47541	HX	BK	Is	PXXA	IS
The Queen Mother					
47542	JX			RXLD	BR
47543	HX			RXLD	BR
47544	JX			IWCA	CD
47546	HX	BK		DCHA	IS
Aviemore Centre					
47547	HX			NSSA	LA
47549	HX	B	I	RXLD	ED
Royal Mail					
47550	HX	BK		DCHA	IS
University of Dundee					
47551	MX	XB		ICCA	BR
47552	MX	XB		ICCA	BR
47553	MX	XB	I	IWCA	CD
47555	HX	B	I	ICHA	CD
The Commonwealth Spirit					
47556	KX			ICCA	BR

Loc No	Dia	SC	Liv	Pool	Dep
47557	KX	B		RXLD	BR
47558	KX			RXLD	BR
Mayflower					
47559	KX	B		RXLD	BR
Sir Joshua Reynolds					
47560	KX	B	I	IWRA	BR
Tamar					
47562	KX	BK		IWCA	ED
Sir William Burrell					
47563	KX	B		PXXA	IS
Womens' Guild					
47564	KX	B		RXLD	BR
Colossus					
47565	KX			RXLD	BR
47566	KX			RXLD	BR
47567	KX			RXLD	BR
Red Star					
47568	KX			RXLD	BR
47569	KX	B		RXLD	ED
47570	KX	B		IWCA	ED
47571	KX			ICCA	CD
47572	KX	B		RXLD	SF
Ely Cathedral					
47573	KX		N	NWRA	OC
The London Standard					
47574	KX			RXLD	SF
Benjamin Gimbert G.C.					
47575	KX			RXLD	BR
City of Hereford					
47576	KX		N	NNEA	SF
King's Lynn					
47577	KX	B		IECA	CD
47578	KX	BK		PXXA	IS
Royal Society of Edinburgh					
47579	KX		N	NNEA	SF
James Nightall G.C.					
47580	KX			RXLD	SF
County of Essex					
47581	KX		N	NNEA	SF
Great Eastern					
47582	KX		N	NWRA	OC
County of Norfolk					
47583	KX		N	NWRA	OC
County of Hertfordshire					
47584	KX			RXLD	BR
County of Suffolk					
47585	KX			RXLD	SF
County of Cambridgeshire					
47586	KX	B		IMLA	CD
47587	KX			NSSA	LA
47588	KX	B	FG	FGWA	TI
47589	KX		I	ICCA	CD
47590	KX			RXLD	BR
Thomas Telford					
47591	MX	XB		ICCA	BR
47592	KX			RXLD	BR
County of Avon					
47593	KX	BK	I	ICCA	ED
Galloway Princess					
47594	KX	B		FMYT	TE
47595	KX	BK		IWCA	ED
Confederation of British Industry					
47596	KX	B,75		FGWA	TI
Aldeburgh Festival					
47597	KX	B		IWCA	ED
47598	KX			NSSA	SF
47599	KX	B,75	FM	FGWA	TI
47600	KX	B,75	FG	FGWA	TI
Dewi Sant. Saint David					

Loc No	Dia	SC	Liv	Pool	Dep	Name
47602	KX		I	ICCA	CD	Glorious Devon
47603	KX			RXLD	BR	County of Somerset
47604	KX	BK		DCHA	ED	Women's Royal Voluntary Service
47605	KX	B		FTLC	CD	
47606	KX		I	ICCA	CD	Odin
47607	KX	B,75	I	ICCA	CD	Royal Worcester
47608	KX			ICCA	CD	
47609	KX	B	I	ICHA	BR	Fire Fly
47610	KX	B		ICCA	CD	
47611	KX		I	IWRA	BR	Thames
47612	KX		I	ICCA	CD	Titan
47613	KX		I	IWRA	BR	North Star
47614	KX	B		IWCA	ED	
47615	KX	75	FG	FGWA	TI	Castell Caerffili. Caerphilly Castle
~~47616~~	KX	B		RXLD	BR	Y Ddraig Goch. The Red Dragon
47617	KX	BK		DCHA	IS	University of Stirling
47618	KX	B	I	IWCA	CD	Fair Rosamund
47619	KX			IWCA	CD	
47620	KX	B	I	ICHA	BR	Windsor Castle

Loc No	Dia	SC	Liv	Pool	Dep	Name
47621	KX		I	IWRA	BR	Royal County of Berkshire
47622	KX	B	I	ICCA	ED	The Institution of Mechanical Engineers
47623	KX			DCWA	OC	Vulcan
47624	KX			RXLD	BR	Cyclops
~~47625~~	KX	B		RXLD	BR	
47626	KX	B		RXLD	BR	Atlas
47627	KX	B		RXLD	BR	City of Oxford
47628	KX		★	DCWA	OC	Sir Daniel Gooch
47629	KX	B		IWCA	BR	
47630	KX	BK		PXXA	IS	
47631	KX	B		RXLD	BR	
47632	KX	B		IWCA	ED	
47633	KX	B		ICCA	ED	Orion
47634	KX			RXLD	BR	Henry Ford
47635	KX	B		PXXA	IS	Jimmy Milne
47636	KX	BK		ICCA	ED	Sir John de Graeme
47637	KX		IS	IWCA	CD	
47638	KX	B		IWCA	CD	County of Kent
47639	KX			IWCA	CD	Industry Year 1986
47640	KX	B		PXXA	IS	University of Strathclyde

Loc No	Dia	SC	Liv	Pool	Dep
47641	KX	BK		PXXA	IS
Fife Region					
47642	KX	B	IS	PXXA	IS
Strathisla					
47643	KX	BK	IS	PXXA	IS
47644	KX	BK		PXXA	IS
The Permanent Way Institution					
47645	KX	B		IWCA	CD
Robert F. Fairlie					
47646	KX			IWCA	CD
47647	KX			IWCA	CD
Thor					
47648	KX			IWCA	CD
47649	KX	B		IWCA	ED

Loc No	Dia	SC	Liv	Pool	Dep
47650	MX	XB		ICCA	BR
47651	MX	XB		ICCA	BR
47652	MX	X		ICCA	BR
47653	MX	X		ICCA	BR
47654	MX	X		ICCA	BR
Finsbury Park					
47655	MX	X		ICCA	BR
47656	MX	X		ICCA	BR
47657	MX	XB		ICCA	BR
47658	MX	X		ICCA	BR
47659	MX	XB		ICCA	BR
47660	MX	X		ICCA	BR
47661	MX	X		ICHA	BR
47662	MX	X		ICHA	BR
47663	MX	X		ICHA	BR
47664	MX	X		ICCA	BR
47665	MX	X		ICCA	BR

CLASS 47/7 TYPE 4 CO-CO

Built: British Railways and Brush Engineering Ltd 1966-67. Modified to this specification by BREL from 1979.
Weight: 118.7 tonnes.
Engine, Dimensions, Brake force, Maximum tractive effort, Train brake: As Class 47/0.
Route availability: 7
Power/control equipment: Six Brush Traction Motors TM64-68 Mk 1A; main generator Brush TG172-50 Mk 1.
Fuel: 1,295gal.
Maximum operating speed: 100mph.
Train heating: Brush Electric alternator BL100-30.
ETH Index: 66.
Diagram: 47-7AX
Standard equipment: Cab/shore radio (B); Headlights (L); One man operation (M); Push-Pull operation (P).

Sectors:
Provincial: **PXXA:** General.
Livery: *Provincial ScotRail.*

Loc No	Dia	SC	Liv	Pool	Dep	Name
47701	AX			PXXA	ED	*Saint Andrew*
47702	AX			PXXA	ED	*Saint Cuthbert*

Loc No	*Dia*	*SC*	*Liv*	*Pool*	*Dep*	*Name*
47703	AX			*PXXA*	ED	*Saint Mungo*
47704	AX			*PXXA*	ED	*Dunedin*
47705	AX			*PXXA*	ED	*Lothian*
47706	AX			*PXXA*	ED	
47707	AX			*PXXA*	ED	*Holyrood*
47708	AX			*PXXA*	ED	*Waverley*
47709	AX			*PXXA*	ED	*The Lord Provost*
47710	AX			*PXXA*	ED	*Sir Walter Scott*
47711	AX			*PXXA*	ED	*Greyfriars Bobby*
47712	AX			*PXXA*	ED	*Lady Diana Spencer*
47714	AX			*PXXA*	ED	*Grampian Region*
47715	AX			*PXXA*	ED	*Haymarket*
47716	AX			*PXXA*	ED	*The Duke of Edinburgh's Award*
47717	AX			*PXXA*	ED	*Tayside Region*

Note: No 47717 was converted by BRML Doncaster from No 47497 during 1988 using some equipment from withdrawn locomotive, fire damaged No 47713.

CLASS 47/9 TYPE 5 CO-CO

Built: British Railways 1964. Modified to this design at BREL Crewe in 1979.
Engine: Ruston-Paxman 12cyl, 4-stroke, 12RK3CT of 3,250hp (2,460kW).
Power/control equipment: Six Brush Traction Motors TM64-68 Mk 1A; main generator Brush BA1101.
Weight: 113.7 tonnes.
Dimensions, Brake force: As Class 47/0.
Maximum tractive effort: 57,325lb (516kN).
Route availability: 6.
Fuel: 1,010gal.
Train brake: Air.
Maximum operating speed: 75mph.
Train heating: Not equipped.
Diagram: 47-9AA.
Standard equipment: Cab/shore radio (B); One man operation (M); Slow speed control (S).

Sector:
Railfreight: **FAWC:** Construction (Stone), Cardiff.
Livery: *Railfreight Construction.* (FA).

Loc No	*Dia*	*SC*	*Liv*	*Pool*	*Dep*
47901	AA		FA	*FAWC*	CF

CLASS 50/0 TYPE 4 CO-CO

Built: English Electric 1967-68.
Engine: English Electric 16cyl, 4-stroke, 16CSVT of 2,700hp (2,014kW).
Weight: 116.9 tonnes.
Dimensions: 68.5ft L × 9.1ft W × 12.8ft H.
Power/control equipment: Six English Electric traction Motors EE538/5A, main generator EE840/4B.
Train brake: Dual Air and Vacuum.
Brake force: 59 tonnes.
Maximum tractive effort: 48,500lb (216kN).
Fuel: 1,055gal.
Maximum operating speed: 100mph.
Train heating: Electric generator, English Electric EE915/1B.
ETH Index: 61.
Diagram: 50-0AX.
Standard equipment: Snowplough brackets (K), Headlights (L), One man operationa (M), Multiple Working (Orange Square, code 2).
Special characteristics: Cab-shore Radio (B).

Sectors:
Departmental: **DCWA:** DCE Western Region.
Network SouthEast: **NSSA:** Solent and Sarum. **NWRA:** Western Region (Thames & Chiltern).
Parcels: **RXXA:** General.
Special livery: *GWR Brunswick Green:* 50007.

Loc No	*Dia*	*SC*	*Liv*	*Pool*	*Dep*	*Name*
50001	AX	B	N	*NSSA*	LA	*Dreadnought*
50002	AX	B	N	*NSSA*	LA	*Superb*
50003	AX	B	N	*NSSA*	LA	*Temeraire*
50004	AX			*DCWA*	LA	*St Vincent*
50005	AX	B	N	*DCWA*	LA	*Collingwood*
50007	AX	B		*DCWA*	LA	*Sir Edward Elgar*
50008	AX			*DCWA*	LA	*Thunderer*
50009	AX			*DCWA*	LA	*Conqueror*
50012	AX			*DCWA*	LA	*Benbow*
50015	AX			*DCWA*	LA	*Valiant*
50016	AX			*DCWA*	LA	*Barham*
50017	AX	B	N	*NSSA*	LA	*Royal Oak*
50018	AX		N	*NSSA*	LA	*Resolution*
50019	AX	B	N	*NSSA*	LA	*Ramillies*
50020	AX			*DCWA*	LA	*Revenge*
50021	AX			*DCWA*	LA	*Rodney*
50023	AX		N	*NWRA*	OC	*Howe*
50024	AX	B	N	*NWRA*	OC	*Vanguard*
50025	AX	B	N	*NWRA*	OC	*Invincible*
50026	AX	B	N	*NWRA*	OC	*Indomitable*
50027	AX	B	N	*NSSA*	LA	*Lion*
50028	AX	B	N	*NSSA*	LA	*Tiger*
50029	AX	B	N	*NSSA*	LA	*Renown*
50030	AX	B	N	*NWRA*	OC	*Repulse*

Loc No	*Dia*	*SC*	*Liv*	*Pool*	*Dep*	*Name*
50031	AX			*NWRA*	OC	*Hood*
50032	AX		N	*NWRA*	OC	*Courageous*
50033	AX			*NWRA*	OC	*Glorious*
50034	AX		N	*NWRA*	OC	*Furious*
50035	AX	B	N	*NWRA*	OC	*Ark Royal*
50036	AX			*NWRA*	OC	*Victorious*
50037	AX		N	*NWRA*	OC	*Illustrious*
50039	AX			*NWRA*	OC	*Implacable*
50040	AX			*NWRA*	OC	*Centurion*
50041	AX	B	N	*NSSA*	LA	*Bulwark*
50042	AX			*DCWA*	LA	*Triumph*
50043	AX	B	N	*NSSA*	LA	*Eagle*
50044	AX	B	N	*NSSA*	LA	*Exeter*
50045	AX			*DCWA*	LA	*Achilles*
50046	AX	B		*NWRA*	OC	*Ajax*
50048	AX	B	N	*NSSA*	LA	*Dauntless*
50050	AX	B	N	*NWRA*	OC	*Fearless*

CLASS 50/1 TYPE 4 CO-CO

Built: English Electric 1968.
Experimental modified Class 50/0 locomotive using bogies and traction motors of Class 37/5 locomotive. Engine derated to 2,450hp.

Maximum operating speed: 80mph.
Standard equipment: As Class 50/0 and Cab/shore Radio (B).
Diagram: 50-1AX.

Sectors:
Railfreight: **FTLL:** China Clay, Laira.
Livery: *Railfreight General.* Fx.

Loc No	*Dia*	*SC*	*Liv*	*Pool*	*Dep*	*Name*
50149	AX		Fx	*FTLL*	LA	*Defiance*

CLASS 56 TYPE 5 CO-CO

Built: 56001-30 at Electroputere (Romania); others at BREL, 1977-84.
Engine: GEC Ruston-Paxman 16cyl, 4-stroke, 16RK3CT of 3,250hp (2,460kW).
Power/control equipment: Six Brush TM73-62 traction motors; main alternator Brush BA1101A.
Dimensions: 63.5ft L × 9.2ft W × 13ft H.
Brake force: 60 tonnes.
Maximum tractive effort: 49,456lb (270kN).
Route availability: 7.
Fuel: 1,150gal.
Train brake: Air.
Maximum operating speed: 80mph.
Train heating: Not equipped.
Diagram: 56-0AA.
Bogies: *Electroputere:* 56001-41/43-60. *BR CP1:* 56042. *BR CP2:* 56061-56135.
Standard equipment: Multiple working (Red Diamond, Code 3), Headlight (L), One man operation (M), Slow speed control (S), Sanding gear.
Special characteristics: Cab-shore radio (B). Remote control (Z).

Sectors:
Railfreight: **FALX:** Construction (Stone), Leicestershire. **FAWC:** Construction (Stone), Cardiff Canton. **FENB:** Coal, Midlands. **FEYA:** Coal, Yorkshire. **FEYB:** Coal, Blyth (Toton).

Loc No	*Dia*	*SC*	*Liv*	*Pool*	*Dep*
56001	AA	B	FA	*FAWC*	CF
Whatley					
56002	AA	B	F	*FENB*	TO
56003	AA	B		*FENB*	TO
56004	AA			*FENB*	TO
56005	AA		F	*FENB*	TO
56006	AA	B	F	*FENB*	TO
56007	AA	B	F	*FENB*	TO
56008	AA	B		*FENB*	TO
56009	AA	B	F	*FENB*	TO
56010	AA	B		*FENB*	TO
56011	AA	B	F	*FENB*	TO
56012	AA			*FENB*	TO
56013	AA	B		*FENB*	TO
56014	AA			*FENB*	TO
56015	AA			*FENB*	TO
56016	AA		F	*FENB*	TO
56017	AA		F	*FENB*	TO
56018	AA	B	F	*FENB*	TO
56019	AA			*FENB*	TO
56020	AA	B		*FENB*	TO
56021	AA	B		*FENB*	TO
56022	AA	B		*FENB*	TO
56023	AA			*FENB*	TO

Loc No	*Dia*	*SC*	*Liv*	*Pool*	*Dep*
56024	AA	B	F	*FENB*	TO
56025	AA	B		*FENB*	TO
56026	AA	B		*FENB*	TO
56027	AA			*FENB*	TO
56028	AA	B	FE	*FENB*	TO
West Burton Power Station					
56029	AA	B		*FEYA*	TO
56030	AA		FE	*FEYA*	TO
56031	AA			*FAWC*	CF
Merehead					
56032	AA			*FAWC*	CF
Sir de Morgannwg. County of South Glamorgan					
56033	AA		F	*FAWC*	CF
56034	AA		F	*FAWC*	CF
Castell Ogwr. Ogmore Castle					
56035	AA		F	*FAWC*	CF
Taff Merthyr					
56036	AA		FP	*FAWC*	CF
56037	AA		F	*FAWC*	CF
Richard Trevithick					

Loc No	Dia	SC	Liv	Pool	Dep
56038	AA		F	FAWC	CF
Western Mail					
56039	AA	B	F	FAWC	CF
56040	AA	B	F	FAWC	CF
Oystermouth					
56041	AA		F	FAWC	CF
56042	AA			FALX	TO
56043	AA		F	FAWC	CF
56044	AA		F	FAWC	CF
56045	AA	B	F	FAWC	CF
56046	AA		F	FAWC	CF
56047	AA	B	F	FEYA	TO
56048	AA			FAWC	CF
56049	AA	B	F	FAWC	CF
56050	AA		F	FAWC	CF
56051	AA		F	FAWC	CF
56052	AA		F	FAWC	CF
56053	AA		FA	FAWC	CF
Sir Morgannwg Ganol. County of Mid Glamorgan					
56054	AA			FEYA	TO
56055	AA		F	FAWC	CF
56056	AA		F	FAWC	CF
56057	AA		F	FAWC	CF
56058	AA	B	F	FALX	TO
56059	AA		F	FALX	TO
56060	AA	B	F	FALX	TO
56061	AA		F	FALX	TO
56062	AA		F	FALX	TO
56063	AA		F	FALX	TO
Bardon Hill					
56064	AA		F	FALX	TO
56065	AA		F	FALX	TO
56066	AA		F	FEYA	TO
56067	AA		F	FEYA	TO
56068	AA		F	FEYA	TO
56069	AA			FEYA	TO
56070	AA			FALX	TO
56071	AA			FEYA	TO
56072	AA	Z		FAWC	CF
56073	AA	Z	FE	FEYA	TO
56074	AA			FEYA	TO
Kellingley Colliery					

Loc No	Dia	SC	Liv	Pool	Dep
56075	AA		F	FEYA	TO
West Yorkshire Enterprise					
56076	AA		F	FEYA	TO
56077	AA		F	FEYA	TO
56078	AA		FA	FALX	TO
56079	AA		F	FEYA	TO
56080	AA			FEYA	TO
56081	AA			FEYA	TO
56082	AA			FEYA	TO
56083	AA		F	FEYA	TO
56084	AA		F	FEYA	TO
56085	AA		F	FEYA	TO
56086	AA		F	FEYA	TO
56087	AA		F	FEYA	TO
56088	AA		F	FEYA	TO
56089	AA		F	FEYA	TO
56090	AA		F	FEYA	TO
56091	AA			FEYA	TO
56092	AA			FEYA	TO
56093	AA			FEYA	TO
56094	AA			FEYA	TO
56095	AA			FEYA	TO
Harworth Colliery					
56096	AA		F	FEYA	TO
56097	AA		F	FEYA	TO
56098	AA			FEYA	TO
56099	AA			FEYA	TO
56100	AA		F	FEYA	TO
56101	AA			FEYA	TO
56102	AA			FEYA	TO
56103	AA			FEYA	TO
56104	AA			FEYA	TO
56105	AA			FEYA	TO
56106	AA			FEYA	TO
56107	AA		F	FEYA	TO
56108	AA		F	FEYA	TO
56109	AA			FEYA	TO
56110	AA			FEYA	TO
56111	AA			FEYB	TO
56112	AA			FEYB	TO
56113	AA			FEYB	TO
56114	AA			FEYB	TO
56115	AA			FEYB	TO
56116	AA			FEYB	TO
56117	AA			FEYB	TO

Loc No	Dia	SC	Liv	Pool	Dep
56118	AA			FEYB	TO
56119	AA			FEYB	TO
56120	AA			FEYB	TO
56121	AA		FE	FEYB	TO
56122	AA		FE	FEYB	TO
Wilton Coal Power					
56123	AA		FE	FEYA	TO
Drax Power Station					
56124	AA			FEYB	TO
Blue Circle Cement					
56125	AA		FE	FEYB	TO
56126	AA			FEYB	TO
56127	AA			FEYB	TO
56128	AA			FEYB	TO
56129	AA			FEYB	TO
56130	AA			FEYB	TO
56131	AA			FEYB	TO
Ellington Colliery					
56132	AA			FEYB	TO
Fina Energy					
56133	AA			FEYB	TO
Crewe Locomotive Works					
56134	AA			FEYB	TO
Blyth Power					
56135	AA		F	FEYB	TO
Port of Tyne Authority					

CLASS 58 TYPE 5 CO-CO

Built: BREL 1983-85.
Engine: GEC Ruston Paxman 12cyl, 4-stroke, 12RK3ACT of 3,300hp (2,460kW).
Power/control equipment: Six Brush TM73-62 traction motors; main alternator Brush BA1101A.
Dimensions: 62.8ft L × 8.9ft W × 13.0ft H.
Brake force: 60 tonnes.
Maximum tractive effort: 60,750lb (329kN).
Route availability: 7.
Train brake: Air.
Maximum operating speed: 80mph.
Train heating: Not equipped.
Diagram: 58-0AA.
Standard equipment: Snowplough brackets (K); Headlights (L); One man operation (M); Slow speed control (S).

Sectors:
Railfreight: **FENA:** Coal, West Midlands. **FENC:** Coal, East Midlands.

Loc No	Dia	SC	Liv	Pool	Dep
58001	AA	B	F	FENA	TO
58002	AA	B	FE	FENC	TO
Daw Mill Colliery					
58003	AA	B	FE	FENA	TO
58004	AA		F	FENA	TO
58005	AA	B	F	FENA	TO
58006	AA		F	FENA	TO
58007	AA	B	F	FENA	TO
58008	AA	B	F	FENC	TO
58009	AA	B	F	FENA	TO
58010	AA	B	F	FENA	TO
58011	AA	B	F	FENA	TO
58012	AA		F	FENA	TO
58013	AA	B	F	FENA	TO
58014	AA	B	FE	FENA	TO
Didcot Power Station					

Loc No	*Dia*	*SC*	*Liv*	*Pool*	*Dep*
58015	AA	B	F	*FENA*	TO
58016	AA		F	*FENC*	TO
58017	AA	B	F	*FENC*	TO
58018	AA	B	FE	*FENC*	TO
High Marnham Power Station					
58019	AA	B	F	*FENC*	TO
58020	AA	B	F	*FENC*	TO
Doncaster Works					
58021	AA	B	F	*FENC*	TO
58022	AA	B	F	*FENC*	TO
58023	AA	B	F	*FENC*	TO
58024	AA	B	F	*FENC*	TO
58025	AA	B	F	*FENC*	TO
58026	AA		F	*FENC*	TO
58027	AA		F	*FENC*	TO
58028	AA	B	F	*FENC*	TO
58029	AA	B	F	*FENC*	TO
58030	AA	B	F	*FENC*	TO
58031	AA		F	*FENC*	TO
58032	AA	B	F	*FENC*	TO
58033	AA		F	*FENC*	TO
58034	AA	B	F	*FENC*	TO
Bassetlaw					
58035	AA		F	*FENC*	TO
58036	AA	B	F	*FENC*	TO
58037	AA		F	*FENC*	TO
58038	AA		F	*FENC*	TO
58039	AA		F	*FENC*	TO
Rugeley Power Station					
58040	AA	B	F	*FENC*	TO
Cottam Power Station					
58041	AA	B	FE	*FENC*	TO
Ratcliffe Power Station					
58042	AA	B	F	*FENC*	TO
Ironbridge Power Station					
58043	AA		F	*FENC*	TO
58044	AA		F	*FENC*	TO
58045	AA		F	*FENC*	TO
58046	AA	B	F	*FENC*	TO
58047	AA		F	*FENC*	TO
58048	AA		F	*FENC*	TO
58049	AA	B	F	*FENC*	TO
Littleton Colliery					
58050	AA		FE	*FENC*	TO
Toton Traction Depot					

CLASS 59 TYPE 5 CO-CO

Privately owned by Foster Yeoman Ltd, Merehead, Somerset

Built: General Motors, USA, 1985.
Engine: General Motors 16cyl, 4-stroke, 645E3C of 3,300hp (2,460kW).
Power/Control equipment: Six EMD D77B traction motors, main alternator EMD AR11 MLD D14A.
Weight: 126 tonnes.
Dimensions: 70.0ft L × 8.7ft W × 12.8ft H.
Brake force: 69 tonnes.
Maximum tractive effort: 122,000lb (573kN).

Sectors:
Private Owner: **CYPO:** Foster Yeoman.
Livery: Foster Yeoman Blue.

Route availability: 7.
Fuel: 990gal.
Train brakes: Air.
Maximum speed: 60mph.
Train heating: Not equipped.
Diagram: 59-0AA.
Standard equipment: Headlight (L); One man operation (M); Multiple working (within Class only), Sanding gear.
Special characteristics: Bell, No 1 end cab front, No 59001.

Loc No	Dia	SC	Liv	Pool	Dep	Name
59001	AA		★	CYPO	HQ	Yeoman Endeavous
~~59002~~	AA		★	CYPO	HQ	Yeoman Enterprise
59003	AA		★	CYPO	HQ	Yeoman Highlander
~~59004~~	AA		★	CYPO	HQ	Yeoman Challenger
~~59005~~			★	CYPO		

Note: Maintained at Merehead by BR staff.

CLASS 60 TYPE 5 CO-CO

Built: Brush Traction 1989-91.
Engine: Mirrlees Blackstone 8cyl, 4-stroke, 8MB875T of 3,100hp (kW).
Power/control equipment: Six Brush traction motors, main alternator
Weight: 126 tonnes.
Dimensions: ft L × ft W × ft H.
Brake Force: tonnes.
Maximum tractive effort: .
Route availability:
Fuel: gal.
Train brake: Air.
Maximum speed: 60mph.
Train heating: Not equipped.
Diagram: 60-0AA.
Standard equipment: Headlight (L), One man operation (M).

Sector:
Railfreight: **FA--:** Construction, Toton; **FP--:** Petroleum, Immingham.

Loc No	Dia	SC	Liv	Pool	Dep
60001	AA			F----	--
60002	AA			F----	--
60003	AA			F----	--
60004	AA			F----	--
60005	AA			F----	--
60006	AA			F----	--
60007	AA			F----	--
60008	AA			F----	--
60009	AA			F----	--
60010	AA			F----	--
60011	AA			F----	--
60012	AA			F----	--
60013	AA			F----	--
60014	AA			F----	--
60015	AA			F----	--
60016	AA			F----	--
60017	AA			F----	--
60018	AA			F----	--
60019	AA			F----	--
60020	AA			F----	--
60021	AA			F----	--
60022	AA			F----	--
60023	AA			F----	--
60024	AA			F----	--
60025	AA			F----	--
60026	AA			F----	--
60027	AA			F----	--
60028	AA			F----	--
60029	AA			F----	--
60030	AA			F----	--
60031	AA			F----	--
60032	AA			F----	--
60033	AA			F----	--
60034	AA			F----	--
60035	AA			F----	--
60036	AA			F----	--

Loc No	Dia	SC	Liv	Pool	Dep
60037	AA			F----	--
60038	AA			F----	--
60039	AA			F----	--
60040	AA			F----	--
60041	AA			F----	--
60042	AA			F----	--
60043	AA			F----	--
60044	AA			F----	--
60045	AA			F----	--
60046	AA			F----	--
60047	AA			F----	--
60048	AA			F----	--
60049	AA			F----	--
60050	AA			F----	--
60051	AA			F----	--
60052	AA			F----	--
60053	AA			F----	--
60054	AA			F----	--
60055	AA			F----	--
60056	AA			F----	--
60057	AA			F----	--
60058	AA			F----	--
60059	AA			F----	--
60060	AA			F----	--
60061	AA			F----	--
60062	AA			F----	--
60063	AA			F----	--
60064	AA			F----	--
60065	AA			F----	--
60066	AA			F----	--
60067	AA			F----	--
60068	AA			F----	--
60069	AA			F----	--
60070	AA			F----	--
60071	AA			F----	--
60072	AA			F----	--
60073	AA			F----	--
60074	AA			F----	--
60075	AA			F----	--
60076	AA			F----	--
60077	AA			F----	--
60078	AA			F----	--
60079	AA			F----	--
60080	AA			F----	--
60081	AA			F----	--
60082	AA			F----	--
60083	AA			F----	--
60084	AA			F----	--
60085	AA			F----	--
60086	AA			F----	--
60087	AA			F----	--
60088	AA			F----	--
60089	AA			F----	--
60090	AA			F----	--
60091	AA			F----	--
60092	AA			F----	--
60093	AA			F----	--
60094	AA			F----	--
60095	AA			F----	--
60096	AA			F----	--
60097	AA			F----	--
60098	AA			F----	--
60099	AA			F----	--
60100	AA			F----	--

CLASS 73/0 TYPE E BO-BO

Built: British Railways 1962.
Dimensions: 53.7ft L × 8.7ft W × 12.5ft H.
Traction motors: Four English Electric EE542A.
Weight: 76.3 tonnes.
Brake force: 31 tonnes.
Route availability: 6.
Maximum operating speed: 80mph.
Train brake: Air, Vacuum and Electro-Pneumatic.
Diagram: 73-0AX (SR Type JA).

DIESEL engine: English Electric 4-cyl, 4-stroke, 4SRKT Mk 2 of 600hp (422kW).
Main generator: English Electric EE824/3D.
Fuel: 340gal.

ELECTRIC supply: Third rail, 660-750V dc; 1,420 (1,060kW) rail hp.
Maximum tractive effort: *Diesel:* 34,100lb (151kN). *Electric:* 42,000lb (186kN).
Train heating: *Diesel:* Preheating only from main generator. *Electric:* 675V dc, 400amps.

ETH Index: *Electric:* 66.
Standard equipment: Multiple working (Blue Star), One man operation (M); Driver-Guard communication; Sanding gear.

Sectors:
Network SouthEast: **NSSB:** Solent and Sarum.
Special livery: *Light blue:* 73004/05.

Loc No	*Dia*	*SC*	*Liv*	*Pool*	*Dep*
73001	AX			*NSSB*	SL
73002	AX			*NSSB*	SL
73003	AX			*NSSB*	SL
73004	AX		★	*NSSB*	SL
The Bluebell Railway					
~~73005~~	AX		★	*NSSB*	SL
Mid-Hants Watercress Line					
73006	AX			*NSSB*	SL

CLASS 73/1 TYPE E BO-BO

Built: English Electric 1965-67.
Dimensions, Route availability, Train brake, Brake force: As Class 73/0.
Traction motors: Four English Electric EE546/1B.
Weight: 76.8 tonnes.
Maximum operating speed: 90mph.
Diagram: 73-1AX (SR Type JB).

DIESEL engine: As Class 73/0.
Main generator: English Electric EE824/5D.
Fuel: 310gal.

ELECTRIC supply: As Class 73/0.
Maximum tractive effort: *Diesel:* 36,000lb (160kN). *Electric:* 40,000lb (179kN).
Train heating: *Diesel:* Not equipped. *Electric:* As Class 73/0. Some to be modified to provide facilities as Class 73/0.
Standard equipment: As Class 73/0 plus flash guards for Gatwick Express service operation.

Sectors:
Departmental: **DCSA:** DCE Southern Region.
Railfreight: **FALS:** Construction (Stone), Stewarts Lane.
InterCity: **IVGA:** Victoria-Gatwick Express.
Network SouthEast: **NSSB:** Solent and Sarum, Stewarts Lane.

Loc No	Dia	SC	Liv	Pool	Dep
73101	AX		I	DCSA	SL
	Brighton Evening Argos				
73103	AX		I	DCSA	SL
73104	AX			NSSB	SL
73105	AX		I	DCSA	SL
	Quadrant				
73106	AX		I	NSSB	SL
73107	AX		I	NSSB	SL
73108	AX		I	DCSA	SL
73109	AX		I	DCSA	SL
73110	AX		I	DCSA	SL
73111	AX		I	NSSB	SL
73112	AX		I	NSSB	SL
73114	AX			DCSA	SL
73117	AX		I	DCSA	SL
	University of Surrey				
73118	AX		I	DCSA	SL
	The Romney Hythe and Dymchurch Railway				
73119	AX		I	DCSA	SL
	Kentish Mercury				
73126	AX		I	DCSA	SL
73128	AX		I	DCSA	SL
73129	AX		I	DCSA	SL
	City of Winchester				
73130	AX		I	DCSA	SL
	City of Portsmouth				
73131	AX		I	DCSA	SL
	County of Surrey				
73132	AX		I	DCSA	SL
73133	AX		I	DCSA	SL
73134	AX		I	DCSA	SL
	Woking Homes 1885-1985				
73135	AX		I	DCSA	SL
73136	AX		I	NSSB	SL
73138	AX			NSSB	SL
73139	AX		I	NSSB	SL
73140	AX			NSSB	SL
73141	AX		I	FALS	SL
73201	AX		I	IVGA	SL
	Broadlands				
73202	AX		I	IVGA	SL
	Royal Observer Corps				
73203	AX		I	IVGA	SL
73204	AX		I	IVGA	SL
	Stewarts Lane 1860-1985				
73205	AX		I	IVGA	SL
	London Chamber of Commerce				
73206	AX		I	IVGA	SL
	Gatwick Express				
73207	AX		I	IVGA	SL
	County of East Sussex				
73208	AX		I	IVGA	SL
	Croydon 1883-1983				
73209	AX		I	IVGA	SL
73210	AX		I	IVGA	SL
	Selhurst				
73211	AX		I	IVGA	SL
	County of West Sussex				
73212	AX		I	IVGA	SL
	Airtour Suisse				

CLASS 81 TYPE A BO-BO

Built: Birmingham Railway C&W 1960-61.
Supply system: Overhead Electric 25kV ac.
Dimensions: 56.5ft L × 8.7ft W × 13.0ft H (Pantograph housed).
Weight: 79.4 tonnes.
Traction motors: Four AEI Type 189 bogie suspension; Alsthom flexible, single reduction gear drive.
Control system: LT tap changing.
Maximum tractive effort: 50,000lb (222kN).
Train brakes: Auto air and air continuous vacuum.
Brake force: 40 tonnes.
Maximum operating speed: 80mph (originally 100mph).
Train heating: Electric, 320kW at 800V ac.
ETH Index: 66.
Diagram: 81-OBX.
Standard equipment: One man operation (M), Sanding gear.

Sectors:
InterCity: **IWCA:** West Coast main line.
Railfreight: **FGXZ:** Distribution (Speedlink) ac locomotives. **FMXX:** Metals, ac locomotives. **FXXL:** General.
Freightliner: **LXXA:** Distribution (Freightliner), General.
Parcels: **RXLE:** General.

Loc No	*Dia*	*SC*	*Liv*	*Pool*	*Dep*	*Loc No*	*Dia*	*SC*	*Liv*	*Pool*	*Dep*
81002	BX			*IWCA*	GW	81010	BX			*LXXA*	GW
81004	BX			*FMXX*	GW	81011	BX			*IWCA*	GW
81005	BX			*IWCA*	GW	81012	BX			*LXXA*	GW
81006	BX			*RXLE*	GW	81013	BX			*FGXZ*	GW
81007	BX			*LXXA*	GW	81017	BX			*FGXZ*	GW
81009	BX			*FMXX*	GW	81019	BX			*FXXL*	GW

CLASS 83 TYPE A BO-BO

Built: English Electric 1961.
Supply system: Overhead Electric 25kV ac.
Dimensions: 52.5ft L × 8.7ft W × 13.0ft H (Pantograph housed).
Weight: 76.4 tonnes.
Traction motors: Four English Electric EE535A bogie suspension; SLM flexible single reduction gear drive.
Control system: LT tap changing.
Maximum tractive effort: 38,000lb.
Train brakes: Auto air and air continuous vacuum.
Brake force: 38 tonnes.
Maximum operating speed: 40mph (originally 100mph).
Train heating: Electric, 320kW at 800V ac.
ETH Index: 66.
Diagram: 83-OAX.
Standard equipment: One man operation (M), Sanding gear.

Sectors:
InterCity: **IWCA:** West Coast main line.
Note: Restricted to operation of empty coaching stock between Euston and Wembley InterCity CSD.

Loc No	*Dia*	*SC*	*Liv*	*Pool*	*Dep*
83009	AX			*IWCA*	WN
83012	AX			*IWCA*	WN

CLASS 85 TYPE A BO-BO

Built: British Railways 1961-64.
Supply system: Overhead Electric 25kV ac.
Dimensions: 56.5ft L × 8.7ft W × 13.0ft H (Pantograph housed).
Weight: 82.5 tonnes.
Traction motors: Four AEI Type 189 bogie suspension; Alsthom flexible, single reduction drive system.
Control system: LT tap changing.
Rectifier: Silicon.
Maximum tractive effort: 50,000lb (222kN).
Train brakes: Auto air and air continuous vacuum.
Locomotive brakes: Straight air, auto air and rheostatic.
Brake force: 41 tonnes.
Maximum operating speed: 100mph (see SC).
Train heating: Electric, 320kW at 800V ac.
ETH Index: 66.
Diagram: 85-0AX.
Standard equipment: One man operation (M), Sanding gear.
Special characteristics: Maximum permitted speed 80mph (80).

Sectors:
Railfreight: **FGXZ:** Distribution (Speedlink) ac locomotives. **FXXL:** General.
InterCity: **IWCA:** West Coast main line.
Freightliner: **LXXA:** Distribution (Freightliner), General.
Network SouthEast: **NXXA:** General.
Parcels: **RXLE:** General.

Loc No	*Dia*	*SC*	*Liv*	*Pool*	*Dep*
85002	AX			*RXLE*	CE
85003	AX			*NXXA*	CE
85004	AX	80		*FGXZ*	CE
85005	AX	80		*IWCA*	CE
85006	AX			*FXXL*	CE
85007	AX	80		*LXXA*	CE
85008	AX	80		*IWCA*	CE
85009	AX	80		*FGXZ*	CE
85010	AX	80		*FGXZ*	CE
85011	AX			*RXLE*	CE
85012	AX	80		*FGXZ*	CE
85013	AX			*FXXL*	CE
85014	AX			*RXLE*	CE
85015	AX	80		*FGXZ*	CE
85016	AX	80		*FGXZ*	CE
85018	AX	80		*FGXZ*	CE
85019	AX			*RXLE*	CE
85020	AX	80		*FGXZ*	CE
85021	AX	80		*FGXZ*	CE
85022	AX			*RXLE*	CE
85023	AX			*RXLE*	CE
85024	AX	80		*FGXZ*	CE
85025	AX			*RXLE*	CE
85026	AX	80		*FGXZ*	CE

Loc No	Dia	SC	Liv	Pool	Dep
85028	AX			*FGXZ*	CE
85030	AX	80		*IWCA*	CE
85031	AX	80		*FGXZ*	CE
85032	AX	80		*FGXZ*	CE
85034	AX	80		*LXXA*	CE
85035	AX			*FGXZ*	CE
85036	AX			*FXXL*	CE
85037	AX	80		*IWCA*	CE
85038	AX	80		*IWCA*	CE
85040	AX	80		*FGXZ*	CE

CLASS 86/1 TYPE A BO-BO

Built: English Electric 1965-66 as Class 86. Modified BREL Crewe 1972.
Supply System: Overhead electric 25kV ac.
Dimensions: 58.5ft L × 8.7ft W × 13.0ft H (Pantograph housed).
Weight: 86.8 tonnes.
Traction Motors: Four GEC type G412AZ, nose suspension, single reduction gear drive.
Control system: LT tap changing.
Performance: 5,000hp continuous rating.
Rectifier: Silicon.
Maximum tractive effort: 58,000lb (258kN).
Train brakes: Auto air and air continuous vacuum.
Locomotive brakes: Straight air, auto air and rheostatic.
Brake force: 40 tonnes.
Route availability: 6.
Maximum operating speed: 110mph.
Train heating: 320kW at 800V ac.
ETH Index: 66 (95 on stock with 600amp wiring.
Diagram: 86-1BX.
Standard equipment: BP9 bogies with flexicoil springs; One man operation (M); Driver/guard communication; Sanding gear.
Special characteristics: Headlight (L).

Sector:
InterCity: **IWCA:** West Coast main line.
Livery: InterCity.

Loc No	Dia	SC	Liv	Pool	Dep	Name
86101	BX	L	I	*IWCA*	WN	*Sir William A. Stanier FRS*
86102	BX		I	*IWCA*	WN	*Robert A. Riddles*
86103	BX	LL	I	*IWCA*	WN	*André Chapelon*

CLASS 86/2 TYPE A BO-BO

Built: British Railways (†) and English Electric 1965-66.
Supply System, Dimensions, Control system, Rectifier, Maximum tractive effort, Train brakes, Locomotive brakes, Brake force, Route availability, Train heating, all as Class 86/1.
Traction Motors: Four AEI type 282AZ, nose suspension, single reduction gear drive.
Performance: 4,040hp continuous rating.
ETH Index: 66.

Diagram	*Weight*	*Max speed*
86-2BX	85.0 tonnes	100mph
86-2CX	86.2 tonnes	100mph
	Ballast weighted bogies	
86-2DX	85.0 tonnes	110mph
86-2EX	86.2 tonnes	110mph
	Ballast weighted bogies	

Standard equipment: One man operation (M); Driver/guard communication; Sanding gear.

Special characteristics: Cab/shore radio (B); Headlight (L); Push-pull (Time Division Multiplex system (P).

Sectors:

InterCity: **IANA:** Anglia Region. **ICCA:** Cross-Country. **ICHA:** Charter. **IWCA:** West Coast main line. **IWCB:** West Coast main line (equipped TDM).

Freightliner: **LXXA:** Railfreight Distribution (Freightliner), General.

Network SouthEast: **NXXA:** General.

Parcels: **RXLE:** General.

Loc No	*Dia*	*SC*	*Liv*	*Pool*	*Dep*	*Name*
86204	BX		I	*ICHA*	WN	*City of Carlisle*
86206	CX			*ICCA*	WN	*City of Stoke on Trent*
86207	BX		I	*ICCA*	WN	*City of Lichfield*
86208	CX		I	*IWCA*	WN	*City of Chester*
86209†	EX	L	I	*IWCA*	WN	*City of Coventry*
86210	CX	L	I	*ICCA*	WN	*City of Edinburgh*
86212	CX		I	*IWCB*	WN	*Preston Guild*
86213	CX	L	I	*RXLE*	WN	*Lancashire Witch*
86214†	BX	L	I	*IANA*	WN	*Sans Pareil*
86215	BX		I	*IANA*	WN	*Joseph Chamberlain*
86216	BX	L	I	*IANA*	WN	*Meteor*
86218	BX		I	*IANA*	WN	*Planet*
86219	CX		I	*IWCB*	WN	*Phoenix*
86220	CX		I	*IANA*	WN	*The Round Tabler*
86221†	CX		I	*IANA*	WN	*BBC Look East*
86223	CX		I	*IANA*	WN	*Norwich Union*
86224†	EX	B	I	*IWCA*	WN	*Caledonian*
86225	DX	BL	I	*RXLE*	WN	*Hardwicke*
86226	BX		I	*IWCA*	WN	*Royal Mail Midlands*
86227†	BX		I	*IANA*	WN	*Sir Henry Johnson*
86228	BX	P	I	*IWCB*	WN	*Vulcan Heritage*
86229†	BX	L	I	*IANA*	WN	*Sir John Betjeman*
86230	BX	L	I	*IANA*	WN	*The Duke of Wellington*
86231†	EX		I	*IWCB*	WN	*Starlight Express*
86232†	BX		I	*IANA*	WN	*Harold Macmillan*
86234	CX		I	*RXLE*	WN	*J. B. Priestley O.M.*
86235	CX		I	*IANA*	WN	*Novelty*

Loc No	Dia	SC	Liv	Pool	Dep	Name
86236†	CX	L	I	IWCA	WN	Josiah Wedgwood. Master Potter 1730-1795
86237	CX		I	IANA	WN	Sir Charles Hallé
86238†	BX	L	I	IANA	WN	European Community
86239	BX	B		IWCA	WN	L. S. Lowry
86240†	CX	PL	I	IWCB	WN	Bishop Eric Treacy
86241†	BX			IWCB	WN	Glenfiddich
86242†	CX		I	RXLE	WN	James Kennedy GC
86243	CX		I	RXLE	WN	The Boys' Brigade
86244	BX		I	IANA	WN	The Royal British Legion
86245	CX	L	I	RXLE	WN	Dudley Castle
86247	CX		I	ICCA	WN	Abraham Darby
86248†	BX	L	I	ICCA	WN	Sir Clwyd — County of Clwyd
86249	BX			NXXA	WN	County of Merseyside
86250	CX	L	I	ICCA	WN	The Glasgow Herald
86251	CX	B	I	IWCA	WN	The Birmingham Post
86252†	BX	B	I	IWCA	WN	The Liverpool Daily Post
86253†	CX		I	ICCA	WN	The Manchester Guardian
86254	CX		I	RXLE	WN	William Webb Ellis
86255	CX		I	ICCA	WN	Penrith Beacon
86256†	CX		I	ICHA	WN	Pebble Mill
86257†	CX	L	I	NXXA	WN	Snowdon
86259†	CX	L	I	IANA	WN	Peter Pan
86260	CX		I	IANA	WN	Driver Wallace Oakes G.C.
86261†	BX		I	NXXA	WN	Driver John Axon G.C.

CLASS 86/4 TYPE A BO-BO

Built: British Railways (†) and English Electric 1965-66.

Supply System, Dimensions, Control system, Rectifier, Maximum tractive effort, Train brakes, Locomotive brakes, Brake force, Route availability, Train heating, all as Class 86/1.

Traction Motors: Four GEC type G412BZ, nose suspension, single reduction gear drive.

Performance: As Class 86/2.

Maximum speed: 100mph.

ETH Index: 66.

Diagram	Weight	
86-4AX	83.0 tonnes	
86-4BX	83.9 tonnes	Ballast weighted bogies

Standard equipment: Flexicoil suspension and SAB wheels; Multiple working only with other locomotives fitted with 36-way jumper cables (Class 86/4 & 87) and others with TDM(P) equipment. One man operation (M); Driver/guard communication; Sanding gear.

Special characteristics: Cab/shore radio (B); Headlight (L).

Sectors:
Railfreight: **FGXZ:** Distribution (Speedlink), ac locomotives. **FMXX:** Metals. **FVXX:** Metals (Automotive).
InterCity: **ICCA:** Cross-Country. **IWCA:** West Coast main line.
Freightliner: **LXXA:** Railfreight Distribution (Freightliner), General.
Network SouthEast: **NXXA:** General.
Parcels: **RXLE:** General.
Special Livery: Electric blue 86426.

Loc No	*Dia*	*SC*	*Liv*	*Pool*	*Dep*	*Name*
86401	BX	LM	N	*NXXA*	WN	
86402	AX	LM		*LXXA*	WN	
86403†	AX	LM	I	*LXXA*	WN	
86404†	AX	LM	I	*LXXA*	WN	
86405	AX	M	I	*IWCA*	WN	
86406†	AX	LM	I	*LXXA*	WN	
86407	AX	LM	I	*LXXA*	WN	*The Institution of Electrical Engineers*
86408	BX	LM	I	*LXXA*	WN	*St John Ambulance*
86409†	AX	LM	I	*LXXA*	WN	
86410†	AX	LM	I	*IWCA*	WN	
86411	AX	M	I	*LXXA*	WN	*Airey Neave*
86412†	AX	LM	I	*ICCA*	WN	*Elizabeth Garrett Anderson*
86413†	BX	LM	I	*FVXX*	WN	*County of Lancashire*
86414	BX	LM	I	*FVXX*	WN	*Frank Hornby*
86415†	BX	LM	I	*FMXX*	WN	*Rotary International*
86416†	AX	LM	I	*LXXA*	WN	*Wigan Pier*
86417	BX	LM	I	*LXXA*	WN	*The Kingsman*
86418	AX	LM	I	*FMXX*	WN	
86419†	AX	LM	I	*IWCA*	WN	
86420†	AX	LM	I	*LXXA*	WN	
86421	BX	LM	I	*LXXA*	WN	*London School of Economics*
86422	AX	LM	I	*FMXX*	WN	
86423	BX	LM	I	*FMXX*	WN	
86424†	AX	LM	I	*IWCA*	WN	
86425	BX	LM	I	*RXLE*	WN	
86426	BX	LM	★	*RXLE*	WN	
86427†	AX	LM	I	*FMXX*	WN	*The Industrial Society*
86428	BX	M	I	*IWCA*	WN	*Aldaniti*
86430†	AX	LM	I	*IWCA*	WN	*Scottish National Orchestra*
86431	BX	M	I	*IWCA*	WN	
86432	BX	M	I	*FMXX*	WN	*Brookside*
86433	BX	M	I	*FMXX*	WN	*Wulfruna*
86434	AX		I	*FGXZ*	WN	*University of London*
86435†	BX		I	*LXXA*	WN	
86436	BX		I	*FGXZ*	WN	
86437†	BX		I	*IWCA*	WN	
86438†	AX	L	I	*LXXA*	WN	
86439	BX	L	I	*ICCA*	WN	

CLASS 86/5 TYPE A BO-BO

Built: British Railways (†) and English Electric 1965-66. Regeared for Freightliner duties at BREL Crewe 1988/89.
Supply System, Dimensions, Traction motors, Control system, Performance, Rectifier, Maximum tractive effort, Train brakes, Locomotive brakes, Brake force, Route availability, Train heating, ETH Index, Standard equipment: all as Class 86/2.

Maximum speed: 75mph.

Diagram	*Weight*	
86-5AX	86.2 tonnes	Ballast weighted bogies
86-5BX	85.0 tonnes	

Special characteristics: Cab/shore radio (B); Headlight (L); Multiple Working (to be equipped).

Sector:
Freightliner: **LNRE:** Railfreight Distribution (Freightliner) West Coast main line ac locomotives.

Loc No	*Dia*	*SC*	*Liv*	*Pool*	*Dep*	*Name*
86501 (86258)†	AX	L	I	*LNRE*	WN	*Talyllyn*
86502 (86222)†	AX	B	Fx	*LNRE*	WN	*Lloyd's List*
86503 (86205)†	AX		F-	*LNRE*	WN	*City of Lancaster*
86504 (86217)	BX	B	F-	*LNRE*	WN	*Halley's Comet*
86505 (86246)	BX		F-	*LNRE*	WN	*Royal Anglian Regiment*
86506 (86233)	AX		F-	*LNRE*	WN	*Laurence Olivier*
86507 ( )						
86508 ( )						
86509 ( )						
86510 ( )						

86609

86632

CLASS 87/0 BO-BO

Built: BREL Crewe. 1973-74.
Supply System: Overhead electric 25kV ac.
Dimensions: 58.5ft L × 8.7ft W × 13.1ft H (Pantograph housed).
Weight: 83.3 tonnes.
Traction Motors: Four GEC type G412AZ fully suspended, single reduction gear drive.
Control system: HT tap changing.
Performance: 5,000hp continuous rating.
Rectifier: Silicon.
Maximum tractive effort: 58,000lb (258kN).
Train brakes: Air.

Locomotive brakes: Air and Rheostatic.
Brake force: 40 tonnes.
Route availability: 6.
Maximum operating speed: 110mph.
Train heating: 460kV A at 800V ac.
ETH Index: 74 (95 on stock with 600amp wiring).
Diagram: 87-0AA.

Standard equipment: Multiple Working with ac locomotives fitted with 36-way jumper cables (Class 86/4 & 87) and other with TDM(P) equipment; Driver/guard communication; Headlights (L); Sanding gear.
Special characteristics: Cab/shore radio (B).

Sectors:
InterCity: **ICCA:** Cross Country. **IWCA:** West Coast main line.
Freightliner: **LXXA:** Railfreight Distribution (Freightliner), General.

Loc No	*Dia*	*SC*	*Liv*	*Pool*	*Dep*	*Name*
87001	AA		I	*IWCA*	WN	*Royal Scot*
87002	AA		I	*IWCA*	WN	*Royal Sovereign*
87003	AA		I	*IWCA*	WN	*Patriot*
87004	AA		I	*IWCA*	WN	*Britannia*
87005	AA		I	*LXXA*	WN	*City of London*
87006	AA		I	*LXXA*	WN	*Glasgow Garden Festival*
87007	AA		I	*IWCA*	WN	*City of Manchester*
87008	AA		I	*IWCA*	WN	*City of Liverpool*
87009	AA		I	*ICCA*	WN	*City of Birmingham*
87010	AA	B	I	*ICCA*	WN	*King Arthur*
87011	AA		I	*IWCA*	WN	*The Black Prince*
87012	AA		I	*IWCA*	WN	*The Royal Bank of Scotland*
87013	AA		I	*LXXA*	WN	*John o'Gaunt*
87014	AA	B	I	*IWCA*	WN	*Knight of the Thistle*
87015	AA		I	*IWCA*	WN	*Howard of Effingham*
87016	AA		I	*IWCA*	WN	*Sir Francis Drake*
87017	AA		I	*IWCA*	WN	*Iron Duke*
87018	AA		I	*IWCA*	WN	*Lord Nelson*
87019	AA		I	*IWCA*	WN	*Sir Winston Churchill*
87020	AA		I	*IWCA*	WN	*North Briton*
87021	AA		I	*IWCA*	WN	*Robert the Bruce*
87022	AA		I	*IWCA*	WN	*Cock o' the North*
87023	AA		I	*IWCA*	WN	*Velocity*
87024	AA		I	*IWCA*	WN	*Lord of the Isles*
87025	AA		I	*IWCA*	WN	*County of Cheshire*
87026	AA		I	*IWCA*	WN	*Sir Richard Arkwright*
87027	AA		I	*IWCA*	WN	*Wolf of Badenoch*
87028	AA		I	*IWCA*	WN	*Lord President*
87029	AA		I	*IWCA*	WN	*Earl Marischal*
87030	AA		I	*IWCA*	WN	*Black Douglas*
87031	AA	B	I	*ICCA*	WN	*Hal o' the Wynd*
87032	AA		I	*ICCA*	WN	*Kenilworth*
87033	AA		I	*IWCA*	WN	*Thane of Fife*
87034	AA		I	*IWCA*	WN	*William Shakespeare*
87035	AA		I	*IWCA*	WN	*Robert Burns*

CLASS 87/1 BO-BO

Built: BREL Crewe 1975.
Supply System, Dimensions, Maximum tractive effort, Train brakes, Locomotive brakes, Brake force, Route availability, Standard equipment, ETH Index: as Class 87/0.
Weight: 79.1 tonnes.
Traction Motors: Four GEC type G412BZ fully suspended, single reduction gear drive.
Control system & Rectifier: Thyristor.
Performance: 4,850hp continuous rating.
Maximum operating speed: 110mph
Train heating: 510kV A at 890V ac.
Diagram: 87-1AA.

Sector:
Railfreight: **FVXX:** Metals (Automotive).

Loc No	*Dia*	*SC*	*Liv*	*Pool*	*Dep*	*Name*
87101	AA			*FVXX*	WN	*Stephenson*

CLASS 89 CO-CO

Built: BREL Crewe (for Hawker-Siddeley) 1986.
Supply System: Overhead electric 25kV ac.
Dimensions: 64.9ft L × 9ft W × 13.0ft H (pantograph housed).
Weight: 104 tonnes.
Traction Motors: Brush.
Control system: Thyristor.
Performance: 5,830hp (4,350kW) continuous rating.
Rectifier: Thyristor.
Maximum tractive effort: 46,200lb (205kN).
Train brakes: Air.
Locomotive brakes: Air and Rheostatic.
Brake force: 50 tonnes.
Route availability: 6.
Maximum operating speed: 125mph.
Train heating: Electric, 510kVA at 890V ac.
ETH Index: 95.
Diagram: 89-0AA.
Standard equipment: Headlight (L); One man operation (M).

Sector:
InterCity: **IECA:** East Coast main line.
Livery: InterCity.

Loc No	*Dia*	*SC*	*Liv*	*Pool*	*Dep*
89001	AA		I	*IECA*	BN

CLASS 90 BO-BO

Built: BREL Crewe 1987-90.
Supply System: Overhead electric 25kV ac.
Dimensions: 61.5ft L × 9ft W × 13ft H (pantograph housed).
Weight: 84.5 tonnes.
Traction Motors: Four GEC type G412BZ, fully suspended, single reduction gear drive.
Control system: Microprocessor, air-cooled Thyristor.
Performance: 4,850hp (3,260kW) continuous rating.
Rectifier: Thyristor.
Maximum tractive effort: 192kN.
Train brakes: Air.
Locomotive brakes: Air and Rheostatic.
Brake force: 40 tonnes.
Route availability: 7.
Maximum operating speed: 110mph.
Train heating: Electric, 510kV A at 890V ac.
ETH Index: 95.
Diagram: 90-OAA
Standard equipment: Push-pull operation (Time Division Multiplex system); Multiple Working with ac locomotives *SC* P; Snowplough brackets (K); Driver/guard communication; Headlights (L); One man operation (M).

Sectors:
Railfreight: **FGXZ**: Distribution (Speedlink). **FMXX**: Metals.
InterCity: **IWCA**: West Coast main line.
Freightliner: **LXXA**: Railfreight Distribution (Freightliner).

Loc No	*Dia*	*SC*	*Liv*	*Pool*	*Dep*	*Name*
~~90001~~	AA	P	I	*IWCA*	WN	
90002	AA	P	I	*IWCA*	WN	
90003	AA	P	I	*IWCA*	WN	
~~90004~~	AA	P	I	*IWCA*	WN	
~~90005~~	AA	P	I	*IWCA*	WN	*Financial Times*
90006	AA	P	I	*IWCA*	WN	
~~90007~~	AA	P	I	*IWCA*	WN	
~~90008~~	AA	P	I	*IWCA*	WN	
~~90009~~	AA	P	I	*IWCA*	WN	
~~90010~~	AA	P	I	*IWCA*	WN	
90011	AA	P	I	*IWCA*	WN	*Chartered Institute of Transport*
90012	AA	P	I	*IWCA*	WN	
90013	AA	P	I	*IWCA*	WN	
~~90014~~	AA	P	I	*IWCA*	WN	
~~90015~~	AA	P	I	*IWCA*	WN	
90016	AA	P	I	*FMXX*	WN	
~~90017~~	AA	P	I	*FMXX*	WN	
~~90018~~	AA	P	I	*IWCA*	WN	
90019	AA	P	I	*IWCA*	WN	
~~90020~~	AA	P		*IWCA*		
~~90021~~	AA	P		*IWCA*		

Loc No	Dia	SC	Liv	Pool	Dep
90022	AA	P		IWCA	
90023	AA	P		FGXZ	
90024	AA	P		IWCA	
90025	AA	P		FGXZ	
90026	AA	P		FGXZ	
90027	AA	P		LXXA	
90028	AA	P		LXXA	
90029	AA	P		LXXA	

CLASS 91 BO-BO

Built: GEC (constructed by BREL Crewe), 1988-90.
Supply system: Overhead electric 25kV ac.
Dimensions: 63.7ft L × 9ft W × 12.3ft H (Pantograph housed).
Weight: 84.1 tonnes.
Traction motors: GEC.
Control system: Microprocessor, air-cooled Thyristor.
Performance: 6,080hp (4,530kN) continuous rating.
Rectifier: Thyristor.
Maximum tractive effort: --lb (--kN).
Train brakes: Air.
Locomotive brakes: Air and Rheostatic.
Brake force: 45 tonnes.
Route availability: 7.
Maximum operating speed: 140mph.
Train heating: Electric, 510kV A at 890V ac.
ETH Index: 95.
Diagram: 91-0AA.
Standard equipment: Push-pull operation (Time Division Multiplex system); Multiple working with ac locomotives *SC* (R); Driver/guard communication; Headlights (L); One man operation (M).

Sector:
InterCity: **IECA:** East Coast main line.
Livery: *InterCity*.

Loc No	Dia	SC	Liv	Pool	Dep
91001	AA	P	I	IECA	BN
91002	AA	P	I	IECA	BN
91003	AA	P	I	IECA	BN
91004	AA	P	I	IECA	BN
91005	AA	P	I	IECA	BN
91006	AA	P	I	IECA	BN
91007	AA	P	I	IECA	BN
91008	AA	P	I	IECA	BN
91009	AA	P	I	IECA	BN
91010	AA	P		IECA	
91011	AA	P		IECA	
91012	AA	P		IECA	
91013	AA	P		IECA	

Loc No	*Dia*	*SC*	*Liv*	*Pool*	*Dep*
91014	AA	P		*IECA*	
91015	AA	P		*IECA*	
91016	AA	P		*IECA*	
~~91017~~	AA	P		*IECA*	
91018	AA	P		*IECA*	
91019	AA	P		*IECA*	
91020	AA	P		*IECA*	
91021	AA	P		*IECA*	
~~91022~~	AA	P		*IECA*	
~~91023~~	AA	P		*IECA*	
91024	AA	P		*IECA*	
91025	AA	P		*IECA*	
91026	AA	P		*IECA*	
91027	AA	P		*IECA*	
91028	AA	P		*IECA*	
91029	AA	P		*IECA*	
91030	AA	P		*IECA*	
91031	AA	P		*IECA*	

InterCity 125 trains. Mk 3A Passenger Carrying Coaching Stock

Each set comprises a rake of between seven and nine Mk 3 coaches including a catering vehicle and a GJ2 (Trailer Guard Standard) having facilities for the travelling Conductor Guard.

Formations are generally semi-permanent to ensure regular maintenance schedules are adhered to, but temporary changes may be effected when a fault is found on a vehicle which cannot be rectified within the scheduled maintenance period. To provide cover a few spare vehicles are held at the main depots.

The coaches are not compatible with standard Mk 3 coaching stock. Movement is restricted to haulage by Class 43 locomotives (Power Cars) or buckeye coupling fitted Class 08 shunting locomotives unless an appropriate barrier coach with buckeye and conventional couplings is provided. To allow haulage of train sets by Push Pull fitted (Time Division Multiplex system) electric locomotives some TGS coaches are being modified with buffers and conventional coupling gear.

Standard data:
Built: BREL Derby Carriage Works 1976-82.
Dimensions: 23.0m L × 2.74m W × 3.81m H.
Maximum speed: 125mph.
Equipment: Air brakes, public address, electric heating and air conditioning, fluorescent and tungsten lighting.
Special characteristics: Public payphone (P). Refurbished (unless applicable to all of type) (R). Reference to smoking/non-smoking accommodation is only made where it is the only significant variation between diagrams.

Sectors:
INTERCITY: **ICC:** Cross Country. **ICH:** Charter. **IEC:** East Coast main line. **IML:** Midland Lines. **IWR:** Western Region.

Livery: All refurbished vehicles (R) carry *INTERCITY* livery, latest outshopped include the Swallow emblem introduced during 1988.

TRB: Trailer Restaurant with Buffet, Unclassified

Diagram: GN4.01.0A.
Weight: 38 tonnes.
Bogies: BT10 and BT10a (one each).
Equipment: Microwave/Microaire electric ovens, Public address transmitter.
Seats: 23.

Veh No	*Dia*	*SC*	*Liv*	*Pool*	*Dep*
40204	OA	R	I	*IWR*	PM
40205	OA	R	I	*IWR*	PM
40206	OA			*IWR*	PM
40207	OA	R	I	*IWR*	PM
40208	OA	R	I	*IWR*	PM
40209	OA	R	I	*IWR*	PM
40210	OA			*IWR*	PM
40211	OA			*IWR*	PM
40212	OA	R	I	*IWR*	PM
40213	OA	R	I	*IWR*	PM

TRUB: Trailer Restaurant Unclassified, Buffet

Diagram: GK4.01.0C.
Weight: 39 tonnes.
Bogies: BT10b and BT10c (one each).
Equipment: Microwave/Microaire electric ovens, Public address transmitter.
Seats: 17.

Veh No	*Dia*	*SC*	*Liv*	*Pool*	*Dep*
40322	OC	R		*IWR*	LA
40323	OC	R		*IWR*	LA
40324	OC	R		*IWR*	LA
40325	OC	R		*IWR*	LA
40326	OC	R		*IWR*	LA
40327	OC	R		*IWR*	LA
40331	OC	R		*IWR*	LA
40355	OC	R		*IWR*	LA

TRSB: Trailer Restaurant Standard with Buffet

Diagram: GK2.02.0B.
Weight: 36 tonnes.
Equipment: Microwave/Microaire electric ovens, Public address transmitter.
Bogies: One each BT10 and BT10a.
Seats: 35.

Veh No	Dia	SC	Liv	Pool	Dep
40401	0B	PR	I	ICC	PM
40402	0B	PR	I	ICC	PM
40403	0B	R	I	ICC	PM
40414	0B	R	I	ICC	LA
40415	0B	PR	I	ICC	LA
40416	0B	R	I	IWR	00
40417	0B	R	I	IWR	00
40418	0B	R	I	IWR	00
40419	0B	R	I	IWR	00
40420	0B	R	I	IWR	PM
40421	0B	P		ICC	PM
40422	0B	R	I	IWR	PM
40423	0B	R	I	IWR	00
40424	0B	R	I	IWR	LA
40425	0B	R	I	ICC	PM
40426	0B	R	I	ICC	LA
40427	0B	R	I	IWR	00
40428	0B			IWR	PM
40429	0B		I	IEC	NL
40430	0B	PR	I	ICC	LA
40431	0B	P		ICC	LA
40432	0B			ICC	LA
40433	0B			ICC	LA
40434	0B			ICC	LA
40435	0B	R	I	IWR	PM
40436	0B	R	I	IWR	00
40437	0B	R	I	IWR	00

TRFK: Trailer Restaurant First (Pullman) with Kitchen

Diagram: GL1.01.0A.
Weight: 37 tonnes.
Equipment: Microwave/Microaire ovens, Public address transmitter.
Bogies: One each BT10 and BT10a.
Seats: 24.

Veh No	Dia	SC	Liv	Pool	Dep
40501	0A	R	I	IEC	NL
40505	0A	R	I	IEC	NL
40511	0A	R	I	IEC	NL

TLUK: Trailer Lounge Unclassifed with Kitchen

Modified from TRFK in 1984. Available for special hire as additional or replacement in standard train.

Diagram: GM4.01.0A.
Weight: 36.5 tonnes.
Equipment: Microwave/Microaire ovens.
Bogies: One each BT10 and BT10a.
Seats: 16 (eight at conference table, eight lounge chairs).
Toilet: 1.

Veh No	Dia	SC	Liv	Pool	Dep
40513	0A	R	I	ICH	BN

TRFM: Trailer Restaurant First, Modular

Modified from TRFB in 1987. Operated in Sheffield-St Pancras 'Master Cutler' service.

Diagram: GK1.02.0A.
Weight: 39 tonnes.
Equipment: Microwave/Microaire ovens (Cuisine 2000 Modular catering); Public address transmitter.
Bogies: One each BT10 and BT10a.
Seats: 17.
Toilet: 1 (staff).

Veh No	*Dia*	*SC*	*Liv*	*Pool*	*Dep*
40619	0A	R	I	*IML*	NL

TRFB: Trailer Restaurant First with Buffet

Diagram	**Weight**	**Bogies (one each)**
GH1.01.0A	38 tonnes	BT10 and BT10a
GK1.01.0B	39 tonnes	BT10b and BT10c

Equipment: Microwave/Microaire ovens; Public address transmitter.
Seats: 17.

Veh No	*Dia*	*SC*	*Liv*	*Pool*	*Dep*
40700	0A	PR	I	*IEC*	NL
40701	0A	PR	I	*IEC*	BN
40702	0A	PR	I	*IEC*	BN
40703	0A	PR	I	*IEC*	BN
40704	0A	R	I	*IEC*	BN
40705	0A	PR	I	*IEC*	BN
40706	0A	PR	I	*IEC*	BN
40707	0A	R	I	*IEC*	BN
40708	0A	R	I	*IEC*	BN
40709	0A	PR	I	*IML*	NL
40710	0A	PR	I	*IEC*	BN
40711	0A	P	I	*IEC*	NL
40712	0A	PR	I	*IEC*	NL
40713	0A	PR	I	*IEC*	NL
40714	0A	PR	I	*IEC*	NL
40715	0A	PR	I	*IEC*	BN
40716	0A	R	I	*IEC*	BN
40717	0A	R	I	*IEC*	BN
40718	0A	PR	I	*IEC*	BN
40720	0A	R	I	*IEC*	BN
40721	0A	R	I	*IEC*	BN
40728	0B	PR	I	*IEC*	NL
40729	0B	R	I	*IEC*	BN
40730	0B	PR	I	*IEC*	NL
40732	0B	PR	I	*IWR*	LA
40733	0B	PR	I	*IEC*	BN
40734	0B	PR	I	*IEC*	BN
40735	0B	P		*IML*	NL
40736	0B	P	I	*IEC*	BN
40737	0B	P	I	*IML*	NL
40738	0B	PR	I	*IML*	NL
40739	0B	PR	I	*IEC*	BN
40740	0B		I	*IEC*	BN
40741	0B	PR	I	*IML*	NL
40742	0B	R	I	*IEC*	BN
40743	0B	P		*IML*	NL
40744	0B	P	I	*IML*	NL
40745	0B	PR	I	*IML*	NL
40746	0B	PR	I	*IML*	NL
40747	0B	P		*IML*	NL

Veh No	*Dia*	*SC*	*Liv*	*Pool*	*Dep*
40748	0B		I	*IML*	NL
40749	0B	PR	I	*IEC*	HT
40750	0B	P		*IML*	NL
40751	0B	PR	I	*IEC*	NL
40752	0B			*IEC*	NL
40753	0B	P	I	*IEC*	NL
40754	0B	R	I	*IEC*	BN
40756	0B	R	I	*IEC*	BN
40757	0B	PR	I	*IWR*	LA

TF: Trailer First

Diagram	**Weight**	**Bogies**	**Variation**
GH1.02.0A	33 tonnes	BT10	
GH1.02.0B	33.5 tonnes	BT10b	
GH1.02.0D	33.5 tonnes	BT10b	Refurbished
GH1.02.0E	33 tonnes	BT10	All non-smoking
GH1.02.0F	33.5 tonnes	BT10b	All non-smoking
GH1.02.1C	33 tonnes	BT10	Converted prototype
GH1.02.1G	33 tonnes	BT10	Converted prototype, all non-smoking
GH1.02.2A	33 tonnes	BT10	Payphone
GH1.02.2B	33.5 tonnes	BT10b	Payphone
GH1.02.2D	33.5 tonnes	BT10b	Refurbished, Payphone
GH1.02.0E	33 tonnes	BT10	All non-smoking, Payphone
GH1.02.3A	34 tonnes	BT10	
GH1.02.3B	34 tonnes	BT10	All non-smoking

Equipment: One table and seat removable for disabled passengers.

Seats: 48.
Toilets: 2.

Veh No	*Dia*	*SC*	*Liv*	*Pool*	*Dep*
41003	2A	PR	I	*IWR*	PM
41004	0E	R	I	*IWR*	PM
41005	2A	PR	I	*IWR*	PM
41006	0E	R	I	*IWR*	PM
41007	2A	PR	I	*IWR*	PM
41008	0E	R	I	*IWR*	PM
41009	2A	PR	I	*IWR*	PM
41010	0E	R	I	*IWR*	PM
41011	2A	PR	I	*IWR*	PM
41012	0E	R	I	*IWR*	PM
41013	2A	P		*IWR*	PM
41014	0E			*IWR*	PM
41015	2A	P	I	*IWR*	PM
41016	0E		I	*IWR*	PM
41017	2A	P	I	*IWR*	PM
41018	0E		I	*IWR*	PM
41019	2A	P		*IWR*	PM
41020	0E			*IWR*	PM
41021	2A	P		*IWR*	PM
41022	0E			*IWR*	PM
41023	2A	PR	I	*IWR*	LA
41024	0E	R	I	*IWR*	LA
41025	2A	PR	I	*IWR*	LA
41026	0E	R	I	*IWR*	LA
41027	2A	PR	I	*IWR*	LA
41028	0E	R	I	*IWR*	LA
41029	2A	PR	I	*IWR*	LA
41030	0E	R	I	*IWR*	LA
41031	2A	PR	I	*IWR*	LA
41032	0E	R	I	*IWR*	LA
41033	2A	PR	I	*IWR*	LA
41034	0E	R	I	*IWR*	LA
41035	0A	PR	I	*IWR*	OO
41036	0E	R	I	*IWR*	OO

Veh No	Dia	SC	Liv	Pool	Dep
41037	2A	PR	I	*IWR*	OO
41038	0E	R	I	*IWR*	OO
41039	0E			*IML*	NL
41040	0E			*IML*	NL
41041	2E	PR	I	*IEC*	NL
41042	0A	R	I	*ICC*	LA
41043	0A	R	I	*IML*	NL
41044	0E	R	I	*IML*	NL
41045	0A	R	I	*IML*	NL
41046	0A	R	I	*IEC*	BN
41047	0A			*IML*	NL
41048	0E			*IML*	NL
41049	0A	R	I	*IML*	NL
41050	0E	R	I	*IML*	NL
41051	0A	R	I	*IML*	NL
41052	0E	R	I	*IML*	NL
41053	0A			*IML*	NL
41054	0E			*IML*	NL
41055	0A	R	I	*IML*	NL
41056	0E	R	I	*IML*	NL
41057	0A	R	I	*IEC*	BN
41058	0E	R	I	*IEC*	BN
41059	0A	R	I	*IEC*	BN
41060	0E	R	I	*IEC*	BN
41061	0A	R	I	*IEC*	BN
41062	0E	R	I	*IEC*	BN
41063	0A	R	I	*IEC*	BN
41064	0E	R	I	*IEC*	BN
41065	0A	R	I	*IML*	NL
41066	2E	P		*IEC*	HT
41067	0A	R	I	*IEC*	NL
41068	0E	R	I	*IEC*	NL
41069	0A	R	I	*IEC*	NL
41070	0E	R	I	*IEC*	NL
41071	0A	R	I	*IEC*	NL
41072	0E	R	I	*IEC*	NL
41073	0A			*IEC*	NL
41074	0E			*IEC*	NL
41075	0A	R	I	*IEC*	BN
41076	0E	R	I	*IEC*	BN
41077	0A			*IEC*	NL
41078	0E			*IEC*	NL
41079	0A	R	I	*IEC*	NL
41080	0E	R	I	*IEC*	NL
41081	0A	R	I	*IEC*	BN
41082	0E	R	I	*IEC*	BN
41083	0A	R	I	*IEC*	BN
41084	0E	R	I	*IEC*	BN
41085	0A	R	I	*IEC*	BN
41086	0E	R	I	*IEC*	BN
41087	0A	R	I	*IEC*	BN
41088	0E	R	I	*IEC*	BN
41089	0A	R	I	*IEC*	BN
41090	0E	R	I	*IEC*	BN
41091	0A	R	I	*IEC*	BN
41092	0E	R	I	*IEC*	BN
41093	0A	R	I	*IEC*	BN
41094	0E	R	I	*IEC*	BN
41095	0A	R	I	*IEC*	BN
41096	0E	R	I	*IEC*	BN
41097	0A	R	I	*IML*	NL
41098	0E	R	I	*IML*	NL
41099	0A	R	I	*IEC*	NL
41100	0E	R	I	*IEC*	NL
41101	0A	R	I	*IEC*	NL
41102	0E	R	I	*IEC*	NL
41103	0A	R	I	*IEC*	NL
41104	0E	R	I	*IEC*	NL
41105	0A	R	I	*IEC*	NL
41106	0E	R	I	*IEC*	NL
41107	0A	R	I	*IEC*	BN
41108	0E	R	I	*IEC*	BN
41109	0A	R	I	*IEC*	BN
41110	0E	R	I	*IEC*	BN
41111	0A	R	I	*IEC*	HT
41112	0E	R	I	*IEC*	HT
41113	0A	R	I	*IEC*	BN
41114	0E			*IEC*	BN
41115	0A	R	I	*IEC*	BN
41116	0E	R	I	*IEC*	BN
41117	0A	R	I	*IML*	NL
41118	0E	R	I	*IEC*	BN
41119	0A	R	I	*IEC*	BN
41120	0E	R	I	*IEC*	BN
41121	2D	PR	I	*IWR*	LA
41122	0D	R	I	*IWR*	LA
41123	2B	PR	I	*IWR*	PM
41124	0F	R	I	*IWR*	PM
41125	0D	R	I	*IWR*	LA
41126	2D	PR	I	*IWR*	LA
41127	2B	PR	I	*IWR*	PM
41128	0F	R	I	*IWR*	PM
41129	2B	PR	I	*IWR*	OO
41130	0F	R	I	*IWR*	OO

Veh No	Dia	SC	Liv	Pool	Dep
41131	2B	PR	I	*IWR*	OO
41132	0F	PR	I	*IWR*	OO
41133	2B	R	I	*IWR*	OO
41134	0F	R	I	*IWR*	OO
41135	2B	PR	I	*IWR*	OO
41136	0F	R	I	*IWR*	OO
41137	0B	P		*IWR*	PM
41138	0F			*IWR*	PM
41139	2B	PR	I	*IWR*	OO
41140	0F	R	I	*IWR*	OO
41141	2B	PR	I	*IWR*	LA
41142	0F	R	I	*IWR*	LA
41143	2B	PR	I	*IWR*	OO
41144	0F	R	I	*IWR*	OO
41145	2B	PR	I	*IWR*	LA
41146	0F	R	I	*IWR*	LA
41147	0B	R	I	*ICC*	PM
41148	0B	R	I	*ICC*	PM
41149	0B	R	I	*IEC*	BN
41150	0F	R	I	*IEC*	BN
41151	0B	PR	I	*IEC*	BN
41152	0F	PR	I	*IEC*	BN
41153	0B	R	I	*IML*	NL
41154	0F	R	I	*IML*	NL
41155	0B		I	*IML*	NL
41156	0F		I	*IML*	NL
41157	0B			*IML*	NL
41158	0F			*IML*	NL
41159	0B	R	I	*ICC*	PM
41160	0B	R	I	*ICC*	PM
41161	0B			*ICC*	PM
41162	0B	R	I	*ICC*	LA
41163	0B	R	I	*ICC*	LA
41164	0B	R	I	*IWR*	LA
41165	0B	R	I	*ICC*	LA
41166	0B			*ICC*	LA
41167	0B			*ICC*	LA
41168	0B			*ICC*	LA
41169	0B			*ICC*	LA
41170	1C	R	I	*IEC*	BN
41171	1C	R	I	*IEC*	BN
41172	1G	R	I	*IEC*	BN
41173	1G	R	I	*IEC*	BN
41174	1C	R	I	*IEC*	BN
41175	0B			*IML*	NL
41176	0A			*IML*	NL

TS: Trailer Standard

Diagram	Weight	Seats	Bogies	Variation
GH2.02.0B	34 tonnes	72	BT10	
GH2.02.0D	35 tonnes	72	BT10	All non-smoking
GH2.02.0E	34 tonnes	72	BT10	All non-smoking
GH2.02.0G	35 tonnes	72	BT10	
GH2.02.0H	34 tonnes	72	BT10	
GH2.02.0J	33.5 tonnes	72	BT10b	
GH2.03.0D	33.5 tonnes	76★	BT10b	Refurbished, non-smoking*
GH2.03.0E	33.5 tonnes	76★	BT10b	Refurbished, non-smoking*
GH2.03.0F	33.5 tonnes	76★	BT10d	Non-smoking
GH2.03.0H	34 tonnes	76★	BT10	Non-smoking
GH2.03.0J	33.5 tonnes	76★	BT10b	Refurbished
GH2.03.0K	34 tonnes	76★	BT10	Refurbished
GH2.03.0L	35 tonnes	76★	BT10	Refurbished, non-smoking
GH2.03.0M	33 tonnes	76★	BT10	Refurbished

*No discernible variation

Toilets: 2.

Veh No	Dia	SC	Liv	Pool	Dep
42003	20D	R★	I	*IWR*	PM
42004	20D	R★	I	*IWR*	PM
42005	20G	R★	I	*IWR*	PM
42006	20D	R	I	*IWR*	PM
42007	20D	R	I	*IWR*	PM
42008	20G	R	I	*IWR*	PM
42009	20D	R★	I	*IWR*	PM
42010	20D	R★	I	*IWR*	PM
42011	20G	R★	I	*IWR*	PM
42012	20D	R★	I	*IWR*	PM
42013	20D	R★	I	*IWR*	PM
42014	20G	R★	I	*IWR*	PM
42015	20D	R	I	*IWR*	PM
42016	20D	R	I	*IWR*	PM
42017	20G	R	I	*IWR*	PM
42018	20D			*IWR*	PM
42019	20D			*IWR*	PM
42020	20G			*IWR*	PM
42021	20D	R	I	*IWR*	PM
42022	20D	R	I	*IWR*	PM
42023	20H	R	I	*IWR*	PM
42024	20E	R	I	*IWR*	PM
42025	20E	R	I	*IWR*	PM
42026	20H	R	I	*IWR*	PM
42027	20E			*IWR*	PM
42028	20E			*IWR*	PM
42029	20E			*IWR*	PM
42030	20E			*IWR*	PM
42031	20E			*IWR*	PM
42032	20H			*IWR*	PM
42033	20E	R	I	*IWR*	LA
42034	20E	R	I	*IWR*	LA
42035	20H	R	I	*IWR*	LA
42036	20E	R	I	*IWR*	LA
42037	20E	R	I	*IWR*	LA
42038	20H	R	I	*IWR*	LA
42039	20E	R	I	*IWR*	LA
42040	20E	R	I	*IWR*	LA
42041	20H	R	I	*IWR*	LA
42042	20E	R	I	*IWR*	LA
42043	20E	R	I	*IWR*	LA
42044	20H	R	I	*IWR*	LA
42045	20E	R★	I	*IWR*	LA
42046	20E	R★	I	*IWR*	LA
42047	20H	R★	I	*IWR*	LA
42048	20E	R	I	*IWR*	LA
42049	20E	R	I	*IWR*	LA
42050	20H	R	I	*IWR*	LA
42051	20E	R	I	*IWR*	OO
42052	20E	R	I	*IWR*	OO
42053	20H	R	I	*IWR*	OO
42054	20E	R	I	*IWR*	OO
42055	20E	R	I	*IWR*	OO
42056	20H	R	I	*IWR*	OO
42057	20E			*IML*	NL
42058	20E			*IML*	NL
42059	20H			*IML*	NL
42060	20E	R	I	*IWR*	LA
42061	20H	R	I	*IWR*	LA
42062	20E	R	I	*IML*	NL
42063	20E	R	I	*IML*	NL
42064	20E	R	I	*IML*	NL
42065	20H	R	I	*IML*	NL
42066	20E	R	I	*IML*	NL
42067	20E	R	I	*IML*	NL
42068	20H	R	I	*IML*	NL
42069	20E			*IML*	NL
42070	20E			*IML*	NL
42071	20E			*IML*	NL
42072	20E	R	I	*IML*	NL
42073	20E	R	I	*IML*	NL
42074	20H	R	I	*IML*	NL
42075	20H	R★	I	*IML*	NL
42076	20E	R	I	*IML*	NL
42077	20E	R	I	*IML*	NL
42078	20H	R★	I	*IML*	NL
42079	20E			*IML*	NL
42080	20H			*IML*	NL
42081	20E	R	I	*IML*	NL
42082	20E	R	I	*IML*	NL
42083	20E	R	I	*IML*	NL
42084	20E			*ICC*	PM
42085	20E			*ICC*	PM
42086	20E			*ICC*	PM
42087	20H			*ICC*	PM
42088	20E	R	I	*ICC*	LA
42089	20E	R	I	*ICC*	LA
42090	20E	R	I	*ICC*	LA
42091	20H	R	I	*ICC*	LA
42092	20E	R	I	*ICC*	LA
42093	20E	R	I	*ICC*	LA
42094	20E	R	I	*ICC*	LA
42095	20H	R	I	*ICC*	LA

IC125 Trailers 42096-42191

Veh No	Dia	SC	Liv	Pool	Dep
42096	20E	R	I	*IWR*	LA
42097	20E	R	I	*IWR*	LA
42098	20E	R	I	*IWR*	LA
42099	20E	R	I	*IWR*	LA
42100	20K	R★	I	*IEC*	NL
42101	20K	R★	I	*IEC*	BN
42102	30K	R★	I	*IEC*	BN
42103	20H	R★	I	*IEC*	BN
42104	20E	R★	I	*IEC*	BN
42105	20H	R★	I	*IEC*	BN
42106	20H	R★	I	*IEC*	BN
42107	20H	R★	I	*IEC*	BN
42108	20E	R	I	*ICC*	LA
42109	20E	R	I	*ICC*	LA
42110	20E	R	I	*ICC*	LA
42111	20E	R	I	*IEC*	BN
42112	20E	R	I	*IEC*	BN
42113	20H	R	I	*IEC*	BN
42115	20E	R	I	*IEC*	BN
42116	20E	R	I	*IEC*	BN
42117	20H	R	I	*IEC*	BN
42118	20H			*IML*	NL
42119	20E	R	I	*IEC*	BN
42120	20E	R	I	*IEC*	BN
42121	20H	R	I	*IEC*	BN
42122	20H	R★	I	*IEC*	BN
42123	20H	R★	I	*IEC*	BN
42124	20E	R★	I	*IEC*	BN
42125	30K	R★	I	*IEC*	BN
42126	20H	R	I	*IML*	NL
42127	20E	R	I	*IEC*	BN
42128	20H	R	I	*IEC*	BN
42129	20B			*IEC*	BN
42130	20E	R★	I	*IEC*	BN
42131	20E	R★	I	*IEC*	NL
42132	20E	R★	I	*IEC*	NL
42133	20H	R★	I	*IEC*	NL
42134	20E	R★	I	*IEC*	BN
42135	20E	R★	I	*IEC*	NL
42136	20E	R★	I	*IEC*	NL
42137	20H	R★	I	*IEC*	NL
42138	20E	R★	I	*IEC*	BN
42139	30H	R★	I	*IEC*	NL
42140	30H	R★	I	*IEC*	NL
42141	30K	R★	I	*IEC*	NL
42143	20E			*IEC*	NL
42144	20E			*IEC*	NL
42145	20H			*IEC*	NL
42146	20E	★	I	*IML*	NL
42147	30H	R★	I	*IEC*	BN
42148	30H	R★	I	*IEC*	BN
42149	30K	R★	I	*IEC*	BN
42150	20E	★	I	*IML*	NL
42151	20E			*IEC*	NL
42152	20E			*IEC*	NL
42153	20H			*IEC*	NL
42154	20H	★	I	*IML*	NL
42155	30H	R★	I	*IEC*	NL
42156	30H	R★	I	*IEC*	NL
42157	30H	R★	I	*IEC*	NL
42158	30D	★	I	*IML*	NL
42159	30H	R★	I	*IEC*	BN
42160	30H	R★	I	*IEC*	BN
42161	30H	R★	I	*IEC*	BN
42162	20E	R★	I	*IEC*	BN
42163	30H	R★	I	*IEC*	BN
42164	20H	R★	I	*IEC*	BN
42165	30H	R★	I	*IEC*	BN
42166	20E	R★	I	*IEC*	BN
42167	20E	R★	I	*IEC*	BN
42168	20E	R★	I	*IEC*	BN
42169	20E	R★	I	*IEC*	BN
42170	20E	R★	I	*IEC*	BN
42171	20E	R★	I	*IEC*	BN
42172	20E	R★	I	*IEC*	BN
42173	20H	R★	I	*IEC*	BN
42174	20H	R★	I	*IEC*	BN
42175	20E	R★	I	*IEC*	BN
42176	20E	R★	I	*IEC*	BN
42177	20E	R★	I	*IEC*	BN
42178	30H	R★	I	*IEC*	BN
~~42179~~	20E	R	I	*IEC*	BN
42180	20E	R	I	*IEC*	BN
~~42181~~	20E	R	I	*IEC*	BN
42182	20E	R★	I	*IEC*	BN
42183	20E	R★	I	*IEC*	BN
42184	20E	R★	I	*IEC*	BN
42185	20E	R★	I	*IEC*	BN
42186	20E	R★	I	*IEC*	BN
42187	20E	R★	I	*IEC*	BN
42188	20E	R★	I	*IEC*	BN
42189	20H	R★	I	*IEC*	BN
42190	20E	R★	I	*IEC*	BN
42191	20E	R★	I	*IML*	NL

Veh No	Dia	SC	Liv	Pool	Dep
42192	20E	R★	I	*IML*	NL
42193	20H	R★	I	*IML*	NL
42194	20B	R★	I	*IEC*	BN
42195	20E	R★	I	*IML*	NL
42196	20E	R★	I	*IWR*	LA
42197	20E	R★	I	*IWR*	LA
42198	20B	R★	I	*IEC*	NL
42199	20H	R★	I	*IEC*	NL
42200	20E	R★	I	*IML*	NL
42201	20E	R★	I	*IEC*	NL
42202	20E	R★	I	*IEC*	NL
42203	20E	R★	I	*IEC*	NL
42204	20H	R★	I	*IEC*	NL
42205	20E	R★	I	*IML*	NL
42206	20E	R★	I	*IEC*	NL
42207	20E	R★	I	*IEC*	NL
42208	20E	R★	I	*IEC*	NL
42209	20H	R★	I	*IEC*	NL
42210	20H	R★	I	*IML*	NL
42211	20E	R★	I	*IEC*	NL
42212	20E	R★	I	*IEC*	NL
42213	20E	R★	I	*IEC*	NL
42214	20H	R★	I	*IEC*	NL
42215	20E	R★	I	*IML*	NL
42216	30H	R★	I	*IWR*	LA
42217	20E	R★	I	*IEC*	BN
42218	20E	R★	I	*IEC*	BN
42219	20H	R★	I	*IEC*	BN
42220	20E	R★	I	*IML*	NL
42221	30H	R★	I	*IWR*	LA
42222	20E	R	I	*IEC*	BN
42223	20E	R	I	*IEC*	BN
42224	20H	R	I	*IEC*	BN
42225	20E	R★	I	*IML*	NL
42226	20E	R★	I	*IEC*	BN
42227	20E	R★	I	*IEC*	HT
42228	20E	R★	I	*IEC*	HT
42229	20H	R★	I	*IEC*	NL
42230	20H	R★	I	*IML*	NL
42231	20B	R★	I	*IEC*	BN
42232	20E			*IEC*	BN
42233	20E			*IEC*	BN
42234	20H			*IEC*	BN
42235	20E			*IML*	NL
42236	20E			*IML*	NL
42237	20E	R★	I	*IEC*	BN
42238	20E	R★	I	*IEC*	BN
42239	20H	R★	I	*IEC*	BN
42240	20E		I	*IML*	NL
42241	20E	R★	I	*IEC*	BN
42242	20E	R★	I	*IEC*	BN
42243	20E	R	I	*IEC*	BN
42244	20H	R	I	*IEC*	BN
42245	20E			*IML*	NL
42246	20E	R★	I	*IEC*	BN
42247	20E	R★	I	*IEC*	BN
42248	20E	R★	I	*IEC*	BN
42249	20H	R★	I	*IEC*	BN
42250	20H			*IML*	NL
42251	30E	R★	I	*IWR*	LA
42252	30D	R★	I	*IWR*	LA
42253	30J	R★	I	*IWR*	LA
42254	20F	R★	I	*ICC*	PM
42255	20F	R★	I	*IWR*	PM
42256	20F	R★	I	*IWR*	PM
42257	20J	R★	I	*IWR*	PM
42258	20F	R★	I	*ICC*	PM
42259	30D	R★	I	*IWR*	LA
42260	30D	R★	I	*IWR*	LA
42261	30J	R★	I	*IWR*	LA
42262	20F	R★	I	*ICC*	PM
42263	20F	R★	I	*IWR*	PM
42264	20F	R★	I	*IWR*	PM
42265	20J	R★	I	*IWR*	PM
42266	20J	R★	I	*ICC*	PM
42267	20F	R★	I	*IWR*	OO
42268	20F	R★	I	*IWR*	OO
42269	20J	R★	I	*IWR*	OO
42270	20F	R★	I	*ICC*	PM
42271	20F	R★	I	*IWR*	OO
42272	20F	R★	I	*IWR*	OO
42273	20J	R★	I	*IWR*	OO
42274	20F	R★	I	*ICC*	PM
42275	20F	R★	I	*IWR*	OO
42276	20F	R★	I	*IWR*	OO
42277	20J	R★	I	*IWR*	OO
42278	20F	R★	I	*ICC*	PM
42279	30D	R★	I	*IWR*	OO
42280	30D	R★	I	*IWR*	OO
42281	30J	R★	I	*IWR*	OO
42282	20J	R	I	*ICC*	PM
42283	20F			*IWR*	PM
42284	20F			*IWR*	PM
42285	20J			*IWR*	PM

Veh No	Dia	SC	Liv	Pool	Dep
42286	20F	R	I	ICC	PM
42287	20F	R★	I	IWR	OO
42288	20F	R★	I	IWR	OO
42289	20J	R★	I	IWR	OO
42290	20F	R	I	ICC	PM
42291	20F	R★	I	IWR	LA
42292	20F	R★	I	IWR	LA
42293	20J	R★	I	IWR	LA
42294	20F	R	I	ICC	PM
42295	20F	R★	I	IWR	OO
42296	20F	R★	I	IWR	OO
42297	20J	R★	I	IWR	OO
42298	20J	R	I	ICC	PM
42299	20F	R★	I	IWR	LA
42300	20F	R★	I	IWR	LA
42301	20J	R★	I	IWR	LA
42302	20F	R	I	ICC	PM
42303	20F	R	I	ICC	PM
42304	20F	R	I	ICC	PM
42305	20J	R	I	ICC	PM
42306	20F			ICC	LA
42307	20F			ICC	LA
42308	20F			ICC	LA
42309	20J			ICC	LA
42310	20F			ICC	LA
42311	20F			ICC	LA
42312	20F			ICC	LA
42313	20J			ICC	LA
42314	20F			ICC	LA
42315	20F			ICC	LA
42316	20F			ICC	LA
42317	20J			ICC	LA
42318	20F			ICC	LA
42319	20F			ICC	LA
42320	20F			ICC	LA
42321	20J			ICC	LA
42322	20J	R	I	ICC	LA
42323	30F	★		IML	NL
42324	30F	★		IEC	NL
42325	30F	R★	I	IML	NL
42326	30F	R★	I	IEC	BN
42327	30F	R★	I	IEC	BN
42328	30F	R★	I	IEC	BN
42329	30F	R★	I	IEC	NL
42330	30F	R★	I	IEC	BN
42331	30F	R★	I	IEC	NL
42332	30F	★		IML	NL
42333	30F	★		IEC	NL
42334	30F	R★	I	IEC	BN
42335	30F	R★	I	IEC	BN
42336	30F	R★	I	IEC	BN
42337	30F	R★	I	IEC	BN
42338	30F	R★	I	IEC	BN
42339	30F	★		IEC	NL
42340	30F	R★	I	IML	NL
42341	30D	★		IEC	BN
42342	30D	R★	I	IWR	LA
42343	30D	R★	I	IWR	LA
42344	30D	R★	I	IWR	LA
42345	30D	R★	I	IWR	LA

TGS: Trailer Guard Standard

Diagram	Weight	Variation
GJ2.01.0A	33.5 tonnes	
GJ2.01.0B	34 tonnes	Additional standard coupling and buffers for ac electric locomotive haulage

Bogies: BT10b
Seats: 63
Equipment: Public address transmitter
Toilets: 1.

Veh No	Dia	SC	Liv	Pool	Dep
44000	0A	R	I	ICC	PM
44001	0A	R	I	IWR	PM
44002	0A	R	I	IWR	PM
44003	0A	R	I	IWR	PM
44004	0A	R	I	IWR	PM
44005	0A	R	I	IWR	PM

Veh No	Dia	SC	Liv	Pool	Dep
44006	0A			*IWR*	PM
44007	0A	R	I	*IWR*	PM
44008	0A	R	I	*IWR*	PM
44009	0A			*IWR*	PM
44010	0A			*IWR*	PM
44011	0A	R	I	*IWR*	LA
44012	0A	R	I	*IWR*	LA
44013	0A	R	I	*IWR*	LA
44014	0A	R	I	*IWR*	LA
44015	0A	R	I	*IWR*	LA
44016	0A	R	I	*IWR*	LA
44017	0A	R	I	*IWR*	00
44018	0A	R	I	*IWR*	00
44019	0A			*IWR*	NL
44020	0A	R	I	*IWR*	LA
44021	0A	R	I	*IML*	NL
44022	0A	R	I	*IML*	NL
~~44023~~	0A			*IML*	NL
44024	0A	R	I	*IML*	NL
44025	0A	R	I	*IML*	NL
44026	0A			*IML*	NL
44027	0A	R	I	*IML*	NL
44028	0A	R	I	*IWR*	LA
44029	0A	R	I	*IWR*	PM
44030	0A	R	I	*IWR*	LA
44031	0A	R	I	*IWR*	PM
44032	0A	R	I	*IWR*	00
44033	0A	R	I	*IWR*	00
44034	0A	R	I	*IWR*	00
44035	0A	R	I	*IWR*	00
44036	0A			*IWR*	PM
44037	0A	R	I	*IWR*	00
44038	0A	R	I	*IWR*	LA
44039	0A	R	I	*IWR*	00
44040	0A	R	I	*IWR*	LA
44041	0A	R	I	*IEC*	BN
44042	0A	R	I	*IEC*	BN
44043	0A	R	I	*IEC*	BN
44044	0A	R	I	*IEC*	BN
44045	0A	R	I	*IEC*	BN
44046	0A	R	I	*IEC*	NL
44047	0A	R	I	*IEC*	NL
44048	0A	R	I	*IEC*	NL
44049	0A			*IEC*	NL
44050	0A	R	I	*IEC*	BN
44051	0A			*IEC*	NL
44052	0A	R	I	*IEC*	NL
44053	0A	R	I	*IEC*	BN
44054	0A	R	I	*IEC*	BN
44055	0A	R	I	*IEC*	BN
44056	0B	R	I	*IEC*	BN
44057	0A	R	I	*IEC*	BN
44058	0A	R	I	*IEC*	BN
44059	0B	R	I	*IEC*	BN
44060	0A	R	I	*IEC*	BN
44061	0A	R	I	*IML*	NL
44062	0A	R	I	*ICC*	PM
44063	0A	R	I	*IEC*	NL
44064	0A	R	I	*IEC*	NL
44065	0A	R	I	*ICC*	PM
44066	0A	R	I	*IEC*	NL
44067	0A	R	I	*IEC*	NL
44068	0A	R	I	*ICC*	PM
44069	0A			*ICC*	PM
44070	0A	R	I	*IEC*	BN
44071	0A	R	I	*IEC*	BN
44072	0A	R	I	*ICC*	LA
44073	0A	R	I	*IEC*	HT
44074	0A			*IEC*	BN
44075	0A	R	I	*IEC*	BN
44076	0A	R	I	*ICC*	LA
44077	0A	R	I	*IEC*	BN
44078	0A	R	I	*IEC*	BN
44079	0A	R	I	*IEC*	BN
44080	0A	R	I	*IEC*	BN
44081	0A	R	I	*IWR*	PM
44083	0A	R	I	*IML*	NL
44084	0A	R	I	*ICC*	LA
44085	0A	R	I	*IML*	NL
44086	0B			*IML*	NL
44087	0A	R	I	*ICC*	LA
44088	0A			*ICC*	LA
44089	0A			*ICC*	LA
44090	0A			*ICC*	LA
44091	0A			*ICC*	LA
44093	0A	R	I	*IEC*	BN
44094	0A			*IML*	NL
44097	0A	R		*IEC*	HT
44098	0B	R		*IEC*	BN
44099	0A	R	I	*IWR*	00
44100	0A			*IML*	NL
44101	0B			*IEC*	BN

IC125 TRAILER CAR FORMATIONS

CLASS 253 WESTERN REGION

Unit		Allocation		GH1	GH1	GN4	GH2	GH2	GH2	GJ2
01	R	*IWR*	PM	41003	41004	40209	42003	42004	42005	44001
02	R	*IWR*	PM	41005	41006	40212	42006	42007	42008	44002
03	R	*IWR*	PM	41007	41008	40213	42009	42010	42011	44003
04	R	*IWR*	PM	41009	41010	40204	42012	42013	42014	44004
05	R	*IWR*	PM	41011	41012	40205	42015	42016	42017	44005
06		*IWR*	PM	41013	41014	40206	42018	42019	42020	44006
07	R	*IWR*	PM	41015	41016	40207	42021	42022	42023	44007
08	R	*IWR*	PM	41017	41018	40208	42024	42025	42026	44008
09		*IWR*	PM	41019	41020	40211	42027	42028	42029	44009
10		*IWR*	PM	41021	41022	40210	42030	42031	42032	44010

Unit		Allocation		GH1	GH1	GK1† GK2*/GK4	GH2	GH2	GH2	GH2	GJ2
11	R	*IWR*	LA	41023	41024	40355	42096	42033	42034	42035	44011
12	R	*IWR*	LA	41025	41026	40323	42097	42036	42037	42038	44012
13	R	*IWR*	LA	41027	41028	40325	42098	42039	42040	42041	44013
14	R	*IWR*	LA	41029	41030	40326	42099	42042	42043	42044	44014
15	R	*IWR*	LA	41031	41032	40327	42216	42045	42046	42047	44015
16	R	*IWR*	LA	41033	41034	40331	42221	42048	42049	42050	44016
17	R	*IWR*	OO	41035	41036	40417*	—	42051	42052	42053	44017
18	R	*IWR*	OO	41037	41038	40419*	—	42054	42055	42056	44018
28	P	*IWR*	LA	41121	41122	40322	42345	42251	42252	42253	44028
29	R	*IWR*	PM	41123	41124	40422*	—	42255	42256	42257	44029
30	R	*IWR*	LA	41126	41125	40324	42344	42259	42260	42261	44030
31	R	*IWR*	PM	41127	41128	40435*	—	42263	42264	42265	44031
32	R	*IWR*	OO	41129	41130	40436*	—	42267	42268	42269	44032
33	R	*IWR*	OO	41131	41132	40437*	—	42271	42272	42273	44033
34	R	*IWR*	OO	41133	41134	40427*	—	42275	42276	42277	44034
35	R	*IWR*	OO	41135	41136	40423*	—	42279	42280	42281	44035
36		*IWR*	PM	41137	41138	40428*	—	42283	42284	42285	44036
37	R	*IWR*	OO	41139	41140	40416*	—	42287	42288	42289	44037
38	P	*IWR*	LA	41141	41142	40732†	42342	42291	42292	42293	44038
39	R	*IWR*	OO	41143	41144	40418*	—	42295	42296	42297	44039
40	P	*IWR*	LA	41145	41146	40757†	42343	42299	42300	42301	44040
41	R	*ICC*	PM	—	41147	40401*	42254	42258	42262	42266	44000
42	R	*ICC*	PM	—	41148	40402*	42270	42274	42278	42282	44062
43	R	*ICC*	PM	—	41159	40403*	42286	42290	42294	42298	44065
44	R	*ICC*	PM	—	41160	40425*	42302	42303	42304	42305	44068
45		*ICC*	PM	—	41161	40421*	42084	42085	42086	42087	44069
46	R	*ICC*	LA	—	41162	40414*	42088	42089	42090	42091	44072

Unit		Allocation		GH1	GH1	GK1† GK2*/GK4	GH2	GH2	GH2	GH2	GJ2
47	R	*ICC*	LA	—	41163	40415*	42092	42093	42094	42095	44076
50	R	*ICC*	LA	—	41042	40424*	42196	42197	42060	42061	44020
51	R	*ICC*	LA	—	41165	40430*	42108	42109	42110	42322	44087
52		*ICC*	LA	—	41166	40431*	42306	42307	42308	42309	44088
53		*ICC*	LA	—	41167	40432*	42310	42311	42312	42313	44089
54		*ICC*	LA	—	41168	40433*	42314	42315	42316	42317	44090
55		*ICC*	LA	—	41169	40434*	42318	42319	42320	42321	44091

Spare coaches *GK2:* (R) 40420, 40426.
GH1: (R) 41164.
GJ2: (R) 44081, 44084, 44099.
Refurbished set/vehicle: R; Refurbished for Pullman service: P.

CLASS 254 EAST COAST & MIDLAND MAIN LINES

Unit		Allocation		GH1	GH1/ GH2*	GH1†/GK1 GH2‡/GL1*	GH1/GH2† GK1*	GH2/ GK1*	GH2	GH2	GH2	GJ2
01	R	*IEC*	BN	41057	41058	40708	—	42335	42111	42112	42113	44041
02	R	*IEC*	BN	41059	41060	40733	—	42336	42115	42116	42117	44042
03	R	*IEC*	BN	41061	41062	40729	—	42337	42119	42120	42121	44043
04	R	*IEC*	BN	41063	41064	40754	—	42328	42123	42124	42125	44044
05	R	*IEC*	BN	41171	41173	40734	—	42338	42178	42127	42128	44045
06	R	*IEC*	NL	41067	41068	40749	—	42331	42131	42132	42133	44046
07	R	*IEC*	NL	41069	41070	40751	—	42339	42135	42136	42137	44047
08	R	*IEC*	NL	41071	41072	40728	—	42329	42139	42140	42141	44048
09		*IEC*	NL	41073	41074	40752	—	42333	42143	42144	42145	44049
10	R	*IEC*	BN	41075	41076	40756	—	42327	42147	42148	42149	44050
11		*IEC*	NL	41077	41078	40753	—	42324	42151	42152	42153	44051
12	R	*IEC*	NL	41079	41080	40700	—	42155	42156	42157	42100	44052
13	R	*IEC*	BN	41081	41082	40701	—	42159	42160	42161	42101	44053
14	R	*IEC*	BN	41083	41084	40702	—	42163	42164	42165	42102	44054
15	R	*IEC*	BN	41085	41086	40703	—	42169	42168	42167	42103	44055
16	R	*IEC*	BN	41087	41088	40706	—	42104	42171	42172	42173	44056
17	R	*IEC*	BN	41089	41090	40705	—	42175	42176	42177	42105	44057
18	R	*IEC*	BN	41091	41092	40704	—	42179	42180	42181	42106	44058
19	R	*IEC*	BN	41093	41094	40707	—	42183	42184	42185	42107	44059
20	R	*IEC*	BN	41095	41096	40736	—	42326	42187	42188	42189	44060
21	P	*IML*	NL	41097	41098	41117†	40619§*	42191	42192	42193	—	44061
22	P	*IEC*	NL	41099	41041	40501*	41100	40711*	42198	42199	—	44063
23	R	*IEC*	NL	41101	41102	40712	—	42201	42202	42203	42204	44064
24	R	*IEC*	NL	41103	41104	40713	—	42206	42207	42208	42209	44066
25	R	*IEC*	NL	41105	41106	40714	—	42211	42212	42213	42214	44067
26	P	*IEC*	BN	41113	41108	41107†	40715*	—	42217	42218	42219	44070
27	R	*IEC*	BN	41109	41110	40716	—	42334	42222	42223	42224	44071

Unit		Allocation		GH1	GH1/ GH2*	GH1†/GK1 GH2‡/GL1*	GH1/GH2† GK1*	GH2/ GK1*	GH2	GH2	GH2	GJ2
28	P	*IEC*	HT	41112	41066	40511*	41111	40730*	42227	42228	—	44073
29		*IEC*	BN	41114	42194*	42231*	42341†	40718*	42232	42233	42234	44098+
30	R	*IEC*	BN	41115	41116	40710	—	42330	42237	42238	42239	44075
31	R	*IEC*	BN	41170	41118	40720	—	42241	42242	42243	42244	44077
32	R	*IEC*	BN	41119	41120	40721	—	42246	42247	42248	42249	44078
33	R	*IEC*	BN	41149	41150	40739	—	42226	42182	42186	42190	44079
34	R	*IEC*	BN	41151	41152	40740	—	42226	42182	42186	42190	44080
35	R	*IML*	NL	41153	41154	40741	—	42195	42200	42205	42210	44083
36	R	*IML*	NL	41155	41156	40748	—	42215	42220	42225	42230	44085
37		*IML*	NL	41157	41158	40743	—	42235	42240	42245	42250	44086
38	R	*IML*	NL	41055	41056	40709	—	42081	42082	42083	42126	44027
39	R	*IML*	NL	41045	41065	40738	—	42062	42066	42067	42068	44022
40		*IML*	NL	41047	41048	40744	—	42069	42070	42071	42118	44023
41	R	*IML*	NL	41049	41050	40745	—	42325	42072	42073	42074	44024
42	R	*IML*	NL	41051	41052	40746	—	42075	42076	42077	42078	44025
43		*IML*	NL	41053	41054	40747	—	42332	42236	42079	42080	44026
44	R	*IEC*	BN	41174	41172	40742	—	42130	42134	42138	42122	44093
45		*IML*	NL	41176	41175	40750	—	42158	42146	42150	42154	44094
46		*IML*	NL	41039	41040	40735	—	42323	42057	42058	42059	44019
47	R	*IML*	NL	41044	41043	40737	—	42340	42063	42064	42065	44021

§Modular catering

Spare coaches *GL1:* (P) 40505.
GM4: 40513 (for private hire).
GK2: (R) 40429.
GK1: (R) 40717, 40739.
GH1: (R) 41044, 41046.
GH2: 42129, (R) 42229.
GJ2: (R) 44097. 44074, 44100, 44101.
+Peterborough set. Buffer fitted GJ2 temporarily in place of No 44074.
Refurbished set/vehicle: R; Refurbished for Pullman service: P.

Service Department Special Purpose Vehicles

Class 97/2 — Type 2 — A1A-A1A

Former Class 31/1 locomotives. Details as Capital Stock Diagram 31-1CX.

Diagram: 97-2DX
Sector: *Departmental:* **DRTC**: Research
Livery: Research Red, white and black

Loco No	*Dia*	*SC*	*Pool*	*Dep*
97204	DX	K	*DRTC*	HQ

Note: Former No 31326

Class 97/2 — ETHEL — 2-2

Electric Train Heating Mobile Generators
Former Class 25/3 locomotives. Not self-propelled.

Built: British Railways Derby 1966, converted at Aberdeen Ferryhill TMD, 1983
Engine: Sulzer 6LDA28B, 6-cyl, 4-stroke of 1,250hp
Dimensions: 50.5ft L×9ft W×12.7ft H
Weight: 63 tonnes
Main generator: AEI RTB 15656
ETH Index: 54
Route availability: 5

Fuel: 500gal
Train brake: Dual air and vacuum
Maximum operating speed: 75mph
Diagram: 97-2BX

Sector: *InterCity:* **ICHA**: Charter
Livery: InterCity

Loco No	*Dia*	*Pool*	*Dep*	*Name*
97251	BX	ICHA	CL	*Ethel 2*
97252	BX	ICHA	OC	*Ethel 3*

Class 97/4 — Type 4 — 1CO-CO1

Former Class 46 locomotives.

Built: British Railways, Derby 1962
Engine: Sulzer 12LDA28B, 12-cyl, 4-stroke of 2,500hp
Dimensions: 67.9ft L×9.1ft W×12.8ft H
Weight: 140 tonnes
Power/Control equipment: Six Brush TM73-68 Mk III traction motors, main generator Brush TG160-60
Route availability: 7
Fuel: 790gal
Train brake: Dual air and vacuum
Brake force: 63 tonnes
Maximum tractive effort: 55,000lb

Maximum operating speed: 90mph
Train heating: Steam generator, Spanner Swirlyflow Mk III, 1,850lb/hr (isolated)
Water tanks: 1,040gal
Diagram: 97-4AX

Sector: *Departmental:* **DRTC**: Research
Special livery: Research Red and blue: 97403

Loco No	*Dia*	*Pool*	*Dep*	*Name*
97403	AX	DRTC	HQ	*Ixion*
97404	AX	DRTC	HQ	(Su Egginton Jct) (for spare equipment only)

Class 97/4 — Type 4 — CO-CO

Former Capital Stock Class 47/4.

Built: British Railways 1964

New Diagram	*Equivalent Diagram*
97-4BX	47-4HX
97-4CX	47-4KX

Maximum speed: 100mph

Sector: *Departmental:* **DRTC**: Research
(NB: Usage on non-RTC duties subject to special DMEE authority.)

Loco No	*Former No*	*Dia*	*SC*	*Pool*	*Dep*
97472	(47472)	BX	B	DRTC	CD
97480	(47480) *Robin Hood*	BX		DRTC	CD
97545	(47545)	BX		DRTC	CD
97561	(47561)	CX	B	DRTC	CD

Class 97/0 — Shunters — 0-6-0

Diagram 97-0A0
Built: Ruston and Hornsby 1959
Engine: Ruston Mk 6 VPHL, 6-cyl, 4-stroke of 165hp
Dimensions: 25ft L×8.5ft W×11ft H
Weight: 30.7 tonnes
Power/Control equipment: BTH traction motor RTA 5041, main generator BTH RTB 6034
Route availability: 1
Maximum tractive effort: 17,000lb
Fuel: 80gal
Maximum operating speed: 20mph
Train brakes: Not equipped
Brake force: 16 tonnes

Sector: *Departmental:* **DCSA**: DCE, Western Region

Diagram 97-0DA
Former Capital Stock Class 08. For details see Diagram 08-0FA
Built: British Railways, Derby, 1959

Sector: *Network SouthEast:* **NXXA**: General, Shunters
Livery: Network SouthEast

Diagram 97-0EV
Former Capital Stock Class 03.
Built: British Railways, Doncaster, 1959
Train brake: Vacuum only

Sector: *Departmental:* **DCSA**: DCE, Southern Region

Diagram 97-0FX
Former Capital Stock Class 09. For details see Diagram 09-0AX
Built: British Railways, Horwich, 1961

Sector: *Departmental:* **DCWA**: DCE Western Region
Livery: Blue, grey cab sides

Loco No	*Dia*	*Pool*	*Dep*	*Name*
97651	A0	DCWA	CF (@ GL)	
97653	A0	DCWA	CF (@ RR)	
97654	A0	DCWA	RG	
97800	DA	NXXA	SG	*Ivor*
97805	EV	DCSA	RY	
97806	FX	DCWA	CF (@ Sudbrook)	

Class 97/7 — Battery Electric — B0-B0

Built: 1974-80 from British Railways 1957 built Class 501 DMBS vehicles
Supply: Third rail 750V dc and 320V dc batteries
Dimensions: 60.6ft L×8ft W×11.6ft H
Weight: 58.9 tonnes
Power/Control equipment: Four GEC WT344A 185hp traction motors, drive spur gear and pinion, compressor GEC DH28
Locomotive brake: Electro-pneumatic and Westinghouse automatic
Brake force: 45 tonnes
Maximum opperating speed: 25mph
Route availability: 4
Design code: 97-7AE

Standard equipment: Single cab, Multiple working within type (operated in consecutively numbered pairs)
Sector: *Departmental:* **DCEA**: DCE Eastern Region. **DCMA**: DCE Midland

Loco No	*Dia*	*Liv*	*Pool*	*Dep*
97701	AE		DCMA	HQ (@ BD)
97702	AE		DCMA	HQ (@ BD)
97703	AE		DCEA	HQ (@ HE)
97704	AE		DCEA	HQ (@ HE)
97705	AE		DCEA	HQ (@ HE)
97706	AE		DCEA	HQ (@ HE)
97707	AE	N	DCEA	HQ (@ HE)
97708	AE	N	DCEA	HQ (@ HE)

Special Purpose Locomotives

The following locomotives have been withdrawn from operating stock but are retained for special uses.

ZZB — Mobile Load Bank — 2-2

Non-self-propelled mobile load bank used for checking 25kV overhead electric wiring after installation before cleared for normal operating stock tests.

Built: North British Loco Co 1960 as Class 84 25kV ac electric locomotive. Converted to DMEE, RTC, Derby
Dimensions: 53.5ft L×8.7ft W×13ft H (pantograph housed)

Equipment: Four GEC WT501 traction motors
Sector: *Departmental:* **DRTC:** Research

No	*Pool*	*Dep*
ADB 968021	DRTC	HQ

ZZR — Traction Training — 1CO-CO1* or BO-BO

The following locomotives have been retained by depots for artisan training. They are not now self-propelled and may not now be in complete condition. Departmental numbers allocated may not have been applied, therefore last running numbers are also given here.

No	*Former No*	*Former class*	*Dep*
ADB 968024	45017	45/0*	TO
ADB 968026	25908	25/9	TO
ADB 968027	25912	25/9	HO
ADB 968028	27024	27/0	ED

LOCOMOTIVE COSTING CENTRES/POOLS/ SUB-SECTORS

The following listings show the *Sector* and *sub-Sector* locomotive Pools corrected to the time of going to press (early February). Although locomotives are allocated to a Traction Maintenance Depot this is solely for the larger repairs and examinations. Operation is now dictated by the Sectors to which locomotives are dedicated. In theory, and increasingly in practice, traction is booked to diagrams which are at least primarily financed by the appropriate sub-Sector and only in emergency situations are they used on other duties. At weekends the passenger Sectors may 'hire' locomotives from other Sectors to cover summer relief work or diversionary services.

Diesel shunters are also now generally funded in a similar manner, but for obvious reasons maintenance has to be less centralised. Thus it is now general practice to allocate the locomotives to a main depot in an Area capable of handling all maintenance whilst they operate, fuel and receive light attention at various Servicing Depots nearer their normal point of duty. *Motive Power Monthly* will continue to provide an updating service for this information as locomotive 'ownership' changes occur and alterations are made to locomotive codes.

CBRE: **BREL '88, Shunters** (unofficial code)

08168 08470

CHUB: **Hunslet-Barclay hire locomotives** (unofficial code)

20041 20060 20083 20101 20209 20219 20224 20225

CRFS: **RFS Engineering** (unofficial code)

08331

CSLA: **Steam locomotives, BRHQ**

98238 98240 98243
98372
98400 98406 98427 98455 98469 98472 98479 98480 98482 98488
98500 98505 98507 98512 98519 98525 98526 98529 98530 98532
98560 98565 98567 98571 98577 98598
98605 98641 98642 98690 98693 98696
98700 98701 98709 98715 98727 98729 98750 98751 98771 98780
98792
98800 98801 98802 98805 98809 98822 98824 98828 98829 98832
98833 98851 98857 98868 98872 98898
98920

CYPO: **Foster Yeoman, Private owner, Class 59, BRHQ**

59001 59002 59003 59004 59005

DBMS: **Departmental, BRML**

08484 08629 08642 08647 08883 08892

DCAA: **Departmental, RCE Anglia**

31127 31165 31173 31181 31186 31187 31190 31191 31219 31224
31231 31250 31263 31268
37140 37216
47346 47366

DCAB: **Departmental, RCE Anglia, Shunters**

08528 08529 08531 08540 08541 08638 08655 08757 08772 08775
08810 08859 08889

DCEA: **Departmental, RCE Eastern**

20030 20064 20096
31118 31123 31170 31208 31221 31242 31247 31278 31281 31282
31283 31285
31431 31432 31439 31441 31444 31447 31449 31452 31453 31456
31458 31469
47329 47331 47332 47344 47348 47352
47417 47418
97703 97704 97705 97706 97707 97708

DCEB: **Departmental, RCE Eastern, Shunters**

08499 08583 08605 08607 08618 08657 08701 08706 08773 08783
08794 08866 08867 08870 08876 08885 08906 08908 08919 08931

DCHA: **Departmental, RCE Scottish Region, Eastfield**

26011 26014 26015 26021 26023 26024 26026 26027 26028 26035
26036 26039
37023 37025 37097 37170 37175 37261 37262
37402 37414
47467 47518 47546 47550 47604 47617

DCHB: **Departmental, RCE Scottish Region, RETB, Snowplough, Eastfield.**

20114 20127 20138

DCMA: **Departmental, RCE Midland Region, Bescot.**

20005 20029 20032 20034 20042 20048 20054 20056 20063 20070
20072 20097 20099 20121 20124 20139 20147 20158 20160 21076
20178 20183 20195 20217
31107 31112 31119 31162 31178 31235 31237 31288 31305 31317
31403 31405 31406 31407 31409 31411 31419 31420 31422 31423
31424 31430 31433 31434 31435 31437 31445 31446 31448 31451
31454 31455 31459 31462 31463 31464 31468
47003 47018 47053 47118
47333 47339 47340 47343 47353 46356 46357 47358
47426 47427 47431 47432 47436 47438 47450 47453
97701 97702

DCMB: Departmental, RCE Midland Region, Shunters

08573 08612 08619 08624 08628 08666 08702 08784 08789 08815
08843 08891 08894 08922 08925 08927

DCQA: Departmental DCE Track Test

31412 31414 31416 31426

DCSA: Departmental, RCE Southern

33002 33004 33006 33013 33015 33023 33026 33030 33065
33107 33110 33117 33118
33201 33207
73101 73103 73105 37107 73108 73109 73110 37111 73114 73117
73118 73119 73126 73128 73129 73131 73132 73133 73135 37138
37139

DCSB: Departmental, RCE Southern, Shunters

08831 08847
09003 09004 09005 09009 09011 09014 09019 09021 09026
99800

DCWA: Departmental, RCE Western

08011
37133 37141 37142 37146 37158 37174 37207 37220 37263 37264
37272
47334 47341
47463 47484 47513 47540 47623 47628
50004 50005 50007 50008 50009 50015 50016 50020 50021 50042
50045
50149
97651 97653 97654
97806

DMEA (ex-DWCQ): Departmental, DMEE Nationwide, BRHQ

20066 20148 20193 20202 20204 20227
26010 26042 26043 26046
31101 31105 31106 31131 31135 31196 31205 31206 31230 31232
31252 31255 31260 31264 31272 31286 31289 31290 31392 31323
31413 31415 31417 31457 31460 31461 31465
33025
33111
73136

DMES (ex-DWCS): Departmental, DMEE Shunters: BRHQ

08393 08411 08417 08440 08506 08561 08565 08587 08632 08652
08653 08682 08692 08710 08712 08733 08763 08770 08787 08793
08797 08798 08813 08839 08877 08900 08907 08910 08913 08921
08941 08942
09007

DRTC: Departmental, Derby, Railway Technical Centre

08814
97204
07403 97404
97472 97480 97545 97561

DXXD: Departmental, for reallocation

08530 08576 08584 08767 08932

FABT (ex-FAMT): Railfreight, Construction (Stone), Tinsley

37380
37411
37676 37677 37678 37679 37680 37681 37682 37683 37684 37685
37686 37687 37688

FACM (ex-FAMM): Railfreight, Construction, Stone, Motherwell

37370 37373 37379

FAGS (ex-FALG): Railfreight, Construction, Stratford

31116 31128 31134 31189 31198 31209 31234 31240 31293 31294
31296 31301 31306 31308 31320 31327
37138 37144 37211 37218 37219
37354
47114 47229
47325 47328 47367

FAMA: Railfreight, Construction (Stone), Thornaby

31184 31215 31229

FAME: Railfreight, Constuction (Stone), Eastfield

47004 47006 47017 47210

FASB (ex-FALS): Railfreight, Construction (Stone), Stewarts Lane

33008 33009 33011 33012 33016 33020 33021 33022 33027 33029
33031 33033 33040 33042 33046 33047 33048 33050 33051 33052
33053 33055 33056 33057 33060 33063 33064
33202 33204 33208 33211

FAWK (ex-FAWC): Railfreight, Construction (Stone), Cardiff

37345
37422 37425
47033 47063 47079
47320
47901
56001 56031 56032 56033 56034 56035 56036 56037 56038 56039
56040 56041 56043 56044 56045 56046 56048 56049 56050 56051
56052 56053 56055 56056 56057 56072

***FAXN** (ex-FALX):* **Railfreight, Construction (Stone), Leicester**

56042 56058 56059 56060 56061 56062 56063 56064 56065 56070
56078

FAZZ: **Railfreight, Construction, Shunters**

08521 08532 08542 08544 08581 08593 08917 08923
09018

***FCCC** (ex-FTLC):* **Railfreight, Chemicals, Crewe**

31138
47050 47186 47227 47228 47229
47322 47323 47365
47423 47425 47439 47440 47441 47442 47445 47446 47447 47449
47454 47456 47485 47491 47531 47532 47605

***FCTY** (ex-FTYT):* **Railfreight, Chemicals, Thornaby**

20008 20118 20119 20122 20137 20144 20156 20165
47301 47302 47303 47304 47305 47361 47362 47363

***FEAK** (ex-FECA):* **Railfreight, Coal, Trainload, Aberthaw, Cardiff**

37701 37702 37703 37704 37796 37797 37798 37799 37800 37301
37802 37803 37887 37889 37894 37895 37896 37897 37898 37899

***FEAN** (ex-FENA):* **Railfreight, Coal, West Midlands**

58001 58003 58004 58005 58006 58007 58009 58010 58011 58012
58013 58014 58015

***FEBN** (ex-FENC):* **Railfreight, Coal, East Midlands**

58002 58008 58016 58017 58018 58019 58020 58021 58022 58023
58024 58025 58026 58027 58028 58029 58030 58031 58032 58033
58034 58035 58036 58037 58038 58039 58040 58041 58042 58043
58044 58045 58046 58047 58048 58049 58050

***FECN** (ex-FENB):* **Railfreight, Coal, Midlands**

56002 56003 56004 56005 56006 56007 56008 56009 56010 56011
56012 56013 56014 56015 56016 56017 56018 56019 56020 56021
56022 56023 56024 56025 56026 56027 56028

***FEDN** (ex-FEYA):* **Railfreight, Coal, Yorkshire, Toton**

56029 56030 56047 56054 56066 56067 56068 56069 56071 56072
56073 56074 56075 56076 56077 56079 56080 56081 56082 56083
56084 56085 56086 56087 56088 56089 56090 56091 56092 56093
59094 56095 56096 56097 56098 56099 56100 56101 56102 56103
56104 56105 56106 56107 56108 56109 56110 56123

***FEEN** (ex-FEYB):* **Railfreight, Coal, Trainload, Blythe**

56111 56112 56113 56114 56115 56116 56117 56118 56119 56120
56121 56122 56124 56125 56126 56127 56128 56129 56130 56131
56132 56133 56134 56135

FEFN (ex-FEND): Railfreight, Coal, East Midlands, Toton

20026 20047 20059 20071 20081 20084 20085 20094 20103 20104
20105 20108 20129 20131 20133 20134 20136 20140 20142 20151
20154 20157 20163 20166 20170 20177 20182 20186 20190 20194
20196 20210 20214 20215

FEGN (ex-FENW): Railfreight, Coal, North-West, Toton

20004 20006 20007 20010 20013 20016 20019 20020 20021 20023
20040 20045 20051 20052 20053 20055 20057 20058 20065 20073
20075 20078 20080 20082 20087 20088 20090 20106 20113 20117
20120 20128 20130 20132 20135 20141 20143 20159 20168 20169
20175 20179 20187 20188 20197 20208

FEOE (ex-FEGA): Railfreight, Coal, Scotland, Eastfield

20192 20198 20199 20205 20206 20211 20212 20213
37165 37229
37375 37376

FEPE (ex-FEGB): Railfreight, Coal, Lothians, Haymarket

26001 26002 26003 26004 26005 26006 26007 26008

FEZZ: Railfreight, Coal, Shunters, General

08434 08436 08610 08791 08893

FGWA: Railfreight, Distribution (Speedlink), Tinsley, Class 47

47002 47005 47012 47016 47049 47052 47060 47095 47097 47098
47102 47107 47110 47117 47120 47124 47142 47143 47144 47145
47146 47147 47150 47152 47156 47157 47188 47200 47201 47203
47204 47205 47206 47207 47209 47211 47213 47214 47215 47217
47218 47219 47220 47225 47226 47231 47234 47236 47237 47238
47241 47245 47249 47256 47258 47270 47279 47280 47283 47284
47285 47286 47287 47288 47289 47290 47292 47293 47296 47297
47298
47306 47307 47308 47309 47310 47311 47312 47313 47314 47315
47316 47317 47321 47337 47338 47360 47370 47371 47372 47375
47376 47377 47378
47421 47474 47588 47599 47600 47615

FGWB: Railfreight, Distribution (Speedlink), Tinsley, Class 37

37003 37009 37013 37015 37029 37031 37058 37059 37062 37063
37065 37066 37071 37072 37073 37095 37096 37098 37101 37185
37194 37198 37242 37251 37270 37271 37285 37298
37352 37353 37355 37356 37357 37378

FGWC: Railfreight, Distribution (Speedlink), Tinsley, Class 31

31102 31108 31110 31113 31125 31126 31132 31142 31144 31145
31146 31147 31149 31155 31158 31159 31160 31163 31164 31166
31171 31174 31180 31248 31257 31259 31271 31284 31309
31402 31466 31467

FGWD: **Railfreight, Distribution (Speedlink), Dover Link-span. Class 33/2. Stewarts Lane**

33203 33205 33206

FGWE: **Railfreight, Distribution (Speedlink), dc Electric, Stewarts Lane**

73001 73002 73003 73004 73006
73106 73140 73141

FGWS: **Railfreight, Distribution (Speedlink), Eastfield**

26025 26031 26032 26034 26037 26038 26040 26041

FGXX: **Railfreight, Distribution (Speedlink), General**

20009 20028 20035 20043 20069 20100 20145 20171 20172 20173
20185 20189 20218 20228
37070 37109 37110 37114 37153 37196 37260
37401 37402 37403 37404 37405 37406 37409 37410 37413 37423
37424
47401 47402

FGXZ: **Railfreight, Speedlink, ac locomotives**

81013 81017
85004 85009 85010 85012 85015 85016 85018 85020 85021 85024
85026 85028 85031 85032 85035 85040
90016 90017 90018

FGZZ: **Railfreight, Shunters, Distribution (Speedlink)**

03170
08388 08389 08397 08399 08405 08407 08410 08418 08419 08445
08447 08448 08454 08460 08466 08481 08489 08492 08495 08496
08498 08507 08510 08514 08516 08517 08519 08523 08526 08533
08539 08569 08570 08577 08580 08582 08589 08590 08591 08599
08620 08622 08627 08630 08631 08637 08649 08654 08656 08659
08661 08664 08672 08675 08690 08693 08695 08699 08700 08703
08705 08711 08713 08724 08725 08732 08737 08738 08739 08750
08754 08755 08778 08780 08781 08786 08792 08795 08799 08800
08802 08803 08819 08825 08826 08827 08832 08834 08838 08849
08853 08856 08881 08882 08887 08904 08905 08911 08912 08935
08937 08938 08939 08947 08948 08953 08956 08958
09001 09010 09015 09022 09024 09025

FHAC (ex-FHHA): **Railfreight, (Coal), Flask, Crewe**

31120 31130 31200 31217 31270 31275 31276 31312 31324

FHBK (ex-FHCC): **Railfreight, Coal, Train-load, Cardiff**

37689 37690 37691 37692 37693 37694 37695 37696 37697 37698
37699

***FHZZ:* Railfreight, Shunters, Coal**

08202 08308 08309 08375 08390 08402 08421 08428 08434 08436
08441 08442 08493 08508 08512 08535 08543 08586 08613 08623
08660 08686 08727 08729 08735 08769 08776 08782 08785 08796
08809 08818 08824 08870 08903 08946
08993 08994 08995

***FJLL (ex-FTLL):* Railfreight, Chemicals (China Clay) Laira. 071088**

37421
37669 37670 37671 37672 37673 37674 37575

***FMCA:* Railfreight, Metals (Steel), Cardiff**

37197 37254 37278 37293
47281
47359

***FMCC:* Railfreight, Metals (Steel), Cardiff**

37901 37902 37903 37904 37905 37906

***FMCH:* Railfreight, Metals (Steel), Cardiff**

37710 37711 37712 37713 37714 37715 37716 37717 37718 37719
37883 37884 37885 37886

***FMGM:* Railfreight, Metals, Ore, Hunterston**

37010 37037 37040 37049 37051 37092 37137 37190 37201 37310
37311 37313 37320 37323 37324 37325 37326

***FMYI:* Railfreight, Metals, Immingham**

20025 20031 20044 20046 20061 20092 20093 20095 20098 20102
20107 20110 20112 20126
37002 37042 37048 37054 37083 37106 37202 37203 37225 37241
37255 37258 37275
37377 37381

***FMYT:* Railfreight, Metals, Thornaby**

37046 37069 37227 37240 37250
37501 37502 37503 37504 37505 37506 37507 37508 37509 37510
37511 37512 37513 37514 37515 37516 37517 37518 37519 37520
37521 37667 37668
47347
47594

***FMXX:* Railfreight, Metals, General**

81004 81009
86415 86418 86422 86423 86427 86432 86433

FMZZ: **Railfreight, Shunters, Metals**

08401 08485 08500 08509 08525 08537 08543 08594 08595 08603
08604 08615 08662 08665 08691 08694 08714 08749 08759 08920
08952 09008 09013

FPGE: **Railfreight, Petroleum and Chemicals, Eastfield**

37035 37080 37113 37118 37188 37191 37232 37245
37359

FPLC: **Railfreight, Petroleum (Oil), Stanlow**

47010 47085 47119 47125 47190 47193 47194 47195 47196 47233
47278
47324 47368

FPLI: **Railfreight, Oil, Chemical, Construction, Immingham**

31154 31156 31170 31185 31188 31199 31201 31203 31207 31210
31212 31221 31223 31225 31233 31238 31243 31249 31273 31284
31299 31302 31304 31319 31322
47054 47115 47212 47221 47222 47223 47224 47276 47294 47295
47299
47319 47336 47373 47374 47379 47380
47411

FPLW: **Railfreight, Petroleum, South Wales**

37078 37215 37221 37248 37280 37294 37306
37350 37371
47094 47197 47198 47227
47318 47326 47327 47369 47381

FPLX: **Railfreight, Petroleum, North Thames**

31124 31152 31168 31311
37705 37706 37707 37708 37709 37888 37890 37891 37892 37893

FPZZ: **Railfreight, Petroleum, Shunters**

08482 08734 08788 08877 08916

FQCK (ex-FQLC): **Railfreight, Distribution (Speedlink), Coal, Cardiff**

37131 37139 37162 37167 37212 37213 37214 37217 37222 37223
37230 37235 37239 37244 37294 37308

FQZZ: **Railfreight, Distribution (Speedlink), Coal, Shunters**

08416 08829

FTZZ: **Railfreight, Chemicals, Shunters**

03162
08423 08449 08463 08511 08575 08588 08663 08740 08743 08745
08751

***FVXX:* Railfreight, Automotive, General**

86413 86414
87101

***FVZZ:* Railfreight, Shunters, Automotive**

08601 08685 08688 08709 08758 08869 08873 08884 08902 08928

***FXXA:* Railfreight, General, for identification**

08515 08747 08771 08886
33019 33035 33039

***FXXL:* Railfreight, Shunters, General**

08479 08532 08608 08646 08650 08668 08671 08756 08760 08779
08801 08804 08835 08837 08848 08850 08895 08896 08940 08945
08954 85006 85013 85036

***FXXS:* Railfreight, General, Stored**

***IANA:* InterCity, Anglia Region, Willesden**

86214 86215 86216 86218 86220 86221 86223 86227 86229 86230
86232 86235 86237 86238 86244 86259 86260

***IANB:* InterCity, Anglia, Shunters**

08658 08752 08868

***ICCA:* InterCity, Cross-Country**

08568 08571 08641 08644 08673 08854
09020
47470 47478 47512 47519 47520 47521 47525 47527 47551 47552
47556 47571 47577 47586 47589 47591 47593 47602 47606 47607
47608 47610 47612 47622 47629 47633 47636 47650 47651 47652
47653 47654 47655 47656 47657 47658 47659 47660 47664 47665
86206 86207 86210 86247 86248 86250 86253 86255
86412 86439
87009 87010 87031 87032

***ICHA:* InterCity Charter**

08556 08929
45106
47500 47508 47509 47555 47609 47620 47661 47662 47663
86204 86856
97251 97252

***IECA:* InterCity East Coast route**

08741 08874 08888 08957

47471 47577

89001

91001 91002 91003 91004 91005 91006 91007 91008 91009 91010

***IMAL:* InterCity Midland Region**

08536

47586

***IVGA:* InterCity, Victoria-Gatwick**

09012

73201 73202 73203 73204 73205 73206 73207 73208 73209 73210

73211 73212

***IWCA:* InterCity West Coast route**

08451 08609 08635 08648 08677 08680 08683 08717 08718 08765

08768 08808 08841 08846 08858 08901 08926 08934

47459 47483 47517 47530 47544 47553 47562 47570 47578 47595

47597 47614 47618 47619 47629 47632 47637 47638 47639 47645

47646 47647 47648 47649

81002 81005 81011

83009 83012

85005 85008 85030 85037 85038

86101 86102 86103

86208 86209 86224 86226 86236 86251 86252

86405 86410 86419 86428 86430 86431 86437

87001 87002 87003 87004 87007 87008 87011 87012 87014 87015

87016 87017 87018 87019 87020 87021 87022 87023 87024 87025

87026 87027 87028 87029 87030 87033 87034 87035

90001 90002 90003 90004 90005 90006 90007 90008 90009 90010

90011 90012 90013 90014 90015 90020 90021 90022 90024

***IWCB:* InterCity West Coast route, TDM trials+BSO. Willesden**

86212 86219 86228 86231 86240 86241

86425

***IWRA:* InterCity Western Region**

08480 08483 08643 08645 08651 08949

47560 47590 47611 47613 47621

***LNRA:* Railfreight, Distribution (Freightliner), Class 37, Stratford**

37004 37012 37019 37038 37047 37053 37055 37057 37074 37075

37077 37087 37100 37104 37107 37116 37128 37154 37178 37209

37238 37252

37358

LNRB: **Railfreight, Distribution (Freightliner), Class 47, Stratford**

47007 47014 47096 47099 47100 47105 47108 47112 47116 47121
47123 47291
47430 47452 47462

LNRC: **Railfreight, Distribution (Freightliner), Class 47, Crewe**

47008 47009 47019 47051 47101 47187
47330 47335 47343 47349 47350 47351 47354 47355 47364
47451 47457 47479 47481

LNRE: **Railfreight, Distribution (Freightliner), ac locomotives, Willesden**

86501 86502 86503 86504 86505 86506 86507 86508 86509 86510

LNRS: **Railfreight, Distribution (Freightliner), Shunters**

08413 08414 08415 08472 08667 08669 08689 08708 08811 08820
08823 08936

LXXA: **Railfreight, Distribution (Freightliner) General**

47189
81007 81010 81012
85007 85034
86402 86403 86404 86406 86407 86408 86409 86411 86416 86417
86420 86421 86435 86438
87005 87006 87013
90027 90028 90029

NNEA: **Network SouthEast, Northwest, Stratford**

47576 47579 47581

NSSA: **Network SouthEast, Solent and Sarum, Laira**

47473 47547 47587 47598
50001 50002 50003 50017 50018 50019 50027 50028 50029 50041
50043 50044 50048

NSSB: **Network SouthEast, Solen and Sarum, Stewarts Lane**

73005
73104 73112 73130 73134

NWRA: **Network SouthEast, Western Region. Old Oak Common**

47573 47582 74583 47598
50023 50024 50025 50026 50030 50031 50032 50033 50034 50035
50036 50037 50039 50040 50046 50050

NXXA: Network SouthEast, General

03179
08670 08696 08698 08715 08828 08830 08845 08914 08933
09006 09016 09023
85003
86249 86257 86261
86401
97800

PCFA: Provincial, Cardiff

08848
37407 37408 37426 37427 37428 37429 37430 37431

PCRA: Provincial, Settle & Carlisle, Immingham, Class 47/4

47406 47407 47413

PEDA: Provincial, Eastfield

47701 47702 47703 47704 47705 47706 47707 47708 47709 47710
47711 47712 47714 47715 47716 47717

PISA: Provincial, Inverness

08753
37412 37415 37416 37417 37418 37419 37420
47460 47461 47469 47492 47541 47563 47630 47635 37640 47641
47642 47643 47644

PTPA: Provincial, North Trans-Pennine. Crewe

47422 47424 47434 47443 47444 47448 47475 47488 47503

PXXA: Provincial, General

03073
08567 08616 08720 08731 08745 08761 08762 08777 08790 08851
08872 08915 08924

RCWE: Parcels, dc Electric, Stewarts Lane

73141

RXLA: Parcels, General, Shunters

08527 08534 08538 08562 08578 08579 08585 08597 08611 08614
08617 08625 08633 08634 08676 08697 08704 08719 08721 08723
08730 08742 08744 08746 08748 08766 08805 08807 08821 08822
08833 08836 08840 08842 08844 08855 08857 08865 08875 08879
08890 08897 08899 08909 08918 08930 08944 08950 08951 08955
09002

RXLB: Parcels, General, Class 31

31400 31404 31408 31410 31418 31421 31425 31427 31428 31429
31438 31442 31443 31450

***RXLD:* Parcels, General, Class 47**

47433 47435 47455 47458 47465 47466 47468 47476 47477 47482
47489 47490 47501 47515 47522 47523 47524 47526 47528 47533
47534 47535 47536 47537 47538 47539 47542 47543 47549 47557
47558 47559 47564 47565 47566 47567 45768 47569 47472 47574
47575 47580 47584 47585 47592 47603 47616 47624 47625 47626
47627 47631 47634

***RXLW:* Parcels, General, ac Electric locomotives**

85002 85011 85014 85019 85022 85023 85025
86213 86225 86234 86242 86243 86245 86254
86425 86426

***RXXA:* Parcels, General**

85022
90019

INTERCITY 125 POWER CARS
COSTING CENTRES/POOLS/SUB-SECTORS

***ICCP:* Cross Country, BRHQ**

43012 43016 43019 43035 43036 43037 43126 43163 43164 43165
43166 43171 43172 43173 43174 43175 43177 43178 43179 43181
43182 43183 43184 43185 43186

***IECP:* East Coast main line. Neville Hill**

43013§ 43014§ 43040 43041 43042 43043 43052 43053 43054 43056
43057 43058 43059 43062 43063 43067 43068 43069 43070 43071
43074 43075 43078 43079 43080 43081 43082 43083 43084§ 43085
43086 43087 43088 43089 43090 43091 43092 43093 43094 43095
43096 43097 43098 43099 43100 43101 43102 43103 43104 43105
43106 43107 43110 43111 43112 43113 43114 43115 43116 43117
43118 43119 43120 43121 43122 43123§ 43154 43155 43156 43157
43159 43160 43194 43195 43196 43197 43198

IMPL: Midland main line. Neville Hill

43038 43019 43044 43045 43046 43047 43048 43049 43050 43051
43055 43060 43061 43064 43065§ 43066 43072 43073 43076 43077
43108 43109 43152 43153 43158 43161 43162 43193

IWRP: Western Region: Bristol Bath Road

43002 43003 43004 43005 43006 43007 43008 43009 43010 43011
43015 43017 43018 43020 43021 43022 43023 43024 43025 43026
43027 43028 43029 43030 43031 43032 43033 43034 43124 43125
43127 43128 43129 43130 43131 43132 43133 43134 43135 43136
43137 43138 43139 43140 43141 43142 43143 43144 43145 43146
43147 43148 43149 43150 43151 43167 43168 43169 43170 43176
43180 43187 43188 43189 43190 43191 43192

(§ Modified for DVT duties)

Privately Owned Steam Locomotives on TOPS – Number Conversion Table

Hist No	*Class*	*Origin*	*TOPS Loco No*	*Name*
1638	16xx	GWR	98238	
3440	City	GWR	98240	*City of Truro*
46443	2MT	LMS	98243	
1000	4P	LMS	98400	
43106	4MT	LMS	98406	
4027	4F	MR	98427	
4555	45xx	GWR	98455	
75069	4MT	BR Std	98469	
5572	45xx	GWR	98472	
80079	4MT	BR Std	98479	
80080	4MT	BR Std	98480	
3882	0-6-0ST		98482	*Barbara*
4588	45xx	GWR	98488	
5000	5MT	LMS	98500	
5305	5MT	LMS	98505	*'Alderman A. E. Draper'*
5407	5MT	LMS	98507	
7812	Manor	GWR	98512	*Erlestoke Manor*
7819	Manor		98519	*Hinton Manor*
5025	5MT	LMS	98525	
925	V	SR	98526	*Cheltenham*
73129	5MT	BR Std	98529	
4930	Hall	GWR	98530	*Hagley Hall*
44932	5MT	LMS	98532	
6960	Hall	GWR	98560	*Raveningham Hall*
2765	6P5F	LMS	98565	
44767	5MT	LMS	98567	*'George Stephenson'*
44871	5MT		98571	*'Sovereign'*
777	N15	SR	98577	*Sir Lamiel*
6998	Hall	GWR	98598	*Burton Agnes Hall*
2005	K1	LNER	98605	
841	S15	SR	98641	
3442	K4	LNER	98642	*The Great Marquess*
5690	6P5F	LMS	98690	*Leander*
5593	6P5F	LMS	98693	*Kolhapur*
5596	6P5F	LMS	98696	*Bahamas*
70000	7P6F	BR Std	98700	*Britannia*
34101	WC	SR	98701	*Hartland*
53809	7F	SDJR	98709	
6115	7P	LMS	98715	*Scots Guardsman*
34027	WC	SR	98727	*Taw Valley*
7029	Castle	GWR	98729	*Clun Castle*
850	LN	SR	98750	*Lord Nelson*
5051	Castle	GWR	98751	*Drysllwyn Castle*
4771	V2	LNER	98771	*Green Arrow*
5080	Castle	GWR	98780	*Defiant*
34092	WC	SR	98792	*City of Wells*
6000	King	GWR	98800	*King George V*
6201	8P	LMS	98801	*Princess Elizabeth*
35005	MN	SR	98805	*Canadian Pacific*
60009	A4	LNER	98809	*Union of South Africa*
3822	2884	GWR	98822	
35028	MN	SR	98828	*Clan Line*
46229	8P	LMS	98829	*Duchess of Hamilton*
532	A2	LNER	98832	*Blue Peter*
8233	8F	LMS	98833	
48151	8F	LMS	98851	
2857	28xx	GWR	98857	
4468	A4	LNER	98868	*Mallard*
4472	A3	LNER	98872	*Flying Scotsman*
4498	A4	LNER	98898	*Sir Nigel Gresley*
92220	9F	BR Std	98920	*Evening Star*

Notes:

The third character of Class 98 locomotive numbers represents the vehicle sub class, and the power classification of the locomotive, '9' are the largest locomotives and '0' are the smallest.

The last two characters of the locomotive number relate to the last two characters of the historic number. (Except when a clash occurs within a particular power range.)

Locomotive names shown between apostrophes, eg: *'George Stephenson'* are not the historic name of the locomotive but have been allocated since preservation and may be currently carried on the locomotive.

Additional Information

The following amendments, advised to 20 February, require to be made to this publication covering changes effected during our production period.

Class 03: **Dimensions:** Add: 03-OCV before 03-ODX:
Train brakes: add: except *Diagram 03-OCV:* Vacuum only.
Sectors: delete *Network SouthEast*, add *Departmental:* **DCSB:** DCE Southern.
Note: add No 03079 formerly officially No 97805.
Add entry: 03079 CV *DCSB* RY.

Class 08: **Sectors:** *Departmental:* add **DCAB:** DCE Anglia. **DCEB:** DCE Eastern. **DXXD:** General, to be allocated. Change **DWCS** to **DMES**.
Provincial: ***Add:*** **PCFA:** General, Cardiff. **PISA:** General, Inverness. *Railfreight:* delete **FXXA** and **LNRS**.
Entries: *Amend* No 08182 to read 08168 and 08335 to read 08331.
Delete (Withdrawn): 08250/58, 08468, 08716, 08898.
Allocations (Depot): 08449-IM, 08534-CL, 08595-DR, 08653-OC, 08745-NL, 08748-CA, 08837-RG, 08838-DY, 08928-BS, 08929-OC, 08947-WN.

Class 09: **Sectors:** *Departmental:* add **DMES:** DMEE, Shunters.
Allocations (Depot): 09007-SL.

Class 20: **Sectors:** Add *Private owner:* **CHUB:** Hunslet-Barclay.
Departmental: Change **DWCQ:** to **DMEA:**.
Railfreight: Change **FEGA:** to **FEOE, FEND** to **FEFN, FENW** to **FEGN, FTYT** to **FCYT**. *Delete:* **FGXX, FMGA.** *Add:* **FEOE:** Coal, Scotland. **FGTE:** Distribution, Eastfield. **FGXI:** Distribution, Immingham. **FGXN:** Distribution, Toton.
Delete (Withdrawn): 20146, 20203.
Allocations (Depot): 20028-TO, 20041-ZQ, 20043-TO, 20060-ZQ, 20069-TO, 20083-ZQ, 20101-ZQ, 20145-ED, 20172/79-TO, 20185-ED, 20208-TO, 20209/19/24/25-ZQ, 20228-ED.

Classes 26/0 and 26/1: **Maximum operating speed:** Amend to 60mph (originally 80mph).
Sectors: *Departmental: Change* **DWCQ** to **DMEA**.
Railfreight: Change: **FEGB** to **FEPE, FGWS** to **FGSE**.

Class 31/1: **Maximum operating speed:** Amend to 60mph.
Sectors: *Departmental: Change:* **DWCQ** to **DMEA**.
Railfreight: Change: **FALG** to **FAGS, FAMA** to **FALY, FGWC** to **FGOT, FHHA** to **FHAC, FPLI** to **FPCI**, **FTLC** to **FCCC. Add: FPFS:** Petroleum, North Thames.
Delete (Withdrawn): 31141/43, 31226/27, 31311.
Allocations (Depot): 31106-CD, 31124-SF, 31135/38-CD, 31149-TI, 31152/68-SF, 31230/52/55-CD, 31257/71/84-TI, 31289-SF, 31290-CD, 31293/96-SF, 31301-SF, 31322-IM.

Class 31/4: **Sectors:** *Departmental: Change:* **DWCQ** to **DMEA**.
Railfreight: Change: **FGWC** to **FGOT**.
Provincial: Delete: **PXXA.**
Allocations: 31403-07/09/10/19/22/23/24/48/51/54/55/59/62/63/64-BS.

Class 33/0: **Maximum operating speed:** Amend to 60mph (originally 85mph).
Sectors: *Departmental: Add:* **DMEA:** DMEE General.
Railfreight: Change: **FALS** to **FASB.** *Delete:* **FPXX.**
Network SouthEast. ***Delete:*** **NSSB.**
Delete (Withdrawn): 33031.
Named: Add: 33025 *Sultan*.
Allocations (Depot): 33064-SL.

Late Information/Notes

Class 33/1: ***Add*** **Maximum operating speed:** 85mph.
Sectors: *Departmental: Add:* **DMEA:** DMEE General.
Network SouthEast: Delete: **NSSB**.
Named: *Delete:* 33114 *Sultan*.

Class 33/2: **Sectors:** *Railfreight: Change:* **FALS** to **FASB, FGWD** to **FGWB.**
Add (Reinstated): 33202 AX Fa *FASB* SL
Delete (Withdrawn): 33209.

Class 37/0: **Sectors:** *Railfreight: Change:* **FEGA** to **FEOE, FGWB** to **FGET, FMCA** to **FMAK, FMYT** to **FMTY, FPGE** to **FPAE, FPLW** to **FPEK, FQLC** to **FQCK**. *Add:* **FAGS:** Construction, Stratford. **FGDS:** (ex-LNRA) Distribution, Stratford. **FGUV:** Distribution, Inverness. *Delete:* **FGXX, FMCH**.
Freightliner: Delete **LNRA** (Now FGDS).
Renumbering: Add: 37303 = 37271, 37304 = 37272, 37306 = 37273, 37308 = 37274, 37374 = 37165.
Add: (Reclassified and renumbered) 37165 KX x F *FEOE* ED.
Move data (Renumbered): 37303, 37271 to 37304 to 37272, 37306 to 37273, 37308 to 37274, 37312 to 37137, 37321 to 37037.
Named: 37275 *Stainless Pioneer*.
Allocations (Depot): 37227/40/50-TE.

Class 37/3: **Sectors:** *Railfreight, Change:* **FAMM** to **FACM, FAMT** to **FABT, FGWB** to **FGET**, Add: **FAWK** Construction (Stone), Cardiff. **FEOE:** Coal, Scotland. **FGDS:** Distribution, Stratford. **FPAE:** Petroleum & Chemicals, Eastfield. **FPLW:** Petroleum, Wales, Cardiff. *Delete:* **FPLX, FQLC.**
Delete (Reclassified): 37374.
Allocations (Depot): 37350/54-CF, 37375/76-ED.

Class 37/4: **Sectors:** *Departmental: Delete* **DCHA.**
Railfreight: Change: **FAWC** to **FAWK**. *Add:* **FABT:** Construction (Stone), Tinsley. **FGTE:** Distribution, Eastfield. **FGUV:** Distribution, Inverness. **FJLL:** Chemicals (China Clay), Laira. *Delete:* **FGXX, FMGA.**
InterCity: Delete: **ICHA, IWCA.**
Provincial: Add: **PCFA:** General, Cardiff. *Delete:* **PXXA.**
Allocations (Depot): 37407/08-CF, 37411-TI, 37412-LA, 37422/25-CF.

Class 37/5: **Sectors:** *Railfreight: Change:* **FAMT** to **FABT, FHCC** to **FHBK, FMYT** to **FMTY, FTLL** to **FJLL.**

Class 37/7: **Sectors:** *Railfreight: Change:* **FECA** to **FEKK, FMCH** to **FMHK, FPLX** to **FPFS.**

Class 37/9: **Sector:** *Railfreight: Change:* **FMCC** to **FMCK.**

Class 43: **Named:** *Add:* 43108 *BBC Television Railwatch*. 43191 *Seahawk*.
43192 *City of Truro*. *Delete:* 43002/61/92/96/98, 43100/01/02/05/07/10/21/26/31/42/88.

Class 45/1: **Delete:** Special Livery.
Delete (Withdrawn): 45106.
Add (Reinstated): 45128 AX *ICHA* TI.

Class 47/0: **Sectors:** *Departmental: Delete:* **DCHA.**
Railfreight: Add: **FAGS:** Construction (Stone), Stratford. **FGBC** (ex-LNRC) Distribution, Crewe. **FGCS** (ex-LNRB) Distribution, Stratford. *Change:* **FAWC** to **FAWK, FGWA** to **FGAT, FPLC** to **FPBC, FPLI** to **FPCI, FPLW** to **FPEK, FTLC** to **FCCC.**
Freightliner: *Delete:* **LNRB** (now FGCS), **LNRC** (now FGBC).
Add (Reinstated): 47145 EX *FGAT* TI
47189 EX *FGBC* CD (sDL)
Delete (Withdrawn): 47235.
Dia: *Change:* **LX:** 47054. **NX:** 47222/24/94.
Allocation (Depot): 47115-IM, 47124-TI, 47186/87-CD, 47229-SF, 47277-CF.

Class 47/3: **Diagram:** ***Sectors:*** *Railfreight: Add:* **FCTY:** Chemicals, Thornaby. **FGBC:** (ex-LNRC) Distribution, Crewe. *Change:* **FALG** to **FAGS, FAWC** to **FAWK, FGWA** to **FGAT, FMYT** to **FMTY, FPLI** to **FPCI, FPLW** to **FPEK, FTLC** to **FCCC.**
Freightliner: Delete **LNRC** (now FGBC).
Dia: *Change:* **BX:** 47319/36/73/74.
Allocations (Depot): 47320-CF.

Class 47/4: **Sectors:** *Departmental, Add:* **DCEA:** DCE, Eastern Region.
Railfreight: Add: **FGBC:** Distribution, Crewe. **FGCS:** Distribution, Stratford. **FGXI:** Distribution, Immingham. **FPCI:** Petroleum, Immingham. *Change:* **FGWA** to **FGAT, FMYT** to **FMTY, FTLC** to **FCCC.**
Provincial: Add **PISA:** General, Inverness. *Delete:* **PXXA.**
Allocations (Depot): 47481-CD, 47515-BR, 47542-ED, 47572/74-BR, 47578-ED, 47580/85-BR, 47596-OC, 47598-LA.

Class 47/7: **Sector:** *Provincial: Add:* ***PEDA*** *General, ScotRail Express, Eastfield. Delete:* **PXXA.**

Class 47/9: **Sector:** *Railfreight: Change:* ***FAWC to FAWK.***

Class 50: **Diagram:** *Add* 50-0BX, Maximum operating speed 60mph.
Sectors: *Delete:* **RXXA.**
Delete (Withdrawn): 50012.
Dia. *Change:* **BX:** 50004/05/07/08/09/15/16/20/21/42/45.

Class 50/1: **Maximum operating speed:** *Change:* 60mph (originally 100mph as Class 50/0).
Sectors: Add *Departmental:* **DCWA:** DCE, Western Region.
Railfreight: Delete.

Class 56: **Sectors:** *Railfreight: Change:* **FALX** to **FAXN, FAWC** to **FAWK, FENB** to **FECN, FEYA** to **FEDN, FEYB** to **FEEN.**
Allocations (Depot): 56072-TO.

Class 58: **Sectors:** *Railfreight: Change:* **FENA** to **FEAN, FENC** to **FEBN.**
Named: *Add:* 58003 *Markham Colliery.*

Class 73/0: **Sectors:** *Add: Railfreight:***FGWE:** Distribution, dc electric locomotives.

Class 73/1: **Sectors:** *Departmental:* **DMEA:** DMEE General. *Railfreight: Add:* **FGWE:** Distribution, dc electric locomotives. *Delete:* ***FALS.***

Class 81: **Delete (Withdrawn):** 81005/06/19.

Class 85: **Delete (Withdrawn):** 85022.

Class 86/2: **Delete (Reclassified and renumbered):** 86239/41.

Class 86/5: **Add data:** 86507 (86239) BX s I *LNRE* WN *L. S. Lowry*
86508 (86241)† BX I *LNRE* WN *Glenfiddich*

Class 87/0: **Renamed:** 87006 *City of Glasgow.*

Class 89: **Named:** 89001 *Avocet.*

Class 90: **Allocations:** 90020-23 -ZQ.

Class 97/0: **Delete (Reclassified):** Diagram 97-0EV and 97805 (see Class 03).

Class 97/7: **Sector:** *Departmental: Add* **DMEX:** DMEE, Battery-electric locomotives. *Delete:* **DCEA, DCMA.**

Late Information/Notes

***Special Purpose Locomotives.* Allocations (Depot):** ADB 968021 -ZQ.
InterCity 125 Coaching Stock.
Reclassified and renumbered: 40228 0A R I *IWR* PM. (ex- 40428). 40724 0A R I *IWR* LA (ex-40324). Delete (Withdrawn): 42126, 44027.
Diagrams: *30E:* 42254/55/56/58/62/63/64/67/68/70/71/72/74/75/76/78/87/88/91/92/95/96/99, 42300
30F: 42341
30H: 42024/25/45/46, 42104/24/27/33/34/38/66-72/75/76/77/83-88/91/92/95-98, 42200-03/05-08/10-13/17/18/22/23/25/26/27/37/38/41/42/46/47/48
30J: 42257/65/66/69/82/89/93/97, 42301
30K: 42023/26/47/78, 42103/05/06/07/22/28/32/73/74/82/89/90/93/99, 42204/09/14/19/24/28-31/39/49
30L: 42003/04/09/10/12/13/21/22
30M: 42005/11/14.
Allocations (Depot): 40741-HT, 40749-NL, 41111/12-NL, 41153/54-HT, 42195-NL, 42205/09-HT, 42227/28-NL, 44020-NL, 44070-HT, 44073-NL, 44083-HT, 44097-BN.
***Formations:* Class 253** In second set headings after 'GK4' add 'GN4§'.
Unit 30: Change 40324 to 40724†.
Unit 36: Add R, change 40428 to 40228§.
Unit 50: Delete 42196, change 44020 to 44084. *Spare:* Delete 44084.
Class 254: Amend units to read:
28 R *IML* NL 41112 41111 40741 -- 42195 42220 42227 42228 44073.
35 P *IEC* HT 41153 41154 40511* 41066* 40749* 42205 42210 -- 44083.
38 *Change:* 42126 and 44027 to read 42196 44020.

SPECIAL CHARACTERISTICS: The following additions are applicable:
B: 37430/31, 47007/08/12/16/18/19/49/50/52/54/60/95/97, 47102/07/20/24/44/56/57/88/93/94/97, 47203-06/09/14/15/17/18/20/26/28/31/33/34/36/37/38/41/45/49/78/80/83/84/85/87-92/96/97/98, 47301/06-09/14/15/19/20/21/36/37/44/47/53/55/58/60/70-73/76, 47406/11/13/17/21/22/25/26/31/32/33/40/43/50/51/52/56/57/59/74/75/79/89/91, 47500/03/15/18/19/30/36/42/43/56/58/66/79/81/89/90/92, 47606/12/13/15/21/24/37/39/47/52/55/56/58/60/62/63/64, 50015, 56004/05/12/14-17/19/27/30/33/37/42/51/54/57/59/61/63-99, 56100-11/13-35, 58004/06/12/16/26/27/31/33/35/37/38/39/43/44/45/47/48/50.
C: 08567/71/83, 08624, 08770, 08800, 08903/06/08.
R: 37430/31.
U: 33211.
X: 47222/24/94, 47319/36/73/74.
60: 50004/05/07/08/09/15/16/20/21/42/45.
The following deletions are advised:
B: 86225.
K: 20118/19/22, 37196.
75: 47596, 47607.
InterCity 125 Coaching Stock:
R: 41021/22, 41137/38, 42030/31/32, 42283/84/85, 44010/36.
·: 42030/31/32, 42283/84/85.

SECTORS: The following have changed Sector/sub-Sector ownership. Where the sub-Sector code only has been changed (as indicated above) a full listing of locomotives involved appears on preceding pages.
CHUB: 20041/60/83, 20101, 20209/19/24/25.
DCAB: 08528/29/31/40/41, 08638, 08757/72/75, 08810/59/89. *DCEB:* 08499, 08583, 08605/07/18/55/57, 08701/06/73/83/94, 08866/67/70/76/85, 08906/08/19/31. *DCMA:* 20056, 20121/78, 31403-07/09/10/19/22/23/24/48/51/54/55/59/62/63/64. *DCMB:* 08624. *DCSA:* 33058, 73107/11/38/39. *DCSB:* 03179. *DCWA:* 47334/41, 50149.
DMEA: 20202, 31289, 31460, 33025, 33111, 73136. *DMES:* 08632/52, 08734/87, 09007. *DMEX:* 97701-08.
DXXD: 08530/76/84, 08767, 08932.

FABT: 37411. *FAGS*: 31189, 31293/96, 31301/20, 47325. *FASB*: 33046/48/52/63/64, 33204. *FAWK*: 37354, 37422/25, 47320. *FAZZ*: 08521/42/44/93, 08923. *FCCC*: 31138, 47186. *FCTY*: 47301-05/61/62/63.
FEAN: 58017. *FEDN*: 56072. *FEGN*: 20088, 20187, 20208. *FEOE*: 37165, 37375/76.
FGAT: 47124. *FGBC*: 47187, 47451/57/79/81. *FGCS*: 47430/52/62. *FGDS*: 37358. *FGOT*: 31149, 31257/71/84.
FGTE: 20145/85, 20228, 37401-06/09/10/13/23/24. *FGUV*: 37070, 37109/10/14/53/96, 37260, 37412/14-20.
FGWE: 73001-04/06, 73106/40/41. *FGXI*: 20009/35, 20171, 47401/02. *FGXN*: 20028/43/69, 20100/72/73/89, 20218. *FGXZ*: 90016/17/18. *FGZZ*: 08413/14/15/72, 08516/39/77, 08659/69/89, 08708/60, 08811/17/20/23/38/78, 08936/47.
FHZZ: 08308/09, 08434/36, 08586, 08880.
FJLL: 37421. *FMTY*: 37227/40/50. *FMZZ*: 08401, 08500/09/25/37/94/95, 08662/65/91, 08714/49.
FPAE: 37359. *FPCI*: 31170, 31221, 31322, 47115, 47221/94, 47411. *FPFS*: 31124/52/68. *FPLW*: 37215/94, 37350, 47277. *FPZZ*: 08871.
FQZZ: 08806.
FTZZ: 08575/88, 08740/43/51.
FVZZ: 08709/58, 08869/73, 08928.
FXXL: 08515, 08837/87.
ICHA: 08929. *IECP*: 43065. *IMLP*: 43043. *IWCA*: 47578. *IWCB*: 86425.
NSSB: 73130/34. *NWRA*: 47596. *NXXA*: 08670, 08715, 08828.
PCFA: 08848, 37407/08/26-31. *PEDA*: 47701-12/14-17. *PISA*: 08753, 47460/61/69/92, 47541/63, 47630/35/40-44. *PXXA*: 08567, 08745, 08872.
RXLA: 08719/66, 08833. *RXLC*: 33101/02/03/06/14. *RXLE*: 86424. *RXXA*: 90019.

InterCity 125 Coaching Stock:
IEC: 40741, 41153/54, 42205/10, 44083, 44100.
IML: 40749, 41111/12, 42196, 42227/28, 44020/73.

LIVERIES: The following revised liveries have been reported:
Departmental: **D:** 31412/52/53.
InterCity: **I:** 43006/08/29/50/73/76/80/91/94, 43106/07/08/10/17/21/29/30/39/42/61/64/65/88/91/92, 47470, 47520/66/70/90, 47619/25, 73104/14/38/40, 90020-23.
Network SouthEast **N:** 03179, 47596/98.
Provincial **Pt:** 47475.
Railfreight: **F-:** 08506, 26008, 37902/03/04/06, 47335/54/65, 47605/15.
Fa: 08542, 08923, 33033/42/63, 33204, 47063, 47114, 56032/50/62.
Fe: 08512, 08791, 26001/07, 31120/30, 31200/17/70/75/76, 31312/24, 37167, 37235/74, 56003/12-15/29/47/69/72/80/84/88/90/92/94/95, 56104/27/28/29, 58006/09/11/12/16/25.
Fg: 08407/60, 08737, 37047/63, 37101/94/98, 37271/72, 37355/56/57, 47052, 47117/50/56/87, 47201/14/41/58.
Fm: 08665, 08920, 37037/49, 37106/37, 37201/02/75/78, 47347.
Fp: 31201/73, 37080, 37215, 47010/54/94, 47336/68.

InterCity 125 Coaching Stock: *InterCity*: **I:** 41021/22, 41137/38, 42030/31/32, 42283/84/85, 44010/36/97/98.

LOCOMOTIVE COSTING CENTRES

Stop Press

Changed codes: FAMA now FALY, FGWA now FGAT, FGWB now FGET, FGWC now FGOT, FGWD now FGWB, FGWS now FGSE, FGXX divided to FGUV, FGTE, FGXI, FGXN; FMCA now FMAK, FMCC now FMCK, FMCH now FMHK, FMTY now FMYT, FPGE now FPAE, FPLC now FPBC, FPLI now FPCI, FPLW now FPEK, FPLX now FPFS, LNRA now FGDS, LNRB now FGCS, LNRC now FGBC, LNRS deleted, added to FGZZ.
New codes: .DMEX: Departmental, DMEE, Battery-electric locomotives; ***FGTE:*** *Distribution, Eastfield;* ***FGUV:*** *Distribution, Inverness;* ***FGXI:*** *Distribution, Immingham;* ***FGXN:*** *Distribution, Toton.*

DMEX: 97701-08. (Delete from DCEA or DMEA)
FALS: delete 33031.

FGTE: 20145/85, 20228, 37401-06/09/23/24.
FGUV: 37070, 37109/10/14/53/96, 37260, 37414-21.
FGXI: 20009/35, 20171, 47401/02.
FGXN: 20028/43/69, 20100/72/73/89, 20218.
FJLL: Delete 37421, Add 37412.
FPLX: Delete 31311.
FXXA to *FXXL:* 08515, 08747/71, 08886.
ICHA: Delete 45106, Add 45128.
IWCA: Delete 81005.
PISA: Delete 37412/15-20.
RXXA: Delete 85022.

BRITISH RAIL
MULTIPLE-UNITS

LONDON

IAN ALLAN LTD

Introduction

New to this edition is the current BR Director of Mechanical Engineering's (DMEE) full Design Classification for each vehicle. Network SouthEast's Regional Traction & Rolling Stock Engineer also has a separate design reference inherited from, and used in conjunction with, all Southern Region-operated electric units. Whilst both are listed herein there are examples where the two records do not agree, in which case this book shows the revised DMEE reference.

The most significant factor during 1988 was the continued growth of passenger traffic which stretched the rolling stock resources of BR. Due to this, although new units were delivered, stock that was in a reasonable condition that was planned for condemnation in fact received a light overhaul at a BRML Level 5 depot.

Regrettably BR continued to experience serious problems with some of its new units. The Pacer DMUs suffered numerous gearbox failures and a programme of replacing many SCG boxes with Voith units, a type proven on BR's Sprinters, has greatly improved availability. Problems with the sliding plug doors caused all Class 155 Super Sprinters to be 'grounded' at Cardiff and Leeds in mid-December. Luckily Metro-Cammell had been ahead of schedule with delivery of Class 156 units and Provincial Sector management was able to draft 20 of these to Cardiff, and make small adjustments elsewhere to cover their duties, some reverting to locomotive-hauled coaches.

By October 1989 sufficient new 'Express' Class 158 units are due to be delivered by BREL '88 Ltd for ScotRail Express (Glasgow/Edinburgh/Aberdeen) services in place of locomotive-hauled trains. Some duties at present formed of Class 156 units will later be operated by Class 158s and cascading will allow old DMUs to be withdrawn. However it will be at least 10 years before all the 1960s-era units can be eliminated, and therefore a limited programme of second life-extension overhauls will commence this year, particularly on Class 108 vehicles.

Network SouthEast received Government authority for new Networker Turbo DMUs for Chiltern Lines duties which will replace Marylebone route Class 115s. Generally NSE is awaiting feasibility studies and Government approval before investing in the Paddington-Oxford, Reading-Tonbridge and Waterloo-Exeter routes.

Subject to Government authority Birmingham's Cross-City line (Lichfield-Redditch) will be electrified and operated by new units. ScotRail's Class 311 and unrefurbished Class 303 units will be replaced by the new Class 320 series on order with BREL at York.

Thameslink's 60 Class 319 EMUs have already proved a tremendous success and a further 20 are on order to cover traffic growth on both sides of the Thames. The new Anglia Class 321 EMUs are being delivered at the rate of two per week and are generally augmented rather than directly replacing old units. The compartment-style Class 302s retained primarily for peak-hour duties will gradually be withdrawn.

By the end of 1988 two Class 442 Wessex Electric units had still to enter service and two more had already been involved in incidents, one as a result of vandalism. Traffic growth meant that BR decided to overhaul three of the Class 432 4-REP tractor units, but one was written off in the Clapham tragedy last December, the worst accident on BR in 20 years. Thus NSE has retained the Class 492/8 and additional Class 438 units on a short-term basis. 'New' stock, in the form of 1938 London Underground life-expired trains, has been purchased for the Isle of Wight and should enter service in 1989 after overhaul and modifications at BRML Eastleigh. Refurbishment of other slam-door Southern Region stock this year is expected to be confined to Class 423 4-VEP units. Kent suburban services are scheduled for new Networker trains in 1991, an order for over 700 vehicles is sure to be subject to very keen tendering by at least BREL and Metro-Cammell, with Brush and GEC seeking type approval of new ac traction motors installed in EMU Nos 7001 and 5920 respectively.

Multiple-units do not have the enthusiastic following of locomotives, but from an economic viewpoint they form the only way forward for BR's short- and medium-distance routes. The future for locomotives on BR will be confined to the long-distance International routes via the Channel Tunnel, East and West Coast main lines, plus freight and engineering duties.

Roger Wood, Editor
March 1989

Sector Codes

Multiple-unit stock is used by five of BR's six Sectors, Railfreight having no normal use for such stock. BR's policy is to allocate all costs of stock to a financial pool to be funded from service income and national and local Government grants. The Pools in use at the time of going to press are:

InterCity

IVGA Gatwick Express

Network SouthEast

NCH Charter services
NGB Gospel Oak-Barking line
NGE Great Eastern lines (Anglia East)
NGN Great Northern lines
NKC Kent Coast routes
NKS Kent suburban routes
NMY Chiltern Lines (Marylebone)
NNE Northeast routes (Anglia West)
NNL North London lines
NNW North Western lines
NSB Surrey and Berkshire
NSL South London lines
NSS Solent and Sarum
NST London, Tilbury & Southend line
NSX Sussex routes
NWR Western Region
NXX Spare
NXXZ Authorised for condemnation

Provincial

This Sector ceased to use area and route codes with effect from 1 April 1989. All stock is financially controlled based on maintenance depot allocation, the cost of work effected at other than home depot being charged to the current recorded DMEE Rolling Stock Library allocation (eg Newton Heath based stock has a Sector code of *PNH* etc.)

PXX Spare
PXXZ Authorised for condemnation

Parcels Sector

RPMA AC electric multiple-units
RPMD DC electric multiple-units
RPXN Diesel multiple-units
RXXX Spare or authorised for condemnation

Departmental

DXXZ Captial stock awaiting transfer to Departmental service, or authorised for condemnation

Special Characteristics

D Additional dc lines collection shoe (Euston-Watford route)
E Express gear ratio on suburban stock
L Headlight/Spotlight fitted
F Facelifted units, not standard to class
G Through gangway fitted, not standard to class
M Driver only operation, cab-signalling centre communication
O Open type accommodation, normally non-corridor compartments
R Radio Electronic Token Block signalling system
V Voith transmission (other SCG)
+ AEC engines (others in class Leyland)
# Asbestos insulation

Liveries

L London & South Sector ('Jaffa-Cake')
M Greater Manchester PTE
N Network SouthEast
P Provincial blue
RR Post Office red
S Strathclyde PTE
***** Special, see class heading

Acknowledgements

This stock is a very difficult area to maintain accuracy of records. The five Regions have, to varying degrees, issued their own records but not ensured that the main BRB records were similarly revised.

The editor wishes to thank the staff of RSL Derby, the responsible officers of the five Regions, and also, Alan, Brian, Dave L, Dave T, Lawrie and Peter for their invaluable assistance.

Level of Repair and Maintenance Facility

In April 1987 BR introduced a new maintenance policy for all traction and coaching stock. Under the scheme, depots and workshops are classified on a scale of 1 to 6, called Levels, determined by the facilities available and work effected at each location.

The larger establishments, Level 5, normally have separate workshops to carry out this category of repair and are not necessarily answerable to the Sector which 'owns' the main depot.

Definition

Level	*Facility*	*Description*
1	Fuel point	Facility for dispensing fuel, oil and water to diesel locomotives and/or DMUs. Minor servicing to EMUs. Manned by unskilled staff.
2	Servicing	Capable of undertaking 'A' exam work and occasional 'B' exams on locomotives and multiple-units together with work arising and brake blocking also full maintenance for diesel shunter locomotives. For coaching stock some cleaning, chemical emission toilet disposal, environmental checks, two daily exams, weekly exams and brake blocking. The facility will have a covered pit, a small store and be manned by skilled staff.
3	Maintenance	This facility will have a Traction and Rolling Stock allocation and be capable of carrying out all levels of exams and the majority of repairs arising. It will have covered pits, staff accomodation, light lifting and jacking facilities. A full range of equipment will be available to meet all exam requirements. Multiple-units and coaching stock all levels of exams, code 'C' cleaning, patch painting and some body repair.
4	Maintenance and repair	As for level 3 but having an additional capability for heavier repairs. The depot will be well equipped with cranes and/or heavy lifting jacks for bogie removal and possibly a wheel lathe.
5	Heavy repair	A facility capable of undertaking unplanned heavy repairs and collision damage. May also have the facility for lower level of classified repair, limited component refurbishment and half life component exchange. Fuelling facilities are not necessarily provided.
6	Workshop	A main workshop with full facilities for undertaking all levels of classified and unclassified repairs.

	Level DMU	EMU		Main Sector(s)	Full Maintenance Classes Allocated
AF	2/5*	2/5*	Ashford, Chart Leacon T&RSMD	N	—
AN	2		Allerton SD	P	—
AY	2		Ayr SD	P	—
BD		4/5*	Birkenhead North EMUD	P	508
BE	1	1	Bedford	N	—
BI		4	Brighton T&RSMD	N	421/1, 421/3, 421/4, 422/1, 422/2, 423/0, 423/1
BM		4	Bournemouth West EMUD	N	423/0, 423/1, 431, 432, 438, 492/8
BQ		4	Bury EMUD	P	504
BP	1		Blackpool	P	—
BR	2		Bristol Bath Road TMD	P	108
BX	2		Buxton TMD	P	108
BY	4	4	Bletchley TMD	N	104(T), 108, 115, 310, 310/1, 313, 317 (321)
CA	4		Cambridge (Coldhams Lane) TMD	R	101, 105, 114, 128
CC		4	Clacton EMUD	N	309/1, 309/2, 309/3, 309/4, 312/0, 312/1, 313
CE		2	Crewe ETD	P	—
CF	4		Cardiff Canton TMD	P	101, 116, 119, 155
	5	5	Cardiff Cathays RSMD	—	
CH	2		Chester TMD	P DMUs to cease asap	101, 108
CK	1	4	Corkerhill SD	P	156
CL	1		Carlisle Upperby RSMD	P	
CP	1		Crewe RSMD (all stored)	P	101, 104, 115, 116, 127
DL	5	5	Doncaster Major Depot, BRML	—	
DY	4		Derby, Etches Park T&RSMD	P	150, 150/1, 151, 154
ED	4		Eastfield, Glasgow TMD	P DMUs to Level 2 soon	101, 104, 107, 108

	Level				Full Maintenance
	DMU	EMU		Main Sector(s)	Classes Allocated
EH	4		Eastleigh T&RSMD	N	205
EM		4	East Ham EMUD	N	302, 308/1, 310
EX	1		Exeter St Davids SD	P	
FR	2	3	Fratton T&RSMD	N	411/5, 412, 421, 423/0, 423/1
GI		2	Gillingham EMUD	N	—
GW		4	Glasgow, Shields EMD	P	303, 311, 314, 318
HA	4		Haymarket TMD	P	101, 107, 108, 110(T), 120, 150/2, 156, (158)
HE		4	Hornsey EMUD		313, 317/1, 317/2
HR		3	Hall Road EMUD	P	507
HT	4		Heaton T&RSMD	P	101, 111(T), 142, 143
IL		4/5*	Ilford EMD	N	302, 305/1, 305/2, 307, 308/1, 308/2, 315, 321
IP	1		Ipswich HS	F	—
LA	4		Laira TMD	P	101, 118, 121, 122
LE	4		Landore TMD	P	101, 108, 116(T), 118(T)
LG		4	Longsight EMD	P	303, 304
LO	2		Longsight TMD	R	127
ME	2		Marylebone TMD	N	—
MN	1		Machynlleth	P	—
NC	4		Norwich, Crown Point T&RSMD	P	101, 111(T), 156
NH	4		Newton Heath TMD	P	100, 101(T), 104, 105, 108, 142, 142/1, 150/2
NL	4/5*		Neville Hill T&RSMD	P	101, 108, 110, 111, 141, 141/1, 142, 144, 150/2, 156
OO	4		Old Oak Common HSTD	N	101, 104, 116, 121
ON		3	Orpington HS	N	—
PB	1		Peterborough SD	N	
PE	1	1	Peterborough CS	R	

	Level DMU	EMU		Main Sector(s)	Full Maintenance Classes Allocated
RE		4	Ramsgate EMUD	N	411/3, 411/4, 411/5, 413/2, 413/3, 414/2, 419, 423/0
RG	4		Reading TMD	N	101, 117, 119
RY		4/5	Ryde, Isle of Wight EMD	N	(483), 485, 486
SG		4/5*	Slade Green T&RSMD	N	415/1, 415/3, 415/4, 416/2, 416/4
SH	—	‡	Strawberry Hill	—	—
SL		4	Stewarts Lane T&RSMD	I	488/2, 488/3, 489
SU	4/5*	4/5*	Selhurst T&RSMD	N	319, 415/3, 415/4, 416/2, 416/3, 455/8
	1		Stirling	—	
TS	4		Tyseley TMD	P	101, 108, 111(T), 115(T), 116, 121, 127(T)
WC		4/5*	Waterloo (Waterloo & City) EMUD	N	487
WD		4	East Wimbledon EMUD	N	414/2, 414/3, 423/0, 455/7, 455/8, 455/9
WN		1	Willesden TMD	N	
ZG	6	6	Eastleigh BRML		
ZH	5	5	Springburn BRML		
ZN		5	Wolverton BRML		
BREL Works:					
ZD			Derby Carriage CEM (under contract)		
ZR			York Carriage		
British Railways Board:					
ZQ			BRB Headquarters (stock on acceptance)		

Sectors:
I: InterCity
P: Provincial Services
N: Network SouthEast
R: Parcels

* Level 5 Workshop for specific work only
‡ Specialist repair workshops

Diesel Multiple-Units

Class 119 — Driving Motor Brake

Built: Gloucester RC&W Co 1958

Diagram	Type	Weight	Seats 1st	Seats Std
DQ3.02.0B	DMBC	37.5t	18	16
DQ2.--.--	DMBS	37.5t	—	34

Engines: Two Leyland 150bhp (112kW) 6-cyl horizontal

Transmission: Four speed epicyclic gearbox/ carden shaft

Dimensions: 19.66m L × 2.74m W × 3.86m H. Gangway within unit

Maximum speed: 70mph

Brakes: Vacuum

AWS: Fitted

Veh No	*Dia*	*SC*	*Liv*	Pool	Dep
51057	2----			*PCH*	CH
51060	3020B			*NSS*	RG
51062	3020B	#	N	*NWR*	RG
51065	3020B	#		*NSB*	RG
51066	3020B		N	*NSS*	RG
51071	2----			*PCH*	CH
51073	3020B		N	*NWR*	RG
51074	3020B			*NWR*	RG
51076	3020B			*NWR*	RG
51079	3020B			*NSS*	RG

Class 119 — Driving Motor

Built: Gloucester RC&W Co 1958

Diagram	Type	Weight	Seats	Toilet
DP2.03.0C	DMS(L)	38.5t	68	2

Engines: Two Leyland 150bhp (112kW) 6-cyl horizontal

Transmission: Four speed epicyclic gearbox/ carden shaft

Dimensions: 19.66m L × 2.74m W × 3.86m H. Gangway within unit

Maximum speed: 70mph

AWS: Fitted

Veh No	*Dia*	*SC*	*Liv*	Pool	Dep
51086	OC			*NWR*	RG
51088	OC			*NSB*	RG
51090	OC	#	N	*NWR*	RG
51094	OC		N	*NSS*	RG
51095	OC	#		*PCH*	CH
51099	OC			*NWR*	RG
51101	OC	#		*PCH*	CH
51103	OC	#		*NSB*	RG
51104	OC		N	*NWR*	RG
51107	OC		N	*NSS*	RG

Class 116 — Driving Motor Brake

Built: British Railways, Derby Carriage Works 1958

Diagram	Type	Weight	Seats	Note
DQ2.30.1A	DMBS	36.5t	65	Gangwayed
DQ2.30.2B	DMBS	36.5t	65	Refurbished and Gangwayed

Engines: Two Leyland 150bhp (112kW) 6-cyl horizontal
Transmission: Four speed epicyclic gearbox/ carden shaft
Dimensions: 20.29m L × 2.82m W × 3.86m H. Gangwayed within unit, with side doors to each seating bay as shown
Maximum speed: 70mph
AWS: Fitted

Veh No	*Dia*	*SC*	*Liv*	Pool	Dep
51128	2B	LG		*PCF*	CF
51129	2B	G		*PTS*	TS
51130	1A	G		*PTS*	TS
51131	2B	G		*PTS*	TS
51132	2B	LG		*PCF*	CF
51133	1A	G		*PTS*	TS
51134	2B	LG		*PCF*	CF
51135	2B	LG		*PCF*	CF
51136	2B	G		*PTS*	TS
51138	2B	G		*PTS*	TS
51139	2B	LG		*PCF*	CF
51140	2B	LG		*PCF*	CF

Series continued with No 53050.

Class 116 — Driving Motor

Built: British Railways, Derby Carriage Works 1958

Diagram	Type	Weight	Seats	Note
DP2.20.1A	DMS	36.5t	89	Gangwayed
DP2.20.2B	DMS	36.5t	89	Refurbished and Gangwayed

Engines: Two Leyland 150bhp (112kW) 6-cyl horizontal
Transmission: Four speed epicyclic gearbox/ carden shaft
Dimensions: 20.29m L × 2.82m W × 3.86m H. Gangwayed within unit, with side doors to each seating bay as shown
Maximum speed: 70mph
Brakes: Vacuum
AWS: Fitted

Veh No	*Dia*	*SC*	*Liv*	Pool	Dep
51141	2B	LG		*PCF*	CF
51142	2B	G		*PTS*	TS
51143	2B	G		*PTS*	TS
51144	2B	G		*PTS*	TS
51145	2B	LG		*PCF*	CF
51146	1A	G		*PTS*	TS
51147	2B	LG		*PCF*	CF
51148	2B	LG		*PCF*	CF

Veh No	Dia	SC	Liv	Pool	Dep
51149	2B	G		PTS	TS
51151	2B	G		PTS	TS
51152	2B	LG		PCF	CF
51153	2B	LG		PCF	CF

Series continued with No 53092.

Class 101 Driving Motor Brake

Built: Metropolitan-Cammell 1958

Diagram	Type	Weight	Seats	Engine	Note
DQ2.02.1A	DMBS	32.5t	52	AEC	—
DQ2.02.2B	DMBS	32.5t	52	AEC	Refurbished
DQ2.02.2E	DMBS	32.5t	52	Leyland	Refurbished
DQ2.32.0A	DMBS	32.5t	49	Leyland	Refurbished

Engines: Two AEC or Leyland 150bhp (112kW) 6-cyl horizontal
Transmission: Four speed epicyclic gearbox/ carden shaft
Dimensions: 18.49m L × 2.82m W × 3.85m H. Gangwayed within unit
Maximum speed: 70mph
Brakes: Vacuum
AWS: Fitted

Veh No	Dia	SC	Liv	Pool	Dep
51174	022E			PHA	HA
51175	022B	†		PNL	NL
51177	022E			PNC	NC
51178	022B	†		PNC	NC
51179	022E			PLA	LA
51180	022E			PNC	NC
51181	022E			PLA	LA
51182	022E			PHA	HA
51183	022E	#		PNL	NL
51184	022E			PNC	NC
51185	022E			PNC	NC
51187	022E			PNC	NC
51188	022E			PNC	NC
51189	022E			PNC	NC
51190	022E			NSS	RG
51191	022E			PNC	NC
51192	022E			PNC	NC
51194	022E			PNC	NC
51197	021A	#		PHT	HT
51201	022E			PNC	NC
51203	022E	#		PHT	HT
51205	022E			PLA	LA
51206	022B	#†		PNH	NH
51207	022E		N	NGE	CA
51208	022E		N	NGE	CA
51210	022E			PHA	HA
51211	320A	L		NSS	RG
51212	022E		N	NWR	OO
51213	022E			PNC	NC
51215	022E	#		PNL	NL
51216	022B	#†		PHT	HT
51217	022B	#†		PHT	HT
51218	022E			PNC	NC
51219	022E			PLA	LA
51220	022E		N	NWR	OO
51221	022E			NWR	OO
51222	022E			PCF	CF
51223	022E			PLA	LA
51224	022E			PED	ED
51225	022E			NWR	OO
51226	320A			NSS	RG
51227	022B	#†		PNH	NH
51228	022E			PHA	HA
51230	022E			PNC	NC
51231	022E			PHA	HA
51234	022E			PHA	HA

Veh No	Dia	SC	Liv	Pool	Dep
51241	022E			PHA	HA
51243	022B	#†		PNH	NH
51244	022E			PHA	HA
51245	022E			PHA	HA
51246	022E			PLA	LA
~~51247~~	022E			PNC	NC
51249	022E		S	PED	ED
51252	022E			PNC	NC
51253	022E			PHA	HA

Series continued with No 51425.

Class 118 — Driving Motor Brake

Built: Birmingham RC&W Co 1960

Diagram	Type	Weight	Seats	Toilet
DQ2.20.0A	DMBS	36.5t	65	—
DQ2.20.1D	DMBS	36.5t	65	Refurbished

Engines: Two Leyland 150bhp (112kW) 6-cyl horizontal
Transmission: Four speed epicyclic gearbox/ carden shaft
Dimensions: 20.45m L × 2.82m W × 3.86m H. Gangwayed within unit, with side doors to each seating bay
Maximum speed: 70mph
Brakes: Fitted
AWS: Fitted

Veh No	Dia	SC	Liv	Pool	Dep
51305	OA	#		PLA	LA
51306	ID			PTS	TS
51307	OA	L		PCF	CF
51310	OA	#		PCF	CF
51312	OA	#		PCF	CF
51314	OA			PTS	TS
51315	OA	#		PCF	CF
51316	ID			PTS	TS

Class 118 — Driving Motor

Built: Birmingham RC&W Co 1960

Diagram	Type	Weight	Seats	Note
DP2.21.0B	DMS	36.5t	89	—
DP2.21.1D	DMS	36.5t	89	Refurbished

Engines: Two Leyland 150bhp (112kW) 6-cyl horizontal
Transmission: Four speed epicyclic gearbox/ carden shaft
Dimensions: 20.45m L × 2.82m W × 3.86m H. Gangwayed within unit, with side doors to each seating bay
Maximum speed: 70mph
Brakes: Vacuum
AWS: Fitted

Veh No	Dia	SC	Liv	Pool	Dep
~~51319~~	OB		N	NWR	OO
51320	OB	#		PLA	LA
51321	ID			PTS	TS
51325	OB	#		PCF	CF
51327	OB	#		PCF	CF
51329	OB			PTS	TS
51330	OB	#		PCF	CF
51331	ID			PTS	TS

Class 117 — Driving Motor Brake

Built: Pressed Steel Co 1959

Diagram	Type	Weight	Seats	Note
DQ2.20.1C	DMBS	36.5t	65	Refurbished

Engines: Two Leyland 150bhp (112kW) 6-cyl horizontal
Transmission: Four speed epicyclic gearbox/ carden shaft
Dimensions: 20.45m L × 2.82m W × 3.86m H. Gangwayed within unit, with side doors to each seating bay
Maximum speed: 70mph
Brakes: Vacuum
AWS: Fitted
Special livery: GWR: 51368

Veh No	*Dia*	*SC*	*Liv*	*Pool*	*Dep*
51332	IC			*NWR*	RG
51333	IC		N	*NWR*	RG
51334	IC			*PTS*	TS
51335	IC		N	*NWR*	RG
51336	IC		N	*NWR*	RG
51337	IC			*NWR*	RG
51338	IC			*PTS*	TS
51339	IC			*PTS*	TS
51340	IC		N	*NWR*	RG
51341	IC		N	*NWR*	RG
51342	IC		N	*NWR*	RG
51343	IC		N	*NWR*	RG
51344	IC		N	*NWR*	RG
51345	IC			*NWR*	RG
51346	IC		N	*NWR*	RG
51347	IC		N	*NWR*	RG
51348	IC			*PTS*	TS
51349	IC		N	*NWR*	RG
51350	IC		N	*NWR*	RG
51351	IC		N	*NWR*	RG
51352	IC			*PTS*	TS
51353	IC			*PTS*	TS
51354	IC		N	*NWR*	RG
51355	IC		N	*NWR*	RG
51356	IC		N	*NWR*	RG
51358	IC		N	*NWR*	RG
51359	IC		N	*NWR*	RG
51360	IC			*PTS*	TS
51361	IC			*NWR*	RG
51362	IC		N	*NWR*	RG
51363	IC			*NWR*	RG
51364	IC			*PTS*	TS
51365	IC			*PTS*	TS
51366	IC		N	*NWR*	RG
51367	IC		N	*NWR*	RG
51368	IC		★	*PTS*	TS
51369	IC			*PTS*	TS
51370	IC			*PTS*	TS
51371	IC			*PTS*	TS
51372	IC			*PTS*	TS
51373	IC			*PTS*	TS

Class 117 — Driving Motor

Built: Pressed Steel Co 1959

Diagram	Type	Weight	Seats	Note
DP2.21.1C	DMS	36.5t	89	Refurbished

Engines: Two Leyland 150bhp (112kW) 6-cyl horizontal
Transmission: Four speed epicyclic gearbox/ carden shaft

Dimensions: 20.45m L × 2.82m W × 3.86m H. Gangwayed within unit, with side doors to each seating bay
Maximum speed: 70mph
Brakes: Vacuum
AWS: Fitted
Special livery: GWR: 51410

Veh No	*Dia*	*SC*	*Liv*	*Pool*	*Dep*
51374	IC			*NWR*	RG
51375	IC		N	*NWR*	RG
51376	IC			*PTS*	TS
51377	IC		N	*NWR*	RG
51378	IC		N	*NWR*	RG
51379	IC			*NWR*	RG
51380	IC			*PTS*	TS
51381	IC		N	*NWR*	RG
51382	IC			*PTS*	TS
51383	IC		N	*NWR*	RG
51384	IC		N	*NWR*	RG
51385	IC		N	*NWR*	RG
51386	IC		N	*NWR*	RG
51387	IC			*NWR*	RG
51388	IC		N	*NWR*	RG
51389	IC		N	*NWR*	RG
51390	IC			*PTS*	TS
51391	IC		N	*NWR*	RG
51392	IC		N	*NWR*	RG
51393	IC			*NWR*	RG
51394	IC			*PTS*	TS
51395	IC			*PTS*	TS
51396	IC		N	*NWS*	RG
51397	IC			*NWR*	RG
51398	IC		N	*NWR*	RG
51399	IC			*NWR*	RG
51400	IC		N	*NWR*	RG
51401	IC		N	*NWR*	RG
51402	IC			*PTS*	TS
51404	IC		N	*NWR*	RG
51405	IC			*NWR*	RG
51406	IC			*PTS*	TS
51407	IC			*PTS*	TS
51408	IC		N	*NWR*	RG
51409	IC			*NWR*	RG
51410	IC		★	*PTS*	TS
51411	IC			*PTS*	TS
51412	IC			*PTS*	TS
51413	IC			*PTS*	TS
51414	IC			*PTS*	TS
51415	IC			*PTS*	TS

Class 108 — Driving Motor Brake

Built: British Railways Derby Carriage Works, 1960

Diagram	**Type**	**Weight**	**Seats**	**Note**
DQ2.13.1A	DMBS	29.5t	52	—
DQ2.13.2B	DMBS	29.5t	52	Refurbished

Engines: Two Leyland 150bhp (112kW) 6-cyl horizontal
Transmission: Four speed epicyclic gearbox/ carden shaft
Dimensions: 19.84m L × 2.82m W × 3.87m H
Maximum speed: 70mph
Brakes: Vacuum
AWS: Fitted

Veh No	*Dia*	*SC*	*Liv*	*Pool*	*Dep*
51416	2B			*PCF*	CF
51417	2B			*PCH*	CH
51418	2B			*PCH*	CH
51419	1A			*PCH*	CH
51420	2B			*PNH*	NH
51421	2B			*PCH*	CH
51422	2B			*PCH*	CH
51424	2B			*PCH*	CH

Series continued with No 51901.

Class 101 — Driving Motor Brake

Built: Metropolitan-Cammell 1959

Diagram	Type	Weight	Seats	Engine	Note
DQ2.02.2E	DMBS	32.5t	52	Leyland	Refurbished
DQ2.32.0A	DMBS	32.5t	49	Leyland	Refurbished

Full details see series commencing No 51174.

Veh No	*Dia*	*SC*	*Liv*	*Pool*	*Dep*
51425	022E			*NSS*	RG
51426	022E			*PHA*	HA
51427	022E			*PNC*	NC
51428	022E			*PNC*	NC
51429	022E			*PNC*	NC
51431	022E			*PNC*	RG
51432	022E			*NSS*	RG
51434	320A			*NSS*	RG
51435	022E			*PNH*	NH
51436	022E	#		*PNL*	NL
51437	022E			*NSB*	RG
51438	022E		N	*NNE*	CA
51442	022E			*PNC*	NC
51443	022E		N	*NWR*	OO
51444	022E		N	*NGE*	CA
51445	022E	L		*PNL*	NL
51446	022E	L		*PNL*	NL
51449	022E	L		*PNH*	NH
51450	022E	L		*PNL*	NL
51454	022E			*PNL*	NL
51455	022E			*PNL*	NL
51456	022E	#		*PNH*	NH
51458	022E			*PHT*	HT
51462	022E	L		*PCF*	CF
51463	022E	L		*PNL*	NL
51465	022E			*PNL*	NL
51467	022E			*PHT*	HT
51468	022E			*PED*	ED

Series continued with No 51795.

Parcels Sector vehicles in this series.

Class 101 — Driving Motor

Built: Metropolitan-Cammell 1959

Diagram	Type	Weight	Seats 1st	Seats Std	Toilets	Note
DP2.10.1D	DMS(L)	32.5t	—	65	1	Mk 3 Bogies
DP2.10.2F	DMS(L)	32.5t	—	65	1	Mk 3 Bogies Refurbished
DP2.10.2H	DMS(L)	32.5t	—	65	1	Mk 2 Bogies Refurbished
DP3.04.2H	DMC(L)	32.5t	12	53	1	Mk 3 Bogies Refurbished
DP3.17.0D	DMC(L)	32.5t	12	46	1	Mk 3 Bogies Refurbished

Engines: Two Leyland 150bhp (112kW) 6-cyl horizontal
Transmission: Four-wheel epicyclic gearbox, carden shaft
Dimensions: 18.49m L × 2.82m W × 3.85m H
Maximum speed: 70mph
Brakes: Vacuum
AWS: Fitted

Veh No	Dia	SC	Liv	Pool	Dep
51495	2101D			PNL	NL
51496	2102F			PHA	HA
51498	3042H			NSS	RG
51499	3170D			NSS	RG
51500	2102H			PNL	NL
51501	3042H			NSS	RG
51503	3170D			NSS	RG
51504	3042H			NSS	RG
51505	2102F			PCF	CF
51506	2102H	LR		PNC	NC
51508	2102H	LR		PNC	NC
51509	2102F			PCF	CF
51510	2101D			PNL	NL
51511	2102F			PCF	CF
51512	2102F			PNL	NL
51513	2102F			PCF	CF
51515	2102H	L		PHT	HT
51516	2102F			PHT	HT
51517	2102H	L		PNL	NL
51519	2102F	L		PNL	NL
51522	2102H	L		PHT	HT
51523	2102H	L#		PNL	NL
51524	2102F			PNL	NL
51526	2102F			PNL	NL
51529	2102F			PNL	NL
51530	2102F	L		PLA	LA
51531	2102F			PHA	HA
51532	2102F	#		PNH	NH
51533	2102F	L		PNL	NL
51538	2102F			PNL	NL

Series continued with No 51803.

Class 108 — Driving Motor

Built: British Railways Derby Carriage Works, 1959

Diagram	Type	Weight	Seats		Toilet	
DP2.26.0A	DMS(L)	28.5t	—	64	1	Refurbished
DP3.11.1B	DMC(L)	28.5t	12	52	1	Refurbished

Engines: Two Leyland 150bhp (112kW) 6-cyl horizontal
Transmission: Four speed epicyclic gearbox/ carden shaft
Dimensions: 18.49m L × 2.79m W × 3.87m H. Gangwayed within unit
Maximum speed: 70mph
Brakes: Vacuum
AWS: Fitted

Veh No	Dia	SC	Liv	Pool	Dep
51561	2260A	L		PLE	LE
51562	2260A	L		PLE	LE
51563	2260A	L		PLE	LE
51565	2260A	L		PLE	LE
51566	2260A	L		PHA	HA
51567	2260A	L		PLE	LE
51568	2260A			PBX	BX
51569	2260A			PBX	BX
51570	2260A			PLA	LA
51571	3111B			NNL	BY
51572	3111B			NNL	BY

Series continued with No 52038.

Class 115 — Driving Motor Brake

Built: British Railways, Derby Carriage Works 1960

Diagram	Type	Weight	Seats	AWS	Note
DQ2.18.0A	DMBS	38.5t	78	Fitted	—
DQ2.18.1A	DMBS	38.5t	78	Fitted	—
DQ2.18.2B	DMBS	39t	78	Fitted	Refurbished
DQ2.18.3B	DMBS	39t	78	—	Refurbished
DQ2.33.1B	DMBS	39t	78	Fitted	Refurbished and Gangwayed

Engines: Two Leyland Albion 230bhp (172kW) 6-cyl horizontal
Transmission: Four speed epicyclic gearbox/ carden shaft
Dimensions: 20.45m L × 2.82m W × 3.87m H. Built non-gangwayed, side doors to each seating bay semi-open. Gangways within unit fitted where shown (G)
Maximum speed: 70mph
Brakes: Vacuum

Veh No	*Dia*	*SC*	*Liv*	*Pool*	*Dep*
51651	331B	G		*NMY*	BY
51652	181A			*NMY*	BY
51653	182B			*NMY*	BY
51654	331B	G		*NMY*	BY
51655	182B			*NMY*	BY
51656	331B	G		*NMY*	BY
51657	331B	G		*NMY*	BY
51658	182B			*NMY*	BY
51659	182B		N	*NMY*	BY
51660	183B			*NMY*	BY
51661	181A			*NMY*	BY
51662	331B	G		*PTS*	TS
51663	182B			*NMY*	BY
~~51664~~	182B			*NMY*	BY
51665	182B			*NMY*	BY
51666	182B		N	*NMY*	BY
51667	182B		N	*NMY*	BY
~~51668~~	181A			*NMY*	BY
51669	182B			*NMY*	BY
51670	182B			*NMY*	BY
51671	181A		N	*NMY*	BY
51673	182B			*NMY*	BY
51674	180A			*NMY*	BY
51675	181A			*NMY*	BY
51676	331B	G		*NMY*	BY
51677	182B			*NMY*	BY
51678	183B	G		*NMY*	BY
51679	331B	G		*NMY*	BY
51680	182B			*NMY*	BY

Series continued with No 51849.

Class 101 — Driving Motor Brake

Built: Metropolitan-Cammelll 1959

Diagram	Type	Weight	Seats	Engine	Note
DQ2.02.2E	DMBS	32.5t	52	Leyland	Refurbished

For full details see series commencing No 51174.

Veh No	Dia	SC	Liv	Pool	Dep
51795	022E			PNL	NL
51798	022E	#		PNH	NH
51799	022E	L		PNL	NL
51800	022E			PHA	HA
51801	022E	L		PNL	NL

Class 101 — Driving Motor

Built: Metropolitan-Cammell 1959

Diagram	Type	Weight	Seats	Toilet	Note
DP2.10.2F	DMS(L)	32.5t	65	1	Mk 3 Bogies Refurbished

For full details see series commencing No 51495.

Veh No	Dia	SC	Liv	Pool	Dep
51803	2102F			PED	ED
51804	2102F			PNL	NL
~~51808~~	2102F	L		PNL	NL

Class 110 — Driving Motor Brake

Built: Birmingham RC&W Co 1961

Diagram	Type	Weight	Seats	Note
DQ2.—.—*	DMBS	32.5t	45	*Official code DQ3.01.0B. Refurbished

Engines: Two Rolls-Royce 130D of 180bhp (134kW), 6-cyl
Transmission: Four speed epicyclic gearbox/ carden shaft
Dimensions: 18.48m L × 2.82m W × 3.84m H. Gangway within unit
Maximum speed: 70mph
Brakes: Vacuum
AWS: Fitted

Veh No	Dia	SC	Liv	Pool	Dep
51809				PNL	NL
51812				PNL	NL
51813				PNL	NL
51817				PNL	NL
51823				PNL	NL
51827				PNL	NL
51828				PNL	NL

Series continued with No 52066.

Class 110 — Driving Motor

Built: Birmingham RC&W Co 1961

Diagram	Type	Weight	Seats	Toilet	Note
DP2.—.—*	DMS	32.5t	66	1	*Official code DP3.13.1B. Refurbished

Engines: Two Rolls-Royce 130D of 180bhp (134kW), 6-cyl
Transmission: Four speed epicyclic gearbox/ carden shaft
Dimensions: 18.48m L × 2.82m W × 3.84m H. Gangway within unit
Maximum speed: 70mph
Brakes: Vacuum
AWS: Fitted

Veh No	Dia	SC	Liv	Pool	Dep
~~51829~~				PNL	NL
51830				PNL	NL
51834				PNL	NL
51835				PNL	NL
51840				PNL	NL
51842				PNL	NL
51843				PNL	NL
51847				PNL	NL

Series continued with No 52077.

Class 115 — Driving Motor Brake

Built: British Railways, Derby Carriage Works 1960

Diagram	Type	Weight	Seats	AWS	Note
DQ2.18.1A	DMBS	38.5t	78	Fitted	
DQ2.18.2B	DMBS	39.0t	78	Fitted	Refurbished
DQ2.18.3B	DMBS	39.0t	78	—	Refurbished
DQ2.33.0A	DMBS	38.5t	78	—	Gangwayed
DQ2.33.1B	DMBS	39.0t	78	Fitted	Gangwayed, Refurbished

For full details see series commencing No 51651.

Veh No	Dia	SC	Liv	Pool	Dep
51849	331B	G		NMY	BY
51851	330A	G		PTS	TS
51852	331B	G		PTS	TS
51853	331B	G		PTS	TS
51854	331B	G		PTS	TS
51855	331B	G		NMY	BY
51856	331B	G		PTS	TS
51857	182B		N	NMY	BY
51858	331B	G		PTS	TS
51859	331B	G		PTS	TS
51860	331B	G		PTS	TS
51862	331B	G		PTS	TS

Veh No	Dia	SC	Liv	Pool	Dep
51863	183B			*NMY*	BY
51865	330A	G		*PTS*	TS
51866	331B	G		*NMY*	BY
51867	330A	G		*PTS*	TS
51868	331B	G		*PTS*	TS
51869	331B	G		*PTS*	TS
51870	330A	G		*PTS*	TS
51871	182B			*NMY*	BY
51872	182B			*NMY*	BY
51873	182B		N	*NMY*	BY
51874	182B			*NMY*	BY
51875	182B			*NMY*	BY
51876	331B	G		*PTS*	TS
51877	331B	G		*PTS*	TS
51878	331B	G		*NMY*	BY
51879	182B		N	*NMY*	BY
51880	331B	G		*PTS*	TS
51883	182B			*NMY*	BY
51884	331B	G		*PTS*	TS
51885	181A			*NMY*	BY
51886	181A			*NMY*	BY
51887	182B			*NMY*	BY
51888	181A			*NMY*	BY
51889	181A		N	*NMY*	BY
51890	182B			*NMY*	BY
51891	182B			*NMY*	BY
51892	331B	G		*PTS*	TS
51893	331B	G		*NMY*	BY
51894	182B			*NMY*	BY
51895	331B	G		*NMY*	BY
51896	182B			*NMY*	BY
51897	331B	G		*PTS*	TS
51898	331B	G		*PTS*	TS
51899	183B			*NMY*	BY
51900	182B		N	*NMY*	BY

Class 108 — Driving Motor Brake

Built: British Railways, Derby Carriage Works 1960

Diagram	**Type**	**Weight**	**Seats**	**Note**
DQ2.13.1A	DMBS	29.5t	52	
DQ2.13.2B	DMBS	29.5t	52	Refurbished

For full details see series commencing No 51416.

Veh No	Dia	SC	Liv	Pool	Dep
51901	2B			*PCH*	CH
51902	2B			*PCH*	CH
51903	2B			*PCH*	CH
51904	2B			*PCH*	CH
51905	2B			*PCH*	CH
51906	2B			*PCH*	CH
51907	2B			*PCH*	CH
51908	2B			*PCH*	CH
51909	2B		N	*NNL*	BY
51911	2B			*PCH*	CH
51912	2B			*NNL*	BY
51913	2B			*PCH*	CH
51914	2B		N	*NNL*	BY
51916	1A			*NNL*	BY
51917	2B			*PCH*	CH
51919	1A	L		*PLE*	LE
51920	1A			*PCH*	CH
51922	1A	L		*PLE*	LE
51924	2B	L		*PLE*	LE
51925	2B			*PHA*	HA
51926	2B			*PHA*	HA
51927	1A			*PCH*	CH
51928	2B	L		*PLE*	LE
51930	2B	L		*PLE*	LE
51931	2B	L		*PLE*	LE
51932	2B			*PLA*	LA
51933	2B			*PLA*	LA
51935	2B			*PBX*	BX
51936	2B			*PHA*	HA
51937	2B			*PTS*	TS
51938	2B			*PBX*	BX
51939	2B			*PLA*	LA

Veh No	Dia	SC	Liv	Pool	Dep	Veh No	Dia	SC	Liv	Pool	Dep
51940	2B			*PLA*	LA	51945	2B			*PBX*	BX
51941	2B			*PBX*	BX	51947	1A	L		*PBX*	BX
51942	2B		N	*NNL*	BY	51948	2B			*PBX*	BX
51943	2B			*PBX*	BX	51950	2B			*PBX*	BX

Class 107 Driving Motor Brake

Built: British Railways, Derby Carriage Works 1960

Diagram	**Type**	**Weight**	**Seats**	**Note**
DQ2.11.1C	DMBS	35t	52	Refurbished

Engines: Two Leyland 150bhp (112kW) 6-cyl horizontal
Transmission: Four speed epicyclic gearbox/ carden shaft
Dimensions: 18.49m L × 2.82m W × 3.87m H. Gangwayed within unit
Maximum speed: 70mph
Brakes: Vacuum
AWS: Fitted

Veh No	Dia	SC	Liv	Pool	Dep	Veh No	Dia	SC	Liv	Pool	Dep
51985	IC			*PHA*	HA	51997	IC		S	*PED*	ED
51986	IC		S	*PED*	ED	51998	IC		S	*PED*	ED
51987	IC		S	*PED*	ED	51999	IC		S	*PED*	ED
51988	IC			*PHA*	HA	52000	IC		S	*PHA*	HA
51989	IC		S	*PED*	ED	52001	IC		S	*PED*	ED
51990	IC		S	*PED*	ED	52004	IC			*PED*	ED
51991	IC			*PHA*	HA	52005	IC		S	*PED*	ED
51992	IC			*PHA*	HA	52006	IC		S	*PED*	ED
51993	IC		S	*PED*	ED	52007	IC		S	*PED*	ED
51994	IC			*PHA*	HA	52008	IC		S	*PED*	ED
51996	IC		S	*PED*	ED	52010	IC		S	*PED*	ED

Class 107 Driving Motor

Built: British Railways, Derby Carriage Works 1960

Diagram	**Type**	**Weight**	**Seats**	**Toilet**	**Note**
DP2.15.1C	DMS(L)	35.5t	65	1	Refurbished

Engines: Two Leyland 150bhp (112kW) 6-cyl horizontal
Transmission: Four speed epicyclic gearbox/ carden shaft
Dimensions: 18.49m L × 2.82m W × 3.87m H. Gangwayed within unit
Maximum speed: 70mph
Brakes: Vacuum
AWS: Fitted

Veh No	Dia	SC	Liv	Pool	Dep
52011	IC			PHA	HA
52012	IC		S	PED	ED
52013	IC			PHA	HA
52015	IC		S	PED	ED
52016	IC			PED	ED
52018	IC		S	PED	ED
52019	IC		S	PED	ED
52020	IC		S	PED	ED
52021	IC		S	PED	ED
52023	IC		S	PED	ED
52024	IC		S	PED	ED
52025	IC		S	PED	ED
52026	IC			PHA	HA
52028	IC			PHA	HA
52029	IC		S	PED	ED
52030	IC			PED	ED
52031	IC		S	PED	ED
52033	IC		S	PED	ED
52034	IC		S	PED	ED
52035	IC			PHA	HA
52036	IC			PHA	HA

Class 108 — Driving Motor

Built: British Railways, Derby Carriage Works 1960

Diagram	Type	Weight	Seats	Toilet	Note
DP2.27.0A	DMS(L)	28.5t	65	1	Refurbished
DP2.27.1B*	DMS(L)	28.5t	65	1	*Unofficial code

For full details see series commencing No 51561.

Veh No	Dia	SC	Liv	Pool	Dep
52038	IB	L		PLE	LE
52039	IB			PBX	BX
52041	IB	L		PLE	LE
52042	IB			PED	ED
52043	IB			PHA	HA
52044	IB	L		PLE	LE
52045	IB	L		PLE	LE
52046	OA	L		PLE	LE
52047	IB			PLA	LA
52048	IB	L		PLE	LE
52049	IB			PBX	BX
52050	IB			PBX	BX
52051	IB			PHA	HA
52053	IB			PHA	HA
52054	IB			PLA	LA
52055	IB	L		PLE	LE
52056	IB			PBX	BX
52057	IB			PLA	LA
52058	IB			PBX	BX
52059	IB			PHA	HA
52060	IB			PBX	BX
52061	OA	L		PLE	LE
52062	OA	L		PBX	BX
52063	IB			PLA	LA
52064	IB			PBX	BX
52065	OA	L		PBX	BX

Class 110 — Driving Motor Brake

Built: Birmingham RC&W Co 1961

Diagram	Type	Weight	Seats	Note
DQ2—	DMBS	32.5t	45	Refurbished. Official code DQ3.01.0B

For full details see series commencing No 51809.

Veh No	*Dia*	*SC*	*Liv*	*Pool*	*Dep*
~~52066~~				*PNL*	NL
52067				*PNL*	NL
52069				*PNL*	NL
52071				*PNL*	NL
52072				*PNL*	NL
52075				*PNL*	NL

Class 110 — Driving Motor

Built: Birmingham RC&W Co 1960

Diagram	**Type**	**Weight**	**Toilet**	**Seats**	**Note**
DP2.—	DMS	32.5t	66	1	Refurbished Official code DP3.13.1B

For full details see series commencing No 51829.

Veh No	*Dia*	*SC*	*Liv*	*Pool*	*Dep*
52077				*PNL*	NL
52080				*PNL*	NL
52081				*PNL*	NL
52082				*PNL*	NL
52084				*PNL*	NL
52085				*PNL*	NL

Class 114 — Driving Motor Brake

Built: British Railways, Derby Carriage Works 1956

Diagram	**Type**	**Weight**	**Seats**	**Note**
DQ2.17.2B	DMBS	38t	62	Refurbished

Engines: Two Leyland Albion 230bhp (172kW) 6-cyl horizontal
Transmission: Four speed epicyclic gearbox/ carden shaft
Dimensions: 20.45m L × 2.82m W × 3.86m H. Gangwayed within unit
Maximum speed: 70mph
Brakes: Vacuum
AWS: Fitted

Veh No	*Dia*	*SC*	*Liv*	*Pool*	*Dep*
53002	2B			*PTS*	TS
53005	2B			*PTS*	TS
53006	2B			*PTS*	TS
53008	2B			*PTS*	TS
53015	2B			*PTS*	TS
53018	2B			*PTS*	TS
53019	2B			*PTS*	TS
53021	2B			*PTS*	TS
53026	2B			*PTS*	TS
53030	2B			*PTS*	TS
53036	2B			*PTS*	TS
53037	2B			*PTS*	TS
53039	2B			*PTS*	TS
53044	2B			*PTS*	TS

Parcels Sector vehicles in this series.

Class 116 — Driving Motor Brake

Built: British Railways, Derby Carriage Works 1957

Diagram	Type	Weight	Seats	Note
DQ2.30.1A	DMBS	36.5t	65	Gangway
DQ2.30.2B	DMBS	36.5t	65	Gangway, Refurbished

For full details see series commencing No 51128 page xx

Veh No	Dia	SC	Liv	Pool	Dep
53050	2B	G		PTS	TS
53053	2B	G		PTS	TS
53054	2B	G		PTS	TS
53055	2B	G		PTS	TS
53056	2B	G		PTS	TS
53058	2B	G		PTS	TS
53060	2B	G		PTS	TS
53061	2B	G		PTS	TS
53071	1A	G		PTS	TS
53073	2B	G		PTS	TS
53079	2B	G		PTS	TS
53080	2B	GL#		PCF	CF
53082	2B	G		PTS	TS
53083	2B	G	N	NGB	OO
53086	2B	GL#		PCF	CF
53089	2B	GL#		PCF	CF
53090	2B	G		PTS	TS

Series continued with No 53818.

Class 116 — Driving Motor

Built: British Railways, Derby Carriage Works 1957

Diagram	Type	Weight	Seats	Note
DP2.20.2B	DMS	36.5t	89	Gangway and Refurbished

For full details see series commencing No 51141.

Veh No	Dia	SC	Liv	Pool	Dep
53092	2B	G		PTS	TS
53093	2B	G		PTS	TS
53101	2B	G		PTS	TS
53102	2B	G		PTS	TS
53106	2B	G		PTS	TS
53114	2B	G		PTS	TS
53116	2B	G		PTS	TS
53122	2B	GL#		PCF	CF
53124	2B	G		PTS	TS
53128	2B	GL#		PCF	CF
53131	2B	GL#		PCF	CF
53132	2B	G		PTS	TS

Class 101 Driving Motor

Built: Metropolitan-Cammell 1956

Diagram	Type	Weight	Engine	Seats	Toilet	Note
DP2.12.2B	DMS(L)	32.5t	AEC	57	1	Refurbished. Mk 2 Bogies
DP2.12.2C	DMS(L)	32.5t	Leyland	57	1	Refurbished. Mk 2 Bogies

Engines: Two AEC or Leyland 150bhp (112kW) 6-cyl horizontal
Transmission: Four speed epicyclic gearbox/ carden shaft
Dimensions: 18.49m L × 2.82m W × 3.85m H.
Maximum speed: 70mph
Brakes: Vacuum
AWS: Fitted

Veh No	*Dia*	*SC*	*Liv*	*Pool*	*Dep*
53139	2B	LR		*PNC*	NC
53141	2B			*PNL*	NL
53146	2C		S	*PED*	ED
53149	2C	LR		*PNC*	NC
53150	2C	LR		*PNC*	NC

Class 101 Driving Motor Brake

Built: Metropolitan-Cammell 1956

Diagram	Type	Weight	Seats 1st	Seats Std	Note	
DQ3.—.2B	DMBC	32.5t	16	33	Leyland	Refurbished. Mk 2 Bogies
DQ2.02.2E	DMBS	32.5t	—	52	Leyland	Refurbished. Mk Bogies

Engines: Two AEC or Leyland 150bhp (112kW) 6-cyl horizontal
Transmission: Four speed epicyclic gearbox/ carden shaft
Dimensions: 18.49m L × 2.82m W × 3.85m H.
Maximum speed: 70mph
Brakes: Vacuum
AWS: Fitted

Veh No	*Dia*	*SC*	*Liv*	*Pool*	*Dep*
53155	3—2B			*NWR*	OO
53157	2022E			*PLA*	LA

Series continued with No 53164.

Class 101 — Driving Motor

Built: Metropolitan-Cammell 1956

Diagram	Type	Weight	Engine	Seats	Toilet	Note
DP2.14.2B	DMS(L)	32.5t	AEC	65	1	Refurbished
DP2.14.2C	DMS(L)	32.5t	Leyland	65	1	Refurbished

Engines: Two AEC or Leyland 150bhp (112kW) 6-cyl horizontal
Transmission: Four speed epicyclic gearbox/ carden shaft
Dimensions: 18.49m L × 2.82m W × 3.85m H.
Maximum speed: 70mph
Brakes: Vacuum
AWS: Fitted

Veh No	*Dia*	*SC*	*Liv*	*Pool*	*Dep*
53158	2C		S	*PED*	ED
53159	2C			*PNL*	NL
53160	2C		S	*PED*	ED
~~53162~~	2C			*PNL*	NL
53163	2B			*PHA*	HA

Series continued with No 53168.

Class 101 — Driving Motor Brake

Built: Metropolitan-Cammell 1957

Diagram	Type	Weight	Seats	Note
DQ2.02.2E	DMBS	32.5t	52	Refurbished. Mk 2 Bogies

For full details see No 53157.

Veh No	*Dia*	*SC*	*Liv*	*Pool*	*Dep*
53164	2E			*PHA*	HA
53165	2E			*PLA*	LA

Class 101 — Driving Motor

Built: Metropolitan-Cammell 1957

Diagram	Type	Weight	Engine	Seats	Toilet	Note
DP2.14.1A	DMS(L)	32.5t	AEC	65	1	—
DP2.14.2B	DMS(L)	32.5t	AEC	65	1	Refurbished
DP2.14.2C	DMS(L)	32.5t	Leyland	65	1	Refurbished

For full details see No 53158.

Veh No	Dia	SC	Liv	Pool	Dep
53168	2C	LR		PNC	NC
53169	2C	#		PNH	NH
53170	2C	LR		PNC	NC
53171	2C			PHA	HA
53176	2C			PHA	HA
53177	2C	LR		PNC	NC
53180	2C	LR		PNC	NC
53181	2C	R		PNC	NC
53182	2C	#		PHT	HT
53185	2C			PED	ED
53186	2B	†		PHA	HA
53187	2B	†		PHA	HA
53188	2C	#		PHT	HT
53189	1A	†		PHA	HA
53193	2C	LR		PNC	NC
53194	2C			PED	ED
53195	2C	#		PHT	HT
53196	2C	#		PHT	HT
53197	2B	†		PHA	HA

Class 101 Driving Motor Brake

Built: Metropolitan-Cammell 1957

Design Code	Type	Weight	Engine	Seats	Note
DQ2.02.2B	DMBS	32.5t	AEC	52	Refurbished
DQ2.02.2E	DMBS	32.5t	Leyland	52	Refurbished

For full details see No 53157.

Veh No	Dia	SC	Liv	Pool	Dep
53198	2E			PED	ED
53200	2E			PLA	LA
53201	2B	†		PNC	NC
53202	2E			PNC	NC
53203	2E			PNC	NC
53204	2E			PNC	NC
53207	2E		N	NGB	OO
53208	2B	†		PNC	NC
53211	2E			PHA	HA
53212	2E			PLA	LA
53214	2B	†#		PNL	NL
53215	2B	†		PHA	HA
53216	2E			PHA	HA
53219	2B	†#		PNH	NH
53222	2E	#		PCH	CH
53223	2E			PLA	LA
53224	2E			PCF	CF
53228	2E			PNC	NC
53229	2B	†		PHT	HT
53231	2E			PNC	NC

Parcels Sector vehicles in this series..

Class 101 Driving Motor

Built: Metropolitan-Cammell 1957

Diagram	Type	Weight	Seats	Note
DP2.13.1C	DMS	32t	52	Refurbished. Mk 2 Bogies

Engines: Two Leyland 150bhp (112kW) 6-cyl horizontal
Transmission: Four speed epicyclic gearbox/ carden shaft
Dimensions: 18.49m L × 2.82m W × 3.85m H.

Maximum speed: 70mph
Brakes: Vacuum
AWS: Fitted

Veh No	Dia	SC	Liv	Pool	Dep
53235	1C	#		PNH	NH
53237	1C	#		PNL	NL
53238	1C	R		PNC	NC
53239	1C			PHA	HA
53240	1C	#		PNH	NH
53241	1C			PED	ED
53242	1C			PHA	HA
53243	1C			PHA	HA
53244	1C			PHA	HA
53245	1C			PHA	HA

Class 101 Driving Motor Brake

Built: Metropolitan-Cammell 1957

Diagram	Type	Weight	Seats	Note
DQ2.03.2B	DMBS	32.5t	44	Refurbished

Engines: Two Leyland 150bhp (112kW) 6-cyl horizontal
Transmission: Four speed epicyclic gearbox/ carden shaft
Dimensions: 18.49m L × 2.82m W × 3.85m H
Maximum speed: 70mph
Brakes: Vacuum
AWS: Fitted

Veh No	Dia	SC	Liv	Pool	Dep
53247	2B			PLA	LA
53248	2B			PLA	LA

Class 101 Driving Motor Brake

Built: Metropolitan-Cammell 1957

Diagram	Type	Engine	Weight	Seats	Note
DQ2.02.2B	DMBS	AEC	32.5t	52	Refurbished, AWS
DQ2.02.2E	DMBS	Leyland	32.5t	52	Refurbished, AWS
DQ2.02.3E	DMBS	Leyland	32.5t	52	Refurbished

For full details see series commencing 53157.

Veh No	Dia	SC	Liv	Pool	Dep
53250	2E			PHA	HA
53251	2B	†#		PNH	NH
53253	2E	#		PHA	HA
53256	3E			PLA	LA
53257	2E	#		PHT	HT

Parcels Sector vehicles in this series.

Class 101 Driving Motor

Built: Metropolitan-Cammell 1957

Diagram	Type	Weight	Seats 1st	Std	Toilets	Note
DP2.10.2H	DMS(L)	32.5t	—	65	1	Refurbished, Mk 2 bogies
DP3.17.0A	DMC(L)	32.5t	12	46	1	Refurbished

For full details see series commencing No 51495.

Veh No	Dia	SC	Liv	Pool	Dep	Veh No	Dia	SC	Liv	Pool	Dep
53260	2102H			PHA	HA	53266	2102H	LR		PNC	NC
53263	2102H	#		PHT	HT	53267	2102H	LR		PNC	NC
53264	2102H			PNH	NH	53268	2102H			PHA	HA
53265	3170A			NSS	RG	53269	2102H			PHA	HA

Class 101 Driving Motor Brake

Built: Metropolitan-Cammell 1957

Diagram	Type	Weight	Engine	Seats	Note
DQ2.02.2B	DMBS	32.5t	AEC	52	Refurbished Mk 2 bogies
DQ2.02.2E	DMBS	32.5t	Leyland	52	Refurbished Mk 2 bogies
DQ2.32.0B	DMBS	32.5t	Leyland	49	Refurbished Mk 2 bogies

For full details see series commencing No 53157.

Veh No	Dia	SC	Liv	Pool	Dep	Veh No	Dia	SC	Liv	Pool	Dep
53290	022B	†		PHA	HA	53309	022B	†#		PCH	CH
53291	022E			PHA	HA	53310	022E			NSS	RG
53293	022E			PNC	NC	53311	022E			NSS	RG
53294	022E			PHA	HA	53312	320B			NSS	RG
53296	022E			NGB	OO	53314	320B			NSS	RG
53303	022B	†#		PCH	CH	53315	022E	L		PLA	LA
53305	022E	LR		PNC	NC	53317	022B	†#		PCH	CH
53306	022E	†		PCH	CH	53318	022E	#		PCH	CH
53307	022E	†		PCH	CH	53319	022E	L		PCF	CF
53308	320B			NSS	RG						

Class 101 Driving Motor

Built: Metropolitan-Cammell 1958

Diagram	Type	Weight	Seats 1st	Std	Toilet	Note
DP2.10.1B	DMS(L)	32.5t	—	65	1	Mk 2 bogies
DP2.10.1D	DMS(L)	32.5t	—	65	1	Mk 3 bogies
DP2.10.2F	DMS(L)	32.5t	—	65	1	Refurbished, Mk 3 bogies
DP2.10.2H	DMS(L)	32.5t	—	65	1	Mk 2 bogies

DP3.04.2F	DMC(L)	32.5t	12	53	1	Refurbished
DP3.04.2H	DMC(L)	32.5t	12	53	1	Mk 3 bogies, Refurbished
DP3.17.0B	DMC(L)	32.5t	12	53	1	Mk 2 bogies, Refurbished

For full details see series commencing No 51495.

Veh No	*Dia*	*SC*	*Liv*	*Pool*	*Dep*
53321	2102H	LR		*PNC*	NC
53322	3042H			*NSS*	RG
53323	2102H			*PCH*	CH
53324	2102H	#		*PCH*	CH
53325	2101B			*PCH*	CH
53326	3170B			*NSS*	RG
53327	3170B			*NSS*	RG
53330	2102F	L		*PLA*	LA
53331	3170B			*NSS*	RG
53332	3170B			*NSS*	RG
53333	3042F			*NSS*	RG
53334	2101D			*PNH*	NH
53335	2102H	L		*PNL*	NL
53336	2102F			*PCH*	CH
53337	2101D	#		*PCH*	CH
53338	2102H	#		*PCH*	CH

Class 100 — Driving Motor Brake

Built: Gloucester RC&W Co 1957

Diagram	**Type**	**Weight**	**Seats**
DQ2.01.1A	DMBS	30.5t	52

Engines: Two AEC 150bhp (112kW) 6-cyl horizontal
Transmission: Four speed epicyclic gearbox/ carden shaft
Dimensions: 18.49m L × 2.82m W × 3.85m H
Maximum speed: 70mph
Brakes: Vacuum
AWS: Fitted

Veh No	*Dia*	*SC*	*Liv*	*Pool*	*Dep*
53355	1A			*PNH*	NH

Class 105 — Driving Motor Brake

Built: Cravens
Parcels Sector vehicles in this series Nos 53361-73.

Class 104 — Driving Motor Brake

Built: Birmingham RC&W Co 1957

Design Code	**Type**	**Weight**	**Seats**
DQ2.05.1A	DMBS	31.5t	52

Engines: Two Leyland 150bhp (112kW) 6-cyl horizontal
Transmission: Four speed epicyclic gearbox/ carden shaft

Dimensions: 18.49m L × 2.82m W × 3.84m H
Maximum speed: 70mph
Brakes: Vacuum
AWS: Fitted

Veh No	*Dia*	*SC*	*Liv*	*Pool*	*Dep*
53421	1A			*PNH*	NH

Series continued with No 53429 below.

Class 104 Driving Motor

Built: Gloucester RC&W Co 1957

Design Code	**Type**	**Weight**	**Seats**	**Toilet**
DP2.09.1A	DMS(L)	31.5t	66	1

Engines: Two Leyland 150bhp (112kW) 6-cyl horizontal
Transmission: Four speed epicyclic gearbox/ carden shaft
Dimensions: 18.49m L × 2.82m W × 3.84m H
Maximum speed: 70mph
Brakes: Vacuum
AWS: Fitted
Window bars fitted: 53425

Veh No	*Dia*	*SC*	*Liv*	*Pool*	*Dep*
53425	1A			*PNH*	NH
53427	IA			*PCP*	CP(s)

Series continued with No 53487.

Class 104 Driving Motor Brake

Built: Birmingham RC&W Co 1957

Design Code	**Type**	**Weight**	**Seats**	**AWS**
DQ2.05.0A	DMBS	31.5t	52	Not fitted
DQ2.05.1A	DMBS	31.5t	52	Fitted

For full details see No 53421 above.
Window bars fitted: 53431/42/43/54/65/66/68/70/72/76

Veh No	*Dia*	*SC*	*Liv*	*Pool*	*Dep*
53429	1A			*NGB*	OO
53431	1A			*PNH*	NH
53437	1A			*NGB*	OO
53439	1A			*PNH*	NH
53442	1A			*PNH*	NH
53443	1A			*PNH*	NH
53444	1A			*PNH*	NH
53447	1A			*PNH*	NH
53451	1A			*PNH*	NH
53454	0A			*PNH*	NH
53455	1A		N	*NGB*	OO
53460	1A			*PCP*	CP(s)
53464	1A			*PNH*	NH
53465	1A			*PNH*	NH
53466	1A			*PNH*	NH
53468	1A			*PNH*	NH
53470	1A			*NGB*	OO
53472	1A			*PED*	ED

Veh No	Dia	SC	Liv	Pool	Dep
53474	1A			*PCP*	CP(s)
53476	1A			*PNH*	NH
53477	1A			*NGB*	00
53478	1A			*DXXZ*	ED
53479	1A			*NGB*	00

Series continued with No 53532.

Class 104 — Driving Motor

Built: Birmingham RC&W Co 1957

Design Code	Type	Weight	Seats	Toilet	AWS
DP2.09.0A	DMS(L)	31.5t	66	1	Not fitted
DP2.09.1A	DMS(L)	31.5t	66	1	Fitted

Window bars fitted: 53493/94/96/99, 53500/11/12/16/28/31

For full details see series commencing No 53425.

Veh No	Dia	SC	Liv	Pool	Dep
53487	1A			*PNH*	NH
53492	1A			*PNH*	NH
53493	1A			*PNH*	NH
53494	1A			*PNH*	NH
53496	1A			*PCP*	CP(s)
53499	0A			*PNH*	NH
53500	1A			*PNH*	NH
53501	1A			*PCP*	CP(s)
53504	1A			*PNH*	NH
53507	1A			*PNH*	NH
53511	1A			*PNH*	NH
53512	1A			*PNH*	NH
53516	1A			*PNH*	NH
53517	1A			*PNH*	NH
53518	1A			*PNH*	NH
53520	1A			*PNH*	NH
53522	1A			*PNH*	NH
53528	0A			*PNH*	NH
53529	1A			*PNH*	NH
53530	1A			*DXXZ*	ED
53531	1A			*PNH*	NH

Class 104 — Driving Motor Brake

Built: Birmingham RC&W Co 1958

Design Code	Type	Weight	Seats	AWS
DQ2.05.0A	DMBS	31.5t	52	Not fitted
DQ2.05.1A	DMBS	31.5t	52	Fitted

For full details see No 53421.

Veh No	Dia	SC	Liv	Pool	Dep
53532	1A			*PNH*	NH
53534	1A			*PNH*	NH
53536	1A			*PNH*	NH
53539	1A			*NGB*	00
53540	1A			*NGB*	00
53541	0A			*PNH*	NH

Class 104 — Driving Motor

Built: Birmingham RC&W Co 1958

Diagram	Type	Weight	Seats
DP2.17.1A	DMS(L)	31.5t	63

For full details see series commencing No 53425

Veh No	*Dia*	*SC*	*Liv*	*Pool*	*Dep*
53556	1A			*PNH*	NH

Class 108 — Driving Motor Brake

Built: British Railways Derby Carriage Works 1958

Diagram	Type	Weight	Seats	Note
DQ2.12.2B	DMBS	29.5t	52	Refurbished

Engines: Two Leyland 150bhp (112kW) 6-cyl horizontal
Transmission: Four speed epicyclic gearbox/ carden shaft
Dimensions: 18.49m L × 2.79m W × 3.87m H
Maximum speed: 70mph
Brakes: Vacuum
AWS: Fitted

Veh No	*Dia*	*SC*	*Liv*	*Pool*	*Dep*
53599	2B			*NNL*	BY
53601	2B	#		*PNL*	NL
53602	2B			*PBR*	BR
53606	2B	#		*PNH*	NH
53607	2B	#		*PNL*	NL
53608	2B			*PBR*	BR
53612	2B			*PBR*	BR
53614	2B			*PBR*	BR
53616	2B			*PBR*	BR
53617	2B			*PCF*	CF
53618	2B			*PBR*	BR
53619	2B			*PBR*	BR
53620	2B			*PBR*	BR
53621	2B			*PBR*	BR
53622	2B			*PBR*	BR
53624	2B			*PCF*	CF
53625	2B	L		*PLE*	LE
53626	2B			*PBX*	BX
53627	2B			*PCF*	CF
53628	2B		N	*NNL*	BY
53629	2B			*PCF*	CF

Series continued with No 53924.

Class 108 — Driving Motor

Built: British Railways, Derby Carriage Works 1958

Diagram	Type	Weight	Seats	Toilet	Note
DQ2.19.0A	DMS(L)	28.5t	62	1	
DQ2.19.1B	DMS(L)	28.5t	62	1	Refurbished

Engines: Two Leyland 150bhp (112kW) 6-cyl horizontal
Transmission: Four speed epicyclic gearbox/ carden shaft
Dimensions: 18.49m L × 2.82m W × 3.85m H.
Maximum speed: 70mph
Brakes: Vacuum
AWS: Fitted

Veh No	*Dia*	*SC*	*Liv*	*Pool*	*Dep*
53630	1B			*PHA*	HA
53631	1B			*PHA*	HA
53632	1B			*PHA*	HA
53633	1B	L		*PLE*	LE
53634	0A			*PBX*	BX
53635	1B			*PCF*	CF
53636	1B			*PBX*	BX
53637	1B			*PLA*	LA
53638	1B			*PLA*	LA
53639	1B			*PLA*	LA
53641	1B			*PHA*	HA
53642	1B			*PHA*	HA
53643	1B			*PHA*	HA
53644	1B			*PHA*	HA
53645	1B			*PHA*	HA
53646	1B			*PLA*	LA

Class 120 Driving Motor

Built: British Railways, Swindon Works 1957

Diagram	**Type**	**Weight**	**Seats**	**Note**	
DP2.04.0A	DMS(L)	37t	68	2	—
DP2.04.1C	DMS(L)	37t	68	2	Refurbished

Engines: Two AEC 150bhp (112kW) 6-cyl horizontal
Transmission: Four speed epicyclic gearbox/ carden shaft
Dimensions: 20.45m L × 2.82m W × 3.84m H.
Maximum speed: 70mph
Brakes: Vacuum
AWS: Fitted

Veh No	*Dia*	*SC*	*Liv*	*Pool*	*Dep*
53658	0A	†		*PHA*	HA
53682	IC	†		*PHA*	HA
53686	IC	†		*PHA*	HA

Class 120 Driving Motor Brake

Built: British Railways, Swindon Works 1957

Diagram	**Type**	**Weight**	**Seats**	**Note**	
DQ2.--.0A	DMBS	36.5t	34	—	DQ3.03.0A
DQ2.--.1B	DMBS	36.5t	34	Refurbished	DQ3.03.1B

Engines: Two AEC 150bhp (112kW) 6-cyl horizontal

Transmission: Four speed epicyclic gearbox/ carden shaft

Dimensions: 20.45m L × 2.82m W × 3.84m H.
Maximum speed: 70mph

Brakes: Vacuum
AWS: Fitted

Veh No	*Dia*	*SC*	*Liv*	*Pool*	*Dep*
53699	1B			*PHA*	HA
53700	0A			*PHA*	HA
53732	1B			*PHA*	HA
53733	1B			*PHA*	HA

Class 101 — Driving Motor

Built: Metropolitan-Cammell 1957

Diagram	**Type**	**Weight**	**Engine**	**Seats 1st**	**Seats Std**	**Toilet**	**Note**
DP2.10.2E	DMS	32.5t	AEC	—	65	1	Refurbished
DP3.04.2H	DMC	32.5t	Leyland	12	53	1	Refurbished

For full details see series commencing No 51495.

Veh No	*Dia*	*SC*	*Liv*	*Pool*	*Dep*
53746	2102E	†		*PHA*	HA
53751	3042H			*NSS*	RG

Class 105 — Driving Motor

Built: Cravens 1957

Diagram	**Type**	**Weight**	**Seats**	**Toilet**
DQ2.11.1B	DMS	30t	63	1

Engines: Two Leyland 150bhp (112kW) 6-cyl horizontal
Transmission: Four speed epicyclic gearbox/ carden shaft

Dimensions: 18.49m L × 2.82m W × 3.77m H.
Maximum speed: 70mph
Brakes: Vacuum
AWS: Not fitted

Veh No	*Dia*	*SC*	*Liv*	*Pool*	*Dep*
53812	1B			*PNH*	NH

Class 116 — Driving Motor Brake

Built: British Railways, Derby Carriage Works 1957

Diagram	**Type**	**Weight**	**Seats**	**Note**
DQ2.19.1A	DMBS	36.5t	65	
DQ2.30.1A	DMBS	36.5t	65	Gangwayed
DQ2.30.2B	DMBS	36.5t	65	Gangwayed and Refurbished

For full details see series commencing No 53050.

Veh No	*Dia*	*SC*	*Liv*	*Pool*	*Dep*
53818	302B	G		*PTS*	TS
53820	302B	G	N	*NGB*	OO
53822	302B	G		*PTS*	TS
53826	302B	G		*PTS*	TS
53827	302B	G		*PTS*	TS
53837	302B	G		*PTS*	TS
53838	302B	G		*PTS*	TS
53843	302B	G#		*PCF*	CF
53844	302B	G		*PTS*	TS
53848	302B	G#		*PCF*	CF
53849	302B	G		*PTS*	TS
53850	302B	G		*PTS*	TS
53853	302B	G		*PTS*	TS
53854	302B	G		*PTS*	TS
53855	302B	G#		*PCF*	CF
53858	302B	G		*PCF*	CF
53863	301A	G		*PTS*	TS
53865	302B	G		*PTS*	TS
53866	302B	G#		*PNH*	NH
53869	302B	G#		*PNH*	NH

Class 116 — Driving Motor

Built: British Railways, Derby Carriage Works 1957

Diagram	**Type**	**Weight**	**Seats**	**Note**
DP2.01.1A	DMS	36.5t	95	
DP2.20.1A	DMS	36.5t	89	Gangwayed
DP2.20.2B	DMS	36.5t	89	Ganwayed and Refurbished

For full details see series commencing No 53092.

Veh No	*Dia*	*SC*	*Liv*	*Pool*	*Dep*
53873	202B	G		*PTS*	TS
53878	202B	G		*PTS*	TS
53880	202B	G		*PTS*	TS
53881	202B	G		*PTS*	TS
53886	202B	G		*PTS*	TS
53887	202B	G#		*PNH*	NH
53890	202B	G#		*PTS*	TS
53891	202B	G		*PTS*	TS
53893	202B	G		*PTS*	TS
53894	202B	G		*PTS*	TS
53897	202B	G		*PTS*	TS
53902	202B	G		*PTS*	TS
53907	202B	G		*PTS*	TS
53908	202B	G#		*PCF*	CF
53911	202B	G#		*PCF*	CF
53916	201A	G		*PTS*	TS
53919	202B	G		*PTS*	TS
53921	202B	G		*PTS*	TS
53922	202B	G#		*PNH*	NH

Class 108 — Driving Motor Brake

Built: British Railways, Derby Carriage Works 1959

Diagram	**Type**	**Weight**	**Seats**	**Note**
DQ2.12.1A	DMBS	29.5t	52	
DQ2.12.2B	DMBS	29.5t	52	Refurbished

For full details see series commencing No 53599.
Special livery: Green: 53964

Veh No	Dia	SC	Liv	Pool	Dep
53924	2B			PCH	CH
53925	1A			PBX	BX
53926	2B	L		PLE	LE
53927	2B			PCH	CH
53928	2B	L		PLE	LE
53929	2B			PCH	CH
53930	1A			PBX	BX
53931	1A			PCH	CH
53932	2B			PBX	BX
53933	1A	L		PHA	HA
53934	2B			PNH	NH
53935	2B	L		PLE	LE
53938	2B			PCH	CH
53939	2B	L		PLE	LE
53940	2B			PCH	CH
53941	2B			PBR	BR
53942	2B	L		PLE	LE
53943	2B			PNH	NH
53944	2B			PNH	NH
53945	2B	L		PLE	LE
53947	2B	L		PLE	LE
53948	2B			PNH	NH
53949	2B			PNH	NH
53950	2B			PHT	HT
53951	1A			PHT	HT
53952	1A			PHT	HT
53953	1A			PHT	HT
53954	1A			PHT	HT
53955	1A			PHT	HT
53956	1A			PHT	HT
53957	1A			PHT	HT
53958	1A			PHT	HT
53959	1A			PHT	HT
53960	1A			PHT	HT
53962	1A			PHT	HT
53963	1A			PHT	HT
53964	1A		★	PCH	CH
53965	1A			PCH	CH
53966	1A			PCH	CH
53968	1A			PCH	CH
53969	2B			PCH	CH
53970	2B			PNH	NH
53971	2B			PNH	NH
53973	2B			PHT	HT
53974	2B			PNH	NH
~~53975~~	2B			PNH	NH
53976	2B			PNH	NH
53977	2B			PNH	NH
53978	2B			PNH	NH
53980	1A			PNH	NH
53981	2B			PNH	NH
53982	2B			PNH	NH
53983	2B			PNH	NH
~~53986~~	2B			PCH	CH
53987	1A			PCH	CH

Class 114 — Driving Trailer

Built: British Railways, Derby Carriage Works 1956

Diagram	Type	Weight	Seats	Toilet	Note
DS2.--.0A	DTS	30t	74	1	Refurbished, Official Diagram DS3.13.3B

Dimensions: 20.45m L × 2.35m W × 3.86m H. Gangwayed within unit
Maximum speed: 70mph
Brakes: Vacuum
AWS: Fitted

Veh No	Dia	SC	Liv	Pool	Dep
54006	0A			PTS	TS
54008	0A			PTS	TS
54009	0A			PTS	TS
54010	0A			PTS	TS
54011	0A			PTS	TS
54012	0A			PTS	TS
54013	0A			PTS	TS
54015	0A			PTS	TS
54019	0A			PTS	TS
54024	0A			PTS	TS
54027	0A			PTS	TS
54039	0A			PTS	TS
54043	0A			PTS	TS
54047	0A		#	PTS	TS

Parcels Sector vehicles in this series.

Class 101 — Driving Trailer

Built: Metropolitan-Cammell 1957

Diagram	Type	Weight	Seats 1st	Seats Std	Toilet	Note
DS2.06.2B	DTS	25.5t	—	65	1	Refurbished
DS3.02.2B	DTC	25.5t	12	53	1	Refurbished

Dimensions: 18.49m L × 2.35m W × 3.85m H. Gangwayed within unit
Maximum speed: 70mph
Brakes: Vacuum
AWS: Fitted

Veh No	Dia	SC	Liv	Pool	Dep
54050	2062B			PNC	NC
54054	2062B			PCP	CPs
54055	2062B			PNC	NC
54056	2062B			PNH	NH
54060	2062B			PNC	NC
54061	2062B			PNH	NH
54062	2062B			PNC	NC
54065	2062B			PNC	NC
54068	3022B		N	NNE	CA
54070	3022B			NWR	OO
54071	2062B			PCP	CP
54073	2062B			PNC	NC
54075	2062B			PNH	NH
54080	2062B			PNC	NC
54081	2062B			PNH	NH
54085	2062B			PNH	NH

Series continued with No 54332.

Class 111 — Driving Trailer

Built: Metropolitan-Cammell 1957

Diagram	Type	Weight	Seats	Toilet	Note
DS2.--.0A	DTS	25.5t	65	1	Refurbished. Official code DS3.12.1B

Dimensions: 18.49m L × 2.35m W × 3.85m H. Gangwayed within unit
Maximum speed: 70mph
Brakes: Vacuum
AWS: Fitted

Veh No	Dia	SC	Liv	Pool	Dep
54091	0A			PCH	CH

Class 108 Driving Trailer

Built: British Railways, Derby Carriage Works 1958

Diagram	Type	Weight	Seats 1st	Seats Std	Toilet	Note
DS2.07.2B	DTS	21.5t	—	65	1	Refurbished
DS3.10.2B	DTC	21.5t	12	53	1	Refurbished

Dimensions: 18.49m L × 2.79m W × 3.87m H. Gangwayed within unit
Maximum speed: 70mph
Brakes: Vacuum
AWS: Fitted

Veh No	*Dia*	*SC*	*Liv*	*Pool*	*Dep*
54191	2072B			*PBR*	BR
54194	3102B			*NNL*	BY
54196	2072B			*PNH*	NH
54197	2072B			*PBR*	BR
54201	2072B			*PBR*	BR
54202	2072B			*PBR*	BR
54203	2072B			*PBR*	BR
54204	2072B			*PBR*	BR
54205	2072B			*PBR*	BR
54207	2072B			*PBR*	BR
54208	2072B			*PBR*	BR
54209	2072B			*PBR*	BR
54210	2027B			*PCF*	CF
54212	2072B			*PCH*	CH
54213	3102B		N	*NMY*	BY
54214	2072B			*PCH*	CH

Class 101 Driving Trailer

Built: Metropolitan-Cammell 1957

Diagram	Type	Weight	Seats	Toilet	AWS	Note
DS2.10.1B	DTS	25.5t	57	1	Not fitted	Refurbished
DS2.10.1C	DTS	25.5t	57	1	Fitted	

Dimensions: 18.49m L × 2.35m W × 3.85m H.
Maximum speed: 70mph
Brakes: Vacuum

Veh No	*Dia*	*SC*	*Liv*	*Pool*	*Dep*
54218	1C			*PNC*	NC
54219	1B			*PCP*	CPs
54220	1C			*PNH*	NH

Class 108 Driving Trailer

Built: British Railways, Derby Carriage Works 1959

Diagram	Type	Weight	Seats 1st	Seats Std	Toilet	Note
DS2.07.1A	DTS	21.5t	—	65	1	
DS2.07.2B	DTS	21.5t	—	65	1	Refurbished
DS2.—.1A*	DTS	22.5t	—	65	1	Official code DS3.11.1A
DS2.—.2B*	DTS	22.5t	—	65	1	Refurbished. Official code DS3.11.2B
DS3.10.1A	DTC	21.5t	12	53	1	
DS3.10.2B	DTC	21.5t	12	53	1	Refurbished
DS3.11.1A*	DTC	22.5t	12	53	1	
DS3.11.2B*	DTC	22.5t	12	53	1	Refurbished

Dimensions: 18.49m L × 2.79m or 2.82m* W × 3.87m H. Gangwayed within unit
Maximum speed: 70mph
Brakes: Vacuum
AWS: Fitted
Special livery: Green 54247

Veh No	Dia	SC	Liv	Pool	Dep
54221	2072B			*PCH*	CH
54222	3102B			*NMY*	BY
54223	3102B			*NMY*	BY
54224	3102B			*NMY*	BY
54225	2072B			*PNH*	NH
54227	2072B			*PHT*	HT
54228	3102B			*NMY*	BY
54230	2072B			*PBR*	BR
54231	2072B			*PCH*	CH
54232	2072B			*PCH*	CH
54235	2071A			*PHT*	HT
54236	2071A			*PHT*	HT
54238	2071A			*PHT*	HT
54239	2071A			*PHT*	HT
54240	2071A			*PHT*	HT
54241	2071A			*PHT*	HT
54242	2071A			*PHT*	HT
54243	2071A			*PHT*	HT
54244	2071A			*PHT*	HT
54245	2071A			*PHT*	HT
54246	2072B			*PNH*	NH
54247	2071A		★	*PCH*	CH
54248	2071A			*PCH*	CH
54249	2071A			*PCH*	CH
54251	2071A			*PCH*	CH
54252	2072B			*PCH*	CH
54253	2072B			*PNH*	NH
54256	2071A			*PNH*	NH
54257	3102B			*NMY*	BY
54258	2072B			*PNH*	NH
54259	3102B			*NMY*	BY
54260	2072B			*PCH*	CH
54261	2072B			*PNH*	NH
54262	2072B			*PHT*	HT
54263	2072B			*PHT*	HT
54264	2072B			*PNH*	NH
54265	2071A			*PHT*	HT
54266	2072B			*PNH*	NH
54267	2072B			*PCF*	CF
54268	2072B			*PNH*	NH
54269	2072B			*PCH*	CH
54270	2071A			*PCH*	CH
54271	3112B			*NNL*	BY
54272	2—1A			*PCH*	CH
54273	2—2B			*PCH*	CH
54274	3112B			*NMY*	BY
54275	2—1A			*PCH*	CH
54276	2—1A			*PCH*	CH
54277	2—2B			*PCH*	CH
54278	2—2B			*PCH*	CH
54279	3112B			*NNL*	BY

Series continued with No 54484.

Class 121 — Driving Trailer

Built: Pressed Steel Co 1960

Diagram	Type	Weight	Seats	Note
DS2.01.1B	DTS	30t	91	Refurbished, Non-Gangwayed
DS2.—.1A	DTS	30t	89	Refurbished, Gangwayed within unit

Dimensions: 20.45m L × 2.82m W × 3.86m H.
Maximum speed: 70mph
Brakes: Vacuum
AWS: Fitted

Veh No	Dia	SC	Liv	Pool	Dep	Veh No	Dia	SC	Liv	Pool	Dep
54280	2011B			*NWR*	OO	54287	2—1A		N	*NWR*	OO
54283	2011B		N	*NWR*	OO	54289	2—1A		N	*NWR*	OO
54284	2011B			*PLA*	LA						

Class 101 Driving Trailer

Built: Metropolitan-Cammell 1958

Diagram	Type	Weight	Seats 1st	Seats Std	Toilet	Note
DS2.06.1A	DTS	25.5t	—	65	1	
DS2.06.2B	DTS	25.5t	—	65	1	Refurbished
DS2.02.2B	DTC	25.5t	12	53	1	Refurbished

For details see series commencing No 54050.
AWS: Fitted

Veh No	Dia	SC	Liv	Pool	Dep	Veh No	Dia	SC	Liv	Pool	Dep
54332	2062B			*PNC*	NC	54370	2062B			*PHT*	HT
54335	2062B			*PNC*	NC	54371	3022B		N	*NWR*	OO
54340	2062B			*PNC*	NC	54372	3022B			*NWR*	OO
54342	2062B			*PNC*	NC	54375	2062B			*PNH*	NH
54343	2062B			*PNC*	NC	54379	2062B			*PNC*	NC
54345	2062B			*PHT*	HTs	54380	2062B			*PNC*	NC
54346	2062B			*PNC*	NC	54381	2062B			*PCP*	CPs
54347	2062B			*PNC*	NC	54382	3022B		N	*NNE*	CA
54348	2062B			*PNC*	NC	54385	3022B		N	*NWR*	OO
54350	2062B			*PCP*	CPs	54387	2062B			*PNC*	NC
54351	2062B			*PNC*	NC	54388	2062B			*PNC*	NC
54352	2062B			*PNC*	NC	54391	2062B			*PHT*	HTs
54354	2062B			*PNC*	NC	54393	2062B			*PNC*	NC
54355	2061A			*PNC*	NC	54396	3022B			*NWR*	OO
54358	3022B			*NNL*	BY	54398	2062B			*PCP*	CPs
54362	2062B			*PNH*	NH	54399	2062B			*PNC*	NC
54363	2062B			*PNC*	NC	54401	2062B			*PCP*	CPs
54365	2062B			*PNL*	NL	54402	3022B		N	*NNE*	CA
54367	2062B			*PCP*	CPs	54405	3022B		N	*NNE*	CA
54368	2062B			*PNC*	NC	54408	2062B			*PNH*	NH
54369	2062B			*PNC*	NC						

Class 108 Driving Trailer

Built: British Railways, Derby Carriage Works 1960

Diagram	Type	Weight	Seats 1st	Seats Std	Toilet	Note
DS2.--.1A*	DTS	22.5t	—	65	1	
DS2.--.2B*	DTS	22.5t	—	65	1	Refurbished, Official Code DS3.11.2B
DS3.11.1A*	DTC	22.5t	12	53	1	
DS3.11.2B*	DTC	22.5t	12	53	1	Refurbished

For full details see series commencing No 54221.

Veh No	*Dia*	*SC*	*Liv*	*Pool*	*Dep*
54484	2—2B			*PCH*	CH
54485	2—2B			*PCH*	CH
54486	2—2B			*PCH*	CH
54487	2—2B			*PCH*	CH
54488	2—2B			*PCH*	CH
54489	2—2B			*PCH*	CH
54490	2—2B			*PCH*	CH
54491	3112B			*NMY*	BY
54492	2—2B			*PBR*	BR
54493	3111A		N	*NNL*	BY
54494	2—2B			*PCH*	CH
54495	3112B			*NMY*	BY
54496	2—2B			*PCH*	CH
54497	2—2B			*PCH*	CH
54498	2—2B			*PCH*	CH
54499	3112B			*NMY*	BY
54500	3112B			*NMY*	BY
54501	2—2B			*PCH*	CH
54503	2—2B			*PNH*	NH
54504	2—1A			*PNH*	NH

Class 122 Driving Motor Brake

Built: Gloucester RC&W Co 1958

Diagram	Type	Weight	Seats	Note
DQ2.22.0A	DMBS	36.5t	65	AWS not fitted
DQ2.22.1B	DMBS	36.5t	65	AWS fitted

Engines: Two AEC 150bhp (112kW) 6-cyl horizontal

Transmission: Four speed epicyclic gearbox/ carden shaft

Dimensions: 20.45m L × 2.82m W × 3.86m H. Non-gangwayed, side doors to each seating bay, driving cab each end

Maximum speed: 70mph

Brakes: Vacuum

Veh No	*Dia*	*SC*	*Liv*	*Pool*	*Dep*
55000	1B			*PLA*	LA
55003	1B			*PLA*	LA
55004	0A	#		*NNL*	BY
55005	1B			*PLA*	LA
55006	1B			*PLA*	LA
55009	1B			*PLA*	LA
55011	0A	#		*NNL*	BY
55012	1B			*PLA*	LA

Class 121 — Driving Motor Brake

Built: Pressed Steel Co 1960

Diagram	Type	Weight	Seats	Note
DQ2.21.1C	DMBS	38t	65	Refurbished

Engines: Leyland 150bhp (112kW) 6-cyl horizontal
Transmission: Four speed epicyclic gearbox/ carden shaft
Dimensions: 20.45m L × 2.82m W × 3.86m H. Non-gangwayed, side doors to each seating bay, driving cab each end
Maximum speed: ??mph
Brakes: Vacuum
AWS: Fitted
Special livery: WMPTE (Midland): 55033

Veh No	*Dia*	*SC*	*Liv*	*Pool*	*Dep*
55020	IC		N	*NWR*	00
55021	IC		N	*NWR*	00
55022	IC		N	*NWR*	00
55023	IC			*NWR*	00
55024	IC			*NWR*	00
55025	IC			*NWR*	00
55026	IC			*PLA*	LA
55027	IC			*NWR*	00
55028	IC		N	*NWR*	00
55029	IC		N	*NWR*	00
55030	IC			*NWR*	00
55031	IC		N	*NWR*	00
55032	IC			*PTS*	TS
55033	IC		★	*PTS*	TS
55034	IC			*PTS*	TS

Railbus and Sprinter vehicles commence on page 56.
Parcels Sector Vehicles in the 559xx series, see pages 72/73.

Class 116 — Trailer

Built: British Railways Derby Carriage Works 1957

Diagram	Type	Weight	Seats	Note
DT2.09.1B	TS	29.5t	98	Refurbished

Dimensions: 19.58m L × 2.82m W × 3.86m H. Gangwayed throughout
Maximum speed: 70mph
Brakes: Vacuum

Veh No	*Dia*	*SC*	*Liv*	*Pool*	*Dep*
59032	1B			*PTS*	TS
59040	1B			*PHT*	HTs

Class 101 Trailer

Built: Metropolitan-Cammell 1956

Diagram	Type	Weight	Seats	Toilet	Note
DT2.01.1B	TS	25.5t	61	1	Refurbished

Dimensions: 18.49m L × 2.82m W × 3.85m H. Gangwayed throughout

Maximum speed: 70mph

Brakes: Vacuum

Veh No	*Dia*	*SC*	*Liv*	*Pool*	*Dep*
59042	1B			*PHA*	HA

Series continued with No 59061.

Class 101 Trailer Brake

Built: Metropolitan-Cammell 1956

Diagram	Type	Weight	Seats	Toilet	Note
DU2.02.1B	TBS	25.5t	45	1	Refurbished

Dimensions: 18.49m L × 2.82m W × 3.85m H. Gangwayed throughout

Maximum speed: 70mph

Brakes: Vacuum

Veh No	*Dia*	*SC*	*Liv*	*Pool*	*Dep*
59049	1B		S	*PED*	ED
59050	1B			*PLE*	LE
59055	1B			*PNC*	NC

Series continued with No 59073.

Class 101 Trailer

Built: Metropolitan-Cammell 1957

Diagram	Type	Weight	Seats	Toilet	Note
DT2.02.1B	TS	25.5t	71	1	Refurbished

For full details see No 59042.

Veh No	*Dia*	*SC*	*Liv*	*Pool*	*Dep*
59061	1B			*PHA*	HA
59065	1B			*PHA*	HA
59072	1B			*PHA*	HA

Series continued with No 59086.

Class 101 — Trailer Brake

Built: Metropolitan-Cammell 1956

Diagram	Type	Weight	Seats	Toilet	Note
DU2.03.1B	TBS	25.5t	53	1	Refurbished

For full details see series commencing No 59049.

Veh No	Dia	SC	Liv	Pool	Dep
59073	1B			*PHA*	HA
59074	1B		S	*PED*	ED
59077	1B			*PNC*	NC
59078	1B			*PNL*	NL
59079	1B			*PNC*	NC
59080	1B			*PHA*	HA
59084	1B			*PNC*	NC
59085	1B			*PNC*	NC

Series continued with No 59092.

Class 101 — Trailer

Built: Metropolitan-Cammell 1957

Diagram	Type	Weight	Seats	Toilet	Note
DT2.01.1B	TS	25.5t	61	1	Refurbished
DT2.28.0A	TS	25.5t	58	1	Refurbished

For full details see No 59042.

Veh No	Dia	SC	Liv	Pool	Dep
59086	011B			*PHA*	HA
59090	011B		S	*PED*	ED
59091	280A			*NSS*	RG

Series continued with No 59101.

Class 101 — Trailer Brake

Built: Metropolitan-Cammell 1957

Diagram	Type	Weight	Seats	Toilet	Note
DU2.02.1B	TBS	25.5t	45	1	Refurbished

For full details see series commencing No 59049.

Veh No	Dia	SC	Liv	Pool	Dep
59092	1B			*PNC*	NC
59093	1B			*PNL*	NL
59095	1B			*PNC*	NC
59096	1B			*PNL*	NL

Series continued with No 59113.

Class 101 Trailer

Built: Metropolitan-Cammell 1957

Diagram	Type	Weight	Seats	Toilet	Note
DT2.02.1B	TS	25.5t	71	1	Refurbished
DT2.28.0A	TS	25.5t	58	1	Refurbished

For full details see No 59042.

Veh No	*Dia*	*SC*	*Liv*	*Pool*	*Dep*
59101	280A			*NSS*	RG
59104	021B			*PHA*	HA
59105	021B			*NSB*	RG
59107	021B			*PHA*	HA

Series continued with No 59302.

Class 101 Trailer Brake

Built: Metropolitan-Cammell 1957

Diagram	Type	Weight	Seats	Toilet	Note
DU2.03.1B	TBS	25.5t	53	1	Refurbished

For full details see series commencing No 59049.

Veh No	*Dia*	*SC*	*Liv*	*Pool*	*Dep*
59113	1B	#		*PHA*	HA

Class 101 Trailer

Built: Metropolitan-Cammell 1958

Diagram	Type	Weight	Seats	Toilet	Note
DT2.20.1D	TS	25.5t	65	1	Refurbished, Mk 4 bogies
DT2.28.0A	TS	25.5t	58	1	Refurbished, Mk 1 bogies
DT2.28.0B	TS	25.5t	58	1	Refurbished, Mk 4 bogies

For full details see series commencing No 59034.

Veh No	*Dia*	*SC*	*Liv*	*Pool*	*Dep*
59115	280A			*NSS*	RG
59116	201D			*PHA*	HA
59117	201D			*NSS*	RG
59118	201D			*PLA*	LA
59124	201D			*PHA*	HA
59125	280B			*NSS*	RG
59128	201D			*NSS*	RG
59130	201D			*PLA*	LA

Series continued with No 59525.

Class 104 — Trailer

Built: Birmingham RC&W Co 1957

Diagram	Type	Weight	Seats	Toilet
DT2.03.1A	DTS	24.5t	69	1
DT2.18.0A	DTS	24.5t	66	1

Dimensions: 18.49m L × 2.82m W × 3.81m H. Gangwayed throughout

Maximum speed: 70mph

Brakes: Vacuum

Veh No	*Dia*	*SC*	*Liv*	*Pool*	*Dep*
59137	180A			*PBX*	BX
59144	180A			*PBX*	BX
59148	180A			*PBX*	BX
59149	180A			*PBX*	BX
59152	180A			*PBX*	BX
59153	180A			*PHA*	HA
59155	180A			*PBX*	BX
59163	180A			*NNL*	BY
59168	180A			*PNL*	NL
59183	180A			*PBX*	BX
59187	180A			*PBX*	BX
59195	031A			*PCP*	CPs
59206	031A			*NNL*	BY
59207	031A			*PBX*	BX

Class 104 — Trailer Brake

Built: Birmingham RC&W Co 1958

Diagram	Type	Weight	Seats	Toilet
DU2.04.0A	TBS	25.5t	51	1

Dimensions: 18.49m L × 2.82m W × 3.81m H. Gangwayed throughout

Maximum speed: 70mph

Brakes: Vacuum

Veh No	*Dia*	*SC*	*Liv*	*Pool*	*Dep*
59228	0A			*PNH*	NH

Class 108 — Trailer Brake

Built: British Railways, Derby Carriage Works 1958

Diagram	Type	Weight	Seats	Toilet
DU2.01.1B	TBS	23.5T	50	1

Dimensions: 18.49m L × 2.79m W × 3.87m H. Gangwayed throughout

Maximum speed: 70mph

Brakes: Vacuum

Veh No	*Dia*	*SC*	*Liv*	*Pool*	*Dep*
59245	1B			*PHA*	HA
59246	1B			*PNL*	NL
59248	1B			*PHA*	HA
59249	1B			*PNL*	NL
59250	1B			*PNL*	NL

Class 101 — Trailer

Built: Metropolitan-Cammell 1957

Diagram	Type	Weight	Seats	Toilet	Note
DT2.02.1B	TS	25.5t	71	1	Refurbished

For full details see series commencing No 59042.

Veh No	*Dia*	*SC*	*Liv*	*Pool*	*Dep*
59302	1B			*PHA*	HA
59303	1B			*PHA*	HA
59304	1B			*PHA*	HA
59305	1B			*PHA*	HA
59306	1B			*NSS*	RG

Class 116 — Trailer

Built: British Railways, Derby Carriage Works 1957

Diagram	Type	Weight	Seats	Note
DT2.15.1B	TS	29t	102	Refurbished
DT2.19.0A	TS	29t	88	Gangwayed
DT2.19.1B	TS	29t	88	Refurbished, Gangwayed

Dimensions: 19.58m L × 2.82m W × 3.86m H. Some gangwayed throughout (G)

Maximum speed: 70mph

Brakes: Vacuum

Veh No	*Dia*	*SC*	*Liv*	*Pool*	*Dep*
59330	91B	G		*PCP*	CPs
59335	91B	G		*PTS*	TS
59344	90A	G		*PTS*	TS
59353	91B	G		*PTS*	TS
59367	51B			*PTS*	TS

Series continued with No 59442.

Class 108 — Trailer

Built: British Railways, Derby Carriage Works 1958

Diagram	Type	Weight	Seats	Toilet	Note
DT2.05.1B	TS	22.5t	68	1	Refurbished
DT2.06.0A*	TS	2.5t	68	1	
DT2.06.1B*	TS	2.5t	68	1	Refurbished

Dimensions: 15.41m L × 2.79m W × 3.87m H. Gangwayed throughout

Maximum speed: 70mph

Brakes: Vacuum

Veh No	*Dia*	*SC*	*Liv*	*Pool*	*Dep*
59380	51B			*PLE*	LE
59381	51B			*PLE*	LE
59382	51B			*PLE*	LE
59383	51B			*PLE*	LE

Veh No	Dia	SC	Liv	Pool	Dep
59384	51B			PLE	LE
59385	51B			PLE	LE
59386	61B			PHA	HA
59387	61B			PHA	HA
59388	60A			PBX	BX
59389	61B			PBX	BX
59390	61B			PBX	BX

Class 119 Trailer

Built: Gloucester RC&W Co 1958

Diagram	Type	Weight	Seats	Toilet
DT2.16.0A	TS	31.5t	60	2

Dimensions: 19.81m L × 2.82m W × 3.86m H. Originally fitted with miniature buffet at one end. Buffet area converted to provide luggage space

Maximum speed: 70mph
Brakes: Vacuum

Veh No	Dia	SC	Liv	Pool	Dep
59416	0A			NWR	RG
59419	0A			NSS	RG
59421	0A		N	NWR	RG
59424	0A			NSB	RG
59425	0A			NSS	RG
59430	0A			NWR	RG
59435	0A		N	NWR	RG
59437	0A		N	NSS	RG

Class 116 Trailer

Built: British Railways Derby Carriage Works 1958

Diagram	Type	Weight	Seats	Note
DT2.19.1B	TS	29t	88	Refurbished and Gangwayed

For full details see series commencing No 59330.

Veh No	Dia	SC	Liv	Pool	Dep
59442	91B	G		PTS	TS
59444	91B	G		PTS	TS
59445	91B	G		PTS	TS
59446	91B	G		PTS	TS
59448	91B	G		PTS	TS

Class 118 Trailer

Built: Birmingham RC&W Co 1960

Diagram	Type	Weight	Seats	Note	
DT2.—.0A	TS	30.5t	70	2	Official code DT3.05.0A
DT2.—.1B	TS	30.5t	70	2	Refurbished. Official code DT3.05.1B

Dimensions: 20.45m L × 2.82m W × 3.86m H. Gangwayed throughout

Maximum speed: 70mph
Brakes: Vacuum

Veh No	Dia	SC	Liv	Pool	Dep
59469	0A			PCF	CF
59473	1B			PTS	TS
59481	0A			PTS	TS
59482	0A			PLA	LA
59483	1B			PTS	TS

Class 117 Trailer

Built: Pressed Steel Co 1959

Diagram	Type	Weight	Seats 1st	Seats Std	Toilet	Note
DT2.—.1C	TS	30.5t	—	70	2	Refurbished. Official code DT3.05.1C
DT3.05.1C	TC	30.5t	22	48	2	Refurbished

Dimensions: 20.45m L × 2.82m W × 3.86m H. Gangwayed througout
Maximum speed: 70mph

Brakes: Vacuum
Special livery: GWR chocolate and cream: 59520

Veh No	Dia	SC	Liv	Pool	Dep
59484	3051C			NWR	RG
59485	3051C		N	NWR	RG
59486	2—1C			PTS	TS
59487	3051C		N	NWR	RG
59488	3051C		N	NWR	RG
59489	3051C			NWR	RG
59490	2—1C			PTS	TS
59491	3051C		N	NWR	RG
59492	2—1C			PTS	TS
59493	3051C		N	NWR	RG
59494	3051C		N	NWR	RG
59495	3051C		N	NWR	RG
59496	3051C		N	NWR	RG
59497	3051C			NWR	RG
59498	3051C		N	NWR	RG
59499	3051C		N	NWR	RG
59500	2—1C			PTS	TS
59501	3051C		N	NWR	RG
59502	3051C		N	NWR	RG
59503	3051C		N	NWR	RG
59504	2—1C			PTS	TS
59505	2—1C			PTS	TS
59506	3051C		N	NWR	RG
59507	3051C		N	NWR	RG
59508	3051C		N	NWR	RG
59509	2—1C			PTS	TS
59510	3051C		N	NWR	RG
59511	3051C		N	NWR	RG
59512	2—1C			PTS	TS
59513	3051C			NWR	RG
59514	3051C		N	NWR	RG
59515	3051C			NWR	RG
59516	2—1C			PTS	TS
59517	2—1C			PTS	TS
59518	3051C		N	NWR	RG
59519	3051C		N	NWR	RG
59520	2—1C		★	PTS	TS
59521	2—1C			PTS	TS
59522	2—1C			PTS	TS

Class 101 Trailer

Built: Metropolitan-Cammell 1959

Diagram	Type	Weight	Seats	Toilet	Note
DT2.02.1B	TS	25.5t	71	1	Refurbished. Mk 1 Bogies
DT2.20.1B	TS	25.5t	65	1	Refurbished. Mk 1 Bogies
DT2.20.1D	TS	25.5t	65	1	Refurbished. Mk 4 Bogies
DT2.28.1C	TS	25.5t	58	1	Refurbished. Mk 1 Bogies

For full details see series commencing No 59032.

Veh No	*Dia*	*SC*	*Liv*	*Pool*	*Dep*	*Veh No*	*Dia*	*SC*	*Liv*	*Pool*	*Dep*
59525	201B			*PHA*	HA	59542	201B		S	*PED*	ED
59526	201B			*NSS*	RG	59543	201D			*NSS*	RG
59530	201D			*NSS*	RG	59561	201D			*PLA*	LA
59532	201B			*PHA*	HA	59565	201D			*PWY*	NL
59536	201D			*PNC*	NC	59570	281C			*NSS*	RG
59539	201D			*PCF*	CF	59571	021B			*PHA*	HA
59540	201B			*NSS*	RG						

Series continued with No 59688.

Class 127 Trailer

Built: British Railways, Derby Carriage Works 1959

Diagram	Type	Weight	Seats	Toilet	Note
DT2.26.0A	TS	30.5t	86	2	
DT2.26.1B	TS	30.5t	86	2	Refurbished

Dimensions: 20.45m L × 2.82m W × 3.86m H. Gangwayed throughout

Maximum speed: 70mph
Brakes: Vacuum

Veh No	*Dia*	*SC*	*Liv*	*Pool*	*Dep*	*Veh No*	*Dia*	*SC*	*Liv*	*Pool*	*Dep*
59589	1B			*PTS*	TS	59604	1B			*PTS*	TS
59590	0A			*PTS*	TS	59606	0A			*PTS*	TS
59591	1B			*PTS*	TS	59607	0A			*PTS*	TS
59592	1B			*PTS*	TS	59608	1B			*PTS*	TS
59593	1B			*PTS*	TS	59609	0A			*PTS*	TS
59594	1B			*PTS*	TS	59610	0A			*PTS*	TS
59595	0A			*PTS*	TS	59611	0A			*PTS*	TS
59596	0A			*PTS*	TS	59612	0A			*PTS*	TS
59597	1B			*PTS*	TS	59613	0A			*PTS*	TS
59598	0A			*PTS*	TS	59614	0A			*PTS*	TS
59600	0A			*PTS*	TS	59615	0A			*PTS*	TS
59602	1B			*PTS*	TS	59616	1B			*PTS*	TS
59603	1B			*PTS*	TS	59617	0A			*PTS*	TS

Class 127 Trailer

Built: British Railways, Derby Carriage Works 1959

Diagram	Type	Weight	Seats	Note
DT2.08.0A	TS	29.5t	106	
DT2.08.1D	TS	29.5t	106	Refurbished
DT2.29.1D	TS	30.5t	98	Refurbished, Gangwayed

Dimensions: 20.45m L × 2.82m W × 3.86m H. Some gangwayed throughout (G)

Maximum speed: 70mph

Brakes: Vacuum

Veh No	*Dia*	*SC*	*Liv*	*Pool*	*Dep*
59621	081D			*PCP*	CPs
59622	080A			*PCP*	CPs
59625	291D	G		*PTS*	TS
59627	080A			*PCP*	CPs
59629	291D	G		*PTS*	TS
59631	080A			*PCP*	CPs
59632	291D	G		*PTS*	TS
59641	291D	G		*PTS*	TS
59643	291D	G		*PTS*	TS
59648	291D	G		*PTS*	TS

Class 115 Trailer

Built: British Railways, Derby Carriage Works 1960

Diagram	Type	Weight	Seats 1st	Seats Std	Toilet	Note
DT2.08.0B	TS	29.5t	—	106		
DT2.08.1C	TS	29.5t	—	106		Refurbished
DT2.27.1B	TS	30.5t	—	70	2	Refurbished
DT2.29.1C	TS	30.5t	—	98		Refurbished, Gangwayed
DT2.—.0A	TS	30.5t	—	66	2	Gangwayed
DT2.—.1B	TS	30.5t	—	66	2	Refurbished, Gangwayed
DT3.03.1B	TC	30.5t	30	40	2	Refurbished

Dimensions: 20.45m L × 2.82m W × 3.86m H. Non-gangwayed, except where shown (G)

Maximum speed: 70mph

Brakes: Vacuum

Veh No	*Dia*	*SC*	*Liv*	*Pool*	*Dep*
59651	2081C			*NMY*	BY
59652	2081C			*NMY*	BY
59653	2080B			*PCP*	CPs
59654	2081C		N	*NMY*	BY
59655	2080B			*NMY*	BY
59656	2080B			*NMY*	BY
59657	2081C			*NMY*	BY
59658	2291C	G		*PTS*	TS
~~59659~~	2081C			*NMY*	BY
59660	2081C			*NMY*	BY
59661	2291C	G		*PTS*	TS
59662	2081C			*NMY*	BY
59663	2081C			*NMY*	BY
59664	3031B			*NMY*	BY
59665	3031B			*NMY*	BY
59666	2271B	D		*PCP*	CPs

Veh No	Dia	SC	Liv	Pool	Dep
59667	3031B			NMY	BY
59668	2—1B	G		PTS	TS
59669	3031B			NMY	BY
59670	2—0A	G		PTS	TS
59671	3031B			NMY	BY
59672	2—1B	G		PTS	TS
59673	2—0A	G		PTS	TS
59674	2—0A	G		PTS	TS
59675	3031B			NMY	BY
59676	3031B			NMY	BY
59677	2—0A	G		PTS	TS
59678	3031B			NMY	BY

Series continued with No 59713.

Class 101 Trailer

Built: Metropolitan-Cammell 1959

Diagram	Type	Weight	Seats	Toilet	Note
DT2.20.1D	TS	25.5t	65	1	Refurbished

For full details see series commencing No 59034.

Veh No	Dia	SC	Liv	Pool	Dep
59688	1D			PHA	HA
59690	1D			PNL	NL

Class 110 Trailer

Built: Birmingham RC&W Co 1961

Diagram	Type	Weight	Seats	Toilet	Note
DT2.07.1B	TS	24.5t	72	1	Refurbished

Dimensions: 18.48m L × 2.82m W × 3.88m H. Gangwayed throughout

Maximum speed: 70mph

Brakes: Vacuum

Veh No	Dia	SC	Liv	Pool	Dep
59694	1B			PNL	NL
59696	1B			PHA	HA
59697	1B			PHA	HA
59701	1B			PHA	HA
59709	1B			PCF	CF
59710	1B			PHA	HA

Series continued with No 59809.

Class 115 Trailer

Built: British Railways, Derby Carriage Works 1960

Diagram	Type	Weight	Seats 1st	Seats Std	Toilet	Note
DT2.08.0B	TS	29.5t	—	106		
DT2.08.1C	TS	29.5t	—	106		Refurbished
DT2.27.1B	TS	30.5t	—	70		Refurbished
DT2.29.1B	TS	30.5t	—	98		Gangwayed
DT2.—.0A	TS	30.5t	—	66	2	Gangwayed
DT2.—.1B	TS	30.5t	—	66	2	Refurbished, Gangwayed
DT3.03.0A	TC	30.5t	30	40	2	
DT3.03.1B	TC	30.5t	30	40	2	Refurbished

For details see series commencing No 59651.

Veh No	*Dia*	*SC*	*Liv*	*Pool*	*Dep*
59713	2291B	G		*PTS*	TS
59715	2081C			*PCP*	CPs
59716	2081C			*PCP*	CPs
59717	2080B			*PCP*	CPs
59719	2—1B	G		*PTS*	TS
59720	2—0A	G		*PTS*	TS
59721	2—0A	G		*PTS*	TS
59722	2—0A	G		*PTS*	TS
59723	2—0A	G		*PTS*	TS
59724	2—0A	G		*PTS*	TS
59725	2081C			*PCP*	CPs
59726	2291C	G		*PTS*	TS
59727	2081C		N	*NMY*	BY
59728	2081C			*NMY*	BY
59729	2081C		N	*NMY*	BY
59731	2081C			*NMY*	BY
59732	2081C		N	*NMY*	BY
59733	2081C			*NMY*	BY
59734	2291C	G		*NNL*	BY
59735	2291C	G		*NNL*	BY
59736	2081C			*NMY*	BY
59737	2081C			*NMY*	BY
59738	2081C			*NMY*	BY
59739	2081C			*NMY*	BY
59740	2081C			*NMY*	BY
59741	2291C	G		*PTS*	TS
59743	2291C	G		*PTS*	TS
59744	2080B			*PCP*	CPs
59745	2270A	G		*PTS*	TS
59746	3031B			*NMY*	BY
59747	3031B			*NMY*	BY
59748	2271B			*PCP*	CPs
59749	3031B			*NMY*	BY
59750	3031B			*NMY*	BY
59751	2270A	G		*PTS*	TS
59752	3030A			*NMY*	BY
59753	2—0A	G		*PTS*	TS
59754	3030A			*NMY*	BY
59755	3031B		N	*NMY*	BY
59756	2—0A	G		*PTS*	TS
59757	2—0A	G		*PTS*	TS
59758	3030A			*NMY*	BY
59759	3031B			*NMY*	BY
59760	2—1B	G		*PTS*	TS
~~59761~~	3031B			*NMY*	BY
59762	3031B		N	*NMY*	BY
59763	3031B			*NMY*	BY
59764	3031B			*NMY*	BY

Class 107 Trailer

Built: British Railways, Derby Carriage Works 1960

Diagram	Type	Weight	Seats	Toilet	Note
DT2.04.0A	TS	28.5t	71	1	
DT2.04.1B	TS	28.5t	71	1	Refurbished

Dimensions: 18.49m L × 2.82m W × 3.87m H. Gangwayed throughout

Maximum speed: 70mph

Brakes: Vacuum

Veh No	Dia	SC	Liv	Pool	Dep
59782	1B		S	PED	ED
59783	1B		S	PED	ED
59784	1B		S	PED	ED
59785	1B		S	PHA	HA
59786	1B		S	PHA	HA
59789	1B			PHA	HA
59790	1B		S	PED	ED
59791	1B			PHA	HA
59792	1B		S	PED	ED
59793	1B		S	PED	ED
59794	0A			PHA	HA
59795	1B			PED	ED
59796	1B			PED	ED
59797	1B			PHA	HA
59798	1B		S	PED	ED
59800	1B			PHA	HA
59801	1B		S	PED	ED
59802	1B		S	PED	ED
59803	1B		S	PED	ED
59804	1B		S	PED	ED
59805	1B			PED	ED
59806	1B		S	PED	ED
59807	1B		S	PED	ED

Class 110 — Trailer

Built: Birmingham RC&W Co 1961

Diagram	Type	Weight	Seats	Toilet	Note
DT2.07.1B	TS	24.5t	72	1	Refurbished

For full details see Series commencing No 59694.

Veh No	Dia	SC	Liv	Pool	Dep
59809	1B			PHA	HA
59810	1B			PHA	HA
59812	1B			PCP	CPs
59817	1B			PHA	HA

Class 111 — Driving Motor

Built: Metropolitan-Cammell 1957-59 (Modified 1982)

Diagram	Type	Weight	Engine	Seats	Toilet	Note
DW2.01.1B	DHS	32t	RR138B	65	1	Refurbished Mk 2 Bogies, official diagram DW3.01.1B
DW2.02.1B	DHS	32t	RR138C	65	1	Refurbished Mk 3 Bogies, official diagram DW3.02.1B

Engine: One Rolls-Royce 180hp (134kW) 6-cyl horizontal
Transmission: Four speed epicyclic gearbox, cardan shaft
Dimensions: 18.49m L × 2.82m W × 3.88m H, Gangwayed within unit.

Maximum speed: 70mph
Brakes: Vacuum
AWS: Fitted

Veh No	Dia	SC	Liv	Pool	Dep
78709	11B			*PNL*	NL
78711	11B			*PNL*	NL
78712	11B			*PNL*	NL
78713	11B			*PNL*	NL
78714	11B			*PNL*	NL
78717	21B			*PNL*	NL
78718	21B			*PNL*	NL
78719	21B			*PNL*	NL
78722	21B			*PNL*	NL

Class 111 — Driving Motor Brake

Built: Metropolitan-Cammell 1957-59 (Modified 1982)

Diagram	Type	Weight	Engine	Seats	Note
DY2.02.1C	DHBS	31t	RR138B	52	Refurbished Mk 2 Bogies
DY2.02.1D	DHBS	31t	RR138B	52	Refurbished Mk 3 Bogies
DY2.03.0A	DHBS	32t	RR138C	52	Refurbished Mk 3 Bogies

Engine: One Rolls-Royce 180hp (134kW) 6-cyl horizontal
Transmission: Four speed epicyclic gearbox, cardan shaft
Dimensions: 18.49m L × 2.82m W × 3.88m H, Gangwayed within unit.
Maximum speed: 70mph
Brakes: Vacuum
AWS: Fitted

Veh No	Dia	SC	Liv	Pool	Dep
78959	21C			*PNL*	NL
78960	21D			*PNL*	NL
78961	21D			*PNL*	NL
78962	21C			*PNL*	NL
78964	21C			*PNL*	NL
78967	30A			*PNL*	NL
78968	30A			*PNL*	NL
78969	30A			*PNL*	NL
78971	30A			*PNL*	NL

RAIL BUSES

Class 140 — 2-CAR

Built: British Rail, Derby Carriage Works, 1981
Development of LEV railbus. Vehicles mounted on 4-wheel underframes, and fitted with folding doors

Diagram	Type	Toilet	Seats
DP2.22.0A	DMSA(L)	1	50
DP2.23.0A	DMSB	—	52

Driving Motor Standard: DMSB
Driving Motor Standard: DMSA(L)
Engine: Leyland TL11 of 200bhp (152kW)
Transmission: Mechanical. SCG 4-speed epicyclic reversable gearbox/cardan shaft
Body: 16.20m L × 2.75m W × 3.91m H. Gangwayed throughout
Weight: 23 tonnes
Brakes: Air
AWS: Fitted
Maximum speed: 70mph

Unit No	SC	Pool	Dep	DMS	DMS(L)
140 001	v	PNL	NL (s)	55500	55501

Classes 141/0 & 141/1 — 2-CAR

Built: Leyland National/BREL Derby Works 1983
Development of Class 140. Modified Leyland bus bodies, mounted on 4-wheel rail chassis — fitted with folding doors. Class 141/1 modified 1988 by Alexander Barclay to operate in multiple with Classes 142-144

Diagram	Class	Type	Gearbox	Seats	Toilet	SC
DP2.28.0A	141/0	DMSA	SCG	50		
DP2.28.—	141/0	DMSA	Voith	50		V
DP2.2-.—	141/1	DMSA	SCG	50		
DP2.29.0A	141/0	DMSB(L)	SGG	44	1	
DP2.29.—	141/0	DMSB(L)	Voith	44	1	V
DP2.2-.—	141/1	DMSB(L)	SGG	44	1	

Driving Motor Standard: DMS
Driving Motor Standard: DMS(L)
Engine: Leyland TL11 of 200bhp (152kW)
Transmission: Mechanical. SCG or Voith 4-speed epicyclic reversable gearbox/cardan shaft
Body: 15.45m L × 2.75m W × 3.91m H. Gangwayed within unit
Weight: 21 tonnes

Brakes: Air
AWS: Fitted
Maximum speed: 75mph
Driving Motor Standard: DMS(L)
Details as above except
Weight: 21.5 tonnes
Livery: *West Yorkshire PTE* Class 141/1: Red and cream; Class 141/0: Green and cream

Class 141/1 Unit No	*Class 141/0 Unit No*	*SC*	*Pool*	*Dep*	*DMS*	*DMS(L)*
141 101	(141 020)		*PNL*	NL	55521	55541
141 102	(141 001)		*PNL*	NL	55502	55522
141 103	(141 002)		*PNL*	NL	55503	55523
141 104	141 003		*PNL*	NL	55504	55524
141 105	(141 004)		*PNL*	NL	55505	55525
141 106	(141 005)		*PNL*	NL	55506	55526
141 107	(141 006)		*PNL*	NL	55507	55527
141 108	141 007		*PNL*	NL	55508	55528
141 109	(141 008)		*PNL*	NL	55509	55529
141 110	(141 009)		*PNL*	NL	55510	55530
141 111	(141 010)		*PNL*	NL	~~55511~~	~~55531~~
141 112	(141 011)		*PNL*	NL	55512	55532
141 113	(141 012)	v	*PNL*	NL	55513	55533
141 114	141 013		*PNL*	NL	55514	55534
141 115	(141 014)		*PNL*	NL	55515	55535
141 116	(141 015)		*PNL*	NL	55516	55536

Unit No	Unit No	SC	Pool	Dep	DMS	DMS(L)
141 117	(141 016)		PNL	NL	55517	55537
141 118	141 017		PNL	NL	55518	55538
141 119	(141 018)		PNL	NL	55519	55539
141 120	(141 019)		PNL	NL	55520	55540

Class 141/0 units not shown in parenthesis not so modified.

Class 142 — 2 CAR — Pacers

Built: Associated Rail Technologies (Leyland/BREL Derby) 1985

Diagram	Type	Gearbox	Weight	Seats	Toilet	SC
DP2.34.0A	DMS	SCG	24.5t	62		
DP2.34.—	DMS	Voith	24.5t	62		V
DP2.35.0A	DMS(L)	SCG	25t	59	1	
DP2.35.—	DMS(L)	Voith	25t	59	1	V

Driving Motor Standard: DMS
Engine: Leyland TL11 of 200bhp (152kW)
Transmission: Mechanical. SCG or Voith 4-speed epicyclic reversable gearbox/cardan shaft
Body: 15.55m L × 2.80m W × 3.86m H. Gangwayed within unit
Brakes: Air

AWS: Fitted
Maximum speed: 75mph
Livery: *Standard* Provincial Blue
Special: Greater Manchester PTE (Orange); 142 001-14
Western England (Brown and Cream): 142 015-27

Unit No	SC	Pool	Dep	DMS	DMS(L)
142 001		PNH	NH	55542	55592
142 002		PNH	NH	55543	55593
142 003		PNH	NH	55544	55594
142 004		PNH	NH	55545	55595
142 005		PNH	NH	55546	55596
142 006		PNH	NH	55547	55597
142 007		PNH	NH	55548	55598
142 008		PNH	NH	55549	55599
142 009		PNH	NH	55550	55600
142 010		PNH	NH	55551	55601
142 011		PNH	NH	55552	55602
142 012		PNH	NH	55553	55603
142 013		PNH	NH	55554	55604
142 014		PNH	NH	55555	55605
142 015		PNH	NH	55556	55606
142 016		PHT	HT	55557	55607
142 017		PNH	NH	55558	55608
142 018		PHT	HT	55559	55609
142 019		PHT	HT	55560	55610
142 020		PHT	HT	55561	55611
142 021		PHT	HT	55562	55612
142 022		PHT	HT	55563	55613
142 023	V	PNH	NH	55564	55614
142 024		PNH	NH	55565	55615
142 025		PHT	HT	55566	55616
142 026	V	PNH	NH	55567	55617
142 027		PNH	NH	55568	55618
142 028		PNH	NH	55569	55619
142 029		PNH	NH	55570	55620
142 030		PNH	NH	55571	55621
142 031		PNH	NH	55572	55622
142 032		PNH	NH	55573	55623
142 033		PNH	NH	55574	55624
142 034		PNH	NH	55575	55625
142 035		PNH	NH	55576	55626
142 036		PNH	NH	55577	55759
142 037		PNH	NH	55578	55628
142 038	V	PNH	NH	55579	55629
142 039	V	PNH	NH	55580	55630
142 040		PNH	NH	55581	55631

Unit No	SC	Pool	Dep	DMS	DMS(L)
142 041	v	PNH	NH	55582	55632
142 042		PNH	NH	55583	55633
142 043	v	PNH	NH	55584	55634
142 044		PNH	NH	55585	55635
142 045	v	PNH	NH	55586	55636
142 046		PNH	NH	55587	55637
142 047		PNH	NH	55588	55752
142 048		PNH	NH	55589	55639
142 049		PNH	NH	55590	55640
142 050	v	PNH	NH	55591	55641
142 051		PNH	NH	55701	55747
142 052		PNH	NH	55702	55748
142 053		PNH	NH	55703	55749
142 054		PNH	NH	55704	55750
142 055		PNH	NH	55705	55751
142 056		PNH	NH	55706	55638
142 057		PNH	NH	55707	55753
142 058		PNH	NH	55708	55754
142 059		PNH	NH	55709	55755
142 060		PNH	NH	55710	55756
142 061		PNH	NH	55711	55757
142 062		PNH	NH	55712	55758
142 063		PNH	NH	55713	55627
142 064		PNH	NH	55714	55760
142 065		PNH	NH	55715	55761
142 066		PNH	NH	55716	55762
142 067		PNH	NH	55717	55763
142 068		PNH	NH	55718	55764
142 069		PNH	NH	55719	55765
142 070		PNL	NL	55720	55766
142 071		PNL	NL	55721	55767
142 072		PNL	NL	55722	55768
142 073		PNL	NL	55723	55769
142 074		PNL	NL	55724	55770
142 075		PNL	NL	55725	55771
142 076		PNL	NL	55726	55772
142 077		PNL	NL	55727	55773
142 078		PNL	NL	55728	55774
142 079		PNL	NL	55729	55775
142 080		PNL	NL	55730	55776
142 081		PNL	NL	55731	55777
142 082		PNL	NL	55732	55778
142 083		PNL	NL	55733	55779
142 084		PNL	NL	55734	55780
142 085		PNL	NL	55735	55781
142 086		PNL	NL	55736	55782
142 087		PNL	NL	55737	55783
142 088		PNL	NL	55738	55784
142 089		PNL	NL	55739	55785
142 090		PNL	NL	55740	55786
142 091		PNL	NL	55741	55787
142 092		PNL	NL	55742	55788
142 093		PNL	NL	55743	55789
142 094		PNL	NL	55744	55790
142 095		PNL	NL	55745	55791
142 096		PNL	NL	55746	55792

Class 143 2-CAR Pacers

Built: Walter Alexander/Andrew Barclay 1985

Diagram	Type	Gearbox	Weight	Seats	Toilet	SC
DP2.36.0A	DMSA	SGC	24t	62	—	
DP2.36.—	DMSA	Voith	24t	62	—	v
DP2.37.0A	DMSB(L)	SGC	24.5t	60	1	
DP2.37.—	DMSB(L)	Voith	24.5t	60	1	v

Driving Motor Standard: DMS
Engine: Leyland TL11 of 200bhp (152kW)
Transmission: Mechanical, SCG or Voith 4-speed epicyclic reversable gearbox/cardan shaft

Body: 15.55m L × 2.70m W × 3.62m H.
Gangwayed within unit
Maximum speed: 75mph
Livery: *Standard*: Provincial Sector (Blue); *Special:* Tyne & Wear PTE (Yellow): 143020-25

Unit No	New Unit No	SC	Pool	Dep	DMS	DMS(L)
143 001		v	*PHT*	HT	55642	55667
143 002		v	*PHT*	HT	55643	55668
143 003			*PHT*	HT	55644v	55669
143 004		v	*PHT*	HT	55645	55670
143 005		v	*PHT*	HT	55646	55671
143 006		v	*PHT*	HT	55647	55672
143 007		v	*PHT*	HT	55648	55673
143 008		v	*PHT*	HT	55649	55674
143 009		v	*PHT*	HT	55650	55675
143 010		v	*PHT*	HT	55651	55676
143 011		v	*PHT*	HT	55652	55677
143 012		v	*PHT*	HT	55653	55678
143 013		v	*PHT*	HT	55654	55679
143 014		v	*PHT*	HT	55655	55680
143 015		v	*PHT*	HT	55656	55681
143 016		v	*PHT*	HT	55657	55682
143 017		v	*PHT*	HT	55658	55683
143 018		v	*PHT*	HT	55659	55684
143 019		v	*PHT*	HT	55660	55685
143 020			*PHT*	HT	55661	55686
143 021			*PHT*	HT	55662	55687
143 022			*PHT*	HT	55663	55688
143 023			*PHT*	HT	55664	55689
143 024			*PHT*	HT	55665	55690
143 025			*PHT*	HT	55666	55691

Class 144 — 2 or 3-CAR — Pacers

Built: Walter Alexander/BREL Derby 1986-88

Diagram	Type	Gearbox	Weight	Seats	Toilet	SC
DP2.40.0A	DMSA	SGC	24t	62		
DP2.40.--	DMSA	Voith	24t	62		v
DP2.41.0A	DMSB(L)	SGC	24.5t	60	1	
DP2.41.--	DMSB(L)	Voith	24.5t	60	1	v
DR2.05.0A	MS	SGC	23.5t	73		

Driving Motor Standard: DMS
Motor Standard: MS
Engine: Leyland TL11 of 200bhp (152kW)
Transmission: Mechanical. SCG or Voith 4-speed epicyclic reversable gearbox/cardan shaft
Body: 16.60m L × 2.70m W × 3.73m H. Gangwayed within unit
Maximum speed: 75mph
Livery: West Yorkshire PTE (red and cream)

Unit No	New Unit No	SC	Pool	Dep	DMS	MS	DMS(L)
144 001			*PNL*	NL	55801		55824
144 002			*PNL*	NL	~~55802~~		~~55825~~
144 003			*PNL*	NL	55803		55826
144 004			*PNL*	NL	55804		55827
144 005			*PNL*	NL	~~55805~~		~~55828~~
144 006			*PNL*	NL	55806		55829
144 007			*PNL*	NL	55807		55830
144 008			*PNL*	NL	55808		55831
144 009		v	*PNL*	NL	55809		55832
144 010		v	*PNL*	NL	55810		55833

Unit No	New Unit No	SC	Pool	Dep	DMS	MS	DMS(L)
144 011		v	*PNL*	NL	55811		55834
144 012		v	*PNL*	NL	55812		55835
144 013		v	*PNL*	NL	55813		55836
144 014			*PNL*	NL	55814	55850	55837
144 015			*PNL*	NL	55815	55851	55838
144 016			*PNL*	NL	55816	55852	55839
144 017			*PNL*	NL	55817	55853	55840
144 018			*PNL*	NL	55818	55854	55841
144 019			*PNL*	NL	55819	55855	55842
144 020			*PNL*	NL	55820	55856	55843
144 021			*PNL*	NL	55821	55857	55844
144 022			*PNL*	NL	~~55822~~	~~55858~~	~~55845~~
144 023			*PNL*	NL	55823	55859	55846

20 METRE SPRINTER

Class 150/0 — 3-CAR

Built: BREL York Works 1984

Three-car prototype suburban unit

Diagram	Type	Weight	Seats	Toilet
DP2.30.0A	DMSA(L)	35.8t	75	1
DP2.31.1A	DMSB	35.6t	79	—
DR2.02.0A	MS	34.4t	84	—

Engine: Cummins NT 855R4 of 285hp (312kW)
Transmission: Voith-Gemeinder
Maximum speed: 75mph
Public address, driver/guard communication, air brakes and AWS fitted
Driving Motor Standard: DMSA(L)
Driving Motor Standard: DMS

Body: 20.06m L × 2.73m W × 3.77m H.
Gangwayed within unit
Motor Standard: MS
Body: 20.18m L × 2.73m W × 3.77m H.
Gangwayed throughout
Livery: Provincial Sector (Blue)

Unit No	SC	Pool	Dep	DMS(L)	MS	DMS
150 001		*PDY*	DY	55200	55400	55300

Class 150/1 — 2 or 3-CAR

Built: BREL York Works 1985

Diagram	Type	Weight	Seats	Toilet	SC
DP2.38.0A	DMSA(L)	36.5t	68	1	
DP2.38.--	DMSA(L)	36.5t	68	1	RETB Socket
DP2.39.0A	DMSB	36.5t	70		

150101-150137

DP2.39.--	DMSB	36.5t	70		RETB Socket
DP2.42.0A	DMSA(L)*	37.5t	73	1	See Class 150/2
DP2.43.0A	DMSB†	36.5t	76		for full details

Engines: Cumins NT 855R5 of 285hp (213kW)
Transmission: Voith-Gemeinder
Body: 20.06m L × 2.73m W × 3.77m H.
Gangwayed within unit
Maximum speed: 75mph

Public address, driver-guard communication, air brakes and AWS fitted
Driving Motor Standard: DMS(L)
Driving Motor Standard: DMS
Livery: Provincial Sector (Blue)

Unit No	*SC*	*Pool*	*Dep*	*DMS(L)*	*DMS(L)** *DMS†*	*DMS*
~~150 101~~		*PDY*	DY	52101		57101
150 102		*PDY*	DY	52102		57102
150 103		*PDY*	DY	52103		57103
150 104		*PDY*	DY	52104		57104
150 105		*PDY*	DY	52105		57105
150 106		*PDY*	DY	52106		57106
150 107		*PDY*	DY	52107		57107
150 108		*PDY*	DY	52108		57108
150 109		*PDY*	DY	52109		57109
~~150 110~~		*PDY*	DY	52110		57110
~~150 111~~		*PDY*	DY	52111		57111
150 112		*PDY*	DY	52112		57112
150 113		*PDY*	DY	52113		57113
150 114		*PDY*	DY	52114		57114
~~150 115~~		*PDY*	DY	52115		57115
150 116	R	*PDY*	DY	52116		57116
150 117	R	*PDY*	DY	52117		57117
150 118	R	*PDY*	DY	52118		57118
150 119	R	*PDY*	DY	52119		57119
150 120	R	*PDY*	DY	52120		57120
150 121	R	*PDY*	DY	52121		57121
150 122	R	*PDY*	DY	52122		57122
150 123		*PDY*	DY	52123		57123
150 124		*PDY*	DY	52124		57124
150 125	R	*PDY*	DY	52125		57125
150 126	R	*PDY*	DY	52126		57126
150 127	R	*PDY*	DY	52127		57127
150 128		*PDY*	DY	52128		57128
150 129	R	*PDY*	DY	52129		57129
~~150 130~~		*PDY*	DY	52130		57130
150 131	R	*PDY*	DY	52131		57131
150 132	R	*PDY*	DY	52132		57132
150 133	R	*PDY*	DY	52133		57133
150 134		*PDY*	DY	52134		57134
150 135	R	*PDY*	DY	52135		57135
150 136	R	*PDY*	DY	52136		57136
150 137	R	*PDY*	DY	52137		57137

Unit No	SC	Pool	Dep	DMS(L)	DMS(L)* DMS†	DMS
150 138	R	*PDY*	DY	52138		57138
150 139	R	*PDY*	DY	52139		57139
150 140	R	*PDY*	DY	52140		57140
150 141	R	*PDY*	DY	52141	57253†	57141
150 142	R	*PDY*	DY	52142	57212†	57142
150 143	R	*PDY*	DY	52143	52205*	57143
150 144	R	*PDY*	DY	52144	52212†	57144
150 145	R	*PDY*	DY	52145		57145
150 146	R	*PDY*	DY	52146	52253*	57146
150 147	R	*PDY*	DY	52147		57147
150 148	R	*PDY*	DY	52148		57148
150 149	R	*PDY*	DY	52149		57149
150 150	R	*PDY*	DY	52150		57150

Class 150/2 — 2-CAR

Built: BREL York Works 1987

Diagram	Type	Weight	Seats	SC
DP2.42.0A	DMSA(L)	37.5t	73	
DP2.42.--	DMSA(L)	37.5t	70	†
DP2.43.0A	DMS	36.5t	76	

Engine: Cummins NT 855R5 of 285bhp (213kW)
Transmission: Voith-Gemeinder
Maximum speed: 75mph
Public address and driver-guard communication fitted

Driving Motor Standard: DMS(L)
Driving Motor Standard: DMS
Dimensions: 20.06m L × 2.73m W × 3.77m H. Gangwayed throughout

Unit No	SC	Pool	Dep	DMS(L)	DMS
150 201		*PNH*	NH	52201	57201
150 202		*PNL*	NL	52202†	57202
150 203		*PNH*	NH	52203	57203
150 204		*PNL*	NL	52204†	57204
150 205		Not formed			
150 206		*PNL*	NL	52206†	57206
150 207		*PNH*	NH	52207	57207
150 208		*PHA*	HA	52208	57208
150 209		*PNH*	NH	52209	57209
150 210		*PNL*	NL	52210†	57210
150 211		*PNH*	NH	52211	57211
150 212		*PNL*	NL (at ZD)	52212†	
150 213		*PNH*	NH	52213	57213
150 214		*PNL*	NL	52214†	57214
150 215		*PNH*	NH	52215	57215
150 216		*PNL*	NL	52216†	57216
150 217		*PNH*	NH	52217	57217
150 218		*PNL*	NL	52218†	57218
150 219		*PNH*	NH	52219	57219
150 220		*PNL*	NL	52220†	57220
150 221		*PNH*	NH	52221	57221
150 222		*PNL*	NL	52222†	57222
150 223		*PNH*	NH	52223	57223
150 224		*PNL*	NL	52224†	57224
150 225		*PNH*	NH	52225	57225
150 226		*PNL*	NL	52226†	57226
150 227		*PNH*	NH	52227	57227
150 228		*PNL*	NL	52228†	57228
150 229		*PNH*	NH	52229	57229
150 230		*PNL*	NL	52230†	57230

150 231	*PNH*	NH	52231	57231
150 232	*PNL*	NL	52232†	57232
150 233	*PNH*	NH	52233	57233
150 234	*PNL*	NL	52234†	57234
150 235	*PNH*	NH	52235	57235
150 236	*PNL*	NL	52236†	57236
150 237	*PNH*	NH	52237	57237
150 238	*PNL*	NL	52238†	57238
150 239	*PNH*	NH	52239	57239
~~150 240~~	*PNL*	NL	52240†	57240
150 241	*PNH*	NH	52241	57241
~~150 242~~	*PNL*	NL	52242†	57242
150 243	*PNH*	NH	52243	57243
150 244	*PNL*	NL	52244†	57244
150 245	*PHA*	HA	52245	57245
150 246	*PNL*	NL	52246†	57246
150 247	*PCF*	CF	52247	57247
150 248	*PNL*	NL	52248†	57248
150 249	*PCF*	CF	52249	57249
150 250	*PNL*	NL	52250†	57250
150 251	*PCF*	CF	52251	57251
150 252	*PNL*	NL	52252†	57252
150 253	Not formed			
150 254	*PNL*	NL	52254†	57254
150 255	*PHA*	HA	52255	57255
150 256	*PNL*	NL	52256†	57256
150 257	*PHA*	HA	52257	57257
150 258	*PNL*	NL	52258†	57258
150 259	*PHA*	HA	52259	57259
150 260	*PNL*	NL	52260†	57260
150 261	*PCF*	CF	52261	57261
150 262	*PNL*	NL	52262†	57262
150 263	*PCF*	CF	52263	57263
150 264	*PHA*	HA	52264	57264
150 265	*PCF*	CF	52265	57265
150 266	*PCF*	CF	52266	57266
150 267	*PCF*	CF	52267	57267
150 268	*PCF*	CF	52268	57268
150 269	*PCF*	CF	52269	57269
150 270	*PCF*	CF	52270	57270
150 271	*PCF*	CF	52271	57271
150 272	*PCF*	CF	52272	57272
150 273	*PCF*	CF	52273	57273
150 274	*PCF*	CF	52274	57274
150 275	*PCF*	CF	52275	57275
150 276	*PCF*	CF	52276	57276
150 277	*PCF*	CF	52277	57277
150 278	*PCF*	CF	52278	57278
150 279	*PCF*	CF	52279	57279
150 280	*PCF*	CF	52280	57280
150 281	*PCF*	CF	52281	57281
150 282	*PCF*	CF	52282	57282
150 283	*PHA*	HA	52283	57283
150 284	*PHA*	HA	52284	57284
150 285	*PHA*	HA	52285	57285

Class 151 — 3-CAR

Built: Metro-Cammell 1985

Diagram	Type	Weight	Seats	Toilet
DP2.32.0A	DMSA(L)	32.4t	68	1
DP2.33.0A	DMSB	32.4t	80	
DR2.04.0A	MS	32.1t	84	

Engines: Cummins NT 855 R4 of 285hp (213kW)
Transmission: Mechanical
Maximum speed: 75mph
Public address, driver-guard communication, air brakes and AWS fitted
Driving Motor Standard: DMSA(L)
Driving Motor Standard: DMSB
Dimensions: 19.98m L × 2.81m W × 3.89m H. Gangwayed within unit.
Motor Second: MS
Dimensions: 19.60m L × 2.81m W × 3.89m H. Gangwayed throughout

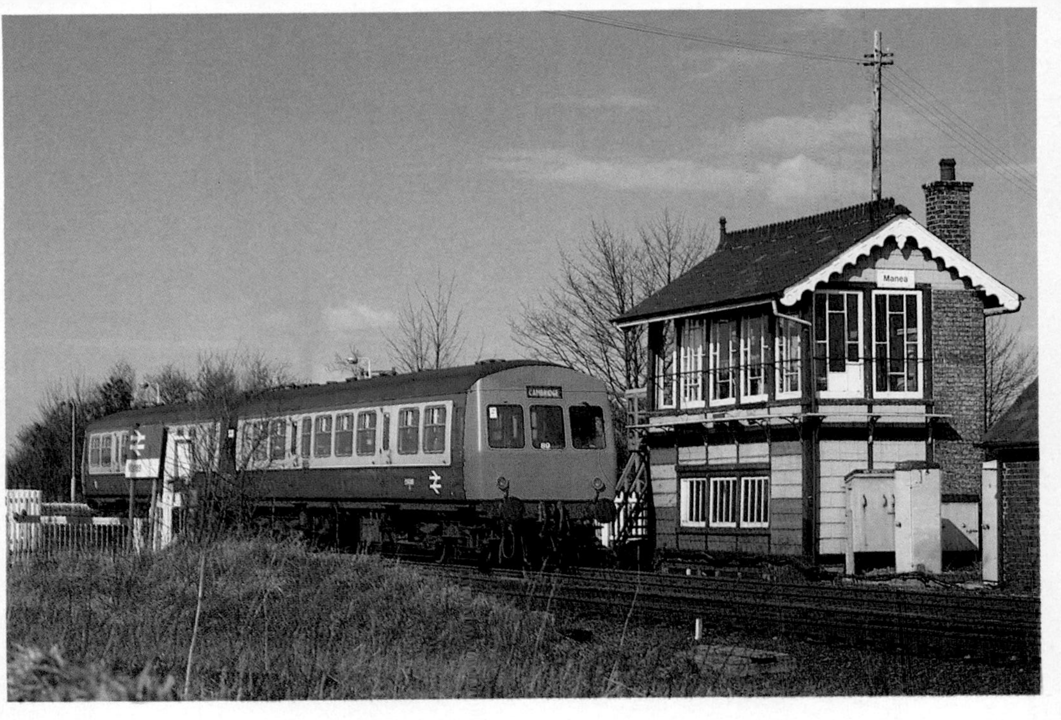

Class 101 DTS No 54089 leads the 11.10 Peterborough-Cambridge at Manea on 4 March 1988. *Bryan Philpott*

Carrying the distinctive Strathclyde PTE livery, Class 107 DMU set No 107444 pauses at Holytown with the 13.26 Glasgow-Edinburgh Waverley on 24 August 1987. *Douglas Young*

The green-liveried Class 108 unit, comprising DMBS vehicle No 53964 and DTS vehicle No 54247, near Carlisle on 22 October 1987. *D. McAlone*

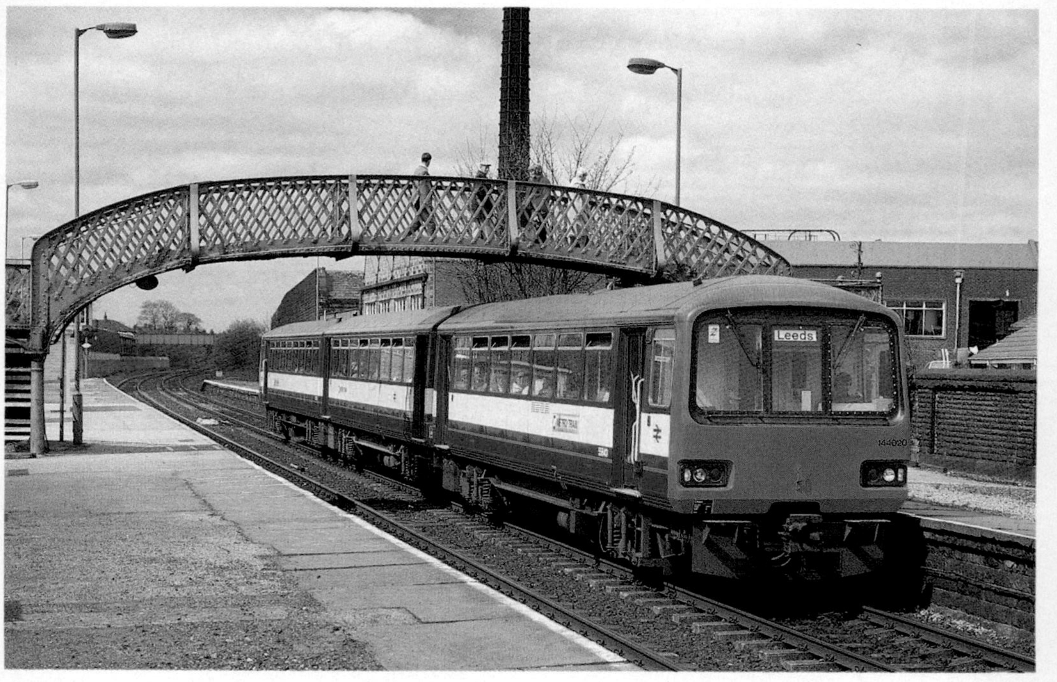

Ten West Yorkshire PTE Class 144 Pacer DMUs have been fitted with centre cars to relieve overcrowding. Here, three-car unit No 144020 leaves Guiseley with the 13.40 Ilkley-Leeds on 23 April 1988. *John E. Oxley*

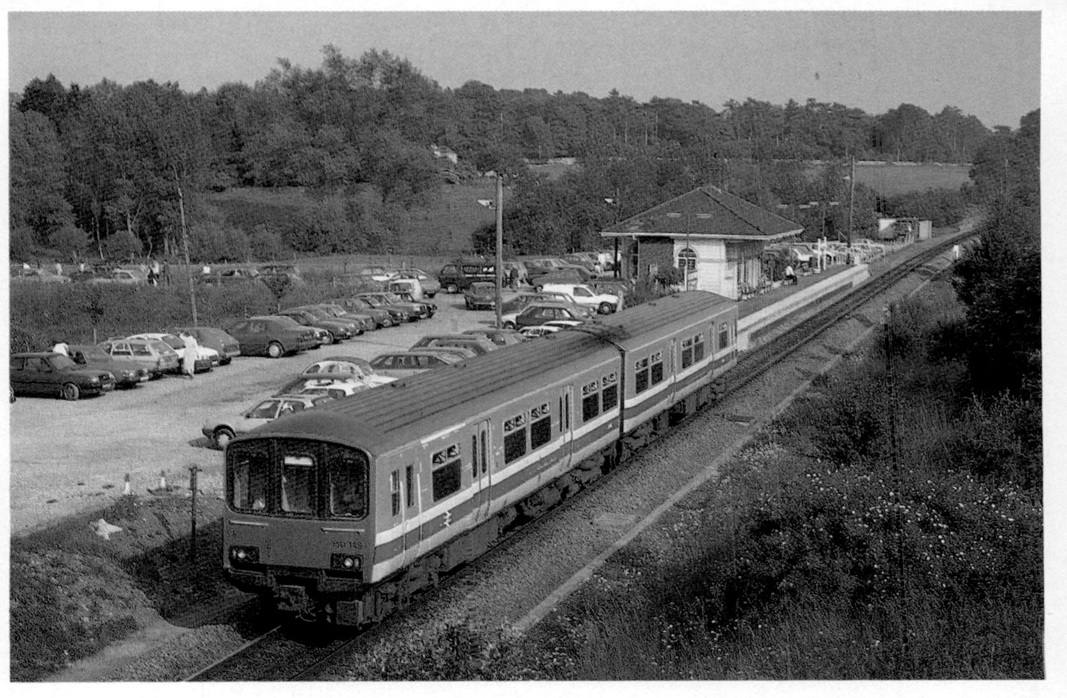

Class 150/1 'Sprinter' DMU No 150148 leaves Charlbury with the 17.36 Oxford-Moreton-in-Marsh on 14 June 1988.
Colin Underhill

The first 'Sprinter' to Bournemouth was Class 155 No 155319 seen here in the New Forest near Beaulieu Road on 25 March 1988. *David Warwick*

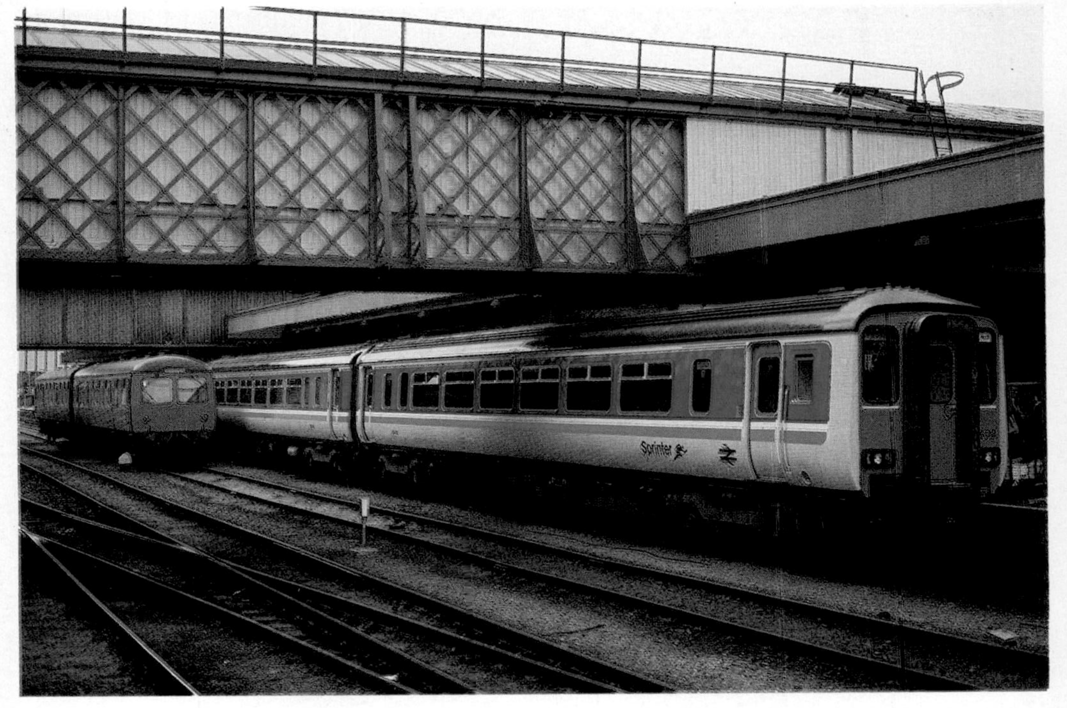

Class 156 'Sprinter' DMU No 156402 at Sheffield on 24 May 1988. *Graham Hudson*

On 14 August 1987, Class 205 DEMU No 205020, still in blue and grey livery, passes Dunbridge with the 15.33 Portsmouth-Salisbury. *David Warwick*

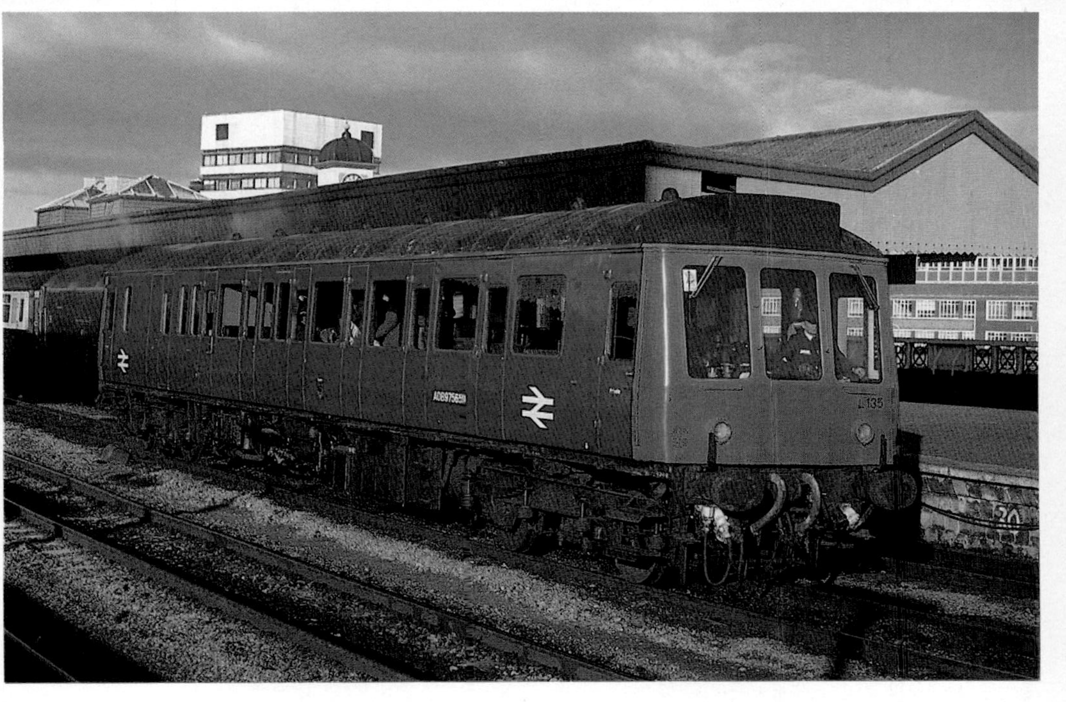

Departmental route-learning saloon No ADB 975659 trundles eastbound through Cardiff Central station on 16 February 1988.
Hugh Ballantyne

Class 310 EMU No 310068, in Network SouthEast livery, approaches Watford Junction with the 10.36 Birmingham-Euston.
John E. Oxley

A morning commuter service from Watford Junction arrives at Euston formed of Class 313 unit No 313006 on 5 July 1988.
Hugh Ballantyne

The 13.56 Luton-Farringdon service, formed of Class 319 'Thameslink' EMU No 319022, calls at Elstree & Borehamwood on Bank Holiday Monday 30 May 1988. *John E. Oxley*

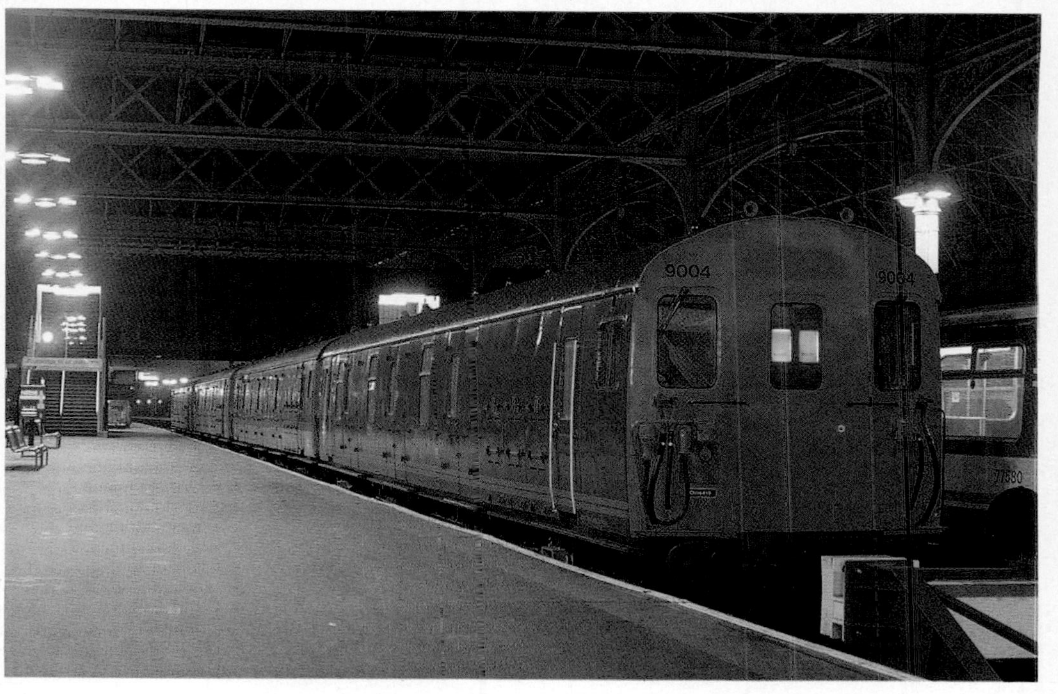

Class 419 MLV No 9004 in Royal Mail red livery, forms part of a parcels service for Redhill at London Bridge on 10 November 1988. *Brian Morrison*

Class 421/3 (4-CIG) unit No 1704 leads the 14.47 Victoria-Hastings at Clapham Junction on 1 April 1988. *John E. Oxley*

Class 442 unit Nos 2421/19 form the 11.45 Waterloo-Poole at Southampton on 5/11/88. *Brian Morrison*

Class 455/8 unit No 5818 leaves Clapham Junction on 1 April 1988. *John E. Oxley*

Unit No	Former Unit No	SC	Pool	Dep	DMS	MS	DMS(L)
151 003	(151 001)		PDY	DY	55202	55402	55302
151 004	(151 002)		PDY	DY	55203	55403	55303

Class 154 — 3-CAR

Built: BREL York Works 1985
Modified at BR EDU, Railway Technical Centre, Derby, 1986, from Class 150 prototype unit No 150002. Public address and driver guard communication fitted. Air conditioning on DMS vehicles

Design Codes	Type	Weight	Seats	Toilet
DP2.46.0A	DMSA(L)	37.9t	58	1
DP2.47.0A	DMSB	37.9t	60	
DR2.03.0A	MS	34.4t	97	

Driving Motor Standard: DMS(L)
Engine: Cummins NTA 855RI of 350hp (275kW)
Transmission: Voith
Body: 20.06m L × 2.73m W × 3.77m H.
Gangwayed within unit
Driving Motor Standard: DMS
Transmission: Twin Disc

Motor Standard: MS
Engine: Rolls-Royce Eagle C6 305R of 350hp (275kW)
Dimensions: 20.18m L × 2.81m W × 3.77m H
Maximum speed: 75mph
Livery: Provincial Sector (Blue)

Unit No	Former Unit No	SC	Pool	Dep	DMS	MS	DMS(L)
154 002	(154 001)		PDY	DY	55201	55401	55301

23 METRE SUPER SPRINTER UNITS

Classes 155/0 & 155/1 — 2-CAR

Built: Leyland National Bus 1987-88
Public address, driver-guard communication, air brakes and AWS fitted

Design Codes	Class	Type	Weight	Seats	Toilet	
DP2.48.0A	155/0	DMS(L)	38.8t	80	1	Wheelchair provision
DP2.48.1B	155/1	DMS(L)	39.4t	80	1	Wheelchair provision
DP2.49.0A	155/0	DMS	37.9t	80		
DP2.49.1B	155/1	DMS	38.6t	80		

Driving Motor Standard: DMSA(L)
Driving Motor Standard: DMSB
Engine: Cummins NT855 R5 of 285hp (213kW)
Transmission: Voith/Gemeinder
Dimensions: 23.21m L × 2.69m W × 3.81m H. Gangwayed throughout

Maximum speed: 75mph
Livery: Class 155/0 *Provincial Sector*: 155301-35
Class 155/1 *Metro Red* (West Yorks PTE): 155341-47

Unit No	*SC*	*Pool*	*Dep*	*DMS*	*DMS(L)*
Class 155/0					
155 301		*PCF*	CF	52301	57301
155 302		*PCF*	CF	52302	57302
155 303		*PCF*	CF	52303	57303
155 304		*PCF*	CF	52304	57304
155 305		*PCF*	CF	52305	57305
155 306		*PCF*	CF	52306	57306
155 307		*PCF*	CF	52307	57307
155 308		*PCF*	CF	52308	57308
155 309		*PCF*	CF	52309	57309
155 310		*PCF*	CF	52310	57310
155 311		*PCF*	CF	52311	57311
155 312		*PCF*	CF	52312	57312
155 313		*PCF*	CF	52313	57313
155 314		*PCF*	CF	52314	57314
155 315		*PCF*	CF	52315	57315
155 316		*PCF*	CF	52316	57316
155 317		*PCF*	CF	52317	57317
155 318		*PCF*	CF	52318	57318
155 319		*PCF*	CF	52319	57319
155 320		*PCF*	CF	52320	57320
155 321		*PCF*	CF	52321	57321
155 322		*PCF*	CF	52322	57322
155 323		*PCF*	CF	52323	57323
155 324		*PCF*	CF	52324	57324
155 325		*PCF*	CF	52325	57325
155 326		*PCF*	CF	52326	57326
155 327		*PCF*	CF	52327	57327
155 328		*PCF*	CF	52328	57328
155 329		*PCF*	CF	52329	57329
155 330		*PCF*	CF	52330	57330
155 331		*PCF*	CF	52331	57331
155 332		*PCF*	CF	52332	57332
155 333		*PCF*	CF	52333	57333
155 334		*PCF*	CF	52334	57334
155 335		*PCF*	CF	52335	57335
Class 155/1					
155 341		*PNL*	NL	52341	57341
155 342		*PNL*	NL	52342	57342
155 343		*PNL*	NL	52343	57343
155 344		*PNL*	NL	52344	57344
155 345		*PNL*	NL	52345	57345
155 346		*PNL*	NL	52346	57346
155 347		*PNL*	NL	52347	57347

Class 156 — 2-CAR

Built: Metropolitan-Cammell 1987-89

Design Codes	**Type**	**Weight**	**Seats**	**Toilet**	**SC**
DP2.44.0A	DMSA(L)	38.6t	79	1	
DP2.44.—	DMSA(L)	38.6t	79	1	RP
DP2.45.0A	DMSB	37.9t	84		
DP2.45	DMSB	37.9t	84		RP

Driving Motor Standard: DMS(L)
Driving Motor Standard: DMS
Engines: Cummins NT 855R5 of 285hp (213kW)
Transmission: Voith/Gemeinder
Dimensions: 23.05m L × 2.73m W × 3.81m H. Gangwayed throughout

Maximum speed: 75mph
Standard livery: *Provincial Sector* (Blue)
156401-
Special livery: *Strathclyde PTE* (Orange)
156——

Unit No	*SC*	*Pool*	*Dep*	*DMS(L)*	*DMS*
156 401		*PNC*	NC	52401	57401
156 402		*PNC*	NC	52402	57402
156 403		*PNC*	NC	52403	57403
156 404		*PNC*	NC	52404	57404
156 405		*PNC*	NC	52405	57405
156 406		*PNC*	NC	52406	57406
156 407		*PNC*	NC	52407	57407
156 408		*PNC*	NC	52408	57408
156 409		*PNC*	NC	52409	57409
156 410		*PNC*	NC	52410	57410
156 411		*PNC*	NC	52411	57411
156 412		*PNC*	NC	52412	57412
156 413		*PNC*	NC	52413	57413
156 414		*PNC*	NC	52414	57414
156 415		*PNC*	NC	52415	57415
156 416		*PNC*	NC	52416	57416
156 417		*PNC*	NC	52417	57417
156 418		*PNC*	NC	52418	57418
156 419		*PNC*	NC	52419	57419
156 420		*PNC*	NC	52420	57420
156 421		*PNC*	NC	52421	57421
156 422		*PNC*	NC	52422	57422
156 423		*PNC*	NC	52423	57423
156 424		*PNC*	NC	52424	57424
156 425		*PNC*	NC	52425	57425
156 426		*PNC*	NC	52426	57426
156 427		*PNC*	NC	52427	57427
156 428		*PNC*	NC	52428	57428
156 429		*PNC*	NC	52429	57429
156 430		*PCK*	CK	52430	57430
156 431		*PCK*	CK	52431	57431
156 432		*PCK*	CK	52432	57432
156 433		*PCK*	CK	52433	57433
156 434		*PCK*	CK	52434	57434
156 435		*PCK*	CK	52435	57435
156 436		*PCK*	CK	52436	57436
156 437		*PCK*	CK	52437	57437
156 438		*PNC*	NC	52438	57438
156 439		*PCK*	CK	52439	57439
156 440		*PNC*	NC	52440	57440
156 441		*PNL*	NL	52441	57441
156 442		*PCK*	CK	52442	57442
156 443		*PNL*	NL	52443	57443
156 444		*PNL*	NL	52444	57444
156 445		*PIS*	IS	52445	57445
156 446		*PIS*	IS	52446	57446
156 447		*PHA*	HA	52447	57447
156 448		*PIS*	IS	52448	57448
156 449		*PIS*	IS	52449	57449
156 450		*PHA*	HA	52450	57450
156 451		*PIS*	IS	52451	57451
156 452		*PIS*	IS	52452	57452
156 453		*PIS*	IS	52453	57453
156 454		*PIS*	IS	52454	57454
156 455		*PIS*	IS	52455	57455
156 456		*PHA*	HA	52456	57456
156 457		*PIS*	IS	52457	57457
156 458		*PIS*	IS	52458	57458
156 459		*PHA*	HA	52459	57459
156 460		*PIS*	IS	52460	57460
156 461		*PHA*	HA	52461	57461
156 462		*P*		52462	57462
156 463		*P*		52463	57463
156 464		*P*		52464	57464
156 465		*P*		52465	57465
156 466		*P*		52466	57466
156 467		*P*		52467	57467
156 468		*P*		52468	57468
156 469		*P*		52469	57469
156 470		*P*		52470	57470
156 471		*P*		52471	57471
156 472		*P*		52472	57472
156 473		*P*		52473	57473
156 474		*P*		52474	57474
156 475		*P*		52475	57475
156 476		*P*		52476	57476
156 477		*P*		52477	57477
156 478		*P*		52478	57478

Unit No	SC	Pool	Dep	DMS(L)	DMS
156 479		P		52479	57479
156 480		P		52480	57480
156 481		P		52481	57481
156 482		P		52482	57482
156 483		P		52483	57483
156 484		P		52484	57484
156 485		P		52485	57485
~~156 486~~		P		~~52486~~	~~57486~~
~~156 487~~		P		52487	57487
156 488		P		52488	57488
156 489		P		52489	57489
156 490		P		52490	57490
156 491		P		52491	57491
156 492		P		52492	57492
156 493		P		52493	57493
156 494		P		52494	57494
156 495		P		52495	57495
156 496		P		52496	57496
156 497		P		52497	57497
156 498		P		52498	57498
156 499		P		52499	57499
156 500		P		52500	57500
156 501		P		52501	57501
156 502		P		52502	57502
156 503		P		52503	57503
156 504		P		52504	57504
156 505		P		52505	57505
156 506		P		52506	57506
156 507		P		52507	57507
156 508		P		52508	57508
156 509		P		52509	57509
156 510		P		52510	57510
156 511		P		52511	57511
156 512		P		52512	57512
156 513		P		52513	57513
156 514		P		52514	57514

23 METRE EXPRESS SPRINTER UNITS

Class 158 — 2 or 3-CAR

Built: BREL Derby Carriage Works 1989-90
Air conditioning, public address, driver-guard communication, air brakes and AWS fitted

Design Codes	Type	Weight	Seats	Toilet
DP2.51.0A	DMSA	38t	74	1
DP2.52.0A	DMSB	38t	72	1
DR2.07.0A	MS	38t	74	2

All seating is officially classified 'Standard'. Sections may be given embellishments appropriate to areas of operation for a higher category.

Driving Motor Standard: DMSA(L)
Driving Motor Standard: DMSB(L)
Motor Standard: MS(L)
Engines: Cummins NT855R5 of 350hp (275kW)
Transmission: Voith-Gemeinder
Dimensions: 22.16m L × 2.70m W × 3.81m H. Gangwayed throughout
Maximum speed: 90mph

Unit No	SC	Pool	Dep	DMS	MS	DMS(L)
158 601		P		52701		57701
158 602		P		52702		57702
158 603		P		52703		57703
158 604		P		52704		57704
158 605		P		52705		57705
158 606		P		52706		57706
158 607		P		52707		57707
158 608		P		52708		57708
158 609		P		52709		57709
158 610		P		52710		57710

Unit No	SC	Pool	Dep	DMS	DMS(L)
158 611		P		52711	57711
158 612		P		52712	57712
158 613		P		52713	57713
158 614		P		52714	57714
158 615		P		52715	57715
158 616		P		52716	57716
158 617		P		52717	57717
158 618		P		52718	57718
158 619		P		52719	57719
158 620		P		52720	57720
158 621		P		52721	57721
158 622		P		52722	57722
158 623		P		52723	57723
158 624		P		52724	57724
158 625		P		52725	57725
158 626		P		52726	57726
158 627		P		52727	57727
158 628		P		52728	57728
158 629		P		52729	57729
158 630		P		52730	57730
158 631		P		52731	57731
158 632		P		52732	57732
158 633		P		52733	57733
158 634		P		52734	57734
158 635		P		52735	57735
158 636		P		52736	57736
158 637		P		52737	57737
158 638		P		52738	57738
158 639		P		52739	57739
158 640		P		52740	57740
158 641		P		52741	57741
158 642		P		52742	57742
158 643		P		52743	57743
158 644		P		52744	57744
158 645		P		52745	57745
158 646		P		52746	57746
158 647		P		52747	57747
158 648		P		52748	57748
158 649		P		52749	57749
158 650		P		52750	57750
158 651		P		52751	57751
158 652		P		52752	57752
158 653		P		52753	57753
158 654		P		52754	57754
158 655		P		52755	57755
158 656		P		52756	57756
158 657		P		52757	57757
158 658		P		52758	57758
158 659		P		52759	57759
158 660		P		52760	57760
158 661		P		52761	57761
158 662		P		52762	57762
158 663		P		52763	57763
158 664		P		52764	57764
158 665		P		52765	57765
158 666		P		52766	57766
158 667		P		52767	57767
158 668		P		52768	57768
158 669		P		52769	57769
158 670		P		52770	57770
158 671		P		52771	57771
158 672		P		52772	57772
158 673		P		52773	57773
158 674		P		52774	57774
158 675		P		52775	57775
158 676		P		52776	57776
158 677		P		52777	57777
158 678		P		52778	57778
158 679		P		52779	57779
158 680		P		52780	57780
158 681		P		52781	57781
158 682		P		52782	57782
158 683		P		52783	57783
158 684		P		52784	57784
158 685		P		52785	57785
158 686		P		52786	57786
158 687		P		52787	57787
158 688		P		52788	57788
158 689		P		52789	57789
158 690		P		52790	57790
158 691		P		52791	57791
158 692		P		52792	57792
158 693		P		52793	57793
158 694		P		52794	57794
158 695		P		52795	57795
158 696		P		52796	57796
158 697		P		52797	57797
158 698		P		52798	57798
158 699		P		52799	57799
158 700		P		52800	57800
158 701		P		52801	57801
158 702		P		52802	57802
158 703		P		52803	57803
158 704		P		52804	57804

Unit No	*SC*	*Pool*	*Dep*	*DMS(L)*	*DMS*
158 705		*P*		52805	57805
158 706		*P*		52806	57806

Note: MS Vehicle numbers 58701-15. Allocation to units to be advised.

PARCELS SECTOR UNITS

Vehicles listed in this section are those reported allocated to the Director of Parcels Sector. Former passenger stock vehicles are having most, if not all, seating removed.

Some single-car units were purpose-built, others are having major modifications including roller-shutter doors.

Class 101 — Driving Motor

Built: Metropolitan-Cammell 1957, to Parcels stock from 1985

Diagram	**Type**	**Weight**	**Engine**	**Note**
DX5.--.2B	DMLV	32.5t	AEC	Refurbished, Official Diagram DQ2.02.2B
DX5.--.2E	DMLV	32.5t	Leyland	Refurbished, Official Diagram DQ2.02.2E

Engines: Two AEC or Leyland 150bhp (112kW) 6-cyl horizontal
Transmission: Four-speed epicyclic gearbox/ carden shaft
Dimensions: 18.49m L × 2.82m W × 3.85m H. Gangwayed within unit
Maximum speed: 70mph
Brakes: Vacuum

Veh No	*Dia*	*SC*	*Liv*	*Pool*	*Dep*
51430	2E			*RXXN*	CA
51439	2E			*RXXN*	CA
51441	2E			*RXXN*	CA
53218	2B			*RXXN*	CA
53221	2E			*RXXN*	CA
53230	2B			*RXXN*	CA
53233	2E			*RXXN*	CA
53255	2E			*RXXN*	CA

Classes 114 and 114/1 — Driving Motor

Built: British Railways, Derby Carriage Works 1956, conversions from passenger stock

Diagram	**Type**	**Weight**	**Engines**	**Note**
DX5.--.2B	DMLV	38t	Albion	Refurbished, Officially Diagram DQ2.17.2B
DX5.13.0A	DMLV	38t	Albion	Roller Shutter Doors
DX5.13.0B	DMLV	38t	TL11	

Engines: Two Leyland Albion 230hp (172kW) 6-cyl horizontal or Leyland TL11 200hp (152kW)
Dimensions: 20.45m L × 2.35m W × 3.86m H

Maximum speed: 70mph
Brakes: Vacuum
AWS: Fitted

Veh No	*Former Veh No*	*Dia*	*SC*	*Liv*	*Pool*	*Dep*
53004		DX5.--.2B	#		*RXXN*	CA
53020		DX5.--.2B	#		*RXXN*	CA
53027		DX5.--.2B	#		*RXXN*	CA
53035		DX5.--.2B			*RXXN*	CA
53038		DX5.--.2B			*RXXN*	CA
53040		DX5.--.2B			*RXXN*	CA
53046		DX5.--.2B			*RXXN*	CA

Class 114/1

Veh No	*Former Veh No*	*Dia*	*SC*	*Liv*	*Pool*	*Dep*
55930	(53010)	DX5.13.0B		RR	*RXXN*	CA
55931	(53040)	DX5.13.0A		RR	*RXXN*	CA
55932	(53032)	DX5.13.0B			*RXXN*	CA

Class 105 — Driving Motor

Built: Cravens 1956, to Parcels stock from 1985

Diagram	**Type**	**Weight**	**AWS**	**Official Diagram**
DX5.--.0B	DMLV	29.5t	Not fitted	DQ2.07.0B
DX5.--.1B	DMLV	29.5t	Fitted	DQ2.07.1B

Engines: Two Leyland 150bhp (112kW) 6-cyl horizontal
Transmission: Four-speed epicyclic gearbox/carden shaft

Dimensions: 18.50m L × 2.82m W × 3.84m H. Gangwayed within unit
Maximum speed: 70mph
Brakes: Vacuum

Veh No	*Dia*	*SC*	*Liv*	*Pool*	*Dep*
53361	1B			*RXXN*	CA
53364	0B			*RXXN*	CA
53365	0B			*RXXN*	CA
53367	1B			*RXXN*	CA
53368	1B			*RXXN*	CA
53373	1B			*RXXN*	CA

Classes 114 and 114/1 — Driving Trailer

Built: British Railways, Derby Carriage Works 1956, conversions from passenger stock commenced 1986

Class	Diagram	Type	Weight	Toilet	Note
114	DX5.—.3B	DTLV	30t	1	Refurbished, Official Diagram DS3.13.3B
114/1	DX5.14.0A	DTLV	30t	1	Roller Shutter Doors

Dimensions: 20.45m L × 2.35m W × 3.86m H

Maximum speed: 70mph

Brakes: Vacuum

Veh No	*Former Veh No*	*Dia*	*SC*	*Liv*	*Pool*	*Dep*
54028		5.—.3B			*RXXN*	CA
54041		5.—.3B			*RXXN*	CA
54042		5.—.3B			*RXXN*	CA
54900	(54034, 55933)	5.14.0A			*RXXN*	CA
54901	(54016)	5.14.0A		RR	*RXXN*	CA
54902	(54036)	5.14.0A			*RXXN*	CA

Class 127 Driving Motor

Built: British Railways, Derby Carriage Works 1959 as DMBS, converted for parcels and newspaper traffic in 1985

Diagram	Type	Weight
DX5.06.0A	DMLV	40t

Engines: Two Rolls-Royce 238bhp (178kW) 8-cyl horizontal

Transmission: Hydro-Torque convertor

Dimensions: 20.45m L × 2.82m W × 3.87m H. Non-gangwayed, side doors. Shutter blind in place of former brake section doors

AWS: Fitted

Livery: Parcels (Blue with red band)

Special Livery: *Green*: 55966/67

Veh No	*Dia*	*SC*	*Liv*	*Pool*	*Dep*
55966	0A		*	*RXXN*	LO
55967	0A		*	*RXXN*	LO
55968	0A			*RXXN*	LO
55969	0A			*RXXN*	LO
55970	0A			*RXXN*	LO
55971	0A			*RXXN*	LO
55972	0A			*RXXN*	LO
55973	0A			*RXXN*	LO
55975	0A			*RXXN*	LO
55976	0A			*RXXN*	LO
55977	0A			*RXXN*	LO
55978	0A			*RXXN*	LO
55979	0A			*RXXN*	LO
55980	0A			*RXXN*	LO
55981	0A			*RXXN*	LO
55982	0A			*RXXN*	LO
55983	0A			*RXXN*	LO
55984	0A			*RXXN*	LO
55985	0A			*RXXN*	LO
55986	0A			*RXXN*	LO
55987	0A			*RXXN*	LO

Class 128 — Driving Motor Luggage Van

Built: Gloucester RC&W Co 1959

Diagram	Type	Weight
DX5.01.0A	DMLV	41.5t
DX5.02.0B	DMLV	40.5t

Engines: Two Leyland Albion 230hp (172kW) 6-cyl horizontal
Transmission: Four-speed epicyclic gearbox/ carden shaft
Dimensions: 20.45m L × 2.82m W × 3.87m H. Driving cab each end
Maximum speed: 70mph
Brakes: Vacuum
AWS: Fitted
Single car can haul a tail load. 55991/92 only gangwayed throughout blanked off
Livery: Post Office Red

Veh No	*Dia*	*SC*	*Liv*	*Pool*	*Dep*
55991	1.0A		RR	*RXXN*	CA
55992	1.0A		RR	*RXXN*	CA
55993	2.0B		RR	*RXXN*	CA
55994	2.0B		RR	*RXXN*	CA
55995	2.0B		RR	*RXXN*	CA

DIESEL-ELECTRIC MULTIPLE-UNITS

Class 203 (SR 4L)

Built: British Rail, Eastleigh Works, 1957 as six-car units. Present formation introduced in 1986

DMEE Diagram	SR Code	Type	Weight	Seats	Toilet
DB2.02.0A	MAIA	DMBS	56t	30	
DH2.02.0A	SBIA	TS(L)	30.5t	60	2

Driving Motor Brake Standard Saloon: DMBS
Engine: English Electric 4-cyl type 4SRKT Mk II of 500bhp
Dimensions: 20.35m L × 2.82m W × 3.86m H. Gangwayed within unit
Brakes: Electro-Pneumatic
AWS: Fitted
Power/Control equipment: Two nose-suspended, axle-hung, traction motors, main generator English Electric Type 824
Livery: Green

Unit No	*Pool*	*Dep*	*DMBS*	*TS*	*TS*	*DMBS*
203 001	*NKC*	SU	60014	60522	60523	60015

NB: 60014 named *St Leonards*

Class 205 (SR 3H)

Built: British Rail Eastleigh Works 1957 as two-car units, trailer added in 1959

Diagram	SR Code	Type	Weight	Seats 1st	Seats Std	Toilet	SC
DB2.03.0A	NA	DMBS	57t	52			
DB2.04.0A	NA1A	DMBS	57t	42			*
DE3.01.0A	VA/VA1A	DTC(L)	32.5t	13	50	2	
DE3.02.0A	VA1C/VA3C	DTC(L)	32.5t	19	50	2	†
DE3.03.0A	VA2B	DTC(L)	34.5t	13	62	2	*
DH2.03.0A	TA/TA1A	TS	30.5t		104		

Motor Brake Standard: DMBS
Engine: English Electric 4-cyl type 4SRKT Mk II of 600hp
Power/Control equipment: Two nose suspended axle hung traction motors, main generator English Electric Type 824
Dimensions: 20.35m L × 2.82m W × 3.86m H. Non gangwayed

Maximum speed: 75mph
Driving Trailer Composite: DTC(L)
Dimensions: as DMBS
Trailer Standard Semi-Open: TS
Dimensions: 20.82m L × 2.82m W × 3.86m H. Non gangwayed

Unit No	Liv	Pool	Dep	DMBS	TS	DTC
205 001	N	*NKC*	SU	60100	60650	60800
205 002		*NKC*	SU	60101	60651	60801
205 008		*NKC*	SU	60120	60657	60820†
205 009		*NKC*	SU	60108	60658	60808†
205 012		*NKC*	SU	60111	60661	60811†
205 015		*NKC*	SU	60114	60664	60814†
205 016		*NKC*	SU	60115	60665	60815†
205 018		*NKC*	SU	60117	60667	60817†
205 023		*NKC*	SU	60122	60668	60822†
205 024		*NKC*	SU	60123	60669	60823
205 025		*NSS*	EH	60124	60670	60824
205 026		*NSS*	EH	60125	60671	60825
205 027		*NSS*	EH	60145*	60672	60826*
205 028		*NSS*	EH	60146*	60673	60827*
205 029	N	*NSS*	EH	60147*	60674	60828*
205 030		*NSS*	EH	60148*	60675	60829*
205 031		*NSS*	EH	60149*	60676	60830*
205 032		*NSS*	EH	60150*	60677	60831*
205 033		*NSS*	EH	60151*	60678	60832*

Class 205/1 (SR 3H (M))

Built: British Railways Eastleigh Works 1957
Refurbished, gangwayed version of Class 205 (3H).
Details as Class 205 except as follows:

Diagram	SR Code	Type	Weight	Seats	Toilet
DB2.03.1C	MB	DMBS	57t	52	
DE2.04.0A	VA	DTS(L)	32.5t	76	2
DH2.03.1B	SE	TS	30.5t	104	

Driving Motor Brake Standard: DMBS
Driving Trailer Standard: DTS(L)
Trailer Standard Open: TS

Unit No	Liv	Pool	Dep	DMBS	TS	DTC
205 101		*NKC*	SU	60110	60660	60810

Class 207 (SR 3D)

Built: British Railways Eastleigh Works, 1962

Diagram	SR Code	Type	Weight	Seats 1st	Seats Std	Toilet
DB2.05.0A	NB	DMBS	57t	42		
DE2.01.0A	VB	DTS	31.5t	76		
DH3.01.0A	TB	TC	31.5t	24	42	1

Motor Brake Standard Open: DMBS
Power/Control equipment: Two nose-suspended axle-hung traction motors, main generator English Electric type 824
Dimensions: 20.35m L × 2.82m W × 3.86m H. Non gangwayed
Brakes: Electro-Pneumatic
AWS: Fitted

Unit No	Liv	Pool	Dep	DMBS	TS	DTC
207 001		*NSX*	SU	60126	60600	60900
207 002		*NSX*	SU	60127	60601	60901
207 004		*NSX*	SU	60129	60603	60903
207 005		*NSS*	EH	60130	60604	60904
207 010		*NSS*	EH	60135	60609	60909
207 011		*NSX*	SU	60139	60610	60910
207 013		*NSS*	EH	60138	60612	60912
207 017		*NSS*	EH	60142	60616	60916

AC ELECTRIC MULTIPLE-UNITS

Class 302 4-Car

Built: British Railways Doncaster and York 1958
Design: BR non-gangwayed
Some units refurbished and fitted with gangways within unit, public address and driver/guard communication 1984/85 (R); some other units modified to open saloon accommodation (O)
Supply: 6.25 and 25kV ac overhead

Traction Motors (MBS): Four 192hp (140kW) dc English Electric
Maximum speed: 75mph
Dimensions: *Driving coaches:* 20.36m L × 2.82m W × 3.86m H. *Trailer coaches:* 20.18m L × 2.82m W × 3.86m H; 3.98m H Pantograph housed on MBS
AWS: Driving coaches fitted

Diagram	*Type*	*Weight*	*Seats 1st*	*Seats Std*	*Toilet*
Motor Brake Standard:					
ED2.05.0A	MBS. Compartment	55t	—	96	—
ED2.16.2C	MBS. Refurbished	55t	—	76	—
ED2.17.0A	MBS. Open	55t	—	82	—

Driving Trailer Standard:

ED2.05.0A	DTS. Compartment	32.5t	—	108	—
EE2.19.0C	DTS. Refurbished	32.5t	—	88	—
EE2.23.0A	DTS. Open	32.5t	—	92	—
Battery Driving Trailer Standard/Composite:					
EF2.01.0A	BDTS. Open	36.5t	—	80	2
EF2.01.0B	BDTS. Open (o units)	36.5t	—	80	2
EF3.03.0C	BDTC. Refurbished	36t	24	52	1
Trailer Standard/Composite:					
EH2.23.0B	TS. Open	30t	—	86	1
EH2.23.0D	TS. Refurbished	30t	—	86	1
EH3.02.0A	TC. Semi-Open	30.5t	19	60	2

Special Livery: *Dark Green:* 302200

Unit No	(old No)	SC	Liv	Pool	Dep	BDTS	MBS	TC	DTS
						EF201	*ED205*	*EM302*	*EE205*
302200	(302207)		★	*NTS*	EM	75091#	61066	70066	75039
						BDTC	**MBS**	**TS**	**DTS**
						EF303	*ED216*	*EH223*	*EE219*
302201		R		*NTS*	EM	75085	61060	70060	75033
302202		R		*NTS*	EM	75086	61061	70061	75034
302203	(302263)	R		*NTS*	EM	75311	61122	70122	75236
302204		R		*NTS*	EM	75088	61063	70063	75036
302205		R		*NTS*	EM	75089	61064	70064	75037
302206		R		*NTS*	EM	75090	61065	70065	75038
302207	(302310)	R		*NTS*	EM	75358	61226	70226	75283
302208	(302308)	R		*NTS*	EM	75356	61224	70224	75281
302209		R		*NTS*	EM	75093	61068	70068	75041
302210		R		*NTS*	EM	75094	61069	70069	75042
302211		R		*NTS*	EM	75095	61070	70070	75043
302212		R		*NTS*	EM	75096	61071	70071	75044
302213		R		*NTS*	EM	75097	61072	70072	75060
302214	(302304)	R		*NTS*	EM	75352	61220	70220	75277
302215		R		*NTS*	EM	75099	61074	70074	75062
302216		R		*NTS*	EM	75100	61075	70075	75063
302217		R	N	*NTS*	EM	75190	61076	70076	75064
302218		R		*NTS*	EM	75191	61077	70077	75065
302219		R		*NTS*	EM	75192	61078	70078	75066
302220		R		*NTS*	EM	75193	61079	70079	75067
302221		R		*NTS*	EM	75194	61080	70080	75068
302222		R		*NTS*	EM	75195	61081	70081	75069
302223	(302293)	R		*NTS*	EM	75341	61209	70209	75266
302224		R		*NTS*	EM	75197	61083	70083	75071
302225		R		*NTS*	EM	75198	61084	70084	75072
302226		R		*NTS*	EM	75199	61085	70085	75073
302227	(302277)	R		*NTS*	EM	75325	61193	70193	75250
302228		R		*NTS*	EM	75201	61087	70087	75075
302229		R		*NTS*	EM	75202	61088	70088	75076

Unit No	(old No)	SC	Liv	Pool	Dep	BDTC	MBS	TS	DTS
302230	(302232)	R		*NTS*	EM	75205	61091	70091	75079

Unit No	(old No)	SC	Liv	Pool	Dep	BDTC	MBS	TS	DTS
						EF201	*ED205*	*EH302*	*EE205*
		0				*EF201*	*ED217*	*EH302*	*EE223*
302231				*NGE*	IL	75204#	61090	70090	75078
302234		0		*NGE*	IL	75207#	61093#	70120	75081
302235				*NSP*	ILs	75208#	61100#	70094	75082
302237				*NSP*	ILs	75333#	61096#	70096	75084
302238				*NSP*	PQs	75360	61097#	70112	75226
302239		0		*NGE*	IL	75287	61098#	70125	75272#
302241				*NGE*	IL	75289#	61094#	70100	75214
302243				*NSP*	PQs	75291#	61102#	70102	75216
302244				*NGE*	IL	75298#	61103#	70103	75217
302245		0		*NTS*	IL	75293#	61104#	70104	75218
302246				*NTS*	IL	75294#	61105#	70105	75219
302247				*NSP*	PQs	75295#	61106#	70106	75220
302248				*NSP*	PQs	75296#	61107#	70107	75221
302249				*NGE*	EM	75297#	61108#	70108	75222
302250	(302300)	0		*NTS*	EM	75348#	61216#	70216	75273#
302251		0		*NTS*	EM	75299#	61110#	70110	75224#
302252		0		*NTS*	IL	75300#	61111#	70111	75225#
302253	(302301)	0		*NTS*	EM	75349#	61217#	70217	75274#
302254		0		*NTS*	EM	75302#	61113#	70113	75227#
302255	(302303)	0		*NTS*	EM	75351#	61219#	70219	75276#
302256		0		*NGE*	IL	75304#	61115#	70115	75229#
302257				*NGE*	IL	75305#	61116#	70116	75230#
302258				*NGE*	IL	75326#	61117#	70117	75231#
302259		0		*NGE*	IL	75307#	61118#	70195#	75232#
302260	(302302)			*NTS*	EM	75321#	61218#	70132#	75246#
302261		0		*NTS*	EM	75309#	61120#	70073	75234#
302262		0		*NTS*	EM	75310	61121#	70131	75235#
302264				*NTS*	EM	75312#	61123#	70123	75254
302265				*NGE*	IL	75313#	61124#	70124	75238#
302267	(302307)			*NTS*	EM	75355#	61223	70223	75280#
302268				*NGE*	IL	75315#	61127#	70127#	75241#
302269				*NGE*	IL	75342#	61128#	70128#	75242#
302270				*NTS*	EM	75318#	61129#	70129#	75243#
302272		0		*NTS*	EM	75320#	61131#	70086#	75245#
302273	(302306)	0		*NTS*	EM	75354#	61222	70202	75279#
302274		0		*NTS*	EM	75322#	61190#	70190#	75247#
302275	(302311)	0		*NTS*	EM	75359#	61227	70227	75284#
302276	(302208)			*NGE*	IL	75092#	61067	70067	75040
302278				*NTS*	EM	75306#	61194#	70194#	75251#
302280		0		*NTS*	EM	75328#	61196#	70196#	75253#
302282				*NTS*	EM	75329#	61198#	70198	75255#
302283		0		*NGE*	IL	75331#	61199#	70130#	75256#

Unit No	(old No)	SC	Liv	Pool	Dep	BDTC	MBS	TS	DTS
302284		0		*NTS*	EM	75332#	61200#	70200	75257#
302285		0		*NGE*	IL	75210#	61201#	70201	75258#
302286				*NTS*	EM	75334#	61202#	70222	75259#
302289				*NGE*	IL	75337#	61205#	70205	75262#
302290				*NGE*	IL	75338#	61206#	70206	75263#
302291				*NSP*	PQs	75339#	61207#	70207	75264#
302292		0		*NTS*	EM	75340	61208	70208	75265
302295				*NSP*	PQs	75343#	61211#	70211	75268#
302296		0		*NTS*	EM	75344#	61212#	70212	75269#
302298		0		*NTS*	EM	75346#	61214#	70214	75271#

Class 302/1 — 3-Car (PCLS)

To be introduced 1989 using non-asbestos insulated coaches converted for conveyance of mail and parcels traffic.

Unit No	Liv	Pool	Dep	BDTV	MBV	DTV
302 ---		*REMA*	IL	—	—	—
302 ---		*REMA*	IL	—	—	—
302 ---		*REMA*	IL	—	—	—

Class 303 — 3-Car

Built: Pressed Steel 1959
Design: BR saloons with sliding doors. Non-gangwayed, unless shown (G). Gangwayed units equipped with public address equipment
Supply: 25kV ac overhead
Traction motors (MBS): Four 207hp (155kW) dc AEI (MV)
Maximum speed: 75mph
Dimensions: 20.18m L × 2.82m W × 3.86m H; 3.98m H Pantograph housed
AWS: Driving coaches fitted

Diagram	*Type*	*Weight*	*Seats*
Motor Brake Standard:			
ED2.01.0A	MBS	56t	70
ED2.--.--	MBS (G)	56t	48
Driving Trailer Standard:			
EE2.06.0A	DTS	34.5t	83
EE2.--.--	DTS (G)	34.5t	56
Battery Driving Trailer Standard:			
EF2.02.0A	BDTS	38t	83
EF2.--.--	BDTS (G)	38t	56

(No Diagram officially issued for Gangwayed units).

Unit No	SC	Liv	Pool	Dep	DTS *EE2*	MBS *ED2*	BDTS *EF2*
303 001	MG	S	*PGW*	GW	75566	61481	75601
303 003	MG	S	*PGW*	GW	75568	61483	75603
303 004	MG	S	*PGW*	GW	75569	61484	75604
303 005	M		*PGW*	GW	75570	61485	75605
303 006	MG	S	*PGW*	GW	75571	61486	75606

Unit No	SC	Liv	Pool	Dep	DTS	MBS	BDTS
303 008	MG	S	*PGW*	GW	75573	61488	75608
303 009	MG	S	*PGW*	GW	75574	61489	75609
303 010	MG	S	*PGW*	GW	75575	61490	75610
303 011	MG	S	*PGW*	GW	75576	61491	75611
303 012	MG	S	*PGW*	GW	75577	61492	75612
303 013	MG	S	*PGW*	GW	75578	61493	75613
303 014	MG	S	*PGW*	GW	75579	61494	75614
303 016	MG	S	*PGW*	GW	75581	61496	75616
303 019	MG	S	*PGW*	GW	75584	61499	75619
303 020	MG	S	*PGW*	GW	75585	61500	75620
303 021	MG	S	*PGW*	GW	75586	61501	75621
303 023	MG	S	*PGW*	GW	75588	61503	75623
303 024	MG	S	*PGW*	GW	75589	61504	75624
303 025	MG	S	*PGW*	GW	75590	61505	75625
303 027	MG	S	*PGW*	GW	75592	61507	75627
303 028	MG	S	*PGW*	GW	75600	61508	75635
303 029	M	S	*PGW*	GW	75594	61509	75629
303 032	MG	S	*PGW*	GW	75597	61512	75632
303 033	MG	S	*PGW*	GW	75595	61860	75817
303 034	MG	S	*PGW*	GW	75599	61514	75634
303 036		M	*PLG*	LG	75746	61812	75802
303 037	MG	S	*PGW*	GW	75747	61813	75803
303 038	MG	S	*PGW*	GW	75748	61814	75804
303 039	M	S	*PGW*	GW	75749	61815#	75805
303 040	MG	S	*PGW*	GW	75750	61816	75806
303 041		M	*PLG*	LG	75751	61817	75807
303 042	M	S	*PGW*	GW	75752	61818	75808
303 043	MG	S	*PGW*	GW	75572	61819	75809
303 045	MG	S	*PGW*	GW	75755	61821	75811
303 046	MG	S	*PGW*	GW	75756	61822	75812
303 047	MG	S	*PGW*	GW	75757	61823	75813
303 048		M	*PLG*	LG	75758	61824	75814
303 049		M	*PLG*	LG	75759	61825	75815
303 050		M	*PLG*	LG	75760	61826	75816
303 052		S	*PGW*	GW	75762	61828	75818
303 053		M	*PLG*	LG	75763	61829	75819
303 054	MG	S	*PGW*	GW	75764	61830	75820
303 055	MG	S	*PGW*	GW	75765	61831	75821
303 056	MG	S	*PGW*	GW	75766	61832	75822
303 057		M	*PLG*	LG	75767	61833	75823
303 058	MG	S	*PGW*	GW	75768	61834	75824
303 060		M	*PLG*	LG	75770	61836	75826
303 061	MG	S	*PGW*	GW	75771	61837	75827
303 062	M		*PGW*	GW	75772	61838	75828
303 063	M	S	*PGW*	GW	75773	61839	75829
303 065	MG	S	*PGW*	GW	75775	61841	75831
303 066		M	*PLG*	LG	75776	61842	75832

Unit No	SC	Liv	Pool	Dep	DTS	MBS	BDTS
303 067		M	*PLG*	LG	75777	61843	75833
303 068		S	*PGW*	GW	75596	61844#	75834
303 069	M	S	*PGW*	GW	75779	61845	75607
303 070	MG	S	*PGW*	GW	75780	61846	75836
303 071	MG	S	*PGW*	GW	75781	61847	75837
303 072		S	*PGW*	GW	75782	61848	75838
303 073	MG	S	*PGW*	GW	75783	61849	75839
303 075	M	S	*PGW*	GW	75785	61851	75841
303 076	M	S	*PGW*	GW	75786	61852	75842
303 077	MG	S	*PGW*	GW	75787	61853	75843
303 078		M	*PLG*	LG	75788	61854	75844
303 079	MG	S	*PGW*	GW	75789	61855	75845
303 080	MG	S	*PGW*	GW	75790	61856	75846
303 082		M	*PLG*	LG	75792	61858	75848
303 083	MG	S	*PGW*	GW	75793	61859	75849
303 085	MG	S	*PGW*	GW	75795	61861	75851
303 086		S	*PGW*	GW	75796	61862#	75852
303 087	MG	S	*PGW*	GW	75797	61863	75853
303 088	MG	S	*PGW*	GW	75798	61864	75854
303 089	MG	S	*PGW*	GW	75799	61865	75855
303 090	MG	S	*PGW*	GW	75800	61866	75856
303 091	MG	S	*PGW*	GW	75801	61867	75857

Class 304 — 3-Car

Built: British Railways Wolverton 1960/61
Design: BR, non-gangwayed saloons
Supply: 25kV ac overhead
Traction motors (MBS): Four 207hp (155kW) dc AEI (BTH)
Maximum speed: 75mph
Dimensions: *Driving coaches:* 20.31m L × 2.82m W × 3.88m H; *MBS:* 20.17m L × 2.82m W × 3.98m H Pantograph housed
AWS: Driving coaches fitted

Diagram	*Type*	*Weight*	*Seats*	*Toilets*
Motor Brake Standard:				
ED2.03.0A	MBS	56t	72	—
ED2.15.0A	MBS	54.5t	82	—
Battery Driving Trailer Standard:				
EF2.03.0A	BDTS	36t	80	2
EF2.04.0A	BDTS	37t	80	2
Driving Trailer Brake Standard:				
EG2.02.0A	DTBS	32t	82	—
EG2.03.0A	DTBS	32.5t	82	—

Unit No	Pool	Dep	DTBS	MBS	BDTS
			EG202	*ED215*	*EF223*
304 001	*PLG*	LG	75645	61045	75045
304 002	*PLG*	LG	75646	61046	75046
304 003	*PLG*	LG	75647	61047	75047
304 004	*PLG*	LG	75648	61048	75048
304 005	*PLG*	LG	75649	61049	75049
304 006	*PLG*	LG	75650	61050	75050
304 007	*PLG*	LG	75651	61051	75051
304 008	*PLG*	LG	75652	61052	75052
304 009	*PLG*	LG	75653	61053	75053
304 010	*PLG*	LG	75654	61054	75054
304 011	*PLG*	LG	75655	61055	75055
304 012	*PLG*	LG	75656	61056	75056

Unit No	Pool	Dep	DTBS	MBS	BDTS
304 013	*PLG*	LG	75657	61057	75057
304 014	*PLG*	LG	75658	61058	75058
304 015	*PLG*	LG	75659	61059	75059
			EG203	*ED203*	*EF204*
304 016	*PLG*	LG	75660	61628	75680
304 017	*PLG*	LG	75661	61629	75681
304 019	*PLG*	LG	75663	61631	75683
304 020	*PLG*	LG	75664	61632	75684
304 021	*PLG*	LG	75665	61633	75685
304 023	*PLG*	LG	75667	61635	75687
304 024	*PLG*	LG	75668	61636	75688
304 027	*PLG*	LG	75671	61639	75691
304 028	*PLG*	LG	75672	61640	75692
304 029	*PLG*	LG	75673	61641	75693
304 030	*PLG*	LG	75674	61642	75694
304 032	*PLG*	LG	75676	61644	75696
304 033	*PLG*	LG	75677	61645	75697
304 034	*PLG*	LG	75678	61646	75698
304 035	*PLG*	LG	75679	61647	75699
304 036	*PLG*	LG	75858	61873	75868
304 037	*PLG*	LG	75859	61874	75869
304 039	*PLG*	LG	75861	61876	75871
304 040	*PLG*	LG	75862	61877	75872
304 041	*PLG*	LG	75863	61878	75873
304 042	*PLG*	LG	75864	61879	75874
304 043	*PLG*	LG	75865	61880	75875
304 045	*PLG*	LG	75867	61882	75877

Class 305/1 — 3-Car

Built: British Railways, York 1960
Design: BR, non-gangwayed saloons
Supply: 6.25 and 25kV ac overhead
Traction motors (MBS): Four 200p (150kW) dc GEC
Maximum speed: 75mph
Dimensions: *Driving coaches:* 20.36m L × 2.82m W × 3.84m H; *MBS:* 20.27m L × 2.82m W × 3.98m H Pantograph housed
AWS: Driving coaches fitted

Diagram	*Type*	*Weight*	*Seats*
Motor Brake Standard:			
ED2.04.0B	MBS	55t	82
Driving Trailer Standard:			
EE2.09.0B	DTS	31.5t	92
Battery Driving Trailer Standard:			
EF2.05.0A	BDTS	35t	92

Unit No	SC	Pool	Dep	BDTS	MBS	DTS
				EF205	*ED204*	*EE209*
305 401	F	*NNE*	IL	75462	61429	75514
305 402	F	*NNE*	IL	75463	61430	75515
305 403	F	*NNE*	IL	75506	61473	75558
305 404	F	*NNE*	IL	75508	61475	75560
305 405	F	*NNE*	IL	75466	61433	75518
305 406	F	*NNE*	IL	75467	61434	75519
305 407	F	*NNE*	IL	75468	61435	75520
305 408	F	*NNE*	IL	75469	61436	75521
305 409	F	*NNE*	IL	75470	61437	75522
305 410	F	*NNE*	IL	75471	61438	75523
305 411	F	*NNE*	IL	75509	61476	75561
305 412	F	*NNE*	IL	75473	61440	75525
305 413	F	*NNE*	IL	75474	61441	75526
305 414	F	*NNE*	IL	75510	61477	75562
305 415	F	*NNE*	IL	75476	61443	75528
305 416	F	*NNE*	IL	75477	61444	75529
305 417	F	*NNE*	IL	75478	61445	75530
305 418		*NNE*	IL	75479	61446	75531
305 419	F	*NNE*	IL	75511	61478	75563
305 420	F	*NNE*	IL	75481	61448	75533
305 421	F	*NNE*	IL	75482	61449	75534
305 422	F	*NNE*	IL	75513	61480	75565

Class 305/2 4-Car

Built: British Railways, Doncaster 1960
Design: BR Saloons, gangwayed within set
Supply: 6.25 and 25kV ac
Traction Motors: Four 205hp (154kW) dc GEC
Maximum speed: 75mph
AWS: All driving coaches fitted
All units refurbished and fitted with public address system and driver/guard communications
Dimensions: *Driving coaches:* 19.88m L × 2.82m W × 3.86m H; *Trailer coaches:* 20.18m L × 2.82m W × 3.86m H; 3.98m H Pantograph housed

Diagram	*Type*	*Weight*	*Seats 1st*	*Seats Std*	*Toilet*
Motor Brake Standard:					
ED2.16.0A	MBS	55t	—	76	—
Driving Trailer Standard:					
EE2.20.0A	DTS	33t	—	88	—
Battery Driving Trailer Composite:					
EF3.04.0A	BDTC	36t	24	52	1
Trailer Standard:					
EH2.23.0A	TS	30t	—	86	1

Unit No	SC	Pool	Dep	DTS *EE220*	TS *EH223*	MBS *ED216*	BDTC *EF304*
305 501		*NNE*	IL	75443	70356	61410	75424
305 502		*NTS*	EM	75444	70357	61421	75425
305 503		*NTS*	EM	75445	70358	61412	75426
305 504		*NTS*	EM	75446	70359	61413	75427
305 505		*NTS*	EM	75447	70360	61414	75435
305 506		*NTS*	EM	75448	70361	61415	75429
305 507		*NTS*	EM	75449	70362	61416	75430
305 508		*NTS*	EM	75450	70363	61417	75431
305 509		*NTS*	EM	75451	70364	61418	75432
305 510		*NTS*	EM	75452	70365	61419	75433
305 511		*NTS*	EM	75453	70366	61420	75434
305 513		*NNE*	IL	75455	70368	61422	75436
305 514		*NNE*	IL	75456	70369	61423	75437
305 515		*NNE*	IL	75457	70370	61424	75438
305 516		*NNE*	IL	75458	70371	61425	75439
305 517		*NNE*	IL	75459	70372	61426	75440
305 518		*NNE*	IL	75460	70373	61427	75441
305 519		*NNE*	IL	75461	70374	61428	75442

Class 305/3 4-Car

Built: British Railways, York 1960. This sub-Class introduced 1988, formed from Class 305/1 units plus TC from Class 302 units (see above for full details). All units facelifted

Diagram	*Type*	*Weight*	*Seats 1st*	*Seats Std*	*Toilet*
Motor Brake Standard:					
ED2.04.0B	MBS	55t	—	82	—
Driving Trailer Standard:					
EE2.09.0B	DTS	33.5t	—	92	—
Battery Driving Trailer Standard:					
EF2.05.0A	BDTS	35t	—	92	—
Trailer Composite:					
EH3.--.-- (No Diagram issued)	TC	30.5t	19	59	1

Unit No	Pool	Dep	BDTS	MBS	TC	DTS
			EF205	*ED204*	*EH3--*	*EE209*
305 521	*NTS*	EM	75464	61431	70098	75516
305 522	*NTS*	EM	75465	61432	70099	75517
305 523	*NTS*	EM	75472	61439	70221	75524
305 524	*NTS*	EM	75475	61442	70118	75527
305 525	*NTS*	EM	75480	61447	70213	75532
305 526	*NTS*	EM	75483	61450	70093	75535
305 527	*NTS*	EM	75507	61474	70204	75559
305 528	*NTS*	EM	75512	61479	70210	75564

Class 306 — 3-Car

Built: Metro-Cammell/BRCW 1949
Design: LNER, Sliding doors, non-gangwayed
Supply: 6.25 and 25kV ac overhead
Traction motors (DMS): Four 207hp (155kW) dc Crompton Parkinson
Maximum speed: 70mph
Special Livery: BR Green

Diagram	*Type*	*Weight*	*Seats*
Driving Motor Standard: *Dimensions:* 19.24m L × 2.82m W × 3.84m H			
EA2.03.0A	DMS	52t	62
Trailer Brake Standard: *Dimensions:* 17.40m L × 2.95m W × 3.98m H Pantograph housed			
EJ2.01.0A	TBS	27t	46
Driving Trailer Standard: *Dimensions:* 19.24m L × 2.82m W × 3.84m H			
EE2.11.0A	DTS	28t	60

Unit No	Pool	Dep	DMS	TBS	DTS
306 017	*NCH*	IL	65217	65417	65617

Note: Unit is available for special hire work only. At all other times it is securely housed at Ilford ETMD.

Class 307 — 4-Car

Built: British Railways, Eastleigh 1956, rebuilt for ac 1960. Refurbished 1981
Design: BR, gangwayed within unit. All units fitted with public address system and driver-guard communication
Supply: 6.25 and 25kV ac overhead
Traction Motors: Four 174hp (130kW) dc GEC
Maximum speed: 75mph
AWS: All driving coaches fitted
Dimensions: *Driving coaches:* 20.31m L × 2.82m W × 3.86m H; *Trailer coaches:* 20.18m L × 2.82m W × 3.86m H 3.98m H Pantograph housed

Diagram	*Type*	*Weight*	*Seats 1st*	*Seats Std*	*Toilet*
Motor Standard:					
EC2.04.0B	MS	47.5t	—	98	—
Driving Trailer Composite:					
EE3.07.0B	DTC	33t	24	52	1
Trailer Standard:					
EH2.22.0B	TS	31t	—	86	1
Battery Driving Trailer Brake Standard:					
EO2.02.0B	BDBS	43t	—	66	—

Unit No	Liv	Pool	Dep	BDBS	MS	TS	DTC
				EO202	*EC204*	*EH222*	*EE307*
307 101		*NGE*	IL	75001	61001	70001	75101
307 102	N	*NGE*	IL	75002	61002	70002	75102
~~307 103~~		*NGE*	IL	75003	61003	70003	75103
307 104		*NGE*	IL	75004	61004	70004	75104
307 105	N	*NGE*	IL	75005	61005	70005	75105
307 106	N	*NGE*	IL	75006	61006	70006	75106
307 107		*NGE*	IL	75007	61007	70007	75107
307 108		*NGE*	IL	75008	61008	70008	75108
307 109		*NGE*	IL	75009	61009	70009	75109
307 110		*NGE*	IL	75010	61010	70010	75110
307 111		*NGE*	IL	75011	61011	70011	75111
307 112		*NGE*	IL	75012	61012	70012	75112
307 113		*NGE*	IL	75013	61013	70013	75113
~~307 114~~		*NGE*	IL	75014	61014	70014	75114
307 115		*NGE*	IL	75015	61015	70015	75115
307 116		*NGE*	IL	75016	61016	70016	75116
307 117	N	*NGE*	IL	75017	61017	70017	75117
307 118		*NGE*	IL	75018	61018	70018	75118
~~307 119~~		*NGE*	IL	75019	61019	70019	75119
307 120		*NGE*	IL	75020	61020	70020	75120
307 121		*NGE*	IL	75021	61021	70021	75121
307 122	N	*NGE*	IL	75022	61022	70022	75122
307 123		*NGE*	IL	75023	61023	70023	75123
307 124		*NGE*	IL	75024	61024	70024	75124
307 125		*NGE*	IL	75025	61025	70025	75125
307 126	N	*NGE*	IL	75026	61026	70026	75126
307 127		*NGE*	IL	75027	61027	70027	75127
307 128		*NGE*	IL	75028	61028	70028	75128
~~307 129~~		*NGE*	IL	75029	61029	70029	75129
307 130	N	*NGE*	IL	75030	61030	70030	75130
307 131		*NGE*	IL	75031	61031	70031	75131
~~307 132~~	N	*NGE*	IL	75032	61032	70032	75132

Class 308/1 — 4-Car

Built: British Railways, 1961
Design: BR gangwayed within set. All units refurbished. (See Class 305/2 for full details.)

Diagram	*Type*	*Weight*	*Seats 1st*	*Seats Std*	*Toilet*
Motor Brake Standard:					
ED2.16.1B	MBS	55t	—	76	—
Driving Trailer Standard:					
EE2.20.0B	DTS	33t	—	88	—
Battery Driving Trailer Composite:					
EF3.04.0B	BDTC	36t	24	52	1
Trailer Standard:					
EH2.23.0A	TS	30t	—	86	1†
EH2.23.0B	TS	30t	—	86	1

† Class 305/2 vehicle

Unit No	Pool	Dep	BDTC	MBS	TS	DTS
			EF304	*ED216*	*EH223*	*EE220*
308 133	*NGE*	IL	75878	61883	70611	75887
308 134	*NGE*	IL	75879	61884	70612	75888
308 135	*NGE*	IL	75880	61885	70613	75889
308 136	*NGE*	IL	75881	61886	70614	75890
~~308 137~~	*NGE*	IL	75882	61887	70615	75891
~~308 138~~	*NGE*	IL	75883	61888	70367†	75892
~~308 139~~	*NGE*	IL	75884	61889	70617	75893
308 140	*NTS*	EM	75885	61890	70618	75894
308 141	*NTS*	EM	75886	61891	70619	75895
308 142	*NTS*	EM	75896	61892	70620	75929
308 143	*NTS*	EM	75897	61893	70621	75930
~~308 144~~	*NTS*	EM	75898	61894	70622	75931
~~308 145~~	*NTS*	EM	75899	61895	70623	75932
~~308 146~~	*NTS*	EM	75900	61896	70624	75933
308 147	*NTS*	EM	75901	61897	70625	75934
308 148	*NTS*	EM	75902	61898	70626	75935
308 149	*NTS*	EM	75903	61899	70627	75936
308 150	*NTS*	EM	75904	61900	70628	75937

Unit No	Pool	Dep	BDTC	MBS	TS	DTS
308 151	*NTS*	EM	75905	61901	70629	75938
308 152	*NTS*	EM	75906	61902	70630	75939
308 153	*NTS*	EM	75907	61903	70631	75940
308 154	*NTS*	EM	75908	61904	70632	75941
308 155	*NTS*	EM	75909	61905	70633	75942
308 156	*NTS*	EM	75910	61906	70634	75943
308 157	*NTS*	EM	75911	61907	70635	75944
308 158	*NTS*	EM	75912	61908	70636	75945
308 159	*NTS*	EM	75913	61909	70637	75946
308 160	*NTS*	EM	75914	61910	70638	75947
308 161	*NTS*	EM	75915	61911	70639	75948
308 162	*NTS*	EM	75916	61912	70640	75949
308 163	*NTS*	EM	75917	61913	70641	75950
308 164	*NTS*	EM	75918	61914	70642	75951
308 165	*NTS*	EM	75919	61915	70643	75952

Class 308/2 — 3-Car (PLCS)

Built: British Railways, 1961. To parcels stock use in 1984 by conversion of DTS to DTLV. Seating not for public use
Design: BR non-gangwayed
Power Supply: 6.25 and 25kV ac

Traction Motors (MLV): Four 192hp (144kW) dc English Electric
Maximum speed: 75mph
AWS: Driving vehicles fitted

Diagram	Type	Weight	Seats	Toilets	Dimensions: L × W × H (m)
Battery Driving Trailer Standard					
EF2.01.0A	BDTS	36.5t	80	2	20.36 × 2.82 × 3.86
EF2.08.0A	BDTS	36.5t	80	2	20.18 × 2.82 × 3.86
Driving Trailer Luggage Van					
EW5.01.0A	DTLV	32t	—		20.36 × 2.82 × 3.86
Motor Luggage Van					
EY5.01.0A	MLV	53t	—		20.18 × 2.82 × 3.98 Pantograph housed

Unit No	Pool	Dep	DTLV	MLV	BDTS
			EW501	*EY501*	*EF208*
308 993	*REMA*	IL	75959	68017	75926
308 994	*REMA*	IL	75960	68018	—
			EW501	*EY501*	*EF201*
308 995	*REMA*	IL	75961	68012	75347

Class 309 — Essex Express 4-Car

Built: British Railways York, 1962
Design: BR, gangwayed throughout. All units refurbished and fitted with public address system
Supply: 6.25 and 25kV ac

Traction Motors: Four 282hp (210kW) dc GEC
Maximum speed: 100mph
AWS: All driving vehicles fitted
Dimensions: 20.18m L × 2.82m W × 3.90m H

Diagram	*Type*	*Weight*	*Seats 1st*	*Seats Std*	*Toilet*	
Driving Motor Brake Standard:						
EB2.07.0A	DMBS	60.5t	—	48	—	Catering Trolley point
Motor Brake Standard:						
ED2.18.0A	MBS	57t	—	48	—	Catering Trolley point
Driving Trailer Standard:						
EE2.29.0A	DTS	32t	—	56	2	
Battery Driving Trailer Standard:						
EF2.16.0A	BDTS	41t	—	60	2	
Battery Driving Trailer Composite:						
EF3.05.0A	BDTC	37.5t	18	32	2	
Trailer Standard/Composite:						
EH2.27.0A	TS	35t	—	64	2	
EH2.28.0A	TS	35t	—	68	—	
EH2.29.0A	TS	35t	—	68	—	
EH3.09.0A	TC	36t	24	28	1	

Class 309/1

Unit No	**Liv**	**Pool**	**Dep**	**DMBS**	**TC**	**TS**	**BDTS**
				EB207	*EH309*	*EH227*	*EF216*
309 601	N	*NGE*	CC	61940	71573	71569	75984
309 602	N	*NGE*	CC	61941	71574	71570	75985
309 603	N	*NGE*	CC	61942	71575	71571	75986
309 604	N	*NGE*	CC	61943	71576	71572	75987
309 605	N	*NGE*	CC	61944	71111	71107	75988
~~309 606~~	N	*NGE*	CC	61945	71112	71108	75989
309 607	N	*NGE*	CC	61946	71113	71109	75990
309 608	N	*NGE*	CC	61947	71114	71110	75991

Class 309/3

Unit No	**Liv**	**Pool**	**Dep**	**BDTC**	**MBS**	**TS**	**DTS**
				EF305	*ED218*	*EH228*	*EE229*
~~309 611~~	N	*NGE*	CC	75637	61932	71754	75976
~~309 612~~	E	*NGE*	CC	75638	61933	71755	75977
~~309 613~~	N	*NGE*	CC	75639	61934∅	71756	75978
~~309 614~~	N	*NGE*	CC	75640	61935	71757	75979
~~309 615~~	N	*NGE*	CC	75641	61936	71758	75980
~~309 616~~	N	*NGE*	CC	75642	61937∅	71759	75981
309 617	N	*NGE*	CC	75643	61938∅	71760	75982
~~309 618~~	N	*NGE*	CC	75644	61939∅	71761	75983
				EF305	*ED218*	*EH229*	*EE229*
~~309 621~~	N	*NGE*	CC	75962	61925	70253	75969
~~309 622~~	N	*NGE*	CC	75963	61926	70254	75970
~~309 623~~	N	*NGE*	CC	75964	61927	70255	75971
309 624	N	*NGE*	CC	75965	61928	70256	75972

Unit No	Liv	Pool	Dep	BDTC	MBS	TS	DTS
309 625	N	*NGE*	CC	75966	61929	70257	75973
~~309 626~~	N	*NGE*	CC	75967	61930	70258	75974
~~309 627~~	N	*NGE*	CC	75968	61931	70259	75975

Class 310 — 4-Car

Built: British Railways Derby, 1965
Design: BR, driving trailers are gangwayed to adjacent vehicle. G=gangwayed within unit, F=Facelifted, interior restyled and public address system fitted as shown
Supply: 25kV ac overhead
Traction Motors: Four 270hp (202kW) dc English Electric

Maximum speed: 75mph
AWS: Fitted to driving vehicles
Dimensions: 20.18m L × 2.82m W *Height:* EF2.14 & all TS: 3.83m; EF2.10, EF2.11, DTS & DTC: 3.86m; MBS: 3.98m Pantograph housed

Diagram	*Type*	*Weight*	*Seats 1st*	*Std*	*Toilet*	
Motor Brake Standard:						
ED2.10.0A	MBS	57t	—	70		
ED2.10.--*	MBS	57t	—	70	—	Facelifted
ED2.19.0A	MBS	57t	—	70	—	Through Gangway
ED2.19.1B	MBS	57t	—	70	—	Through Gangway
Driving Trailer Standard/Composite:						
EE2.37.0A	DTS	34.5t	—	75	2	Facelifted
EE3.06.0A	DTC	34.5t	25	43	2	
EE3.06.1B	DTC	34.5t	25	43	2	Facelifted
Battery Driving Trailer Standard:						
EF2.10.1B	BDTS	34.5t	—	68	2	Facelifted
EF2.11.0A	BDTS	37.5t	—	80	2	
EF2.11.1B	BDTS	37.5t	—	80	2	Facelifted
EF2.11.2C	BDTS	37.5t	—	80	2	
EF2.14.1B	BDTS	35t	—	75	2	Facelifted
Trailer Standard:						
EH2.08.0A	TS	31.5t	—	100	—	
EH2.08.--*	TS	31.5t	—	100	—	Facelifted
EH2.32.0A	TS	31.5t	—	98	—	Through Gangway
EH2.32.1B	TS	31.5t	—	98	—	Through Gangway

*Official diagrams not issued

Class 310/0

Unit No	SC	Liv	Pool	Dep	BDTS *EF21*	MBS *ED21*	TS *EH2*	DTC *EE306*
310 046	GF	N	*NGE*	EM	76130 *11B*	62071 *90A*	70731 *320A*	76180 *1B*
310 047	GF	N	*NGE*	EM	76131 *11B*	62072 *90A*	70732 *320A*	76181 *1B*

Unit No	SC	Liv	Pool	Dep	BDTS	MBS	TS	DTC
310 048†			*PBY*	BY	76132 *10A*	62073 *00A*	70733 *080A*	76182 *0A*
310 049		N	*NGE*	EM	76133 *10A*	62074 *00A*	70734 *080A*	76183 *0A*
310 050	GF	N	*NNE*	EM	76134 *11B*	62075 *90A*	70735 *320A*	76184 *1B*
310 051			*NNW*	BY	76135 *10A*	62076 *00A*	70736 *080A*	76185 *0A*
310 052	GF	N	*NNE*	EM	76136 *11B*	62077 *90A*	70737 *320A*	76186 *1B*
310 053†			*PBY*	BY	76137 *10A*	62078 *00A*	70738 *080A*	76187 *0A*
310 054†			*PBY*	BY	76138 *10A*	62079 *00A*	70739 *080A*	76188 *0A*
310 056	GF	N	*NGE*	EM	76140 *11B*	62081 *00A*	70741 *080A*	76190 *1B*
310 057		N	*NGE*	EM	76141 *10A*	62082 *00A*	70742 *080A*	76191 *0A*
310 058	GF	N	*NGE*	EM	76142 *11B*	62083 *90A*	70743 *320A*	76192 *1B*
310 059	GF	N	*NGE*	EM	76143 *11B*	62084 *0--*	70744 *08--*	76205 *1B*
310 060			*NGE*	EM	76144 *10A*	62085 *00A*	70745 *080A*	76194 *0A*
310 061	GF	N	*NGE*	EM	76145 *11B*	62086 *90A*	70746 *320A*	76195 *1B*
310 062†			*PBY*	BY	76146 *10A*	62087 *00A*	70747 *080A*	76196 *0A*
310 063†			*PBY*	BY	76147 *10A*	62088 *00A*	70748 *080A*	76197 *0A*
310 064	GF	N	*NNE*	EM	76148 *11B*	62089 *90A*	70749 *320A*	76198 *1B*
310 065	GF	N	*NNE*	EM	76149 *11B*	62090 *90A*	70750 *320A*	76199 *1B*
310 066	GF	N	*NNE*	EM	76228 *01B*	62091 *90A*	70751 *320A*	76200 *1B*
310 067	GF	N	*NNE*	EM	76151 *11B*	62092 *90A*	70752 *320A*	76201 *1B*
310 068	GF	N	*NGE*	EM	76152 *11B*	62093 *90A*	70753 *320A*	76202 *1B*
310 069	GF	N	*NGE*	EM	76153 *11B*	62094 *90A*	70754 *320A*	76203 *1B*
310 070	GF	N	*NGE*	EM	76154 *11B*	62095 *90A*	70755 *320A*	76204 *1B*
310 074			*NGE*	EM	76158 *10A*	62099 *00A*	70759 *080A*	76208 *0A*
310 075	GF	N	*NNE*	EM	76159 *11B*	62100 *90A*	70760 *320A*	76209 *1B*
310 077	GF	N	*NNE*	EM	76161 *11B*	62102 *90A*	70762 *320A*	76211 *1B*
310 079		N	*NNE*	EM	76163 *10A*	62104 *00A*	70764 *080A*	76213 *0A*
310 080	GF	N	*NNE*	EM	76164 *11B*	62105 *90A*	70765 *320A*	76214 *1B*
310 081			*NGE*	EM	76165 *10A*	62106 *00A*	70766 *080A*	76215 *0A*
310 082	GF	N	*NNE*	EM	76166 *11B*	62107 *90A*	70767 *320A*	76216 *1B*
310 083		N	*NGE*	EM	76167 *10A*	62108 *00A*	70768 *080A*	76217 *0A*
310 084	GF	N	*NNE*	EM	76168 *11B*	62109 *90A*	70769 *320A*	76218 *1B*
310 085	GF	N	*NNE*	EM	76169 *11B*	62110 *90A*	70770 *320A*	76219 *1B*
310 086	F		*NNW*	BY	76170 *11B*	62111 *0--*	70771 *08--*	76220 *1B*
310 087	GF	N	*NNE*	EM	76171 *11B*	62112 *90A*	70772 *320A*	76221 *1B*
310 088		N	*NNE*	EM	76172 *10A*	62113 *00A*	70773 *080A*	76222 *0A*
310 089		N	*NNE*	EM	76173 *10A*	62114 *00A*	70774 *080A*	76223 *0A*
310 091	GF	N	*NNE*	EM	76175 *11B*	62116 *90A*	70776 *320A*	76225 *1B*
310 092	GF	N	*NNE*	EM	76176 *11B*	62117 *90A*	70777 *320A*	76226 *1B*
310 093	F		*NGE*	EM	76177 *11B*	62118 *0--*	70778 *08--*	76227 *1B*
310 094	GF	N	*NNE*	EM	76998 *41B*	62119 *90A*	70780 *320A*	76193 *1B*
310 095		N	*NNE*	EM	76179 *10A*	62120 *00A*	70779 *080A*	76229 *0A*

† Class 310/0 units for conversion to Class 310/1 during 1989/90.

Class 310/1

Unit No	Old No	SC	Liv	Pool	Dep	BDTS	MBS	TS	DTS
						EF2112C	*ED2191B*	*EH2321B*	*EE2370A*
310 101	(310 073)	GF	P	*PBY*	BY	76157	62098	70758	76207
310 102	(310 055)	GF	P	*PBY*	BY	76139	62080	70740	76189
310 103	(310 076)	GF	P	*PBY*	BY	76160	62101	70761	76210
310 104	(310 078)	GF	P	*PBY*	BY	76162	62103	70763	76212
310 105	(310 090)	GF	P	*PBY*	BY	76174	62115	70775	76224
310 106	(310 072)	GF	P	*PBY*	BY	76156	62097	70757	76206
310 107	(310)	GF	P	*PBY*					
310 108	(310)	GF	P	*PBY*					
310 109	(310)	GF	P	*PBY*					
310 110	(310)	GF	P	*PBY*					
310 111	(310)	GF	P	*PBY*					

Class 311 3-Car

Built: Cravens 1967
Design: BR, saloons with sliding doors, non-gangwayed
Supply: 25kV ac overhead (built also for 6.25kV ac)
Traction motors (MBS): Four 222hp dc AEI
Maximum speed: 75mph
Dimensons: 20.18m L × 2.82m W × 3.86m H; *MBS:* 3,98m H, pantograph housed

AWS: Fitted to driving vehicles

Diagram	*Type*	*Weight*	*Seats*
Motor Brake Standard			
ED2.11.0A	MBS	58t	70
Driving Trailer Standard:			
EE2.14.0A	DTS	34.5t	83
Battery Driving Trailer Standard:			
EF2.12.0A	BDTS	37.5t	83

Unit No	SC	Liv	Pool	Dep	DTS	MBS	BDTS
					EE2.14	*ED2.11*	*EF2.12*
311 092		S	*PGW*	GW	76403	62163	76422
311 097			*PGW*	GW	76408	62168	76427
311 098	M	S	*PGW*	GW	76409	62169	76428
311 099	M		*PGW*	GW	76410	62170	76429
311 102	M		*PGW*	GW	76413	62173	76432
311 103	M		*PGW*	GW	76414	62174	76433
311 104	M		*PGW*	GW	76415	62175	76434
311 105	M	S	*PGW*	GW	76416	62176	76435
311 107	M		*PGW*	GW	76418	62178	76437
311 108	M		*PGW*	GW	76419	62179	76438
311 109	M	S	*PGW*	GW	76420	62180	76439
311 110	M		*PGW*	GW	76421	62181	76440

Class 312 — 4-Car

Built: BREL York 1975
Design: BR, saloons, gangwayed within units. Public address system fitted.
Supply: 25kV ac overhead (Class 312/1 originally also fitted 6.25kV ac)
Traction motors: Four 270hp (202kW) dc GEC
Maximum speed: 90mph
Dimensons: 20.18m L × 2.82m W × 3.86m H; *MBS:* 3.98m H, pantograph housed
Headlight and AWS: Fitted to driving vehicles

Diagram	*Type*	*Weight*	*Seats 1st*	*Std*	*Toilet*
Motor Brake Standard					
ED2.12.0B	MBS	56t	—	68	
ED2.13.0A	MBS	55.5t	—	68	
ED2.13.0B*	MBS	55.5t	—	68	
ED2.14.0B	MBS	55.5t	—	68	
Driving Trailer Composite					
EE3.05.1D	DTC	33t	25	47	
EE3.05.2B	DTC	33t	25	47	
EE3.05.2C*	DTC	33t	25	47	
Battery Driving Trailer Standard					
EF2.13.0C	BDTS	35t	—	84	1
EF2.13.1A	BDTS	35t	—	84	1
EF2.13.1B*	BDTS	35t	—	84	1
Trailer Second					
EH2.09.0C	TS	30.5t	—	98	
EH2.19.1A	TS	30.5t	—	98	
EH2.19.1B*	TS	30.5t	—	98	

*Unofficial codes, not yet issued

Class 312/0

Unit No	SC	Liv	Pool	Dep	BDTS *EF2130C*	MBS *ED2120B*	TS *EH2090C*	DTC *EE3051D*
~~312 701~~	F	N	*NGE*	CC	76949	62484	71168	78000
~~312 702~~	F	N	*NGE*	CC	76950	62485	71169	78001
~~312 703~~	F	N	*NGE*	CC	76951	62486	71170	78002
~~312 704~~	F		*NGE*	CC	76952	62487	71171	78003
~~312 705~~	F		*NGE*	CC	76953	62488	71172	78004
~~312 706~~	F	N	*NGE*	CC	76954	62489	71173	78005
~~312 707~~	F	N	*NGE*	CC	76955	62490	71174	78006
~~312 708~~	F	N	*NGE*	CC	76956	62491	71175	78007
~~312 709~~	F	N	*NGE*	CC	76957	62492	71176	78008
~~312 710~~	F	N	*NGE*	CC	76958	62493	71177	78009
312 711	F	N	*NGE*	CC	76959	62494	71178	78010
312 712	F	N	*NGE*	CC	76960	62495	71179	78011
312 713	F	N	*NGE*	CC	76961	62496	71180	78012
~~312 714~~	F	N	*NGE*	CC	76962	62497	71181	78013
~~312 715~~	F	N	*NGE*	CC	76963	62498	71182	78014
312 716	F	N	*NGE*	CC	76964	62499	71183	78015
312 717	F	N	*NGE*	CC	76965	62500	71184	78016
~~312 718~~	F	N	*NGE*	CC	76966	62501	71185	78017

Unit No	SC	Liv	Pool	Dep	BDTS	MBS	TS	DTC
312 719	F	N	*NGE*	CC	76967	62502	71186	78018
312 720	F	N	*NGE*	CC	76968	62503	71187	78019
312 721	F	N	*NGE*	CC	76969	62504	71188	78020
312 722	F	N	*NGE*	CC	76970	62505	71189	78021
312 723	F	N	*NGE*	CC	76971	62506	71190	78022
312 724	F	N	*NGE*	CC	76972	62507	71191	78023
312 725	F	N	*NGE*	CC	76973	62508	71192	78024
312 726	F	N	*NGE*	CC	76974	62509	71193	78025
					EF2130C	*ED2140B*	*EH2090C*	*EE3051D*
312 727	F	N	*NGE*	CC	76994	62657	71277	78045
312 728	F	N	*NGE*	CC	76995	62658	71278	78046
312 729	F		*NGE*	CC	76996	62659	71279	78047
312 730	F	N	*NGE*	CC	76997	62660	71280	78048

Unit Nos 312727-30 modified from Class 312/2 and renumbered from Unit Nos 312201-04 during 1988

CLASS 312/1

Unit No	SC	Liv	Pool	Dep	BDTS *EF213*		MBS *ED213*		TS *EH219*		DTC *EE305*	
312 781	F	N	*NGE*	CC	76975	*1B*	62510	*0B*	71194	*1B*	78026	*2C*
312 782			*NGE*	CC	76976	*1A*	62511	*0A*	71195	*1A*	78027	*2B*
312 783			*NGE*	CC	76977	*1A*	62512	*0A*	71196	*1A*	78028	*2B*
312 784	F	N	*NGE*	CC	76978	*1B*	62513	*0B*	71197	*1B*	78029	*2C*
312 785	F	N	*NGE*	CC	76979	*1B*	62514	*0B*	71198	*1B*	78030	*2C*
312 786			*NGE*	CC	76980	*1A*	62515	*0A*	71199	*1A*	78031	*2B*
312 787			*NGE*	CC	76981	*1A*	62516	*0A*	71200	*1A*	78032	*2B*
312 788	F	N	*NGE*	CC	76982	*1B*	62517	*0B*	71201	*1B*	78033	*2C*
312 789	F	N	*NGE*	CC	76983	*1B*	62518	*0B*	71202	*1B*	78034	*2C*
312 790			*NGE*	CC	76984	*1A*	62519	*0A*	71203	*1A*	78035	*2B*
312 791	F	N	*NGE*	CC	76985	*1B*	62520	*0B*	71204	*1B*	78036	*2C*
312 792	F	N	*NGE*	CC	76986	*1A*	62521	*0A*	71205	*1A*	78037	*2B*
312 793	F	N	*NGE*	CC	76987	*1B*	62522	*0B*	71206	*1B*	78038	*2C*
312 794	F	N	*NGE*	CC	76988	*1B*	62523	*0B*	71207	*1B*	78039	*2B*
312 795	F	N	*NGE*	CC	76989	*1B*	62524	*0B*	71208	*1B*	78040	*2C*
312 796			*NGE*	CC	76990	*1A*	62525	*0A*	71209	*1A*	78041	*2B*
312 797			*NGE*	CC	76991	*1A*	62526	*0A*	71210	*1A*	78042	*2B*
312 798	F	N	*NGE*	CC	76992	*1B*	62527	*0B*	71211	*1B*	78043	*2C*
312 799			*NGE*	CC	76993	*1B*	62528	*0A*	71212	*1A*	78044	*2B*

Class 313 — 3-Car

Built: BREL York 1976
Design: BR with sliding doors, gangwayed withing units and end doors. Driver/guard and public address systems fitted. Pressure and heating ventilation
Supply: 25kV ac overhead and 750V dc third rail
Traction motors (DMS & BDMS): Four 110hp (82.5kW) GEC G310AZ
Maximum speed: On 25kV: 70mph; on 750V (third rail) 30mph

Dimensons: *Driving coaches:* 19.80m L × 2.82m W × 3.58m H; *Trailer coach:* 19.92m L × 2.82m W ×3.98m H, pantograph housed
AWS: Fitted to driving vehicles

Diagram	*Type*	*Weight*	*Seats*
Driving Motor Standard			
EA2.04.0A	DMS	36t	74
EA2.04.0B	DMS	36t	74†
†Steel body, others aluminium			
Trailer Second, Pantograph			
EH2.10.0A	TS(P)	31t	84
Battery Driving Motor Second			
EI2.01.0A	BDMS	37.5t	74

Unit No	SC	Liv	Pool	Dep	DMS	TS(P)	BDMS
Class 313/1							
					EA2040A	*EH2100A*	*EI2010A*
313 001	D	N	*NNW*	BY	62529	71213	62593
313 002	D	N	*NNL*	BY	62530	71214	62594
313 003	D	N	*NNW*	BY	62531	71215	62595
313 004	D	N	*NNW*	BY	62532	71216	62596
313 005	D	N	*NNW*	BY	62533	71217	62597
313 006	D	N	*NNW*	BY	62534	71218	62598
313 007	D	N	*NNW*	BY	62535	71219	62599
313 008	D	N	*NNW*	BY	62536	71220	62600
313 009	D	N	*NNW*	BY	62537	71221	62601
313 010	D	N	*NNW*	BY	62538	71222	62602
313 011	D	N	*NNW*	BY	62539	71223	62603
313 012	D	N	*NNW*	BY	62540	71224	62604
313 013	D	N	*NNW*	BY	62541	71225	62605
313 014	D	N	*NNW*	BY	62542	71226	62606
313 015	DM	N	*NGN*	HE	62543	71227	62607
313 016	DM	N	*NGN*	HE	62544	71228	62608
313 017	DM	N	*NGN*	HE	62545	71229	62609
Class 313/0							
313 018	M	N	*NGN*	HE	62546	71230	62610
313 019	M		*NGN*	HE	62547	71231	62611
313 020	M		*NGN*	HE	62548	71232	62612
313 021	M		*NGN*	HE	62549	71233	62613
313 022	M	N	*NGN*	HE	62550	71234	62614
313 023	M		*NGN*	HE	62551	71235	62615
313 024	M	N	*NGN*	HE	62552	71236	62616
313 025	M		*NGN*	HE	62553	71237	62617

Unit No	SC	Liv	Pool	Dep	DMS	TS(P)	BDMS
313 026	M		*NGN*	HE	62554	71238	62618
313 027	M	N	*NGN*	HE	62555	71239	62619
313 028	M	N	*NGN*	HE	62556	71240	62620
313 029	M	N	*NGN*	HE	62557	71241	62621
313 030	M		*NGN*	HE	62558	71242	62622
313 031	M		*NGN*	HE	62559	71243	62623
313 032	M		*NGN*	HE	62560	71244	62624
313 033	M	N	*NGN*	HE	62561	71245	62625
313 034	M		*NGN*	HE	62562	71246	62626
313 035	M	N	*NGN*	HE	62563	71247	62627
313 036	M	N	*NGN*	HE	62564	71248	62628
313 037	M		*NGN*	HE	62565	71249	62629
					EA2040B	*EH2100A*	*EI2010A*
313 038	M	N	*NGN*	HE	62566	71250	62630
					EA2040A	*EH2100A*	*EI2010A*
313 039	M	N	*NGN*	HE	62567	71251	62631
313 040	M		*NGN*	HE	62568	71252	62632
313 041	M		*NGN*	HE	62569	71253	62633
313 042	M		*NGN*	HE	62570	71254	62634
313 043	M		*NGN*	HE	62571	71255	62635
313 044	M		*NGN*	HE	62572	71256	62636
313 045	M		*NGN*	HE	62573	71257	62637
313 046	M		*NGN*	HE	62574	71258	62638
313 047	M		*NGN*	HE	62575	71259	62639
313 048	M	N	*NGN*	HE	62576	71260	62640
313 049	M		*NGN*	HE	62577	71261	62641
313 050	M		*NGN*	HE	62578	71262	62642
313 051	M		*NGN*	HE	62579	71263	62643
313 052	M		*NGN*	HE	62580	71264	62644
313 053	M		*NGN*	HE	62581	71265	62645
313 054	M		*NGN*	HE	62582	71266	62646
313 055	M		*NGN*	HE	62583	71267	62647
313 056	M		*NGN*	HE	62584	71268	62648
313 057	M		*NGN*	HE	62585	71269	62649
313 058	M		*NGN*	HE	62586	71270	62650
313 059	M		*NGN*	HE	62587	71271	62651
313 060	M		*NGN*	HE	62588	71272	62652
313 096			*NGE*	CC	62589	71273	62653
313 097			*NGE*	CC	62590	71274	62654
313 098			*NGE*	CC	62591	71275	62655
313 099			*NGE*	CC	62592	71276	62656

Class 314 — 3-Car

Built: BREL York 1979
Design: BR, saloons with sliding doors gangwayed within unit and end doors. Public address system fitted. Pressure and heating ventilation
Supply: 25kV ac overhead
Traction motors: (**DMS**) Four 110hp (82.5kW) GEC 6310AZ or Brush TM61-53, interchangeable
Maximum speed: 75mph
Dimensons: *Driving coaches:* 19.80m L × 2.82m W × 3.58m H; *Trailer vehicle:* 19.92m L × 2.82m W ×3.98m H pantograph housed
AWS: Driving vehicles fitted

Diagram	*Type*	*Weight*	*Seats*	
Driving Motor Standard				
EA2.06.0A	DMS	34.5t	68	
EA2.06.0B	DMS	34.5t	68	Emergency tool box
Trailer Second, Pantograph				
EH2.11.0A	TS	33t	76	

Unit No	SC	Liv	Pool	Dep	DMS *EA2060A*	TS(P) *EH2110A*	DMS *EA2060B*
314 201		S	*PGW*	GW	64583	71450	64584
314 202	M	S	*PGW*	GW	64585	71451	64586
314 203		S	*PGW*	GW	64587	71452	64588
314 204		S	*PGW*	GW	64589	71453	64590
314 205	M	S	*PGW*	GW	64591	71454	64592
314 206		S	*PGW*	GW	64593	71455	64594
314 207	M	S	*PGW*	GW	64595	71456	64596
314 208	M	S	*PGW*	GW	64597	71457	64598
314 209	M	S	*PGW*	GW	64599	71458	64600
314 210		S	*PGW*	GW	64601	71459	64602
314 211	M	S	*PGW*	GW	64603	71460	64604
314 212	M	S	*PGW*	GW	64605	71461	64606
314 213	M	S	*PGW*	GW	64607	71462	64608
314 214	M	S	*PGW*	GW	64609	71463	64610
314 215	M	S	*PGW*	GW	64611	71464	64612
314 216	M	S	*PGW*	GW	64613	71465	64614

Class 315 — 4-Car

Built: BREL York 1980
Design: BR, saloons with sliding doors, gangwayed within units and end doors. Driver/guard communication and public address system fitted. Pressure and heating ventilation
Supply: 25kV ac
Traction motors: (**DMS**) Four 110hp (82.5kW) GEC 310AZ or Brush TM61-53, interchangeable
Maximum speed: 75mph
Dimensons: *Driving coaches:* 19.80m L × 2.82m W × 3.58m H; *Trailer coaches:* 20.18m L × 2.82m W ×3.58m H, pantograph housed

AWS: Driving vehicles fitted

Diagram	*Type*	*Weight*	*Seats*	
Driving Motor Standard				
EA2.07.0A	DMS	35t	74	
EA2.07.0B	DMS	35t	74	Emergency tool box
Trailer Standard				
EH2.16.0A	TS	25.5t	86	
EH2.17.0A	TS	32t	84	Pantograph

NSE Classification: *Class 315/0:* Units 315842-61 (GEC equipment); *Class 315/1:* Units 315801-41 (Brush equipment)

Unit No	SC	Liv	Pool	Dep	DMS *EA2070A*	TS *EH2160A*	TS(P) *EH2170A*	DMS *EA2070B*
315 801	M		*NGE*	IL	64461	71281	71389	64462
315 802	M		*NGE*	IL	64463	71282	71390	64464
315 803	M		*NGE*	IL	64465	71283	71391	64466
315 804	M		*NGE*	IL	64467	71284	71392	64468
315 805	M		*NGE*	IL	64469	71285	71393	64470
315 806			*NGE*	IL	64471	71286	71394	64472
315 807			*NGE*	IL	64473	71287	71395	64474
315 808			*NGE*	IL	64475	71288	71396	64476
315 809			*NGE*	IL	64477	71289	71397	64478
315 810			*NGE*	IL	64479	71290	71398	64480
315 811			*NGE*	IL	64481	71291	71399	64482
315 812		N	*NGE*	IL	64483	71292	71400	64484
315 813			*NGE*	IL	64485	71293	71401	64486
315 814			*NGE*	IL	64487	71294	71402	64488
315 815			*NGE*	IL	64489	71295	71403	64490
315 816		N	*NGE*	IL	64491	71296	71404	64492
315 817		N	*NGE*	IL	64493	71297	71405	64494
315 818		N	*NGE*	IL	64495	71298	71406	64496
315 819		N	*NGE*	IL	64497	71299	71407	64498
315 820		N	*NGE*	IL	64499	71300	71408	64500
315 821		N	*NGE*	IL	64501	71301	71409	64502
315 822			*NGE*	IL	64503	71302	71410	64504
315 823		N	*NGE*	IL	64505	71303	71411	64506
315 824		N	*NGE*	IL	64507	71304	71412	64508
315 825		N	*NGE*	IL	64509	71305	71413	64510
315 826			*NGE*	IL	64511	71306	71414	64512
315 827			*NGE*	IL	64513	71307	71415	64514
315 828		N	*NGE*	IL	64515	71308	71416	64516
315 829		N	*NGE*	IL	64517	71309	71417	64518
315 830		N	*NGE*	IL	64519	71310	71418	64520
315 831		N	*NGE*	IL	64521	71311	71419	64522
315 832		N	*NGE*	IL	64523	71312	71420	64524
315 833		N	*NGE*	IL	64525	71313	71421	64526
315 834		N	*NGE*	IL	64527	71314	71422	64528
315 835			*NGE*	IL	64529	71315	71423	64530
315 836		N	*NGE*	IL	64531	71316	71424	64532
315 837		N	*NGE*	IL	64533	71317	71425	64534
315 838		N	*NGE*	IL	64535	71318	71426	64536
315 839		N	*NGE*	IL	64537	71319	71427	64538

Unit No	SC	Liv	Pool	Dep	DMS	TS	TS(P)	DMS
315 840		N	*NGE*	IL	64539	71320	71428	64540
~~315 841~~		N	*NGE*	IL	64541	71321	71429	64542
315 842		N	*NGE*	IL	64543	71322	71430	64544
~~315 843~~		N	*NGE*	IL	64545	71323	71431	64546
~~315 844~~		N	*NGE*	IL	64547	71324	71432	64548
~~315 845~~		N	*NGE*	IL	64549	71325	71433	64550
~~315 846~~		N	*NGE*	IL	64551	71326	71434	64552
315 847		N	*NGE*	IL	64553	71327	71435	64554
~~315 848~~		N	*NGE*	IL	64555	71328	71436	64556
315 849		N	*NGE*	IL	64557	71329	71437	64558
~~315 850~~		N	*NGE*	IL	64559	71330	71438	64560
~~315 851~~		N	*NGE*	IL	64561	71331	71439	64562
~~315 852~~		N	*NGE*	IL	64563	71332	71440	64564
315 853		N	*NGE*	IL	64565	71333	71441	64566
315 854		N	*NGE*	IL	64567	71334	71442	64568
~~315 855~~		N	*NGE*	IL	64569	71335	71443	64570
315 856		N	*NGE*	IL	64571	71336	71444	64572
~~315 857~~		N	*NGE*	IL	64573	71337	71445	64574
~~315 858~~		N	*NGE*	IL	64575	71338	71446	64576
~~315 859~~		N	*NGE*	IL	64577	71339	71447	64578
315 860		N	*NGE*	IL	64579	71340	71448	64580
315 861		N	*NGE*	IL	64581	71341	71449	64582

Class 317 — 4-Car

Built: BREL Derby and York 1981
Design: BR, saloons with sliding doors, gangwayed throughout. Public address and Driver/guard communication system fitted. Pressure and heating ventilation. Equipped for driver-only operation
Supply: 25kV ac overhead
Traction motors: (**MS**) Four 332hp (249kW) GEC G315BZ
Maximum speed: 90mph
Dimensions: *Driving coaches:* 20.13m L × 2.82m W × 3.77m H; *Trailer coaches:* 20.18m L × 2.82m W ×3.77m H, pantograph housed
Toilets: Class 317/0 units are fitted with gravity toilets due to tunnel use

Diagram	*Type*	*Weight*	*Seats* *1st*	*Std*	*Toilets*
Motor Standard					
EC2.02.0A	MS	49t	—	79	
EC2.05.0A	MS	49t	—	79	
EC2.08.0A	MS	49t	—	79	
Driving Trailer Standard					
EE2.16.0A	DTS(A)	29.5t	—	74	
EE2.17.0A	DTS(B)	29.5t	—	74	
EE2.24.0A	DTS(A)	29.5t	—	74	
EE2.25.0A	DTS(B)	29.5t	—	74	
EE2.32.0A	DTS(B)	29.5t	—	71	
EE2.35.0A	DTS(B)	29.5t	—	70	
Trailer Composite					
EH3.07.0A	TC	29t	22	46	2
EH3.08.0A	TC	28.3t	22	46	2

CLASS 317/0

Unit No	SC	Liv	Pool	Dep	DTS	MS	TC	DTS
					EE2160A	*EC2020A*	*EH3070A*	*EE2350A*
317 301		N	*NNW*	BY	77024	62661	71577	77048
317 302		N	*NNW*	BY	77001	62662	71578	77049
317 303		N	*NNW*	BY	77002	62663	71579	77050
317 304		N	*NNW*	BY	77003	62664	71580	77051
317 305		N	*NNW*	BY	77004	62665	71581	77052
317 306		N	*NNW*	BY	77005	62666	71582	77053
317 307		N	*NNW*	BY	77006	62667	71583	77054
317 308		N	*NNW*	BY	77007	62668	71584	77055
317 309		N	*NNW*	BY	77008	62669	71585	77056
317 310		N	*NNW*	BY	77009	62670	71586	77057
317 311		N	*NNW*	BY	77010	62671	71587	77058
317 312		N	*NNW*	BY	77011	62672	71588	77059
317 313		N	*NNW*	BY	77012	62673	71589	77060
317 314		N	*NNW*	BY	77013	62674	71590	77061
317 315		N	*NNW*	BY	77014	62675	71591	77062
317 316		N	*NNW*	BY	77015	62676	71592	77063
317 317		N	*NNW*	BY	77016	62677	71593	77064
317 318		N	*NNW*	BY	77017	62678	71594	77065
317 319		N	*NNW*	BY	77018	62679	71595	77066
317 320		N	*NNW*	BY	77019	62680	71596	77067
317 321		N	*NNW*	BY	77020	62681	71597	77068
317 322		N	*NNW*	BY	77021	62682	71598	77069
317 323		N	*NNW*	BY	77022	62683	71599	77070
317 324		N	*NNW*	BY	77023	62684	71600	77071
317 325		N	*NNW*	BY	77000	62685	71601	77072
317 326		N	*NNW*	BY	77025	62686	71602	77073
317 327		N	*NNW*	BY	77026	62687	71603	77074
317 328		N	*NNW*	BY	77027	62688	71604	77075
317 329		N	*NNW*	BY	77028	62689	71605	77076
317 330		N	*NNW*	BY	77029	62690	71606	77077
317 331		N	*NNW*	BY	77030	62691	71607	77078
317 332		N	*NNW*	BY	77031	62692	71608	77079
317 333		N	*NNW*	BY	77032	62693	71609	77080
317 334		N	*NNW*	BY	77033	62694	71610	77081

CLASS 317/1

Unit No	SC	Liv	Pool	Dep	DTS	MS	TC	DTS
					EE2160A	*EC2080A*	*EH3080A*	*EE2350A*
317 335		N	*NGN*	HE	77034	62695	71611	77082
317 336		N	*NGN*	HE	77035	62696	71612	77083
					EE2160A	*EC2080A*	*EH3080A*	*EE2320A*
317 337		N	*NGN*	HE	77036	62697	71613	77084
317 338		N	*NGN*	HE	77037	62698	71614	77085
317 339		N	*NGN*	HE	77038	62699	71615	77086

Unit No	SC	Liv	Pool	Dep	DTS	MS	TC	DTS
317 340		N	*NGN*	HE	77039	62700	71616	77087
317 341		N	*NGN*	HE	77040	62701	71617	77088
317 342		N	*NGN*	HE	77041	62702	71618	77089
317 343		N	*NGN*	HE	77042	62703	71619	77090
317 344		N	*NGN*	HE	77043	62704	71620	77091
317 345			*NGN*	HE	77044	62705	71621	77092
					EE2160A	*EC2020A*	*EH3080A*	*EE2170A*
317 346		N	*NGN*	HE	77045	62706	71622	77093
317 347		N	*NGN*	HE	77046	62707	71623	77094
					EE2160A	*EC2080A*	*EH3080A*	*EE2320A*
317 348		N	*NGN*	HE	77047	62708	71624	77095

CLASS 317/2

Unit No	SC	Liv	Pool	Dep	DTS	MS	TC	DTS
					EE2240A	*EC2050A*	*EH3080A*	*EE2250A*
317 349		N	*NGN*	HE	77200	62846	71734	77220
317 350			*NGN*	HE	77201	62847	71735	77221
317 351		N	*NGN*	HE	77202	62848	71736	77222
317 352			*NGN*	HE	77203	62849	71739	77223
317 353			*NGN*	HE	77204	62850	71738	77224
317 354		N	*NGN*	HE	77205	62851	71737	77225
317 355			*NGN*	HE	77206	62852	71740	77226
317 356			*NGN*	HE	77207	62853	71742	77227
317 357			*NGN*	HE	77208	62854	71741	77228
317 358			*NGN*	HE	77209	62855	71743	77229
317 359		N	*NGN*	HE	77210	62856	71744	77230
317 360		N	*NGN*	HE	77211	62857	71745	77231
317 361			*NGN*	HE	77212	62858	71746	77232
317 362			*NGN*	HE	77213	62859	71747	77233
317 363			*NGN*	HE	77214	62860	71748	77234
317 364			*NGN*	HE	77215	62861	71749	77235
317 365		N	*NGN*	HE	77216	62862	71750	77236
317 366		N	*NGN*	HE	77217	62863	71752	77237
317 367		N	*NGN*	HE	77218	62864	71751	77238
317 368		N	*NGN*	HE	77219	62865	71753	77239
317 369		N	*NGN*	HE	77280	62886	71762	77284
317 370		N	*NGN*	HE	77281	62887	71763	77285
317 371		N	*NGN*	HE	77282	62888	71764	77286
317 372		N	*NGN*	HE	77283	62889	71765	77287

Class 318 — 3-Car

Built: BREL Derby and York 1986
Design: BR saloons, with sliding doors, gangwayed throughout. Driver only operation, Driver/guard and public address sytems fitted
Supply: 25kV ac overhead
Traction motors (DMS): Four 332hp (249kW) GECG 315 BZ
Dimensions: *Driving coaches:* 20.13m L × 2.82m W × 3.77m H; *Trailer coach:* 20.18m L × 2.82m W × 3.78m H. Pantograph housed
AWS: Driving vehicles fitted

Diagram	*Type*	*Weight*	*Seats*	*Toilets*
Motor Standard				
EC2.07.0A	MS	50.9t	79	—
Driving Trailer Standard:				
EE2.27.0A	DTS (A)	30.1t	66	1 Invalid area
EE2.28.0A	DTS (B)	29.6t	71	—

Unit No	Liv	Pool	Dep	DTS	MS	DTS
				EE2270A	*EC2070A*	*EE2280A*
318 250	S	*PGW*	GW	77240	62866	77260
318 251	S	*PGW*	GW	77241	62867	77261
318 252	S	*PGW*	GW	77242	62868	77262
318 253	S	*PGW*	GW	77243	62869	77263
318 254	S	*PGW*	GW	77244	62870	77264
318 255	S	*PGW*	GW	77245	62871	77265
318 256	S	*PGW*	GW	77246	62872	77266
318 257	S	*PGW*	GW	77247	62873	77267
318 258	S	*PGW*	GW	77248	62874	77268
318 259	S	*PGW*	GW	77249	62875	77269
318 260	S	*PGW*	GW	77250	62876	77270
318 261	S	*PGW*	GW	77251	62877	77271
318 262	S	*PGW*	GW	77252	62878	77272
318 263	S	*PGW*	GW	77253	62879	77273
318 264	S	*PGW*	GW	77254	62880	77274
318 265	S	*PGW*	GW	77255	62881	77275
318 266	S	*PGW*	GW	77256	62882	77276
318 267	S	*PGW*	GW	77257	62883	77277
318 268	S	*PGW*	GW	77258	62884	77278
318 269	S	*PGW*	GW	77259	62885	77279
318 270	S	*PGW*	GW	77288	62890	77289

Class 319 — 4-Car

Built: BREL York 1987 for Thameslink cross-London duties from Bedford to Brighton and Orpington via Snow Hill tunnel
Design: BR, Saloons, with sliding doors, gangwayed within unit and emergency end doors
Supply: 25kV ac overhead, 750V dc third rail
Traction motors: Four 332hp (249kW) GEC G315 BZ
Dimensions: 20.18m L × 2.82m W × 3.77m H; **MS** 3.78m H Pantograph housed
Maximum Speed: 100mph

Diagram	*Type*	*Weight*	*Seats*	*Toilet*
Motor Standard				
EC2.09.0A	MS	49.2t	81	—
Driving Trailer Standard:				
EE2.33.0A	DTS (A)	28.2t	81	—
EE2.34.0A	DTS (B)	28.1t	78 incl 8 tip-up	—
Trailer Standard:				
EH2.34.0A	TS	31t	76	2

Unit No	Liv	Pool	Dep	BDTS *EE2340A*	MS *EC2090A*	TS *EH2340A*	DTS *EE2330A*
319 001	N	*NML*	SU	77290	62891	71772	77291
319 002	N	*NSX*	SU	77292	62892	71773	77293
319 003	N	*NSX*	SU	77294	62893	71774	77295
319 004	N	*NSX*	SU	77296	62894	71775	77297
319 005	N	*NSX*	SU	77298	62895	71817	77299
319 006	N	*NSX*	SU	77300	62896	71777	77301
319 007	N	*NSX*	SU	77302	62897	71778	77303
319 008	N	*NSX*	SU	77304	62898	71779	77305
319 009	N	*NSX*	SU	77306	62899	71780	77307
319 010	N	*NSX*	SU	77308	62900	71781	77309
319 011	N	*NSX*	SU	77310	62901	71782	77311
319 012	N	*NML*	SU	77312	62902	71783	77313
319 013	N	*NML*	SU	77314	62903	71784	77315
319 014	N	*NML*	SU	77316	62904	71785	77317
319 015	N	*NML*	SU	77318	62905	71786	77319
319 016	N	*NML*	SU	77320	62906	71787	77321
319 017	N	*NML*	SU	77322	62907	71788	77323
319 018	N	*NML*	SU	77324	62908	71789	77325
319 019	N	*NML*	SU	77326	62909	71790	77327
319 020	N	*NML*	SU	77328	62910	71791	77329
319 021	N	*NML*	SU	77330	62911	71792	77331
319 022	N	*NML*	SU	77332	62912	71793	77333
319 023	N	*NML*	SU	77334	62913	71794	77335
319 024	N	*NML*	SU	77336	62914	71795	77337
319 025	N	*NML*	SU	77338	62915	71796	77339
319 026	N	*NML*	SU	77340	62916	71797	77341
319 027	N	*NML*	SU	77342	62917	71798	77343
319 028	N	*NML*	SU	77344	62918	71799	77345
319 029	N	*NML*	SU	77346	62919	71800	77347
319 030	N	*NML*	SU	77348	62920	71801	77349
319 031	N	*NML*	SU	77350	62921	71802	77351
319 032	N	*NML*	SU	77352	62922	71803	77353
319 033	N	*NML*	SU	77354	62923	71804	77355
319 034	N	*NML*	SU	77356	62924	71805	77357
319 035	N	*NML*	SU	77358	62925	71806	77359
319 036	N	*NML*	SU	77360	62926	71807	77361
319 037	N	*NML*	SU	77362	62927	71808	77363
319 038	N	*NML*	SU	77364	62928	71809	77365
319 039	N	*NML*	SU	77366	62929	71810	77367
319 040	N	*NML*	SU	77368	62930	71811	77369
319 041	N	*NML*	SU	77370	62931	71812	77371
319 042	N	*NML*	SU	77372	62932	71813	77373
319 043	N	*NML*	SU	77374	62933	71814	77375
319 044	N	*NML*	SU	77376	62934	71815	77377
319 045	N	*NML*	SU	77378	62935	71816	77379

Unit No	Liv	Pool	Dep	BDTS	MS	TS	DTS
319 046	N	*NML*	SU	77380†	62936	71776	77381†
319 047	N	*NML*	SU	77430	62961	71866	77431
319 048	N	*NML*	SU	77432	62962	71867	77433
319 049	N	*NML*	SU	77434	62963	71868	77435
319 050	N	*NML*	SU	77436	62964	71869	77437
319 051	N	*NML*	SU	77438	62965	71870	77439
319 052	N	*NML*	SU	77440	62966	71871	77441
319 053	N	*NML*	SU	77442	62967	71872	77443
319 054	N	*NML*	SU	77444	62968	71873	77445
319 055	N	*NML*	SU	77446	62969	71874	77447
319 056	N	*NML*	SU	77448	62970	71875	77449
319 057	N	*NML*	SU	77450	62971	71876	77451
319 058	N	*NML*	SU	77452	62972	71877	77453
319 059	N	*NML*	SU	77454	62973	71878	77455
319 060	N	*NML*	SU	77456	62974	71879	77457
319 061	N	*NML*					
319 062	N	*NML*					
319 063	N	*NML*					
319 064	N	*NML*					
319 065	N	*NML*					
319 066	N	*NML*					
319 067	N	*NML*					
319 068	N	*NML*					
319 069	N	*NML*					
319 070	N	*NML*					
319 071	N	*NML*					
319 072	N	*NML*					
319 073	N	*NML*					
319 074	N	*NML*					
319 075	N	*NML*					
319 076	N	*NML*					
319 077	N	*NML*					
319 078	N	*NML*					
319 079	N	*NML*					
319 080	N	*NML*					

† BDTS and DTS vehicles in reverse positions.

Class 320 — 3-Car

New units for Strathclyde (Glasgow) PTA
Built: BREL York (due 1990)
Design: BR, saloons with sliding doors, gangwayed within unit. Equipped for one man operation and public address system
Supply: 25kV ac overhead
Traction motors: Four 332hp (249kW) Brush
Maximum speed: 100mph

Dimensions: *Driving coaches:* 19.95m L × 2.82m W × 3.78m H; *Trailer coach:* 19.92m L × 2.82m W × 3.78m H (Pantograph housed within body height)
AWS: Driving vehicles fitted

Diagram	*Type*	*Weight*	*Seats*	*Toilet*
Motor Standard Pantograph:				
EC	MS	49.2t	81	—
Driving Trailer Standard:				
EE2	DTS (A)	38.2t	74	1
EE2	DTS (B)	38.2t	78	—

Unit No	Liv	Pool	Dep	DTS *EE2*	MS *EC2*	DTS *EE2*
320 01	S	*PGW*				
320 02	S	*PGW*				
320 03	S	*PGW*				
320 04	S	*PGW*				
320 05	S	*PGW*				
320 06	S	*PGW*				
320 07	S	*PGW*				
320 08	S	*PGW*				
320 09	S	*PGW*				
320 10	S	*PGW*				
320 11	S	*PGW*				
320 12	S	*PGW*				
320 13	S	*PGW*				
320 14	S	*PGW*				
320 15	S	*PGW*				
320 16	S	*PGW*				
320 17	S	*PGW*				
320 18	S	*PGW*				
320 19	S	*PGW*				
320 20	S	*PGW*				
320 21	S	*PGW*				
320 22	S	*PGW*				

Class 321 — 4-Car

Built: BREL York 1988
Design: BR, saloons with sliding doors, gangwayed within unit. Equipped for one man operation, driver/guard communication and public address system
Supply: 25kV ac overhead
Traction Motors: Four 332hp (249kW) Brush
Maximum speed: 100mph
Dimensions: *Driving coaches:* 19.95m L × 2.82m W × 3.78m H; *Trailer coaches:* 19.92m L × 2.82m W × 3.78m H (Pantograph housed within body height)
AWS: Driving vehicles fitted

Diagram	*Type*	*Weight*	*Seats 1st*	*Seats Std*	*Toilet*
Motor Standard, Pantograph:					
EC2.10.0A	MS	49.2t	—	81	—
Battery Driving Trailer Standard:					
EE2.36.0A	DTS	28.2t	—	78	—
Driving Trailer Composite:					
EE3.08.0A	DTC	28.2t	19	58	—
Trailer Standard:					
EH2.35.0A	TS	31t	—	76	2

Unit No	Liv	Pool	Dep	BDTS *EE236*	MS *EC210*	TS *EH235*	DTC *EE308*
321 301	N	*NNE*	IL	77853	62975	71880	78049
~~321 302~~	N	*NNE*	IL	77854	62976	71881	78050
321 303	N	*NNE*	IL	77855	62977	71882	78051
~~321 304~~	N	*NNE*	IL	77856	62978	71883	78052
~~321 305~~	N	*NNE*	IL	77857	62979	71884	78053
~~321 306~~	N	*NNE*	IL	77858	62980	71885	78054

Unit No	Liv	Pool	Dep	BDTS	MS	TS	DTC
321 307	N	*NNE*	IL	77859	62981	71886	78055
321 308	N	*NNE*	IL	77860	62982	71887	78056
321 309	N	*NNE*	IL	77861	62983	71888	78057
321 310	N	*NNE*	IL	77862	62984	71889	78058
321 311	N	*NNE*	IL	77863	62985	71890	78059
321 312	N	*NGE*	IL	77864	62986	71891	78060
321 313	N	*NGE*	IL	77865	62987	71892	78061
321 314	N	*NGE*	IL	77866	62988	71893	78062
321 315	N	*NGE*	IL	77867	62989	71894	78063
321 316	N	*NGE*	IL	77868	62990	71895	78064
321 317	N	*NGE*	IL	77869	62991	71896	78065
321 318	N	*NGE*	IL	77870	62992	71897	78066
321 319	N	*NGE*	IL	77871	62993	71898	78067
321 320	N	*NGE*	IL	77872	62994	71899	78068
321 321	N	*NGE*	IL	77873	62995	71900	78069
321 322	N	*NGE*	IL	77874	62996	71901	78070
321 323	N	*NGE*		77875	62997	71902	78071
321 324	N	*NGE*		77876	62998	71903	78072
321 325	N	*NGE*		77877	62999	71904	78073
321 326	N	*NGE*		77878	63000	71905	78074
321 327	N	*NGE*		77879	63001	71906	78075
321 328	N	*NGE*		77880	63002	71907	78076
321 329	N	*NGE*		77881	63003	71908	78077
321 330	N	*NGE*		77882	63004	71909	78078
321 331	N	*NGE*		77883	63005	71910	78079
321 332	N	*NGE*		77884	63006	71911	78080
321 333	N	*NGE*		77885	63007	71912	78081
321 334	N	*NGE*		77886	63008	71913	78082
321 335	N	*NGE*		77887	63009	71914	78083
321 336	N	*NGE*		77888	63010	71915	78084
321 337	N	*NGE*		77889	63011	71916	78085
321 338	N	*NGE*		77890	63012	71917	78086
321 339	N	*NGE*		77891	63013	71918	78087
321 340	N	*NGE*		77892	63014	71919	78088
321 341	N	*NGE*		77893	63015	71920	78089
321 342	N	*NNW*		77894	63016	71921	78090
321 343	N	*NNW*		77895	63017	71922	78091
321 344	N	*NNW*		77896	63018	71923	78092
321 345	N	*NNW*		77897	63019	71924	78093
321 346	N	*NNW*		77898	63020	71925	78094
321 347	N	*N*					
321 348	N	*N*					
321 349	N	*N*					
321 350	N	*N*					
321 351	N	*N*					
321 352	N	*N*					
321 353	N	*N*					

Unit No	Liv	Pool	Dep	BDTS	MS	TS	DTC
321 354	N	*N*					
321 355	N	*N*					
321 356	N	*N*					
321 357	N	*N*					
321 358	N	*N*					
321 359	N	*N*					
321 360	N	*N*					
321 361	N	*N*					
321 362	N	*N*					
321 363	N	*N*					
321 364	N	*N*					
321 365	N	*N*					
321 366	N	*N*					
321 367	N	*N*					
321 368	N	*N*					
321 369	N	*N*					
321 370	N	*N*					
321 371	N	*N*					
321 372	N	*N*					
321 373	N	*N*					
321 374	N	*N*					
321 375	N	*N*					
321 376	N	*N*					

Class 322 — 4-Car

New units for Stansted Airport link service
Built: BREL York (due 1989)
Design: BR, saloons with sliding doors, gangwayed within unit. Equipped for one man operaiton, driver/guard and public address systems
Supply: 25kV ac overhead
Traction motors (MBS): Four 332hp (249kW) Brush
Maximum speed: 100mph
Dimensions: *Driving coaches:* 19.95m L × 2.82m W × 3.78m H. *Trailer coaches:* 19.92m L × 2.82m W × 2.78m H. (Pantograph housed within body height)

Diagram	*Type*	*Weight*	*Seats 1st*	*Seats Std*	*Toilets*
Motor Sandard, Pantograph:					
EC2.	MS	49.2t			
Battery Driving Trailer Standard:					
EE2.	DTS	28.5t			
Driving Trailer Composite:					
EE3.	DTC	28.5t			
Trailer Standard:					
EH2.	TS	31t			2

Unit No	Liv	Pool	Dep	BDTS	MS	TS	DTC
				EE2	*EC2*	*EH2*	*EE3*
322 01	N	*N*					
322 02	N	*N*					

Unit No	Liv	Pool	Dep	BDTS	MS	TS	DTC
322 03	N	*N*					
322 04	N	*N*					
322 05	N	*N*					

DC ELECTRIC MULTIPLE UNITS

Class 421 4-CIG 4-Car

Built: *Class 421/1:* British Railways York 1964.
Class 421/2: BREL York 1970
Design: BR gangwayed throughout. Driver-guard communication fitted
Power supply: 750/850V dc third rail
Traction motors (MBS): Four 250hp (185kW) dc English Electric
Maximum speed: 90mph
Dimensions: 20.19m L × 2.82m W × 3.86m H
AWS: Driving vehicles fitted

DMEE Diagram	*SR Design*	*Type*	*Weight*	*Seats 1st*	*Std*	*Toilets*
Motor Brake Standard, Pantograph:						
ED2.60.0A	EA	MBS	49t	—	56	
ED2.60.1B	EA1A	MBS	49t	—	56	
ED2.60.2B	EA2A	MBS	49t	—	56	
Driving Trailer Composite (Compartment/Saloon):						
EE3.63.3B	FA1A	DTC	36t	24	28	2
EE3.63.4B	FA2A	DTC	36t	24	28	2
EE3.63.5A	FA	DTC	36t	24	28	2
EE3.64.4B	FA1A	DTC	35.5t	18	36	2
EE3.64.5B	FA2A	DTC	35.5t	18	36	2
EE3.64.6A	FA	DTC	35.5t	18	36	2
EE3.71.0B†. See Class 423						
Trailer Standard:						
EH2.75.0A	BO	TS	31.5t	—	72	
EH2.75.1B	BO1A	TS	31.5t	—	72	

Class 421/1

Fitted with electric parking brake.

Unit No	SC	Liv	Pool	Dep	DTC *EE36*		MBS *ED2600A*	TS *EH275*		DTC *EE36*	
1100			*NSX*	BI	76125	*46A*	62066	71051	*1B*	76071	*35A*
1105	F		*NSX*	BI	76080	*46A*	62021	70699	*0A*	76039	*35A*
1110	F	N	*NSX*	BI	76085	*46A*	62026	70704	*0A*	76031	*46A*
1111	F	N	*NSX*	BI	76086	*46A*	62027	70705	*0A*	76032	*35A*
1114	F	N	*NSX*	BI	76089	*46A*	62030	70708	*0A*	76035	*35A*
1116	F	N	*NSX*	BI	76091	*46A*	62032	70710	*0A*	76037	*35A*

Unit No	SC	Liv	Pool	Dep	DTC	MBS	TS	DTC
1118	F	N	*NSX*	BI	76026 *35A*	62034	70712 *0A*	76093 *46A*
1123	F		*NSX*	BI	76119 *46A*	62060	70717 *0A*	76065 *35A*
1127	F		*NSX*	BI	76102 *46A*	62043	70721 *0A*	76048 *35A*

Class 421/2

Not fitted with electric parking brake.

Unit No	Liv	Pool	Dep	DTC	MBS	TS	DTC
				EE3645B	*ED2602B*	*EH2751B*	*EE3634B*
1201	N	*NSX*	BI	76751	62389	71069	76822
1202	N	*NSX*	BI	76752	62390	71070	76823
1203	N	*NSX*	BI	76753	62391	71071	76824
1204	N	*NSX*	BI	76754	62392	71072	76825
1205	N	*NSX*	BI	76755	62393	71073	76826
1206	N	*NSX*	BI	76756	62394	71074	76827
1208	N	*NSS*	FR	76758	62396	71076	76829
1209	N	*NSS*	FR	76759	62397	71077	76830
1210	N	*NSS*	FR	76760	62398	71078	76831
1211	N	*NSS*	FR	76761	62399	71079	76832
1212	N	*NSS*	FR	76762	62400	71080	76833
1213	N	*NSS*	FR	76763	62401	71081	76834
1214	N	*NSS*	FR	76764	62402	71082	76835
1215	N	*NSS*	FR	76765	62403	71083	76836
1216		*NSS*	FR	76766	62404	71084	76266N†
1217		*NSS*	FR	76767	62405	71085	76838
1218	N	*NSS*	FR	76768	62406	71086	76839
1219		*NSS*	FR	76769	62407	71087	76840
1220		*NSS*	FR	76770	62408	71088	76841
1221		*NSS*	FR	76771	62409	71089	76842
1222		*NSS*	FR	76772	62410	71090	76843
1223		*NSS*	FR	76773	62411	71091	76844
1224		*NSS*	FR	76774	62412	71092	76845
1225		*NSS*	FR	76775	62413	71093	76846
1226		*NSS*	FR	76776	62414	71094	76847
				EE3644B	*ED2601B*	*EH2751B*	*EE3633B*
1238		*NSS*	FR	76582	62288	70968	76612
1241		*NSS*	FR	76585	62291	70971	76615
1243		*NSS*	FR	76587	62293	70973	76617
1244	N	*NSS*	FR	76588	62294	70974	76618
1245	N	*NSS*	FR	76589	62295	70975	76619
1246	N	*NSS*	FR	76590	62296	70976	76620
1247	N	*NSS*	FR	76591	62297	70977	76621
1249	N	*NSS*	FR	76593	62299	70979	76623
1252	N	*NSS*	FR	76596	62302	70982	76626
1253	N	*NSS*	FR	76597	62303	70983	76627

Unit No	Liv	Pool	Dep	DTC	MBS	TS	DTC
1254		*NSS*	FR	76598	62304	70984	76628
1255	N	*NSS*	FR	76599	62305	70985	76629
1256	N	*NSS*	FR	76600	62306	70986	76630
1257	N	*NSS*	FR	76601	62307	70987	76631
1258	N	*NSX*	BI	76566	62282	70988	76576
1259	N	*NSX*	BI	76603	62309	70989	76633
1260	N	*NSX*	BI	76604	62310	70990	76634
1261	N	*NSX*	BI	76605	62311	70991	76635
1262	N	*NSX*	BI	76606	62312	70992	76636
1263		*NSX*	BI	76607	62313	70993	76637
1264		*NSX*	BI	76608	62314	70994	76638
1266	N	*NSX*	BI	76610	62316	70996	76640
				EE3645B	*ED2602B*	*EH2751B*	*EE3634B*
1268	N	*NSX*	BI	76718	62356	71036	76789
1269	N	*NSX*	BI	76719	62357	71037	76790
1270	N	*NSX*	BI	76720	62358	71038	76791
1271	N	*NSX*	BI	76721	62359	71039	76792
1272		*NSX*	BI	76722	62360	71040	76793
1274		*NSX*	BI	76724	62362	71042	76795
1275	N	*NSX*	BI	76725	62363	71043	76796
1276	N	*NSX*	BI	76726	62364	71044	76797
1277	N	*NSX*	BI	76727	62365	71045	76798
1278	N	*NSX*	BI	76728	62366	71046	76799
1279	N	*NSX*	BI	76729	62367	71047	76800
1280	N	*NSX*	BI	76730	62368	71048	76801
1281	N	*NSX*	BI	76731	62369	71049	76802
1282	N	*NSX*	BI	76732	62370	71050	76803
1284	N	*NSX*	BI	76734	62372	71052	76805
1285	N	*NSX*	BI	76735	62373	71053	76806
1286	N	*NSX*	BI	76736	62374	71054	76807
1287	N	*NSX*	BI	76737	62375	71055	76808
1288	N	*NSX*	BI	76738	62376	71056	76809
1289	N	*NSX*	BI	76739	62377	71057	76810
1290	N	*NSX*	BI	76740	62378	71058	76811
1291	N	*NSX*	BI	76741	62379	71059	76812
1292	N	*NSX*	BI	76742	62380	71060	76813
1293	N	*NSX*	BI	76743	62381	71061	76814
1294	N	*NSX*	BI	76744	62382	71062	76815
1295	N	*NSX*	BI	76745	62383	71063	76816
1296	N	*NSX*	BI	76746	62384	71064	76817
1297	N	*NSX*	BI	76747	62385	71065	76818
1298	N	*NSX*	BI	76748	62386	71066	76819
1299	N	*NSX*	BI	76749	62387	71067	76820
1300	N	*NSX*	BI	76750	62388	71068	76821

Class 411 — 4-CEP 4-Car

Built: British Railways, Eastleigh 1956
Introduced: 1975. Prototype refurbished unit
Design: BR gangwayed throughout, driver/guard communitcation and public address equipment fitted
Supply: 750/850V dc third rail
Traction motors (DMS): Two 250hp (185kW) dc English Electric
Maximum speed: 90mph
Dimensons: 20.34m L × 2.82m W × 3.83m H
AWS: Fitted to driving vehicles

DMEE Diagram	*SR Design*	*Type*	*Weight*	*Seats 1st*	*Seats Std*	*Toilets*
Driving Motor Standard						
EA2.61.1A	AK1A	DMS	41.5t	—	64	
EA2.62.1A	AL1K	DMS	41.5t	—	64	
EA2.63.0A	A0	DMS	41t	—	64	
EA2.63.1A*	A01A	DMS	41t	—	64	
EA2.64.0A	AK	DMS	41t	—	64	
EA2.64.1A	AM	DMS	41t	—	64	
EA2.64.2B	AM1A	DMS	41t	—	64	
EA2.64.3A	AL	DMS	41t	—	64	
EA2.64.4B	AN	DMS	41t	—	64	
EA2.64.5A	AN1A	DMS	41t	—	64	
Trailer Standard						
EH2.77.0A	BX3D	TS	31.5t	—	64	2
EH2.82.0A	BZ	TS	31.5t	—	64	2
EH2.82.1A	BX	TS	31.5t	—	64	2
EH2.82.2A	BX1A	TS	31.5t	—	64	2
EH2.82.4A*	BX1B	TS	31.5t	—	64	2
EH2.84.0A	BX4E	TS	33.5t	—	64	2
Trailer Brake Composite: (Compartment)						
EJ3.60.0A	BW3D	TBC	31.5t	24	6	2
EJ3.61.0A	BY	TBC	31.5t	24	6	2
EJ3.61.1A	BW	TBC	31.5t	24	6	2
EJ3.61.2A	BW1A	TBC	31.5t	24	6	2
EJ3.61.4A*	BW1B	TBC	31.5t	24	6	2

*Unofficial code

CLASS 411/3

Prototype refurbished unit, modified 1975

Unit No	SC	Liv	Pool	Dep	DMS	TBC	TS	DMS
					EA261	*EJ360*	*EH277*	*EA262*
1500		L	*NKC*	RE	61389	70345	70302	61388

Class 411/4

Unit No	SC	Liv	Pool	Dep	DMS	TBC	TS		DMS
					EA2630A	*EJ3610A*	*EH28*		*EA2631A*
~~1501~~			*NKC*	RE	61041	70041	70034	*20A*	61042
1502		L	*NKC*	RE	61040	70040	70036	*20A*	61039
1503		L	*NKC*	RE	61033	70037	70033	*20A*	61034
1504		L	*NKC*	RE	61043	70042	71712	*40A*	61037
1505		N	*NKC*	RE	61044	70039	70035	*20A*	61038

Unit No	SC	Liv	Pool	Dep	DMS		TBC		TS		DMS	
					EA264		*EJ361*		*EH28*		*EA2643*	
1506			*NKC*	RE	61349	*0A*	70325	*1A*	70282	*21A*	61348	*3A*
1507			*NKC*	RE	61363	*0A*	70332	*1A*	70289	*21A*	61362	*3A*
1508			*NKC*	RE	61305	*0A*	70303	*1A*	70260	*21A*	61304	*3A*
1509			*NKC*	RE	61335	*0A*	70318	*1A*	70275	*21A*	61334	*3A*
1510			*NKC*	RE	61365	*0A*	70333	*1A*	70290	*21A*	61364	*3A*
1511			*NKC*	RE	61367	*0A*	70334	*1A*	70291	*21A*	61366	*3A*
1512		L	*NKC*	RE	61321	*0A*	70311	*1A*	70268	*21A*	61320	*3A*
1513			*NKC*	RE	61796	*1A*	70321	*1A*	70278	*21A*	61340	*3A*
~~1514~~			*NKC*	RE	61327	*0A*	70314	*1A*	70271	*21A*	61326	*3A*
1515		L	*NKC*	RE	61345	*0A*	70323	*1A*	70280	*21A*	61344	*3A*
1516			*NKC*	RE	61319	*0A*	70310	*1A*	70267	*21A*	61318	*3A*
1517		L	*NKC*	RE	61317	*0A*	70309	*1A*	70266	*21A*	61316	*3A*
1518		L	*NKC*	RE	61333	*0A*	70317	*1A*	70274	*21A*	61332	*3A*
1519		L	*NKC*	RE	61403	*0A*	70352	*1A*	70516	*22A*	61402	*3A*
1520		L	*NKC*	RE	61343	*0A*	70327	*1A*	70284	*21A*	61380	*3A*
1521		L	*NKC*	RE	61353	*0A*	70324	*1A*	70281	*21A*	61352	*3A*
1522		L	*NKC*	RE	61347	*0A*	70341	*1A*	70665	*24A*	61346	*3A*
1523		L	*NKC*	RE	61383	*0A*	70342	*1A*	70299	*21A*	61382	*3A*
1524		L	*NKC*	RE	61309	*0A*	70305	*1A*	70262	*21A*	61308	*3A*
1525		L	*NKC*	RE	61235	*0A*	70238	*1A*	70232	*21A*	61236	*3A*
1526		L	*NKC*	RE	61239	*0A*	70240	*1A*	70234	*21A*	61240	*3A*
~~1527~~		L	*NKC*	RE	61237	*0A*	70239	*1A*	70233	*21A*	61238	*3A*
1528		L	*NKC*	RE	61379	*0A*	70340	*1A*	70297	*21A*	61378	*3A*
1529		L	*NKC*	RE	61355	*0A*	70328	*1A*	70285	*21A*	61354	*3A*
1530		L	*NKC*	RE	61331	*0A*	70316	*1A*	70273	*21A*	61330	*3A*
1531		L	*NKC*	RE	61233	*0A*	70237	*1A*	70231	*21A*	61234	*3A*
~~1532~~		L	*NKC*	RE	61391	*0A*	70346	*1A*	71626	*40A*	61390	*3A*
1533		L	*NKC*	RE	61393	*0A*	70347	*1A*	71627	*40A*	61385	*3A*
1534		L	*NKC*	RE	61405	*0A*	70353	*1A*	71628	*40A*	61404	*3A*
1535		L	*NKC*	RE	61397	*0A*	70349	*1A*	71629	*40A*	61396	*3A*
1536		L	*NKC*	RE	61399	*0A*	70350	*1A*	71631	*40A*	61398	*3A*
1537		L	*NKC*	RE	61229	*0A*	70235	*1A*	70229	*21A*	61230	*3A*
1538		L	*NKC*	RE	61307	*0A*	70304	*1A*	70261	*21A*	61306	*3A*
1539		L	*NKC*	RE	61401	*0A*	70351	*1A*	71632	*40A*	61400	*3A*
1540		L	*NKC*	RE	61870	*1A*	70343	*1A*	70300	*21A*	61384	*3A*
1541		L	*NKC*	RE	61409	*0A*	70355	*1A*	71633	*40A*	61408	*3A*
1542		L	*NKC*	RE	61395	*0A*	70348	*1A*	71634	*40A*	61394	*3A*

Unit No	SC	Liv	Pool	Dep	DMS		TBC		TS		DMS	
~~1543~~		L	*NKC*	RE	61323	*0A*	70312	*1A*	70269	*21A*	61322	*3A*
1544		L	*NKC*	RE	61315	*0A*	70308	*1A*	70265	*21A*	61314	*3A*
~~1545~~		L	*NKC*	RE	61359	*0A*	70330	*1A*	70287	*21A*	61358	*3A*
1546		L	*NKC*	RE	61357	*0A*	70329	*1A*	70286	*21A*	61356	*3A*
1547		L	*NKC*	RE	61329	*0A*	70315	*1A*	70272	*21A*	61328	*3A*
~~1548~~		L	*NKC*	RE	61375	*0A*	70338	*1A*	70295	*21A*	61374	*3A*
~~1549~~		L	*NKC*	RE	61339	*0A*	70320	*1A*	70277	*21A*	61338	*3A*
1550		L	*NKC*	RE	61313	*0A*	70307	*1A*	70264	*21A*	61312	*3A*
~~1551~~		L	*NKC*	RE	61325	*0A*	70313	*1A*	70270	*21A*	61324	*3A*
1552		L	*NKC*	RE	61373	*0A*	70337	*1A*	70294	*21A*	61372	*3A*
1553		L	*NKC*	RE	61351	*0A*	70306	*1A*	70263	*21A*	61350	*3A*
~~1554~~		L	*NKC*	RE	61369	*0A*	70335	*1A*	70292	*21A*	61368	*3A*
~~1555~~		L	*NKC*	RE	61311	*0A*	70326	*1A*	70283	*21A*	61310	*3A*
~~1556~~		L	*NKC*	RE	61371	*0A*	70336	*1A*	70293	*21A*	61370	*3A*
~~1557~~		L	*NKC*	RE	61337	*0A*	70331	*1A*	70288	*21A*	61360	*3A*
1558		L	*NKC*	RE	61361	*0A*	70319	*1A*	70276	*21A*	61336	*3A*
1559		L	*NKC*	RE	61377	*0A*	70339	*1A*	70296	*21A*	61376	*3A*
1560		N	*NSS*	FR	61387	*0A*	70344	*2A*	70301	*21A*	61386	*3A*
1561		N	*NSS*	FR	61231	*0A*	70604	*2A*	70230	*21A*	61232	*3A*
1562		N	*NSS*	RE	61407	*0A*	70236	*1A*	70241	*22A*	61406	*3A*
1563		L	*NKC*	RE	61740	*1A*	70575	*2A*	70526	*22A*	61741	*4B*
1564		L	*NKC*	RE	61788	*1A*	70599	*2A*	70550	*22A*	61789	*4B*
1565		L	*NKC*	RE	61762	*1A*	70586	*2A*	71711	*40A*	61763	*4B*
~~1566~~		L	*NKC*	RE	61722	*1A*	70566	*2A*	70517	*22A*	61723	*4B*
1567		L	*NKC*	RE	61786	*1A*	70598	*2A*	70549	*22A*	61787	*4B*
~~1568~~		L	*NKC*	RE	61766	*1A*	70588	*2A*	70539	*22A*	61767	*4B*
1569		L	*NKC*	RE	61782	*1A*	70596	*2A*	70547	*22A*	61783	*4B*
1570		L	*NKC*	RE	61738	*1A*	70574	*2A*	70525	*22A*	61739	*4B*
1571		L	*NKC*	RE	61806	*1A*	70608	*2A*	71636	*40A*	61807	*4B*
~~1572~~		L	*NKC*	RE	61734	*1A*	70572	*2A*	70523	*22A*	61735	*4B*
~~1573~~		L	*NKC*	RE	61726	*1A*	70568	*2A*	70519	*22A*	61727	*4B*
1574		L	*NKC*	RE	61792	*1A*	70601	*2A*	71635	*40A*	61793	*4B*
1575		L	*NKC*	RE	61768	*1A*	70583	*2A*	70540	*22A*	61769	*4B*
1576		L	*NKC*	RE	61770	*1A*	70590	*2A*	70541	*22A*	61771	*4B*
1577		L	*NKC*	RE	61718	*1A*	70564	*2A*	70515	*22A*	61719	*4B*
1578		L	*NKC*	RE	61700	*1A*	70555	*2A*	70506	*22A*	61701	*4B*
1579		L	*NKC*	RE	61772	*1A*	70591	*2A*	70542	*22A*	61773	*4B*
1580		L	*NKC*	RE	61756	*1A*	70589	*2A*	70534	*22A*	61757	*4B*
1581		L	*NKC*	RE	61784	*1A*	70597	*2A*	70548	*22A*	61785	*4B*
1582		L	*NKC*	RE	61748	*1A*	70603	*2A*	71630	*40A*	61797	*4B*
1583		L	*NKC*	RE	61746	*1A*	70578	*2A*	70529	*22A*	61747	*4B*
1584		L	*NKC*	RE	61752	*1A*	70581	*2A*	70532	*22A*	61753	*4B*
1585		L	*NKC*	RE	61710	*1A*	70560	*2A*	70511	*22A*	61711	*4B*
1586		L	*NKC*	RE	61714	*1A*	70562	*2A*	70513	*22A*	61715	*4B*
1587		L	*NKC*	RE	61764	*1A*	70587	*2A*	71625	*40A*	61765	*4B*
1588		L	*NKC*	RE	61720	*1A*	70044	*2A*	70520	*22A*	61721	*4B*
1589		L	*NKC*	RE	61742	*1A*	70576	*2A*	70527	*22A*	61743	*4B*

Unit No	SC	Liv	Pool	Dep	DMS		TBC		TS		DMS	
1590		L	*NKC*	RE	61696	*1A*	70553	*2A*	70504	*22A*	61697	*4B*
1591		L	*NKC*	RE	61790	*1A*	70600	*2A*	70551	*22A*	61791	*4B*
1592		L	*NKC*	RE	61778	*1A*	70594	*2A*	70545	*22A*	61779	*4B*
1593		L	*NKC*	RE	61730	*1A*	70570	*2A*	70521	*22A*	61731	*4B*
1594		L	*NKC*	RE	61754	*1A*	70582	*2A*	70533	*22A*	61755	*4B*
1595		L	*NKC*	RE	61704	*1A*	70557	*2A*	70508	*22A*	61705	*4B*
1596		L	*NKC*	RE	61716	*1A*	70563	*2A*	70514	*22A*	61717	*4B*
1597		L	*NKC*	RE	61708	*1A*	70559	*2A*	70510	*22A*	61709	*4B*
1598		L	*NKC*	RE	61780	*1A*	70595	*2A*	70546	*22A*	61781	*4B*
1599		L	*NKC*	RE	61706	*1A*	70558	*2A*	70509	*22A*	61707	*4B*
1600		L	*NKC*	RE	61724	*1A*	70567	*2A*	70518	*22A*	61725	*4B*
1601		L	*NKC*	RE	61776	*1A*	70593	*2A*	70544	*22A*	61777	*4B*
1602		L	*NKC*	RE	61958	*2B*	70565	*2A*	70279	*21A*	61959	*5A*
1603			*NKC*	RE	61728	*1A*	70569	*2A*	70298	*21A*	61729	*4B*
1604			*NKC*	RE	61732	*1A*	70571	*2A*	70522	*22A*	61733	*4B*
1605			*NKC*	RE	61712	*1A*	70561	*2A*	70512	*22A*	61713	*4B*
1606			*NKC*	RE	61694	*1A*	70552	*2A*	70503	*22A*	61695	*4B*
1607		N	*NKC*	RE	61698	*1A*	70554	*2A*	70505	*22A*	61699	*4B*
1608			*NKC*	RE	61960	*2B*	70659	*4A*	70666	*24A*	61961	*5A*
1609		L	*NKC*	RE	61744	*1A*	70577	*2A*	70528	*22A*	61745	*4B*
1610		L	*NKC*	RE	61750	*1A*	70580	*2A*	70531	*22A*	61751	*4B*
1611		L	*NKC*	RE	61758	*1A*	70584	*2A*	70537	*22A*	61759	*4B*
1612		L	*NKC*	RE	61794	*1A*	70602	*2A*	70535	*22A*	61795	*4B*
1613		L	*NKC*	RE	61760	*1A*	70585	*2A*	70536	*22A*	61761	*4B*
1614		L	*NBT*	RE	61702	*1A*	70556	*2A*	70507	*22A*	61703	*4B*
1615		L	*NBT*	RE	61956	*2B*	70657	*4A*	70664	*24A*	61957	*5A*
1616		L	*NBT*	RE	61950	*2B*	70654	*4A*	70543	*22A*	61951	*5A*
1617		L	*NBT*	RE	61800	*1A*	70605	*2A*	70661	*24A*	61801	*4B*
1618		L	*NBT*	RE	61868	*1A*	70043	*2A*	70663	*24A*	61869	*4B*
1619		L	*NBT*	RE	61952	*2B*	70655	*4A*	70662	*24A*	61953	*5A*
1620		N	*NBT*	RE	61948	*2B*	70653	*4A*	70660	*24A*	61949	*5A*
1621		N	*NBT*	RE	61810	*1A*	70610	*2A*	70524	*22A*	61811	*4B*

Class 421 — 4-CIG 4-Car

Built: Class 421/3: British Railways York 1964; **Class 421/4:** BREL York 1970

Facelifted 1985-89
For full details see Class 421

DMEE Diagram	*SR Design*	*Type*	*Weight*	*Seats 1st*	*Seats Std*	*Toilets*
Motor Brake Standard						
ED2.64.0A	EA3B	MBS	49t	—	56	
ED2.64.1B	EA5B	MBS	49t	—	56	
ED2.64.2C*	EA4B	MBS	49t	—	56	

Driving Trailer Composite: (Compartment/Saloon)					
EE3.69.0A	FA4B	DTC	35.5t	18 36	2
EE3.69.1A	FA6B	DTC	35.5t	18 36	2
EE3.69.2B*	FA5B	DTC	35.5t	18 36	2
EE3.69.3C*	FA7B	DTC	35.5t	18 36	2
EE3.69.4D*	FA8B	DTC	35.5t	18 36	2
Trailer Standard					
EH2.87.0A	B02B	TS	31.5t	— 72	
EH2.87.1A	B04B	TS	31.5t	— 72	
EH2.87.2B	B03B	TS	31.5t	— 72	
EH2.87.3C	B04B	TS	31.5t	— 72	†

*Official codes not issued

Class 421/3

Equipped with electronic parking brake

Unit No	SC	Liv	Pool	Dep	DTC	MBS	TS	DTC
					EE3690A	*ED2640A*	*EH2870A*	*EE3690A*
1701		N	*NSX*	BI	76087	62028	70706	76033
1702		N	*NSX*	BI	76101	62042	70720	76047
1703		N	*NSX*	BI	76097	62038	70716	76043
1704		N	*NSX*	BI	76092	63033	70711	76038
1705		N	*NSX*	BI	76076	62017	70695	76022
1706		N	*NSX*	BI	76094	62035	70713	76040
1707		N	*NSX*	BI	76084	62025	70703	76030
1708		N	*NSX*	BI	76110	62051	70729	76056
1709		N	*NSX*	BI	76103	62044	70722	76049
1710		N	*NSX*	BI	76078	62019	70697	76024
1711		N	*NSX*	BI	76114	62055	71766	76060
1712			*NSX*	BI	76079	62020	70698	76025
1713			*NSX*	BI	76128	62069	71767	76074
1714			*NSX*	BI	76028	62018	70696	76023
1715			*NSX*	BI	76082	62023	70701	76077
1716		N	*NSX*	BI	76100	62041	71768	76046
1717		N	*NSX*	BI	76083	62024	70702	76029
1718		N	*NSX*	BI	76081	62022	70700	76027
					EE3690A	*ED2643C*	*EH2870A*	*EE3690A*
1719		N	NSX	BI	76116	62057	70719	76062
					EE2690A	*ED2640A*	*EH2870A*	*EE3690A*
1720		N	*NSX*	BI	76098	62039	71769	76044
1721		N	*NSX*	BI	76090	62031	70709	76036
1722		N	*NSX*	BI	76106	62047	70725	76052
1723		N	*NSX*	BI	76107	62048	70726	76053
1724		N	*NSX*	BI	76120	62061	71770	76066
1725		N	*NSX*	BI	76088	62029	70707	76034
1726		N	*NSX*	BI	76109	62050	70728	76055
1727		N	*NSX*	BI	76111	62052	70730	76057

Unit No	SC	Liv	Pool	Dep	DTC	MBS	TS	DTC
					EE3692B	*ED2642C*	*EH2872B*	*EE3692B*
1728		N	*NSX*	BI	76099	62040	70718	76045
1729		N	*NSX*	BI	76104	62045	70723	76050
1730		N	*NSX*	BI	76105	62046	70724	76113
1731		N	*NSX*	BI	76095	62036	70714	76041
					EE3693C	*ED2642C*	*EH2872B*	*EE3693C*
1732		N	*NSX*	BI	76096	62037	70715	76042

Class 421/4

Unit No	SC	Liv	Pool	Dep	Former Unit No	DTC	MBS	TS	DTC
						EE3691A	*ED2641B*	*EH2871A*	*EE3691A*
1801			*NSX*	BI	—	76777	62415	71095	76848
1802			*NSX*	BI	—	76779	62417	71097	76850
1803			*NSX*	BI	—	76780	62418	71098	76851
1804			*NSX*	BI	—	76778	62416	71096	76849
1805			*NSX*	BI	—	76782	62420	71100	76853
1806			*NSX*	BI	—	76783	62421	71101	76854
1807		N	*NSX*	BI	—	76784	62422	71102	76855
1808		N	*NSX*	BI	—	76785	62423	71103	76856
1809		N	*NSX*	BI	—	76786	62424	71104	76857
1810		N	*NSX*	BI	—	76787	62425	71105	76858
1811		N	*NSX*	BI	—	76781	62419	71099	76852
1812		N	*NSX*	BI	—	76757	62395	71075	76828
1813		N	*NSX*	BI	—	76789	62430	71106	76860
						EE3694D	*ED2641B*	*EH2871A*	*EE3694D*
1814		N	*NSS*	FR	(1251)	76595	62301	70981	76625
1815		N	*NSS*	FR	(1240)	76584	62290	70970	76614
1816		N	*NSS*	FR	(1237)	76581	62287	70967	76611
1817		N	*NSS*	FR	(1239)	76583	62289	70969	76613
1818		N	*NSS*	FR	(1267)	76717	62355	71035	76788
1819		N	*NSS*	FR	(1273)	76723	62361	71041	76794
1820		N	*NSS*	FR	(1242)	76586	62292	70972	76616
1821		N	*NSS*	FR	(1248)	76592	62298	70978	76622
1822		N	*NSS*	FR	(1250)	76594	62300	70980	76624
						EE3694D	*ED2641B*	*EH2873C*	*EE3694D*
1823		N	*NSS*	FR	(2207)	76567	62283	71926	76577
1824		N	*NSS*	FR	(2201)	76561	62277	71927	76571
1825		N	*NSS*	FR	(2202)	76562	62278	71928	76572

†Coach Nos 71826/27/28 formerly TRBS Nos 69315/30/31 respectively

Class 431 4REP 4-Car

Built: British Railways, York 1966
Design: BR, gangwayed throughout, Driver/guard communication equipped
Supply: 750/850V dc third rail
Traction Motors (DMS): Two 365hp (300kW) dc English Electric EE546
Maximum speed: 90mph
Dimensions: 20.35m L × 2.83m W × 3.90m H
AWS: Driving vehicles fitted
Note: Tractor unit to work in conjunction with Class 438 TC units. Reformed from Class 432 4-REP during 1988/89

DMEE Diagram	*SR Design*	*Type*	*Weight*	*Seats 1st*	*Seats Std*	*Toilets*
Driving Motor Standard:						
EA2.60.1A	AJ	DMS	55.5t	—	64	—
Trailer Composite (Compartment):						
EH3.--.2B	BU2B	TC	33.5t	36	8	2
Trailer Brake Standard (Compartment):						
EJ2.60.0A	BT	TBS	35.5t	—	32	1 PA fitted

*Unofficial code

Unit No	Old No	Liv	Pool	Dep	DMS *EA260*	TBS *EJ260*	TC *EH3--*	DMS *EA260*
1901	(2001 R)	N	*NSS*	BM	62141	70830	71163	62142
1902	(2007 R)	N	*NSS*	BM	62154	70824	70845	62153

Class 422 4-BIG 4-Car

Built: British Railways, York 1965
Design: BR, gangwayed throughout. All refurbished. Driver/guard communication and public address equipment fitted
Supply: 750/850V dc third rail
Traction Motors: Four 250hp (185kW) dc English Electric
Maximum speed: 90mph
Dimensions: 20.19m L × 2.82m W × 3.86m H
AWS: Driving vehicles fitted

DMEE Diagram	*SR Design*	*Type*	*Weight*	*Seats 1st*	*Seats Std*	*Toilet*
Motor Brake Standard:						
ED2.60.0A	EA	MBS	49t	—	56	—
ED2.60.1B	EA1A	MBS	49t	—	56	—

Driving Trailer Composite (Compartment):						
EE3.63.3B	FA1A	DTC	36t	24	28	2
EE3.63.5A	FA	DTC	36t	24	28	2
EE3.64.4B	FA1A	DTC	35.5t	18	36	2
EE3.64.6A	FA	DTC	35.5t	18	36	2
Trailer Brake Standard:						
EN2.60.0A	BP	TBS	35t	—	40	—
EN2.60.1B	BP1A	TBS	35t	—	40	—

Class 422/1

Fitted with electric parking brakes

Unit No	Liv	Pool	Dep	DTC	MBS	TRBS	DTC
				EE3646A	*ED2600A*	*EN2600A*	*EE3635A*
2101	N	*NSX*	BI	76063	62054	69302	76059
2102	N	*NSX*	BI	76129	62064	69312	76069
2103	N	*NSX*	BI	76124	62065	69313	76070
2104	N	*NSX*	BI	76117	62058	69306	76051
2105	N	*NSX*	BI	76121	62062	69310	76067
2106	N	*NSX*	BI	76118	62059	69307	76064
2107	N	*NSX*	BI	76122	62063	69311	76068
2108	N	*NSX*	BI	76127	62068	69316	76073
2109	N	*NSX*	BI	76123	62070	69318	76075
2110	N	*NSX*	BI	76115	62056	69304	76061
2111	N	*NSX*	BI	76112	62053	69301	76058
				EE3646A	*ED2600A*	*EN2601B*	*EE3635A*
2112	N	*NSX*	BI	76126	62067	69333	76072

Class 422/2

Not fitted with electric parking brakes.

Unit No	Liv	Pool	Dep	DTC	MBS	TRBS	DTC
				EE3644B	*ED2601B*	*EN2601B*	*EE3633B*
2203		*NSX*	BI	76563	62279	69332	76573
2204		*NSX*	BI	76564	62280	69336	76574
2205		*NSX*	BI	76565	62281	69339	76575
2206		*NSX*	BI	76602	62308	69338	76632
2208		*NSX*	BI	76568	62284	69334	76578
2209	N	*NSX*	BI	76569	62285	69335	76579
2210	N	*NSX*	BI	76570	62286	69337	76580

Class 412/3 — 4-BEP 4-Car

Built: British Railways, Eastleigh 1961
Design: BR, gangwayed throughout. Driver/guard communication and public address equipment fitted. Refurbished 1982
Supply: 750/850V dc third rail
Traction Motors (DMS): Two 250hp (185kW) dc English Electric
Maximum speed: 90mph
Dimensions: 20.34m L × 2.82m W × 3.83m H
AWS: Driving coaches fitted

DMEE Diagram	*SR Design*	*Type*	*Weight*	*Seats 1st*	*Std*	*Toilet*
Driving Motor Standard:						
EA2.64.1A	AM	DMS	41t	—	64	—
EA2.64.2B	AM1A	DMS	41t	—	64	—
EA2.64.4B	AN	DMS	41t	—	64	—
EA2.64.5A	AN1A	DMS	41t	—	64	—
Trailer Brake Composite (Corridor):						
EJ3.61.1A	BW	TBC	31.5t	24	6	2
EJ3.61.2A	BW1A	TBC	31.5t	24	6	2
EJ3.61.4A*	BW1B	TBC	31.5t	24	6	2
Trailer Buffet Standard:						
EN2.61.0A	BL3C	TBS	35.5t	—	33	1

*Unofficial code

Unit No	**Liv**	**Pool**	**Dep**	**DMS** *EA264*	**TBC** *EJ361*	**TRBS** *EN261*	**DMS** *EA264*
~~2301~~	N	*NSS*	FR	61804 *1A*	70607 *2A*	69341	61805 *4B*
~~2302~~	N	*NSS*	FR	61774 *1A*	70592 *2A*	69342	61775 *4B*
2303	N	*NSS*	FR	61954 *2B*	70656 *4A*	69343	61955 *5A*
~~2304~~	N	*NSS*	FR	61736 *1A*	70573 *2A*	69344	61737 *4B*
~~2305~~		*NSS*	FR	61798 *1A*	70354 *1A*	69345	61799 *4B*
2306		*NSS*	FR	61808 *1A*	70609 *2A*	69346	61809 *4B*
~~2307~~		*NSS*	FR	61802 *1A*	70606 *2A*	69347	61803 *4B*

Class 442 — 5-WES 5-Car

Built: BREL, Derby-Litchurch Lane 1987
WESSEX ELECTRIC UNITS
Design: BR, gangwayed Mk3. Power operated swing-plug doors. Sliding doors each end of driving trailers. Air conditioned
Supply: 750/850V dc third rail
Traction Motors (MBLS): Four 365hp (300kW) dc English Electric EE546
Maximum speed: 100mph
Dimensions: 22.15m L × 2.74m W × 3.81m H
AWS: Driving coaches fitted

DMEE Diagram	*SR Design*	*Type*	*Weight*	*Seats 1st*	*Std*	*Toilet*
Motor Buffet Luggage Standard (Modular Catering):						
ED2.65.0A	EC	MBLS	51t	—	14	—
ED2.65.1B*	EC	MBLS	51t	—	14	—
Additional seating in buffet lounge area						
Driving Trailer Standard/First:						
EE2.73.0A	FE	DTS	34t	—	78	1
EE1.60.0A	FD	DTF	34t	50	—	1
Trailer Standard:						
EH2.88.0A	BV	TS	34t	—	80	2
EH2.89.0A	BV-1A	TS	34t	—	78	2 Wheelchair position

*Official code not issued

Unit No	**Liv**	**Pool**	**Dep**	**DTF**	**TS**	**MBLS**	**TS**	**DTS**
				EE1600A	*EH2880A*	*ED2650A*	*EH2890A*	*EE2730A*
~~2401~~	N	*NSS*	BM	77382	71818	62937	71842	77406
2402	N	*NSS*	BM	77383	71819	62938	71843	77407
~~2403~~	N	*NSS*	BM	77384	71820	62939	71844	77408
~~2404~~	N	*NSS*	BM	77385	71821	62940	71845	77409
~~2405~~	N	*NSS*	BM	77386	71822	62941	71846	77410
2406	N	*NSS*	BM	77387	71823	62942	71847	77411
~~2407~~	N	*NSS*	BM	77388	71824	62943	71848	77412
2408	N	*NSS*	BM	77389	71825	62944	71849	77413
2409	N	*NSS*	BM	77390	71826	62945	71850	77414
2410	N	*NSS*	BM	77391	71827	62946	71851	77415
2411	N	*NSS*	BM	77392	71828	62947	71852	77416
~~2412~~	N	*NSS*	BM	77393	71829	62948	71853	77417
				EE1600A	*EH2880A*	*ED2651B*	*EH2890A*	*EE2730A*
~~2413~~	N	*NSS*	BM	77394	71830	62949	71854	77418
~~2414~~	N	*NSS*	BM	77395	71831	62950	71855	77419
~~2415~~	N	*NSS*	BM	77396	71832	62951	71856	77420
~~2416~~	N	*NSS*	BM	77397	71833	62952	71857	77421
~~2417~~	N	*NSS*	BM	77398	71834	62953	71858	77422
~~2418~~	N	*NSS*	BM	77399	71835	62954	71859	77423
2419	N	*NSS*	BM	77400	71836	62955	71860	77424
2420	N	*NSS*	BM	77401	71837	62956	71861	77425
2421	N	*NSS*	BM	77402	71838	62957	71862	77426
2422	N	*NSS*	BM	77403	71839	62958	71863	77427
~~2423~~	N	*NSS*	BM	77404	71840	62959	71864	77428
~~2424~~	N	*NSS*	BM	77405	71841	62960	71865	77429

Class 492 5-TCB 5-Car

Built: British Railways York 1966. Present formation introduced in 1986-88 from Class 438 4-TC adding TRB to Class 432 4-REP units
Design: BR gangwayed throughout. Driver/guard and public address equipment fitted
Supply: From Class 431, 432 or locomotive
Maximum speed: 90mph
AWS: Driving vehicles fitted
Dimensions: 22.15m L × 2.74m W × 3.81m H

DMEE Diagram	*SR Design*	*Type*	*Weight*	*Seats 1st*	*Seats Std*	*Toilets*
Driving Trailer Standard						
EE2.66.0A	FC	DTS	32.5t	—	64	
EE2.66.1A	FC1A	DTS	32.5t	—	64	
Trailer First: (Compartment)						
EH1.60.0A	BU	TF	33.5t	42	—	2
EH1.60.1B	BU1A	TF	33.5t	42	—	2
Trailer Brake First/Standard: (Compartment)						
EJ1.60.1B	BR1A	TBF	35.5t	24	—	1
EJ2.60.0A	BT	TBS	35.5t	—	32	1
Trailer Buffet Unclass						
EN4.63.0A	BS1A	TRB	35t	—	23	2
Built 1974						

Unit No	Old No	SC	Liv	Pool	Dep	DTS *EE266*	TF *EH160*	TRB *EN463*	TBF/TBS	DTC *EE266*
2804	(8009 R)			*NSS*	BM	76286 *0A*	70846 *0A*	69024 *#*	70820 *EJ2*	76285 *0A*
2807	(8033 R)			*NSS*	BM	76945 *1A*	70854 *0A*	69022	71156 *EJ1*	76946 *1A*
2809	(8031 R)			*NSS*	BM	76329 *0A*	71164 *1B*	69023 *#*	70842 *EJ2*	76330 *0A*

Class 423/0 4-VEP 4-Car

Built: British Railways Derby and York 1967
Design: BR gangwayed throughout. Driver-guard communication fitted
Power Supply: 750/850V dc
Traction motors: Four 250hp (185kW) English Electric
Maximum speed: 90mph
Dimensions: 20.18m L × 2.82m W × 3.84m H
AWS: Driving vehicles fitted

DMEE Diagram	SR Design	Type	Weight	Seats 1st	Std	Toilet
Motor Brake Standard						
ED2.61.0A	EB	MBS	49t	—	58	
ED2.61.1A	EB1A	MBS	49t	—	58	
ED2.62.0A	EB2A	MBS	49t	—	58	
ED2.63.0A	EV1A	MBS	49t	—	58	
ED2.63.1A	EB2A	MBS	49t	—	58	
ED2.63.2A	EB3A	MBS	49t	—	58	
ED2.63.3A	EB4A	MBS	49t	—	58	
ED2.63.5A	EB6A	MBS	49t	—	58	
Driving Trailer Composite: (Compartment/Saloon)						
EE3.63.4B† See Class 421/2 (not N)						
EE3.65.1A	FB	DTC	32.5t	24	38	1
EE3.66.1A	FB3A	DTC	35t	24	34	1
EE3.67.4A	FB	DTC	35.5t	24	38	1
EE3.67.6A	FB3A	DTC	35.5t	24	38	1
EE3.68.1B	FB1B	DTC	35.5t	18	46	1
EE3.68.2B	FB3B	DTC	35.5t	18	46	1
EE3.68.3B	FB2B	DTC	35.5t	18	46	1
EE3.71.0A	FB	DTC	32.5t	18	46	1
EE3.71.0B	FB4B	DTC	32.5t	18	46	1
Trailer Standard						
EH2.76.0A	BQ	TS	31.5t	—	98	
EH2.78.0A	BQ	TS	31.5t	—	90	
EH2.83.0A	BQ	TS	31.5t	—	98	

Unit No	SC	Liv	Pool	Dep	DTC *EE3710*		MBS *ED2610A*	TS *EH2760A*	DTC *EE3710*	
3001		N	*NSS*	BM	76230	*B*	62121	70781	76231	*B*
3002			*NSS*	BM	76233	*A*	62122	70782	76232	*A*
3003		N	*NSS*	BM	76234	*A*	62123	70783	76235	*A*
3005		N	*NSS*	BM	76239	*A*	62125	70785	76238	*A*
3006		N	*NSS*	BM	76241	*B*	62126	70786	76240	*B*
3007		N	*NSS*	BM	76243	*A*	62127	70787	76242	*A*
3008		N	*NSS*	BM	76244	*A*	62128	70788	76245	*A*
3009		N	*NSS*	BM	76246	*B*	62129	70789	76247	*B*
3010		N	*NSS*	BM	76369	*B*	62130	70790	76249	*B*
3011		N	*NSS*	BM	76251	*B*	62131	70791	76250	*B*
3012		N	*NSS*	BM	76252	*B*	62132	70792	76253	*B*
3013		N	*NSS*	BM	76255	*B*	62133	70793	76254	*B*
3014		N	*NSS*	BM	76257	*B*	62134	70794	76248	*B*
3015		N	*NSS*	BM	76258	*B*	62135	70795	76259	*B*
3016		N	*NSS*	BM	76261	*B*	62136	70796	76260	*B*
3017		N	*NSS*	BM	76262	*A*	62137	70797	76263	*A*
3018		N	*NSS*	BM	76265	*B*	62138	70875	76264	*B*
3019		N	*NSS*	BM	76267	*B*	62139	70799	76837†	*B*
3020		N	*NSS*	BM	76269	*B*	62140	70800	76268	*B*

Unit No	SC	Liv	Pool	Dep	DTC		MBS	TS	DTC	
					EE3710		*ED2611A*	*EH2760A*	*EE3710*	
3026		N	*NSX*	BI	76344	*B*	62187	70877	76343	*B*
3030		N	*NSS*	BM	76352	*B*	62191	70881	76351	*B*
3032		N	*NSS*	BM	76356	*B*	62193	70883	76355	*B*
3034		N	*NSS*	BM	76360	*B*	62195	70885	76359	*B*
3035		N	*NSS*	BM	76362	*B*	62196	70890	76361	*B*
3037		N	*NSS*	BM	76366	*B*	62198	70888	76365	*B*
3046		N	*NSS*	BM	76384	*A*	62207	70897	76383	*A*
					EE3674A		*ED2611A*	*EH2830A*	*EE3674A*	
3058			*NSS*	FR	76446		62219	70909	76445	
					EE36		*ED2631A*	*EH2830A*	*EE36*	
3067			*NSS*	WDs	76464	*76A*		70918	76463	*76A*
3068		N	*NSS*	FR	76466	*82B*	62229	70919	76370	*82B*
3069			*NSS*	WD	76468	*76A*	62230	70920	76467	*76A*
					EE3676A		*ED2631A*	*EH2760A*	*EE3710A*	
3070			*NSS*	WD	76470		62231	70900	76339	
					EE36		*ED2631A*	*EH2830A*	*EE36*	
3071		N	*NSS*	WD	76472	*82B*	62232	70922	76471	*82B*
3072			*NSS*	WD	76474	*76A*	62233	70923	76473	*76A*
3073			*NSS*	WD	76476	*76A*	62234	70924	76475	*76A*
3074			*NSS*	WD	76478	*76A*	62235	70925	76477	*76A*
3075		N	*NSS*	WD	76480	*82B*	62236	70926	76479	*82B*
3076			*NSS*	WD	76482	*76A*	62237	70927	76481	*76A*
3077		N	*NSS*	WD	76484	*82B*	62238	70928	76483	*82B*
3078		N	*NSS*	WD	76486	*82B*	62239	70929	76485	*82B*
3080		N	*NSX*	BI	76490	*82B*	62241	70931	76489	*82B*
3083			*NSX*	BI	76496	*82B*	62244	70934	76495	*82B*
3084			*NSX*	BI	76498	*76A*	62245	70935	76497	*76A*
3085			*NSX*	BI	76500	*76A*	62246	70936	76499	*76A*
3086			*NSX*	BI	76502	*76A*	62247	70937	76501	*76A*
3087			*NSX*	BI	76504	*76A*	62248	70938	76503	*76A*
					EE3661A		*ED2620A*	*EH2780A*	*EE3661A*	
3088			*NSX*	BI	76506		62249	70939	76505	
3089			*NSX*	BI	76508		62250	70940	76507	
3090			*NSX*	BI	76510		62251	70941	76509	
3091		N	*NSX*	BI	76512		62252	70942	76511	
3092		N	*NSX*	BI	76514		62253	70943	76513	
3093		N	*NSX*	BI	76516		62254	70944	76515	
3094		N	*NSX*	BI	76518		62255	70945	76517	
3095		N	*NSX*	BI	76520		62256	70946	76519	
3096		N	*NSX*	BI	76522		62257	70947	76521	
3097		N	*NSX*	BI	76524		62258	70948	76523	

Unit No	SC	Liv	Pool	Dep	DTC		MBS	TS	DTC	
					EE3651A		*ED2620A*	*EH2780A*	*EE3661A*	
3098			*NSX*	BI	76364		62259	70949	76525	
					EE3661A		*ED2620A*	*EH2780A*	*EE3661A*	
3099		N	*NSX*	BI	76528		62260	70950	76527	
					EE36		*ED2632A*	*EH2830A*	*EE36*	
3107		N	*NSX*	BI	76544	*82B*	62268	70958	76543	*82B*
3109			*NSX*	BI	76548	*76A*	62270	70960	76547	*76A*
3110			*NSX*	BI	76550	*76A*	62271	70961	76549	*76A*
3111			*NSX*	BI	76552	*76A*	62272	70962	76551	*76A*
3112		N	*NSX*	BI	76554	*81B*	62273	70963	76553	*81B*
3113		N	*NSB*	WD	76556	*81B*	62274	70964	76555	*81B*
3114		N	*NSX*	WD	76558	*81B*	62275	70965	76557	*81B*
3115		N	*NSX*	WD	76560	*81B*	62276	70966	76559	*81B*
					EE36		*ED2633A*	*EH2830A*	*EE36*	
3116		N	*NSX*	WD	76641	*81B*	62317	70997	76642	*81B*
3117		N	*NSX*	WD	76643	*81B*	62318	70998	76644	*81B*
3118		N	*NSX*	WD	76645	*81B*	62319	70999	76646	*81B*
3119		N	*NSX*	WD	76647	*81B*	62320	71000	76648	*81B*
3120			*NSX*	WD	76649	*75A*	62321	71001	76650	*75A*
3121		N	*NSX*	WD	76651	*81B*	62322	71002	76652	*81B*
3122			*NSX*	WD	76653	*75A*	62323	71003	76654	*75A*
3123		N	*NSX*	WD	76655	*81B*	62324	71004	76656	*81B*
3124			*NSX*	WD	76657	*75A*	62325	71005	76658	*75A*
3125		N	*NSX*	WD	76659	*81B*	62326	71006	76660	*81B*
3126			*NSX*	WD	76661	*75A*	62327	71007	76662	*75A*
3127			*NSX*	WD	76663	*75A*	62328	71008	76664	*75A*
3128			*NSX*	WD	76665	*75A*	62329	71009	76666	*75A*
3129			*NSX*	WD	76667	*75A*	62330	71010	76668	*75A*
3130			*NSX*	WD	76669	*75A*	62331	71011	76670	*75A*
3131			*NSX*	WD	76671	*75A*	62332	71012	76672	*75A*
3132			*NSX*	WD	76673	*75A*	62333	71013	76674	*75A*
3133			*NSX*	WD	76675	*75A*	62334	71014	76676	*75A*
3134		N	*NSX*	BI	76677	*81B*	62335	71015	76678	*81B*
3135		N	*NSX*	BI	76679	*81B*	62336	71016	76680	*81B*
3136			*NSX*	BI	76681	*75A*	62337	71017	76682	*75A*
3137		N	*NSX*	BI	76683	*81B*	62338	71018	76684	*81B*
3138		N	*NSX*	BI	76685	*81B*	62339	71019	76686	*81B*
3139		N	*NSX*	BI	76687	*81B*	62340	71020	76688	*81B*
					EE3681B		*ED2633A*	*EH2760A*	*EE3710B*	
3140		N	*NSX*	BI	76689		62341	70887	76363	
					EE3681B		*ED2633A*	*EH2830A*	*EE3681B*	
3141		N	*NSB*	WD	76691		62342	71022	76692	

Unit No	SC	Liv	Pool	Dep	DTC	MBS	TS	DTC
3142		N	*NSB*	WD	76693	62343	71023	76694
3143			*NSB*	WD	76695	62344	71024	76696
3144		N	*NSB*	WD	76697	62345	71025	76698
3145			*NSS*	BM	76699	62346	71026	76700
3146		N	*NSS*	BM	76701	62347	71027	76702
3147		N	*NSS*	BM	76703	62348	71028	76704
3148		N	*NKC*	RE	76705	62349	71029	76706
3149		N	*NKC*	RE	76707	62350	71030	76708
3150		N	*NKC*	RE	76709	62351	71031	76710
3151			*NKC*	RE	76711	62352	71032	76712
					EE3682B	*ED2633A*	*EH2830A*	*EE3681B*
3152		N	*NKC*	RE	76465	62353	71033	76714
					EE3681B	*ED2633A*	*EH2830A*	*EE3681B*
3153		N	*NKC*	RE	76715	62354	71034	76716
					EE36838	*ED2635A*	*EH2830A*	*EE3683B*
3154		N	*NKC*	RE	76861	62435	71115	76862
3155		N	*NKC*	RE	76863	62436	71116	76864
3156		N	*NKC*	RE	76865	62437	71117	76866
3157		N	*NKC*	RE	76867	62438	71118	76868
3158		N	*NKC*	RE	76869	62439	71119	76870
3159		N	*NKC*	RE	76871	62440	71120	76872
3160		N	*NKC*	RE	76873	62441	71121	76874
3161		N	*NKC*	RE	76875	62442	71122	76876
3162		N	*NKC*	RE	76877	62443	71123	76878
3163		N	*NKC*	RE	76879	62444	71124	76880
3164		N	*NKC*	RE	76881	62445	71125	76882
3165		N	*NKC*	RE	76883	62446	71126	76884
3166		N	*NKC*	RE	76885	62447	71127	76886
3167		N	*NKC*	RE	76887	62448	71128	76888
3169		N	*NKC*	RE	76891	62450	71130	76892
3170		N	*NKC*	RE	76893	62451	71131	76894
3171		N	*NKC*	RE	76895	62452	71132	76896
3172		N	*NKC*	RE	76897	62453	71133	76998
3173		N	*NKC*	RE	76899	62454	71134	76900
3174			*NKC*	RE	76901	62455	71135	76902
3175		N	*NKC*	RE	76903	62456	71136	76904
3176		N	*NKC*	RE	76905	62457	71137	76906
3177		N	*NKC*	RE	76907	62458	71138	76908
3178		N	*NKC*	RE	76909	62463	71139	76910
3179		N	*NKC*	RE	76911	62460	71140	76912
3180		N	*NKC*	RE	76913	62461	71141	76914
3181		N	*NKC*	RE	76915	62462	71142	76916
3182		N	*NKC*	RE	76917	62459	71143	76918
3183		N	*NKC*	RE	76919	62464	71144	76920

Unit No	SC	Liv	Pool	Dep	DTC	MBS	TS	DTC
3184		N	*NKC*	RE	76921	62465	71145	76922
3185		N	*NKC*	RE	76923	62466	71146	76924
3186		N	*NKC*	RE	76925	62467	71147	76926
3187		N	*NKC*	RE	76927	62468	71148	76928
3188		N	*NKC*	RE	76929	62469	71149	76930
3189		N	*NKC*	RE	76931	62470	71150	76932
3190		N	*NKC*	RE	76933	62471	71151	76934
3191		N	*NKC*	RE	76935	62472	71152	76936
3192		N	*NKC*	RE	76937	62473	71153	76938
3193		N	*NKC*	RE	76939	62474	71154	76940
3194		N	*NKC*	RE	76941	62475	71155	76942

Class 413 — 4-CAP 4-car

Built: BR, Eastleigh 1957. Present formations introduced 1982 by pairing Class 414 stock.
Design: BR, non-gangwayed. Driver/guard communication fitted. Controls of power cars not used
Supply: 750/850V dc
Traction Motors (MBS, MLS): Two 250hp (185kW) English Electric

Maximum speed: 90mph
Dimensions: *Motor coaches:* 20.04m L × 2.82m W × 3.86m H (over Periscopes). *Driving coaches:* 20.44m L × 2.82m W × 3.77m H
AWS: See below

DMEE Diagram	*SR Design*	*Type*	*Weight*	*Seats 1st*	*Seats Std*	*Toilet*	*AWS*
Motor Brake Standard:							
EB2.69.2B	CQ2B	MBS	42t	—	84	—	—
EB2.69.3B	CQ3A	MBS	42t	—	84	—	—
EB2.69.6B	CQ3A	MBS	42t	—	84	—	Isolated
EB2.70.0A	CR	MBS	42t	—	84	—	—
EB2.70.3A	CR	MBS	42t	—	84	—	Isolated
Motor Luggage Standard (MLS): Details as MBS above							
Driving Trailer Composite/Standard (Compartment/Saloon):							
EE2.21.1A	DX	DTS	32.5t	—	69	2	Fitted
EE2.22.1A	DZ	DTS	32.5t	—	69	2	Fitted
EE3.61.2A	DX	DTC	32.5t	19	50	2	Fitted
EE3.61.3A*	DX1A	DTC	32.5t	19	50	2	Fitted
EE3.62.3A	DZ	DTC	32.5t	19	50	2	Fitted

*Official code not issued

Class 413/2

Unit No	Liv	Pool	Dep	DTC *EE361*	MBS *EB269*	MLS *EB269*	DTS *EE2211A*
3201	N	*NKC*	RE	77120 *3A*	65398 *2B*	65401 *3B*	77123

Unit No	Liv	Pool	Dep	DTC	MBS	MLS	DTS
3202	N	*NKC*	RE	77118 *2A*	65396 *3B*	65412 *3B*	77134
3203	N	*NKC*	RE	77117 *2A*	65395 *6B*	65424 *3B*	77146
3204	N	*NKC*	RE	77132 *2A*	65410 *6B*	65420 *6B*	77142
3205		*NKC*	RE	77135 *2A*	65413 *3B*	65422 *3B*	77144
3206		*NKC*	RE	77141 *2A*	65419 *6B*	65423 *6B*	77145
3207		*NKC*	RE	77126 *2A*	65404 *3B*	65428 *3B*	77150
3208		*NKC*	RE	77147 *2A*	65425 *3B*	65429 *3B*	77151
3209		*NKC*	RE	77129 *2A*	65407 *6B*	65430 *6B*	77152
3210		*NKC*	RE	77124 *2A*	65402 *3B*	65434 *3B*	77156
3211		*NKC*	RE	77115 *2A*	65393 *3B*	65427 *3B*	77149
3212		*NKC*	RE	77128 *2A*	65406 *3B*	65433 *3B*	77155
3213		*NKC*	RE	77119 *2A*	65397 *3B*	65432 *3B*	77154

Class 413/3

Unit No	Liv	Pool	Dep	DTC	MBS	MLS	DTS
				EE3622A	*EB270*	*EB270*	*EE2211A*
3301	N	*NKC*	RE	75373	61253 *0A*	61255 *0A*	75375
3302		*NKC*	RE	75361	61241 *0A*	61244 *0A*	75364
3303		*NKC*	RE	75370	61250 *3A*	61252 *0A*	75372
3304		*NKC*	RE	75402	61282 *3A*	61283 *3A*	75403
3305		*NKC*	RE	75399	61279 *3A*	61302 *3A*	75422
3306		*NKC*	RE	75374	61254 *0A*	61256 *3A*	75376
3307		*NKC*	RE	75378	61258 *0A*	61271 *0A*	75391
3308		*NKC*	RE	75366	61246 *3A*	61264 *3A*	75384
3309		*NKC*	RE	75371	61251 *0A*	61257 *0A*	75377
3310		*NKC*	RE	75363	61243 *0A*	61259 *3A*	75386
3311		*NKC*	RE	75411	61291 *0A*	61297 *3A*	75417

Class 423/1 — 4-VEP 4-Car

For full details see Class 423 4-VEP. Facelifted and Public address fitted: BRML Eastleigh, 1988-90.

DMEE Diagram	*SR Design*	*Type*	*Weight*	*Seats 1st*	*Std*	*Toilet*
Motor Brake Standard:						
ED2.--.0A*	ED6A	MBS	c49t	—	76	—
ED2.--.1A*	ED1A	MBS	c49t	—	76	—
ED2.--.2A*	ED2A	MBS	c49t	—	76	—
Driving Trailer Composite (Compartment):						
EE3.71.5B*	FB5B	DTC	32.5t	18	46	1
EE3.71.7B*	FB7B	DTC	32.5t	18	46	1
Trailer Standard:						
EH2.83.1B*	BQ1B	TS	31.5t	—	96	—

*Official Codes not yet issued

3401-19 to be formed from Unit Nos 3001/02/03/05-20.

Unit No	Old Unit No	Liv	Pool	Dep	DTC	MBS		TS	DTC
					EE3717B	*ED2-0A*		*EQ2831B*	*EE3717B*
3421	(3168)	N	*NKC*	RE	76889	62449		71129	76890
					EE3715B	*ED2-*		*EQ2831B*	*EE3715B*
3422	(3040)	N	*NKC*	RE	76372	62201	*1A*	70891	76371
3423	(3061)	N	*NKC*	RE	76452	62222	*2A*	70912	76451
3424	(3031R)	N	*NKC*	RE	76354	62185	*1A*	70882	76353
3425	(3023R)	N	*NSS*	BM	76338	62192	*1A*	70874	76337
3426	(3047)	N	*NSS*	BM	76386	62208	*1A*	70898	76385
3427	(3041R)	N	*NSS*	BM	76374	62184	*1A*	70892	76373
3428	(3062)	N	*NSS*	BM	76454	62223	*2A*	70913	76453
3429	(3021R)	N	*NSS*	BM	76334	62202	*1A*	70872	76333
3430	(3028)	N	*NSB*	WD	76348	62189	*1A*	70879	76347
3431	(3064R)	N	*NSB*	WD	76458	62182	*1A*	70915	76457
3432	(3054R)	N	*NSB*	WD	76400	62225	*2A*	70905	76399
3433	(3057R)	N	*NSB*	WD	76444	62215	*1A*	70908	76443
3434	(3066R)	N	*NSB*	WD	76462	62218	*1A*	70917	76461
3435	(3025R)	N	*NSX*	BI	76342	62228	*2A*	70876	76341
3436	(3029R)	N	*NSX*	BI	76350	62186	*1A*	70880	76349
3437	(3027R)	N	*NSX*	BI	76346	62190	*1A*	70878	76345
3438	(3100R)	N	*NSX*	BI	76530	62262	*2A*	70951	76329
3439	(3055R)	N	*NSX*	BI	76402	62227	*2A*	70906	76401
3440	(3102R)	N	*NSX*	BI	76534	62188	*1A*	70953	76533
3441	(3043R)	N	*NSX*	BI	76378	62261	*2A*	70894	76377
3442	(3081R)	N	*NSX*	BI	76492	62216	*1A*	70932	76491
3443	(3082R)	N	*NSX*	BI	76494	62263	*2A*	70933	76493
3444	(3038R)	N	*NSX*	BI	76368	62204	*1A*	70889	76367
					EE3715B	*ED2-2A*		*EQ2831C*	*EE3715B*
3445	(3060R)	N	*NKC*	RE	76450	62242		70911	76449
3446	(3101R)	N	*NKC*	RE	76532	62243		70952	76531
3447	(3044R)	N	*NKC*	RE	76380	62199		70895	76379
3448	(3042R)	N	*NKC*	RE	76376	62221		70886	76375
3449	(3022R)	N	*NKC*	RE	76336	62205		70873	76335
3450	(3065R)	N	*NKC*	RE	76460	62203		70916	76459
3451	(3079)	N	*NKC*	RE	76488	62240		70930	76487
3452	(3024R)	N	*NKC*	RE	76340	62183		71021	76690
3453	(3045R)	N	*NKC*	RE	76382	62226		70896	76381
3454	(3049R)	N	*NKC*	RE	76390	62200		70798	76389
3455	(3048R)	N	*NSS*	FR	76388	62206		70899	76387
3456	(3063R)	N	*NSS*	FR	76456	62210		70914	76455
3457	(3050R)	N	*NSS*	FR	76392	62197		70901	76391
3458	(3051R)	N	*NSS*	FR	76394	62209		70902	76393
3459	(3052R)	N	*NSS*	FR	76396	62224		70903	76395
3460	(3105)	N	*NSX*	BI	76540	62211		70956	76539

Unit No	Old Unit No	Liv	Pool	Dep	DTC	MBS	TS	DTC
3461	(3104)	N	*NSX*	BI	76538	62212	70955	76537
3462	(3103R)	N	*NSX*	BI	76536	62213	70954	76535
3463	(3053R)	N	*NSX*	BI	76398	62266	70904	76397
3464	(3056R)	N	*NSX*	BI	76442	62265	70907	76441
3465	(3106R)	N	*NSX*	BI	76542	62264	70957	76541
3466	(3067)	N	*NSS*	WD	76464	62214	70918	76463
3467	(3158)	N	*NSS*	FR	76446	62217	70909	76445
3468	(3059)	N	*NSS*	FR	76448	62267	70910	76447
3469	(3108)	N	*NSX*	BI	76546	62219	70958	76545
3470	(3083)	N	*NSX*	BI	76496	62220	70934	76495
3471	(3084)	N	*NSX*	BI	76498	62269	70935	76497
3472		N				62244		
3473		N				62245		
3474								
3475								
3476								
3477								
3478								
3479								
3480								
3481								
3482								
3483								
3484								
3485								
3486								
3487								
3488								
3489								
3490								
3491								
3492								
3493								
3494								
3495								
3496								
3497								
3498								
3499								
3500								
3501								
3502								
3503								
3504								
3505								
3506								
3507								

Unit No	Old Unit No	Liv	Pool	Dep	DTC	MBS	TS	DTC
3508								
~~3509~~								
3510								

Unit Nos 3511-91 to be formed from Class 423/0 1990 onwards.

Class 414 — 2-HAP 2-Car

Built: British Railways Eastleigh 1958
Design: BR non-gangwayed
Power supply: 750/850V dc third rail
Traction motors (DMBS): Two 250hp (185kW) English Electric
Maximum speed: 90mph
Dimensions: *Motor coaches:* 20.04m L × 2.82m W × 3.86m H (over periscopes); *Trailer coaches:* 20.44m L × 2.82m W × 3.77m H
AWS: All vehicles fitted

DMEE Diagram	*SR Design*	*Type*	*Weight*	*Seats 1st*	*Seats Std*	*Toilet*
Driving Motor Brake Standard (Semi-Open)						
EB2.69.6B	CQ3A	DMBS	42t	—	84	
EB2.70.1B	CU	DMBS	42t	—	84	
EB2.70.3A	CR	DMBS	42t	—	84	
Driving Trailer Composite (Compartment/Saloon)						
EE3.61.2A	DX	DTC	32.5t	19	50	2
EE3.62.1B	DAD	DTC	32.5t	19	50	2
EE3.62.3A	DZ	DTC	32.5t	19	50	2

Class 414/2

Unit No	SC	Liv	Pool	Dep	DMBS	DTC
					EE2696B	*FE3612A*
4201			*NSB*	WD	65405	77127

Class 414/3

Unit No	SC	Liv	Pool	Dep	DMBS	DTC
					EE2703A	*EE3623A*
~~4301~~			*NSB*	WD	61249	75369
4302			*NSB*	WD	61260	75379
~~4303~~			*NSB*	WD	61261	75381
4304			*NSB*	WD	61262	75382
~~4305~~			*NSB*	WD	61268	75388
4306			*NSB*	WD	61270	75390
4307			*NSB*	WD	61273	75393
4308			*NSB*	WD	61275	75395
4309			*NSB*	WD	61276	75396
4310			*NSB*	WD	61278	75398
4311			*NSB*	WD	61287	75407
4312			*NSB*	WD	61288	75408
4313			*NSB*	WD	61290	75410

Unit No	SC	Liv	Pool	Dep	DMBS	DTC
4314			*NSB*	WD	61294	75414
4315			*NSB*	WD	61295	75415
4316			*NSB*	WD	61296	75416
4317			*NSB*	WD	61298	75418
4318			*NSB*	WD	61300	75420
4319			*NSB*	WD	61303	75423
					EB2701B	*EE3621B*
4320				WD	61654	75706
4321				WD	61668	75720
4322		N		WD	61683	75735

Class 465 'NETWORKER 1'

A new fleet of suburban trains for Network SouthEast London-Kent services is due to be ordered during 1989 for deliveries commencing in late 1990. Equipment and seating trials are being conducted in Class 455/9 unit No 5920 and Class 457 unit No 7001.

Class 415 4-EPB 4-Car

Built: Southern Region Eastleigh 1951
Design: SR non-gangwayed
Supply: 750/850V dc third rail
Traction motors (DMBS): Two 250hp (185kW) English Electric (E Express gear ratio)
Maximum speed: 75mph (E 90mph)
Dimensions: See below
AWS: Driving vehicles fitted

Driving Motor Brake Standard

Classes 415/1 & 415/5

DMEE Diagram	*SR Design*	*Type*	*Weight*	*Seats*		*Dimensions L × W × H m (over periscopes where fitted)*
EB2.66.2A	CP	DMBS	40t	82		19.23 × 2.82 × 3.99
EB2.66.3A	CP1A	DMBS	40t	82		19.23 × 2.82 × 3.99
EB2.66.4A*	CP3A	DMBS	40t	82		19.23 × 2.82 × 3.99
EB2.66.5A*	CP4A	DMBS	40t	82		19.23 × 2.82 × 3.99
EB2.67.1A	CP1AS	DMBS	40t	84	(semi-open)	19.23 × 2.82 × 3.99
EB2.69.4A	CQ	DMBS	42t	84		20.03 × 2.82 × 3.86
EB2.69.5A	CQ1A	DMBS	42t	84		20.03 × 2.82 × 3.86

Class 415/4 (Facelifted)

DMEE Diagram	*SR Design*	*Type*	*Weight*	*Seats*	*Dimensions L × W × H m (over periscopes where fitted)*
EB2.77.1A*	CX	DMBS	40t	82	19.23 × 2.82 × 3.99

EB2.77.2A*	CX2A	DMBS	40t	82		19.23 × 2.82 × 3.99
EB2.77.3A*	CX3A	DMBS	40t	82		19.23 × 2.82 × 3.99
EB2.77.4A*	CX4A	DMBS	40t	82		19.23 × 2.82 × 3.99
EB2.77.5A*	CX5A	DMBS	40t	82		19.23 × 2.82 × 3.99
EB2.77.6A*	CX6A	DMBS	40t	82		19.23 × 2.82 × 3.99
EB2.78.0A	CX1A	DMBS	40t	82		19.23 × 2.82 × 3.99

Trailer Standard

Class 415/5 (Compartment)

DMEE Diagram	*SR Design*	*Type*	*Weight*	*Seats*		*Dimensions L × W × H m*
EH2.67.0A	DU	TS	28t	108	(9 compt)	18.96 × 2.82 × 3.77
EH2.67.1B	DU1A	TS	28t	108	(9 compt)	18.96 × 2.82 × 3.77
EH2.68.0A	DU	TS	28t	120	(10 compt)	18.96 × 2.82 × 3.77
EH2.68.1B	DU1A	TS	28t	120	(10 compt)	18.96 × 2.82 × 3.77
EH2.68.2C*	DU3A	TS	28t	120	(10 compt)	18.96 × 2.82 × 3.77

Class 415/1

DMEE Diagram	*SR Design*	*Type*	*Weight*	*Seats*		*Dimensions L × W × H m*
EH2.70.0A	DS	TS	27t	102		18.96 × 2.82 × 3.77
EH2.70.1A*	DS1A	TS	27t	102		18.96 × 2.82 × 3.77

Class 415/4 (Facelifted)

DMEE Diagram	*SR Design*	*Type*	*Weight*	*Seats*		*Dimensions L × W × H m*
EH2.79.0A	DAK1B	TS	26t	102		18.96 × 2.82 × 3.77
EH2.79.0B	DAK1B	TS	26t	102	Non-smoking	18.96 × 2.82 × 3.77
EH2.79.3A*	DAK3A	TS	26t	102		18.96 × 2.82 × 3.77
EH2.79.3B*	DAK3B	TS	26t	102		18.96 × 2.82 × 3.77
EH2.80.1B	DAK1B	TS	28t	102	Non-smoking	18.96 × 2.82 × 3.77
EH2.80.1C*	DAK1B	TS	28t	102		18.96 × 2.82 × 3.77
EH2.80.2B*	DAK2B	TS	28t	102	Non-smoking	18.96 × 2.82 × 3.77
EH2.80.3A*	DAK3A	TS	28t	102		18.96 × 2.82 × 3.77
EH2.80.3B*	DAK3B	TS	28t	102		18.96 × 2.82 × 3.77
EH2.81.0A	DAK1A	TS	27t	102		18.96 × 2.82 × 3.77
EH2.81.1A	DAK2A	TS	27t	102		18.96 × 2.82 × 3.77
EH2.81.2B	DAH	TS	27t	102	Prototype	18.96 × 2.82 × 3.77
EH2.81.2D	DAH	TS	27t	102	Prototype, non-smoking	18.96 × 2.82 × 3.77
EH2.81.3A*	DAK3A	TS	27t	102		18.96 × 2.82 × 3.77
EH2.81.3B*	DAK3B	TS	27t	102		18.96 × 2.82 × 3.77
EH2.81.4A*	DAK4A	TS	27t	102		18.96 × 2.82 × 3.77

*Official codes not issued

Class 415/1

Unit No	SC	Liv	Pool	Dep	DMBS	TS	TS	DMBS
					EB2662A	*EH2700A*	*EH2700A*	*EB2662A*
5104			*NKS*	SG	14207	15409	15157	14208
5107			*NKS*	SG	14213	15153	15235	14214
5113			*NKS*	SG	14225	15376	15241	14226
5114			*NKS*	SG	14227	15426	15242	14228
					EB2662A	*EH2701A*	*EH2700A*	*EB2662A*
5115			*NKS*	SG	14230	15350	15243	14229
					EB2662A	*EH2700A*	*EH2700A*	*EB2662A*
5121			*NKS*	SG	14242	15247	15249	14241
5124			*NKS*	SG	14248	15248	15252	14247
5126			*NKS*	SG	14252	15244	15254	14376
5131			*NKS*	SG	14261	15412	15259	14262
5133			*NKS*	SG	14265	15132	15261	14266
					EB2695A	*EH2700A*	*EH2700A*	*EB2662A*
5134			*NKS*	SG	65383	15444	15262	14268
					EB2662A	*EH2700A*	*EH2700A*	*EB2662A*
5138			*NKS*	SG	14275	15423	15266	14276
5139			*NKS*	SG	14277	15442	15267	14278
5145			*NKS*	SG	14290	15158	15273	14289
5146			*NKS*	SG	14291	15133	15274	14292
5148			*NKS*	SG	14296	15343	15276	14295
5150			*NKS*	SG	14099	15370	15278	14299
5153			*NKS*	SG	14305	15256	15281	14306
5154			*NKS*	SG	14308	15279	15282	14307
5155			*NKS*	SG	14309	15107	15283	14310
5156			*NKS*	SG	14311	15272	15334	14312
5157			*NKS*	SG	14313	15381	15335	14314
5159			*NKS*	SG	14317	15105	15337	14318
5160			*NKS*	SG	14319	15268	15338	14320
5163			*NKS*	SG	14325	15260	15341	14326
5166			*NKS*	SG	14331	15253	15344	14332
5168			*NKS*	SG	14335	15340	15346	14336
					EB2694A	*EH2700A*	*EH2700A*	*EB2662A*
5169			*NKS*	SG	65303	15109	15347	14338
					EE2662A	*EH2700A*	*EH2700A*	*EE2662A*
5170			*NKS*	SG	14339	15245	15348	14340
5173			*NKS*	SG	14345	15116	15120	14346
5174			*NKS*	SG	14348	15138	15352	14347
5176			*NKS*	SG	14352	15396	15354	14351
5177			*NKS*	SG	14354	15257	15355	14353

Unit No	SC	Liv	Pool	Dep	DMBS	TS	TS	DMBS
~~5182~~			*NKS*	SG	14364	15357	15360	14363
5185			*NKS*	SG	14369	15277	15363	14370
5189			*NKS*	SG	14377	15339	15367	14378
5190			*NKS*	SG	14380	15361	15368	14379
5191			*NKS*	SG	14381	15108	15369	14382
5194			*NKS*	SG	14388	15275	15372	14387
5195			*NKS*	SG	14389	15239	15373	14390
5196			*NKS*	SG	14392	15399	15374	14391
5201			*NKS*	SG	14402	15126	15379	14401
5202			*NKS*	SG	14404	15362	15380	14403
~~5209~~			*NKS*	SG	14418	15395	15397	14417
5210			*NKS*	SG	14420	15263	15398	14419
5213			*NKS*	SG	14425	15353	15401	14426
					EB2663A	*EH2700A*	*EH2700A*	*EB2663A*
5217			*NKS*	SG	14434	15366	15405	14433
					EB2663A	*EH2700A*	*EH2700A*	*EB2662A*
~~5220~~			*NKS*	SG	14439	15349	15408	14260
					EB2663A	*EH2700A*	*EH2700A*	*EB2663A*
5222			*NKS*	SG	14490	15421	15410	14444
5223			*NKS*	SG	14446	15427	15411	14445
5226			*NKS*	SG	14451	15280	15414	14452
5228			*NKS*	SG	14455	15415	15416	14456
					EB2662A	*EH2700A*	*EH2700A*	*EB2663A*
5229			*NKS*	SG	14333	15435	15417	14457
					EB2663A	*EH2700A*	*EH2700A*	*EB2663A*
5230			*NKS*	SG	14460	15110	15418	14459
5231			*NKS*	SG	14461	15264	15419	14462
5232			*NKS*	SG	14464	15422	15420	14463
					EB2662A	*EH2700A*	*EH2700A*	*EB2663A*
5240			*NKS*	SG	14103	15425	15428	14480
					EB2663A	*EH2700A*	*EH2700A*	*EB2663A*
~~5242~~			*NKS*	SG	14483	15402	15430	14484
					EB2662A	*EH2700A*	*EH2700A*	*EB2663A*
~~5243~~			*NKS*	SG	14405	15375	15356	14485
					EB2663A	*EH2700A*	*EH2700A*	*EB2663A*
~~5248~~			*NKS*	SG	14492	15443	15436	14510

Unit No	SC	Liv	Pool	Dep	DMBS	TS	TS	DMBS
					EB2694A	*EH2700A*	*EH2700A*	*EB2694A*
5261			*NKS*	SG	65300	15154	15413	65310
					EB2671A	*EH2700A*	*EH2700A*	*EB2671A*
5264	E		*NKS*	SG	14522	15258	15147	14523

Unit No	Former No	SC	Liv	Pool	Dep	DMBS	TS	TS	DMBS
						EB2662A	*EH2700A*	*EH2700A*	*EB2662A*
5265	(5001)			*NKS*	SG	14001	15429	15101	14002
5266	(5020)			*NKS*	SG	14039	15234	15382	14040
5267	(5027)			*NKS*	SG	14053	15123	15127	14042
5268	(5035)			*NKS*	SG	14069	15113	15135	14070
5269	(5039)			*NKS*	SG	14078	15118	15139	14094
5270	(5040)			*NKS*	SG	14080	15122	15140	14079
5271	(5042)			*NKS*	SG	14083	15130	15142	14084
5272	(5044)			*NKS*	SG	14087	15345	15144	14088
5273	(5045)			*NKS*	SG	14090	15129	15145	14089
5274	(5046)			*NKS*	SG	14091	15364	15146	14092
5275	(5049)			*NKS*	SG	14098	15271	15149	14097
5276	(5051)			*NKS*	SG	14101	15143	15151	14102
						EB2662A	*EH2700A*	*EH2700A*	*EB2663A*
5277	(5052)			*NKS*	SG	14104	15103	15152	144208

Class 415/4

Built: 1951, facelifted 1979-86

Design: Driver-guard communication and public address system fitted

Unit No	SC	Liv	Pool	Dep	DMBS		TS		TS		DMBS	
					EB2772A		*EH2812B*		*EH2812D*		*EB2772A*	
5401	E		*NSL*	SU	14556		15449		15450		14521	
					EB2772A		*EH2810A*		*EH2790B*		*EB2771A*	
5402			*NSL*	SU	14449		15464		15465		14407	
					EB27		*EH28B*		*EH28*		*EB27*	
5403			*NSL*	SU	14286	*71A*	15174	*01C*	15221	*01B*	14285	*71A*
5404			*NSL*	SU	14435	*80A*	15036	*01B*	15406	*10A*	14436	*80A*
5405			*NSL*	SU	14470	*72A*	15053	*01B*	15216	*10A*	14469	*72A*
5406			*NSL*	SU	14303	*71A*	15230	*01B*	15285	*10A*	14356	*71A*
5407			*NSL*	SU	14428	*71A*	15392	*01B*	15060	*10A*	14427	*71A*
5408			*NSL*	SU	14297	*71A*	15227	*01B*	15313	*10A*	14298	*71A*
5409			*NSL*	SU	14494	*72A*	15065	*01B*	15047	*10A*	14206	*71A*
5410			*NSL*	SU	14540	*72A*	15386	*01B*	15304	*10A*	14528 E	*71A*
5411			*NSL*	SU	14475	*72A*	15056	*01B*	15192	*10A*	14476	*72A*

Unit No	SC	Liv	Pool	Dep	DMBS		TS		TS		DMBS	
					EB2771A		*EH2790B*		*EH2810A*		*EB2772A*	
5412			*NSL*	SU	14415		15451		15452		14304	
					EB27		*EH28*		*EH2810A*		*EB27*	
5413			*NSL*	SU	14396	*71A*	15326	*01B*	15191		14395	*71A*
5414			*NSL*	SU	14441	*72A*	15039	*01B*	15182		14442	*72A*
5415			*NSL*	SU	14465	*72A*	15040	*01B*	15051		14466	*72A*
5416			*NSL*	SU	14421	*71A*	15389	*01B*	15324		14422	*71A*
5417			*NSL*	SU	14478	*72A*	15057	*01B*	15041		14477	*72A*
5418			*NSL*	SU	14443	*72A*	15063	*01B*	15219		14282	*71A*
5419			*NSL*	SU	14473	*72A*	15055	*01B*	15058		14474	*72A*
5420			*NSL*	SU	14240	*71A*	15198	*01B*	15202		14239	*71A*
5421			*NSL*	SU	14500	*72A*	15068	*01B*	15073		14499	*72A*
5422			*NSL*	SU	14467	*72A*	15209	*01B*	15050		14468	*72A*
5423			*NSL*	SU	14511	*72A*	15074	*01B*	15212		14512	*72A*
5424			*NSL*	SU	14447	*72A*	15042	*01B*	15052		14448	*72A*
					EB2772A		*EH2790B*		*EH2810A*		*EB2775A*	
5425	E		*NSL*	SU	14538		15453		15454		14570	
					EB27		*EH28*		*EH28*		*EB27*	
5426			*NSL*	SU	14517	*72A*	15077	*01B*	15066	*10A*	14518	*72A*
5427			*NSL*	SU	14453	*72A*	15045	*01B*	15046	*10A*	14454	*72A*
5428			*NSL*	SU	14430	*73A*	15393	*01B*	15061	*10A*	14429	*73A*
5429			*NSL*	SU	14410	*71A*	15333	*01B*	15383	*10A*	14409	*71A*
5430			*NSL*	SU	14496	*72A*	15438	*01B*	15437	*10A*	14509	*72A*
5431			*NSL*	SU	14423	*71A*	15390	*01B*	15400	*10A*	14424	*71A*
5432			*NSL*	SU	14486	*72A*	15044	*01B*	15447	*10A*	14416	*71A*
5433			*NSL*	SU	14472	*72A*	15054	*01B*	15424	*10A*	14471	*72A*
5434			*NSL*	SU	14498	*72A*	15067	*02B*	15455	*11A*	14497	*72A*
5435			*NSL*	SU	14491	*72A*	15403	*01B*	15431	*10A*	14267	*71A*
5436			*NSL*	SU	14534	*72A*	15456	*01B*	15457	*10A*	14543	*72A*
5437			*NSL*	SU	14411	*71A*	15384	*01B*	15394	*10A*	14412	*71A*
5438			*NSL*	SU	14530	*72A*	15459	*02B*	15458	*11A*	14547	*72A*
5439			*NSL*	SU	14487	*72A*	15062	*01B*	15432	*10A*	14488	*72A*
5440			*NSL*	SU	14514	*72A*	15075	*01B*	15445	*10A*	14513	*72A*
5441			*NSL*	SU	14397	*71A*	15327	*01B*	15377	*10A*	14398	*71A*
5442			*NSL*	SU	14537	*72A*	15460	*02B*	15461	*11A*	14554	*72A*
5443			*NSL*	SU	14504	*72A*	15070	*10A*	15440	*01B*	14503	*72A*
5444			*NSL*	SU	14535	*72A*	15463	*11A*	15462	*02B*	14553	*72A*
5445			*NSL*	SU	14527	*72A*	15020	*01B*	15351	*10A*	14529	*72A*
					EB2772A		*EH2810A*		*EH2790B*		*EB2772A*	
5446	E		*NSL*	SU	14531		15466		15467		14541	
5447			*NSL*	SU	14532		15468		15469		14550	
5448			*NSL*	SU	14539		15470		15471		14548	

Unit No	SC	Liv	Pool	Dep	DMBS		TS		TS		DMBS	
					EB2772A		*EH2810A*		*EH2810B*		*EB2772A*	
~~5449~~			*NSL*	SU	14438		15037		15407		14437	
					EB27		*EH279*		*EH279*		*EB27*	
5450			*NSL*	SU	14533	*76A*	15472	*3B*	15473	*3A*	14552	*76A*
~~5451~~	E		*NSL*	SU	14526	*76A*	15474	*3A*	15475	*3B*	14551	*76A*
~~5452~~			*NKS*	SG	14536 E	*76A*	15477	*3A*	15476	*3B*	14563	*75A*
5453	E		*NKS*	SG	14545	*76A*	15479	*3B*	15478	*3A*	14525	*76A*
5454	E		*NKS*	SG	14555	*76A*	15481	*3A*	15480	*3B*	14524	*76A*
					EB27		*EH28*		*EH28*		*EB27*	
~~5455~~			*NKS*	SG	14062	*74A*	15023	*03B*	15027	*03A*	14054	*74A*
~~5456~~			*NKS*	SG	14481	*75A*	15001	*03A*	15059	*03B*	14482	*75A*
5457			*NKS*	SG	14501	*75A*	15439	*14A*	15069	*03B*	14502	*75A*
~~5458~~			*NKS*	SG	14431	*74A*	15034	*03B*	15404	*13A*	14432	*74A*
~~5459~~			*NKS*	SG	14506	*75A*	15441	*14A*	15071	*03B*	14505	*75A*
~~5460~~			*NKS*	SG	14516	*75A*	15446	*14A*	15076	*03B*	14515	*75A*
~~5461~~			*NKS*	SG	14520	*75A*	15448	*14A*	15078	*03B*	14519	*75A*
~~5462~~			*NKS*	SG	14021	*74A*	15011	*03B*	15111	*13A*	14022	*74A*
5463			*NKS*	SG	14037	*74A*	15019	*03B*	15119	*13A*	14038	*74A*
5464			*NKS*	SG	14081	*74A*	15166	*03B*	15159	*03A*	14082	*74A*
~~5465~~			*NKS*	SG	14236	*74A*	15196	*03B*	15208	*03A*	14350	*74A*
~~5466~~			*NKS*	SG	14004	*74A*	15002	*03B*	15220	*03A*	14003	*74A*
5467			*NKS*	SG	14006	*74A*	15003	*03B*	15177	*03A*	14005	*74A*
5468			*NKS*	SG	14211	*74A*	15332	*03A*	15184	*03B*	14212	*74A*
~~5469~~			*NKS*	SG	14007	*74A*	15004	*03B*	15201	*03A*	14008	*74A*
5470			*NKS*	SG	14315	*74A*	15286	*03B*	15215	*03A*	14316	*74A*
~~5471~~			*NKS*	SG	14255	*74A*	15206	*03B*	15231	*03A*	14256	*74A*
5472			*NKS*	SG	14508	*75A*	15295	*03B*	15169	*03A*	14458	*75A*
~~5473~~			*NKS*	SG	14493	*75A*	15029	*03B*	15170	*03A*	14058	*74A*
~~5474~~			*NKS*	SG	14065	*74A*	15033	*03B*	15224	*03A*	14066	*74A*
~~5475~~			*NKS*	SG	14019	*74A*	15010	*03B*	15048	*03A*	14020	*74A*
~~5476~~			*NKS*	SG	14016	*74A*	15316	*03B*	15319	*03A*	14015	*74A*
~~5477~~			*NKS*	SG	14013	*74A*	15180	*03B*	15233	*03A*	14057	*74A*
~~5478~~			*NKS*	SG	14059	*74A*	15030	*03B*	15167	*03A*	14060	*74A*
~~5479~~			*NKS*	SG	14322	*74A*	15289	*03B*	15317	*03A*	14321	*74A*
5480			*NKS*	SG	14264	*74A*	15210	*03B*	15291	*03A*	14263	*74A*
~~5481~~			*NKS*	SG	14330	*74A*	15293	*03B*	15226	*03A*	14329	*74A*
5482			*NKS*	SG	14017	*74A*	15009	*03B*	15297	*03A*	14018	*74A*
~~5483~~			*NKS*	SG	14052	*74A*	15175	*03B*	15329	*03A*	14051	*74A*
~~5484~~			*NKS*	SG	14061	*74A*	15031	*03B*	15308	*03A*	14046	*74A*
~~5485~~			*NKS*	SG	14105	*74A*	15178	*03B*	15185	*03A*	14106	*74A*
~~5486~~			*NKS*	SG	14071	*74A*	15161	*03B*	15125	*13A*	14072	*74A*
~~5487~~			*NKS*	SG	14361	*74A*	15309	*03B*	15359	*13A*	14362	*74A*
~~5488~~			*NKS*	SG	14386	*74A*	15321	*03B*	15371	*13A*	14385	*74A*
~~5489~~			*NKS*	SG	14024	*74A*	15012	*03B*	15112	*13A*	14023	*74A*
5490			*NKS*	SG	14205	*74A*	15433	*13B*	15128	*13A*	14056	*74A*

Unit No	SC	Liv	Pool	Dep	DMBS		TS		TS		DMBS	
5491			*NKS*	SG	14029	*74A*	15136	*13B*	15115	*13A*	14030	*74A*
5492			*NKS*	SG	14223	*74A*	15246	*13B*	15240	*13A*	14224	*74A*
5493			*NKS*	SG	14028	*74A*	15237	*13B*	15114	*13A*	14027	*74A*
5494			*NKS*	SG	14073	*74A*	15236	*13B*	15137	*13A*	14074	*74A*
5495			*NKS*	SG	14095	*74A*	15265	*13B*	15148	*13A*	14096	*74A*
5496			*NKS*	SG	14400	*74A*	15336	*13B*	15378	*13A*	14399	*74A*
5497			*NKS*	SG	14246	*74A*	15104	*13B*	15251	*13A*	14245	*74A*

Class 415/5

Unit No	Old Unit Nos	SC	Liv	Pool	Dep	DMBS *EB266*		TS *EH26*		TS *EH26*		DMBS *EB266*	
5501	(5125/5166)			*NKS*	SG	14250	*2A*	15015	*80A*	15294	*81B*	14249	*2A*
5502	(5183/5190)			*NKS*	SG	14366	*2A*	15311	*81B*	15318	*81B*	14365	*2A*
5503	(5140/5160)			*NKS*	SG	14359	*2A*	15218	*81B*	15288	*81B*	14279	*2A*
5504	(5038/5174)			*NKS*	SG	14076	*2A*	15163	*81B*	15302	*81B*	14075	*2A*
5505	(5162/5168)			*NKS*	SG	14323	*2A*	15290	*81B*	15296	*81B*	14324	*2A*
5506	(5151/5154)			*NKS*	SG	14302	*2A*	15229	*81B*	15232	*81B*	14301	*2A*
5507	(5171/5220)			*NKS*	SG	14341	*2A*	15299	*81B*	15038	*70A*	14342	*2A*
5508	(5018/5039)			*NKS*	SG	14036	*2A*	15018	*80A*	15164	*81B*	14035	*2A*
5509	(5119/5121)			*NKS*	SG	14238	*2A*	15197	*81B*	15199	*81B*	14237	*2A*
5510	(5172/5115)			*NKS*	SG	14344	*4A*	15193	*82C*	15084	*71B*	14343	*5A*
5511	(5016/5173)			*NKS*	SG	14031	*2A*	15016	*80A*	15301	*81B*	14032	*2A*
5512	(5105/5145)			*NKS*	SG	14210	*2A*	15183	*81B*	15223	*81B*	14209	*2A*
5513	(5179/5182)			*NKS*	SG	14357	*2A*	15307	*81B*	15310	*81B*	14358	*2A*
5514	(5184/5202)			*NKS*	SG	14367	*2A*	15312	*81B*	15330	*81B*	14368	*2A*
5515	(5207/5209)			*NKS*	SG	14413	*2A*	15385	*81B*	15387	*81B*	14414	*2A*
5516	(5032/5133)			*NKS*	SG	14063	*2A*	15032	*80A*	15211	*81B*	14064	*2A*
5517	(5022/5040)			*NKS*	SG	14043	*2A*	15022	*80A*	15165	*81B*	14044	*2A*
5518	(5147/5194)			*NKS*	SG	14294	*2A*	15225	*81B*	15322	*81B*	14293	*2A*
5519	(5137/5139)			*NKS*	SG	14274	*2A*	15320	*81B*	15217	*81B*	14383	*2A*
5520	(5111/5195)			*NKS*	SG	14221	*2A*	15189	*81B*	15323	*81B*	14222	*2A*
5521	(5135/5210)			*NKS*	SG	14050	*2A*	15213	*81B*	15388	*81B*	14270	*2A*
5522	(5197/5243)			*NKS*	SG	14394	*2A*	15325	*81B*	15306	*81B*	14393	*2A*
5523	(5116/5126)			*NKS*	SG	14232	*2A*	15194	*81B*	15204	*81B*	14231	*2A*
5524	(5144/5156)			*NKS*	SG	14287	*2A*	15222	*81B*	15284	*81B*	14288	*2A*
5525	(5136/5231)			*NKS*	SG	14272	*2A*	15214	*81B*	15049	*80A*	14271	*2A*
5526	(5187/5213)			*NKS*	SG	14374	*2A*	15315	*81B*	15391	*81B*	14349	*2A*
5527	(5117/5170)			*NKS*	SG	14234	*2A*	15195	*81B*	15298	*81B*	14233	*2A*
5528	(5129/5177)			*NKS*	SG	14257	*2A*	15207	*81B*	15305	*81B*	14258	*2A*
5529	(5043/5051)			*NKS*	SG	14085	*2A*	15168	*81B*	15176	*81B*	14086	*2A*
5530	(5101/5261)			*NKS*	SG	14201	*2A*	15179	*81B*	15081	*80A*	14202	*2A*
5531	(5005/5159)			*NKS*	SG	14010	*2A*	15005	*70A*	15287	*81B*	14009	*2A*
5532	(5013/5035)			*NKS*	SG	14025	*2A*	15013	*80A*	15160	*81B*	14026	*2A*

Class 415 — 4-Car

Built: British Railways Eastleigh 1960, facelifted 1982-4
Design: BR non-gangwayed
Driver-guard communication and public address systems fitted
Power Supply: 750/850V dc third rail

Traction Motors (DMBS): Two 250hp (185kW) English Electric. (E Express gear ratio).
Maximum speed: 75mph. *Classs 415/7:* 90mph.
Dimensions: See below.
AWS: Driving vehicles fitted.

DMEE Diagram	*SR Design*	*Type*	*Weight*	*Seats*	*Dimensions L × W × H (m)*
Driving Motor Brake Standard:					
EB2.71.3A*	CAA	DMBS	41t	84	20.04 × 2.82 × 3.86
EB2.72.3A*	CAB	DMBS	41t	84	20.04 × 2.82 × 3.86
Trailer Standard:					
EH2.71.2A*	DAN	TS	29.5t	112	20.43 × 2.82 × 3.77
EH2.71.2B*	DAN2B	TS	29.5t	112	20.43 × 2.82 × 3.77
EH2.71.3A*	DAO	TS	29.5t	112	20.43 × 2.82 × 3.77

*Official codes not issued.

Class 415/6

Unit No	Liv	Pool	Dep	DMBS *EB2713A*	TS *EH2712A*	TS *EH2713A*	DMBS *EB2723A*
~~5601~~		*NKS*	SG	61550	70409	70410	61551
5602	N	*NKS*	SG	61582	70441	70442	61583
~~5603~~		*NKS*	SG	61538	70397	70398	61539
~~5604~~		*NKS*	SG	61588	70447	70448	61589
~~5605~~		*NKS*	SG	61540	70399	70400	61541
~~5606~~		*NKS*	SG	61536	70395	70396	61537
5610		*NKS*	SG	61566	70425	70426	61567
~~5611~~		*NKS*	SG	61570	70429	70430	61571
5612		*NKS*	SG	61542	70401	70402	61543
5613		*NKS*	SG	61532	70391	70392	61533
~~5614~~		*NKS*	SG	61546	70405	70406	61547
5615		*NKS*	SG	61612	70471	70472	61613
~~5616~~		*NKS*	SG	61576	70435	70436	61577
5617		*NKS*	SG	61592	70451	70452	61593
~~5618~~		*NKS*	SG	61584	70443	70444	61585
5619		*NKS*	SG	61562	70421	70422	61563
5620		*NKS*	SG	61602	70461	70462	61603
~~5621~~		*NKS*	SG	61520	70380	70379	61521
5622		*NKS*	SG	61560	70419	70420	61561

Class 415/7

Unit No	Old Unit No	SC	Liv	Pool	Dep	DMBS	TS	TS	DMBS
						EB2713A	*EH2712A*	*EH2713A*	*EB2723A*
5623	—	E		*NKC*	RE	61578	70437	70438	61579
5624	—	E		*NKC*	RE	61572	70431	70432	61573
						EB2713A	*EH2712B*	*EH2713A*	*EB2723A*
5625	—	E		*NKC*	RE	61608	70455	70468	61609
						EB2713A	*EH2712A*	*EH2713A*	*EB2723A*
5626	(5607)	E	N	*NKC*	RE	61590	70449	70450	61591
5627	(5608)	E		*NKC*	RE	61600	70460	70459	61601
5628	(5609)	E		*NKC*	RE	61604	70464	70463	61605

Class 455 — 4-Car

Built: BREL York 1982
Design: BR with sliding doors, gangwayed throughout. All equipped with pressure heating and ventilation, driver-guard communication and public address equipment.
Power supply: 750V dc third rail

Traction motors (MS): Four 205hp (155kW) dc GEC 507-20J. *Diagram EC211:* Two 220hp (165kW) ac GEC G350. (Converted from Class 210 TS at RTC, Derby, 1988).
Maximum speed: 75mph
AWS: Driving vehicles fitted

DMEE Diagram	*SR Design*	*Type*	*Weight*	*Seats*	*Electrical Equipment*	*Dimensions L × W × H (m)*
Motor Standard:						
EC2.03.0A	YA	MS	45.6t	84	GEC	19.92 × 2.82 × 3.77
EC2.03.0B*	YA1A	MS	45.6t	84	GEC	19.92 × 2.82 × 3.77
EC2.03.0C*	YA2A	MS	45.6t	84	GEC	19.92 × 2.82 × 3.77
EC2.03.1A	YA3A	MS	45.6t	84	Brush	19.92 × 2.82 × 3.77
EC2.06.0A	YA4B	MS	45.6t	84	Brush	19.92 × 2.82 × 3.77
EC2.06.1A*	YA5B	MS	45.6t	84	Brush	19.92 × 2.82 × 3.77
EC2.06.2A*	YA6B	MS	45.6t	84	Brush	19.92 × 2.82 × 3.77
EC2.11.0A	—	MS	—	84	GEC	19.92 × 2.82 × 3.77
Driving Trailer Standard:						
EE2.18.0A	ZA	DTS	29.5t	74	—	19.92 × 2.82 × 3.77
EE2.18.0B*	ZB	DTS	29.5t	74	—	19.92 × 2.82 × 3.77
EE2.18.1A*	ZA-1A	DTS	29.5t	74	—	19.92 × 2.82 × 3.77
EE2.26.0A	ZB-1A	DTS	29.5t	74	—	19.92 × 2.82 × 3.77
Trailer Standard:						
EH2.19.0A	XB1A	TS	25.5t	86	—	19.92 × 2.82 × 3.58
EH2.19.2B*	XB2B	TS	25.5t	86	—	19.92 × 2.82 × 3.58
EH2.21.0A	XC	TS	27.1t	84	—	19.92 × 2.82 × 3.77
EH2.21.1A*	XC1A	TS	27.1t	84	—	19.92 × 2.82 × 3.77
EH2.24.0A	XC2B	TS	27.1t	84	—	19.92 × 2.82 × 3.77

† *Modified interiors. Experimental for Class 465 Networker EMUs.*
‡ Experimental Dot-Matrix indicators on interior and exterior.
* Official codes not issued.

Class 455/7

Phase III units

Unit No	Liv	Pool	Dep	DTS	MS	TS	DTS
				EE2180B	*EC2031A*	*EH2190A*	*EE2180B*
5701	N	*NSB*	WD	77727	62783	71545	77728
5702	N	*NSB*	WD	77729	62784	71547	77730
5703	N	*NSB*	WD	77731	62785	71540	77732
5704		*NSB*	WD	77733	62786	71548	77734
5705		*NSB*	WD	77735	62787	71565	77736
5706		*NSB*	WD	77737	62788	71534	77738
5707		*NSB*	WD	77739	62789	71536	77740
5708		*NSB*	WD	77741	62790	71560	77742
5709		*NSB*	WD	77743	62791	71532	77744
5710		*NSB*	WD	77745	62792	71566	77746
5711		*NSB*	WD	77747	62793	71542	77748
5712		*NSB*	WD	77749	62794	71546	77750
5713		*NSB*	WD	77751	62795	71567	77752
5714		*NSB*	WD	77753	62796	71539	77754
5715		*NSB*	WD	77755	62797	71535	77756
5716		*NSB*	WD	77757	62798	71564	77758
5717		*NSB*	WD	77759	62799	71528	77760
5718		*NSB*	WD	77761	62800	71557	77762
5719		*NSB*	WD	77763	62801	71558	77764
5720		*NSB*	WD	77765	62802	71568	77766
				EE2180B	*EC2031A*	*EH2192B*	*EE2180B*
5721		*NSB*	WD	77767	62803	71553	77768
5722		*NSB*	WD	77769	62804	71533	77770
5723		*NSB*	WD	77771	62805	71526	77772
5724		*NSB*	WD	77773	62806	71561	77774
5725		*NSB*	WD	77775	62807	71541	77776
5726		*NSB*	WD	77777	62808	71556	77778
5727		*NSB*	WD	77779	62809	71562	77780
5728		*NSB*	WD	77781	62810	71527	77782
5729		*NSB*	WD	77783	62811	71550	77784
5730		*NSB*	WD	77785	62812	71551	77786
5731		*NSB*	WD	77787	62813	71555	77788
5732		*NSB*	WD	77789	62814	71552	77790
5733		*NSB*	WD	77791	62815	71549	77792
5734		*NSB*	WD	77793	62816	71531	77794
5735		*NSB*	WD	77795	62817	71563	77796
5736		*NSB*	WD	77797	62818	71554	77798
5737		*NSB*	WD	77799	62819	71544	77800
5738		*NSB*	WD	77801	62820	71529	77802
5739		*NSB*	WD	77803	62821	71537	77804
5740		*NSB*	WD	77805	62822	71530	77806
5741		*NSB*	WD	77807	62823	71559	77808

Unit No	Liv	Pool	Dep	DTS	MS	TS	DTS
5742		*NSB*	WD	77809	62824	71543	77810
5743		*NSB*	WD	77811	62825	71538	77812

Class 455/8

Phase I Units

Unit No	Liv	Pool	Dep	DTS	MS	TS	DTS
				EE2180A	*EC2030A*	*EH2210A*	*EE2180A*
5801	N	*NSL*	SU	77579	62709	71637	77580
5802	N	*NSL*	SU	77581	62710	71638	77582
5803	N	*NSL*	SU	77583	62711	71639	77584
5804	N	*NSL*	SU	77585	62712	71640	77586
5805	N	*NSL*	SU	77587	62713	71641	77588
5806	N	*NSL*	SU	77589	62714	71642	77590
				EE2180A	*EC2030B*	*EH2210A*	*EE2180A*
5807	N	*NSL*	SU	77591	62715	71643	77592
				EE2180A	*EC2030A*	*EH2210A*	*EE2180A/ EE2181A**
5808	N	*NSL*	SU	77593	62716	71644	77594
5809	N	*NSL*	SU	77595	62717	71645	77596
5810	N	*NSL*	SU	77597	62718	71646	77598
5811	N	*NSL*	SU	77599	62719	71647	77600
5812	N	*NSL*	SU	77601	62720	71648	77602
5813	N	*NSL*	SU	77603	62721	71649	77604
5814	N	*NSL*	SU	77605	62722	71650	77606
5815	N	*NSL*	SU	77607	62723	71651	77608
5816	N	*NSL*	SU	77609	62724	71652	77610
5817	N	*NSL*	SU	77611	62725	71653	77612
5818	N	*NSL*	SU	77613	62726	71654	77614
5819	N	*NSL*	SU	77615	62727	71655	77616
5820	N	*NSL*	SU	77617	62728	71656	77618
5821	N	*NSL*	SU	77619	62729	71657	77620
5822	N	*NSL*	SU	77621	62730	71658	77622
5823	N	*NSL*	SU	77623	62731	71659	77624
5824‡	N	*NSL*	SU	77637	62732	71660†	77626
5825	N	*NSL*	SU	77627	62733	71661	77628
5826	N	*NSL*	SU	77629	62734	71662	77680*
5827	N	*NSL*	SU	77631	62735	71663	77632
5828	N	*NSL*	SU	77633	62736	71664	77634
5829	N	*NSL*	SU	77635	62737	71665	77636
5830	N	*NSL*	SU	77625	62743	71666	77638
5831	N	*NSL*	SU	77639	62739	71667	77640
5832	N	*NSL*	SU	77641	62740	71668	77642
5833	N	*NSL*	SU	77643	62741	71669	77644
5834	N	*NSL*	SU	77645	62742	71670	77646

Unit No	Liv	Pool	Dep	DTS	MS	TS	DTS
5835	N	*NSL*	SU	77647	62738	71671	77648
5836	N	*NSL*	SU	77649	62744	71672	77650
5837	N	*NSL*	WD	77651	62745	71673	77652
5838	N	*NSL*	WD	77653	62746	71674	77654
5839	N	*NSL*	WD	77655	62747	71675	77656
5840	N	*NSL*	WD	77657	62748	71676	77658
5841	N	*NSL*	WD	77659	62749	71677	77660
5842	N	*NSL*	WD	77661	62750	71678	77662
5843	N	*NSL*	WD	77663	62751	71679	77664
5844	N	*NSL*	WD	77665	62752	71680	77666
5845	N	*NSL*	WD	77667	62753	71681	77668
5846	N	*NSL*	WD	77669	62754	71682	77670
5847	N	*NSL*	WD	77671	62755	71683	77672
5848	N	*NSL*	WD	77673	62756	71684	77674
5849	N	*NSL*	WD	77675	62757	71685	77676

Class 455/8

Phase II Units

Unit No	Liv	Pool	Dep	DTS	MS	TS	DTS
				EE2181A	*EC2030C*	*EH2211A*	*EE2181A/ EE2180A**
5850†	N	*NSL*	SU	77677	62758	71686	77678
5851	N	*NSL*	WD	77679	62759	71687	77630*
5852	N	*NSL*	WD	77681	62760	71688	77682
5853	N	*NSL*	WD	77683	62761	71689	77684
5854	N	*NSL*	WD	77685	62762	71690	77686
5855	N	*NSL*	WD	77687	62763	71691	77688
5856	N	*NSL*	WD	77689	62764	71692	77690
5857	N	*NSL*	WD	77691	62765	71693	77692
5858	N	*NSL*	WD	77693	62766	71694	77694
5859	N	*NSL*	WD	77695	62767	71695	77696
5860	N	*NSL*	WD	77697	62768	71696	77698
5861	N	*NSL*	WD	77699	62769	71697	77700
5862		*NSL*	WD	77701	62770	71698	77702
5863		*NSL*	WD	77703	62771	71699	77704
5864	N	*NSL*	WD	77705	62772	71700	77706
5865		*NSL*	WD	77707	62773	71701	77708
5866		*NSL*	WD	77709	62774	71702	77710
5867		*NSL*	WD	77711	62775	71703	77712
5868	N	*NSL*	WD	77713	62776	71704	77714
5869	N	*NSL*	WD	77715	62777	71705	77716
5870		*NSL*	WD	77717	62778	71706	77718
5871		*NSL*	WD	77719	62779	71707	77720
5872†	N	*NSL*	WD	77721	62780	71708	77722
5873		*NSL*	WD	77723	62781	71709	77724
5874		*NSL*	WD	77725	62782	71710	77726

Class 455/9

Phase IV Units

Unit No	Liv	Pool	Dep	DTS	MS	TS	DTS
				EE2260A	*EC2060A*	*EH2240A*	*EE2260A*
5901		*NSL*	WD	77813	62826	71714	77814
5902		*NSL*	WD	77815	62827	71715	77816
5903		*NSL*	WD	77817	62828	71716	77818
5904		*NSL*	WD	77819	62829	71717	77820
5905		*NSL*	WD	77821	62830	71718	77822
5906		*NSL*	WD	77823	62831	71719	77824
5907		*NSL*	WD	77825	62832	71720	77826
5908		*NSL*	WD	77827	62833	71721	77828
5909		*NSL*	WD	77829	62834	71722	77830
5910		*NSL*	WD	77831	62835	71723	77832
5911		*NSL*	WD	77833	62836	71724	77834
				EE2260A	*EC2062A*	*EH2240A*	*EE2260A*
5912		*NSL*	WD	77835	62837	71725	77836
				EE2260A	*EC2060A*	*EH2240A*	*EE2260A*
5913		*NSL*	WD	77837	62838	71726	77838
5914		*NSL*	WD	77839	62839	71727	77840
5915		*NSL*	WD	77841	62840	71728	77842
				EE2260A	*EC2061A*	*EH2240A*	*EE2260A*
5916		*NSL*	WD	77843	62841	71729	77844
5917		*NSL*	WD	77845	62842	71730	77846
5918		*NSL*	WD	77847	62843	71731	77848
5919		*NSL*	WD	77849	62844	71732	77850

Unit No	Liv	Pool	Dep	DTS	MS	MS	DTS
				EE2260A	*EC2060A*	*EC2110A*	*EE2260A*
5920	N	*NSL*	WD	77851	62845	67400	77852

Note: Vehicle 67400 renumbered from 60400

Class 456 — 2-Car

To be built: BREL, York 1989/90
Design: BR with sliding doors, gangwayed. similar to Class 455
24 units. Full details to be announced

Class 416 — 2-EPB 2-Car

Built: British Railways, Eastleigh 1953
Design: BR, non-gangwayed
Supply: 750V dc third rail
Traction Motors: Two 250hp (185kW) dc English Electric
Maximum speed: 75mph
Dimensions: *Motor vehicles:* 20.03m L × 2.82m W × 3.86m H. *Trailer vehicles:* 20.44m L × 2.82m W × 3.86m H
AWS: All vehicles fitted

DMEE Diagram	*SR Design*	*Type*	*Weight*	*Seats*	*Dimensions L × W × H (m)*
Driving Motor Brake Standard:					
Class 416/2					
EB2.69.4A	CQ	DMBS	42t	84 (Semi-open)	20.03 × 2.82 × 3.86
EB2.69.5A	CQ1A	DMBS	42t	84 (Semi-open)	20.03 × 2.82 × 3.86
EB2.--.0A*	CQ	DMBS	42t	82 (Open)	20.03 × 2.82 × 3.86
Class 416/3					*Over periscopes*
EB2.77.2A*	CX2A	DMBS	40t	82	19.10 × 2.82 × 3.98
EB2.77.5A*	CX5A	DMBS	40t	82	19.10 × 2.82 × 3.98
EB2.77.6A*	CX6A	DMBS	40t	82	19.10 × 2.82 × 3.98
Class 416/4					
EB2.80.0A	CY	DMBS	42t	82	20.03 × 2.82 × 3.86
EB2.80.1A*	CY2A	DMBS	42t	82	20.03 × 2.82 × 3.86
EB2.81.0A	CY3B	DMBS	42t	79	20.03 × 2.82 × 3.86
Driving Trailer Standard:					
Class 416/2					
EE2.64.1A	DV	DTS	32.5t	102 (Semi-Compt)	20.44 × 2.82 × 3.86
EE2.--.0A*	DV	DTS	32.5t	94 (Semi-Open)	20.44 × 2.82 × 3.86
Class 416/3					*Over periscopes*
EE2.69.0A	DAL	DTS	30t	92	19.10 × 2.82 × 3.98
EE2.69.1A*	DAL-1A	DTS	30t	92	19.10 × 2.82 × 3.98
Class 416/4					
EE2.71.0A	DAM1A	DTS	30.5t	92	20.44 × 2.82 × 3.86
EE2.71.1A*	DAM	DTS	30.5t	92	20.44 × 2.82 × 3.86
EE2.74.0A	DAM3B	DTS	30.5t	90	20.44 × 2.82 × 3.86
EE2.74.1B	DAM	DTS	32.5t	90	20.44 × 2.82 × 3.86

*Official codes not issued

Class 416/2

Unit No	Pool	Dep	DMBS *EB2694A*	DTS *EE2641A*
~~6202~~	*NKS*	SG	65301	77501
~~6203~~	*NKS*	SG	65302	77502
~~6205~~	*NKS*	SG	65304	77504
~~6207~~	*NKS*	SG	65306	77506
6212	*NKS*	SG	65326	77511
~~6213~~	*NKS*	SG	65327	77512
6217	*NKS*	SG	65331	77516
6218	*NKS*	SG	65332	77517
6221	*NKS*	SG	65335	77520
6222	*NKS*	SG	65336	77521

Unit No	Pool	Dep	DMBS	DTS
6223	*NKS*	SG	65337	77522
6224	*NKS*	SG	65338	77523
6225	*NKS*	SG	65339	77524
6226	*NKS*	SG	65340	77525
6227	*NKS*	SG	65341	77526
			EB2--0A	*EE2641A*
6229	*NKS*	SG	65343	77528
6230	*NKS*	SG	65344	77529
6231	*NKS*	SG	65345	77530
6235	*NKS*	SG	65349	77534
6236	*NKS*	SG	65350	77535
6237	*NKS*	SG	65351	77536
			EB2--0A	*EE2--0A*
6238	*NKS*	SG	65352	77537
			EB2694A	*EE2641A*
6239	*NKS*	SG	65353	77538
			EB2--0A	*EE2--0A*
6240	*NKS*	SG	65354	77539
			EB2694A	*EE2641A*
6241	*NKS*	SG	65355	77540
6243	*NKS*	SG	65357	77542
6244	*NKS*	SG	65358	77543
6245	*NKS*	SG	65359	77544
6247	*NKS*	SG	65361	77546
6249	*NKS*	SG	65363	77548
6251	*NKS*	SG	65365	77550
6253	*NKS*	SG	65367	77552
6255	*NKS*	SG	65369	77554
6256	*NKS*	SG	65370	77555
6257	*NKS*	SG	65371	77556
			EB2695A	*EE2641A*
6259	*NKS*	SG	65373	77558
6260	*NKS*	SG	65374	77559
6261	*NKS*	SG	65375	77560
6262	*NKS*	SG	65376	77561
6263	*NKS*	SG	65377	77562
6264	*NKS*	SG	65378	77563
6265	*NKS*	SG	65379	77564
6267	*NKS*	SG	65381	77566
6268	*NKS*	SG	65382	77567
			EB2694A	*EE2641A*
6269	*NKS*	SG	65307	77568
			EB2695A	*EE2641A*
6270	*NKS*	SG	65384	77569
6271	*NKS*	SG	65385	77570
6272	*NKS*	SG	65386	77571
6273	*NKS*	SG	65387	77572
6274	*NKS*	SG	65388	77573
6275	*NKS*	SG	65389	77574
6276	*NKS*	SG	65390	77575
6277	*NKS*	SG	65391	77576
6278	*NKS*	SG	65392	77577

Class 416/3

Built: 1955-59, facelifted 1983-84. Driver/guard communication and public address equipment fitted. Units 6313-28 ftted with window bars for North London line service

Unit No	Liv	Pool	Dep	MBS	DTS
				EB277	*EE2690A*
6301		*NSL*	SU	14577 *2A*	16121
6302		*NSL*	SU	14580 *2A*	16124
6303		*NSL*	SU	14576 *2A*	16120
6304		*NSL*	SU	14589 *2A*	16133
6305		*NSL*	SU	14587 *2A*	16131
6306		*NSL*	SU	14571 *2A*	16115
				EB277	*EE2691A*
6307		*NSL*	SU	14573 *5A*	16117
6308		*NSL*	SU	14564 *5A*	16108
6309		*NSL*	SU	14562 *5A*	16106
6310		*NSL*	SU	14574 *5A*	16118
6311		*NSL*	SU	14565 *5A*	16109
6312		*NSL*	SU	14579 *5A*	16123
6313		*NNL*	SU	14558 *5A*	16102
6314		*NNL*	SU	14586 *5A*	16130
6315		*NNL*	SU	14590 *5A*	16134
6316		*NNL*	SU	14559 *5A*	16103
6317		*NNL*	SU	14578 *5A*	16122
6318		*NNL*	SU	14566 *5A*	16110
6319		*NNL*	SU	14568 *5A*	16112
6320		*NNL*	SU	14561 *5A*	16105
6321		*NNL*	SU	14283 *2A*	16128
6322		*NNL*	SU	14575 *5A*	16119
6323		*NNL*	SU	14581 *5A*	16125
6324		*NNL*	SU	14560 *5A*	16104

Unit No	Liv	Pool	Dep	MBS	DTS
6325		*NNL*	SU	14567 *5A*	16111
6326		*NNL*	SU	14546 *6A*	16129
6327		*NNL*	SU	14572 *5A*	16116
6328		*NNL*	SU	14582 *5A*	16126
6329		*NSL*	SU	14542 *2A*	16114
6330		*NSL*	SU	14588 *5A*	16132
6331		*NSL*	SU	14583 *5A*	16127
6332		*NSL*	SU	14569 *5A*	16113
6333		*NSL*	SU	14557 *5A*	16101
6334		*NSL*	SU	14546 *6A*	16107

Class 416/4

Built: 1953, facelifted 1985-86. Driver/guard communication and public address equipment fitted. Units 6401-09 modified with extra end doorways

Unit No	Liv	Pool	Dep	MBS	DTS
				EB2810A	*EE2740A*
6401	N	*NKS*	SG	65346	77531
6402	N	*NKS*	SG	65362	77547
6403		*NKS*	SG	65356	77541
6404		*NKS*	SG	65329	77514
6405		*NKS*	SG	65347	77532
6406		*NKS*	SG	65305	77505
6407		*NKS*	SG	65330	77515
6408		*NKS*	SG	65342	77527
				EB2810A	*EE2741B*
6409		*NKS*	SG	65309	77113
				EB2800A	*EE2711A*
6410		*NKS*	SG	65334	77519
6411		*NKS*	SG	65333	77518
6412		*NKS*	SG	65364	77549
				EB2801A	*EE2710A*
6413		*NKS*	SG	65372	77557
				EB2800A	*EE2711A*
6414		*NKS*	SG	65368	77553
6415		*NKS*	SG	65348	77533
6416		*NKS*	SG	65328	77513
6417		*NKS*	SG	65366	77551
6418		*NKS*	SG	65360	77545

Class 457 — 4-Car

Built: BREL Derby 1982. Former Class 210 Diesel-Electric Multiple-Unit stock modified at RTC, Derby, 1988. (TS No 71733 see Class 455/9.)
Design: BR with sliding doors, gangwayed throughout. Public address system
Supply: 750V dc third rail

Traction motors: (**DMS**) Two 220hp (165kW) three phase ac Brush
Maximum speed: 75mph
Dimensions: *Driving vehicles:* 19.83m L × 2.82m W × 3.77m H; *Trailer vehicles:* 19.92m L × 2.82m W × 3.77m H
AWS: Driving vehicles fitted

DMEE Diagram	*SR Design*	*Type*	*Weight*	*Seats*
Driving Motor Standard				
EA2.09.0A	—	DMS(A)	29t	74
EA2.09.1B	—	DMS(B)	29t	74

Trailer Standard

EH2.24.0A	XC2B	TS	27.1t	84
EH2.36.0A	—	TS	26.5t	84

Unit No	SC	Liv	Pool	Dep	DMS *EA2090A*	TS *EH2360A*	TS *EH2240A*	DMS *EA2090B*
7001		N	*NSB*	WD	67300	67401	71733	67301

Note: 67300/01, 67401 renumbered from 60300/01, 60401 during 1988

Class 447 — 4-Car

PRIVATE OWNER — BATTERSEA LEISURE GROUP
To be built: BREL York 1990
Four units based on the Class 319 design for 750/850V dc third rail supply only. To operate service between London Victoria and a new Battersea Leisure Centre

Vehicle Nos: BLL 99470-BLL 99481

Class 438/0 — 4-TC 4-Car

TRAILER UNITS
Built: British Railways York 1966
Design: BR gangwayed throughout. Driver-guard and public address equipment fitted
Maximum speed: 90mph
Dimensions: 22.15m L × 2.74m W × 3.81m H
AWS: Driving vehicles fitted

DMEE Diagram	*SR Design*	*Type*	*Weight*	*Seats 1st*	*Seats Std*	*Toilet*
Driving Trailer Standard						
EE2.66.0A	FC	DTS	32.5t	—	64	
Trailer Brake Standard: (Compartment)						
EJ2.60.0A	BT	TBS	35.5t	—	32	1
Trailer First/Composite: (Compartment)						
EH1.60.0A	BU	TF	33.5t	42	—	2
EH3.—.1A*	BU	TC	33.5t	30	16	2
EH3.—.2B*	BU	TC	33.5t	36	8	2

* Unofficial codes

Unit No	SC	Liv	Pool	Dep	DTS *EE2660A*	TF/TC *EH1600A/EH3–*	TBS *EJ2600A*	DTS *EE2660A*
~~8001~~		N	*NSS*	BM	76270	70844 *2B*	70812	76332
8004		N	*NSS*	BM	76275	70847 *0A*	70815	76276
8006		N	*NSS*	BM	76280	70849 *0A*	70817	76279
8007			*NSS*	BM	76281	70850 *0A*	70818	76282
8010		N	*NSS*	BM	76288	70853 *2B*	70821	76287

Unit No	SC	Liv	Pool	Dep	DTS	TF/TC	TBS	DTS
8012		N	*NSS*	BM	76292	70858 *2B*	70828	76291
8014			*NSS*	BM	76295	70857 *0A*	70825	76296
8015		N	*NSS*	BM	76297	70855 *1A*	70823	76298
8017		N	*NSS*	BM	76302	70860 *2B*	70826	76301
8018		N	*NSS*	BM	76303	70861 *2B*	70829	76304
8020			*NSS*	BM	76307	70863 *0A*	70831	76308
8021			*NSS*	BM	76309	70864 *0A*	70832	76310
8023		N	*NSS*	BM	76313	70866 *2B*	70834	76314
8026			*NSS*	BM	76319	70869 *0A*	70837	76320
8027		N	*NSS*	BM	76321	70870 *2B*	70838	76322
8028			*NSS*	BM	76324	70871 *0A*	70839	76323

Class 488 — RAILAIR 2- & 3-Car

TRAILER UNITS
Built: BREL Derby and Eastleigh, 1984
Design: BR rebuilt Mk 2f stock built 1973, gangwayed throughout. Air conditioned. Public address equipment fitted

Maximum speed: 90mph
Dimensions: 20.38m L × 2.84m W × 3.79m H
Livery: InterCity Gatwick Express

DMEE Diagram	*SR Design*	*Type*	*Weight*	*Seats 1st*	*Seats Std*	*Toilet*
Trailer Standard:						
EH2.85.0A	BC	TS	35t	—	56	1
Trailer First/Standard Handbrake:						
EP1.01.1A	BA	TFH	35t	41	—	1 Payphone
EP2.01.0A	BB	TSH	35t	—	56	1

Class 488/2

Unit No	Pool	Dep	TFH *EP1011A*	TSH *EP2010A*
8201	*IVG*	SL	72500	72638
8202	*IVG*	SL	72501	72617
8203	*IVG*	SL	72502	72640
8204	*IVG*	SL	72503	72641
8205	*IVG*	SL	72504	72628
8206	*IVG*	SL	72505	72629
8207	*IVG*	SL	72506	72642
8208	*IVG*	SL	72507	72643
8209	*IVG*	SL	72508	72644
8210	*IVG*	SL	72509	72635

Class 488/3

Unit No	Pool	Dep	TSH *EP2010A*	TS *EH2850A*	TSH *EP2010A*
8302	*IVG*	SL	72602	72701	72604
8303	*IVG*	SL	72603	72702	72608
8304	*IVG*	SL	72606	72703	72611
8305	*IVG*	SL	72605	72704	72609
8306	*IVG*	SL	72607	72705	72610
8307	*IVG*	SL	72612	72706	72613
8308	*IVG*	SL	72614	72707	72615
8309	*IVG*	SL	72616	72708	72639
8310	*IVG*	SL	72618	72709	72619
8311	*IVG*	SL	72620	72710	72621
8312	*IVG*	SL	72622	72711	72623
8313	*IVG*	SL	72624	72712	72625
8314	*IVG*	SL	72626	72713	72627
8315	*IVG*	SL	72636	72714	72645

Unit No	Pool	Dep	TSH	TS	TSH
8316	*IVG*	SL	72630	72715	72631
8317	*IVG*	SL	72632	72716	72633
8318	*IVG*	SL	72634	72717	72637
8319	*IVG*	SL	72646	72718	72647

Class 419 DMLV

Built: British Railways, Eastleigh 1959
Design: BR non-gangwayed. Driving cab each end. These vehicles can work singly, hauling a limited load, or in multiple with EP-type stock. They are equipped with traction batteries for working on non-electrified quay lines at Dover and Folkestone
Power Supply: 750/850V dc third rail or batteries
Traction Motors: Two 250hp (185kW) dc English Electric
Maximum speed: 90mph
Dimensions: 20.45m L × 2.82m W × 3.86m H (over periscopes)

DMEE Diagram	*SR Design*	*Type*	*Weight*
Driving Motor Luggage Van:			
EX5.60.0B*	AF	DMLV	45.5t
EX5.60.1C*	AF1A	DMLV	45.5t

*Official codes not issued

Unit No	Liv	Pool	Dep	DMLV
				EX5600B
9001	L	*RPMD*	RE	68001
9002		*RPMD*	RE	68002
				EX5601C
9003	L	*RPMD*	RE	68003
9004	RR	*RPMD*	RE	68004
9005	L	*RPMD*	RE	68005
9006	L	*NBT*	RE	68006
9007	L	*RPMD*	RE	68007
9008	L	*RPMD*	RE	68008
9009	RR	*RPMD*	RE	68009
9010	L	*NBT*	RE	68010

Class 489 DMLV RAILAIR

Built: BREL, Eastleigh 1984
Design: BR converted from Class 414 DMBS vehicles built 1958. Gangwayed at one end. Public address transmitter equipment
Supply: 750/850V dc third rail
Traction Motors: Two 250hp (185kW) dc English Electric
Maximum speed: 90mph
AWS: Fitted
Dimensions: 20.45m L × 2.82m W × 3.86m H
Livery: InterCity Gatwick Express

DMEE Diagram	*SR Design*	*Type*	*Weight*
Driving Motor Luggage Van:			
EX5.61.0A	AQ	DMLV	45t

Unit No	Pool	Dep	DMLV
			EX5610A
9101	*IVG*	SL	68500
9102	*IVG*	SL	68501
9103	*IVG*	SL	68502
9104	*IVG*	SL	68503

Unit No	Pool	Dep	DMLV
~~9105~~	*IVG*	SL	68504
9106	*IVG*	SL	68505
9107	*IVG*	SL	68506
9108	*IVG*	SL	68507
~~9109~~	*IVG*	SL	68508
9110	*IVG*	SL	68509

Class 482

An order for 20 Motor Standard coaches is to be placed during 1989 for Network SouthEast Waterloo and City line.

Class 483

Built: Metro-Cammell 1938
Purchased from London Underground 1988 for operation on Network SouthEast Isle of Wight services. Sixteen vehicles to be overhauled at BRML Eastleigh Works to form two-car units
Design: London Transport tube with sliding doors. Cab end-doors sealed, inner-end doors for emergency egress. Fitted with driver/guard communication and public address equipment

Power supply: 630V dc third rail
Traction motors (DMBS):
Dimensions: 15.94m L × 2.60m W × 2.88m H
AWS: Fitted

Driving Motor Brake Second

DMEE	*SR*			
Diagram	*Design*	*Type*	*Weight*	*Seats*
EB2.--.--	CV	DMBS	27.45t	42

Unit No	SC	Liv	Pool	Dep	DMBS *EB2*	DMBS *EB2*
483001		N	*NSS*			
483002		N	*NSS*			
483003		N	*NSS*			
483004		N	*NSS*			
483005		N	*NSS*			
483006		N	*NSS*			
483007		N	*NSS*			
483008		N	*NSS*			

Note: Full details to be advised

Classes 485 & 486 — 5-VEC & 2-TIS

5- and 2-Car Units (Isle of Wight)
Introduced: 1967, rebuilt from london Transport stock built 1935
Design: LT with sliding doors end doors throughout, sealed on cab ends of DMBS vehicles. Fitted with driver-guard communication and public address equipment

Supply: 630V dc third rail
Traction motors (DMBS): Two 240hp (178kW) dc English Electric EE507
Maximum speed: 30mph
AWS: Fitted to DMBS coaches

DMEE Diagram	*SR Design*	*Type*	*Weight*	*Seats*	*Dimensions L × W × H*
Driving Motor Brake Standard					
EB2.61.2A	CV2A	DMBS	32t	26	16.19 × 2.69 × 2.90
EB2.61.2B	CV2B	DMBS	32t	26	16.19 × 2.69 × 2.90
EB2.61.2C	CV2C	DMBS	32t	26	16.19 × 2.69 × 2.90
EB2.61.3A	CV3A	DMBS	32t	26	16.19 × 2.69 × 2.90
EB2.61.3B	CV3B	DMBS	32t	26	16.19 × 2.69 × 2.90
EB2.61.4A	CV4A	DMBS	32t	26	16.19 × 2.69 × 2.90
EB2.61.4B	CV4B	DMBS	32t	26	16.19 × 2.69 × 2.90
Driving Trailer Standard					
EE2.60.0B	DAE1A	DTS	17t	38	15.82 × 2.69 × 2.90
EE2.60.2A	DAF2A	DTS	17t	38	15.82 × 2.69 × 2.90
EE2.60.3A	DAF3A	DTS	17t	38	15.82 × 2.69 × 2.90 Driving compartment not used
Trailer Standard					
EH2.61.1A	DAF1A	TS	18t	42	15.69 × 2.69 × 2.90
EH2.61.1B	DAF1B	TS	18t	42	15.69 × 2.69 × 2.90

All codes not yet official
Formations shown may be varied to suit local operating requirements
i De-icing equipment in unused driving cab

Class 485

Unit No	SC	Liv	Pool	Dep	DMBS	TS	TS	TS	DMBS
					EB2612B	*EE2603A*	*EH2611B*	*EE2603A*	*EB2612C*
485041			*NSS*	RY	1 N	27 N	92	26 N	2
					EB2614B	*EH2611B*	*EH2611B*	*EE2603A*	*EB2614A*
485042			*NSS*	RY	3 N	95 N	47	29 N	4 N
					EB2612A	*EE2602A*	*EE2603A*	*EH2611B*	*EB2612C*
485043			*NSS*	RY	5 N	31 i N	32 N	43	6
					EB2614B	*EH2611B*	*EE2603A*	*EH2611A*	*EB2614A*
485044		N	*NSS*	RY	7	44	33	49	8
					EB2613B	*EH2611B*	*EE2603A*	*EH2611B*	*EB2613A*
485045		N	*NSS*	RY	9	94	34	93	10

Class 486

Unit No	SC	Liv	Pool	Dep	DMBS	DTS
					EB2614B	*EE2600B*
486031		N	*NSS*	RY	11	28

Class 487

Waterloo & City Line Units
Built: English Electric 1940
Design: SR with sliding doors, tube size vehicles end doors throughout. Trains formed of up to 2 Motors and 3 Trailers. Driver-guard communication equipment fitted
Supply: 750/850V dc third rail
Traction Motors: Two 190hp (140kW) dc English Electric
Maximum Speed: 40mph
Dimensions: 14.86m L × 2.64m W × 2.92m H

AWS: Not fitted
Livery: Network and Allied-Lyons sponsorship logo as shown N

DMEE Diagram	*SR Design*	*Type*	*Weight*	*Seats*
Driving Motor Brake Standard				
EB2.60.0B*	CS	DMBS	29t	40
EB2.60.1B*	CW1A	DMBS	29t	40
Trailer Standard				
EH2.60.0B*	DAG	TS	20t	52

*Unofficial codes

DMBS

No	SC	Liv	Pool	Dep
EB2600B				
51		N	*NSB*	WC
53		N	*NSB*	WC
54		N	*NSB*	WC
55			*NXX*	WC (s)
56		N	*NSB*	WC
EB2601B				
57		N	*NSB*	WC
EB2600B				
58		N	*NSB*	WC
59		N	*NSB*	WC
60		N	*NSB*	WC
61		N	*NSB*	WC
62		N	*NSB*	WC

TS

No	SC	Liv	Pool	Dep
EH2600B				
71			*NXX*	WC (s)
72		N	*NSB*	WC
73		N	*NSB*	WC
74		N	*NSB*	WC
75		N	*NSB*	WC
76		N	*NSB*	WC
77		N	*NSB*	WC
78		N	*NSB*	WC
79			*NXX*	WC (s)
80		N	*NSB*	WC
81		N	*NSB*	WC
83		N	*NSB*	WC
84		N	*NSB*	WC
85		N	*NSB*	WC
86		N	*NSB*	WC

Class 504 2-CAR

Built: British Railways Wolverton 1959
Design: BR, non-gangwayed
Supply: 1,200V dc, third rail side contact
Traction motors (DMBS): Four 141hp (90kW) dc English Electric
Maximum Speed: 65mph

AWS: All fitted

Diagram	*Type*	*Weight*	*Seats*
Driving Motor Brake Standard			
EB2.04.0A	DMS	50t	84
Driving Trailer Standard			
EE2.15.1A	DTS	33t	94

Dimensions: 20.31m L × 2.82m W × 3.84m H

Note: Unit numbers are not always carried, but formations are normally maintained

Unit No	SC	Liv	Pool	Dep	DMBS	DTS
					EB2040A	*EB2151A*
504 444			*PBQ*	BQ	65444	77165
504 445		M	*PBQ*	BQ	65445	77166
504 446		M	*PBQ*	BQ	65446	77167
504 447			*PBQ*	BQ	65447	77168
504 449		M	*PBQ*	BQ	65449	77170
504 450		M	*PBQ*	BQ	65450	77171
504 451		M	*PBQ*	BQ	65451	77172
504 452			*PBQ*	BQ	65452	77173
504 453		M	*PBQ*	BQ	65453	77174
504 454			*PBQ*	BQ	65454	77175
504 455		M	*PBQ*	BQ	65455	77176
504 456		M	*PBQ*	BQ	65456	77177
504 457		M	*PBQ*	BQ	65457	77178
504 458		M	*PBQ*	BQ	65458	77179
504 459			*PBQ*	BQ	65459	77180
504 460		M	*PBQ*	BQ	65460	77181
504 461		M	*PBQ*	BQ	65461	77182

Class 507 — 3-Car

Built: BREL, York 1978
Design: BR saloon with sliding doors, driver/guard and public address equipment. Units 507.001-008 fitted with de-icing equipment
Supply: 600/750V dc
Traction Motors: Four 110hp (82.5kW) dc GEC G310AZ
Maximum speed: 75mph
Unit No 507009 experimentally equipped additionally with magnetic track brakes. Unit normally used on Wirral Line services

Dimensions: *Motor coaches:* 20.20m L × 3.02m W × 3.58m H. *Trailer coaches:* 19.92m L × 3.02m W × 3.58m H

Diagram	*Type*	*Weight*	*Seats*
Driving Motor Standard:			
EA2.01.0A	DMS	35.5t	74
Trailer Standard:			
EH2.05.0A	TS	25.5t	86
EH2.05.0B	TS	25.5t	86
Battery Driving Motor Standard:			
EI2.02.0A	BDMS	37t	74

Unit No	Liv	Pool	Dep	BDMS	TS	DMS
				EI2020A	*EH2050B*	*EA2010A*
507 001		*PHR*	HR	64367	71342	64405
507 002		*PHR*	HR s	64368	71343	64406
507 003		*PHR*	HR	64369	71344	64407
507 004		*PHR*	HR	64370	71345	64408
507 005		*PHR*	HR	64371	71346	64409
507 006		*PHR*	HR	64372	71347	64410
507 007		*PHR*	HR	64373	71348	64411
507 008		*PHR*	HR	64374	71349	64412
				EI2020A	*EH2050A*	*EA2010A*
507 009		*PHR*	HR	64375	71350	64413
507 010		*PHR*	HR	64376	71351	64414
507 011		*PHR*	HR s	64377	71352	64415

Unit No	Liv	Pool	Dep	BDMS	TS	DMS
507 012		*PHR*	HR	64378	71353	64416
507 013		*PHR*	HR	64379	71354	64417
507 014		*PHR*	HR	64380	71355	64418
507 015		*PHR*	HR	64381	71356	64419
507 016		*PHR*	HR	64382	71357	64420
507 017		*PHR*	HR	64383	71358	64421
507 018		*PHR*	HR	64384	71359	64422
507 019		*PHR*	HR	64385	71360	64423
507 020		*PHR*	HR	64386	71361	64424
507 021		*PHR*	HR	64387	71362	64425
507 022		*PHR*	HR	64388	71363	64426
507 023		*PHR*	HR	64389	71364	64427
507 024		*PHR*	HR	64390	71365	64428
507 025		*PHR*	HR	64391	71366	64429
507 026		*PHR*	HR	64392	71367	64430
507 027		*PHR*	HR	64393	71368	64431
507 028		*PHR*	HR	64394	71369	64432
507 029		*PHR*	HR	64395	71370	64433
507 030		*PHR*	HR	64396	71371	64434
507 031		*PHR*	HR	64397	71372	64435
507 032		*PHR*	HR	64398	71373	64436
507 033		*PHR*	HR	64399	71374	64437

Class 508 3-CAR

Built: BREL, York 1979
Design: BR saloon, with sliding doors, gangwayed within unit and end doors, driver-guard communication and public address equipment
Power Supply: 750/850V dc third rail
Traction Motors (DMS & BDMS): Four 110hp (82.5kW) dc GEC G310AZ or Brush TM61-53 (Interchangeable)
Maximum Speed: 75mph
Dimensions: *Driving coaches:* 20.20m L × 2.82m W × 3.58m H; *Trailer coach:* 19.92m L × 2.82m W × 3.58m H

AWS: Driving coaches fitted

Diagram	*Type*	*Weight*	*Seats*
Driving Motor Standard			
EA2.08.0A	DMS	36t	74
Trailer Standard			
EH2.18.0A	TS	26.5t	86
EH2.--.0A*	TS	26.5t	82
Battery Driving Motor Standard			
EI2.03.0A	BDMS	36.5t	74

*Official diagram not issued

Unit No	SC	Liv	Pool	Dep	BDMS *EI2030A*	TS *EH2—0A*	DMS *EA2080A*
508 101			*PBD*	BD	64692	71483	64649
508 102			*PBD*	BD	64693	71484	64650
508 103			*PBD*	BD	64694	71485	64651
508 104			*PBD*	BD	64695	71486	64652

Unit No	SC	Liv	Pool	Dep	BDMS	TS	DMS
508 105			*PBD*	BD	64696	71487	64653
508 106			*PBD*	BD	64697	71488	64654
508 107			*PBD*	BD	64698	71489	64655
508 108			*PBD*	BD	64699	71490	64656
508 109			*PBD*	BD	64700	71491	64657
508 110			*PBD*	BD	64701	71492	64658
508 111			*PBD*	BD	64702	71493	64659
508 112			*PBD*	BD	64703	71494	64660
					EI2030A	*EH2—0A*	*EA2080A*
508 113			*PBD*	BD	64704	71495	64661
508 114			*PBD*	BD	64705	71496	64662
508 115			*PBD*	BD	64706	71497	64663
508 116			*PBD*	BDs	64707	71498	64680
508 117			*PBD*	BD	64708	71499	64665
508 118			*PBD*	BD	64709	71500	64666
508 119			*PBD*	BD	64710	71501	64667
					EI2030A	*EH2180A*	*EA2080A*
508 120			*PBD*	BD	64711	71502	64668
					EI2030A	*EH2—0A*	*EA2080A*
508 121			*PBD*	BD	64712	71503	64669
508 122			*PBD*	BD	64713	71504	64670
508 123			*PBD*	BD	64714	71505	64671
508 124			*PBD*	BD	64715	71506	64672
508 125			*PBD*	BD	64716	71507	64673
508 126			*PBD*	BD	64717	71508	64674
508 127			*PBD*	BD	64718	71509	64675
508 128			*PBD*	BD	64719	71510	64676
508 129			*PBD*	BD	64720	71511	64677
508 130			*PBD*	BD	64721	71512	64678
508 131			*PBD*	BD	64722	71513	64679
508 132			*PBD*	BD	64723	71514	64664
508 133			*PBD*	BD	64724	71515	64681
508 134			*PBD*	BD	64725	71516	64682
508 135			*PBD*	BD	64726	71517	64683
508 136			*PBD*	BD	64727	71518	64684
508 137			*PBD*	BD	64728	71519	64685
508 138			*PBD*	BD	64729	71520	64686
508 139			*PBD*	BD	64730	71521	64687
508 140			*PBD*	BD	64731	71522	64688
508 141			*PBD*	BD	64732	71523	64689
508 142			*PBD*	BD	64733	71524	64690
508 143			*PBD*	BD	64734	71525	64691

NB: Units 508134-43 normally operate on Hall Road (HR) duties from Kirkdale depot.

Spare Vehicles. Network SouthEast EMU Stock

Vehicle No	Type	Class	DMEE Diagram	SR Design
61035	MBS	411/4	EA2.63	AP
61342	MBS	411/5	EA2.64	AL
70995	TS	421/2	EH2.75	BO-IA
76108	DTC	421/1	EE3.64	FA
76331	DTS	438	EE2.66	FC
76339	DTC	423	EE3.65	FB
76639	DTC	423	EE3.63.3B	

Service Department Multiple-Unit Stock

SECTOR: *DMEX:* Director of Mechanical and Electrical Engineering.
DRTC: Director of Research.

(Note: Specification codes A-R are shown for cross-reference purposes only for this publication).

DIESEL-ELECTRIC MULITPLE-UNITS

Spec	*Built*	*Type*	*Dimensions L×W×H (m)*	*Weight*	*Max speed*	*Brake*
A	BR Eastleigh 1958	Trailer	20.34×2.74×3.87	31.5t	75mph	Air
B1	BR Eastleigh 1956	Driving Motor	15.94×2.74×3.87	55t	75mph	Air
	Engine: English Electric 4SRKT Mk II, 4cyl, 500hp (375kW) *Traction Motors:* Two nose-suspended, axle-hung. *Main Generator:* EE Type 824.					
B2	BR Eastleigh 1956	Trailer	15.94×2.74×3.87	55t	75mph	Air

DIESEL-MECHANICAL MULITIPLE UNITS

The following vehicles have a number of common features which are summarised as follows:
Engines: (where fitted) Two AEC or Leyland 150hp (114kW) 6cyl, horizontal, except:
Spec **Q:** One Cummins NT855 R5 285hp (213kW)
Spec **R:** Two Rolls-Royce 130D of 180hp (134kW) 6cyl
Transmission: Four-speed epicyclic gearbox, carden shaft. Spec **Q:** Voith.
Maximum speed: 70mph, except Spec **Q:** 75mph.

Spec	*Built*	*Type*	*Dimensions L×W×H (m)*	*Weight*	*Engines*	*Gangway*
C1	BR Derby 1954	Driving Motor B	18.49×2.82×3.85	27t	AEC	Within unit
C2	BR Derby 1954	Driving Trailer	18.49×2.82×3.85	21t	—	Within unit
D	BR Derby 1956	Driving Motor B	18.49×2.82×3.85	—	AEC	Twin-cab
E	Gloucester RCW 1958	Driving Motor B	20.45×2.82×3.86	36.5t	AEC	Twin-cab
F1	Pressed Steel 1960	Driving Motor B	20.45×2.82×3.86	38t	Leyland	Twin-cab
F2	Pressed Steel 1960	Driving Trailer	20.45×2.82×3.86	30t	—	—
G1	Park Royal 1957	Driving Motor B	18.49×2.82×3.85	34t	AEC	Within unit
G2	Park Royal 1957	Driving Trailer	18.49×2.82×3.85	27t	—	Within unit
H1	Gloucester RCW 1957	Driving Motor B	18.49×2.82×3.85	30.5t	AEC	Within unit
H2	Gloucester RCW 1957	Driving Trailer	18.49×2.82×3.85	25.5t	—	Within unit
I	BR Derby 1958	Trailer	19.58×2.82×3.87	28.5t	—	—

K1	Cravens 1956	Driving Motor B	18.49×2.82×3.84	30t	Leyland	Within unit
K2	Cravens 1956	Driving Trailer	18.49×2.82×3.84	23t	—	Within unit
M1	Metro Cammell 1957-59	Driving Motor B	18.49×2.82×3.85	32.5t	Leyland	Within unit
M2	Metro Cammell 1957-59	Driving Motor	18.49×2.82×3.85	32.5t	Leyland	Within unit
N	Pressed Steel 1960	Driving Trailer	20.45×2.82×3.86	29.5t	—	—
P	Wickham 1958	Driving Motor	10.97×2.72×3.84	11t	AEC	Railbus
Q	BREL York 1987	Driving Motor	20.06×2.73×3.77	36.5t	Cummins	Within unit
R1	BRCW 1961	Driving Motor B	18.48×2.82×3.84	32.5t	RR	Within unit
R2	BRCW 1961	Driving Motor	18.48×2.82×3.84	32.5t	RR	Within unit

Veh No	*Former No*	*Spec*	*Type*	*Pool*	*Depot*	*Use*
DB975007	(79018)	C1	QWV(DMB)	DMEX	RG	2-car Ultrasonic Test Train
DB975008	(79612)	C2	QXV(DT)	DMEX	RG	2-car Ultrasonic Test Train
RDB975010	(79900)	D	QWV(DMB)	DRTC	ZQ	RTC Test Coach *Iris*
TDB975023	(55001)	E	QWV(DMB)	DMEX	TS	Route Learning
TDB975025	(60755)	A	QXV(T)	DMEX	SL	SR General Manager's Saloon
TDB975042	(55019)	E	QWV(DMB)	DMEX	TS	Route Learning
RDB975089	(50396)	G1	QWV(DMB)	DRTC	ZQ	RTC Laboratory 5 Trim
RDB975090	(56162)	G2	QXV(DT)	DRTC	ZQ	RTC Laborary No 4
DB975349	(51116)	H1	QWV(DMB)	DMEX	CA	2-car unit RCE Inspection Saloon (a)
RDB975386	(60750)	A	QXV(T)	DRTC	ZQ	RTC (Tilt Tests)
DB975539	(56101)	H2	QXV(DT)	DMEX	CA	2-car unit RCE Inspection Saloon (a)
DB975637	(56300)	H2	QXV(DT)	DMEX	CA	2-car unit RCE Inspection Saloon (b)
TDB975659	(55035)	F1	QWV(DMB)	DMEX	OO	Route Learning. Set No L135
DB975664	(51122)	H1	QWV(DMB)	DMEX	CA	2-car unit RCE Inspection Saloon (b)
RDB975964	(59466)	I	QXV(T)	DMEX	ZD	Stores Van
ADB977048	(56142)	K2	QXV(DT)	DMEX	BX	Sandite spray
ADB977052	(56145)	K2	QXV(DT)	DMEX	TS	Sandite spray
TDB977123	(51286)	K1	QWV(DMB)	DMEX	CA	2-car Route Learning unit, (c)
TDB977124	(51296)	K1	QWV(DMB)	DMEX	CA	2-car Route Learning unit, (d)
TDB977125	(56444)	K2	QXV(DMB)	DMEX	CA	2-car Route Learning unit, (c)
TDB977126	(56445)	K2	QXV(DMB)	DMEX	CA	2-car Route Learning unit, (d)
ADB977342	(53475)	L	QWV(DMB)	DRTC	ZQ	RTC Carriage wash test vehicle
ADB977376	(60002)	B1	QWA(DMB)	DMEX	SU	3-car unit SR Sandite train, Unit 066
ADB977377	(60504)	B2	QXA(T)	DMEX	SU	3-car unit SR Sandite train, Unit 066
ADB977379	(60003)	B1	QWA(DMB)	DMEX	SU	3-car unit SR Sandite train, Unit 066
DB977391	(51433)	M1	QWV(DMB)	DRTC	ZQ	2-car unit RTC Track Assessment train
DB977392	(53167)	M1	QWV(DMB)	DRTC	ZQ	For RTC Track Assessment train
DB977393	(53246)	M1	QWV(DMB)	DRTC	ZQ	2-car unit RTC Track Assessment train
TDB977466	(54286)	N	QXV(DT)	DMEX	CF	Sandite trailer coach
TDB977486	(54285)	N	QXV(DT)	DMEX	LA	Sandite trailer coach
TDB977535	(53259)	M1	QWV(DMB)	DMEX	HT	2-car Sandite unit, (f)
TDB977536	(53295)	M1	QWV(DMB)	DMEX	HT	2-car Sandite unit, (f)
ADB977607	(51464)	M1	QWV(DMB)	DMEX	ED	2-car Route Learning/Sandite unit, (g)
ADB977608	(51525)	M1	QWV(DM)	DMEX	ED	2-car Route Learning/Sandite unit, (g)
ADB977611	(51824)	R1	QWV(DMB)	DMEX	NL	2-car Sandite train (j)
ADB977612	(51838)	R1	QWV(DM)	DMEX	NL	2-car Sandite train (j)
ADB977613	(51826)	R1	QWV(DMB)	DMEX	NL	2-car Sandite train (k)
ADB977614	(52076)	R1	QWV(DM)	DMEX	NL	2-car Sandite train (k)
ADB977615	(54281)	F2	QXV(DT)	DMEX	LA	Sandite trailer coach
RDB999507	—	P	QWV(DM)	DRTC	ZQ	RTC Laboratory Track Recorder
DB999600	—	Q	QWA(DM)	DRTC	ZQ	2-car RTC Track Recording Train, (h)
DB999601	—	Q	QWA(DM)	DRTC	ZQ	2-car RTC Track Recording Train, (h)

ELECTRIC MULTIPLE UNIT VEHICLES

Most of the following continue to operate as a 'multiple-unit' of two or more vehicles. Unit numbers in brackets are class numbers, not carried on the vehicle as part of the unit identity. The first three vehicles listed are now in Service Stock use but have not been officially recorded by the BRB, DMEE, Rolling Stock Library. All vehicles are formerly Capital Stock and in most cases seating has been removed and replaced by special equipment appropriate to the vehicles current use. Rail Cleaning units can be used for either De-Icing fluid or Sandite (leaf removal) applications.

Units listed take electricity supply from ac overhead lines at 6.25 and 25kV or dc third rail at 630/750/850V as indicated under Vehicle Type. Traction Motors are all dc manufactured by English Electric (EE), or General Electric Company (GEC).

Diagram	*Built*	*Vehicle type*	*ex-Class*	*Dimensions L×W×H (m)*	*Weight*	*Max*	*Motors*	*Gangway*
ED2.04.0A	1960	AC Motor Brake	305/1	20.27×2.82×3.98	55t	75	4 GEC 200hp	—
EE2.09.1B	1960	AC Driving Trailer	305/1	20.36×2.82×3.84	31.5t	75	—	—
EF2.05.0A	1960	AC Batt Driving Trailer	305/1	20.36×2.82×3.84	35t	75	—	—
EZ5.02.0A	1939	DC Driving Motor Brake	402	19.53×2.74×3.99	44t	70	2 EE 275hp	—
EZ5.03.0A	1940	DC Driving Motor Brake	4-LAV	19.51×2.74×3.99	44t	70	2 EE 275hp	—
EZ5.04.0A	1957	DC Driving Motor Brake	501	18.47×2.82×3.86	47t	70	4 GEC 185hp	—
EZ5.04.1B	1957	DC Driving Motor Brake	501	18.47×2.90×3.86	48t	70	4 GEC 185hp	—
EZ5.06.0A	1957	DC Driving Trailer	501	18.47×2.82×3.86	30t	70	—	—
EZ5.06.1B	1957	DC Driving Trailer	501	18.47×2.90×3.86	30.5t	70	—	—
EZ5.12.0A	1948	DC Driving Motor Brake	405	19.23×2.74×3.99	39t	70	2 EE 250hp	—
EZ5.15.0A	1958	DC Driving Motor Brake	412	19.23×2.74×3.98	40t	90	2 EE 250hp	—
EZ5.16.0A	1958	DC Driving Trailer	412	19.23×2.74×3.98	30t	75	2 EE 250hp	—
EZ5.20.0A	1946	DC Trailer	4-SUB	19.99×2.74×3.99	29t	70	—	—
EZ5.22.2C	1957	DC Driving Motor Brake	414/2	20.42×2.82×3.86	42t	90	2 EE 250hp	—
EZ5.23.0A	1957	DC Driving Trailer	414/2	20.42×2.82×3.86	32.5t	90	—	—
EZ5.25.0A	1953	DC Driving Motor Brake	416/2	20.04×2.82×3.86	40.5t	75	2 EE 250hp	—
EZ5.25.0B	1953	DC Driving Motor Brake	416/2	20.04×2.82×3.86	40.5t	75	2 EE 250hp	—
EZ5.26.0A	1954	DC Driving Trailer	416/2	20.44×2.82×3.86	32.5t	75	—	—
EZ5.28.0A	1967	AC Driving Trailer	302	20.36×2.82×3.86	32.5t	75	—	—
EZ5.29.0A	1967	AC Motor Brake	302	20.27×2.82×3.86	55t	75	4 EE 192hp	
EZ5.--	1966	DC Driving Trailer	438	20.35×2.82×3.86	32.5t	90	—	Throughout

Veh No	*Former No*	*Dia/type*	*Unit No*	*Pool*	*Depot*	*Use*
61463	—	ED2040A(MB)	305935	DMEX	IL	ECML Driver Instruction unit
75496	—	EF2050A(BDT)	305935	DMEX	IL	ECML Driver Instruction unit
75548	—	EE2091B(DT)	305935	DMEX	IL	ECML Driver Instruction unit
ADB975027	(61162)	EZ5040A(DMB)	(930)	DMEX	SH	R&D Test Car
ADB975032	(75165)	EZ5060A(DT)	(930)	DMEX	SH	R&D Test Car *Mars*
ADB975586	(10907)	EZ5120A(DMB)	(930)004	DMEX	EH	Rail Cleaning Unit
ADB975587	(10908)	EZ5120A(DMB)	(930)004	DMEX	EH	Rail Cleaning Unit
ADB975588	(10981)	EZ5120A(DMB)	(930)005	DMEX	WD	Rail Cleaning Unit
ADB975589	(10982)	EZ5120A(DMB)	(930)005	DMEX	WD	Rail Cleaning Unit
ADB975590	(10833)	EZ5120A(DMB)	(930)006	DMEX	WD	Rail Cleaning Unit
ADB975591	(10834)	EZ5120A(DMB)	(930)006	DMEX	WD	Rail Cleaning Unit
ADB975592	(10993)	EZ5120A(DMB)	(930)007	DMEX	GI	Rail Cleaning Unit
ADB975593	(12659)	EZ5120A(DMB)	(930)007	DMEX	GI	Rail Cleaning Unit
ADB975594	(12658)	EZ5120A(DMB)	(930)003	DMEX	SU	Rail Cleaning Unit
ADB975595	(10994)	EZ5120A(DMB)	(930)003	DMEX	SU	Rail Cleaning Unit
ADB975596	(10844)	EZ5120A(DMB)	(930)008	DMEX	GI	Rail Cleaning Unit
ADB975597	(10987)	EZ5120A(DMB)	(930)008	DMEX	GI	Rail Cleaning Unit
ADB975598	(10989)	EZ5120A(DMB)	(930)009	DMEX	BI	Rail Cleaning Unit
ADB975599	(10990)	EZ5120A(DMB)	(930)009	DMEX	BI	Rail Cleaning Unit
ADB975600	(10988)	EZ5120A(DMB)	(930)010	DMEX	BI	Rail Cleaning Unit

ADB975601	(10843)	EZ5120A(DMB)	(930)010	DMEX	BI	Rail Cleaning Unit
ADB975602	(10991)	EZ5120A(DMB)	(930)011	DMEX	RE	Rail Cleaning Unit
ADB975603	(10992)	EZ5120A(DMB)	(930)011	DMEX	RE	Rail Cleaning Unit
ADB975604	(10939)	EZ5120A(DMB)	(930)012	DMEX	FR	Rail Cleaning Unit
ADB975605	(10940)	EZ5120A(DMB)	(930)012	DMEX	FR	Rail Cleaning Unit
ADB975896	(11387)	EZ5120A(DMB)	(930)013	DMEX	RE	Rail Cleaning Unit
ADB975897	(11388)	EZ5120A(DMB)	(930)013	DMEX	RE	Rail Cleaning Unit
ADB977068	(14549)	EZ5150A(DMB)	(931)019	DMEX	SG	Stores unit
ADB977069	(16029)	EZ5160A(DMB)	(931)019	DMEX	SG	Stores unit
ADB977290	(65318)	EZ5250A(DMB)	(931)018	DMEX	SG	Stores unit
ADB977291	(65324)	EZ5250A(DMB)	(931)018	DMEX	SG	Stores unit
ADB977296	(65319)	EZ5250B(DMB)	(932)050	DMEX	SH	RSD Test unit
ADB977297	(77108)	EZ5260A(DT)	(932)050	DMEX	SH	RSD Test unit
ADB977304	(65317)	EZ5250A(DMB)	(936)021	DMEX	WD	Traction shunting unit
ADB977305	(65322)	EZ5250A(DMB)	(936)021	DMEX	WD	Traction shunting unit
DB977335	(76277)	EZ5 (DT)	—	DRTC	ZQ	RTC Track Recording Train
DB977336	(76278)	EZ5 (DT)	—	DRTC	ZQ	RTC Track Recording Train
ADB977345	(61178)	EZ5041B(DMB)	(936)001	DMEX	BD	Rail Cleaning unit
ADB977346	(75178)	EZ5061B(DT)	(936)001	DMEX	BD	Rail Cleaning unit
ADB977347	(61180)	EZ5041B(DMB)	(936)002	DMEX	BD	Rail Cleaning unit
ADB977348	(75180)	EZ5061B(DT)	(936)002	DMEX	BD	Rail Cleaning unit
ADB977349	(61183)	EZ5041B(DMB)	(936)003	DMEX	BD	Rail Cleaning unit
ADB977350	(75183)	EZ5061B(DT)	(936)003	DMEX	BD	Rail Cleaning unit
ADB977362	(10392)	EZ5200A(T)	(930)	DMEX	BI	De-Icing coach
ADB977363	(10399)	EZ5200A(T)	(930)	DMEX	FR	De-Icing coach
ADB977364	(10400)	EZ5200A(T)	(930)	DMEX	RE	De-Icing coach
ADB977365	(10726)	EZ5020A(DMB)	(930)001	DMEX	SU	Rail Cleaning unit
ADB977366	(10500)	EZ5030A(DMB)	(930)002	DMEX	BM	Rail Cleaning unit
ADB977367	(10497)	EZ5030A(DMB)	(930)002	DMEX	BM	Rail Cleaning unit
ADB977368	(10499)	EZ5030A(DMB)	(930)002	DMEX	SU	Rail Cleaning unit
ADB977385	(61148)	EZ5041B(DMB)	(936)148	DMEX	WN	Rail Cleaning unit
ADB977386	(75189)	EZ5061B(DT)	(936)148	DMEX	WN	Rail Cleaning unit
ADB977505	(65321)	EZ5250B(DMB)	(932)053*	DMEX	SH	RSD Test unit
ADB977506	(65323)	EZ5250B(DMB)	(932)054*	DMEX	SH	RSD Test unit
ADB977507	(77110)	EZ5260A(DT)	(932)053	DMEX	SH	RSD Test unit
ADB977508	(77112)	EZ5260A(DT)	(932)054	DMEX	SH	RSD Test unit
ADB977531	(14047)	EZ5120A(DMB)	(930)015	DMEX	SU	Sandite unit
ADB977532	(14048)	EZ5120A(DMB)	(930)015	DMEX	SU	Sandite unit
ADB977533	(14273)	EZ5120A(DMB)	(930)016	DMEX	SU	Sandite unit
ADB977534	(14384)	EZ5120A(DMB)	(930)016	DMEX	SU	Sandite unit
ADB977559	(65313)	EZ5250A(DMB)	(931)026	DMEX	SU	Stores unit
ADB977560	(65320)	EZ5250A(DMB)	(931)026	DMEX	SU	Stores unit
ADB977566	(65312)	EZ5250A(DMB)	(931)017	DMEX	SU	Stores unit
ADB977567	(65314)	EZ5250A(DMB)	(931)017	DMEX	SU	Stores unit
ADB977598	(75080)	EZ5280A(DT)	(937)996	DMEX	IL	Rail Cleaning unit
ADB977599	(61073)	EZ5290A(MB)	(937)996	DMEX	IL	Rail Cleaning unit
ADB977600	(75061)	EZ5280A(DT)	(937)996	DMEX	IL	Rail Cleaning unit
ADB977601	(75211)	EZ5280A(DT)	(937)997	DMEX	IL	Rail Cleaning unit
ADB977602	(61228)	EZ5290A(MB)	(937)997	DMEX	IL	Rail Cleaning unit
ADB977603	(75035)	EZ5280A(DT)	(937)997	DMEX	IL	Rail Cleaning unit
ADB977604	(75077)	EZ5280A(DT)	(937)998	DMEX	IL	Rail Cleaning unit
ADB977605	(61062)	EZ5290A(MB)	(937)998	DMEX	IL	Rail Cleaning unit
ABD977606	(75070)	EZ5280A(DT)	(937)998	DMEX	IL	Rail Cleaning unit
ADB977609	(65414)	EZ5222C(DMB)	(930)022	DMEX	WD	Rail Cleaning unit
ADB977610	(77130)	EZ5230A(DT)	(930)022	DMEX	WD	Rail Cleaning unit

*When ADB977505 and ADB977506 run together Unit No to be 055.

Additional Information

The following information updates this publication with notified changes by mid-March 1989.

DIESEL MULTIPLE-UNITS

DELETE (Withdrawn):

51458, 51522, 51809, 52084, 53026/37, 53214/51, 53866/69, 53922, 54013/19, 54375, 59096, 59113, 78722, 78967/69.

SPECIAL CHANGES:

Class 101: *Reinstated, Add:* 51520 2102F *PNL* NL.
Class 114: Delete: 53015/18, 54009/15 (to Parcels stock).
Class 141: 141003 renumbered 141104.
Classes 155/0 and 155/1: Not in public service pending modifications.
Class 158: *add footnote:* Unit Nos 158707-75 ordered January 1989.

SECTOR CODES:

NSB: 51060/62/66/73/74/76/79/86/90/94/99, 51104/07/90, 51211/26, 51425/31/32/34/98/99, 51501/03/04, 59091, 59101/15/17/25/28, 59416/19/21/25/30/35/37, 59526/30/40/43/70.
NNE: 51207/08, 51444.
NSX: 205008/09/12/15/16/18/23/24, 205101.

SECTOR & DEPOT CODE CHANGES (New allocations):

PCF CF: 51449, 53240, 53887, 150233/35/43, 156420/38/48/52/54/55/61-73.
PCH CH: 53626/34/36.
PLA LA: 55004/11 (at Tyseley waiting orders).
PHA HA: 150260, 156445/47/49/50/53/56/74.
PIS IS: 156446/57/58/77/78.
PNH NH: 142071, 150202/04/06/10/16/18/22.
PNL NL: 51197, 51243, 51456/58, 51522, 53162/69/95/96, 53229/35, 53606, 54196, 142050, 150264, 156451/59/60/75/76/79-83.
PTS TS: 53980-83, 54246/53/56/66.
PXXZ: 52043, 53355, 53427/60/74/96, 53501/56, 53812, 54054/71, 54350/98, 54401, 59330, 59748/86, 59812.
PXXZ CP(s): 53355, 53500/18/56, 53812.
Stored: Add to allocation '(s)': 52043, 53427, 54071.

DIAGRAM NUMBER CHANGES:

***DQ2.02.2B:* 51203.**

SPECIAL CHARACTERISTICS (Add):

†: 51197, 51203, 53139/41.
#: 51446/50/54/55/58/67/95, 51510/15/16/17/19/22/24/26/29/38, 51795, 51801/04, 53141/59/62, 53229, 53335, 59096, 59690.
R 55200, 55300, 150124/28/30.
RP 156445/46/47/50/53/56/57/58/77/78.
V 142015-19/21/24/25/27/34/35/36/47/48/60/71.

LIVERIES (Add):
N: 51332/45/74/87, 51572, 51680, 51912, 53155, 53479, 53539/99, 54194, 54271, 54358, 55023, 59206, 59305, 59484/97, 59565, 59735/36/39, 205030.

PARCELS STOCK

Class 114 Add:
55928 (53018) DX5.13.0B RR *RPXN* CA.
55929 (53015) DX5.13.0B RR *RPXN* CA.
54903 (54009) DX5.14.0A RR *RPXN* CA.
54904 (54015) DX5.14.3B RR *RPXN* CA.

Sector Code on all DMUs *RXXN* to now read *RPXN*.

ELECTRIC MULTIPLE UNITS

New Class 320: Unit Nos to read 320301-320322, coach numbers DTS 77899-77920, MS 63021-63042, DTS 77921-77944.
Seats to read: MS and DTS(A): each 79.

Delete, Withdrawn: 302231/35/37/38/41/43/48/55/76, 8021, ADB 975027.

Renumbered and reclassified: Unit Nos 310048, 310053, 310054, 310062, 310063 officially now 310109, 310108, 310110, 310107, 310111 respectively. (p88 delete footnote).

SECTOR CODES:
NGE: 302245/52.
NNE: 321312-19.
NNL: 321336-46.
RPMA: 308993/94/95.

SECTOR & DEPOT CODES:
NGE IL: 302264/70/82.
NKS SG: 5451.
NNL BY: 321320/21.
NSL SU: 5837.
NTS EM: 308133-39.
NXX PQ(s): 302246/49/54/60/68/69/89/90/91/95, 307101/06.
NXX Shoeburyness(s): 302284.
PXX GW(s): 303005/71.
Stored (s): 1280/95, 3441.

DIAGRAM NUMBERS:
Class 413: *DTC to DTS, Seats 69-*
*EE2.72.1A:** 77120.
EE2.21.1A: 77117/18/32/35.
EE2.22.1A: 75373.

Class 415/7: *EB2.71.0J*: 61572/78, 61600.
EB2.71.2J: 61590, 61604/08.
EB2.72.0H: 61573/79, 61601.
EB2.72.2H: 61591, 61605/09.
EH2.71.0E: 70431/37/49/60/64.
EH2.71.1E: 70432/38/50/59/63/68.

SET FORMATIONS:

302269: add 75216 in place of 75242.

302990		*RPMA*	IL	75082	61090	75084	
302991		*RPMA*	IL	75221		75211	

308994: add 75927 (BDTS).
2306 delete 69346.

2308	(1562R)	*NSS*	FR	61407	70236	69346	61406

3466 to 3471 add 'R' to old unit numbers.
3467 to read (3058R).

3472	(3085R)	*NSX*	BI	76500	62244	70936	76499
3473	(3086R)	*NSX*	BI	76502	62245	70937	76501
3474					62246		
3475					62247		

LIVERIES:
Network SouthEast: N: 305502, 307111/20/25, 308135/49, 309612 (delete E), 312799, 1217/20/21/41/64, 4303/21, 5485/86, 5606, 6308, 6403/05; delete 307106, 6401.

SPECIAL CHARACTERISTICS:
F: add 312799.

***Motive Power Monthly* — June 1989**

A full depot by depot listing of all DMU stock, including formations of conventional stock, correct to 1 April 1989 will be included in the above magazine, on sale 8 May 1989.

Also included will be an up to date depot allocation summary for all EMUs.

BRITISH RAIL

HAULED COACHING STOCK

Edited by L. J. Bowles

LONDON

IAN ALLAN LTD

The Coaching Stock of British Railways

This is the fourth edition of the Ian Allan ABC listing in detail the loco-hauled stock owned by British Railways. Also included are details of stock owned privately which is permitted to run on the BR system.

1988 has been a year of considerable change to the hauled coaching stock fleet. During the year, the InterCity 125 fleet was reclassified to comprise Locomotives and Hauled Coaches, thereby boosting the hauled stock totals by 712 vehicles. However since, with certain well-publicised exceptions, the IC125s remain a distinct operating unit of their own, with neither locomotives nor coaches being used with other types, the fleet has remained listed together in the *abc British Rail Locomotives.*

Construction of Mk 3 Driving Van Trailers (DVTs) at BREL Derby Litchurch Lane (to run on the West Coast main line) and Mk 4 coaches at Metro-Cammell (which are to take over East Coast main line duties from IC125s from mid-1989) has commenced. Building of the bodyshells for the Mk 4s has been sub-contracted to BREL Derby although 56 bodies are now to be built at Breda, in Italy. The first vehicles, Mk 3 DVTs, came off the production line late in 1988, and the first Mk 4 coach was sent to the Research Division at Derby RTC in January 1989. The introduction to service of these vehicles will be the main development in 1989. Refurbishing of the Mk 3 fleet is almost complete, and that of the Mk 2f fleet continues, as do conversions to update the catering fleet.

In the Provincial Sector, the introduction of Sprinter DMUs has seen the end of most loco-hauled services (in addition to the withdrawal of many first generation DMUs). The aim is the elimination of loco-hauled passenger trains in the near future. Late in the year, the Vale of Rheidol Railway (whose stock operated for sector PMW) was sold to the Brecon Mountain Railway, thus eliminating narrow gauge vehicles from the BR passenger fleet.

By contrast, Network SouthEast is busily engaged on updating its fleet by facelifting late Mk 1 and early Mk 2 open coaches, with new moquette seating, revised interior decor and the fitting of a PA system, creating a very attractive vehicle destined for several years further use — indeed, some early Mk 2s with a good potential life are being brought in from Provincial.

The Parcels Sector suffered further considerable withdrawals during 1988 following the loss of newspaper-carrying contracts, and the upgrading and renumbering of NCVs came to an abrupt halt. Two types of stock were completely withdrawn during the year — NAV (basic BG) and NPV (the CCT, the last passenger-rated 4-wheeled vehicles on BR, only one van remaining in Exhibition stock).

InterCity livery has continued to be applied, with front rank stock receiving a revised lettering style compatible with the InterCity 'Swallow' livery. NSE has replaced the mid-shade of blue with a rather darker version, and this has now become more widespread. However, no further hauled coaches have appeared in the Provincial (Trans-Pennine) livery as new Express DMUs are due to be used from mid-1990s. The original West Highland line green and cream-liveried set, operated by InterCity Charter sub-Sector, has been replaced by more modern vehicles, and the last steam-heat set, used with steam locomotives and painted in Great Western-style colours, was withdrawn in 1988.

Finally, the International Train has not yet entered public service and, sadly, it is not now expected that the travelling public will be able to sample this innovative stock on BR.

Design

During 1988 construction commenced on the first examples of the new Mk 4 design. The design characteristics have been fully described in the Ian Allan magazine *Modern Railways*. This, and Mk 3 stock, is built by integral methods.

Standard stock prior to Mk 3 was mostly of all-steel constuction on under-frames of two standard lengths: 57ft (short) and 63ft (long). One van (now withdrawn) had a body of glass fibre. Frames for some stock were fabricated at one works and taken to another for completion. These dual-built vehicles are indicated and the frame builder precedes the body builder.

All stock is carried on two four-wheel bogies apart from one in the royal train which uses six-wheel bogies and a 4-wheeled exhibition van. Initially BR bogies were all of the B1 or the similar but heavier B2 type, after which the Commonwealth type became standard for a time. Several other types were tried in service but did not survive except for the Gresley design which is still to be seen under some electric multiple units. In 1963 the Swindon-designed B4 and its heavy-duty counterpart B5 became standard and remained so until the BT5, BT10 and other very similar types were introduced for the Mk 3 stock and for multiple units. The latest types are designated in numerical series prefixed by 'BP' (powered) or by 'BT' (trailer).

Equipment has been installed in recent years to allow the guard and catering steward to address passengers. The transmitter is naturally installed in brake-vans and catering cars. More recently some gangwayed brake-vans have been fitted with a device which allows the driver and guard to converse. This is always an addition to the public address system and is not be be confused with the clear-call type of communication long a feature of multiple units.

All locomotive-hauled trains are now heated by electricity. Most coaches so equipped are able to take ac or dc at 1,000 volts and can carry 600 amps through their connecting jumpers. The earliest Southern Region stock was insulated only for 750 volts (the third-rail maximum) and in common with other Regions was wired for 400 amps. Some coaches of Mk 2d and Mk 2e design are not able to take power from the types of locomotive which take power from their transmission systems with a wide fluctuation of voltage, while some others may take only ac International systems which differ from that of British Railways and some stock is fitted with a switch which allows it to work with UIC standard stock. The power taken by a vehicle is indicated by its ETH index. If this figure for each vehicle of a train is added together and compared with the index of the locomotive it can be seen whether the stock can be used as intended. The index of a vehicle wired for 600 amps carries the suffix 'X' (usually shown here by an asterisk).

Details such as these are included in the headings of the various types of stock, variations are shown in a sub-heading or against the vehicle numbers.

Numbering

Stock is numbered in one series between 1 and 99999 and each vehicle was allotted prefix letters (E, M, S, SC or W) to denote its regional allocation. No number — whether it be a locomotive, coaching stock or freight stock — is duplicated unless it carries a prefix which is part of its identity, eg: the older freight stock, track maintenance machines and privately-owned stock.

With the introduction of Sector ownership, prefixes are being discontinued.

Sector Allocations:

Whilst the last few years has seen BR reorganised into Sectors — InterCity, Provincial and Network SouthEast for passenger services, Parcels and Railfreight — hauled coaching stock has remained Regionally based, with, from late 1983, the addition of depot allocations.

However, from the 1987/88 financial year all BR Capital stock is allocated specifically to these Sectors and in this edition the ownership for all stock has been listed by an official code after the number.

Passenger Sectors

SECTOR CODES

InterCity

IXX	General
IXXZ	General, for condemnation
IAN	Anglia
ICC	Cross Country
ICH	Charter
ICHH	Charter – Hold for future use
IEC	East Coast main line
IML	Midland main line
IWC	West Coast main line
IWR	Western Region main line

Network SouthEast

NXX	General
NXXZ	General, for condemnation
NNW	LNW Outer Suburban
NSS	Solent and Sarum
NWR	Western Suburban
NNE	London Anglia Outer Suburban

Provincial

PCR	Settle & Carlisle
PCW	Cotswolds
PDC	Devon & Cornwall
PEX	Excursions & Special Traffic
PLC	Lancashire & Cheshire
PMX	LMR cross country
PNS	ScotRail, North Scotland
PSP	Spare
PSY	South Yorkshire, Lincolnshire and Humberside
PSW	ScotRail, West
PSX	ScotRail, InterCity
PTP	North Trans-Pennine
PWH	ScotRail, West Highland line
PWX	WR cross country
PWY	West Yorkshire
PXX	General
PXXZ	General, for condemnation

With effect from 1 April 1989, the codes for this sector's stock are scheduled to be revised. The second and third letters will match the two-letter depot code.

Parcels Sector

RNPE Newspaper, Eastern Region
RNPM Newspaper, London Midland Region
RNPS Newspaper, Southern Region
RNPW Newspaper, Western Region
RPOC Post Office, General Van Pool
RPOE Post Office, Eastern Region
RPOM Post Office, London Midland Region
RPOW Post Office, Western Region
RPOZ Post Office, Scottish Region
RPSP Parcels, Red Star
RPXB Parcels, General, NDX
RPXC Parcels, General, NDV
RPXD Parcels, General, NJV, NKV
RPXE Parcels, General, NJA, NJX
RPXG Parcels, General, Courier
RPXH Gangwayed Brake, NEA 100mph, NHA 110mph Eastern Region
RPXM Gangwayed Brake, NEA 100mph, NHA 110mph London Midland Region
RPXT Parcels, General, NDV, Southern Region
RPXW Gangwayed Brake, NEA 100mph, NHA 110mph Western Region
RPXZ Gangwayed Brake, NEA 100mph, NHA 110mph Scottish Region
RPXX Parcels, General

InterCity Sector
ICH Charter
IWC West Coast main line

These codes are not carried on the vehicle, and are given for readers guidance only. Official codes and alterations as they occur will be announced in *Motive Power Monthly* magazine. Until January 1989, RPSP and RPX- series used the letter X as the second character and these codes (RRSP, RXXB to RXXZ) are used herein.

DXXZ For transfer to Departmental Service stock

Vehicle Type & Design Codes

Overall dimensions of BR Standard Hauled Stock (length×width).

Mk 1 (passenger)	20.45×2.82m
Mk 2, 2a	20.45×2.82m
Mk 2b-2f	20.63×2.82m
Mk 3, 3a, 3b	23.00×2.75m
Mk 4	23.40×2.74m
Mk 1 (non-passenger)	see class headings

Mk 1 coaches are 3.90m high, Mks 2, 2a and 2b are 3.86m, Mk 2c are 3.84m, 2d and 2e are 3.79m and Mk 3 are 3.8m high.

The two-letter codes for hauled stock are listed below:

AA Gangwayed Corridor
AB Gangwayed Corridor Brake
AC Gangwayed Open (2+2 seating)
AD Gangwayed Open (2+1 seating)
AE Gangwayed Open Brake
AF Gangwayed Driving Open Brake
AG Open with Miniature Buffet
AH Buffet/Kitchen
AI Open Coach, 2+2 seating, Gangwayed one end only
AJ Restaurant/Kitchen with Buffet
AL Open Coach, 2+2 seating Disabled facilities
AN Miniature Buffet
AO Privately owned
AP Pullman with Kitchen
AQ Pullman Parlour
AR Pullman Parlour Brake
AS Sleeping Car
AT Royal Train Coach

AU	Sleeping Car with Pantry	NL	General Utility Van, News, Gangway fitted
NA	Gangwayed Brake	NM	General Utility Van, News, Non-Gangwayed
NB	High Security Non-Gangwayed Brake	NN	Courier vehicle
NC	Gangwayed Brake, News	NS	Post Office Sorting Van
ND	Gangwayed Brake, dual heated, 90mph	NT	Post Office Stowage Van
NE	Gangwayed Brake, 100mph	NU	Post Office Brake Stowage Van
NF	Non-gangwayed Brake	NV	Two-tier Motor-car Van
NH	Gangwayed Brake 110mph	NX	General Utility Van, Motorail
NJ	General Utility Van, EW	NY	Exhibition Van
NK	General Utility Van, Brute		

These codes are followed by a figure to indicate class of the vehicle viz 1: First, 2: Second, 3: First and Second or 4: Either Class. Non passenger vehicles carry 5.

On passenger vehicles, the fourth character indicates the type of vehicle viz 1: Mk 1; Z: Mk 2; A-F: Mk 2a-2f; G: Mk 3, 3a; H: Mk 3b, Mk 4.

On non-passenger vehicles the suffix letter denotes the type of train brake fitted. Three-letter codes without the character 5 are now being displayed on the vans and they are utilised in this book. The brake type suffix letters are detailed below but not all apply to coaching stock.

A	Air Braked	P	Vacuum Piped
B	Air Braked and Vacuum Piped	Q	Air Piped
E	Electro-pneumatic	R	Dual Piped
F	Vacuum Braked (A.F.I.)	V	Vacuum Braked
G	Vacuum Braked (A.F.I.) & Air Piped	W	Vacuum Braked & Air Piped
H	Dual Braked (A.F.I.)	X	Dual Braked
O	No train brake		

Loading Gauge

On coach ends of Mk 1 and Mk 2 vehicles, the large figures 'C1' are carried, with the corresponding figures 'C3' being carried on Mk 3s (and IC125 coaches). These indicate the route availability restrictions which apply to the coaches. 'C1' indicates universal availability (with certain minor exceptions), whilst C3 indicates that these long vehicles cannot travel over lines where clearances are limited and curvature is sharp.

Certain Mk 1 coaches allocated to the SR in the 1960s also carry a small circular plate denoting 'Restriction 4', which indicates the same restrictions as 'C1'.

Abbreviations

It is an unfortunate necessity to use these so that the details may be included in a reasonably small space. The following are applicable throughout the book but additional ones are used for each section and are detailed in the notes which precede the tabulated numbers of their own section.

a	Air Braked	Int.	Introduced
AWS	Automatic Warning System	PA or p	Public Address equipment
x	Dual braked	PT or q	PA Transmitter
DG or g	Driver/Guard communication	R	Refurbished
f	750-volt electric heating	UIC	International Union of Railways
F	Facelifted	v	Vacuum Braked

Liveries

BR's standard liveries are blue and grey for passenger-rated stock and plain blue for non-passenger vehicles. Where whole classes or lots are in other liveries, this is stated in the headings. Where individual vehicles are concerned, the following symbols are used.

I	InterCity livery (beige, dark brown with red band)
S	ScotRail livery (beige, dark grey with blue stripe)
N	Network SouthEast livery (white, blue, red and grey bands)
RR	Post Office red livery
P	Trans Pennine livery (blue and white, light blue stripe)

Certain standard Mk 1 coaches are painted in other uses. These vehicles are listed in the class headings. Other liveries are in use on multiple-unit stock and private owner vehicles.

Level of Repair and Maintenance Facility

In April 1987 BR introduced a new maintenance policy for all traction and coaching stock. Under the scheme, depots and workshops are classified on a scale of 1 to 6, called Levels, determined by the facilities available and work effected at each location.

The larger establishments, Level 5, normally have separate workshops to carry out this category of repair and are not necessarily answerable to the Sector which 'owns' the main depot.

Definition

Level	*Facility*	*Description*
1	Fuel point	Facility for dispensing fuel, oil and water to diesel locomotives and/or DMUs. Minor servicing to EMUs. Manned by unskilled staff.
2	Servicing	Capable of undertaking 'A' exam work and occasional 'B' exams on locomotives and multiple-units together with work arising and brake blocking; also full maintenance for diesel shunter locomotives. For coaching stock some cleaning, chemical emission toilet disposal, environmental checks, two daily exams, weekly exams and brake blocking. The facility will have a covered pit, a small store and be manned by skilled staff.

Depot Codes

Level	Facility	Description
3	Maintenance	This facility will have a Traction and Rolling Stock allocation and be capable of carrying out all levels of exams and the majority of repairs arising. It will have covered pits, staff accommodation, light lifting and jacking facilities. A full range of equipment will be available to meet all exam requirements. Multiple-units and coaching stock all levels of exams, code 'C' cleaning, patch painting and some body repair.
4	Maintenance and repair	As for level 3 but having an additional capability for heavier repairs. The depot will be well equipped with cranes and/or heavy lifting jacks for bogie removal and possibly a wheel lathe.
5	Heavy repair	A facility capable of undertaking unplanned heavy repairs and collision damage. May also have the facility for lower level of classified repair, limited component refurbishment and half life component exchange. Fuelling facilities are not necessarily provided.
6	Workshop	A main workshop with full facilities for undertaking all levels of classified and unclassified repairs.

	Level LHCS	Level PCLS		Main Sector(s)
AB	2		Aberdeen Ferryhill TMD	P/I
BI		1	Brighton T&RSMD	N
BJ		4	Bristol, Marsh Junction	R
BM	2		Bournemouth West EMUD	N
BN	4		Bounds Green T&RSMD	I/R
CA	3	4	Cambridge (Coldhams Lane) TMD	R
CF	4		Cardiff Canton TMD	P
	5	5	Cardiff Cathays RSMD	—
CL	3	1	Carlisle Upperby RSMD	P
		‡	Carlisle Currock RSMD	
CP		1	Crewe RSMD	R
DL		5	Doncaster Major Depot, BRML	—
EC	4	1	Edinburgh, Craigentinny T&RSMD	I/P
EH	4	4	Eastleigh T&RSMD	N/R
EN	4	2	Euston Downside CS	1
HT	4	4	Heaton T&RSMD	P/R
IL		4	Ilford EMUD	R
IP		2	Ipswich	R
IS	4	1	Inverness TMD	P
LA	4		Laira TMD	I/N/P

	Level LHCS	PCLS		Main Sector(s)
LL	4		Liverpool, Edge Hill CS	I
MA	4	4	Longsight CSMD	I/R
MV		1	Manchester Red Bank CS	R
NC	4	4	Norwich, Crown Point T&RSMD	P
NL	4	4	Neville Hill T&RSMD	I/P
OM	4	4	Old Oak Common T&RSMDs	I/N/R
OY	4	4	Oxley (Wolverhampton) CSMD	I
PC	4	4	Polmadie CSMD	P
PE		4	Peterborough CS	R
PH	2		Perth (SRPS)	I
PY		3	Pylle Hill, Bristol	R
RE		1	Ramsgate EMUD	N
TF	1	1	Thornton Fields	I/N/R
WB	4	4	Wembley CSMD	
ZG	6	6	Eastleigh BRML	
ZH	5	5	Springburn BRML	
ZN	5	5	Wolverton BRML	

BREL Works:

ZD	6	6	Derby Carriage (CEM under contract)	
ZR	6	6	York Carriage	

Private Works:

ZB		5	RFS Industries, Doncaster	

Headquarters:

ZQ			British Railways Board. Includes all Private Owner vehicles and new stock on acceptance	

Sectors:
I: InterCity
N: Network SouthEast
P: Provincial
R: Parcels

‡ Specialist repair workshops

BR Standard Number Series

PFK AP1Z

Pullman Parlour with Kitchen, Mk. 2 — AP101

Introduced: 1966
Weight: 41 tonnes
Seats: 1st, 18
Brakes: Air
Heating: Pressure Heating & Ventilation (AC only)
ETH Index: 6

Bogies: B5
Toilets: 2 (1 staff only)
Maximum speed: 100mph
Standard equipment: Liquid Gas Cooking

InterCity Pullman livery

Derby 30755/66

504	*ICH*	EN	*Ullswater*
506	*ICH*	EN	*Windermere*

PFP AQ1Z

Pullman Parlour Mk. 2. — AQ101

Introduced: 1966
Weight: 35 tonnes
Seats: 1st, 36
Brakes: Air
Heating: Pressure Heating & Ventilation (AC only)
ETH Index: 5

Bogies: B4
Toilets: 2
Maximum Speed: 100mph

InterCity Pullman livery

Derby 30754/66

546	*ICH*	EN	*Coniston Water*
548	*ICH*	EN	*Grasmere*
549	*ICH*	EN	*Bassenthwaite Lake*
550	*ICH*	EN	*Rydal Water*
551	*ICH*	EN	*Buttermere*
552	*ICH*	EN	*Ennerdale Water*
553	*ICH*	EN	*Crummock Water*

PFB — AR1Z

Pullman Brake Mk.2 — AR101

Introduced: 1966
Weight: 35 tonnes
Seats: 1st, 30
Brakes: Air
Heating: Pressure Heating & Ventilation (AC only)
ETH Index: 4

Bogies: B4
Toilets: 1
Maximum Speed: 100mph

InterCity Pullman livery

Derby 30753/66

586	*ICH*	EN	*Derwent Water*

These former Manchester Pullman cars were refurbished and air-braked during 1986/87 and re-entered service for the InterCity Charter fleet carrying Lakeland names.

RFO — AJ1F

Restaurant Lounge First Mk 2f AJ104 —

Introduced: 1988 by modification from AD1F and AD2F
Weight: 33.5 tonnes
Seats: 1st, 26
Brakes: Air
Heating: Full air conditioning
ETH Index: 5X
Bogies: B4
Toilets: 2

Maximum speed: 100mph
Standard equipment: Public Address and transmitter fitted
Mk 2f FOs and SOs refurbished and converted by the addition of miniature buffet equipment with a fixed boiler and microwave oven as a further development, with fixed seating, 6700-08, AN2D series.
InterCity livery.

1200	*IWC*	WB	1208	*IWC*	WB	1216	*IWK*	LA
1201	*IWC*	PC	1209	*IWC*	WB	1217	*IWK*	LA
1202	*IWC*	WB	1210	*ICC*	MA	1218	*IWR*	LA
1203	*IWC*	PC	1211	*ICC*	MA	1219	*ICC*	MA
1204	*IWC*	WB	1212	*ICC*	MA	1220	*ICC*	MA
1205	*IWC*	WB	1213	*ICC*	MA	1221	*ICC*	MA
1206	*IWC*	WB	1214	*ICC*	MA			
1207	*IWC*	WB	1215	*ICC*	MA			

RBR — AJ41

Restaurant Buffet with Kitchen — AJ403

Introduced: 1956
Weight: 39 tonnes
Seats: 23 chairs
Brakes: Air (Dual: x)
ETH Index: 2 (2X-1663/65/66/70/71/72/75/78/80/84/90/93)
Bogies: Commonwealth
Toilets: 0

Maximum speed: 100mph
Standard equipment: Liquid Gas Cooking
Special features: Public address only (p) or Public address and transmitter (q) fitted as indicated.

All built as RB but are now refurbished with fluorescent lighting and reclassified RBR.

Pressed Steel 30628/60-1

1644	l	*ICH*	BN	1659	lq	*ICH*	BN	~~1683~~	lq	*IAN*	NC
1645	lq	*ICH*	BN	1663	lx	*ICH*	BN	1684	xq	*ICC*	OY
1646	lq	*ICH*	BN	1665	x	*ICC*	MA	1686	lq	*IAN*	NC
1647	lq	*IAN*	NC	1666	lx	*ICH*	BN	1687		*ICC*	MA
1648	lq	*ICC*	MA	1667	lx	*ICH*	BN	1688	l	*ICC*	MA
1649	q	*ICC*	MA	1670	x	*ICC*	OY	~~1689~~	l	*IAN*	NC
1650	q	*ICC*	MA	1671	x	*ICC*	MA	1691	l	*IAN*	NC
1651	lp	*ICC*	MA	1672	lx	*ICH*	BN	~~1692~~	lq	*IAN*	NC
1652	lq	*ICC*	MA	1673	q	*ICC*	MA	1693	x	*ICH*	BN
1653	lq	*ICC*	OY	1674	lp	*ICH*	BN	1694		*ICC*	MA
1654	p	*ICC*	MA	1675	lx	*ICH*	BN	1695		*ICC*	MA
1655	lq	*ICC*	MA	1678	lx	*ICH*	OM	1696	lq	*IAN*	NC
1656	l	*ICC*	MA	1679	lq	*ICH*	BN	1697	lq	*IAN*	NC
1657	q	*ICC*	OY	1680	x	*ICC*	OY	1698	l	*ICH*	BN
1658	lp	*ICC*	OY	1681	lq	*IAN*	NC	1699	lq	*IAN*	NC

RMB — AN21

Open Standard with Miniature Buffet — AN202 or AN203

Introduced: 1957
Weight: 38 tonnes
Seats: 44
Brakes: Dual (Vacuum [v] or Air [a] as marked)
ETH Index: 3 (3X: 1813-16/33/80)
Bogies: Commonwealth (B4, B5 as marked)
Toilets: 2

Maximum Speed: 100mph
Standard equipment: Liquid Gas Cooking
Special features: Public Address (p) or Public Address and Transmitter (q) as indicated

All are refurbished with fluorescent lighting.
AN208 further facelifted internally

York 30485/57 **AN202**

1805	laB4p	*ICC*	PC

Wolverton 30520/60 **AN203**

1813	p	*ICC*	MA	1816	p	*IWC*	EN	1833	l	*IAN*	NC
1815		*IXX*	BN	1832	l	*ICC*	MA				

Wolverton 30567/60 **AN202** (1842 AN208)

1838		*ICC*	MA	1845		*IWC*	EN	1850	vB5	*NNE*	CA
1842	Np	*NNE*	CA	1848	lp	*ICC*	MA				

Wolverton 30670/61-2 **AN203**

1853	l	*ICC*	PC	1859		*ICHH*	PH	1863	p	*ICC*	MA
1854	lvp	*ICC*	PC	1860	l	*ICC*	MA	1864	p	*ICC*	MA
1857	p	*IXX*	EN	1861	p	*ICHH*	BN				

Wolverton 30702/62 **AN203**

1865	Nv	*NNE*	CA	1870	la	*IAN*	NC	1878	ap	*ICC*	MA
1867	laq	*ICC*	MA	1871	Np	*NNE*	CA	1879	lap	*ICC*	MA
1868	lap	*IAN*	NC	1875	lap	*ICC*	MA	1880	a	*IWC*	EN
1869	la	*IAN*	NC	1876	la	*ICC*	MA	1882	ap	*ICC*	MA

RBR AJ41

Unclassified Restaurant — AJ414

Introduced: 1957 as RU with 33 chairs
Weight: 38 tonnes or 39 tonnes (1959-84)
Seats: 23 fixed chairs
Brakes: Air (Dual [x])
ETH Index: 2 (2X: 1923/24/47/48/53)
Bogies: B4/B5 or Commonwealth (1959-84)
Toilets: 0

Maximum speed: 100mph
Standard equipment: Liquid Gas cooking
Special features: Public Address (p) or Public Address and Transmitter (q) as indicated

All are refurbished with fluorescent lighting

Ashford/Swindon 30476/58

1923	lx	*ICC*	MA
1924	lx	*ICC*	MA

Ashford/Swindon 30575/60

1944	p	*ICC*	MA	1947	x	*ICC*	MA	1954	q	*ICC*	MA
1945	q	*ICC*	MA	1948	lx	*ICH*	OM	1956	p	*ICC*	OY
1946	q	*ICC*	MA	1953	x	*IWR*	OM				

Ashford/Swindon 30632/60-1

1959	lq	*ICC*	OY	1966	lq	*ICC*	MA	1972	q	*ICC*	OY
1961	q	*ICC*	OY	1969	lq	*ICC*	MA	1973	lq	*ICC*	OY
1962	q	*ICC*	OY	1970	q	*ICC*	OY	1981	lp	*ICC*	OY
1965	q	*IXX*	OM	1971	lq	*ICC*	OY	1984	q	*ICC*	MA

SLSC AU51

Sleeper Support Coach, Mk 1 — AU501

Introduced: 1988 by modifying BCK built 1964
Weight: 36 tonnes
Berths: Details not yet available
Brakes: Air
ETH Index: 3
Bogies: Commonwealth

Toilets: 1
Maximum speed: 100mph
Standard equipment: Fitted with berths for the use of staff on Charted Trains. Coaches retain 5 compartments. Fluorescent lighting. InterCity livery.

Derby 30732/64

2833	*ICH*	BN
2834	*ICH*	BN

Royal Train Vehicles

Whether one vehicle is attached to a standard regular train or a special train is required for a full Royal party the following stock is available. All maintenance and interior attention is the responsibility of BRML at Wolverton in a secure separate building under the charge of ICH Sector. In the interests of national security only limited information can be published on this fleet.

No	Use	Built/ Converted	Former No	Weight	Toilet	Brake	Air Con	EH Index	Bogies	Design Code
2900	*Saloon*	W 30130/55		42t		Air	★	5X	B5	AT501
2901	*Saloon*	W 30131/57		42t		Air	★	5X	B5	AT503
2902	*Dining Saloon*	W 30129/56	499	43t		Air	★	3X	B5	AT502
2903	*Saloon*	D 30848/72 W 30886/77	11001	37t	1 CET	Air	★	9X	BT5	AT525

2904	*Saloon*	D 30847/72 W 30887/77	12001	37t	1 CET	Air	★	15X	BT5	AT526
2905	*Sleeper Power Brake*	D 30790/69 W 30888/77	14105	46t	1 CET	Air	PHV	5X	B5	AT527
2906	*Sleeper*	D 30790/69 W 30889/77	14112	35t	1 CET	Air	PHV	4X	B4	AT528
2907	*Restaurant/Kitchen*	A/S 30633/61	325	38t	1	Air		2X	B5	AT517
2911	*Special Saloon*	W /20 W /82	45000	36t		Dual		PHV	B4	AT530
2914	*Sleeper*	D 31002/84		43t	2	Air	★	6X	BT10	AT531
2915	*Sleeper*	D 31002/84		43t	2	Air	★	6X	BT10	AT531
2916	*Dining & Royal Household*	D 30884/76 W 31059/86	40515	37t		Air	★	3	BT10 BT10A	AT537
2917†	*Household Staff Diner*	D 30884/76 W /	40512			Air	★	6X	BT10 BT10A	AT532
2918†	*Lounge Sleeper*	D 30884/76 W /	40518			Air	★	6X	BT10 BT10A	AT532
2919†	*Saloon/Diner/Sleeper*	D 30884/76 W /	40514			Air	★	6X	BT10 BT10A	AT532
2920	*Generator*	D 30790/69 W 31044/88	17109	48t	1	Air		2X	B5	AT536
2921†	*Escort Vehicle*	D 30790/69 W /	17107	32t	1	Air	PHV	4	B4	AT5
2922	*Sleeper*	D/W 31035/86		38t	3	Air	★	10X	BT10 BT10A	AT534
2923	*Sleeper/Lounge*	D/W 31036/86		38t	3	Air	★	10X	BT10 BT10A	AT535

† Not yet ready for service ★ Equipment fitted W=Wolverton D=Derby A=Ashford S=Swindon

PHV=Pressure Heating and Ventilation *Liquid Gas Cooking* 2902/06/07/12

Electric Cooking 2904 *Wooden framing* 2910

British standard and adaptor gangways 2911-12

CET=Controlled emission toilet

FO AD11

Open First Mk. 1. — AD103

Introduced: 1951
Weight: 33 tonnes or 36 tonnes (3107 on)
Seats: 1st, 42
Brakes: Air. Vacuum (v) or Dual (x) as marked
ETH Index: 3
Bogies: B4 or Commonwealth (3107 on)
Toilets: 2
Maximum speed: 100mph

Special characteristics: 3097, 3107/11/14/15/18/19/20/23/24/27/31-35/40/43/46-50 are refurbished and form the VIP FO fleet, and 3121/36/41 are undergoing refurbishing for this fleet. 3096 is the reserve vehicle. All VIP vehicles have PA and individual table lamps. Fluorescent lighting is fitted to 3097 and 3107 on.

3135/36/41/43/44/46/47/48 formerly SOs 3601/05/08/09/02/06/04/10 respectively before refurbishing

Doncaster 30091/54

3045	lv	*ICHH*	BN

BRCW 30576/59

3096	lv	*ICH*	BN	3098	v	*ICH*	PH
3097	l	*ICH*	BN	3100	v	*ICH*	PH

Swindon 30697/62-3

3107	lx	*ICH*	BN	3118	lx	*ICH*	BN	3123	l	*ICH*	BN
3111	lx	*ICH*	BN	3119	lx	*ICH*	BN	3124	l	*ICH*	BN
3114	lx	*ICH*	BN	3120	lx	*ICH*	BN	3127	l	*ICH*	BN
3115	lx	*ICH*	BN	3121	l	*ICH*	BN				

Swindon 30717/63

3131	lx	*ICH*	BN	3136	l	*ICH*	CL	3146	l	*ICH*	BN
3132	lx	*ICH*	BN	3140	lx	*ICH*	BN	3147	l	*ICH*	BN
3133	lx	*ICH*	BN	3141	l	*ICH*	CL	3148	l	*ICH*	BN
3134	lx	*ICH*	BN	3143	l	*ICH*	BN	3149	l	*ICH*	BN
3135	l	*ICH*	BN	3144	l	*ICH*	BN	3150	l	*ICH*	BN

FO — AD1D

Open First, Mk. 2d. — AD105

Introduced: 1971
Weight: 34 tonnes
Seats: 1st, 42
Brakes: Air
Heating: Full air conditioning
ETH Index: 5

Bogies: B4
Toilets: 2
Maximum speed: 100mph
Standard equipment: Public Address fitted
Special characteristics: Day/night lighting fitted for Nightrider: 3170, 3208

Derby 30821/71-2

3170		*ICH*	OM	3186	I	*IAN*	NC	3202	I	*ICC*	MA
3171	I	*IML*	DY	3187	I	*ICH*	BN	3203	I	*ICH*	MA
3172	I	*IAN*	NC	3188	I	*IAN*	NC	3204		*ICH*	OM
3173	I	*ICH*	BN	3189		*ICH*	OM	3205		*ICH*	OM
3174	I	*IAN*	NC	3190	I	*ICH*	MA	3206		*ICH*	OM
3175	I	*ICH*	EN	3191		*ICH*	OM	3207	I	*ICH*	OM
3176	I	*ICH*	OM	3192	I	*ICC*	MA	3208	I	*ICH*	OM
3177	I	*IEC*	NL	3193	I	*ICH*	OM	3209	I	*ICH*	BN
3178	I	*ICH*	BN	3194	I	*IML*	DY	3210		*ICH*	OM
3179	I	*ICH*	BN	3195	I	*ICH*	MA	3211	I	*ICH*	OM
3180	I	*ICH*	OM	3196	I	*ICH*	MA	3212	I	*ICH*	MA
3181	I	*ICH*	BN	3197	I	*ICH*	BN	3213	I	*ICH*	OM
3182	I	*IAN*	NC	3198		*ICH*	OM	3215		*ICH*	OM
3183	I	*IAN*	NC	3199		*ICH*	OM	3216		*ICH*	OM
3184	I	*ICH*	BN	3200	I	*ICH*	OM				
3185		*ICH*	OM	3201	I	*ICH*	MA				

FO — AD1E

Open First, Mk. 2e. — AD106

Introduced: 1972
Weight: 34 tonnes
Seats: 1st, 42 († 1st: 41)
Brakes: Air
Heating: Full air conditioning
ETH Index: 5

Bogies: B4
Toilets: 2
Maximum Speed: 100mph
Standard equipment: Public Address fitted
Special characteristics: Day/night lighting: 3255/58
†Wheelchair accommodation

Derby 30843/72-3

3221	†I	*IAN*	NC	3239	I	*ICC*	MA	3258		*ICH*	OM
3222		*ICH*	OM	3240		*ICH*	MA	3259	†I	*IAN*	NC
3223		*ICH*	OM	3241		*ICH*	OM	3260	I	*ICH*	BN
3224	I	*ICC*	MA	3242	†I	*IAN*	NC	3261	†I	*IAN*	NC
3225	I	*ICH*	MA	3244	†I	*IAN*	NC	3262	I	*IAN*	NC
3226	I	*ICH*	OM	3245	S	*PSE*	EC	3263	I	*ICH*	BN
3227	I	*ICH*	OM	3246	†I	*IAN*	NC	3264		*ICH*	OM
3228	I	*ICC*	MA	3247	S	*PSX*	EC	3265	S	*PSX*	EC
3229	I	*ICH*	MA	3248	S	*PSX*	EC	3266	I	*IAN*	NC
3230	I	*ICH*	MA	3249		*IAN*	NC	3267		*ICH*	OM
3231	I	*ICC*	MA	3250	†I	*IAN*	NC	3268	I	*ICH*	MA
3232	†I	*IAN*	NC	3251	†I	*IAN*	NC	3269	I	*ICH*	OM
3233	I	*ICH*	OM	3252	†I	*IAN*	NC	3270		*ICH*	OM
3234	†I	*IAN*	NC	3253		*ICH*	OM	3271	I	*ICC*	MA
3235		*ICH*	OM	3254	I	*ICH*	BN	3272		*ICH*	OM
3236	I	*ICC*	MA	3255		*ICH*	OM	3273	I	*ICC*	MA
3237	I	*ICC*	MA	3256	†I	*IAN*	NC	3274	I	*ICH*	OM
3238		*ICH*	OM	3257	†I	*IAN*	NC	3275		*ICH*	OM

FO — AD1F

Open First, Mk. 2f. — AD107

Introduced: 1973
Weight: 33.5 tonnes
Seats: 1st, 42
Brakes: Air. 3284 has disc brakes
Heating: Full Air Conditioning
ETH Index: 5X
Bogies: B4
Toilets: 2
Maximum Speed: 100mph

Standard equipment: Public Address fitted
Special features: 3358/59/83/97, 3434/39 are fitted with video equipment. Day/night lighting: 3388, 3428/29
3359 seats 39F
Nightrider stock: 3277/80/90, 3303/12/31/36/38/44/54/66/67/72/83/88/97, 3408/28/29/32/39
R: Refurbished, InterCity livery

Derby 30845/73

3277		*IWC*	WB	3292	R	*IWC*	OY	3304	R	*IWC*	OY
3278		*IWC*	WB	3293		*IWC*	MA	3309		*IWC*	PC
3279	R	*IWC*	MA	3295	R	*IWC*	OY	3312		*IWC*	WB
3280		*IWC*	PC	3296		*IWC*	WB	3313	R	*IWC*	OY
3284	S	*PSX*	EC	3299	R	*IWC*	OY	3314		*IWC*	MA
3285	R	*IWC*	OY	3300	R	*IWC*	OY	3318		*IWC*	WB
3290		*IWC*	PC	3303		*IWC*	WB				

Derby 30859/73-4.

No.		Operator	Livery
3322		IWC	PC
3325	R	IWC	OY
3326	R	IWC	OY
3330	R	IWC	OY
3331		IWC	WB
3333	R	IWC	OY
3334	R	IWC	OY
3336		IWC	WB
3337	R	IWC	OY
3338		IWC	PC
3340	R	IWC	OY
3344		IWC	PC
3345	R	IWC	OY
3348	R	IWC	OY
3350	R	IWC	OY
3351	R	IWC	MA
3352		IWC	MA
3353	R	IWC	OY
3354	R	ICC	OY
3356	R	IWC	MA
3358	R	IWC	OY
3359	R	IWC	OY
3360	R	IWC	OY
3362	R	IWC	MA
3363	R	IWC	OY
3364	R	IWC	MA
3366	R	IWC	OY
3367		IWC	WB
3368	R	IWC	OY
3369	R	IWC	OY
3372		IWC	EN
3373	R	IWC	OY
3374	R	IWC	OY
3375	R	IWC	OY
3378		IWC	EN
3379	R	IWC	OY
3381	R	IWC	OY
3383		IWC	PC
3384	R	IWC	OY
3385	R	IWC	OY
3386	R	IWC	OY
3387	R	IWC	OY
3388	R	IWC	OY
3389	R	IWC	OY
3390	R	IWC	MA
3391		IWC	PC
3392	R	IWC	OY
3395	R	IWC	OY
3397	R	IWC	OY
3399	R	IWC	OY
3400	R	IWC	OY
3402	R	IWC	OY
3408		IWC	WB
3411	R	IWC	OY
3414	R	IWC	OY
3416	R	IWC	OY
3417	R	IWC	OY
3424	R	IWC	OY
3425	R	IWC	OY
3426	R	IWC	OY
3428	R	IWC	OY

Derby 30873/74-5

No.		Operator	Livery
3429	R	IWC	OY
3431	R	IWC	OY
3432		IWC	PC
3433	R	IWC	OY
3434	R	IWC	OY
3438	R	IWC	OY
3439		IWC	PC

TSO/SO AC21/AD21

Tourist Open Standard — AC204 or Open Standard AD201

Introduced: 1951
Weight: 33 tonnes
Seats: 64 (TSO) or 48 (SO)
Brakes: Vacuum (exceptions see lot headings)
ETH Index (where equipped): 4 or 4S (750V)
Bogies: B1 or Commonwealth (4918 on) with B4 and Commonwealth (CW) fitted as shown to individual vehicles
Toilets: 2
Maximum Speed: 100mph (90mph B1 bogies)
Special Livery: West Highland (green and cream) WH as marked
Special features: PA (p) fitted as marked
F Facelifted
R Refurbished

The majority of these were built to design code AC204 but most survivors are to diagram AC201 and these are noted against the lots concerned. Four lots have arm-rests and seat 48S, with the type and design codes SO, AD201. These are designated Open Standard.

Doncaster 30043/53, Air Brake, Electric heat (750V) Commonwealth Bogies

3749		*ICH*	CL							

York 30079/53, Vacuum brake

3754		*PEX*	PC	3767	WH	*ICH*	BN	3771	*PEX*	IS
3766	WH	*ICH*	BN	3769		*PEX*	PC			

Eastleigh 30086/54-5 Vacuum brake, (3918-24 are Ashford/Eastleigh, Air brake, Electric heat (750V)

3918	CW	*IXXZ*	CL	3924	CW	*ICH*	CL	3961	*PEX*	PC
3919	CW	*ICH*	CL	3950		*PEX*	PC			
3923	CW	*ICH*	CL	3958		*PEX*	PC			

York 30090/54, Air brake, Electric heat (750V), Commonwealth bogies

3991		*ICHH*	CL							
3993		*ICHH*	CL							

Ashford/Swindon 30149/56-7. Air brake, Electric heat (750V) Commonwealth Bogies

4058		*ICHH*	CL	4076		*ICHH*	CL			
4066		*ICHH*	CL							

Eastleigh 30121/55. SO, AD201

4366		*PSP*	HT							

Ashford/Swindon 30219/57. Air brake, Electric heat (BR/UIC). Commonwealth bogies.

4376		*ICHH*	CL	4393		*ICHH*	CL			
4392		*ICHH*	CL							

BRCW 30226/56-7

4419	WH	*ICH*	BN	4422		*ICH*	PH	4435 WH	*ICH*	BN
4420		*PEX*	PC	4425		*ICH*	PH			

BRCW. 30227/57. SO, AD201

4478		*PWH*	PC	4483		*PWH*	PC	4485	*PWH*	PC
4479		*PWH*	PC	4484		*PSP*	HT			

York 30376/57. SO, AD201.

4779		*PWH*	PC
4785		*PSP*	HT
4786		*PSP*	HT
4787		*PSP*	HT
4789		*PSP*	HT
4790		*PSP*	HT
4795		*PWH*	PC
4796		*PSP*	HT
4798		*PWH*	PC
4802		*PSP*	HT
4804		*PSP*	HT
4805		*PSP*	HT
4809		*PWH*	PC

BRCW 30473/59. SO, AD201.

4816		*PWH*	PC
4821		*PSP*	HT
4822	B4	*PSP*	HT
4823	B4	*PSP*	HT
4824	B4	*PSP*	HT
4826	B4	*PSP*	HT
4828	B4	*PSP*	HT
4829	B4	*PSP*	HT

Wolverton 30506/59. AC201. Dual brake, Fluorescent lighting

4830		*NNW*	EN
4831		*PNS*	IS
4832		*PNS*	IS
4834		*NNW*	EN
4836		*PNS*	IS

Wolverton 30525/59-60. AC201 Vacuum brake, Fluorescent lighting. B4 bogies (Dual braked [x] and B1 bogies as marked)

4842	x	*ICH*	MA
4843		*PSP*	PC
4844	BI	*ICH*	PH
4845		*ICH*	OY
~~4846~~	Np	*NNW*	EN
4847		*NNW*	EN
4848	N	*NNW*	EN
4849	N	*NNW*	EN
~~4852~~	NFp	*NNW*	EN
4853	NFp	*NNW*	EN
4854		*NNW*	EN
4855		*ICH*	OY
4856	x	*ICH*	MA
4857		*ICH*	OY
4858	x	*ICH*	MA
4860	x	*ICH*	MA
4861		*ICH*	OY
4862	N	*NNW*	EN
4864	BI	*PEX*	IS
4866	Np	*NNW*	EN
4867	Np	*NNW*	EN
4869	x	*ICH*	MA
4871	BI	*ICH*	PH
~~4873~~	N	*NNW*	EN
4875	N	*NNW*	EN
4876		*NNW*	EN
4880	N	*NNW*	EN
4884		*ICH*	BN
4885		*PEX*	IS
4886		*ICH*	OY
4888		*NNW*	EN
~~4891~~	N	*NNW*	EN
4894		*ICH*	OM
4895	N	*NNW*	EN
4899	N	*NNW*	EN

Wolverton 30646/61. AC201. Fluorescent lighting
All built with Commonwealth bogies but B1's substituted on most. B4 and CW bogies now fitted as marked

4900	WH	*ICH*	BN
4901	Ncw	*NNW*	EN
4902	B4	*PNS*	IS
4903		*PEX*	PC
4904		*PEX*	PC
4905		*NSS*	EH
4906		*PEX*	PC
4907		*PEX*	IS
4908	Ncw	*NNW*	EN
4909	B4	*PEX*	IS
~~4910~~		*NSS*	EH
4911	WH	*ICH*	BN
4912	WH	*ICH*	BN
4913	Ncw	*NNW*	EN
4915	B4	*PEX*	PC
4916	B4	*PNS*	IS
4917	Ncw	*NNW*	EN

Wolverton 30690/61-2. AC201. Fluorescent lighting, Commonwealth bogies, Vacuum brake except Dual (x)
R Refurbished, InterCity livery except 5009

4918		ICH	OY
4919	R	ICH	OY
4920	NFp	NNW	EN
4922		ICH	OY
4923	N	NNW	EN
4924		ICH	OY
4925		ICH	OM
4926	N	NNW	EN
4927	R	ICH	OY
4928		ICH	OY
4929	N	NNW	EN
4930	R	ICH	OY
4931	N	NNW	EN
4932		ICH	OY
4933	N	NNW	EN
4934		ICH	OY
4935	N	NNW	EN
4936	p	NNW	EN
4937		ICH	OY
4938		ICH	OY
4939		ICH	OM
4940	N	NNW	EN
4943	N	NNW	EN
4944		IST	OY
4945	Np	NNW	EN
4946	R	ICH	OY
4947		ICH	OY
4948		ICH	OY
4949		ICH	OY
4950	N	NNW	EN
4951	Np	NNW	EN
4952		ICH	OY
4953	Np	NNW	EN
4954		ICH	OY
4955	Np	NNW	EN
4956		ICH	OM
4958		ICH	OY
4959		ICH	BN
4960		ICH	OY
4961	R	ICH	OY
4962		ICH	OY
4963		ICH	OY
4964		ICH	OY
4965		ICH	OY
4966	R	ICH	OY
4973	N	NNW	EN
4974		ICH	BN
4975	Np	NNW	EN
4976		ICH	OM
4977		ICH	OM
4978		ICH	OY
4979	R	ICH	OY
4980	N	NNW	EN
4981		ICH	OY
4982		ICH	OY
4983		ICH	OM
4984		ICH	OY
4985	N	NNW	EN
4986		ICH	OY
4987		ICH	OY
4988		ICH	OY
4989	NFp	NNW	EN
4990	Np	NNW	EN
4991		ICH	OY
4992	p	NNW	EN
4993		ICH	OY
4994		NNW	EN
4995		ICH	OY
4996	R	ICH	OY
4997		ICH	OY
4998		ICH	OY
4999		ICH	OY
5000	Np	NNW	EN
5001	R	ICH	OY
5002		ICH	OY
5003	Np	NNW	EN
5004		ICH	OY
5005		ICH	OY
5006	Np	NNW	EN
5007		ICH	OM
5008	R	ICH	OY
5009	R	ICH	OY
5010		ICH	OM
5023		ICH	OM
5024	N	NNW	EN
5025		ICH	OM
5027		ICH	OM
5028	★	ICH	MA
5029		ICH	OM
5030		ICH	OY
5031		ICH	OY
5032	x	ICH	MA
5033		ICH	BN
5035	x	ICH	MA
5036		ICH	OY
5037		ICH	OY
5038	x	ICH	MA
5039	Np	NNW	EN
5040	x	ICH	MA
5041		ICH	OY
5042	x	ICH	MA
5043		NNW	EN
5044	Fp	ICH	OM

TSO AC2Z

Tourist Open Standard, Mk. 2 — AC205

Introduced: 1965
Weight: 32.5 tonnes
Bogies: B4
Toilets: 2

Seats: 64
Brakes: Vacuum. ([a] Air as marked)
Heating: Pressure heating and Ventilation
ETH Index: 4

Maximum speed: 100mph
Special characteristics: All air braked vehicles are wired for the former push/pull operation on the Edinburgh-Glasgow service.
Facelifted: 5105/36/62/99, 5208/16

Derby 30751/65-67

5070		*PCR*	CL
5072		*PCR*	CL
5073		*NWR*	OM
5076		*PCR*	CL
5080		*NWR*	OM
5085		*NNE*	CA
5086	N	*NWR*	OM
5087	N	*NWR*	OM
5088		*PCR*	CL
5090		*NNE*	CA
5097		*PCR*	CL
5099		*PCR*	CL
5104	N	*NWR*	OM
5105		*NNE*	CA
5112	N	*NWR*	OM
5113	N	*NWR*	OM
5114		*PCR*	CL
5118	N	*NWR*	OM
5124		*PNS*	IS
5125		*PCR*	CL
5128		*PCR*	CL
5131		*PCR*	CL
5132		*PNS*	IS
5133		*PNS*	IS
5135		*PNS*	IS
5136	N	*NNE*	CA
5138		*NWR*	OM
5139		*PNS*	IS
5140	N	*NNE*	CA
5141		*NNE*	CA
5142	a	*ICC*	PC
5143		*PNS*	IS
5144	a	*PTP*	NL
5145		*PNS*	IS
5146	Sa	*PSE*	EC
5147	Pa	*PTP*	HT
5148		*PNS*	IS
5149		*PNS*	IS
5150	N	*NWR*	OM
5151		*PNS*	IS
5152	Sa	*PSE*	EC
5153	Sa	*PSE*	EC
5154		*PNS*	IS
5155		*PNS*	IS
5156		*PNS*	IS
5157	N	*NWR*	OM
5158	N	*NWR*	OM
5159	N	*NWR*	OM
5160	Pa	*PTP*	HT
5161	N	*NWR*	OM
5162	N	*NGE*	CA
5163		*PNS*	IS
5165	N	*NWR*	OM
5166		*PNS*	IS
5167	N	*NWR*	OM
5170		*PNS*	IS
5171	N	*NNE*	CA
5172	N	*NNE*	CA
5173	N	*NWR*	OM
5174		*PNS*	IS
5175	N	*NNE*	CA
5176	Sa	*PSE*	EC
5177	N	*NWR*	OM
5178	N	*NWR*	OM
5179	N	*NWR*	OM
5180	N	*NWR*	OM
5181	N	*NNE*	CA
5182	a	*PTP*	NL
5183	N	*NWR*	OM
5184	N	*NWR*	OM
5186	N	*NWR*	OM
5187	a	*ICC*	PC
5189	a	*PTP*	NL
5191		*PNS*	IS
5192	Pa	*PTP*	HT
5193		*PNS*	IS
5194		*NWR*	OM
5196		*PNS*	IS
5197	Sa	*PSE*	EC
5198	N	*NWR*	OM
5199	N	*NNE*	CA
5200		*NNE*	CA
5201		*PNS*	IS
5204		*NNE*	CA
5205	N	*NWR*	OM
5207	N	*PNS*	IS
5208	N	*NNE*	CA
5209	N	*NWR*	OM
5210	N	*NWR*	OM
5211	N	*NNE*	CA
5212		*PNS*	IS
5213	N	*NWR*	OM
5214	N	*NWR*	OM
5215	N	*NNE*	CA
5216	N	*NNE*	CA
5217		*PNS*	IS
5219		*NNE*	CA
5220	N	*NNE*	CA
5221		*PNS*	IS
5222	N	*NNE*	CA
5224		*NNE*	CA
5225	N	*NWR*	OM
5226	N	*NWR*	OM
5228	N	*NWR*	OM

SO AD2Z

Open Standard, Mk 2 — AD203

Introduced: 1966
Weight: 32.5 tonnes
Seats: 48
Brakes: Vacuum ([a] Air as marked)
Heating: Pressure heating and Ventilation

ETH Index: 4
Bogies: B4
Toilets: 2
Maximum speed: 100mph
Special features: Public address (p)

Derby 30752/66

5230		*PWH*	PC	5239		*PWH*	PC	5248	Na	*PTP*	NL
5231		*PWH*	PC	5240		*PWH*	PC	5249		*PWH*	PC
5232		*PWH*	PC	5241		*PWH*	PC	5251	pa	*PWX*	CF
5233		*PWH*	PC	5243		*PWH*	PC	5252	pa	*PWX*	CF
5234		*PWH*	PC	5244		*PWH*	PC	5253	pa	*PWX*	CF
5235		*PWH*	PC	5245	Na	*PWX*	CF	5254	pa	*PWX*	CF
5236		*PWH*	PC	5246	a	*PWX*	CF	5255	pa	*PTP*	NL
5237		*PWH*	PC	5247	a	*PWX*	CF	5256	Npa	*PTP*	NL

TSO AC2A

Tourist Open Standard, Mk 2a — AC206

Introduced: 1967
Weight: 32.5 tonnes
Seats: 64
Brakes: Air
Heating: Pressure heating and Ventilation

ETH Index: 4
Bogies: B4
Toilets: 2
Maximum speed: 100mph

Derby 30776/67-8.

5257		*PSW*	PC	5270		*PSX*	IS	5284		*PMX*	DY
5258		*PMX*	DY	5271		*PSX*	IS	5286		*IWC*	WB
5259		*IWC*	BN	5272		*PSX*	IS	5287		*IWR*	OM
5260		*PTP*	NL	5273		*PSX*	IS	5288		*PWY*	NL
5261		*NSS*	LA	5274		*PSX*	IS	5290	N	*NSS*	LA
5262	N	*PSW*	PC	5275		*NWR*	OM	5291	P	*PTP*	HT
5263	N	*NSS*	LA	5276	N	*NSS*	LA	5292		*PSX*	IS
5264	N	*NWR*	OM	5277		*PSX*	IS	~~5293~~		*NWR*	OM
5265	N	*NSS*	LA	5278	N	*NSS*	LA	5294		*PWY*	NL
5266		*PMX*	DY	5279		*PSX*	IS	5295		*PWX*	CF
5267		*PSW*	PC	5281		*NWR*	OM	5296		*PCR*	CL
5268		*PWX*	CF	5282		*PSX*	IS	5298	P	*PTP*	HT
5269		*PSX*	IS	5283	P	*PTP*	HT	5299		*PWY*	NL

5300		*PSX*	IS
5301	P	*PTP*	HT
5302	N	*NSS*	LA
5303	N	*NSS*	LA
5304		*IAN*	NC
5306		*PMX*	DY
5307		*PSX*	IS
5308		*NSS*	LA
5309		*NWR*	OM
5310		*PWY*	NL
5311	P	*PTP*	HT
5312	N	*NSS*	LA
5314		*ICC*	MA
5315		*PSW*	PC
5316	P	*PTP*	HT
5317		*PWY*	NL
5318		*PSX*	IS
5321	P	*PTP*	HT
5322	N	*NSS*	LA
5323	P	*PTP*	HT
5325		*PSX*	IS
5326	N	*NWR*	OM
5327		*PSX*	IS
5329	P	*PTP*	HT
5330		*PSX*	IS
5331	N	*NSS*	LA
5333		*PSX*	IS
5335	N	*NSS*	LA
5336		*NSS*	LA
5337		*PMX*	DY
5338		*IML*	DY
5339		*IML*	DY
5340	P	*PTP*	HT
5341	N	*NWR*	OM
5342		*PWX*	CF
5343	P	*PTP*	HT
5345		*NSS*	LA

Derby 30787/68.

5346		*NWR*	OM
5347	P	*PTP*	HT
5349		*PSW*	EC
5350	N	*NSS*	LA
5351	P	*PTP*	HT
5352		*PCR*	CL
5353		*PSW*	EC
5354	N	*NWR*	OM
5355	N	*NSS*	LA
5356		*ICC*	PC
5357		*IWC*	WB
5359	P	*PWX*	CF
5360	N	*NWR*	OM
5361		*NSS*	LA
5362	N	*NSS*	LA
5363		*PWY*	NL
5364		*IML*	DY
5365	P	*PTP*	HT
5366	N	*NWR*	OM
5367		*ICC*	PC
5368		*IWC*	WB
5369		*IWC*	WB
5370		*ICC*	MA
5371		*NSS*	LA
5372		*IWC*	WB
5373	N	*NSS*	LA
5374		*PCR*	CL
5375		*PSY*	DY
5376		*NWR*	OM
5378		*NWR*	OM
5379	P	*PTP*	HT
5381	N	*NSS*	LA
5382		*ICC*	MA
5383		*PCR*	CL
5384		*NSS*	LA
5385		*PSY*	DY
5386	N	*NWR*	OM
5387	P	*PTP*	HT
5388		*PWY*	NL
5389		*NSS*	LA
5391	P	*PTP*	HT
5392		*PSX*	IS
5393		*PSX*	IS
5394		*PSX*	IS
5395	P	*IML*	DY
5396	P	*PTP*	HT
5397		*PMX*	DY
5398	N	*NSS*	LA
5399		*PSY*	NL
5400		*IWC*	WB
5401		*PSX*	IS
5402		*PCR*	CL
5403		*IAN*	NC
5404	N	*NSS*	LA
5406	P	*PTP*	HT
5408	N	*NSS*	LA
5409	P	*PTP*	HT
5410	N	*NSS*	LA
5412	N	*NWR*	OM
5413		*PCR*	CL
5414	P	*PTP*	HT
5415		*ICC*	MA
5416	P	*PMX*	DY
5417		*IWR*	OM
5418	N	*NSS*	LA
5419	N	*NSS*	LA
5420	N	*NSS*	LA
5421	P	*PMX*	DY
5422		*IML*	DY
5423	N	*ICC*	PC
5424		*PMX*	DY
5425	P	*PTP*	HT
5426		*PCR*	CL
5427		*PSW*	EC
5429		*PWX*	CF
5430		*IWR*	OM
5431	P	*PTP*	HT
5432	P	*PTP*	HT
5433	N	*NSS*	LA

TSO AC2B

Tourist Open Standard, Mk 2b — AC207

Introduced: 1969
Weight: 32.5 tonnes
Seats: 62
Brakes: Air
Heating: Pressure heating and Ventilation
ETH Index: 4
Bogies: B4
Toilets: 2
Maximum speed: 100mph

Derby 30791/69

5434	N	*PMX*	DY	5455	N	*NSS*	LA	5477	N	*NSS*	LA
5435	N	*NSS*	LA	5456	N	*NWR*	OM	5478		*IWC*	WB
5436		*NSS*	LA	5457	N	*NWR*	OM	5479	P	*PTP*	HT
5437		*PSW*	PC	5458	N	*NSS*	LA	5480		*NSS*	LA
5438	N	*ICC*	MA	5459		*NSS*	LA	5481		*NSS*	LA
5439	N	*NSS*	LA	5461		*NSS*	LA	5482	N	*NSS*	LA
5440		*PCR*	CL	5462	N	*NSS*	LA	5483	P	*PSY*	NL
5442	N	*NWR*	OM	5463	P	*PTP*	HT	5484	N	*NSS*	LA
5443	N	*NSS*	LA	5464		*NSS*	LA	5486		*IWC*	WB
5444	N	*NWR*	OM	5465	N	*NSS*	LA	5487		*IML*	DY
5445		*PSW*	EC	5466	N	*NSS*	LA	5488		*PSW*	EC
5446	N	*NSS*	LA	5467		*IXX*	OM	5489		*PCR*	CL
5447	N	*NSS*	LA	5468	N	*NSS*	LA	5490	N	*NSS*	LA
5448	N	*NSS*	LA	5470	N	*NWR*	OM	5491	N	*NWR*	OM
5449	N	*NSS*	LA	5471	N	*NSS*	LA	5492	N	*NSS*	LA
5450	N	*NSS*	LA	5472	N	*NSS*	LA	5493	N	*NWR*	OM
5451	N	*NSS*	LA	5473		*PWX*	CF	5494	N	*NWR*	OM
~~5452~~	N	*NWR*	OM	5474	N	*NSS*	LA	5495	N	*NSS*	LA
5453	N	*NSS*	LA	5475	N	*NSS*	LA	5496		*NSS*	LA
5454	N	*NSS*	LA	~~5476~~		*IWR*	OM	5497	N	*NSS*	LA

TSO AC2C

Tourist Open Standard, Mk 2c — AC208

Introduced: 1969
Weight: 32 tonnes
Seats: 62
Brakes: Air
Heating: Pressure heating and Ventilation
ETH Index: 4
Bogies: B4
Toilets: 2
Maximum speed: 100mph
Standard equipment: All Public address except 5552

30 coaches of this batch were converted to Micro-Buffet cars in 1980/1 and renumbered 6500-29.

Derby 30795/69-70

5500		IWC	EN
5501		IWC	EN
5502		IWC	EN
5505		ICC	PC
5508		IWC	EN
5509		ICC	PC
5512		IWC	EN
5515		IWC	EN
5517		IWC	EN
5519		ICC	MA
5520	P	PTP	HT
5522		ICC	PC
5523		NSS	LA
5524		IWC	EN
5525	N	NSS	LA
5526		IWC	EN
5527		ICC	PC
5529		ICC	MA
5530		IWC	EN
5532		ICC	PC
5533		IWC	EN
5536		ICC	MA
5539		ICC	PC
5540		ICC	MA
5541		ICC	PC
5542		IWC	WB
5546		ICC	MA
5548		ICC	PC
5549		IWC	EN
5550		ICC	MA
5552		IWC	EN
5554		ICC	PC
5557		ICC	PC
5560		ICC	PC
5561		ICC	MA
5565		IWC	EN
5566		ICC	PC
5569		IWC	EN
5572		IWC	EN
5574		ICC	MA
5576		ICC	MA
5581		ICC	MA
5582		IAN	NC
5584		IWC	EN
5585		IAN	NC
5586		ICC	PC
5589		ICC	MA
5590		IWC	EN
5591		IWC	EN
5594		ICC	MA
5595		IWC	EN
5596		ICC	PC
5597		ICC	MA
5600		IWC	EN
5601		ICC	MA
5604		ICC	MA
5605		IWC	EN
5607		IWC	EN
5609		ICC	MA
5610		IWC	EN
5613		ICC	MA
5614	P	PTP	HT
5615		IWC	EN

TSO AC2D

Tourist Open Standard, Mk. 2d — AC209

Introduced: 1971
Weight: 33.5 tonnes
Seats: 62
Brakes: Air
Heating: Full air conditioning
ETH Index: 5
Bogies: B4

Toilets: 2
Maximum speed: 100mph
Standard equipment: Public address fitted

20 coaches of this batch were converted to Micro-Buffet cars in 1980/1 and renumbered 6600-19.

Derby 30822/71

5616	I	IAN	NC
5617	I	IAN	NC
5618	I	ICC	MA
5619	I	IAN	NC
5620	I	ICC	MA
5621	I	IAN	NC
5623	S	PSX	EC
5624	I	IAN	NC
5625	I	IAN	NC
5626	I	IAN	NC
5628	I	IAN	NC
5629	I	IAN	NC
5630	I	IAN	NC
5631	I	IAN	NC
5632	I	IAN	NC
5633	I	IAN	NC
5634	I	IAN	NC
5636	I	IAN	NC
5637		ICC	MA
5638	I	ICC	MA
5639		ICC	MA
5640	I	IAN	NC
5642		ICC	MA
5643	I	IAN	NC

5645	I	*IAN*	NC	5677	I	*ICC*	MA	5712	I	*IAN*	NC
5646		*ICC*	MA	5678	I	*ICC*	MA	5713	I	*IAN*	NC
5647		*ICC*	MA	5679	I	*IAN*	NC	5714	I	*IAN*	NC
5648	I	*IAN*	NC	5680	I	*IAN*	NC	5715	I	*IAN*	NC
5650	I	*ICC*	MA	5681	I	*IAN*	NC	5716	s	*PSX*	EC
5651	I	*IAN*	NC	5682	I	*ICC*	MA	5717	I	*ICC*	MA
5652	I	*IAN*	NC	5684	I	*ICC*	MA	5718	I	*IAN*	NC
5653	s	*PSX*	EC	5685	I	*IAN*	NC	5719	I	*ICC*	MA
5654	I	*IAN*	NC	5686	I	*IAN*	NC	5722	I	*IAN*	NC
5657	I	*IAN*	NC	5687	I	*ICC*	MA	5723	I	*IAN*	NC
5658		*ICC*	MA	5689	I	*ICC*	MA	5724	I	*IAN*	NC
5659	s	*PSX*	EC	5690		*ICC*	MA	5726	s	*PSX*	EC
5660		*ICC*	MA	5692	I	*IAN*	NC	5727	I	*IAN*	NC
5661	I	*IAN*	NC	5693	I	*IAN*	NC	5728	I	*ICC*	MA
5662	s	*PSX*	EC	5694	s	*PSX*	EC	5729	I	*IAN*	NC
5663	s	*PSX*	EC	5695		*ICC*	MA	5730	I	*IAN*	NC
5665	I	*IAN*	NC	5699		*ICC*	MA	5731	I	*IAN*	NC
5666	I	*IAN*	NC	5700	I	*IAN*	NC	5732	I	*IAN*	NC
5667		*ICC*	MA	5701	I	*ICC*	MA	5734	I	*ICC*	MA
5668	I	*IAN*	NC	5703	I	*IAN*	NC	5735	I	*IAN*	NC
5669	I	*ICC*	MA	5704		*ICC*	MA	5737	I	*IAN*	NC
5670	I	*ICC*	MA	5705	I	*IAN*	NC	5738	I	*ICC*	MA
5671	s	*PSX*	EC	5706	I	*ICC*	PC	5739	I	*IAN*	NC
5672	I	*IAN*	NC	5707	I	*IAN*	NC	5740	s	*PSX*	EC
5673	s	*PSX*	EC	5708		*ICC*	MA	5742	I	*IAN*	NC
5674	I	*IAN*	NC	5709		*ICC*	MA	5743	I	*ICC*	MA
5675	I	*ICC*	MA	5710	I	*IAN*	NC				
5676	I	*IAN*	NC	5711	s	*PSX*	EC				

TSO AC2E

Tourist Open Standard, Mk. 2e — AC210

Introduced: 1972
Weight: 34 tonnes
Seats: 64
Brakes: Air
Heating: Full air conditioning
ETH Index: 5

Bogies: B4
Toilets: 2
Maximum speed: 100mph
Standard equipment: Public address fitted
Special feature: Day/night lighting 5872

Derby 30837/72.

5744	I	*ICC*	MA	5749	I	*ICC*	MA	5754	I	*ICC*	MA
5745	I	*ICC*	PC	5750	I	*IWR*	LA	5755	I	*ICC*	PC
5746	I	*ICC*	MA	5751	I	*ICC*	PC	5756	I	*IWR*	LA
5747	I	*ICC*	PC	5752	I	*ICC*	MA	5757	I	*ICC*	PC
5748		*ICC*	MA	5753	I	*ICC*	PC	5758	I	*ICC*	PC

5759	I	*ICC*	MA
5760	I	*ICC*	PC
5761	I	*ICC*	PC
5762	I	*ICC*	PC
5763	I	*ICC*	MA
5764	I	*ICC*	MA
5765	I	*ICC*	MA
5766	I	*ICC*	PC
5767	I	*ICC*	PC
5768	I	*ICC*	MA
5769	I	*ICC*	MA
5770	I	*ICC*	MA
5771	I	*ICC*	PC
5772	I	*ICC*	MA
5773	I	*ICC*	MA
5774	I	*ICC*	MA
5775	I	*ICC*	PC
5776	I	*ICC*	MA
5777	I	*ICC*	MA
5778	I	*ICC*	MA
5779	I	*ICC*	MA
5780		*ICC*	MA
5781	I	*ICC*	PC
5782	I	*ICC*	MA
5783	I	*ICC*	MA
5784	I	*ICC*	MA
5785	I	*ICC*	MA
5786	I	*ICC*	PC
5787	I	*ICC*	MA
5788	I	*ICC*	MA
5789		*ICC*	MA
5790	I	*ICC*	PC
5791	I	*ICC*	MA
5792		*ICC*	MA
5793	I	*ICC*	MA
5794		*ICC*	MA
5795	I	*ICC*	PC
5796	I	*ICC*	PC
5797	I	*ICC*	PC
5798	I	*ICC*	MA
5799	I	*IWR*	LA
5800	I	*ICC*	PC
5801		*ICC*	MA
5802	I	*ICC*	PC
5803	I	*ICC*	PC
5804	I	*ICC*	MA

Derby 30844/72-3.

5809	I	*ICC*	PC
5810	I	*ICC*	PC
5811	I	*ICC*	PC
5812	I	*ICC*	MA
5813	I	*ICC*	PC
5814	I	*ICC*	MA
5815	I	*IWR*	LA
5816	I	*ICC*	MA
5817	I	*ICC*	MA
5818	I	*ICC*	PC
5819	I	*ICC*	PC
5820	I	*ICC*	PC
5821		*ICC*	MA
5822	I	*ICC*	PC
5823		*ICC*	MA
5824		*ICC*	MA
5825	I	*ICC*	PC
5826		*ICC*	MA
5827	I	*ICC*	PC
5828	I	*ICC*	PC
5829	I	*ICC*	PC
5830	I	*ICC*	PC
5831	I	*ICC*	PC
5832	I	*ICC*	PC
5833	I	*ICC*	PC
5834	I	*ICC*	PC
5835	I	*ICC*	PC
5836	I	*ICC*	MA
5837	I	*ICC*	PC
5838	I	*ICC*	PC
5839	I	*ICC*	PC
5840	I	*ICC*	PC
5841	I	*ICC*	PC
5842	I	*ICC*	MA
5843	I	*ICC*	PC
5844	I	*ICC*	PC
5845	I	*ICC*	PC
5846	I	*ICC*	MA
5847	I	*ICC*	MA
5848	I	*ICC*	MA
5849	I	*ICC*	MA
5850	I	*ICC*	MA
5851	I	*ICC*	MA
5852	I	*ICC*	PC
5853	I	*ICC*	MA
5854	I	*ICC*	MA
5855	I	*IWR*	LA
5856	I	*ICC*	MA
5857	I	*ICC*	MA
5858	I	*ICC*	MA
5859	I	*ICC*	PC
5860	I	*ICC*	MA
5861	I	*ICC*	PC
5862	I	*ICC*	MA
5863	I	*ICC*	MA
5864	I	*ICC*	MA
5865	I	*ICC*	MA
5866	I	*ICC*	MA
5867	I	*ICC*	PC
5868	I	*ICC*	OY
5869	I	*ICC*	PC
5870	I	*ICC*	OY
5871	I	*ICC*	OY
5872	I	*IWR*	LA
5873	I	*ICC*	MA
5874	I	*ICC*	MA
5875	I	*ICC*	PC
5876	I	*ICC*	PC
5877	I	*ICC*	MA
5878	I	*ICC*	PC
5879	I	*IWR*	LA
5880	I	*ICC*	PC
5881		*IWR*	LA
5882	I	*ICC*	MA
5883	I	*ICC*	PC
5884	I	*ICC*	PC
5885	I	*ICC*	MA
5886	I	*ICC*	MA
5887	I	*ICC*	MA
5888		*ICC*	MA
5889	I	*ICC*	PC
5890	I	*ICC*	PC
5891	I	*ICC*	PC
5892	I	*ICC*	MA
5893		*ICC*	PC
5894	I	*ICC*	MA
5895	I	*ICC*	MA
5896	I	*ICC*	PC
5897		*ICC*	MA
5898	I	*ICC*	PC

5899	I	*ICC*	MA	5902	I	*ICC*	MA	5905	I	*ICC*	MA
5900	I	*ICC*	PC	5903	I	*ICC*	MA	5906	I	*ICC*	PC
5901	I	*ICC*	PC	5904	I	*ICC*	MA	5907	I	*ICC*	MA

TSO AC2F

Tourist Open Standard, Mk. 2f — AC211

Introduced: 1973
Weight: 33.5 tonnes
Seats: 64
Brakes: Air
Heating: Full air conditioning
ETH Index: 5X
Bogies: B4
Toilets: 2
Standard equipment: IC 70 seats except (†) standard Mk 2. Public address fitted

Maximum speed: 100mph
Special features: Wheelchair accommodation (62 seats): 5918/43/48/88, 6001/27/35/45/52/63, 6176. Day/night lighting: 5921/24/28/36/51/59/64/68/75/78, 6010/47/73, 6112/13/39/44/59. Nightrider stock: 5921/27/51, 6047
R Refurbished, InterCity livery
D Disabled toilet
67 coaches of this type have been converted to Class 488 EMU stock.

Derby 30846/73.

5908	R	*IWC*	OY	5926	R	*IWC*	MA	5944		*IWC*	MA
5910	I	*IWC*	OY	5927		*IWC*	PC	5945	R	*IWC*	MA
5911	R	*IWC*	OY	5928	I	*IWC*	PC	5946	R	*IWC*	OY
5912	R	*IWC*	OY	5929		*IWC*	WB	5947		*IWC*	WB
5913	R	*IWC*	OY	5930	R	*IWC*	OY	5948	R	*IWC*	MA
5914	R	*IWC*	OY	5931		*IWC*	WB	5949		*ICC*	MA
5915	R	*IWC*	OY	5932		*IWC*	WB	5950		*IWC*	WB
5916	R	*IWC*	WB	5933	R	*IWC*	OY	5951		*IWC*	PC
5917		*IWC*	WB	5934		*IWC*	WB	5952		*IWC*	WB
5918	R	*IWC*	MA	5935		*IWC*	WB	5953		*IWC*	WB
5919	R	*IWC*	OY	5936		*IWC*	PC	5954	R	*IWC*	OY
5920	R	*IWC*	OY	5937	R	*IWC*	OY	5955	R	*IWC*	OY
5921		*IWC*	PC	5939	R	*IWC*	OY	5956	R	*IWC*	OY
5922		*IWC*	WB	5940	R	*IWC*	MA	5957		*IWC*	WB
5924		*IWC*	PC	5941	R	*IWC*	OY	5958	R	*IWC*	OY
5925	R	*IWC*	OY	5943	R	*IWC*	OY				

Derby 30860/73-4.

5959		*IWC*	PC	5964		*IWC*	PC	5969		*IWC*	MA
5960	R	*IWC*	MA	5965		*IWC*	WB	5971		*IWC*	WB
5961	R	*IWC*	MA	5966		*IWC*	WB	5973		*IWC*	WB
5962	R	*IWC*	OY	5967		*IWC*	WB	5975	†I	*IWC*	PC
5963	R	*IWC*	MA	5968		*IWC*	PC	5976	R	*IWC*	MA

5977	R	*IWC*	OY
5978	†I	*IWC*	PC
5980	R	*IWC*	OY
5981	R	*IWC*	OY
5983	R	*IWC*	MA
5984	†R	*IWC*	OY
5985	R	*IWC*	OY
5986	R	*IWC*	OY
5987	†R	*IWC*	OY
5988	RD	*IWC*	OY
5989		*IWC*	WB
5991	R	*IWC*	OY
5993	†R	*ICC*	MA
5994	†I	*IWC*	WB
5995		*IWC*	WB
5996	R	*IWC*	OY
5997	R	*IWC*	OY
5998	R	*IWC*	OY
5999		*IWC*	WB
6000	R	*IWC*	OY
6001	R	*IWC*	OY
6002	R	*IWC*	OY
6005	†R	*IWC*	MA
6006	R	*IWC*	OY
6008	R	*IWC*	OY
6009	R	*IWC*	OY
6010		*IWC*	PC
6011	R	*IWC*	MA
6012	†R	*IWC*	OY
6013	†R	*IWC*	OY
6014	R	*IWC*	OY
6015	R	*IWC*	OY
6016	R	*IWC*	OY
6018	†I	*IWC*	PC
6021	R	*IWC*	MA
6022		*IWC*	MA
6024	R	*IWC*	OY
6025	†I	*IWC*	WB
6026	†R	*IWC*	OY
6027	RD	*IWC*	MA
6028	R	*IWC*	OY
6029	R	*IWC*	OY
6030	R	*IWC*	OY
6031	R	*IWC*	OY
6034	R	*IWC*	OY
6035	R	*IWC*	OY
6036	†I	*IWC*	WB
6037	R	*IWC*	OY
6038	R	*IWC*	OY
6041	R	*IWC*	OY
6042	R	*IWC*	OY
6043	R	*IWC*	MA
6045	R	*IWC*	MA
6046	R	*IWC*	OY
6047	†	*IWC*	PC
6049	R	*IWC*	OY
6050	R	*IWC*	OY
6051	†R	*IWC*	OY
6052	I	*IWC*	OY
6053	†I	*IWC*	WB
6054	R	*IWC*	OY
6055	R	*IWC*	OY
6056	R	*IWC*	OY
6057	R	*IWC*	OY
6059	R	*IWC*	OY
6060	†R	*IWC*	OY
6061	†R	*IWC*	MA
6062	†R	*IWC*	OY
6063	R	*IWC*	OY
6064	R	*IWC*	OY
6065	R	*IWC*	OY
6066	R	*IWC*	OY
6067	R	*IWC*	OY
6073		*IWC*	PC
6100	†I	*IWC*	WB
6101	R	*IWC*	OY
6102	R	*IWC*	MA
6103	R	*IWC*	OY
6104	R	*IWC*	OY
6105	R	*IWC*	OY
6106	R	*IWC*	MA
6107	R	*IWC*	OY
6110	RD	*IWC*	MA
6111	R	*IWC*	OY
6112	R	*IWC*	PC
6113		*IWC*	PC
6115	R	*IWC*	OY
6116	R	*IWC*	OY
6117	R	*IWC*	OY
6119	R	*IWC*	OY
6120	R	*IWC*	OY
6121	R	*IWC*	OY
6122	R	*IWC*	OY
6123		*IWC*	WB
6124	R	*IWC*	OY
6134	R	*IWC*	OY
6135	R	*IWC*	OY
6136	R	*IWC*	MA
6137	R	*IWC*	OY
6138	R	*IWC*	MA
6139	†I	*IWC*	PC
6141		*IWC*	MA
6142	†I	*IWC*	PC
6144	†	*IWC*	PC
6145	†R	*IWC*	MA
6146	†R	*IWC*	OY
6147	†R	*IWC*	OY
6148	†R	*IWC*	WB
6149	†	*ICC*	MA
6150	†R	*IWC*	WB
6151	†I	*IWC*	WB
6152	†I	*IWC*	WB
6153	†R	*IWC*	WB
6154	†R	*IWC*	WB
6155	†I	*IWC*	PC
6157	†	*IWC*	WB
6158	†R	*ICC*	MA
6159	†R	*IWC*	PC
6160	†R	*IWC*	WB
6161	†I	*IWC*	OY
6162	R	*IWC*	MA
6163	R	*IWC*	OY
6164	R	*IWC*	OY
6165	R	*IWC*	OY
6166	R	*IWC*	MA
6167	R	*IWC*	OY
6168	R	*IWC*	OY
6170	R	*IWC*	OY

Derby 30874/74-5.

6171	†R	*IWC*	OY
6172	†R	*IWC*	OY
6173	†R	*IWC*	OY
6174	†R	*IWC*	OY
6175	†R	*IWC*	OY
6176	†R	*IWC*	OY

~~6177~~	†R	*IWC*	OY	6180	†	*IWC*	PC	6183	†R	*IWC*	OY
6178	†	*IWC*	MA	~~6181~~	†R	*IWC*	OY	6184	†I	*IWC*	PC
6179	†R	*IWC*	OY	6182	†R	*IWC*	OY				

SALOON AD4

Open Standard Saloon — AD401

Introduced: 1987 by conversion from Class 101 DMU. Driving trailer No 54356, 54367
Weight: 25 tonnes
Seats: Unclassed: 42
Brakes: Vacuum
Bogies: Madison
Toilets: 1
Maximum speed: 70mph
Standard equipment: PA fitted
Special livery: West Highland (green and cream). Named 'Hebridean Observation Saloon'
6301 under conversion

Metro Cammell 30468/58

6300	*PNS*	IS
6301		

SO AD2C

Open Standard Mk. 2c — AD205

Introduced: 1982 by conversion from FO
Weight: 33 tonnes
Seats: Standard 42
Brakes: Air
Heating: Pressure heating and Ventilation
ETH Index: 4
Bogies: B4
Toilets: 2
Maximum speed: 100mph
Standard equipment: Public address fitted

Derby 30810/70.

6400	*PSY*	DY	6410	*PSP*	OY	6415	*PSY*	DY
6405	*IXX*	LL	6413	*PMX*	OY			
6406	*IXX*	LL	6414	*PSY*	DY			

Mk 2f AN1F RLF lounge first vehicle No 1205 at Wolverhampton on 23 September 1988. *Chris Morrison*

Mk 1 AN21 RMB No 1832 at Bristol Temple Meads on 17 August 1988. *John Augustson*

Mk 1 AJ41 RBR No 1953 at Carlisle. *John Augustson*

Mk 2e AD1E FO No 3195 at Exeter St Davids on 19 August 1988. *John Augustson*

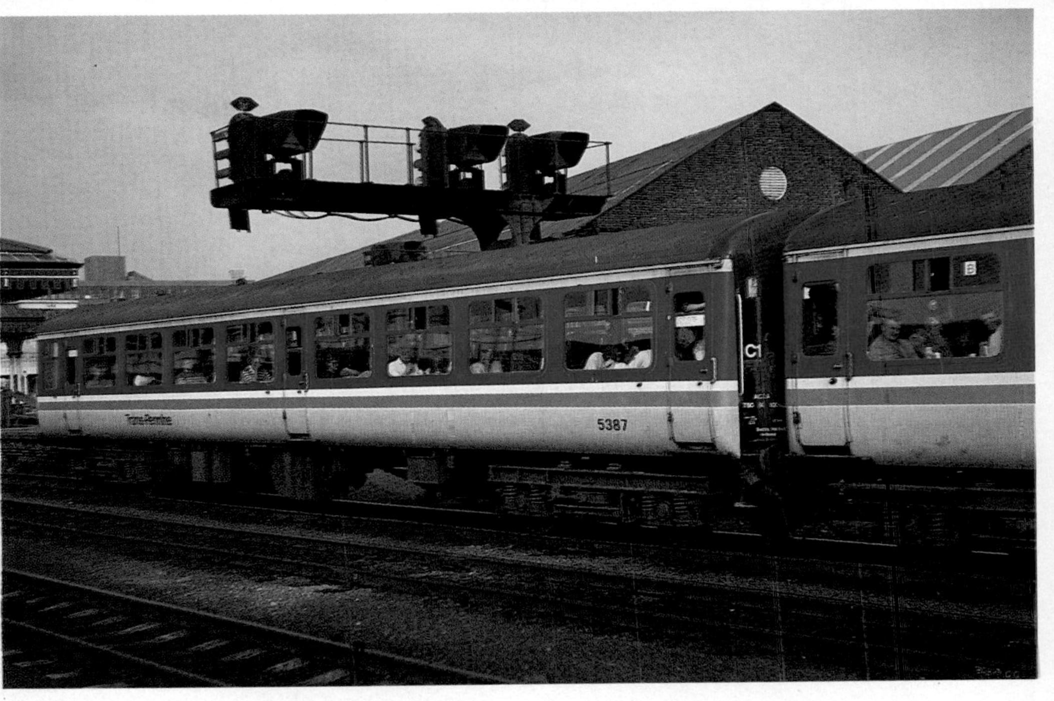

Mk 2a AC2A TSO No 5387 in Provincial Sector 'Trans-Pennine' livery at York, formed in the 16.17 Newcastle-Liverpool on 1 August 1988. *David Masterman*

Mk 2d AG2D TSO(T) No 6604 at Perth station. *John Augustson*

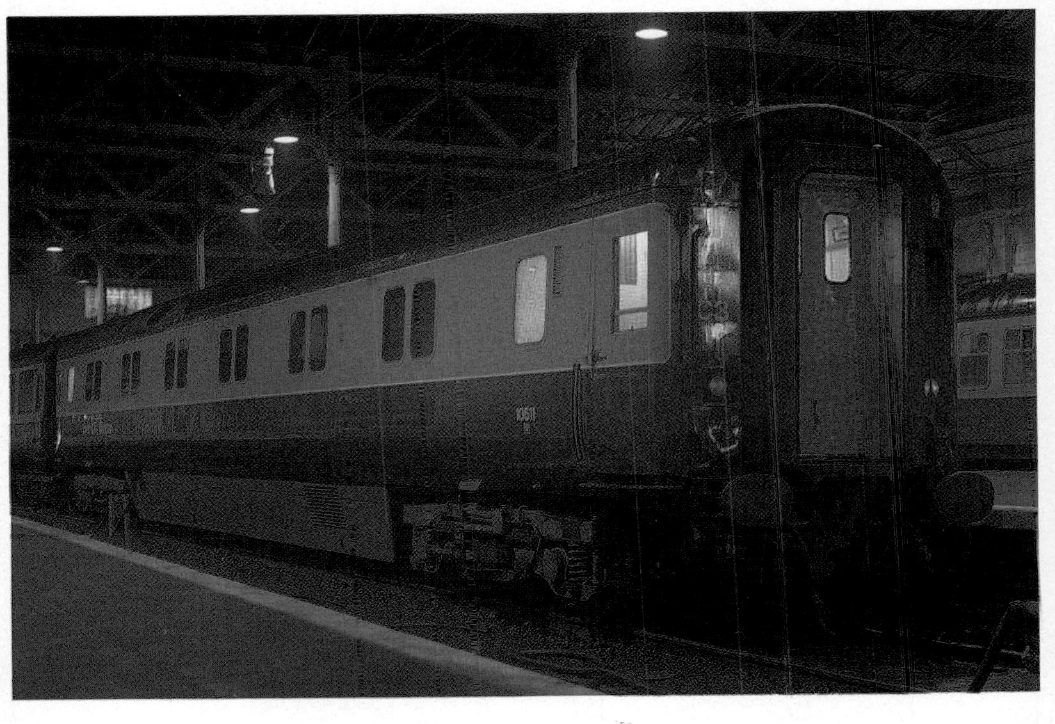

Mk 3a AU4G SLEP No 10611. *David Masterman*

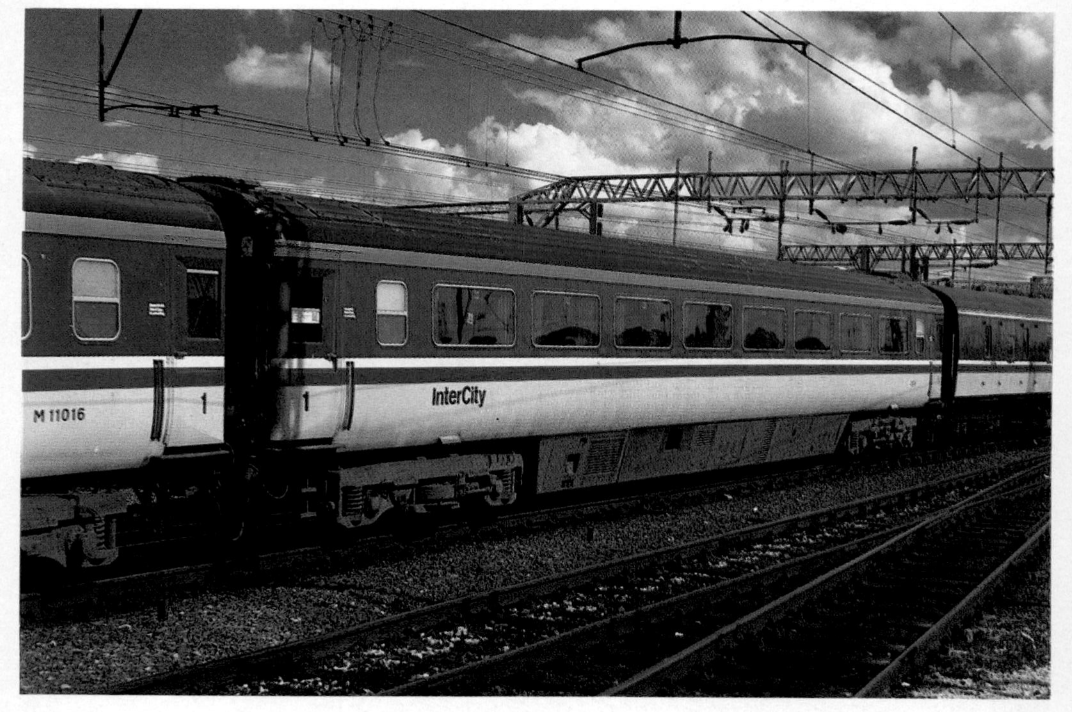

Mk 3b AD1H FO No 11065 in InterCity livery at Crewe on 5 July 1988. *John Augustson*

This Mk 3a AC2G TSO, No 12024, is marshalled in a 'ScotRail Express' formation at Edinburgh Haymarket on 10 June 1988.
John Augustson

Mk 2d AA1D corridor first No 13596 at Exeter St Davids. *John Augustson*

The occupants of Mk 2 AB1Z BFK No 17042 are treated to Class 89 haulage at Doncaster on 17 September 1988.
John Augustson

Mk 2c AB1C BFK No 17132, in Network SouthEast livery, at Exeter St Davids on 20 August 1988. *John Augustson*

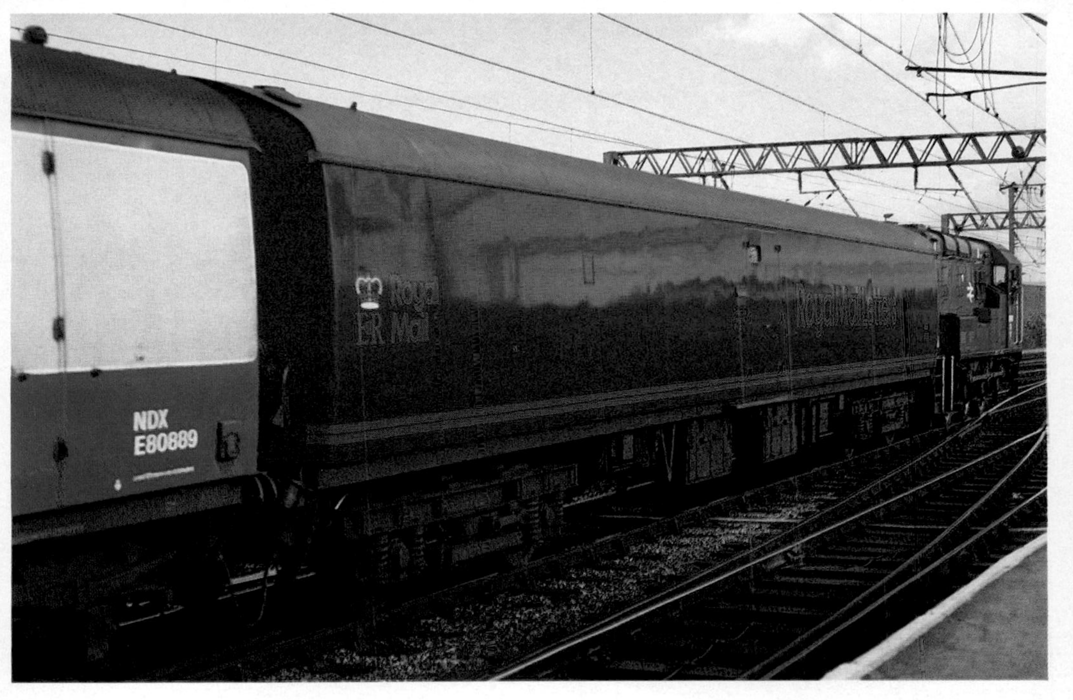

Carrying Royal Mail red livery, NS5 POS No 80331 is seen at Carlisle on 22 September 1987. *John Augustson*

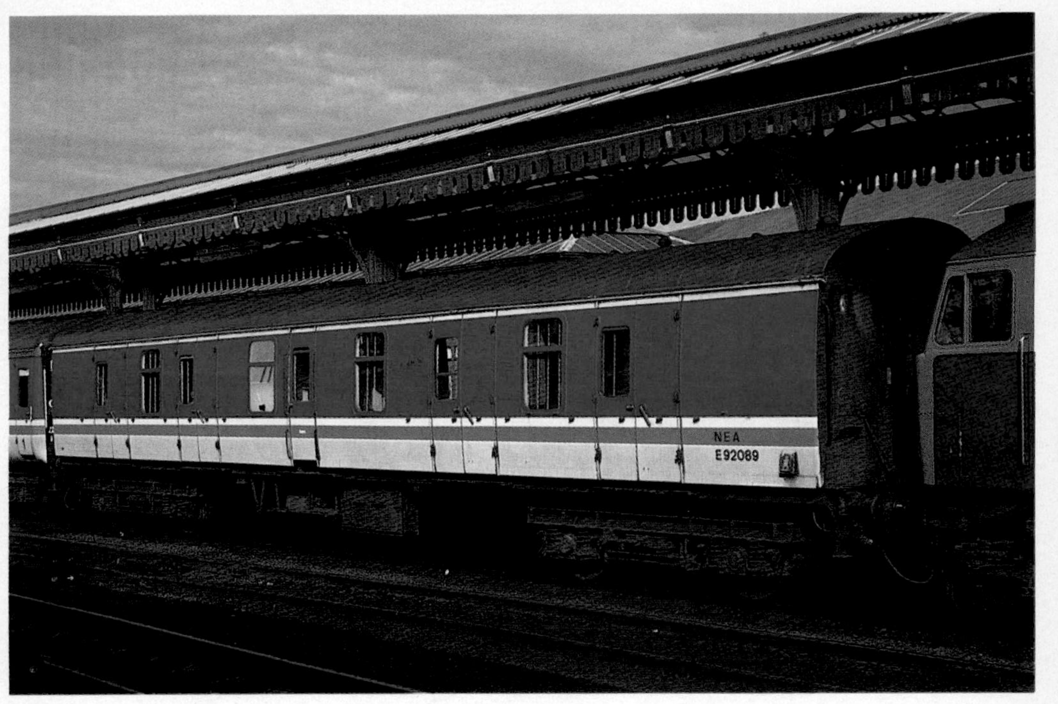

NE5 BG No 92089 in Provincial Sector livery at York on 1 August 1988. *David Masterman*

Mk 3 DVT No 82101 is seen at Wembley InterCity Depot on 8 November 1988. *Brian Morrison*

This floodlit scene shows Mk 2f AF2F DBSO No 9713 leading the 20.00 to Glasgow Queen Street at Edinburgh Waverley on 29 October 1987. *Mike Jones*

SO AD2F

Open Standard Mk. 2f — AD206

Introduced: 1985 by conversion from FO
Weight: 33.5 tonnes
Seats: 42
Brakes: Air
Heating: Full air conditioning
ETH Index: 5X
Bogies: B4
Toilets: 2
Maximum speed: 100mph
Standard equipment: Public address fitted
Special characteristics: Nightrider stock: 6464/65

Derby 30845/73. lot 30859/73

6420	*IWC*	WB	6425	*IWC*	WB	6429	*IWC*	WB
6423	*IWC*	WB	6427	*IWC*	WB	6431	*IWC*	WB
6424	*IWC*	WB	6428	*IWC*	WB	6434	*IWC*	WB

Derby 30859/73-4

6435	*IWC*	WB	6442	*IWC*	WB	6449	*IWC*	WB
6436	*IWC*	WB	6443	*IWC*	WB	6450	*IWC*	WB
6437	*IWC*	WB	6446	*IWC*	WB	6451	*IWC*	WB
6439	*IWC*	WB	6447	*IWC*	WB	6452	*IWC*	WB
6440	*IWC*	WB	6448	*IWC*	WB			

Derby 30873/74-5

6454	*IWC*	WB
6455	*IWC*	WB

Derby 30845/73

6458	*IWC*	WB	6461	*IWC*	WB
6460	*IWC*	WB			

Derby 30859/74

6463	*IWC*	WB	6465	*IWC*	WB
6464	*IWC*	WB			

TSO(T) AG2C

Micro-Buffet, Mk. 2c — AG201

Introduced: 1980 by conversion from TSO
Weight: 32 tonnes
Seats: 55
Brakes: Air
Heating: Pressure heating and Ventilation
ETH Index: 4
Bogies: B4
Toilets: 1
Maximum speed: 100mph
Standard equipment: Public address fitted
One seating bay removed and replaced by counter with space for trolley and standing area. Adjacent toilet altered to store and steward's washing area.

Derby 30795/69-70

6500	N	*NSS*	LA	6511		*IML*	DY	6520		*IML*	DY
6501	N	*NSS*	LA	6512		*NSS*	LA	6521	N	*NSS*	LA
6502	N	*NSS*	LA	6513		*NSS*	LA	6522	N	*NSS*	LA
6503		*NSS*	LA	6514		*PSX*	IS	6523		*ICC*	MA
6504		*NSS*	LA	6515		*PWY*	NL	6524		*ICC*	MA
6506		*ICC*	MA	6516		*IWR*	OM	6526		*PWY*	NL
6508		*ICC*	MA	6517		*NSS*	LA	6527		*NSS*	LA
6509		*IWR*	OM	6518		*PSX*	IS	6528		*PSY*	NL
6510		*PSX*	IS	6519		*PSX*	IS	6529		*PSY*	NL

TSO(T) AG2D

Micro-Buffet, Mk. 2d — AG202

Introduced: 1980 by conversion from TSO
Weight: 33.5 tonnes
Seats: 55
Brakes: Air
Heating: Full air conditioning
ETH Index: 5
Bogies: B4
Toilets: 1
Maximum speed: 100mph
Standard equipment: Public address fitted
Converted as AG2C. 6602/10/11/12/15 further converted to AN207 below

Derby 30822/71.

6600	I	*ICC*	MA	6607		*PSX*	EC	6616	I	*IWR*	LA
6601	S	*PSX*	EC	6608	I	*ICC*	MA	6617	I	*IWR*	LA
6603		*PNS*	IS	6609	I	*IWR*	LA	6618	I	*ICC*	MA
6604	S	*PSX*	EC	6613	S	*PSX*	EC	6619	S	*PSX*	EC
6605	S	*PSX*	EC	6614	S	*PSX*	EC				

RMBT AN2D

Micro-Buffet, Mk. 2d. — AN207

Introduced: 1985 by conversion from AG2D
Weight: 33.5 tonnes
Seats: 47
Brakes: Air
Heating: Full air conditioning
ETH Index: 6
Bogies: B4
Toilets: 1
Maximum speed: 100mph
Modifications: Public address fitted
AG2D coach further modified by the fitting of fixed Boiler and Microwave Oven.
Renumbered in 1986.
All InterCity livery

Derby 30822/71

6652	*IWC*	WB	~~6661~~	*IWC*	EN	6665	*IWC*	WB
6660	*IWC*	WB	6662	*IWC*	EN			

RLB AN1F

Restaurant Lounge First Buffet, Mk 2f — AN101

Introduced: 1987 by conversion from AD1F
Weight: 33.5 tonnes
Seats: 1st, 26 (loose)
Brakes: Air
Heating: Full air conditioning
ETH Index: 5X
Bogies: B4
Toilets: 1
Maximum speed: 100mph
Standard equipment: Public address and telephone fitted
Mk 2f FOs refurbished and converted by the addition of miniature buffet equipment as a development of AN2D series
All InterCity livery

Derby 30859/73-74 or 30845/73 (6703-07)

6700	*IWC*	WB	6703	*IWC*	EC	6706	*IWC*	WB
6701	*IWC*	EC	6704	*IWC*	WB	6707	*IWC*	WB
6702	*IWC*	WB	6705	*IWC*	WB	6708	*IWC*	WB

CK AA31

Corridor Composite — AA301 or AA302

Introduced: 1952
Weight: 34 tonnes
Bogies: Commonwealth (B1 as marked)
Toilets: 2

Seats: 1st, 24; **Std,** 18 or **1st,** 24; **Std,** 24 (AA302)
Brakes: Vacuum
ETH Index: 3 or (4)7199-7219

Maximum speed: 100mph (B1 bogies: 90mph)
Special features: g fluorescent lights, p public address fitted
7196 have been converted from 24F 18S to 24F 24S since 1984

Met Cam. 30471/58

7074	B1	*PDC*	LA

Derby 30665/61

7153	N	*NNW*	EN	7165	Np	*NNW*	EN	7188		*PWX*	EN
7154		*PWX*	CF	7166	N	*NNW*	EN	7190		*NNW*	EN
7156	N	*NNW*	EN	7167	N	*NNW*	EN	7195	N	*NNW*	EN
7158	N	*NNW*	EN	7168		*NNW*	EN	7196		*PSP*	NL
7162		*PSP*	NL	7172	Np	*NNW*	EN				

Derby 30666/61. AA302

7199		*PSP*	NL	7212	g	*NNW*	EN	7214	g	*NNW*	EN
7209		*PDC*	CF	7213	N g	*NNW*	EN	7219	Ng	*NNW*	EN

Derby 30729/63. Commonwealth bogies

7232	p	*NNW*	EN	7235	N	*NNW*	EN	7238		*PSP*	HT
7233		*PSP*	HT	7237	N	*NNW*	EN				

CK AA3C

Corridor Composite Mk2c. — AA304

Introduced: 1985 by downgrading from FK
Weight: 34 tonnes
Seats: 1st, 24; **Standard,** 18
Brakes: Air
Heating: Pressure heating and ventilation

ETH Index: 4
Bogies: B4
Toilets: 2
Maximum speed: 100mph

Derby 30797/69-70.

7550	*PSX*	IS	7553	*PSX*	IS	7561	*PSX*	IS
7551	*PSX*	IS	7558	*PSX*	IS			

BSO(T) AH21

Brake Micro-Buffet, Mk. 1 — AH201

Introduced: 1979 by conversion from BSO
Weight: 36 tonnes
Seats: 31
Brakes: Dual
ETH Index: 3
Bogies: B1
Toilets: 1
Maximum speed: 90mph

Doncaster 30170/55-6

9016	*PSP*	PC

BSO(T) AH2Z

Brake Micro-Buffet, Mk. 2 — AH203 (9100/01) or AH204 (9102-07)

Introduced: 1983 and 1986 by conversion from Mk 2 BSO
Weight: 32 tonnes
Seats: 31 (9100/01) or 27 (9102-07)
Brakes: Vacuum
Heating: Pressure heating and ventilation
ETH Index: 4
Bogies: B4
Toilets: 1
Maximum speed: 100mph

Derby 30757/66.

9100	*PNS*	IS
9101	*PNS*	IS
9102	*PWH*	PC
9103	*PWH*	PC
9104	*PWH*	PC
9105	*PWH*	PC
9106	*PWH*	PC
9107	*PWH*	PC

BSO AE21

Brake Open Standard, Mk. 1. — AE201

Introduced: 1955
Weight: 33.5 tonnes
Seats: 39
Brakes: Dual
ETH Index: 3
Bogies: B1
Toilets: 1
Maximum speed: 90mph

Doncaster 30170/55

9227	*ICHH*	PH

BSO — AE2Z

Brake Open Standard, Mk. 2. — AE203

Introduced: 1966
Weight: 32 tonnes
Seats: 31
Brakes: Vacuum (Air: a)
Heating: Pressure heating and ventilation
ETH Index: 4
Bogies: B4
Toilets: 1
Maximum speed: 100mph
Modifications: 9397, 9400/02 were wired for the former push/pull operation on Edinburgh-Glasgow services. 9400/02 retain disc air brakes
Facelifted: 9396

Derby 30757/66.

9382	N	*NWR*	OM	9391		*NNE*	CA	9400	a	*ICH*	IS
9384		*NNE*	CA	9392		*PCR*	CL	9409	N	*NNE*	CA
9385		*PCR*	CL	9393		*PSW*	IS	9410		*PCR*	CL
9386		*PCR*	CL	9394		*PCR*	CL	9412	a	*PSX*	EC
9388		*PSW*	IS	9396	N	*NNE*	CA	9413		*ICH*	OY
~~9390~~	N	*NNE*	CA	9397	a	*PSX*	IS	9414		*PSW*	IS

BSO — AE2A

Brake Open Standard, Mk. 2a. — AE204

Introduced: 1967
Weight: 32 tonnes
Seats: 31
Brakes: Air
Heating: Pressure heating and ventilation
ETH Index: 4
Bogies: B4
Toilets: 1
Maximum speed: 100mph

Derby 30777/67

9417	*PMX*	DY	9420	*PMX*	DY	9423	*PSX*	IS
9418	*PSW*	PC	9421	*IXX*	OM	9424	*PSX*	IS
9419	*PWX*	CF	9422	*PWX*	CF	9425	*PMX*	DY

Derby 30788/68.

9426	*PWX*	CF	9431	*PSX*	IS	9436	*PSW*	PC
9427	*IWR*	OM	9432	*IXXH*	OM	9437	*PCR*	CL
9428	*PSY*	DY	9434	*PSX*	IS	9438	*IWR*	OM
9429	*IXXH*	OM	9435	*PWX*	CF			

BSO — AE2C

Brake Open Standard, Mk. 2c. — AE205

Introduced: 1970
Weight: 32.5 tonnes
Seats: 31
Brakes: Air
Heating: Pressure heating and ventilation
ETH Index: 4

Bogies: B4
Toilets: 1
Maximum speed: 100mph
Special characteristics: Public address transmitter fitted: q as marked

Derby 30798/70-1

9439		*ICC*	MA	9443	q	*IML*	DY	9447	q	*IML*	DY
9440	q	*PSX*	EC	9444		*PSX*	IS	9448		*PCR*	CL
9441	q	*ICH*	MA	9445		*PSX*	IS				
9442		*PMX*	DY	9446	q	*PSX*	IS				

Derby 30820/70.

9449		*PSW*	EC	9459		*IXX*	CL	9469		*ICH*	MA
9450	q	*IXX*	EN	9460		*PSX*	IS	9471	q	*IXX*	EC
9451	q	*PSX*	IS	9461		*ICH*	OM	9472	q	*ICH*	OM
9452		*PSY*	DY	9462		*PCR*	CL	9473	q	*IWC*	EN
9453	q	*IWC*	EN	9463		*PSX*	IS	~~9474~~		*ICH*	MA
9454	q	*ICH*	OM	9464		*ICC*	MA	9475	q	*IWC*	EN
9455	q	*IXXH*	OM	9465		*IXX*	EC	9476	q	*ICH*	MA
9456	q	*ICH*	MA	9466	q	*IXX*	EC	9477	q	*IXX*	OM
9457	q	*ICH*	MA	9467		*ICC*	MA	9478		*ICH*	OM
9458	p	*PSY*	NL	9468		*IXX*	EN				

BSO — AE2D

Brake Open Standard, Mk. 2d. — AE206

Introduced: 1971
Weight: 34 tonnes
Seats: 31
Brakes: Air
Heating: Full air conditioning
ETH Index: 5

Bogies: B4
Toilets: 1
Maximum speed: 100mph
Standard equipment: Driver/Guard communication and Public address transmitter fitted.

Derby 30824/71

9479	I	*IAN*	NC
9480	I	*IWC*	MA
9481	I	*ICH*	OM
9482	I	*IWC*	MA
9483	I	*IAN*	NC
9484		*ICH*	OM
9485	I	*IAN*	NC
9486	I	*IAN*	NC
9487	I	*IAN*	NC
9488	I	*IAN*	NC
9489	I	*IAN*	NC
9490	I	*ICH*	OM
9492	I	*IAN*	NC
9493	I	*IAN*	NC
9494	I	*IAN*	NC
9495	I	*IAN*	NC

BSO AE2E

Brake Open Standard, Mk. 2e. — AE207

Introduced: 1972
Weight: 33.5 tonnes
Seats: 32
Brakes: Air
Heating: Full air conditioning
ETH Index: 5
Bogies: B4
Toilets: 1
Maximum speed: 100mph
Standard equipment: Driver/Guard communication and Public address transmitter fitted.

Derby 30838/72

9496	I	*IWC*	PC
9497	I	*IWC*	PC
9498	I	*IWR*	LA
9499		*IWR*	LA
9500	I	*IWC*	OY
9501	I	*IWC*	PC
9502	I	*IWC*	PC
9503	I	*IWC*	PC
9504	I	*IWC*	MA
9505	I	*IWC*	OY
9506	I	*IWR*	LA
9507	I	*IWC*	PC
9508		*ICH*	OM
9509		*IWC*	MA

BSO AE2F

Brake Open Standard, Mk. 2f. — AE208

Introduced: 1974
Weight: 33 tonnes
Seats: 32
Brakes: Air
Heating: Full air conditioning
ETH Index: 5X
Bogies: B4
Toilets: 1
Maximum speed: 100mph
Standard equipment: Driver/Guard communication and Public address transmitter fitted
Special characteristics: 9516 has an experimental hydro-kinetic brake, now isolated
R Refurbished, InterCity livery
Nightrider stock: 9521/37
Day/night lighting: 9516/20/21/24/26/37

Derby 30861/74.

9513	R	*IWC*	WB	9524	R	*IWC*	WB	9533	I	*IWC*	WB
9516	R	*IWC*	PC	9525	R	*IWC*	WB	9537	R	*IWC*	PC
9520	R	*IWC*	PC	9526	R	*IWC*	PC	9538	I	*IWC*	WB
9521	R	*IWC*	OY	9527	R	*IWC*	WB	9539	R	*IWC*	WB
9522	I	*IWC*	MA	9529	R	*IWC*	WB				
9523	R	*IWC*	PC	9531	R	*IWC*	WB				

DBSO AF2F

Driving Brake Open Standard, Mk. 2f. — AF201

Introduced: 1979/80 and 1984/85/86 by conversion from BSO built Derby 30861/74
Weight: 33 tonnes
Seats: 32
Brakes: Air
Heating: Full air conditioning
ETH Index: 5X
Bogies: B4
Toilets: 1
Maximum speed: 100mph
Standard equipment: Driver/Guard communication, Public address transmitter, AWS and cowcatchers fitted
Special features: 9707 is fitted with video equipment
All ScotRail livery

Glasgow 30937/79-80/84/85/86

9701	*PSX*	EC	9707	*PSX*	EC	9712	*PSX*	EC
9702	*PSX*	EC	9708	*PSX*	EC	9713	*PSX*	EC
9703	*PSX*	EC	9709	*PSX*	EC	9714	*PSX*	EC
9704	*PSX*	EC	9710	*PSX*	EC			
9705	*PSX*	EC	9711	*PSX*	EC			

RFM AJ1G

Restaurant First Modular, Mk.3a — AJ103 or AJ101 (10200/01)

Introduced: 1984 by conversion from TRUK, FO or RFB
Weight: 40.6 tonnes (AJ101) or 39.8 tonnes
Seats: 1st, 22 or 24 (10200/01)
Brakes: Air
Heating: Full air conditioning
ETH Index: 14X (10200/01: 16X)
Bogies: BT10/BT10a (one of each)
Toilets: 0
Maximum speed: 125mph
Standard equipment: Electric and microwave cooking
Public address and (except 10200/01) transmitter fitted

The prototype conversions, 10200/01, seat 24. The production batches were introduced in 1987 with a revised layout, seating 22. Numbers 10239/43/44 not used as they clashed with Class 405 EMU coaches. All refurbished, in InterCity livery

Derby 30884/76-77 Converted from HST TRUK

10200	*IWC*	OY	10204	*IEC*	BN	10208	*IWC*	WB
10201	*IWC*	OY	10205	*IEC*	BN	10209	*IWC*	WB
10202	*IEC*	BN	10206	*IEC*	BN	10210	*IWC*	WB
10203	*IEC*	BN	10207	*IWC*	WB	10211	*IWC*	WB

Derby 30878/75 Converted from FO

10212	*IWC*	WB	10218	*IWC*	WB	10224	*IWC*	WB
10213	*IWC*	WB	10219	*IWC*	WB	10225	*IWC*	WB
10214	*IWC*	WB	10220	*IWC*	WB	10226	*IWC*	WB
10215	*IWC*	WB	10221	*IWC*	WB	10227	*IWC*	WB
10216	*IWC*	WB	10222	*IWC*	WB	10228	*IWC*	WB
10217	*IWC*	WB	10223	*IWC*	WB	10229	*IWC*	WB

Derby 30890/79-80 Converted from RFB

10230	*IWC*	WB	10241	*IWC*	OY	10253	*IWC*	OY
10231	*IWC*	WB	10242	*IWC*	OY	10254	*IWC*	OY
10232	*IWC*	WB	10245	*IWC*	OY	10255	*IWC*	OY
10233	*IWC*	WB	10246	*IWC*	OY	10256	*IWC*	OY
10234	*IWC*	WB	10247	*IWC*	OY	10257	*IWC*	OY
10235	*IWC*	WB	10248	*IWC*	OY	10258	*IWC*	OY
10236	*IWC*	OY	10249	*IWC*	OY	10259	*IWC*	OY
10237	*IWC*	OY	10250	*IWC*	OY	10260	*IWC*	OY
10238	*IWC*	OY	10251	*IWC*	OY			
10240	*IWC*	OY	10252	*IWC*	OY			

RFM AJ1H

Restaurant First Modular, Mk 4 — AJ105

Introduced: 1989
Weight: 45.5 tonnes
Seats: 1st: 20
Brakes: Air
Heating: Full air conditioning
ETH Index: 6X
Bogies: BT41
Toilets: 2
Maximum speed: 140mph
Standard equipment: Public address and transmitter fitted. Electric and microwave cooking

Metro Cammell 31045/89

10300	*IEC*	10312	*IEC*	10324	*IEC*
10301	*IEC*	10313	*IEC*	10325	*IEC*
10302	*IEC*	10314	*IEC*	10326	*IEC*
10303	*IEC*	10315	*IEC*	10327	*IEC*
10304	*IEC*	10316	*IEC*	10328	*IEC*
10305	*IEC*	10317	*IEC*	10329	*IEC*
10306	*IEC*	10318	*IEC*	10330	*IEC*
10307	*IEC*	10319	*IEC*	10331	*IEC*
10308	*IEC*	10320	*IEC*	10332	*IEC*
10309	*IEC*	10321	*IEC*	10333	*IEC*
10310	*IEC*	10322	*IEC*		
10311	*IEC*	10323	*IEC*		

SLEP AU4G

Sleeper, either Class with Pantry, Mk. 3a. — AU401

Introduced: 1981
Weight: 43.5 tonnes
Berths: 1st: 12 or **Std:** 24
Brakes: Air
Heating: Full air conditioning

ETH Index: 7X
Bogies: BT10C
Toilets: 2 (Controlled emission)
Maximum speed: 125mph
Special features: Short-swing link bogies: L

Derby 30960/81-2

10500	I	*ICH*	BN	10521		*IEC*	BN	10543		*IWC*	WB
10501	I	*IWC*	WB	10522	I	*IWC*	WB	10544		*IWC*	WB
10502	I	*IWC*	EC	10523		*IWC*	EC	10545	IL	*ICC*	EC
10503	I	*ICH*	BN	10525		*IEC*	BN	10546	I	*IWC*	WB
10504		*IWC*	WB	10526	L	*IWC*	EC	10547	I	*IWC*	WB
10506	I	*IWC*	WB	10527	I	*IWC*	WB	10548		*IWC*	WB
10507	I	*IWC*	WB	10529	I	*IWC*	WB	10549	I	*IWC*	WB
10508		*IWC*	WB	10530		*IWC*	WB	10550	I	*IWC*	WB
10509		*IEC*	BN	10531	I	*IWC*	WB	10551	I	*IWC*	WB
10510		*IWC*	WB	10532	IL	*IWC*	EC	10552		*IEC*	BN
10511		*IEC*	BN	10533	I	*IWC*	WB	10553	I	*IWC*	WB
10512		*IWC*	EC	10534	I	*IWC*	WB	10554	L	*ICC*	EC
10513		*IWC*	WB	10535		*IWC*	WB	10555	IL	*IWC*	EC
10514	I	*ICH*	BN	10536	I	*IWC*	WB	10556		*IWR*	LA
10515	I	*IWC*	WB	10537		*IWC*	EC	10557	I	*IWC*	EC
10516	I	*IWC*	WB	10538		*IWC*	WB	10558		*IWR*	LA
10517		*IEC*	BN	10539	IL	*IWC*	EC	10559	I	*IWC*	WB
10518		*IEC*	BN	10540		*IWC*	WB	10560		*IWC*	EC
10519		*IWC*	WB	10541	I	*ICC*	EC	10561	I	*IWC*	WB
10520	IL	*IWC*	EC	10542	I	*IWC*	WB	10562	I	*IWC*	WB

No.		Pool	Depot
10563	I	*IWC*	WB
10564		*IWR*	LA
10565	I	*IWC*	WB
10566		*IWC*	WB
10567		*IWC*	WB
10568		*IWC*	WB
10569	L	*IWC*	WB
10570		*IWR*	LA
10571		*IWC*	WB
10572		*IWC*	WB
10573	I	*IWC*	WB
10574	I	*ICH*	BN
10575	I	*ICH*	BN
10576		*PSX*	EC
10577		*PSX*	EC
10578	I	*PSX*	EC
10579	I	*PSX*	EC
10580		*IWC*	WB
10581		*PSX*	EC
10582	I	*IWC*	WB
10583		*IWC*	WB
10584	I	*IWC*	WB
10585		*IWR*	LA
10586		*IWR*	LA
10587	I	*IWR*	LA
10588		*IWR*	LA
10589		*IWC*	WB
10590	I	*IWC*	WB
10591		*IWC*	EC
10592		*ICC*	EC
10593	I	*IWC*	EC
10594	I	*IWR*	LA
10595		*ICC*	EC
10596	I	*IWC*	WB
10597	I	*IWC*	EC
10598		*IWC*	WB
10599		*IWC*	WB
10600		*IWC*	WB
10601		*IWC*	WB
10602		*IWC*	WB
10603	I	*IWR*	LA
10604		*IWC*	WB
10605	I	*IWC*	WB
10606		*IWC*	WB
10607	I	*IWC*	WB
10608		*IWC*	WB
10609		*PSX*	EC
10610	I	*ICC*	EC
10611		*IEC*	BN
10612		*ICC*	EC
10613		*ICC*	EC
10614		*ICC*	EC
10615		*IEC*	BN
10616		*ICC*	EC
10617		*ICC*	EC
10618		*IEC*	BN
10619		*IEC*	BN

SLE AS4G

Sleeper, either Class, Mk. 3a. — AS404

Introduced: 1981
Weight: 43 tonnes
Berths: 1st: 13 or **Std:** 26
Brakes: Air
Heating: Full air conditioning
ETH Index: 6X
Bogies: BT10A
Toilets: 2 (Controlled emission)
Maximum speed: 125mph
Special features: Short-swing link bogies: L

Derby 30961/81-2.

No.		Pool	Depot
10646	I	*ICH*	BN
10647		*IWC*	WB
10648		*IWC*	WB
10649		*IWC*	WB
10650		*IWC*	WB
10651	I	*IWC*	WB
10653		*IWC*	WB
10654		*IEC*	BN
10655	I	*IWC*	WB
10656	I	*IWC*	WB
10657	I	*IWC*	WB
10658	I	*IWR*	WB
10660	I	*IWC*	WB
10661	I	*ICH*	BN
10662		*ICH*	BN
10663	L	*ICC*	EC
10665		*IWC*	WB
10666	L	*ICC*	EC
10668		*IWC*	WB
10670		*IWC*	WB
10671		*IWC*	WB
10672		*IWC*	WB
10673		*IWC*	EC
10674		*IWC*	EC
10675	I	*IWC*	WB
10678		*IWC*	EC
10679		*IWC*	EC
10680	IL	*IWC*	EC
10682	I	*IWC*	EC
10683	I	*IWC*	WB
10684	IL	*IWC*	EC
10685	IL	*IWC*	EC
10686		*IWR*	WB
10687		*IWC*	WB
10688		*IWC*	WB
10689		*IWC*	WB
10690		*IWC*	WB
10691		*IWC*	WB
10692	I	*IWC*	WB

10693	IL	*IWC*	EC	10708	IL	*IWC*	WB	10720	I	*IWC*	EC
10696	I	*IWC*	WB	10709		*IWC*	WB	10722		*IWC*	WB
10697	IL	*IWC*	EC	10710	I	*IWC*	WB	10723		*IEC*	BN
10699	L	*ICC*	EC	10711		*IWC*	WB	10724	I	*ICH*	BN
10700		*IWC*	WB	10712		*ICC*	EC	10725	I	*ICH*	BN
10701		*IWC*	WB	10713		*IWC*	WB	10726	I	*ICH*	BN
10702	I	*IWC*	EC	10714		*IWC*	WB	10727	I	*ICH*	BN
10703	I	*IWC*	EC	10715	I	*IWC*	WB	10728		*ICH*	BN
10704	IL	*IWC*	EC	10716	IL	*IWC*	WB	10729		*ICH*	BN
10705	I	*IWC*	WB	10717	IL	*IWC*	WB	10730	I	*IWC*	WB
10706		*IEC*	BN	10718	L	*ICC*	EC	10731	I	*IWC*	WB
10707	I	*IWC*	WB	10719	L	*ICC*	EC	10732	I	*IWC*	WB

10664/67/69/76/77/81/94/95/98, 10721 are on six year lease to Danish State Railways (DSB) from 1987.

FO AD1G

Open First, Mk. 3a. — AD108

Introduced: 1975
Weight: 33 tonnes
Seats: 1st, 48
Brakes: Air
Heating: Full air conditioning
ETH Index: 6X

Bogies: BT10
Toilets: 2
Maximum speed: 125mph
Standard equipment: Public address fitted
Special feature: 11021 has BT15 bogies, 11058 has BT5 bogies, D: Disabled toilet

Derby 30878/75. All Refurbished in InterCity livery

11011	D	*IWC*	WB	11027	*IWC*	WB	11042		*IWC*	WB
11013		*IWC*	WB	11028	*IWC*	WB	11044		*IWC*	WB
11016		*IWC*	WB	11029	*IWC*	WB	11045		*IWC*	WB
11017		*IWC*	WB	11030	*IWC*	WB	11046		*IWC*	WB
11018		*IWC*	WB	11031	*IWC*	WB	11048		*IWC*	WB
11019		*IWC*	WB	11033	*IWC*	WB	11052		*IWC*	WB
11020		*IWC*	WB	11036	*IWC*	WB	11054		*IWC*	WB
11021		*IWC*	WB	11037	*IWC*	WB	11055		*IWC*	WB
11023		*IWC*	WB	11038	*IWC*	WB	11058		*IWC*	WB
11024		*IWC*	WB	11039	*IWC*	WB	11060		*IWC*	WB
11026		*IWC*	WB	11040	*IWC*	WB				

FO — AD1H

Open First and Pullman, Mk. 3b. — AD110

Introduced: 1984
Weight: 34.6 tonnes
Seats: 1st, 48
Brakes: Air
Heating: Full air conditioning
ETH Index: 6X
Bogies: BT10

Toilets: 2
Maximum speed: 125mph
Standard equipment: Public address fitted

All InterCity livery except 11073-94 InterCity Pullman.
Names in brackets not currently carried

Derby 30982/84-5

Open First

No.			No.			No.		
11064	*IWC*	WB	11067	*IWC*	WB	11070	*IWC*	WB
11065	*IWC*	WB	11068	*IWC*	WB	11071	*IWC*	WB
11066	*IWC*	WB	11069	*IWC*	WB	11072	*IWC*	WB

Pullman

No.			Name	No.			Name
11073	*IWC*	WB	*William Ewart Gladstone*	11084	*IWC*	WB	*William Roscoe*
11074	*IWC*	WB	*Thomas Brassey*	11085	*IWC*	WB	*Sir John Barbirolli*
11075	*IWC*	WB		11086	*IWC*	WB	*Henry Doulton*
11076	*IWC*	WB	*John Lennon*	11087	*IWC*	WB	*(Sir William Fairbairn)*
11077	*IWC*	WB	*Sir Richard Arkwright*	11088	*IWC*	WB	*Sir John Brunner*
11078	*IWC*	WB	*John Owens*	11089	*IWC*	WB	*George Stubbs*
11079	*IWC*	WB	*Francis Egerton*	11090	*IWC*	WB	
11080	*IWC*	WB	*(Emmeline Pankhurst)*	11091	*IWC*	WB	*Sir Stanley Matthews*
11081	*IWC*	WB	*Elizabeth Gaskell*	11092	*IWC*	WB	*Ernest Rutherford*
11082	*IWC*	WB	*James Joule*	11093	*IWC*	WB	*LS Lowry*
11083	*IWC*	WB	*Kitty Wilkinson*	11094	*IWC*	WB	*Arnold Bennett*

Open First

No.			No.			No.		
11095	*IWC*	WB	11098	*IWC*	WB	11101	*IWC*	WB
11096	*IWC*	WB	11099	*IWC*	WB			
11097	*IWC*	WB	11100	*IWC*	WB			

FO — AD1H

First Open and Pullman, Mk. 4 — AD111

Introduced: 1989
Weight: 39.7 tonnes
Seats: 1st or Pullman, 46
Brakes: Air
Heating: Full air conditioning
ETH Index: 6X

Bogies: BT41
Toilets: 1
Maximum speed: 140mph
Standard equipment: Public address fitted. The distinction between 1st and Pullman is in the level of service provided on individual trains

Metro Cammell 31046/89

Number	Operator
11200	*IEC*
11201	*IEC*
11202	*IEC*
11203	*IEC*
11204	*IEC*
11205	*IEC*
11206	*IEC*
11207	*IEC*
11208	*IEC*
11209	*IEC*
11210	*IEC*
11211	*IEC*
11212	*IEC*
11213	*IEC*
11214	*IEC*
11215	*IEC*
11216	*IEC*
11217	*IEC*
11218	*IEC*
11219	*IEC*
11220	*IEC*
11221	*IEC*
11222	*IEC*
11223	*IEC*
11224	*IEC*
11225	*IEC*
11226	*IEC*
11227	*IEC*
11228	*IEC*
11229	*IEC*
11230	*IEC*
11231	*IEC*
11232	*IEC*
11233	*IEC*
11234	*IEC*
11235	*IEC*
11236	*IEC*
11237	*IEC*
11238	*IEC*
11239	*IEC*
11240	*IEC*
11241	*IEC*
11242	*IEC*
11243	*IEC*
11244	*IEC*
11245	*IEC*
11246	*IEC*
11247	*IEC*
11248	*IEC*
11249	*IEC*
11250	*IEC*
11251	*IEC*
11252	*IEC*
11253	*IEC*
11254	*IEC*
11255	*IEC*
11256	*IEC*
11257	*IEC*
11258	*IEC*
11259	*IEC*
11260	*IEC*
11261	*IEC*
11262	*IEC*
11263	*IEC*

CO — AD3G

Open Composite Mk. 3a — AD301

Introduced: 1986 by modifying FO
Weight: 33 tonnes
Seats: 1st, 24; **Std,** 35

Bogies: BT10
Toilets: 2
Maximum speed: 125mph

Brakes: Air
Heating: Full air conditioning
ETH Index: 6X

All ScotRail livery

No.	Livery	Depot
11905	*PSX*	EC
11906	*PSX*	EC
11907	*PSX*	EC
11908	*PSX*	EC
11909	*PSX*	EC
11910	*PSX*	EC
11922	*PSX*	EC

TSO — AC2G

Tourist Open Standard, Mk. 3a. — AC212, AC213★

Introduced: 1975
Weight: 33 tonnes
Seats: 72, 76★, 74D
Brakes: Air
Heating: Full air conditioning
ETH Index: 6X

Bogies: BT10
Toilets: 2
Maximum speed: 125mph
Special features: 12010/62 have BT15 bogies, 12139 has one BT10a bogie and 12140 has experimental SIG bogies. Disabled toilets: D

Derby 30877/75-77

No.		Livery	Depot
12004	S	*PSX*	EC
12005	S	*PSX*	EC
12007	S	*PSX*	EC
12008	S	*PSX*	EC
12009	R★	*IWC*	WB
12010	R	*IWC*	WB
12011	S	*PSX*	EC
12012	S	*PSX*	EC
12013	S	*PSX*	EC
12014	S	*PSX*	EC
12015	S	*PSX*	EC
12016	S	*PSX*	EC
12017	S	*PSX*	EC
12019	S	*PSX*	EC
12020	S	*PSX*	EC
12021	S	*PSX*	EC
12022	S	*PSX*	EC
12023	S	*PSX*	EC
12024	S	*PSX*	EC
12025	S	*PSX*	EC
12026	S	*PSX*	EC
12027	S	*PSX*	EC
12028	S	*PSX*	EC
12029	S	*PSX*	EC
12030	S	*PSX*	EC
12031	S	*PSX*	EC
12032	R	*IWC*	WB
12033		*IWC*	WB
12034	R	*IWC*	WB
12035	R★	*IWC*	WB
12036	R	*IWC*	WB
12037	R	*IWC*	WB
12038	R	*IWC*	WB
12040	R	*IWC*	WB
12041	R	*IWC*	WB
12042	R	*IWC*	WB
12043	R★	*IWC*	WB
12044	R	*IWC*	WB
12045	R	*IWC*	WB
12046	R	*IWC*	WB
12047	RD	*IWC*	WB
12048	R	*IWC*	WB
12049	R	*IWC*	WB
12050	R	*IWC*	WB
12051	S	*PSX*	EC
12052	R★	*IWC*	WB
12053	R	*IWC*	WB
12054	RD	*IWC*	WB
12055	R	*IWC*	WB
12056	R	*IWC*	WB
12057	R★	*IWC*	WB
12058	R	*IWC*	WB
12059	R★	*IWC*	WB
12060	R	*IWC*	WB
12061	R	*IWC*	WB
12062	R	*IWC*	WB
12063	R	*IWC*	WB
12064	R	*IWC*	WB
12065	R	*IWC*	WB
12066	R	*IWC*	WB
12067	R	*IWC*	WB
12068	R	*IWC*	WB
12069	R	*IWC*	WB
12070	R★	*IWC*	WB
12071	R	*IWC*	WB
12072	R	*IWC*	WB
12073	R	*IWC*	WB
12075	R	*IWC*	WB
12076	R	*IWC*	WB
12077	R	*IWC*	WB
12078	R	*IWC*	WB
12079	R	*IWC*	WB

No.	Notes	Owner	Operator
12080	R★	*IWC*	WB
12081	R	*IWC*	WB
12082	R	*IWC*	WB
12083	R	*IWC*	WB
12084	R	*IWC*	WB
12085	R★	*IWC*	WB
12086	R	*IWC*	WB
12087	R★	*IWC*	WB
12088	RD	*IWC*	WB
12089	R	*IWC*	WB
12090	R	*IWC*	WB
12091	R	*IWC*	WB
12092	R	*IWC*	WB
12093	R	*IWC*	WB
12094	R	*IWC*	WB
12095	R★	*IWC*	WB
12096	R	*IWC*	WB
12097	R★	*IWC*	WB
12098	R★	*IWC*	WB
12099	R	*IWC*	WB
12100		*IWC*	WB
12101	R	*IWC*	WB
12102	R	*IWC*	WB
12103	R	*IWC*	WB
12104	R	*IWC*	WB
12105	R	*IWC*	WB
12106	R	*IWC*	WB
12107	R	*IWC*	WB
12108	R	*IWC*	WB
12109	R	*IWC*	WB
12110	R	*IWC*	WB
12111	★	*IWC*	WB
12112	RD	*IWC*	WB
12113	R	*IWC*	WB
12114	R	*IWC*	WB
12115	R	*IWC*	WB
12116	R	*IWC*	WB
12117	R	*IWC*	WB
12118	R★	*IWC*	WB
12119	R	*IWC*	WB
12120	R	*IWC*	WB
12121	R	*IWC*	WB
12122	RD	*IWC*	WB
12123	R	*IWC*	WB
12124	R	*IWC*	WB
12125	R	*IWC*	WB
12126	R★	*IWC*	WB
12127	R	*IWC*	WB
12128	R	*IWC*	WB
12129	R	*IWC*	WB
12130	R	*IWC*	WB
12131	R	*IWC*	WB
12132		*IWC*	WB
12133	R	*IWC*	WB
12134	R	*IWC*	WB
12135	R	*IWC*	WB
12136	R	*IWC*	WB
12137	R	*IWC*	WB
12138	R	*IWC*	WB
12139	R	*IWC*	WB
12140	RD	*IWC*	WB
12141	R	*IWC*	WB
12142		*IWC*	WB
12143	R	*IWC*	WB
12144	R	*IWC*	WB
12145	R	*IWC*	WB
12146	R	*IWC*	WB
12147	R	*IWC*	WB
12148	R	*IWC*	WB
12149	R	*IWC*	WB
12150	R	*IWC*	WB
12151	R	*IWC*	WB
12152	R	*IWC*	WB
12153	R	*IWC*	WB
12154	R	*IWC*	WB
12155	R	*IWC*	WB
12156	R	*IWC*	WB
12157	R	*IWC*	WB
12158	R	*IWC*	WB
12159	R	*IWC*	WB
12160	R	*IWC*	WB
12161		*IWC*	WB
12163	R	*IWC*	WB
12164	R	*IWC*	WB
12165	R	*IWC*	WB
12166	R	*IWC*	WB
12167	R	*IWC*	WB
12168	R*	*IWC*	WB

TSOE — AI2H

Tourist Open Standard-End coach, Mk 4 — AI201

Introduced: 1989
Weight: 39.5 tonnes
Seats: 74
Brakes: Air
Heating: Full air conditioning
ETH Index: 6X

Bogies: BT41
Toilets: 2
Maximum speed: 140mph
Standard equipment: These vehicles are to be marshalled next to the locomotive and therefore have no gangway at one end. Public address fitted

Metro Cammell 31047/89

12200	*IEC*	12211	*IEC*	12222	*IEC*
12201	*IEC*	12212	*IEC*	12223	*IEC*
12202	*IEC*	12213	*IEC*	12224	*IEC*
12203	*IEC*	12214	*IEC*	12225	*IEC*
12204	*IEC*	12215	*IEC*	12226	*IEC*
12205	*IEC*	12216	*IEC*	12227	*IEC*
12206	*IEC*	12217	*IEC*	12228	*IEC*
12207	*IEC*	12218	*IEC*	12229	*IEC*
12208	*IEC*	12219	*IEC*	12230	*IEC*
12209	*IEC*	12220	*IEC*	12231	*IEC*
12210	*IEC*	12221	*IEC*		

TSOD AL2H

Tourist Open Standard — Disabled, Mk 4 — AL201

Introduced: 1989
Weight: 39.4 tonnes
Seats: 72 with wheelchair space
Brakes: Air
Heating: Full air conditioning
ETH Index: 6X
Bogies: BT41
Toilets: 1 (Disabled)
Maximum speed: 140mph
Standard equipment: Public address fitted

Metro Cammell 31048/89

12300	*IEC*	12311	*IEC*	12322	*IEC*
12301	*IEC*	12312	*IEC*	12323	*IEC*
12302	*IEC*	12313	*IEC*	12324	*IEC*
12303	*IEC*	12314	*IEC*	12325	*IEC*
12304	*IEC*	12315	*IEC*	12326	*IEC*
12305	*IEC*	12316	*IEC*	12327	*IEC*
12306	*IEC*	12317	*IEC*	12328	*IEC*
12307	*IEC*	12318	*IEC*	12329	*IEC*
12308	*IEC*	12319	*IEC*	12330	*IEC*
12309	*IEC*	12320	*IEC*		
12310	*IEC*	12321	*IEC*		

TSO AC2H

Tourist Open Standard, Mk 4 — AC214

Introduced: 1989
Weight: 39.9 tonnes
Seats: 74
Brakes: Air
Heating: Full air conditioning
ETH Index: 6X
Bogies: BT41
Toilets: 2
Maximum speed: 140mph
Standard equipment: Public address fitted

Metro Cammell 31049/89

12400	IEC	12431	IEC	12462	IEC
12401	IEC	12432	IEC	12463	IEC
12402	IEC	12433	IEC	12464	IEC
12403	IEC	12434	IEC	12465	IEC
12404	IEC	12435	IEC	12466	IEC
12405	IEC	12436	IEC	12467	IEC
12406	IEC	12437	IEC	12468	IEC
12407	IEC	12438	IEC	12469	IEC
12408	IEC	12439	IEC	12470	IEC
12409	IEC	12440	IEC	12471	IEC
12410	IEC	12441	IEC	12472	IEC
12411	IEC	12442	IEC	12473	IEC
12412	IEC	12443	IEC	12474	IEC
12413	IEC	12444	IEC	12475	IEC
12414	IEC	12445	IEC	12476	IEC
12415	IEC	12446	IEC	12477	IEC
12416	IEC	12447	IEC	12478	IEC
12417	IEC	12448	IEC	12479	IEC
12418	IEC	12449	IEC	12480	IEC
12419	IEC	12450	IEC	12481	IEC
12420	IEC	12451	IEC	12482	IEC
12421	IEC	12452	IEC	12483	IEC
12422	IEC	12453	IEC	12484	IEC
12423	IEC	12454	IEC	12485	IEC
12424	IEC	12455	IEC	12486	IEC
12425	IEC	12456	IEC	12487	IEC
12426	IEC	12457	IEC	12488	IEC
12427	IEC	12458	IEC	12489	IEC
12428	IEC	12459	IEC		
12429	IEC	12460	IEC		
12430	IEC	12461	IEC		

FK AA11

Corridor First, Mk. 1. — AA101

Introduced: 1951
Weight: 34 tonnes
Seats: 1st, 42
Brakes: Vacuum (Dual: x as marked)
ETH Index: 3

Bogies: See individual lots
Toilets: 2
Maximum speed: 100mph
Special features: g: Fluorescent lights
R Refurbished, InterCity livery

Ashford/Swindon. 30381/58 B4 bogies

13225	Rx	*ICH*	BN
13227	Rx	*ICH*	BN
13228	Rx	*ICH*	BN
13229	Rx	*ICH*	BN
~~13230~~	Rx	*ICH*	BN
~~13233~~		*NWR*	OM
13236	R	*ICH*	BN
~~13237~~	R	*ICH*	BN

Swindon 30667/62. Commonwealth bogies

13303		*ICHH*	OM
13306		*ICHH*	OM
13308	N	*NWR*	OM
13313		*ICHH*	CL
13314	R	*ICH*	BN
~~13316~~		*ICHH*	BN
13318	R	*ICH*	BN
13320		*ICHH*	CL
13321	R	*ICHH*	CL
~~13324~~	Ng	*NWR*	OM
~~13325~~		*ICHH*	CL
13326		*ICHH*	BN
13328	Ng	*NWR*	OM
13329	Ng	*NWR*	OM
13331	Ng	*NWR*	OM
13335		*ICHH*	CL
13341	I	*ICH*	OY
13342		*ICH*	OY
13343	R	*ICH*	BN
13344		*ICH*	PH

FK AA1A

Corridor First, Mk.2a. — AA106

Introduced: 1968
Weight: 32 tonnes
Seats: 1st, 42
Brakes: Air (Vacuum: V as marked)
Heating: Pressure heating and ventilation

ETH Index: 4
Bogies: B4
Toilets: 2
Maximum speed: 100mph

Derby 30774/68

13435	Nv	*NWR*	OM
13436	Nv	*NNE*	CA
13437	Nv	*NWR*	OM
13438	Nv	*NWR*	OM
~~13440~~	Nv	*NWR*	OM
13441	Nv	*NWR*	OM
13442	Nv	*NWR*	OM
13443	Nv	*NWR*	OM
13444	Nv	*NWR*	OM
13445	P	*PTP*	HT
13446	v	*NWR*	OM
13447	Nv	*NNE*	CA
13450	v	*NNE*	CA
13451	P	*PTP*	HT
13456		*PSX*	EC
13459	N	*NSS*	EH
13461		*PSX*	EC
13462	N	*NWR*	OM
13463	P	*PTP*	HT

Derby 30785/68

13467	N	*NSS*	EH
13470	Nv	*NNE*	CA
13473	N	*NSS*	EH
~~13474~~	Nv	*NNE*	CA
~~13475~~	v	*NWR*	OM

FK AA1B

Corridor First, Mk.2b. — AA107

Introduced: 1969
Weight: 33.5 tonnes
Seats: 1st, 42
Brakes: Air
Heating: Pressure heating and ventilation

ETH Index: 4
Bogies: B4
Toilets: 2
Maximum speed: 100mph

Derby 30789/69.

13479	N	*NSS*	LA	~~13493~~		*NWR*	OM	13507	N	*NSS*	EH
13482	N	*NSS*	EH	13499	N	*NSS*	EH	13513	N	*NSS*	EH
13488	N	*NWR*	OM	~~13502~~	N	*NWR*	OM				

FK AA1C

Corridor First, Mk.2c. — AA108

Introduced: 1969
Weight: 34 tonnes
Seats: 1st, 42
Brakes: Air
Heating: Pressure heating and ventilation
ETH Index: 4

Bogies: B4
Toilets: 2
Maximum speed: 100mph
Standard equipment: PA fitted to all except 13514/25

Derby 30797/69-70

13514	N	*NSS*	EH	13519	P	*PTP*	HT	13526		*NSS*	LA
13516		*PTP*	HT	13520	P	*PTP*	HT	13527	P	*PTP*	HT
13517		*NWR*	OM	13525	N	*NSS*	EH	13532	P	*PTP*	HT

FK AA1D

Corridor First, Mk.2d. — AA109

Introduced: 1971
Weight: 35 tonnes
Seats: 1st, 42
Brakes: Air
Heating: Full air conditioning

ETH Index: 5
Bogies: B4
Toilets: 2
Maximum speed: 100mph
Standard equipment: Public address fitted

Derby 30825/71-2.

13562	I	*ICC*	MA
13563		*ICC*	MA
13564	I	*IWR*	OM
13565	I	*ICC*	MA
13566	I	*ICC*	MA
13567	I	*IWR*	OM
13568	I	*ICC*	PC
13569	I	*ICC*	PC
13571	I	*ICC*	PC
13572		*ICC*	MA
13574	I	*ICC*	MA
~~13575~~		*ICC*	MA
13576		*ICH*	MA
13577	I	*ICH*	OM
13578	I	*ICC*	PC
13579	I	*ICH*	OM
~~13580~~	I	*ICC*	MA
13581	I	*ICC*	MA
13582	I	*ICC*	PC
13583	I	*ICH*	OM
13584	I	*ICH*	OM
13585	I	*ICC*	MA
13586	I	*ICH*	OM
13587	I	*ICC*	MA
13588	I	*ICC*	PC
13589	I	*ICH*	OM
13590	I	*ICH*	MA
13591	I	*ICC*	MA
13592	I	*ICC*	MA
13593	I	*ICC*	MA
13594	I	*ICH*	OM
13595	I	*ICH*	OM
13596	I	*ICC*	PC
13597		*ICH*	MA
13598	I	*ICC*	MA
13599		*ICC*	MA
~~13600~~		*ICC*	MA
13601	I	*ICC*	PC
13602	I	*ICC*	PC
~~13603~~	I	*ICC*	PC
~~13604~~	I	*ICC*	MA
~~13605~~		*ICC*	MA
13606		*ICC*	PC
~~13607~~		*ICC*	MA
13608		*ICC*	MA
~~13609~~	I	*ICC*	MA
13610	I	*ICC*	MA

BFK — AB11

Brake Corridor First, Mk.1. — AB101

Introduced: 1959
Weight: 34 tonnes or 36 tonnes (17015-26)
Seats: 1st, 24
Brakes: Vacuum (Dual: x as marked)
ETH Index: 2
Bogies: See individual batches

Toilets: 1
Maximum speed: B1 bogies 90mph, Commonwealth bogies 100mph
Special features: Fluorescent lights: g.
R Refurbished, InterCity livery

Ashford/Swindon 30218/59-60. B1 bogies.

17003		*PNS*	IS
17005		*PNS*	IS

Ashford/Swindon 30382/60. B1 bogies.

17007		*ICH*	OM

On loan to MNLPS see 99782

Swindon 30668/61. Commonwealth bogies.

17015	Rx	*ICH*	BN
17022		*PNS*	IS

Swindon 30718/63. Commonwealth bogies.

17023	Rx	*ICH*	BN
17025	g	*ICCH*	CL

BFK — AB1Z

Brake Corridor First, Mk.2. — AB102

Introduced: 1966
Weight: 32 tonnes
Seats: 1st, 24
Brakes: Vacuum
Heating: Pressure heating and ventilation

ETH Index: 4
Bogies: B4
Toilets: 1
Maximum speed: 100mph

Derby 30756/66.

No.				No.				No.			
17030		*PWX*	ZQ	17040	N	*NWR*	OM	17051		*ICH*	OY
17031		*ICH*	OY	17041		*ICH*	OY	17052		*ICH*	OY
17035		*PWX*	CF	17042	I	*ICH*	BN	17054		*ICH*	OY
17037	I	*ICH*	BN	17043		*ICH*	OY	17055		*PNS*	PC
17038		*PNE*	HT	17047		*ICH*	OY				
17039		*PWH*	PC	17048		*PNE*	HT				

BFK — AB1A

Brake Corridor First, Mk.2a — AB103

Introduced: 1967
Weight: 32 tonnes
Seats: 1st, 24
Brakes: Air (Vacuum: v as marked)
Heating: Pressure heating and ventilation
ETH Index: 4

Bogies: B4
Toilets: 1
Maximum speed: 100mph
Special features: Public address: p as marked
17089/90/92 were numbered 35502/03/01 respectively until reverting to original identity in 1988

Derby 30775/67-8.

No.				No.				No.			
17056		*NSS*	LA	17063		*NSS*	LA	17072		*NSS*	LA
17057		*NSS*	LA	17064	Nv	*NWR*	OM	17073	N	*NSS*	LA
17058	N	*NWR*	OM	17066	v	*ICH*	OY	17074		*NSS*	LA
17059	v	*PNS*	PC	17068	Nv	*NWR*	OM	17075		*ICC*	MA
17060	v	*NWR*	OM	17069	N	*NSS*	LA	17076	N	*NSS*	LA
17062	N	*NWR*	OM	17070		*NSS*	LA	17077	N	*NWR*	OM

Derby 30786/68.

No.				No.				No.			
17079	N	*NSS*	LA	17089	Nv	*NWR*	OM	17098		*ICC*	MA
17080	N	*NSS*	LA	17090	Nv	*NWR*	OM	17099	v	*PNS*	PC
17081	N	*NSS*	LA	17091	v	*NWR*	OM	17100		*ICC*	MA
17082	Np	*NSS*	LA	17092	Nv	*NWR*	OM	17101	v	*ICH*	OY
17085	Nv	*NWR*	OM	17093	I	*ICH*	BN	17102		*ICC*	MA
17086	N	*NSS*	LA	17096	N	*NSS*	LA	17103	v	*ICH*	OY
17088		*NSS*	LA	17097	N	*NSS*	LA				

BFK — AB1C

Brake Corridor First, Mk.2c. — AB105

Introduced: 1969
Weight: 32 tonnes
Seats: 1st, 24
Brakes: Air
Heating: Pressure heating and ventilation
ETH Index: 4
Bogies: B4
Toilets: 1
Maximum speed: 100mph
Special features: Public address transmitter fitted: q as marked

Derby 30796/69-70.

17113	q	*IWC*	EN	17123	q	*ICC*	PC	17132	N	*NSS*	LA
17114	N	*NSS*	LA	17124	q	*IWC*	EN	17133		*ICC*	MA
17115		*NSS*	LA	17125	q	*ICC*	PC	17134	lq	*ICC*	MA
17117	lq	*ICH*	BN	17126	lq	*ICC*	MA	17135	l	*IAN*	NC
17118	N	*NWR*	OM	17127	q	*PSX*	IS	17136		*ICH*	BN
17119	q	*IWC*	EN	17128		*PSX*	IS	17137	q	*ICC*	PC
17120		*NSS*	LA	17129	lq	*ICC*	PC	17138	lq	*ICC*	MA
17121	q	*NSS*	LA	17130	lq	*ICC*	MA				
17122	lq	*ICC*	PC	17131	q	*ICC*	PC				

BFK — AB1D

Brake Corridor First, Mk.2d. — AB106

Introduced: 1971
Weight: 33 tonnes
Seats: 1st, 24
Brakes: Air
Heating: Full air conditioning
ETH Index: 5
Bogies: B4
Toilets: 1
Maximum speed: 100mph
Standard equipment: Public address transmitter fitted
Special features: Driver/Guard communication: 17139-43/45-54/57/62/64/66/67/69-72

Derby 30823/71-2

17139		*ICC*	PC	17146	l	*ICC*	MA	17153	l	*IAN*	NC
17140	l	*ICC*	MA	17147	l	*ICC*	MA	17154	l	*IAN*	NC
17141	l	*ICC*	MA	17148	l	*IAN*	NC	17155	l	*ICH*	OM
17142	l	*ICC*	MA	17149	l	*IAN*	NC	17156	l	*ICC*	MA
17143	l	*IAN*	NC	17150	l	*ICC*	MA	17157	l	*ICC*	MA
17144	l	*IWR*	LA	17151	l	*ICC*	PC	17158	l	*IAN*	NC
17145	l	*IAN*	NC	17152		*ICC*	MA	17159		*ICC*	MA

17160		*ICC*	PC	~~17165~~	I	*ICC*	MA	17170	I	*ICC*	PC
17161	I	*IAN*	NC	17166	I	*ICC*	PC	17171	I	*ICC*	PC
17162	I	*ICC*	PC	17167	I	*ICC*	PC	17172	I	*ICC*	PC
~~17163~~		*IWR*	LA	17168	I	*IWR*	LA				
~~17164~~	I	*ICC*	MA	17169	I	*ICC*	MA				

BFO — AE1H

Brake Open First, Mk. 3b. — AE101

Introduced: 1985
Weight: 34 tonnes
Seats: 1st, 36
Brakes: Air
Heating: Full air conditioning
ETH Index: 6X
Bogies: BT10
Toilets: 1
Maximum speed: 125mph
Standard equipment: Public address transmitter fitted. Hydraulic Parking Brakes
All InterCity livery

Derby 30990/85

~~17173~~	*IWC*	WB	~~17175~~	*IWC*	WB
17174	*IWC*	WB			

SK — AA21

Corridor Standard. — AA201 or AA202

Introduced: 1951
Weight: 34 tonnes
Seats: 48 (AA201) or 64 (AA202★)
Brakes: Vacuum
Bogies: See individual lots
Toilets: 2
Maximum speed: 90mph. Commonwealth and B4: 100mph
Special features: g fluorescent lights
Some AA201 vehicles have been modified to AA202 since 1984
R Refurbished
Renumbered from 25284-26022.

Wolverton 30349/57. Modified B1 bogies

18284		*PNS*	IS	18288		*PNS*	IS	18303		*PNS*	IS
18287	★	*PWX*	CF	18293		*PSP*	NL				

Wolverton 30350/57. B1 bogies

18414		*PSP*	HT

Wolverton 30426/57-8. AA202 (18568 AA201)
B4 bogies except where marked

18568	B1	*PSP*	HT
18597	g	*PLC*	LL
18601	Ng	*NWR*	OM
18602	Ng	*NWR*	OM
18603	Ng	*NWR*	OM
18604	Ng	*NWR*	OM
18605	Ng	*NWR*	OM
18608	Ng	*NWR*	OM
18610		*PDC*	LA
18611	Ng	*NWR*	OM
18613	g	*PWX*	CF
18616	Ng	*NWR*	OM
18622	Ng	*NWR*	OM
18624		*PSP*	NL
18626		*PSP*	NL
18627	Ng	*NWR*	OM

Derby 30685/61-2. Commonwealth bogies

18704	N*g	*NWR*	OM
18706	N*g	*NWR*	OM
18709	N*g	*NWR*	OM
18711	N*g	*NWR*	OM
18714	N*g	*NWR*	OM
18715	N*g	*NWR*	OM
18716	*g	*PWX*	CF
18717	N*g	*NWR*	OM
18726	*	*PWX*	CF
18727	N*g	*NWR*	OM
18728		*NNW*	EN
18729	N*g	*NWR*	OM
18730	N*g	*NWR*	OM
18733	*	*PWX*	CF
18738		*PLC*	LL
18743		*NNW*	EN
18744	*	*PSP*	NL
18749		*PSP*	NL
18750	*	*PLC*	LL
18752		*NNW*	EN
18758		*PCR*	CL
18759		*PSP*	HT
18760	*	*PSP*	NL
18762		*PNS*	IS
18769		*NNW*	EN
18771		*NNW*	EN
18774		*PSP*	NL
18775	N*g	*NWR*	OM
18783		*PLC*	LL
18784	N*g	*NWR*	OM
18788	N*g	*NWR*	OM
18789	N*g	*NWR*	OM
18792	N*g	*NWR*	OM
18794	N*g	*NWR*	OM
18805	N*g	*NWR*	OM
18809	*	*PLC*	LL
18813		*PSP*	NL
18814	N*g	*NWR*	OM
18817		*PCR*	CL
18818	N*g	*NWR*	OM
18819		*ICH*	OM
18820	*g	*PWX*	CF
18822		*PCR*	CL
18823		*PSP*	HT
18825		*PLC*	LL
18826		*PSP*	NL
18835	*g	*PLC*	LL
18838		*PSP*	NL
18844		*PSP*	HT
18848		*PSP*	NL
18849		*PLC*	LL
18863		*NNW*	EN
18868		*PCR*	CL
18869		*NNW*	EN
18872		*PNS*	IS
18875	N*g	*NWR*	OM
18881		*PCR*	CL
18888		*PSP*	NL
18892		*PCR*	CL
18894		*PCR*	CL
18901		*ICH*	OM

Derby 30686/62. Commonwealth bogies. AA202.
Fluorescent lighting.

18911		*PWX*	CF
18921	N	*NWR*	OM
18925	N	*NWR*	OM
18926		*PWX*	CF
18931	N	*NWR*	OM
18933	N	*NWR*	OM
18935	N	*NWR*	OM
18936	N	*NWR*	OM
18937	N	*NWR*	OM
18938	N	*NWR*	OM
18940	N	*NWR*	OM
18941	N	*NWR*	OM
18943	N	*NWR*	OM
18945	N	*NWR*	OM
18947		*PLC*	LL
18951		*PWX*	CF
18952	N	*NWR*	OM
18955	N	*NWR*	OM
18956		*DXXZ*	CF
18957		*PWX*	CF
18958	N	*NWR*	OM
18959	N	*NWR*	OM
18960	N	*NWR*	OM
18967	N	*NWR*	OM
18968	N	*NWR*	OM
18970	N	*NWR*	OM

Derby 30719/62. Commonwealth bogies.

18977	*ICH*	OM	18997	N	*NWR*	OM	19015	*	*PWX*	CF
18983	*PCR*	CL	18998		*PCR*	CL	19017		*PSP*	HT
18987	*PLC*	LL	19011		*ICH*	OM	19018		*PSP*	NL
18994	*IXXZ*	OM	19012		*PLC*	LL	19022	*g	*NWR*	OM
18996	*PSP*	NL	19014		*ICH*	OM				

Type continued with 24895

SK — AA2A

Corridor Standard, Mk 2a. — AA209

Introduced: 1985 by modification from FK and renumbering
Weight: 32 tonnes
Seats: 42
Brakes: Air
Heating: Pressure heating and ventilation
ETH Index: 4
Bogies: B4
Toilets: 2
Maximum speed: 100mph

Derby 30774/68

19452	*PMX*	DY	19455	*PMX*	DY	19460	*IXX*	LL
19454	*IXX*	LL	19458	*PMX*	DY			

Derby 30785/68

19464	*IXX*	LL	19469	*IXX*	LL
19465	*IXX*	LL			

SK — AA2B

Corridor Standard Mk 2b. — AA207

Introduced: 1985 by modification from FK and renumbering
Weight: 33.5 tonnes
Seats: 42
Brakes: Air
Heating: Pressure heating and ventilation
ETH Index: 4
Bogies: B4
Toilets: 2
Maximum speed: 100mph

Derby 30789/69

19478	*IXX*	LL	19489	*PMX*	OY	19500	*PMX*	OY
19486	*PMX*	DY	19497	*ICHH*	ZQ	19512	*IXX*	OY

SK AA2C

Corridor Standard Mk 2c. — AA208

Introduced: 1985 by modification from FK and renumbering
Weight: 34 tonnes
Seats: 42
Brakes: Air
Heating: Pressure heating and ventilation

ETH Index: 4
Bogies: B4
Toilets: 2
Maximum speed: 100mph
Standard equipment: Public address fitted

Derby 30797/69-70

19522	*PMX*	DY	19536	*PMX*	DY	19548	*PMX*	DY
19523	*PMX*	DY	19537	*IXX*	LL	19549	*PMX*	DY
19529	*PMX*	OY	19540	*IXX*	LL	19555	*PMX*	NL
19534	*IXX*	LL	19545	*PMX*	NL	19556	*PMX*	NL

BCK AB31

Brake Corridor Composite. — AB301 or AB302

Introduced: 1954
Weight: 34 tonnes
Seats: 1st, 12; **Std,** 18 (AB301) or **1st,** 12; **Std,** 24 (AB302)
Brakes: See individual batches

ETH Index: 3
Bogies: Commonwealth except B1 where marked
Toilets: 2
Maximum speed: 100mph (B1 bogies 90mph)
Special livery: West Highland green and cream: 21241

Met Cam 30132/54-5 Vacuum brake, BI Bogies

21034 on loan to MNLPS — see 99781

Swindon 30669/61-2 Vacuum brakes

21240	*ICH*	OM	21242	*ICH*	BN	21247	*ICH*	OM
21241	*ICH*	BN	21246	*ICH*	EN			

Derby 30732/64. AB302 Air brake

21265	B1	*NSS*	EH	~~21268~~	B1	*ICH*	CL	21274	B1	*NSS*	EH
21266	B1	*ICH*	BN	21269		*ICC*	EC				

SK AA21

Corridor Standard — AA201

Type continued from 19022
Derby 30153/55-6

24895		*PSW*	PC

BSK AB21

Brake Corridor Standard — AB201

Introduced: 1951
Weight: 34 tonnes
Seats: 24 or 32 (AB202)
Brakes: Vacuum
ETH Index: 2 (lot 30229 is ETH 2S, 750-volt)
Bogies: See batches
Toilets: 1

Maximum speed: 90mph (Commonwealth and B4 bogies: 100mph)
Special features: Some AB201 coaches have been converted to AB202 since 1984 — these are marked★
g fluorescent lights
R Refurbished
PPublic Address fitted

Wolverton 30095/55. B1 Bogies

34538		*PSP*	PC

Wolverton 30156/55. B1 bogies

34663		*PSP*	HT	34674		*PSP*	HT
34668		*PSP*	PC	34681		*PSP*	NL

Gloucester R.C.W. 30233/56-7. B1 bogies

35053	★	*PWX*	CF

Roberts 30386/57-8. B1 bogies

35116		*ICH*	PH
35120	★	*PDC*	LA

Wolverton 30427/58-9. B4 bogies

35184	★	*PXXZ*	LL	35204	★g	*PWX*	CF
35195	★g	*PDC*	LA	35210		*ICH*	OM

Gloucester R.C.W. 30573/60. B4 bogies

35284		*PDC*	LA
35290	Np	*NNW*	EN

Wolverton 30699/62-3. Commonwealth bogies

35300		IXX	CL
35305		IXX	CL
35306		PSP	IS
35309		ICH	OM
35317	Np	NNW	EN
35320		PSP	DY
35321	*g	PWX	CF
35329	N	NNW	EN
35330		PCR	CL
35332		IXX	CL
35333		PLC	LL
35336		PWX	CF
35339	N	NNW	EN
35340		PNS	IS
35342	N	PCR	CL
35343		PSP	PC

Wolverton 30728/63. Commonwealth bogies

35447	p	NNW	EN
35448		ICH	OM
35449		ICH	OY

Wolverton 30721/63. Commonwealth bogies

35450		ICH	OM
35451		IXX	CL
35452	p	NNW	EN
35453		PSP	PC
35454	R	ICH	OY
35455	N	NNW	EN
35457		PMX	NL
35460		PSP	HT
35463		IXX	CL
35464	Np	NWR	OM
35465	N	ICH	OY
35467		ICH	OY
35468		IXX	CL
35469		ICH	OM
35470		PXXZ	LA
35471	N*g	NWR	OM
35472		PCR	CL
35473		PLC	LL
35474	N*	NWR	OM
35475	*g	NWR	OM
35476		ICH	OM
35478		ICH	OY
35479	Np	NNW	EN
35480	*g	PWX	CF
35481		ICH	OY
35482	*g	PWX	CF
35483		PSP	IS
35486		IXX	CL

BSK AB2A

Brake Corridor Standard, Mk 2a — AB204

Introduced: 1985 by modifying BFK and renumbering
Weight: 32 tonnes
Seats: 24
Brakes: Vacuum
Heating: Pressure heating and ventilation
ETH Index: 4
Bogies: B4
Toilets: 1
Maximum speed: 100mph

Derby 30786/68

35500	N	NWR	OM

RK AK51

Restaurant Kitchen, Mk 1 — AK501

Introduced: 1988 by modifying RBR and renumbering
Weight: To be announced
Seats: 0
Brakes: Dual

ETH Index: To be announced
Bogies: Commonwealth
Toilets: 0
Cooling: Liquid gas

Pressed Steel 30628/61

80041	I	*ICH*	BN

PARCELS STOCK

BG NN5

Riding and Toilet Van — NN503

Introduced: 1986
Body: 19.66×2.82m
Weight: 37 tonnes
Seats: Staff 6
Brakes: Dual except; Vacuum only
ETH Index: 2
Bogies: Commonwealth except B4 as marked

Toilets: 1
Maximum speed: 100mph
Standard equipment: Roller shutter doors fitted
Converted at Cardiff Cathays from BSK by removal of all but six seats (one compartment) and toilet. For building details see batches as built

80200	V	*RXXG*	OM
80201	V	*RXXG*	DY
80202	V	*RXXG*	OM
80203	VB4	*RXXG*	DY
80204		*RXXG*	EN
80205	V	*RXXG*	HT
80206		*RXXG*	EN
80207		*RXXG*	EN
80208		*RXXG*	EN
80209	V B4	*RXXG*	HT
80210	V B4	*RXXG*	HT
80211		*RXXG*	HT
80212		*RXXG*	CA
80213		*RXXG*	EN
80214		*RXXG*	HT
80215	B4	*RXXG*	CA
80216		*RXXG*	EN
80217		*RXXG*	CA
80218		*RXXG*	MA
80219	B4	*RXXG*	CA
80220	B4	*RXXG*	HT
80221		*RXXG*	EN
80222		*RXXG*	EN
80223		*RXXG*	CA
80224		*RXXG*	OM
80225		*RXXG*	OM

POS NS5

Post Office Sorting Van — NS501-506, 531

Introduced: 1959
Body: 19.66×2.82m
Weight: See batches
Brakes: Dual except vacuum where marked
Heating: 80319-95 have Pressure heating and ventilation
ETH Index: See batches
Bogies: B5 except B2 as marked
Toilets: 1
Maximum speed: 100mph (B2 bogies 90mph)
Load: 5T (3 tonnes: 80319-27, 6 tonnes: 80339-55, 7½ tonnes: 80356-80)
Special features: Fluorescent lighting: 80356-95
RR Royal Mail red livery

Wolverton 30486/59. 36 tonnes. ETH: 3X. NS501

80300	B2VRR	*RPOM*	MA	80302	B2VRR	*RPOM*	MA	80304	B2VRR	*RPOE*	CA
80301	B2V	*RPOM*	MA	80303	RR	*RPOE*	CA	80305	B2VRR	*RPOE*	CA

Wolverton 30487/59. 36 tonnes. ETH: 3. NS502

80306	B2VRR	*RPOM*	DY	80308	RR	*RPOE*	NC
80307	B2VRR	*RPOE*	CA				

Wolverton 30661/61. 37 tonnes. ETH: 3. NS501

80309	RR	*RPOE*	CA	80311	B2V	*RPOE*	HT	80313	B2VRR	*RPOE*	HT
80310	B2VRR	*RPOE*	HT	80312	B2VRR	*RPOE*	HT	80314	RR	*RPOE*	HT

Wolverton 30662/61. 36 tonnes. ETH: 3X. NS501

80315	VRR	*RPOE*	HT
80316	RR	*RPOE*	NC

Wolverton 30663/61. 36 tonnes. ETH: 3X. NS501

80318	RR	*RPOE*	NC

York 30778/68-9. 39 tonnes. ETH: 4. NS504

80319	RR	*RPOE*	CA	80322	RR	*RPOE*	HT	80325	RR	*RPOM*	DY
80320	RR	*RPOE*	HT	80323	RR	*RPOE*	HT	80326		*RPOM*	DY
80321	RR	*RPOZ*	EC	80324	RR	*RPOE*	HT	80327	RR	*RPOM*	DY

York 30779/68-9. 35 tonnes. ETH: 4. NS505

80328	RR	*RPOZ*	EC	80332	RR	*RPOE*	HT	80336	RR	*RPOE*	HT
80329	RR	*RPOM*	MA	80333	RR	*RPOE*	HT	80337	RR	*RPOE*	HT
80330	RR	*RPOE*	HT	80334	RR	*RPOM*	MA	80338	RR	*RPOM*	WB
80331	RR	*RPOE*	HT	80335	RR	*RPOE*	HT				

York 30780/68-9. 38 tonnes. ETH: 4. NS506

80339	RR	*RPOM*	WB	80345	RR	*RPOW*	PM	80351	RR	*RPOM*	DY
80340	RR	*RPOM*	MA	80346	RR	*RPOW*	PM	80352	RR	*RPOE*	NC
80341	RR	*RPOM*	WB	80347	RR	*RPOM*	WB	80353	RR	*RPOM*	WB
80342	RR	*RPOM*	WB	80348		*RPOM*	WB	80354	RR	*RPOM*	WB
80343		*RPOM*	MA	80349	RR	*RPOM*	DY	80355	RR	*RPOM*	MA
80344		*RPOM*	WB	80350	RR	*RPOE*	NC				

York 30839/72-3. 37 tonnes. ETH: 4X. NS503

80356	RR	*RPOM*	WB	80365	RR	*RPOE*	HT	80374	RR	*RPOM*	MA
80357	RR	*RPOM*	WB	80366	RR	*RPOM*	WB	80375	RR	*RPOM*	MA
80358	RR	*RPOW*	PM	80367		*RPOM*	WB	80376	RR	*RPOM*	WB
80359		*RPOW*	PM	80368		*RPOM*	WB	80377	RR	*RPOM*	WB
80360	RR	*RPOW*	PM	80369		*RPOM*	WB	80378	RR	*RPOM*	WB
80361	RR	*RPOW*	PM	80370	RR	*RPOM*	WB	80379	RR	*RPOW*	OM
80362	RR	*RPOE*	HT	80371	RR	*RPOM*	WB	80380	RR	*RPOM*	MA
80363	RR	*RPOE*	HT	80372	RR	*RPOM*	WB				
80364	RR	*RPOE*	HT	80373	RR	*RPOM*	WB				

Wolverton 30900/77. 34.5 tonnes. ETH: 4X. NS531
Rebuilds of SK built Wolverton 30155/55-6

80381	RR	*RPOW*	OM	80386	RR	*RPOW*	OM	80391		*RPOW*	OM
80382	RR	*RPOW*	OM	80387	RR	*RPOW*	OM	80392		*RPOW*	OM
80383	RR	*RPOW*	OM	80388	RR	*RPOW*	OM	80393	RR	*RPOW*	OM
80384	RR	*RPOW*	OM	80389	RR	*RPOW*	OM	80394	RR	*RPOW*	OM
80385	RR	*RPOW*	OM	80390	RR	*RPOW*	OM	80395		*RPOM*	MA

POT NT5

Post Office Stowage Van — NT501-505, 521

Introduced: 1959
Body: 19.66×2.82m
Weight: See batches
Brakes: Dual except v; vacuum as marked
Heating: 80415-39 Pressure heating and Ventilation
ETH Index: See batches

Bogies: B5 except B2 as marked
Toilets: 1
Maximum speed: 100mph (B2 bogies: 90mph)
Load: 8 tonnes (2 tonnes: 80403-06/11, 3 tonnes: 80407-10, 7½ tonnes: 80425-39)
Special features: Fluorescent lighting: 80425-30
RR Royal Mail red livery

Wolverton 30488/59. 35 tonnes ETH: 3. NT502

80400		*RPOM*	WB	80402	RR	*RPOM*	WB
80401		*RPOM*	WB				

Mk 3 AS4G SLE No 10730 in revised InterCity livery at Wolverton on 1 October 1988. *Michael McGowan*

Mk 4 AC214 TSO No 12403 nearing completion at BREL Derby Carriage Works, Litchurch Lane. *Brian Morrison*

Mk 2a AB1A BFK No 17093 with the InterCity Charter sub-Sector set outside Ilford 'B' shop on 9 March 1988. *Brian Morrison*

Mk 3 NZ5 Driving Van Trailer at Wembley InterCity depot, showing its striking side profile, on 22 January 1989. *Michael J. Collins*

York. 35 tonnes ETH: 3. NT503
Rebuilt from BSK built Roberts 30143/54

80403	RR	*RPOM*	MA

York. 35 tonnes ETH: 3 or 3X★. NT503 (80407-10 are NT501)
Rebuilt from BSK built Met. Cam. 30229/56-7

80404	RR	*RPOM*	MA
80405	RR	*RPOM*	MA
80406	RR	*RPOM*	MA
80407	VB2★RR	*RPOE*	CA
80408	VB2★RR	*RPOE*	CA
80409	VB2	*RPOW*	OM
80410	VB2RR	*RPOW*	OM
80411	★RR	*RPOW*	PM
80412	★RR	*RPOM*	MA
80413	★RR	*RPOW*	PM
80414	★	*RPOW*	MA

York 30781/68. 34 tonnes ETH: 4. NT505

80415	RR	*RPOM*	WB
80416	RR	*RPOM*	WB
80417	RR	*RPOM*	WB
80418	RR	*RPOM*	WB
80419	RR	*RPOM*	WB
80420		*RPOE*	HT
80421	RR	*RPOE*	HT
80422	RR	*RPOE*	HT
80423		*RPOW*	OM
80424		*RPOM*	WB

York 30840/73. 35 tonnes ETH: 4X. NT504

80425		*RPOM*	WB
80426	RR	*RPOW*	PM
80427	RR	*RPOW*	PM
80428	RR	*RPOM*	WB
80429	RR	*RPOM*	WB
80430	RR	*RPOM*	WB

Wolverton 30901/76. 34.5 tonnes ETH: 4X. NT521 (80435/36/37 NT504)
Rebuilt from SK built Wolverton 30155/55-6

80431	RR	*RPOM*	DY
80432	RR	*RPOE*	HT
80433	RR	*RPOE*	HT
80434	RR	*RPOE*	HT
80435		*RPOW*	OM
80436	RR	*RPOW*	OM
80437	RR	*RPOW*	OM
80438		*RPOM*	DY
80439	RR	*RPOM*	DY

B.POT — NU5

Post Office Brake Storage Van — NU501-502

Introduced: 1959
Body: 19.66×2.82m
Weight: 34 tonnes
Brakes: See batches
ETH Index: See batches
Bogies: See batches
Toilets: 1
Maximum speed: 90mph (B5 bogies; 100mph)
Load: 8 tonnes
RR Royal Mail red livery

Wolverton 30489/59. NU501 B2 bogies Vacuum Brakes ETH:3X

80450	RR	*RPOW*	OM
80451		*RPOW*	OM
80452	RR	*RPOW*	OM
80453	RR	*RPOW*	OM
80454		*RPOW*	OM
80455		*RPOW*	OM

York 30782/68. NU502 B5 bogies, Dual brakes ETH:4

80456	RR	*RPOM*	WB	80458	RR	*RPOM*	WB
80457	RR	*RPOM*	WB				

BG — NB5 NC5 ND5

Gangwayed Brake — NB501, NC501, ND501

Introduced: 1951
Body: 18.50×2.82m
Weight: 32 tonnes
Brakes: Vacuum or Dual
ETH Index: See below
Bogies: B2 or B1 — see below
Toilets: 0
Maximum speed: 90mph
Modifications: All basic BGs (NA) are now withdrawn: the three remaining variants are **NB** — High security mail vans, **NC** — Newspaper Packing Van (normally painted all blue) and **ND** — Dual heated BG.

NBV are Vacuum brake, ETH Index 1, B2 bogies. They have had the gangways removed and are B instead of BG.

NCV are Vacuum brake, ETH Index 3 or 3X, B1 bogies, fluorescent lighting *except* Vacuum brake, B2 bogies, tungsten lighting (80682/95, 80780, 84029)

NDV/NDX are Vacuum/Dual brake, ETH Index 1 or 1X★, B2 bogies (B1★).

NE vehicles have been renumbered 92000 upwards and some NCV have been fitted with Commonwealth bogies and renumbered 95200 upwards (DB) or 95300 upwards (VB).

RR Royal Mail red livery.

† Renumbering scheduled to 953xx series.

Derby 30009/52-3

80501	DV★	*RXXT*	EH	80513	†CV★	*RNPM*	MA
80512	DV★	*RXXC*	CA	80514	DV	*RPOM*	LL

Derby 30039/54

80537	DV★	*RXXC*	CA	80551	DV★	*RXXC*	DY	80565	DV★	*RXXC*	CA
80549	DV★	*RXXC*	BJ	80554	DV★	*RXXC*	CA				

Wolverton 30040/54-5

80570	DV★	*RXXC*	CA	80582	DV★	*RXXT*	EH	80592	DV★	*RXXC*	MA
80571	DV★	*RXXC*	CA	80583	DV★	*RXXC*	DY	80596	DV★	*RXXC*	CA
80576	DV★	*RXXC*	MA	80589	DV★	*RXXC*	MA				
80580	DV★	*RXXC*	CA	80590	DV★	*RXXC*	DY				

York 30046/54

80608	DV★	*RXXC*	DY
80613	†CV★	*RNPW*	BJ
80623	DV★	*RXXC*	CA
80631	†CV★	*RNPW*	BJ
80646	DV★	*RXXC*	NC
80649	†CV★	*RNPE*	HT
80650	DV★	*RXXC*	CA
80653	DV★	*RXXC*	CA
80654	DV★	*RXXC*	CA
80658	DV★	*RXXC*	NC
80663	DV★	*RXXC*	BJ
80664	DV★	*RXXC*	OM
80668	DV★	*RXXC*	BJ
80669	DV★	*RXXC*	OM
80670	DV★	*RXXC*	OM
80671	DV★	*RXXC*	OM

Met. Cam. 30136/55

80674	DV★	*RXXC*	CA
80680	DV★	*RXXC*	DY
80682	†CV	*RNPW*	BJ
80693	DV★	*RXXC*	HT
80695	CV	*RNPS*	EH
80699	DV★	*RXXC*	MA
80700	DX	*RXXB*	IS
80701	DX	*RXXB*	MA
80707	DV★	*RXXC*	OM
80709	DV★	*RXXC*	OM
80710	DV★	*RXXC*	OM
80716	DV★	*RXXC*	BJ
80720	†CV★	*RNPM*	MA

B.R.C.W. 30140/55-6

80728	DV★	*RXXC*	DY
80730	DV★	*RXXC*	DY
80736	DV★	*RXXC*	HT
80737	DX	*RXXB*	LL
80742	DV★	*RXXC*	HT
80743	DV★	*RXXC*	HT
80748	DV★	*RXXT*	EH
80754	DV★	*RXXC*	BJ
80756	DV★	*RXXC*	HT
80761	DV★	*RXXC*	HT
80763	DV★	*RXXC*	HT
80767	CV★	*RNPW*	BJ
80768	CV★	*RNPW*	BJ
80769	DV★	*RXXC*	BJ
08775	CV	*RNPM*	MA
80780	CV★	*RNPW*	BJ
80781	DX	*RXXB*	HT
80782	CV★	*RNPW*	BJ
80789	CV	*RNPM*	MA
80790	DX	*RXXB*	HT
80794	DV★	*RXXC*	HT
80795	DV★	*RXXC*	BJ

Cravens 30144/55

80804	DV★	*RXXC*	NC
80805	DX	*RXXB*	HT
80806	DV★	*RXXC*	HT
80810	DV★	*RXXC*	BJ
80820	DV★	*RXXC*	HT
80824	DV★	*RXXC*	HT
80831	DV★	*RXXC*	HT
80834	DX	*RXXB*	MA
80835	DV★	*RXXC*	CA
80837	DV★	*RXXC*	CA
80843	DX	*RXXB*	MA
80850	DV★	*RXXT*	EH
80851	DV★	*RXXC*	CA
80852	DV★	*RXXC*	CA

Pressed Steel 30162/56-7
80861 — White band livery

80859	DX★	*RXXB*	LL
80861	DX★	*RXXB*	HT
80868	DX★RR	*RXXB*	EC
80885	DX★	*RXXB*	MA
80886	DX	*RXXB*	MA
80889	DX★	*RXXB*	MA
80892	DX★	*RXXB*	MA
80893	DX	*RXXB*	MA
80926	DX	*RXXB*	HT
80945	DX	*RXXB*	CA
80962	DX	*RXXB*	PC

York 30173/56

80965	DV★	*RXXC*	IS
80966	†CV★	*RNPE*	CA
80967	DV★	*RXXC*	CA
80972	DV★	*RXXC*	CA
80976	DV★	*RXXC*	DY
80981	DV★	*RXXC*	CA
80985	DV★	*RXXC*	CA
80988	DX	*RXXB*	HT
80994	DV★	*RXXC*	CA

Type continued with 84010.

DVT NZ5

Driving Van Trailer, Mk 3 — NZ502

Introduced: 1988
Body: 18.83×2.74m
Weight: 43.7 tonnes
Brakes: Air
ETH Index: 6X
Bogies: T4

Toilets: 0
Maximum speed: 125mph
Load: 8.0 tonnes
Standard equipment: Guards compartment and Driving cab with Driver-Guard communication and Public Address Transmitter fitted.

Derby 31042/89

~~82101~~	*IWC*	ZQ	82119	*IWC*	82137	*IWC*
82102	*IWC*	ZQ	~~82120~~	*IWC*	82138	*IWC*
82103	*IWC*	ZQ	~~82121~~	*IWC*	82139	*IWC*
~~82104~~	*IWC*	ZQ	82122	*IWC*	~~82140~~	*IWC*
82105	*IWC*		82123	*IWC*	82141	*IWC*
~~82106~~	*IWC*		~~82124~~	*IWC*	82142	*IWC*
~~82107~~	*IWC*		~~82125~~	*IWC*	~~82143~~	*IWC*
~~82108~~	*IWC*		~~82126~~	*IWC*	82144	*IWC*
~~82109~~	*IWC*		~~82127~~	*IWC*	82145	*IWC*
~~82110~~	*IWC*		82128	*IWC*	82146	*IWC*
~~82111~~	*IWC*		~~82129~~	*IWC*	82147	*IWC*
82112	*IWC*		82130	*IWC*	~~82148~~	*IWC*
~~82113~~	*IWC*		82131	*IWC*	82149	*IWC*
82114	*IWC*		82132	*IWC*	82150	*IWC*
~~82115~~	*IWC*		82133	*IWC*	82151	*IWC*
82116	*IWC*		82134	*IWC*	82152	*IWC*
82117	*IWC*		82135	*IWC*		
82118	*IWC*		82136	*IWC*		

DVT NZ5

Driving Van Trailer, Mk 4 — NZ501

Introduced: 1989
Body: 18.59×2.73m
Weight: 43.5 tonnes
Brakes: Air
ETH Index: 6X
Bogies: BT41

Toilets: 0
Maximum speed: 140mph
Load: 8.0 tonnes
Standard equipment: Guards compartment and Driving cab, with Driver-Guard communication and Public Address Transmitter fitted.

Metro-Cammell 31043/89

~~82200~~	*IEC*	82211	*IEC*	82222	*IEC*
82201	*IEC*	82212	*IEC*	82223	*IEC*
82202	*IEC*	82213	*IEC*	82224	*IEC*
82203	*IEC*	82214	*IEC*	82225	*IEC*
82204	*IEC*	82215	*IEC*	82226	*IEC*
82205	*IEC*	82216	*IEC*	82227	*IEC*
82206	*IEC*	82217	*IEC*	82228	*IEC*
82207	*IEC*	82218	*IEC*	82229	*IEC*
82208	*IEC*	82219	*IEC*	82230	*IEC*
82209	*IEC*	82220	*IEC*	82231	*IEC*
82210	*IEC*	82221	*IEC*		

BG NB5 NC5 ND5

Type continued from 80994

York 30173/56

84010	DX	*RXXB*	CA
84012	†CV	*RNPW*	BJ

Cravens 30224/56
84029 has 3 roller shutter doors

84015	DV⋆	*RXXC*	NC	84026	DX	*RXXB*	MA	84041	†CV	*RNPM*	MA
84016	DV⋆	*RXXC*	BJ	84029	†CV	*RNPW*	BJ	84044	DX	*RXXB*	MA
84020	DV⋆	*RXXC*	BJ	84036	DV⋆	*RXXC*	DY	84051	DX	*RXXB*	EN
84024	DV⋆	*RXXC*	DY	84037	DV⋆	*RXXC*	DY				

Met. Cam. 30228/57-8

84057	DV⋆	*RXXC*	OM	84108	DV	*RXXC*	BJ	84137	DV	*RXXC*	HT
84065	DV⋆	*RXXC*	DY	84109	DV	*RXXC*	BJ	84141	DV⋆	*ICH*	CA
~~84082~~	DV⋆	*RXXC*	DY	84111	DV	*RXXC*	BJ	84143	DV	*RXXC*	MA
84084	DV⋆	*RXXC*	OM	84112	†CV	*RNPW*	BJ	84145	DV	*RXXC*	CA
84086	DV	*RXXC*	MA	84114	DV	*RXXC*	BJ	84146	DV	*RXXC*	CA
84093	DV	*RXXC*	CA	84119	†CV	*RNPE*	HT	84147	DV	*RXXC*	CA
84098	DV	*RXXC*	MA	84121	DV	*RXXC*	OM	~~84151~~	DV	*RXXC*	DY
~~84099~~	DX	*RXXB*	MA	84129	†CV⋆	*RNPE*	HT	84152	DV	*RXXC*	IS
84100	†CV	*RNPE*	HT	84133	DV	*RXXC*	MA	84159	DV⋆	*RXXC*	CA
84104	DX	*RXXB*	MA	84134	DX	*RXXB*	MA	84160	DV	*RXXC*	BJ
84106	DV⋆	*RXXC*	CA	84135	†CV	*RNPM*	MA	84162	DV	*RXXC*	BJ

Cravens 30234/56-7

84181	†CV★	*RNPM*	MA
84185	DV	*RXXC*	MA
84190	DV	*RXXC*	OM
84191	DV★	*RXXC*	MA
84193	DV★	*RXXC*	HT
84194	DV	*RXXC*	CA
84195	DV★	*RXXC*	DY
84197	DV	*RXXC*	MA
84200	DX	*RXXB*	MA
84202	DV	*RXXC*	MA
84203	DV	*RXXC*	DY
84204	DV	*RXXC*	MA

Pressed Steel 30163/57
84215 — White band livery

84211	DX★	*RXXB*	PC
84212	DX★	*RXXB*	CA
84215	DX★	*RXXB*	CA
84217	DX★	*RXXB*	PC
84234	DX★	*RXXB*	HT
84239	DX★	*RXXB*	CA
84240	DX★	*RXXB*	MA
84242	DX★	*RXXB*	MA
84250	DX★	*RXXB*	HT
84251	DX★	*RXXB*	IS
84252	DX★	*RXXB*	CA
84261	DX★	*RXXB*	MA
84262	DX★	*RXXB*	CA

Pressed Steel 30232/57

84273	DX	*RXXB*	HT
84274	DX	*RXXB*	MA
84279	DV	*RXXC*	BJ
84280	DX	*RXXB*	MA
84281	DV	*RXXB*	MA
84286	DV	*RXXC*	MA
84287	DV	*RXXC*	BJ
84289	DX	*RXXB*	HT
84290	DV	*RXXC*	BJ
84296	DV	*RXXC*	MA
84298	DV	*RXXC*	MA
84301	DV	*RXXC*	MA
84302	DV	*RXXC*	MA

Pressed Steel 30400/57-8.
84382/87, 84461/77 were renumbered from 80460-63 in 1987 and are without gangways
84322, 84404 — White band livery

84313	DX	*RXXB*	HT
84318	DV	*RXXC*	DY
84319	DV	*RXXC*	MA
84320	DX	*RXXB*	CA
84322	DX	*RXXB*	MA
84325	DX	*RXXB*	CA
84328	DV	*RXXC*	MA
84330	DV	*RXXC*	IS
84331	DV	*RXXT*	EH
84332	DV	*RXXC*	MA
84339	DX	*RXXB*	MA
84342	DV	*RXXC*	BJ
84344	DV	*RXXC*	MA
84346	DX	*RXXB*	MA
84347	DV	*RXXC*	BJ
84350	DV	*RXXC*	MA
84351	DX	*RXXB*	EC
84352	DX	*RXXB*	IS
84354	DX★	*RXXB*	CA
84356	DV	*RXXC*	MA
84361	DV	*RXXC*	BJ
84363	DX	*RXXB*	CA
84364	DV	*RXXC*	MA
84366	DV	*RXXC*	MA
84370	DX★	*RXXB*	CA
84371	DV	*RXXC*	MA
84373	DV	*RXXC*	DY
84380	DX	*RXXB*	EN
84382	BV	*RPOM*	EN
84386	DV	*RXXT*	EH
84387	BV	*RPOM*	EN
84388	DX	*RXXB*	EN
84390	DV	*RXXC*	DY
84395	DV	*RXXT*	EH
84399	DX	*RXXB*	EN
84402	DV	*RXXT*	EH
84404	DX	*RXXB*	EN
84406	DV	*RXXC*	MA
84408	DV	*RXXC*	BJ
84412	DV	*RXXT*	EH
84415	DV	*RXXT*	EH
84416	DV	*RXXT*	EH
84419	DX	*RXXB*	EN
84420	DX	*RXXB*	PC
84421	DV	*RXXT*	EH
84422	DV	*RXXT*	EH
84427	DX	*RXXB*	EN
84428	DV	*RXXC*	BJ
84430	DX	*RXXB*	EN
84433	DV	*RXXT*	EH
84434	DV	*RXXC*	BJ
84435	DV	*RXXT*	EH
84436	DV	*RXXT*	EH
84439	DV	*RXXC*	MA
84445	DX	*RXXB*	CA
84447	DV	*RXXC*	BJ
84449	DV	*RXXC*	EN
84456	DX	*RXXB*	EN
84458	DX	*RXXB*	CA
84461	BV	*RPOM*	EN
84462	DV	*RXXC*	BJ
84464	DV	*RXXT*	EH
84467	DV	*RPOM*	LL
84469	DX	*RXXB*	EN
84472	DX	*RXXB*	EN
84475	DX	*RXXB*	EN
84477	BV	*RPOM*	EN

Pressed Steel 30484/58

84499	DX	*RXXB*	LL
84501	DX	*RXXB*	MA
84510	DX	*RXXB*	EN
84512	DX	*RXXB*	EN
84515	DX	*RXXB*	EN
84519	DV	*RXXC*	MA
84531	DX	*RXXB*	EN
84543	DV	*RXXC*	MA
84547	DV	*RXXC*	EN
84552	DV	*RXXC*	BJ
84554	DV	*RXXC*	BJ
84558	DV	*RXXC*	OM

Gloucester R.C.W. 30715/62

84577	DX	*RXXB*	EC
84590	DX	*RXXB*	EN

Gloucester R.C.W. 30725/62-3

84619	DV	*RXXC*	EN

BG NE5 NH5

Gangwayed Brake. — NE501 or NH501

Introduced: 1983 by renumbering from BG series
Body: 17.24×2.82m
Weight: 32 tonnes
Brakes: Air (NEA, NHA) or Dual (NEX, NHX)
ETH Index: 1 or 1X*
Bogies: B4 or Commonwealth (92308 onwards)
Toilets: 0
Maximum speed: NE vans are maximum speed 100mph BGs refitted with B4 or Commonwealth bogies.
NH vans have B4 bogies specially maintained to run at 110mph.
Special equipment: g: Driver/Guard communication and Public address transmitter fitted.
p: Public address equipment fitted.
q: Public address transmitter fitted

Met. Cam 30136/55

92000	I EAg	*RXXM*	OY

Pressed Steel 30162/56-7

92001	I HA★g	*RXXM*	WB
92002	I EX★g	*RXXM*	WB
92003	I EX★g	*RXXM*	WB
92004	I EX★g	*RXXM*	WB
92005	I EX★g	*RXXM*	WB
92006	I HA★g	*RXXM*	WB
92007	EX★g	*RXXM*	WB
92008	I HA★g	*RXXM*	WB
92009	I EX★g	*RXXM*	MA
92010	EX★g	*RXXM*	MA
92011	I HA★g	*RXXM*	WB
92012	I EA★g	*RXXM*	WB
92013	I EX★g	*RXXM*	WB
92014	I EX★g	*RXXM*	LL
92015	I EX★q	*RXXM*	LL
92016	I EX★g	*RXXM*	LL
92017	I EX★q	*RXXM*	WB
92018	EX★q	*RXXM*	WB
92019	I EX★g	*RXXM*	WB
92020	EX★g	*RXXM*	WB
92021	EX★q	*RXXM*	WB
92022	EX★g	*RXXM*	WB

York 30173/56

92023	I EA★g	*RXXM*	WB

Cravens 30224/56

92025	I HA★g	*RXXM*	WB

Met. Cam. 30228/57-8

92026	I HA★g	*RXXM*	WB
92027	I HA★g	*RXXM*	WB
92028	I HA★g	*RXXM*	WB
92029	I HA★g	*RXXM*	WB
92031	I HA★g	*RXXM*	WB
92032	I HA★g	*RXXM*	WB
92033	I HA★g	*RXXM*	WB
92034	I HA★g	*RXXM*	WB
92035	I EA★g	*RXXM*	MA
92036	I HA★g	*RXXM*	WB
92037	I HA★g	*RXXM*	WB
92038	I HA★g	*RXXM*	WB
92039	I HA★	*RXXM*	WB

Cravens 30234/56

92040	I EA★g	*RXXM*	WB

Pressed Steel 30163/57

92041	EAq	*RXXM*	WB
92042	EAq	*RXXH*	NC
92043	EAq	*RXXM*	WB
92044	P EAq	*RXXH*	HT
92045	EAq	*RXXM*	WB
92046	I HA★g	*RXXM*	WB
92047	EAq	*RXXZ*	PC
92048	I HA★g	*RXXM*	WB
92049	EAq	*RXXZ*	PC
92050	I EAg	*RXXM*	OY
92051	EAq	*RXXM*	WB
92052	EAq	*RXXM*	WB
92053	EAq	*RXXM*	WB
92054	EAq	*RXXZ*	PC
92055	I EAg	*RXXM*	OY
92056	EAq	*RXXM*	WB
92057	I EAg	*RXXM*	WB
92058	P EAq	*RXXH*	HT
92059	EAq	*RXXM*	MA
92060	EAq	*RXXM*	MA
92061	I EA	*RXXH*	NC
92062	EAq	*RXXM*	WB
92063	I EA★g	*RXXM*	MA
92064	EAq	*RXXM*	MA
92065	EAq	*RXXM*	WB
92066	EAq	*RXXM*	WB
92067	EAq	*RXXM*	WB
92068	I EAq	*RXXZ*	PC
92069	EAq	*RXXM*	WB
92070	EAq	*RXXM*	WB
92071	EAq	*RXXM*	MA
92072	EAq	*RXXM*	WB
92073	EAq	*RXXM*	WB
92074	EAq	*RXXM*	MA
92075	I EA	*RXXM*	MA
92076	EAq	*RXXM*	EN
92077	EAq	*RXXW*	LA
92078	EAq	*RXXM*	MA
92079	EAq	*RXXM*	MA
92080	I EAq	*RXXM*	OY
92081	I EAq	*RXXM*	MA
92082	EAq	*RXXM*	EN

Pressed Steel 30323/57

92083	EAq	*RXXZ*	PC
92084	EAq	*RXXZ*	PC
92086	I EAq	*RXXH*	NC
92087	I EXg	*RXXM*	WB
92088	I EAq	*RXXH*	NC
92089	P EAq	*RXXH*	HT
92090	EAg	*RXXZ*	PC
92091	I EAq	*RXXH*	NC
92092	P EAq	*RXXH*	HT
92093	EAq	*RXXW*	LA

Pressed Steel 30400/57-8

92094	I EAq	*RXXM*	OY
92095	EAq	*RXXM*	MA
92096	EAq	*RXXM*	WB
92097	EAq	*RXXM*	WB
92098	I HA★g	*RXXM*	WB
92099	EX★g	*RXXM*	WB
92100	EAq	*RXXW*	LA
92101	EAq	*RXXM*	WB
92102	EAq	*RXXM*	WB
92103	EXq	*RXXH*	CA
92104	EAq	*RXXM*	WB
92105	EAq	*RXXZ*	PC
92106	EXq	*RXXH*	NC
92107	EXq	*RXXH*	CA
92108	I EAq	*RXXM*	OY
92109	EAq	*RXXM*	WB
92110	EX★g	*RXXH*	CA
92111	I HA★g	*RXXM*	WB
92112	EXq	*RXXH*	CA
92113	EAq	*RXXM*	MA
92114	I HAg	*RXXM*	WB
92115	EAq	*RXXM*	OY
92116	I EAg	*RXXM*	OY
92117	EXq	*RXXH*	CA
92118	I EAq	*RXXM*	WB
92119	EXq	*RXXH*	CA
92120	EX	*RXXH*	CA
92121	EXg	*RXXM*	WB
92122	EXg	*RXXM*	WB
92123	EAq	*RXXZ*	PC
92124	EX	*RXXM*	WB
92125	EAq	*RXXM*	OY
92126	I EAg	*RXXM*	OY
92127	EXg	*RXXM*	WB
92128	I EAq	*RXXH*	NC
92129	EAq	*RXXZ*	PC
92130	I EAq	*RXXZ*	PC
92131	EAq	*RXXW*	LA
92132	EAq	*RXXZ*	PC
92133	EAq	*RXXZ*	PC
92134	EAq	*RXXM*	WB
92135	I EAq	*RXXZ*	PC
92136	EAq	*RXXW*	LA
92137	P EAq	*RXXH*	HT
92138	EAq	*RXXW*	LA

92139	EAq	*RXXM*	MA
92140	EAq	*RXXM*	MA
92141	EAq	*RXXZ*	PC
92142	EAq	*RXXM*	MA
92143	EAq	*RXXZ*	PC
92144	EAq	*RXXZ*	PC
92145	EAq	*RXXM*	EN

Pressed Steel 30484/58

92146	I HA★g	*RXXM*	WB
92147	EAq	*RXXM*	MA
92148	EAq	*RXXM*	WB
92149	EX	*RXXH*	CA
92150	EXq	*RXXM*	WB
92151	I EAq	*RXXM*	OY
92152	EAq	*RXXM*	OY
92153	I EX★g	*RXXM*	WB
92154	EXq	*RXXH*	CA
92155	I EA★g	*RXXM*	WB
92156	EX★g	*RXXM*	WB
92157	EX★q	*RXXM*	WB
92158	EA	*RXXZ*	PC
92159	I HA★g	*RXXM*	WB
92160	EXq	*RXXH*	CA
92161	EAq	*RXXM*	WB
92162	EAq	*RXXM*	WB
92163	EAq	*RXXM*	MA
92164	I EAq	*RXXM*	OY
92165	EAq	*RXXM*	WB
92166	I EAq	*RXXM*	MA
92167	I HA★g	*RXXM*	WB
92168	EAq	*RXXZ*	PC
92169	EX	*RXXM*	WB
92170	EXq	*RXXM*	WB
92171	EXq	*RXXH*	CA
92172	I EAg	*RXXM*	OY
92173	EXq	*RXXH*	CA
92174	I HA★g	*RXXM*	WB
92175	I EAq	*RXXM*	OY
92176	EXq	*RXXM*	WB
92177	EAq	*RXXM*	MA

Gloucester R.C.W. 30715/62

92178	EXq	*RXXM*	WB
92179	EXq	*RXXM*	WB
92180	EAq	*RXXM*	WB
92181	EXq	*RXXM*	WB
92182	EXq	*RXXW*	OM
92183	I EA★g	*RXXM*	WB
92184	EAq	*RXXM*	WB
92185	I EAq	*RXXM*	OY

Gloucester R.C.W. 30716/62

92186	EAq	*RXXM*	OY
92187	EAq	*RXXM*	EN
92188	EAq	*RXXM*	WB
92189	EXq	*RXXM*	WB
92190	EAq	*RXXM*	WB
92191	EAq	*RXXM*	WB
92192	EXq	*RXXM*	WB
92193	I EAq	*RXXM*	OY
92194	I EAg	*RXXM*	MA
92195	EAq	*RXXM*	WB
92196	I EAq	*RXXM*	OY
92197	I EAq	*RXXM*	OY

Gloucester R.C.W. 30725/62-3

92198	EAq	*RXXM*	MA
92199	EAq	*RXXM*	WB
92200	EXq	*RXXH*	CA
92201	EXq	*RXXM*	MA
92202	I EA	*RXXM*	OY
92203	I EAg	*RXXM*	OY
92204	P EAq	*RXXH*	HT
92205	EAq	*RXXM*	WB
92206	EX	*RXXM*	WB
92207	EXq	*RXXM*	WB

The following were converted from 1983 from existing NAV's (92208-57) or from 1985 from NDV (92308-65/83) or NDX (92366-82). All are NEX and have B4 bogies (92208-57) or Commonwealth (92308-83).
92208-38 were converted at Wolverton, 92239-57 at Swindon, 92308-39 at Glasgow, 92340-65/83 at Derby Litchurch Lane and 92366-82 at Swindon.

92208	I	*RXXH*	CA
92209		*RXXH*	CA
92210		*RXXH*	CA
92211		*RXXH*	CA
92212		*RXXH*	CA
92213		*RXXH*	CA
92214		*RXXH*	CA
92215		*RXXH*	CA
92216		*RXXM*	EN
92217		*RXXM*	EN
92218		*RXXM*	EN
92219		*RXXM*	EN
92220		*RXXM*	EN
92221		*RXXM*	EN
92222		*RXXM*	EN
92223		*RXXM*	EN
92224		*RXXM*	EN
92225		*RXXM*	EN
92226		*RXXM*	EN
92227		*RXXM*	EN
92228		*RXXM*	EN
92229		*RXXM*	EN
92230		*RXXH*	CA
92231		*RXXM*	EN

No.		Code	Depot
92232		*RXXM*	EN
92233		*RXXM*	EN
92234		*RXXM*	MA
92235		*RXXM*	EN
92236	N	*RXXW*	OM
92237		*RXXM*	EN
92238		*RXXM*	MA
92239		*RXXM*	EN
92240		*RXXM*	EN
92241		*RXXM*	EN
92242		*RXXM*	EN
92243		*RXXM*	EN
92244		*RXXM*	EN
92245		*RXXM*	EN
92246		*RXXM*	EN
92247		*RXXH*	HT
92248	P	*RXXH*	HT
92249		*RXXH*	CA
92250		*RXXH*	HT
92251		*RXXH*	NC
92252		*RXXH*	CA
92253		*RXXH*	CA
92254		*RXXH*	CA
92255		*RXXH*	CA
92256		*RXXH*	CA
92257		*RXXH*	NC
92308	★	*RXXM*	MA
92309	★	*RXXM*	EN
92310		*RXXM*	MA
92311		*RXXM*	MA
92312		*RXXM*	MA
92313	★	*RXXH*	HT
92314	★	*RXXH*	CA
92315	N★	*RXXW*	OM
92316	P★	*RXXH*	CA
92317	★	*RXXH*	CA
92318	★	*RXXH*	CA
92319	N★	*RXXW*	OM
92320	★	*RXXH*	HT
92321	★	*RXXM*	EN
92322	★	*RXXM*	EN
92323	★	*RXXH*	HT
92324	N	*RXXW*	OM
92325		*RXXH*	CA
92326		*RXXH*	CA
92327	★	*RXXH*	CA
92328	★	*RXXH*	HT
92329	★	*RXXH*	CA
92330	★	*RXXH*	CA
92331		*RXXM*	MA
92332	★	*RXXH*	CA
92333	★	*RXXH*	CA
92334	★	*RXXH*	CA
92335	★	*RXXH*	CA
92336	★	*RXXM*	EN
92337	★	*RXXM*	EN
92338		*RXXM*	MA
92339		*RXXM*	EN
92340	★	*RXXW*	OM
92341		*RXXM*	MA
92342		*RXXM*	EN
92343		*RXXM*	MA
92344	★	*RXXH*	CA
92345	★	*RXXM*	EN
92346		*RXXH*	CA
92347		*RXXH*	CA
92348	★	*RXXH*	CA
92349		*RXXM*	MA
92350	★	*RXXH*	CA
92351		*RXXH*	CA
92352		*RXXM*	MA
92353		*RXXH*	HT
92354		*RXXW*	OM
92355		*RXXH*	CA
92356		*RXXM*	MA
92357		*RXXM*	MA
92358		*RXXM*	MA
92359		*RXXM*	MA
92360		*RXXH*	CA
92361		*RXXH*	CA
92362		*RXXM*	MA
92363		*RXXM*	MA
92364	★	*RXXH*	CA
92365		*RXXM*	MA
92366		*RXXH*	HT
92367	q★	*RXXH*	CA
92368		*RXXH*	CA
92369	★	*RXXH*	CA
92370		*RXXH*	CA
92371	★	*RXXH*	CA
92372		*RXXH*	CA
92373		*RXXH*	CA
92374		*RXXH*	CA
92375		*RXXH*	CA
92376		*RXXH*	CA
92377	★	*RXXH*	HT
92378		*RXXH*	CA
92379	★	*RXXH*	HT
92380	★	*RXXH*	CA
92381		*RXXH*	CA
92382		*RXXH*	CA
92383		*RXXH*	CA

GUV — NK5, NJ5, NX5

General Utility Van — NK501, NJ501 or nX501

Introduced: 1956
Body: 18.50×27.00m
Weight: 30 tonnes
Brakes: Vacuum
Bogies: B2 (B1 and B5 as indicated)
Toilets: 0
Maximum speed: 90mph (B5: 100mph)
Standard equipment: Screw coupled

The details above are the 'standard' vehicle which is also fitted with hinged beams for Brute traffic. Deviations from these details are noted, as are the two type variants recognised by TOPS codes:

NJ501 are Electrically wired and Steam piped (now unused. 93706 is Electrically wired only) and have hinged beams: **ETH Index:** 0 or 0X★

NX501 are reserved for Motorail traffic

NL501 and **NM501**, **502** are Newspaper Packing Vans now renumbered 94001 upwards (qv)

Blue and grey livery: 93159, 93349, 93475/95, 93635/56/63/65.

Pressed Steel 30417/58-9

93078	KV	*RXXD*	MA	93191	KV	*RXXD*	DY	93300	KV	*RXXD*	MA
93079	KV	*RXXD*	HT	93192	JX	*RXXE*	CA	93301	KV	*RXXD*	BJ
93081	JX	*RXXE*	MA	93193	KV	*RXXD*	CA	93304	KV	*RXXD*	CA
93084	JX	*RXXE*	MA	93195	JV★	*RXXD*	CF	93306	KV	*RXXD*	CA
93086	KV	*RXXD*	HT	93205	JX	*RPOC*	PY	93307	KV	*RXXD*	CA
93090	KV	*RXXD*	CA	93207	JV★B1	*RXXD*	BJ	93308	KV	*RXXD*	CA
93091	JX	*RXXE*	MA	93210	JX	*RPOC*	PY	93319	KV	*RXXD*	CA
93093	KV	*RXXD*	MA	93212	JX	*RPOC*	PY	93321	KV	*RXXD*	CA
93100	KV	*RXXD*	MA	93214	KV	*RXXD*	CA	93323	JX★	*RXXE*	DY
93104	JX★B1	*RPOC*	PY	93217	KV	*RXXD*	CA	93325	KV	*RXXD*	BJ
93105	KV	*RXXD*	DY	93234	KV	*RXXD*	DY	93329	KV	*RXXD*	CA
93107	KV	*RRSP*	MA	93235	JX	*RPOC*	PY	93330	KV	*RXXD*	CA
93110	JX	*RPOC*	PY	93236	JV★	*RXXD*	BJ	93336	KV	*RXXD*	CA
93112	JX★B1	*RXXE*	CA	93239	KV	*RXXD*	CA	93338	KV	*RXXD*	CA
93115	KV	*RXXD*	MA	93241	KV	*RXXD*	CA	93339	KV	*RXXD*	CA
93117	KV	*RXXD*	MA	93242	KV	*RXXD*	CA	93343	KV	*RXXD*	CA
93122	JX	*RPOC*	PY	93249	JX	*RXXE*	OM	93345	JV★	*RXXD*	OM
93126	JX	*RPOC*	PY	93251	JV★B1	*RXXD*	BJ	93347	JX	*RPOC*	PY
93131	JV★	*RXXD*	CF	93253	KV	*RXXD*	BJ	93348	KV	*RXXD*	CA
93134	JX	*RPOC*	PY	93255	JX★B1	*RXXE*	OM	93349	JV★	*RXXD*	OM
93135	JV★B1	*RXXD*	BJ	93257	KV	*RXXD*	MA	93353	JX	*RPOC*	PY
93138	KV	*RXXD*	HT	93258	JV★B1	*RXXD*	BJ	93356	KV	*RXXD*	BJ
93140	KV	*RXXD*	CA	93262	JX	*RPOC*	PY	93359	KV	*RXXD*	DY
93141	JX	*RPOC*	PY	93263	JX	*RPOC*	PY	93362	JX	*RPOC*	PY
93142	JX	*RXXE*	OM	93265	JX	*RPOC*	PY	93367	JV★ B1	*RXXD*	MA
93143	JX	*RPOC*	PY	93267	JV★B1	*RXXD*	CF	93370	JV★ B1	*RXXD*	OM
93148	KV	*RXXD*	CA	93269	JX	*RXXE*	OM	93374	KV	*RXXD*	MA
93160	JX	*RPOC*	PY	93272	KV	*RXXD*	BJ	93375	JV★ B1	*RXXD*	CF
93163	JV★B1	*RXXD*	BJ	93273	JV★	*RXXD*	BJ	93376	JX	*RPOC*	PY
93165	JX	*RPOC*	PY	93277	JX★B1	*RPOC*	PY	93379	JV★ B1	*RXXD*	CF
93166	JX	*RXXE*	OM	93278	JV★B1	*RXXD*	CF	93385	XX★ B5	*IWC*	EN
93167	JX	*RPOC*	PY	93284	JV★B1	*RXXD*	OM	93386	KV	*RXXD*	MA
93172	JX	*RPOC*	PY	93287	KV	*RXXD*	MA	93388	JV★ B1	*RXXD*	CF
93174	JX	*RPOC*	PY	93291	KV	*RXXD*	DY	93390	KV	*RXXD*	MA
93176	JV★B1	*RXXD*	BJ	93292	JV★B1	*RXXD*	OM	93391	KV	*RXXD*	DY
93180	KV	*RXXD*	HT	93293	JX	*RPOC*	PY	93393	JX	*RXXE*	OM
93185	JV★B1	*RXXD*	BJ	93295	KV	*RXXD*	BJ	93394	JV★ B1	*RXXD*	MA
93187	KV	*RXXD*	CA	93298	KV	*RXXD*	BJ	93395	JX	*RXXE*	OM

93396	JX	RPOC	PY
93398	KV	RXXD	DY
93401	JV★ B1	RXXD	OM
93406	KV	RXXD	BJ
93407	JX	RXXE	DY
93411	JX	RXXE	DY
93412	KV	RXXD	BJ
93413	KV	RXXD	BJ
93416	JX	RXXE	NC
93417	KV	RXXD	DY
93419	JV★ B1	RXXD	BJ
93421	KV	RXXD	MA
93426	JX	RXXE	DY
93429	JX	RXXE	OM
93431	JV★ B1	RXXD	BJ
93446	JV★	RXXD	BJ
93450	JV★	RXXD	BJ
93455	KV	RXXD	HT
93458	KV	RXXD	BJ
93459	KV	RXXD	HT
93462	JX★ B1	RPOC	PY
93463	KV	RXXD	HT
93464	KV	RXXD	HT
93465	KV	RXXD	HT
93468	JX★ B1	RXXE	DY
93472	KV	RXXD	BJ
93474	JV★	RXXD	BJ
93475	KV	RXXD	BJ
93476	KV	RXXD	MA
93478	JV★ B1	RXXD	OM
93479	KV	RXXD	DY
93482	KV	RXXD	HT
93485	JX	RXXE	DY
93490	JV★ B1	RXXD	CF
93495	JV★	RXXD	OM
93498	KV	RXXD	MA
93499	JX	RPOC	PY

Doncaster 30343/57

93502	KV	RXXD	MA
93504	KV	RXXD	MA
93506	KV	RXXD	MA
93508	JV★ B1	RXXD	OM
93511	JV★ B1	RXXD	CF
93512	KV	RXXD	CF
93514	JV★ B1	RXXD	DY
93515	JV★	RXXD	CF
93516	KV	RXXD	CF
93518	JX	RXXE	OM
93519	KV	RRSP	MA

York/St. Rollox 30402/58-60

93521	JX	RXXE	DY
93523	JX★BI	RPOC	PY
93525	JV★BI	RXXD	MA
93529	JV★BI	RXXD	DY
93533	KV	RXXD	DY
93534	JX★BI	RPOC	PY
93536	JV★	RXXD	CF
93538	KV	RXXD	DY
93539	JX★BI	RPOC	PY
93541	JV★BI	RXXD	DY
93542	KV	RXXD	HT
93546	KV	RXXD	MA
93549	KV	RXXD	DY
93550	KV	RXXD	MA
93554	KV	RRSP	MA
93556	JV★BI	RXXD	CF
93557	JV★BI	RXXD	MA
93560	JX	RXXE	EN
93562	JV★BI	RXXD	MA
93563	JV★BI	RXXD	CF
93571	JX	RPOC	PY
93573	KV	RXXD	HT
93576	JX★BI	RXXE	NC
93578	JX★BI	RXXE	OM
93579	KV	RXXD	MA
93581	JX★BI	RXXE	NC
93585	JV★BI	RXXD	DY
93590	JX	RXXE	NC
93595	KV	RRSP	MA
93596	JV★BI	RXXD	OM
93600	JX	RXXE	OM
93601	KV	RXXD	MA
93604	JX	RXXE	OM
93606	JX	RPOC	PY
93607	JX	RPOC	PY
93610	JX	RPOC	PY
93617	KV	RXXD	MA
93618	KV	RXXD	MA
93622	JV★BI	RXXD	CF
93623	KV	RXXD	DY
93624	JV★BI	RXXD	CF
93630	JV★BI	RXXD	CF
93631	JV★BI	RXXD	CF
93633	JV★BI	RXXD	CF
93634	KV	RXXD	DY
93635	KV	RXXD	HT
93640	KV	RXXD	CF
93643	JV★	RXXD	OM
93644	KV	RXXD	CF
93647	KV	IWC	EN
93648	JXBI	RXXE	EN
93652	KV	RXXD	CF

Pressed Steel 30565/59.

93656	JV★	RXXD	OM
93660	JV★	RXXD	OM
93663	KV	RXXD	HT
93664	KV	RXXD	HT
93667	KV	RXXD	CF
93668	JX★BI	RXXE	OM
93673	JX	RXXE	OM
93675	JX	RXXE	OM
93677	JV★BI	RXXD	CF
93680	KV	RXXD	MA
93681	KV	RRSP	MA
93683	JV★BI	RXXD	DY
93684	KV	RXXD	CF
93687	KV	RXXD	CF
93692	JX★BI	RXXE	OM
93694	JX	NSS	EH
93696	KV	RXXD	HT
93701	JV★BI	RXXD	MA
93706	JV	RXXD	MA
93710	JV	RXXD	CF
93711	JV	RXXD	CF

93713	JV	*RXXD*	CF
93714	JV	*RXXD*	CF
93715	JV	*RXXD*	CF
93717	JV	*RXXD*	CF
93720	JV	*RXXD*	CF
93722	JV	*RXXD*	CF
93723	JV	*RXXD*	CF
93725	JV	*RXXD*	BJ
93726	JV	*RXXD*	BJ
93727	JV	*RXXD*	BJ
93728	JV	*RXXD*	BJ
93756	KV	*IWC*	EN
93762	JX★	*RPOC*	PY
93764	JX★	*RXXE*	EN
93765	KV	*RXXD*	MA
93767	KV	*RXXD*	HT
93769	KV	*RXXD*	HT
93775	JX★	*RPOC*	PY
93776	KV	*RXXD*	HT
93778	KV	*RXXD*	MA
93779	KV	*RXXD*	CF
93781	KV	*RXXD*	CA
93782	KV	*IWC*	EN
93784	KV	*RXXD*	MA
93788	KV	*RXXD*	CA
93791	KV	*RXXD*	CA
93792	KV	*RXXD*	MA
93793	KV	*RXXD*	CA
93795	KV	*RXXD*	CA
93798	JX★	*RPOC*	PY
93800	KV	*RXXD*	CA
93801	KV	*RXXD*	MA
93807	KV	*RXXD*	HT
93811	KV	*RXXD*	CF
93815	KV	*RXXD*	MA
93820	JX★	*RPOC*	PY
93822	KV	*RXXD*	CF
93823	JV	*RXXD*	MA
93824	KV	*RXXD*	MA
93829	KV	*RXXD*	MA
93830	JV★	*RXXD*	BJ
93834	KV	*RXXD*	MA

Pressed Steel 30616/59-60

93836	JX	*RPOC*	PY
93843	KV	*RXXD*	MA
93844	JX	*RXXE*	MA
93846	KV	*RXXD*	MA
93847	JV★BI	*RXXD*	BJ
93849	JV★BI	*RXXD*	BJ
93851	KV	*RXXD*	CA
93852	JX★BI	*NSS*	EH
93853	KV	*RXXD*	CA
93854	JV★BI	*RXXD*	BJ
93855	JV★BI	*RXXD*	MA
93857	JV★BI	*RXXD*	BJ
93858	KV	*RXXD*	DY
93859	JV★BI	*RXXD*	MA
93860	JXBI	*RXXE*	MA
93863	KV	*RXXD*	MA
93864	JX	*RXXE*	MA
93875	KV	*RXXD*	MA
93877	KV	*RXXD*	MA
93880	KV	*IWC*	EN
93881	JV★BI	*RXXD*	BJ
93883	KV	*RXXD*	MA
93886	JV★BI	*RXXD*	CA
93887	JV★BI	*RXXD*	BJ
93888	KV	*RXXD*	MA
93889	JV★BI	*RXXD*	MA
93893	JV★BI	*RXXD*	BJ
93896	KV	*RXXD*	MA
93897	JX★BI	*RXXE*	MA
93901	KV	*RXXD*	MA
93904	KV	*RXXD*	MA
93905	JV★BI	*RXXD*	BJ
93907	KV	*RXXD*	MA
93910	KV	*RXXD*	MA
93911	JV★BI	*RXXD*	BJ
93914	JX★BI	*RXXE*	EN
93915	JV★BI	*RXXD*	CA
93919	KV	*RXXD*	MA
93922	KV	*RXXD*	DY
93925	KV	*RXXD*	CA
93927	KV	*RXXD*	DY
93930	KV	*RXXD*	MA
93931	KV	*RXXD*	MA
93932	KV	*RXXD*	MA
93933	KV	*RXXD*	MA
93935	JV★BI	*RXXD*	MA
93937	KV	*RXXD*	MA
93941	KV	*RXXD*	MA
93942	JX★BI	*RXXE*	MA
93943	KV	*RXXD*	DY
93944	KV	*RXXD*	MA
93948	KV	*RXXD*	MA
93950	JV★BI	*RXXD*	MA
93952	JV★BI	*RXXD*	MA
93955	JV★	*RXXD*	OM
93956	JX★BI	*RXXE*	NC
93957	KV	*RXXD*	MA
93962	JV★BI	*RXXD*	CA
93969	JX	*RXXE*	EN
93973	JV★BI	*RXXD*	BJ
93976	KV	*RXXD*	MA
93978	KV	*RXXD*	MA
93979	JV★BI	*RXXD*	BJ
93980	KV	*RXXD*	MA
93982	JV★BI	*RXXD*	MA

PVG NL5

Gangwayed Newspaper Packing Van. — NL501

Introduced: 1977 by conversion from GUV
Body: 18.50×2.70m
Weight: 34.5 tonnes
Brakes: Dual
ETH Index: 3X

Bogies: B5 (Roller-bearing fitted B1 bogies as marked)
Toilets: 1
Maximum speed: 100mph (B1 bogies: 90mph)
Standard equipment: Fluorescent lighting

Doncaster or Wolverton (94001-7/19/20) 30922/77-8

No.	Bogies	Livery	Depot
94001	BI	*RNPW*	BJ
94002		*RNPW*	OM
94003		*RNPW*	OM
94004		*RNPM*	WB
94005		*RNPW*	OM
94006		*RNPW*	OM
94007		*RNPW*	OM
94008		*RNPW*	OM
94009		*RNPW*	OM
94010	BI	*RNPW*	OM
94011		*RNPW*	OM
94012		*RNPW*	OM
94013		*RNPE*	HT
94015		*RNPM*	MA
94016		*RNPM*	MA
94017		*RNPM*	MA
94018		*RNPE*	HT
94019		*RNPM*	MA
94020		*RNPM*	WB
94021		*RNPW*	OM
94022		*RNPE*	HT
94023		*RNPM*	MA
94024		*RNPM*	MA
94025		*RNPM*	MA
94026		*RNPM*	MA
94027	BI	*RNPM*	WB
94028	BI	*RNPW*	BJ
94029		*RNPW*	OM
94030		*RNPW*	OM
94031		*RNPW*	OM
94032		*RNPW*	OM
94033		*RNPW*	OM
94034		*RNPW*	OM

PVG NM5

Non-Gangwayed Newspaper Packing Vans NM501 (94051-56) or NM502

Introduced: 1985 by renumbering from GUV
Body: 18.50×2.70m
Weight: 30 tonnes
Brakes: Vacuum
ETH Index: 3X (94051/52/53/56 are 3S)

Bogies: B2
Toilets: 0
Maximum speed: 90mph
Standard equipment: Fluorescent lighting.

No.	Livery	Depot
94050	*RNPE*	CA
94051	*RNPE*	CA
94052	*RNPE*	CA
94053	*RNPE*	CA
94056	*RNPE*	CA
94057	*RNPE*	CA
94058	*RNPE*	CA
94061	*RNPE*	CA
94062	*RNPE*	CA
94068	*RNPM*	DY
94071	*RNPM*	DY
94075	*RNPM*	DY
94076	*RNPM*	DY
94077	*RNPM*	MA
94078	*RNPM*	MA

Newspaper Van NC5

Gangwayed Newspaper Packing Van — NC501

Introduced: 1985 by renumbering from BG series
Body: 18.50×2.82m
Weight: 32-35 tonnes
Brakes: Dual
ETH Indices: 1:95212/14/17
1X: 95200/02/03/05/08/15/18/20
3: 95209/10/19/22
3X: 95204/07/13
3S: 95201/06/11/16/21/23

Bogies: Commonwealth
Toilets: 0
Maximum speed: 100mph
Standard equipment: Fluorescent lighting
Converted at York

95200	*RNPE*	CA
95201	*RNPS*	EH
95202	*RNPE*	CA
95203	*RNPE*	CA
95204	*RNPM*	EN
95205	*RNPW*	OM
95206	*RNPS*	EH
95207	*RNPW*	OM
95208	*RNPW*	OM
95209	*RNPM*	EN
95210	*RNPE*	CA
95211	*RNPS*	EH
95212	*RNPM*	EN
95213	*RNPE*	CA
95214	*RNPM*	EN
95215	*RNPW*	OM
95216	*RNPS*	EH
95217	*RNPM*	EN
95218	*RNPW*	OM
95219	*RNPM*	EN
~~95220~~	*RNPW*	OM
95221	*RNPS*	EH
95222	*RNPW*	OM
95223	*RNPS*	EH

Newspaper Van NC5

Gangwayed Newspaper Van — NC501

Introduced: 1987 by renumbering from BG series
Body: 18.50×2.82m
Weight: 32 tonnes
Brakes: Vacuum
ETH Indices: 3X (3: 95300/02/05/06/10/15/23/25/26/31/33/38/39, 3S: 95304, 1: 95307)
Bogies: Commonwealth
Toilets: 0

Maximum speed: 100mph
Standard equipment: Fluorescent lights fitted except to 95300/02/04/07/08/15/27/37/40/42.
Special features: 95306 has 3 roller shutter doors.
Those vehicles with allocations are in stock, the others remain in general BG series awaiting fitting with Commonwealth bogies and renumbering.

Number	Code	Depot
95300	*RNPM*	MA
95301		
95302		
95303	*RNPM*	MA
95304	*RNPS*	EH
95305	*RNPE*	HT
95306		
95307	*RNPE*	HT
95308	*RNPE*	HT
95309		
95310	*RNPS*	EH
95311		
95312	*RNPE*	HT
95313		
95314		
95315		
95316		
95317		
95318		
95319		
95320		
95321	*RNPM*	MA
95322		
95323		
95324		
95325		
95326		
95327		
95328		
95329	*RNPE*	HT
95330		
95331		
95332	*RNPM*	MA
95333		
95334		
95335		
95336		
95337		
95338		
95339		
95340		
95341		
95342		

Motorail Van NX5

General Utility Van — NX501

Introduced: 1987 by renumbering from GUV series
Body: 18.50×2.82m
Weight: 30 tonnes
Brakes: Air or Dual (x)
Bogies: Commonwealth (B2, B5 or SR as marked)
Toilets: 0

Maximum speed: 100mph (90mph B2 or SR)
Livery: I: InterCity. B: Blue and grey. Others Rail Blue

96160 awaits renumbering from the GUV series.

Number	Notes	Code	Depot
96100	B5	*IWC*	EN
96101	B5	*IWC*	EN
96102	B5	*IWC*	EN
96103	B5	*IWC*	EN
96104	B5	*IWC*	EN
96110		*IWC*	EN
96111		*IWC*	EN
96112		*IWC*	EN
96130	BB2	*IWC*	EN
96131		*IWC*	EN
96132	I	*IWC*	EN
96133	B	*IWC*	EN
96134	B	*IWC*	EN
96135	I	*IWC*	EN
96136	I	*IWC*	EN
96137	SR	*IWC*	EN
96138		*ICC*	EC
96139	SR	*ICC*	EC
96140		*ICC*	EC
96141		*ICC*	EC
96150	xB5	*IWC*	EN
96151	BxB5	*IWC*	EN
96152	BxB5	*IWC*	EN
96153	BxB5	*IWC*	EN
96154	BxB5	*IWC*	EN
96155	BxB5	*IWC*	EN
96156	BxB5	*IWC*	EN
96157	xB5	*IWC*	EN
96158	xB5	*IWC*	EN
96159	BxB5	*IWC*	EN
96160	xB5		
96161	xBS	*IWC*	EN
96170	Bx	*IWC*	EN
96171	Bx	*IWC*	EN
96172	Bx	*IWC*	EN
96173	x	*IWC*	EN
96174	x	*IWC*	EN
96175	Bx	*IWC*	EN
96176	Bx	*IWC*	EN
96185	Bx	*IWR*	OM
96186	x	*IWR*	OM
96187	x	*IWC*	EN
96188	Ix	*IWC*	EN
96189	IxB2	*IWC*	EN
96190	Ix	*IWR*	OM
96191	Bx	*IWC*	EN
96192	Ix	*IWC*	EN
96193	x	*IWC*	EN
96194	x	*IWC*	EN
96195	x	*IWC*	EN

Carflat NG5

Carflat. — NG501 (96259-62) or NG502

Introduced: 1985 by transfer from freight stock
Dimensions: 20.37×2.60m
Weight: 21 tonnes
Brakes: Vacuum
Bogies: B1

Toilets: 0
Maximum speed: 90mph
Notes: Converted from Mk 1 Coach underframes
Freight series lot numbers 3679/68-69 or 3757/71 (96258-62)
Carrying capacity 10 tonnes

96250	*ICH*	EN	96256	*ICH*	EN	96262	*ICH*	EN
96251	*ICH*	EN	96257	*ICH*	EN	96263	*ICH*	EN
96252	*ICH*	EN	96258	*ICH*	EN	96264	*ICH*	EN
96253	*ICH*	EN	96259	*ICH*	EN	96265	*ICH*	EN
96254	*ICH*	EN	96260	*ICH*	EN			
96255	*ICH*	EN	96261	*ICH*	EN			

The International Train

BREL unveiled its Demonstration train of vehicles based on the BR Mk 3 body during September 1986. It is aimed at the export market.

Since ownership remains with BREL, Private Owner series numbers have been issued.

All vehicles measure 22.57×2.74m and are carried on BT10 series bogies passed to run at 110mph. Full air conditioning and air brakes are fitted. PT is fitted to 99520 and PA to the rest.

Vehicles maintained at BREL Carriage Works, Litchurch Lane, Derby.

Other details are as follows:

No	Type	Seats 1st	Seats 2nd	Seats U/c	Toilets	Weight tonnes	ETH index	Design code	Notes
99520	BFK	20	—	—	1	37.5	5X	A01.27.0A	Includes 6-seat lounge
99521	FO	54	—	—	2	38.5	6X	A01.28.0A	
99522	FO	54	—	—	2	38.5	6X	A01.28.0B	
99523	RUM	—	—	24	—	39.5	15X	A04.21.0A	
99524	TSO	—	76	—	2	38.5	5X	A02.38.0A	2 saloons with videos
99525	TSO	—	76	—	2	38.5	6X	A02.38.1B	Vending machine fitted
99526	TSO	—	76	—	2	38.5	5X	A02.38.2C	
99527	TSO	—	76	—	2	38.5	5X	A02.38.2C	
99528	TSO	—	76	—	2	38.5	5X	A02.38.2A	
99529	TSO	—	76	—	2	38.5	5X	A02.38.2A	

99524-29 have various seating layouts
The original demonstration coach has now been allocated No 99519, but no further details are available.

Exhibition Van NY5

Introduced: 1970 by converting Mk 1 stock
Body: 20.45×2.82m
Weight: 34 tonnes, except, 99630 (34.5 tonnes), 99641/42 (36 tonnes), 99632/33/43/44/54-59 (33.5 tonnes), 99648 (15 tonnes) or 99649/50 (32 tonnes)
All allocated to SA, all sector *ICH*

Brakes: See lists
Heating: All except 99648 (unheated) now electric from shore supply.
Bogies: See lists
Toilets: 0, except 99602 (8)

Number	Former number	Original lot	Conv	Brakes	Bogies	Design code
99601	34577	Wolverton 30095/55	1970	VB	B2	NY503
99602	21145	Roberts 30187/55	1972	VB	B2	NY502
99620	34692	Wolverton 30156/55	1975	DB	SR Mk IV	NY503
99621	34697	Wolverton 30156/55	1972	DB	SR Mk IV	NY503
99622	34584	Wolverton 30095/53	1972	VBAP	SR Mk IV	NY503
99623	34700	Wolverton 30156/55	1972	DB	B2	NY503
99624	34084	Derby 30003/52	1972	VBAP	SR Mk IV	NY503
99625	34693	Wolverton 30156/55	1973	DB	SR Mk IV	NY503
99629	25972	Derby 30686/62	1979	DB	SR Mk IV	NY515
99630	34695	Wolverton 30156/55	1979	DB	SR Mk IV	NY504
99631	1018	Wolverton 30647/61	1979	DB	CW	NY517
99632	4329	BRCW 30207/56	1981	VB	B1	NY522
99633	3827	Afd/Elh 30054/53	1981	VB	B1	NY522
99634	25317	Wolverton 30349/57	1981	VB	B1	NY520
99635	25637	Wolverton 30426/58	1981	VB	B1	NY520
99636	25646	Wolverton 30426/58	1981	VB	B1	NY526
99637	15854	Met Cam 30221/56	1981	VB	B1	NY521

All allocated to SA, all sector *ICH*

Number	Former number	Original lot	Conv	Brakes	Bogies	Design code
99641	1036	Wolverton 30647/61	1980	ABVP	CW	NY517
99642	1040	Wolverton 30647/61	1980	ABVP	CW	NY517
99643	4272	BRCW 30207/56	1981	VB	B1	NY522
99644	3852	York 30080/53	1981	VB	B1	NY522
99645	1765	Psd Steel 30636/61	1981	VB	CW	NY523
99646	1766	Psd Steel 30636/61	1981	VB	CW	NY523
99647	34629	GRCW 30142/55	1981	VB	B1	NY504
99648	B787017	Psd Steel 3413/63	1981	DB	4 whl	NY525

Number	Former number	Original lot	Conv	Brakes	Bogies	Design code
99649	80502	Derby 30009/52	1981	VB	B2	NY524
99650	80830	Cravens 30144/55	1983	VB	B2	NY524
99657	4569	York 30243/56	1986	VB	B1	NY522
99658	4592	York 30243/56	1986	VB	B1	NY522
99659	4518	York 30243/56	1986	VB	B1	NY522
99661	80510	Derby 30009/53	1986	VB	B1	NY524

99657/58/59 are in GW chocolate and cream livery and were transferred from Departmental stock where they were numbered ADB977217/18/16.
99602 is a toilet vehicle with eight cubicles. 99621-25 are Continental vehicles and 99625 is gangwayed at one end only.
99648 is a 20-tonne Ferry Van which also carried the International number 21 70 21 40 144-3.
The vans converted in 1981 were not officially taken into stock until 1983.

Public address is fitted to 99601/23.
New lot numbers were issued for 99601/02 (Swindon 30841/72-73), 99620-25 (Swindon 30842/72-75), 99629/30/31 (Stewarts Lane 30950/51/52 respectively, 1979) and 99641/42 (Stewarts Lane 30971/80).
Tungsten lighting except 99601/02/21-24/41/42 fluorescent and 99648 unlit.

Preserved Private Owner Operational

The stock listed here is currently authorised to operate in service on BR lines.

Prefix	Number	Identity	Year	Type	Company	Brake	Heating	Seats	Design code
PWDS	99030	34666	1955	BSK	BR	VB	DH	32S	A0231
MRC	99040		1960	BCK	BR	VB	DH	12F18S	A0311
MCA	99052	41	1892	Saloon	CR	VB	SH	21F	A0102
Operated by THR									
MCA	99053	9004	1930	Saloon	GW	VB	SH	25F	A0103
STRM	99054	24287, 9195	1938	RB	LNER	VB	SH	30U	A0402
MCA	99056	34612	1955	BSK	BR	VB	SH	24S	A0202
STRM	99064	45005	1942	Royal Sal	LMS	DB	SH	5F	A0115
SNG	99080	21096	1956	BCK	BR	VB	SH	12F, 18S	A0311
PES	99090	35131	1958	BSK	BR	VB	DH	32S	A0231
SGST	99103	80972	1949	Saloon	GW	VB	SH	20F	A0119
SGST	99106	9001	1940	Saloon	GW	VB	SH	20F	A0125
SGST	99108	17018	1961	BFK	BR	DB	DH	24F	A01
PULR	99120	21236	1961	BCK	BR	VB	DH	12F, 18S	A03
PULR	99121	3105/121	1962	FO	BR	VB	DH	42F	A0120
PULR	99122	3106/122	1962	FO	BR	VB	DH	42F	A0122
PULR	99123	3109/123	1962	FO	BR	VB	DH	42F	A0122
PULR	99124	3110/124	1962	FO	BR	VB	DH	42F	A0122

Prefix	Number	Identity	Year	Type	Company	Brake	Heating	Seats	Design code
PULR	99125	3113/125	1962	FO	BR	VB	DH	42F	A0122
PULR	99126	3116/126	1962	FO	BR	VB	DH	42F	A0122
PULR	99127	3117/127	1962	FO	BR	VB	DH	42F	A0122
PULR	99128	3130/128	1962	FO	BR	VB	DH	42F	A0122
PULR	99129	21272/129	1964	BCK	BR	VB	DH	12F, 24S	A03
PULR	99130	17013/130	1964	BFK	BR	VB	DH	24F	A01
PULR	99131	1999/131	1945	Saloon	LNER	DB	EH	12F	A0133

99121-28 are named *Julia, Helen, Grace, Frances, Eileen, Diane, Carol* and *Beryl* respectively. 99131 was TDE 902260

Prefix	Number	Identity	Year	Type	Company	Brake	Heating	Seats	Design code
SVR	99240	6913	1934	BCK	GW	VB	SH	12F, 32S	A0313
PWDS	99304	21256	1963	BCK	BR	VB	SH	12F18S	A0311
SLOA	99335	335	1960	PKS	BR (Pullman)	VB	DH(PHV)	30F	A0121
SLOA	99347	347	1960	PPS	BR (Pullman)	VB	DH(PHV)	42F	A0120
SLOA	99348	348	1960	PPS	BR (Pullman)	VB	DH(PHV)	42F	A0120
SLOA	99349	349	1960	PPS	BR (Pullman)	VB	DH(PHV)	42F	A0120
SLOA	99350	350	1960	PPS	BR (Pullman)	VB	DH(PHV)	42F	A0120
SLOA	99351	351	1960	PPS	BR (Pullman)	VB	DH(PHV)	42F	A0120
SLOA	99352	352	1960	PPS	BR (Pullman)	VB	DH(PHV)	42F	A0120
SLOA	99353	353	1960	PPS	BR (Pullman)	VB	DH(PHV)	42F	A0120
SLOA	99354	354 *Hadrian Bar*	1960	BAR	BR (Pullman)	VB	DH(PHV)	24S	A0130
SLOA	99355	21249/355	1962	BCK	BR	VB	DH	12F, 18S	A0311
SLOA	99356	21245/356	1962	BCK	BR	VB	DH	12F, 18S	A0311
SLOA	99357	3112/357	1962	FO	BR	VB	DH	42F	A0122
PULR	99358	3108/358	1962	FO	BR	VB	DH	42F	A0122
VSOE	99530	*Perseus* (301)	1951	PFP	Pullman	AB	EH	26F	A0414
VSOE	99531	*Phoenix* (302)	1952	PFP	Pullman	AB	EH	26F	A0415
VSOE	99532	*Cygnus* (308)	1951	PFP	Pullman	AB	EH	26F	A0414
VSOE	99533	70741, 7	1943	BG	LNER	AB	EH	—	A0504
VSOE	99534	*Ibis* (245)	1928	PFK	Pullman	AB	EH	20F	A0417
VSOE	99535	*Minerva* (213)	1928	PFB	Pullman	AB	EH	26F	A0418
VSOE	99536	*Zena* (254)	1929	PFP	Pullman	AB	EH	24F	A0419
VSOE	99537	*Audrey* (280)	1932	PFK	Pullman	AB	EH	20F	A0420
VSOE	99538	34991, 9	1957	BSK (BG)	BR	AB	EH	—	A0231
VSOE	99539	*Ione* (243)	1929	PFK	Pullman	AB	EH	20F	A0416
VSOE	99540	3069, 1	1955	FO	BR	AB	EH	42F	A0122
VSOE	99541	*Lucille* (243)	1928	PFP	Pullman	AB	EH	24F	A0419
TRTS	99710	18767	1961	SK	BR	VB	DH	48S	A0237
TRTS	99711	18857	1961	SK	BR	VB	DH	48S	A0237
TRTS	99712	18893	1962	SK	BR	VB	DH	48S	A0237
TRTS	99713	19013	1962	SK	BR	VB	DH	48S	A0237
TRTS	99714	7187	1961	CK	BR	VB	DH	24F, 18S	A0309
TRTS	99715	35337	1962	BSK	BR	VB	DH	24S	A0228
TRTS	99716	18808	1961	SK	BR	VB	DH	48S	A0237
TRTS	99717	18837	1961	SK	BR	VB	DH	48S	A0237

Private Owner

Prefix	Number	Identity	Year	Type	Company	Brake	Heating	Seats	Design code
TRTS	99718	18862	1961	SK	BR	VB	DH	48S	A0237
TRTS	99719	7191	1961	CK	BR	VB	DH	24F, 18S	A0309
TRTS	99720	35461	1963	BSK	BR	VB	DH	24S	A0228
MNLP	99781	21034	see entry in Capital stock						
MNLP	99782	17007	see entry in Capital stock						
COWS	99792	17019	1961	BFK	BR	VB	DH	24F	A0134
SCR	99808	27389	1947	TO	LMS	VB	DH	56S	A0227
SCR	99810	4215	1956	TSO	BR	VB	SH	64S	A0232
SCR	99813	4224	1954	TSO	BR	VB	SH	64S	A0235
SCR	99818	1730	1960	RBR	BR	DB	DH	23U	A0422
NRMY	99950	35362	1962	BSK	BR	VB	SH	24S	A0228
THR	99880	5159	1891	Saloon	LNWR	VB	SH	12F	A0131
THR	99881	807	1912	Saloon	GNR	VB	SH	19F	A0132
THR	99882	19169, 10000	1963	FK (ex-SK)	BR	VB	SH	8F	A0129
THR	99883	2108	1960	SLF	BR	VB	SH	10F	A0130
THR	99884	19208	1963	FK (ex-SK)	BR	VB	SH	6F	A0129
THR	99885	2110	1960	SLF	BR	VB	SH	8F	A0130
THR	99886	35407	1963	BG (ex-BSK)	BR	VB	SH	—	A0507
THR	99887	2127	1961	SLF	BR	VB	DH(PHV)	11F	A0123

COWS — City of Wells, Society
MCA — William McAlpine, c/o Steamtown, Carnforth
MNLP — Merchant Navy Locomotive Preservation Society, c/o Bulmer Railway Centre
MRC — Midland Railway Centre, Butterley
NRMY — National Railway Museum, York
PES — Princess Elizabeth Society
PULR — Pullman Rail, c/o Steamtown, Carnforth (maintained at Bounds Green)
SCR — Scottish Railway Preservation Society, Falkirk
SGST — Standard Gauge Steam Trust, Tyseley
SLOA — Steam Locomotive Operators Association (operated by PULR)
SNG — A4 Locomotive Society, c/o Steamtown, Carnforth
STRM — Steamtown Railway Museum, Carnforth
SVR — Severn Valley Railway, Bewdley
THR — Thomas Hill, Rotherham (Great Scottish & Western Railway Co Ltd, London SW11)
TRTS — Train Tours, Manchester
VSOE — Sea Containers Ltd (Venice-Simplon-Orient Express)
WDS — D. Smith, Midland Railway Centre, Butterley

The following are the former numbers of vehicles in this booklet that have been converted from another type and renumbered but not shown elsewhere.

	0	1	2	3	4	5	6	7	8	9
1200	6459	6445	6446	3291	3401	6438	3319	6422	3393	6457
1210	6462	3305	6453	3419	6433	3377	3302	6444	3332	3418
1220	6432	3371								
2830	–	–	–	21270	21267	–	–	–	–	–
6300	54356	54367								
6400	3167					3154	3156			
6410	3164			3157	3161	3155		–	3276	–
6420	3282	3283	3328	3288	3289	3294	–	3298	3306	3307
6430	3310	3311	3315	3317	3320	3323	3324	3327	3329	3339
6440	3342	–	3349	3355	3357	3361	3365	3376	3394	3396
6450	3403	3404	3423	3427	3430	3435	3436	3437	3281	3287
6460	3301	3316	3405	3410	3380	3422				
6500	5603	5547	5602	5510	5598	5553	5608	–	5511	5513
6510	5518	5587	5534	5538	5528	5556	5551	5499	5503	5544
6520	5599	5558	5611	5568	5564	–	5537	5563	5592	5579
6600	5688	5697	–	5691	5656	5741	–	5635	5696	5698
6610	–	–	–	5702	5725	–	5720	5733	5644	5655
6650	–	–	5622*	–	–	–	–	–	–	–
6660	5627*	5736*	5641*	–	–	5721*	–	–	–	–

*Built as above, but numbered 6602/10/11/12/15 respectively before their current numbers

	0	1	2	3	4	5	6	7	8	9
6700	3347	3346	3421	3308	3341	6430	6421	6418	3370	
7550	13550	13551	–	13553	–	–	–	–	13558	–
7560	–	13561								
9010	–	–	–	–	–		9237			
9100	9405	9398	9383	9389	9401	9404	9406	9407		
9700		9528	9510	9517	9512	9519	–	9511	9530	9515
9710	9518	9534	9532	9535	9536					
10200	40519	40520	40504	40506	40502	40503	40507	40516	40517	40508
10210	40510	40509	11049	11050	11034	11032	11041	11051	11053	11047
10220	11056	11012	11063	11043	11062	11014	11015	11057	11035	11059
10230	10021	10016	10027	10013	10004	10015	10018	10022	10017	–

	0	1	2	3	4	5	6	7	8	9
10240	10003	10009	10002	–	–	10019	10014	10011	10005	10012
10250	10020	10024	10008	10026	10006	10010	10028	10007	10023	10025
10260	10001									
11900	–	–	–	–	–	11005	11006	11007	11008	11009
11910	11010	–	–	–	–	–	–	–	–	–
11920	–	–	11022							
19450	–	–	13452	–	13454	13455	–	–	13458	–
19460	13460	–	–	–	13464	13465	–	–	–	13469
19470	–	–	–	–	–	–	–	–	13478	–
19480	–	–	–		–	–	13486	–	–	13489
19490	–	–	–	–	–	–	–	13497	–	–
19500	13500	–	–	–	–	–	–	–	–	–
19510	–	–	13512	–	–	–	–	–	–	–
19520	–		13522	13523	–	–	–	–	–	13529
19530	–	–	–		13534		13536	13537		–
19540	13540		–			13545			13548	13549
19550	–	–	–	–	–	13555	13556	–	–	–
35500	17094									
80040		1690								

Non-Passenger Stock.

	0	1	2	3	4	5	6	7	8	9
80200	35303	35311	35462	35287	35297	35312	35304	35466	35341	35279
80210	35282	35296	35307	35316	35323	35292	35295	35299	35197	35201
80220	35276	35321	35315	35331	35291					
80380	–	25112	25109	25053	25078	25083	25099	25045	25088	25103
80390	25047	25089	25082	25118	25156	25056				
80400	–	–	–	–	35014	35009	35022	35015	35018	35019
80410	35001	35003	35002	35004	35005					
80430	–	25104	25071	25150	25119	25117	25077	25068	25139	25127
92000	80723	80855	80858	80864	80867	80876	80878	80880	80895	80897
92010	80900	80903	80910	80916	80923	80927	80930	80940	80941	80944
92020	80950	80956	80958	80971	–	81023	81060	81061	81064	81077
92030	–	81102	81117	81123	81142	81150	81158	81165	81173	81175
92040	81186	81205	81207	81208	81209	81210	81214	81216	81218	81219
92050	81220	81221	81222	81223	81224	81225	81226	81227	81228	81229

	0	1	2	3	4	5	6	7	8	9
92060	81230	81231	81232	81233	81236	81237	81238	81243	81244	81245
92070	81246	81249	81253	81254	81255	81256	81257	81258	81259	81260
92080	81263	81264	81265	81266	81268	–	81282	81283	81284	81303
92090	81305	81308	81309	81312	81367	81375	81377	81378	81381	81383
92100	81391	81392	81394	81400	81401	81405	81409	81410	81411	81413
92110	81426	81432	81440	81442	81443	81444	81450	81451	81452	81454
92120	81455	81457	81459	81460	81465	81470	81471	81473	81478	81479
92130	81480	81481	81482	81484	81485	81486	81487	81488	81490	81491
92140	81492	81493	81494	81495	81496	81497	81498	81500	81506	81509
92150	81514	81516	81518	81520	81522	81525	81529	81532	81533	81534
92160	81537	81538	81539	81540	81541	81546	81550	81553	81555	81556
92170	81559	81560	81562	81565	81567	81568	81569	81572	81574	81580
92180	81581	81582	81585	81588	81589	81591	81595	81597	81598	81599
92190	81600	81601	81602	81604	81606	81607	81609	81611	81613	81614
92200	81615	81618	81620	81621	81622	81623	81624	81627	84403	80873
92210	84466	81267	80937	81321	81504	80911	81376	80877	84314	84285
92220	80924	80888	80887	80932	81277	80891	80879	84337	80921	80902
92230	81423	80860	80870	80890	84336	80908	80909	80738	84563	81170
92240	80703	80943	80857	84489	84248	80939	80929	84536	80935	84511
92250	81235	84425	80959	80936	80894	80871	81424	80955	–	–
92300	–	–	–	–	–	–	–	–	80784	84043
92310	84105	84453	84548	80992	80777	80848	80980	80836	80847	84055
92320	84166	84566	80771	80832	84087	80791	84270	80842	80999	84001
92330	80995	84365	80845	80982	80973	80973	84045	84140	84524	84530
92340	84059	84316	84397	84505	84154	84083	84091	84326	84075	84178
92350	84049	84174	84182	84323	84353	84517	84535	84136	84393	84275
92360	84431	84463	84188	84294	84030	84122	84551	84293	84334	80960
92370	84324	80856	84362	84528	84317	84335	84374	80928	84340	80914
92380	84247	84476	84561	84429						
94000	–	86438	86651	86281	86156	86845	86202	86572	86838	86144
94010	86151	86437	86082	86790	–	86484	86317	86467	86170	86098
94020	86220	86204	86718	86221	86106	86377	86732	86703	86733	86740
94030	86746	86747	86730	86731	86200					
94050	93771	93708	93709	93716	–	–	93804	93137	93530	–
94060	–	93763	93803	–	–	–	–	–	86424	–
94070	–	86544	–	–	–	86841	93842	93862	93971	
95200	84019	80875	80667	80621	80947	80620	80561	80560	80667	84047
95210	80731	80949	84179	80826	84360	80643	84542	84385	80675	80946
95220	80717	84153	80774	80933						
95300	80689	80613	80695	80614	84345	80863	84029	84124	84161	80966
95310	84292	80775	80503		80631	80682	80720	80780	84181	80768
95320		80525	80767	84100	80782	84012	84041		84129	84341

	0	1	2	3	4	5	6	7	8	9
95330	80649	84112	84014	84119					80789	84135
95340	80513									
96100	93734	93741	93743	93744	93745					
96110	93738	93742	93750							
96130	93736	93737	93754	93685	93691	93755	93735	93748	93749	93751
96140	93752	93753								
96150	93097	93286	93324	93327	93331	93334	93337	93344	93351	93355
96160	93385	93443								
96170	93159	93326	93363	93440	93453	93628	93641			
96180	–	–	–	–	–	93083	93087	93168	93320	93447
96190	93448	93665	93669	93874	93949	93958				
99600	–	34577	21145	–	–	–	–	–	–	–
99620	34692	34697	34584	34700	34084	34693	–	–	–	25972
99630	34965	1018	4329	3827	25317	25637	25646	15854	21221	–
99640	–	1036	1040	4272	3852	1765	1766	34629	787017	80502
99650	80830	–	–	–	–	–	4298	4569	4592	4518
99660	–	80510								

Late News

Stock Alterations to 28 January 1989

New: 82105-ZQ.

The first of the Mk 4 coaches, 12201, has been delivered to Derby RSD for trials.

Withdrawn: 3367 (sold), 3918, 18994, 35184.

Withdrawal authorised: 5302.

Transferred to Departmental Service: 3749, 3919/23/24/91/93, 4058/66, 4376/92/93, 9016 to ADB977623-34 (Class 90 Training Train).

Reallocated, Inter-Regional: E-M: 92042, 92118-OY. M-E: 5695-NC. M-SC: 5772, 5888-PC, 84099-IS, 92080, 92197-EC.
SC-M: 5747/62-MA. S-M: 4905/10-EN.
All stock allocated to CA and NC is now allocated to Anglia Region (A).

Reallocated, Regional: 1215/19-21, 3403-OY, 5456-LA, 93131/95, 93267/78, 93375/79/88, 93490, 93511/12/15/16/36/56, 93622/24/30/31/33/40/44/52/67/77/84/87, 93710/11/13-15/17/20/22/23/79, 93811/22-BJ.

Sectors: *IAN:* 1870, 5695. *ICC:* 10578. *IWC:* 3354. *IXX:* 93784, 93834/43/63/75, 93910/37/44/78/80. *NSS:* 5456, 6526. *NNW:* 4905/10, 7188, 7214,. *PSX:* 10595. *RPXM:* 92042, 92128. *RPXX:* 94507. *RPXZ:* 92080, 92197.

Converted: *SO-FO (AD107):* 3403 ex-6450.

Refurbished: 12033, 12100/11/32/42/61 (all InterCity livery).

Modified: *Commonwealth bogies:* 96130.
Payphones fitted: 3354, 11083-90/92-94/96-99, 11100/01.
Wheelchair accommodation: 5949, 6141/49.
Disabled toilet: 12142.
Seating: Std: 76 Diagram AC213 (★): 12036/45/47/55/56/58/60/63/64/66-69/71/72/73/76/77/78/81/82/83/86/89/94/96/99, 12101/06/07/12/13/19/20/22/23/27/30-34/36/46/48/49/50/52/55/56/58/63/64/67.

Liveries: *InterCity* (I): 3403, 5695, 5949, 6141. *NSE* (N): 4876, 5043, 5436, 6517/27.